European History for AS Level

GERMANY 1866 - 1945

Steve Eddy & Tony Lancaster
Edited by Steve Lancaster

Causeway Press

Contents

Unit 5   The Nazis in power   193-229

Unit 6   The Nazification of Germany   230-86

Maps of Germany in 1933

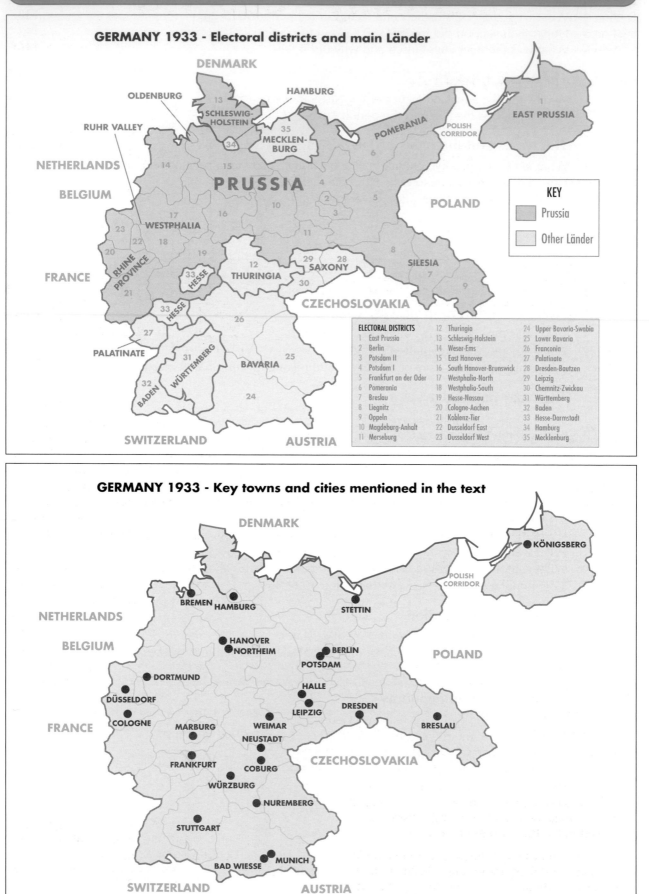

GERMANY 1933 - Electoral districts and main Länder

DENMARK

OLDENBURG

HAMBURG

13

SCHLESWIG-HOLSTEIN

35

34

MECKLEN-BURG

POMERANIA

POLISH CORRIDOR

1

EAST PRUSSIA

RUHR VALLEY

NETHERLANDS

BELGIUM

14

15

PRUSSIA

4

2

3

5

6

POLAND

KEY

Prussia

Other Länder

17

16

23

22

18

WESTPHALIA

11

20

RHINE PROVINCE

19

8

SILESIA

FRANCE

33

HESSE

THURINGIA

12

29

28

SAXONY

7

9

21

30

CZECHOSLOVAKIA

33

HESSE

26

27

PALATINATE

31

WÜRTTEMBERG

BAVARIA

25

32

BADEN

24

SWITZERLAND

AUSTRIA

ELECTORAL DISTRICTS		
1 East Prussia	12 Thuringia	24 Upper Bavaria-Swabia
2 Berlin	13 Schleswig-Holstein	25 Lower Bavaria
3 Potsdam II	14 Weser-Ems	26 Franconia
4 Potsdam I	15 East Hanover	27 Palatinate
5 Frankfurt an der Oder	16 South Hanover-Brunswick	28 Dresden-Bautzen
6 Pomerania	17 Westphalia-North	29 Leipzig
7 Breslau	18 Westphalia-South	30 Chemnitz-Zwickau
8 Liegnitz	19 Hesse-Nassau	31 Württemberg
9 Oppeln	20 Cologne-Aachen	32 Baden
10 Magdeburg-Anhalt	21 Koblenz-Tier	33 Hesse-Darmstadt
11 Merseburg	22 Dusseldorf East	34 Hamburg
	23 Dusseldorf West	35 Mecklenburg

GERMANY 1933 - Key towns and cities mentioned in the text

DENMARK

KÖNIGSBERG

NETHERLANDS

BELGIUM

POLISH CORRIDOR

BREMEN

HAMBURG

STETTIN

POLAND

HANOVER

NORTHEIM

BERLIN

POTSDAM

DORTMUND

HALLE

DÜSSELDORF

LEIPZIG

DRESDEN

COLOGNE

MARBURG

WEIMAR

BRESLAU

FRANCE

NEUSTADT

FRANKFURT

COBURG

CZECHOSLOVAKIA

WÜRZBURG

NUREMBERG

STUTTGART

BAD WIESSE

MUNICH

SWITZERLAND

AUSTRIA

UNIT 1 Germany 1866-1914

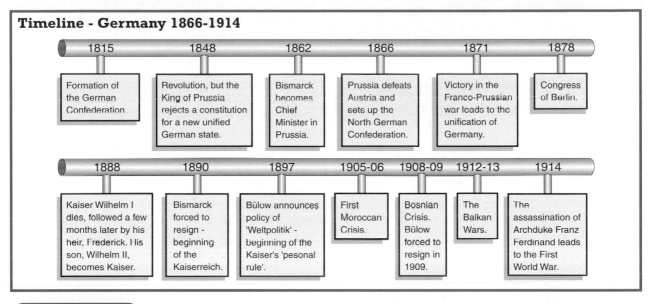

Timeline - Germany 1866-1914

1815	1848	1862	1866	1871	1878
Formation of the German Confederation.	Revolution, but the King of Prussia rejects a constitution for a new unified German state.	Bismarck becomes Chief Minister in Prussia.	Prussia defeats Austria and sets up the North German Confederation.	Victory in the Franco-Prussian war leads to the unification of Germany.	Congress of Berlin.

1888	1890	1897	1905-06	1908-09	1912-13	1914
Kaiser Wilhelm I dies, followed a few months later by his heir, Frederick. His son, Wilhelm II, becomes Kaiser.	Bismarck forced to resign - beginning of the Kaiserreich.	Bülow announces policy of 'Weltpolitik' - beginning of the Kaiser's 'pesonal rule'.	First Moroccan Crisis.	Bosnian Crisis. Bülow forced to resign in 1909.	The Balkan Wars.	The assassination of Archduke Franz Ferdinand leads to the First World War.

Introduction

At the beginning of the 19th century, the name 'Germany' described not a unified state but a loose confederation of 39 separate states. Pressure to unify began to build in the mid-19th century and, under the leadership of the Prussian Chief Minister, Otto von Bismarck, German unification was completed at the end of the Franco-Prussian War of 1870-71. The first part of this unit examines the events leading up to unification and the debate over the role played by Bismarck. For the first 19 years after unification, Bismarck remained German Chancellor (Prime Minister). While there is no doubt that he was a key political figure during the period he remained Chancellor, historians are divided about the contribution he made. Some have portrayed him as a man of great political skill and vision. Others are less positive in their analyses. Some point out, for example, that, in its early years, the unified German state underwent substantial economic and social change. The way in which Bismarck reacted to this change, they argue, only stored up problems for the

future. In 1888, the first Emperor, Kaiser Wilhelm I, died and was succeeded by the Crown Prince, Frederick. A few months later, however, Frederick also died and was succeeded by his son, Wilhelm II. Unlike Wilhelm I, Wilhelm II was determined to take an active role in policy-making. This soon brought him into conflict with Bismarck and, in 1890, Bismarck was forced to resign. The period from Bismarck's resignation to the end of the First World War is often described as the 'Kaiserreich'. Some historians see this as a period in which policy - both domestic and foreign - was dominated by the Kaiser. Others, however, suggest that the Kaiser's power was constrained by his advisers and ministers as well as by external forces beyond his control. The second part of the unit looks at the development of domestic policy and the nature of the political system under first Bismarck and then Kaiser Wilhelm II. The final part of the unit focuses on foreign policy, examining the key developments in the period 1871-1914.

UNIT SUMMARY

Part 1 looks at the key events leading to the unification of Germany in 1871. It also analyses the historical debate over the role Bismarck played in the build-up to unification.

Part 2 examines the political system first under Bismarck and then under Kaiser Wilhelm II. It looks, in particular, at the debate over the extent

to which these two men directed German domestic policy.

Part 3 focuses on the development of foreign policy in the period 1871-1914. It examines the approach adopted both by Bismarck and his successors.

1 The unification of Germany

Key issues

1. Why did the German states remain disunited before 1871?

2. How important was Bismarck in bringing about a united Germany in 1871?

1.1 Why did the German states remain disunited before 1871?

Germany in the early 19th century

At the beginning of the 19th century, the name 'Germany' described not a unified state but a loose confederation made up of 39 separate states. These states were still part of the Holy Roman Empire (HRE) and have been described as:

'A bewildering patchwork of several hundred semi-independent territories which had existed for over a thousand years.' (Whaley 2001, p.15)

Napoleon I destroyed the HRE in 1806 and his own defeat in 1815 led to the formation of the German Confederation, composed of 39 states (see Box 1.1). The Confederation remained a collection of sovereign states with their own rulers and systems of government. Even when the process of German unification had begun in the 1860s:

'Localism and regionalism were of decisive importance in defining the framework within which politicians had to work.' (John 1991, p.17)

John also emphasises that the German states still varied greatly in 'their levels of social and economic development, religious affiliations and administrative and institutional arrangements' (John 1991, p.16).

The German Confederation's political system

The German Confederation provided no effective unifying political institutions. It did, though, have a central executive body, the 'Bundestag' or 'Diet' (Assembly) which met at Frankfurt and was attended by representatives (ambassadors) appointed by each of the 39 states. The President of the Diet was the Austrian representative. Before any action could be taken by the Diet, it had to have the agreement of

---

BOX 1.1   **The German Confederation**

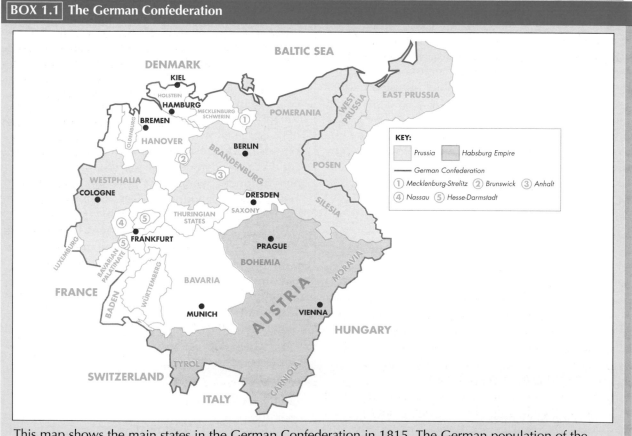

This map shows the main states in the German Confederation in 1815. The German population of the Austrian Habsburg Empire was 9.5 million, but Austria also controlled vast non-Germanic possessions in Italy, Hungary, Poland, Bohemia and Moravia (later Czechoslovakia), Croatia and Slovenia. Prussia, under its Hohenzollern monarchy, had a German-speaking population of 8 million, but also controlled non-German minorities, such as Poles in East Prussia.

all the representatives. This was a recipe for inaction:

'Total agreement was seldom forthcoming, for the representatives were more concerned with safeguarding the interests of their states than working for the Confederation as a whole.' (Stiles & Farmer 2001, p.9)

Under the influence of the conservative Austrians, the Diet was most active in putting down political dissent within the Confederation. The individual states in the Confederation had what Christopher Clark describes as 'a diverse array of constitutional arrangements'. Some had their own Parliaments. In all, however:

'Suffrage was limited to males who met certain legal and economic qualifications and voting was indirect.' (Clark 2001, p.50)

German nationalists (people who wanted a unified German state ruled by one central government) had little chance of mounting effective opposition to their princely rulers:

'Liberal nationalists bemoaned the limitations imposed on political development by the plethora of small states, in which conservative princes and élites retained their dominance.' (John 2001, p.17)

Economic and social factors

Historians agree that the development of a more modern, industrialised economy in Germany after 1815 did, to some extent, create conditions for greater unity in the German Confederation. As the population grew rapidly in most states of the Confederation, agricultural output increased and industry began to develop. A railway network was created in spite of the difficulty of building it across so many state borders. Germany became more urbanised. The Zollverein (customs union) was set up in 1834 under Prussian leadership (Austria remained outside, see below). This broke down customs barriers between the German states and stimulated economic development. However, it is easy to overestimate the economic factors leading to greater unity. Robert Lee suggests that:

'Individual states fought for their own narrow interests and often pursued different approaches to specific issues, such as the development of the railway network, the introduction of freedom of trade or tariff policy. Federal states maintained a particularist approach...the economic unification of Germany had still not been achieved by 1871.' (Lee 2001, pp.82-3 & pp.89-90)

The economic modernisation of Germany produced changes in the class structure, in particular the growth of the middle class. It was from this class that most nationalists were drawn. According to Christopher Clark (2001, p.52), most were 'professionals, academics, men involved in commerce and manufacture'. Nevertheless, forces of conservatism continued to be influential. Aristocratic landowners remained strong in most states. Clark argues that they 'idealised "traditional order" and supported 'paternalistic and localised structures of authority.' (Clark 2001, p.56). In the first half of the 19th century, the majority of German people still worked on the land. Most were poor. In many cases they had only recently emerged from serfdom. Their horizons remained highly localised. An industrial working class, another possible force for change, was only just starting to establish itself.

Another source of division in German society was religion. In the North and East, Protestant religion dominated, while the southern states and the Rhineland were predominantly Roman Catholic. Of the two dominant German states in the Confederation, Prussia was predominantly Protestant while Austria was Catholic.

The rivalry between Prussia and Austria

Most historians agree that the rivalry between Prussia and Austria in the first half of the 19th century was an important block on unification. This point is developed in Box 1.2.

BOX 1.2 The rivalry between Prussia and Austria

At the level of political and military history, Prussia and Austria were the principal actors within Germany up to 1866. No new, unified German state could come into existence unless both Austria and Prussia agreed. For the first half of the 19th century, Austria was seen as the more powerful of the two, though increasingly Prussia challenged this position. Most of the rulers of the medium-sized and smaller German states saw the preservation of their power best protected by the maintenance of the German Confederation under Austrian leadership. They were suspicious of Prussia, concerned about its expansion at their expense. German nationalists, however, were divided over whether to support a greater Germany (Grossdeutsch), led by Austria or a 'little Germany' (Kleindeutsch) under Prussian leadership. Some feared the domination of a united Germany by the conservative, authoritarian Prussian monarchy. Others believed that Austria would put the interests of its huge empire, much of it non-German, before the interests of German unity. The rivalry of Austria and Prussia for the leadership in Germany was finally resolved by force in 1866 (see below).
Adapted from Breuilly 2001.

The failure of the 1848 Revolution

The first serious attempt to create a new national German state ended in failure. In 1848, the overthrow of King Louis Philippe in France led to a wave of revolutionary activity throughout Europe. In Germany, there were uprisings in many states and the King of Bavaria was overthrown. In response to discontent, German princes allowed the election of a German National Assembly. Since this met in Frankfurt, it was known as the Frankfurt Parliament. It was also known as the 'Professors' Parliament' as it was dominated by members of the middle class. Although the Frankfurt Parliament drew up a constitution for a new unified German state with the Prussian King, Friedrich Wilhelm, at its head, Friedrich Wilhelm rejected it out of hand, saying that he would accept such a crown only from his fellow princes, not 'from the gutter'. In May and June 1849, the position of the Prussian monarchy and the other German rulers was finally re-established by the use of force. There followed an attempt by Prussia to challenge the political dominance of Austria in the German Confederation, the aim being, historians agree, to unite Germany under Prussian leadership. In May 1849, Friedrich Wilhelm IV persuaded the rulers of Saxony and Hanover to join him in a 'League of Three Kings'. This was then expanded to include the rulers of 17 other states, resulting in the 'Erfurt Union' (named after its place of origin). At first, Austria (which was excluded) was preoccupied with putting down the revolutions within its boundaries. With the internal revolutions subdued, however, Austrian pressure on Prussia led to the abandonment of the Erfurt Union at a meeting at Olmutz in 1850. The German Confederation was restored under the political leadership of Austria at what became known as the 'humiliation of Olmutz'.

1.2 How important was Bismarck in bringing about a united Germany in 1871?

Historians on Bismarck

Many historians have seen Otto von Bismarck (see Box 1.3) as the key figure in the unification of Germany after he became Chief Minister in Prussia in 1862. For example, a leading German historian, Thomas Nipperdy, opens the second volume of his history of Germany with:

'In the beginning there was Bismarck.' (quoted in Feuchtwanger 2001, p.14)

Gordon Craig, at the beginning of his book, asks: 'Is it a mistake to begin with Bismarck?' and goes on to suggest that it is not (Craig 1978, p.1). Other historians, however, are less inclined to take the 'Great Man' view of history. Mommsen, for example, quotes with approval the words of Bismarck himself:

'I, at least, am not so presumptuous as to believe that history can be made by the likes of us. It is my task to observe history's currents and to steer my ship within them. I cannot guide the currents

themselves, let alone create them.'(Mommsen 1995, p.4)

Breuilly also expresses doubts:

'Bismarck is usually regarded as the master of each moment. I am sceptical.' (Breuilly 1996, p.10)

The debate by historians on Bismarck's overall career continues and his role in the unification of Germany throws light on the discussion.

Bismarck's career to 1862

Bismarck was a Prussian aristocrat, a Junker, born into a landowning East Prussian family. Historians agree that Junkers were generally the most conservative class in Prussia, ardent supporters of the monarchy and expected to serve as officers in the Prussian army.

When Bismarck entered politics he appeared to conform to these conservative ideas. In 1848-49, he worked against the ideas of those who supported the Frankfurt Parliament:

'[He] sprang to prominence as a man of the extreme right. He wanted to defeat the revolution and restore the absolute monarchy. He was rewarded for the role he played and, in 1851, was appointed Prussian envoy to the Diet of the restored German Confederation at Frankfurt.' (Feuchtwanger 2001, p.15)

As Feuchtwanger goes on to suggest, however:

'[Bismarck quickly] moved away from the views of his conservative Prussian associates who had sponsored his appointment to Frankfurt.' (Feuchtwanger 2001, p.15)

Bismarck's stance

For the conservatives, the various German monarchs had to stick together and, in particular, Prussia and Austria had to find ways of working with one another. Bismarck, however, became convinced that Prussia should dominate in Germany:

'[Bismarck's] overriding concern at Frankfurt was to counteract Austria's attempts to continue her leading role in Germany and to insist on Prussia's right to equality.' (Stiles & Farmer 2001, p.58)

He recognised that the rivalry of Austria and Prussia 'might sooner or later have to be resolved by war. Prussia might have to consider an alliance with France, now under Napoleon III. To Prussian conservatives, Napoleon I had been the revolution incarnate and his nephew, Napoleon III was no less so' (Feuchtwanger 2001, p.15). Bismarck also showed the gulf between himself and conservatives in his changing views towards liberal nationalists in Prussia:

'The middle-class liberals who were the mainstay of the German national movement might become useful allies of the monarchy and the aristocracy. As the events of 1848 had shown, they were as

BOX 1.3 Otto von Bismarck 1815-1898

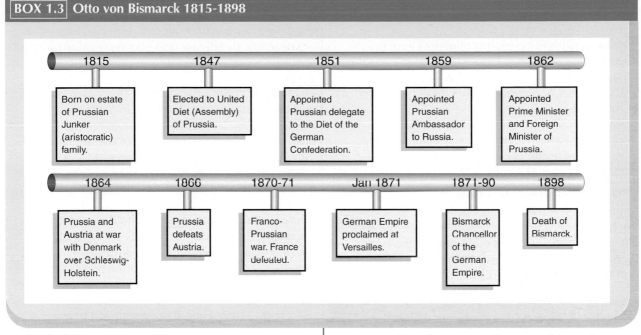

1815	1847	1851	1859	1862
Born on estate of Prussian Junker (aristocratic) family.	Elected to United Diet (Assembly) of Prussia.	Appointed Prussian delegate to the Diet of the German Confederation.	Appointed Prussian Ambassador to Russia.	Appointed Prime Minister and Foreign Minister of Prussia.

1864	1866	1870-71	Jan 1871	1871-90	1898
Prussia and Austria at war with Denmark over Schleswig-Holstein.	Prussia defeats Austria.	Franco-Prussian war. France defeated.	German Empire proclaimed at Versailles.	Bismarck Chancellor of the German Empire.	Death of Bismarck.

afraid of the masses as the aristocracy.'
(Feuchtwanger 2001, p.16)

So, both in foreign and domestic policy Bismarck showed a flexibility that differentiated his policies from conservatives:

'He was often described as a "typical Junker", which he was not. He was too clever, too enterprising and too non-conformist for that.'
(Stiles & Farmer 2001, p.55)

As Waller suggests:

'Most historians have now consigned the view of Bismarck as a reactionary to history's dustbin.'
(Waller 1998, p.42)

Bismarck's rise to power in 1862

Bismarck was appointed to the post of Chief Minister of Prussia in 1862 to settle a constitutional crisis that had arisen over army reforms. In 1859, the army was mobilised in case Prussia became involved in the war between Austria and France over Italy. This mobilisation suggested to the new King, Wilhelm I (he became King of Prussia in 1861) and the army chiefs that the army was suffering from various defects. As a result, the King appointed Albrecht von Roon as Minister of War and Roon proposed the following reforms:

- an increase in the numbers of conscripts called up each year
- reorganisation of army regiments
- increased service in the front line and the reserve
- a reduced period in the Landwehr (militia of older men who had completed their military service).

The liberals, who made up the majority in the Prussian Parliament, accepted the need for a strong army. But, they objected to the cost of the reforms and to the weakening of the Landwehr whose officers came from the middle class and which was seen more as a 'people's army'. As a result, the liberals refused to vote for the increased funds needed for the army reforms. The King and the army chiefs argued that the military matters were their concern and that the opposition of Parliament was a threat to their control of the army. The result was a stalemate which was only broken when Roon suggested that Bismarck, then ambassador in Paris, be called in to deal with the crisis:

'Bismarck withdrew the budget but collected the taxes, arguing that, in the event of a stand-off between Crown and Parliament, the executive must continue to run the country on the basis of laws already passed. Parliament rejected this novel theory [the 'constitutional gap'] but, as it also rejected extra-parliamentary resistance such as a tax boycott, Bismarck overrode the opposition.'
(Breuilly 2001a, p.144)

Bismarck treated opposition politicians and journalists extremely roughly and, although he got his way, remained deeply unpopular with liberal-nationalists. This unpopularity increased when he sided with Russia over the suppression of the Polish revolt in 1863. It was a stroke of luck, namely the Schleswig-Holstein issue (see below), 'that enabled Bismarck to escape from this unpromising situation' (Breuilly 2001a, p.145).

Bismarck's foreign policy, 1862-71

Bismarck's ideas on foreign policy have often been described by the word 'realpolitik' - policy which is based on the realistic interests of the state and which takes no account of ethical or ideological factors (see, for example, Waller 1997, Chapter 2). Most historians now agree that, by the time he came to power in 1862:

'[Bismarck] had no master plan for German unification. His main interest was advancing the interests of Prussia and the German national cause played a secondary role in his thinking.' (Goodlad 2000, p.21)

It was in Prussia's interest to replace Austria as the dominant power in Germany and Bismarck took advantage of a number of favourable factors to achieve this end.

1. The Schleswig-Holstein Issue

In the 1860s, Schleswig and Holstein were German duchies (areas ruled by a Duke). Schleswig-Holstein is located in the North of Germany on the border with Denmark. The Schleswig-Holstein Issue is outlined in Box 1.4.

BOX 1.4   The Schleswig-Holstein Issue

Schleswig and Holstein were two duchies ruled by the Danish Crown. Holstein was German-speaking and a member of the German Confederation. Schleswig had both German and Danish speakers and was not in the Confederation. Danish nationalists claimed Schleswig. German nationalists insisted on the indivisibility of the duchies. The succession of Christian IX to the Danish throne on the death of Frederick VII in November 1863 did not give him the right to rule over the duchies, but Christian IX signed a charter incorporating Schleswig into Denmark (ie making it part of Denmark). German nationalists responded by demanding the title of Duke of Schleswig-Holstein be granted to Frederick, Duke of Augustenburg. He would then bring both duchies into the German Confederation. The rivalry of Danish and German nationalists over the duchies had led to war in 1848. At the end of it, an international treaty, the Treaty of London (1852), had laid down that, when Christian became King of Denmark, he would rule the duchies but not incorporate them into Denmark. When he violated the treaty, German nationalists called for action against Denmark. Some of the smaller states of the German Confederation sent an army into Holstein to install the son of the Duke of Augustenburg as its ruler. Danish nationalists called for the incorporation of both duchies into Denmark. While neither Prussia nor Austria could accept the action of Denmark, they were both unhappy about the duchies becoming independent states, out of their control under Augustenburg. The result was a military alliance between Prussia and Austria (agreed in January 1864) and a war against Denmark. In July 1864, Denmark was defeated and in the subsequent Treaty of Vienna (signed in October 1864) Schleswig-Holstein was handed over to the joint rule of Prussia and Austria.

Adapted from Breuilly 2001a and Carr 1991.

The war against Denmark did not solve the Schleswig-Holstein problem, however. Austrian-Prussian joint rule was difficult, especially for Austria:

'For political, military and geographical reasons, Austria remained the junior partner.' (Kitchen 1996, p.197)

Increasingly Austria came to see that it had 'gained nothing by supporting Bismarck in Schleswig-Holstein' (Carr 1991, p.96). Austrian hopes of preventing Prussian domination of the duchies, the only reason for intervention in this distant area, seemed remote. Also, Austria's intervention weakened its position in the German Confederation. In an attempt to restore its prestige in the Confederation, Austria revived the Augustenburg claim to the Duchies.

'Friction developed over the administration of the duchies and relations between the two powers deteriorated sharply.' (Carr 1991, p.97)

War seemed possible but, in 1865 under the terms of the 'Gastein Convention', it was agreed that in future the duchies would be administered separately. Austria would administer Holstein and Prussia would administer Schleswig. The crisis was defused, but, in less than a year, Prussia and Austria were at war after a further crisis over the control of the duchies. Stiles and Farmer point out that:

'Historians have argued for over a century about Bismarck's motives and his aims in dealing with the Schleswig-Holstein affair. Had Bismarck used the Schleswig-Holstein crisis, as he later claimed, to manoeuvre Austria into open confrontation with Prussia as a way of settling the problem of leadership in Germany? Or did he have no clear policy at the time except to "allow events to ripen"?' (Stiles & Farmer 2001, p.66)

Historians remain divided on this issue.

2. War with Austria 1866

Less than a year after the agreement at Gastein, Prussia and Austria were at war (June-July,1866). The immediate cause of war was Austria's breach of the terms of the Gastein Convention. The war lasted only seven weeks, ending in victory for Prussia on 3 July at the decisive battle of Koniggratz (also called Sadowa). It was a decisive moment in German history because Prussia's victory settled the long standing struggle for supremacy in German affairs in Prussia's rather than Austria's favour.

Later, Bismarck claimed that this outcome was a result of his careful planning. But, historians who have examined the events leading to the war with Austria do not now generally accept Bismarck's view. Lothar Gall's view is typical:

'In reality, what Bismarck did in 1866, for all his shrewd calculations, was to stake everything on a single card in a game in which, besides the skill, chance and luck tipped the scales at the crucial moment.' (Gall 1986, pp.275-76)

The Treaty of Prague (signed in August 1866) led to the creation of a new German state - the North German Confederation - under Prussian leadership. Prussia took control of large areas in the North, gaining 4.5 million inhabitants. All other German states north of the River Main came into the new organisation. The four German states south of the Main - Bavaria, Württemberg, Baden and Hesse-Darmstedt (see map in Box 1.1) - remained independent. The idea of a Little Germany (Kleindeutsch), led by Prussia, had triumphed. Two-thirds of all Germans (excluding Austrian Germans) were now part of the North German Confederation.

3. The Franco-Prussian War 1870-71
According to Gall:

'[Bismarck] was only too well aware that in both domestic and foreign policy he had to traverse an area of considerable danger and risk...His policy was dominated by his awareness of the incompleteness of the overall situation.' (Gall 1986, pp.332-33)

In Germany, the southern states remained outside the new North German Confederation. In foreign policy, France had been alarmed by the speed of Prussian victory in 1866 and had been left empty-handed as a result:

'Napoleon had hoped that Austria and Prussia would bleed one another white and that he could deal with the convalescents at his leisure. Clearly, the strengthened Germany that emerged was unwelcome; a yet more consolidated Germany could be dangerous. Napoleon, therefore, desired to stop further German unification.' (Waller 1997, p.31)

Bismarck's policy after 1866 was seen by earlier historians as the last phase of a carefully worked out plan. This view was often based on Bismarck's own later claims. In 1892, for example, Bismarck said:

'We could not have set up the German Reich without having defeated France. The war with France was a necessary conclusion.'

His close associate, Bucher, claimed that Bismarck 'laid a trap for France' (quoted in Taylor 1961, pp.121-2). Most modern historians argue that there is a less dramatic or clear-cut explanation of events between the two wars of 1866 and 1870. They argue that the war with France played into Bismarck's hands - see Box 1.5.

The crisis of 1870
The bare facts of the crisis in Franco-Prussian relations that led to war in 1870 can be stated simply. The crisis arose over the offer, in July 1870, of the vacant Spanish throne to a member of the Prussian royal family, Prince Leopold of Hohenzollern. France, alarmed at a further extension of Prussian power, demanded that Leopold's candidature be withdrawn. This was accepted by Wilhelm I and Leopold withdrew. However, the

---

BOX 1.5 Prussian policy, 1866-70

Bismarck hoped to bring the remaining southern German states into a unified Germany, but by peaceful, gradual means. In 1866, the four southern states signed defensive military pacts with Prussia agreeing that, in the event of war, they would fight with Prussia. Also, they were members of the Zollverein (customs union) and tied to Prussia economically. Bismarck tried to strengthen these ties by creating a 'Zollparlament' (Parliament) with elected representatives from all members, a strategy which required patience and restraint. While it is true that these tactics did not lead to voluntary unity with the southern states by 1870, it appears that Bismarck was still prepared to be patient. In 1869, he wrote that 'German unity is no ripe fruit at this time: the ability to wait while conditions develop is a necessity of practical politics'. In the event, it was war with France that finally led to unification. A crisis in Franco-Prussian relations came as early as 1867. After his failure to gain territory in 1866, Napoleon III negotiated with the Dutch for the sale of Luxemburg. The Dutch agreed, subject to Prussian agreement. There was a massive popular outcry in Germany against the proposed arrangement. Bismarck used this outcry to stop the Dutch from selling. Napoleon III was outwitted and ended up empty-handed again. The Luxemburg Incident showed that Bismarck remained cautious in his dealings with France. Had Bismarck really wanted war with France, there was an ideal opportunity in 1867. In France, the Luxemburg Incident had important consequences. Before the Incident, Napoleon was prepared to accept great changes in Germany. After it, however, Napoleon was bitterly disillusioned with Bismarck. Hopes of a Prussian alliance were buried and anti-Prussian advisers gained the upper hand. They reverted to the old policy of keeping Germany weak and divided. As a result, when a new crisis arose in 1870, relations between France and Prussia were far less cordial than they had been in 1866.

Adapted from Craig 1978.

French then demanded a guarantee that Leopold's name never be put forward again. This was refused and the French declared war on Prussia on 19 July 1870.

It is the story behind this outline that has led to historical debate over Bismarck's role in the crisis and whether he planned for a war with France. Two questions arise:

(i) Did Bismarck know about the Hohenzollern candidacy for the Spanish throne before it was made public?
At the time, he denied that he did, but documents released after 1945 make it clear that he was not telling the truth:

'The documents make it clear that Bismarck lied. He had known of the matter from the outset and advised support for the candidacy.' (Breuilly 2001a, pp.153-54)

(ii) Did Bismarck deliberately toughen Wilhelm I's refusal to guarantee that Leopold's candidacy should never be revived?

Wilhelm's reply was sent by telegram to Bismarck first, with permission to send it on to the press. The King was staying at Bad Ems, a health spa, and so the telegram became known as the 'Ems Telegram'. Bismarck shortened the telegram, making it read much more abruptly and sharply:

'The publication of the amended telegram caused eruptions in France. The French newspapers and crowds demanded war. Napoleon, urged on by his wife, his ministers, the Chamber of Deputies and public opinion, declared war on Prussia on 19 July 1870.' (Stiles & Farmer 2001, p.86)

The Franco-Prussian War, 1870-71 (July 1870-January 1871)

The Franco-Prussian War, like that of 1866, was short and ended in a decisive victory for the Prussian army. France was without allies. Austria and Italy seemed possible sources of help, but neither saw any reason to risk war. Russia remained neutral, only prepared to enter the war on Prussia's side if Austria aided France. Bismarck helped to heighten Britain's suspicions about Napoleon III's ambitions. He revealed, in the *Times* newspaper, some documents which showed French interest in the acquisition of Belgium, a country whose independence had been guaranteed by Britain in 1839. French military strength was generally overestimated at the time:

'All depended on the rival armies and here the Prussians proved indisputably superior. French mobilisation was much less efficient. By contrast, within 15 days of the declaration of war, three German armies (of well over 300,000 men) were advancing into the Saarland and Alsace.' (Kennedy 1989, p.240)

The decisive battle was fought at Sedan in September 1870 and it ended with the surrender of Napoleon and over 100,000 French troops. When news of the humiliating surrender reached Paris, a revolutionary government set up a republic (the Second French Republic). As a result, the war dragged on, with Paris under siege, until January 1871.

The final unification

Victory in the Franco-Prussian war led directly to the final unification of Germany and the declaration of the new German Empire on 18 January 1871. At a ceremony held in the splendour of the Hall of Mirrors at the Palace of Versailles, Wilhelm I of Prussia was declared Kaiser (Emperor) of Germany. The four southern German states had been persuaded to join the new Germany:

'A great wave of white-hot patriotic fervour swept the country as a whole including the south.' (Carr 1991, p.115)

The armed conflict with France ended with an armistice in late January 1871 and a peace treaty, the Treaty of Frankfurt, was signed in May - see Box 1.6.

BOX 1.6 | The Treaty of Frankfurt

The Treaty of Frankfurt was much harsher than the Treaty of Prague of 1866. The French had to pay £200,000 and the provinces of Alsace and Lorraine were annexed (taken under German control). The terms were harsh because Bismarck believed that French defeat, irrespective of the peace terms, turned France into an irreconcilable enemy. As a result, he wanted to ensure that it could pose no threat to Germany in the future. The Prussian Chief of Staff, Moltke, believed that the provinces of Alsace-Lorraine were of vital strategic importance in the case of renewed conflict. The fortress at Metz, in Moltke's view, was worth the equivalent of an army of 120,000 men. Critics at the time and since have pointed out that the annexations would remain a source of potential conflict between France and Germany and prevent any possibility of real reconciliation between the two countries.

Adapted from Stiles & Farmer 2001.

MAIN POINTS - Sections 1.1 - 1.2

- In the mid-19th century, Germany was not a unified state. It was a confederation of 39 independent states.
- Economic and social factors played a part in the drive towards unification, as did the rivalry between Austria and Prussia.
- The first attempt to build a unified state came in 1848-49. It was a failure.
- Many historians have seen Otto von Bismarck as the key figure in the unification of Germany after he became Chief Minister in Prussia in 1862. But there is some debate over his role.

- Although Bismarck was a junker, he held unorthodox beliefs. His main aim was to ensure that Prussia dominated Germany.
- Bismarck became Prussian Chief Minister in 1862. The key events leading to unification were - (1) The Schleswig-Holstein Issue (2) the war with Austria in 1866 (3) the Luxembourg Incident (4) the crisis of 1870.
- Prussian victory in the Franco-Prussian war led directly to the final unification of Germany and the declaration of the new German Empire on 18 January 1871.

Activity 1.1 Bismarck and the unification of Germany

ITEM 1 The Schleswig-Holstein Issue

(1) Did Bismarck have a blueprint?

(i) 'It was Bismarck's turn to outmanoeuvre Austria. The crisis in Schleswig-Holstein provided him with the perfect opportunity. From the outset, Bismarck intended to annex the duchies. By the summer of 1865, Bismarck was determined to go to war with Austria.'

(Kitchen 1996, p.197)

(iii) 'The compromise Convention of Gastein, which partitioned the duchies between Prussia and Austria, contained the seeds of future conflict between them, although it is not clear, even at this stage, whether Bismarck was actively seeking to manufacture a conflict.'

(McKinnon-Bell & Cawood 2001, p.10)

(ii) 'Bismarck was satisfied that by 1866 Prussia would be strong enough to challenge Austria. He set the diplomatic stage for that challenge, as well as trying out his new army, by his skillful manipulation of the dispute between Germany and Denmark over Schleswig-Holstein. To act jointly with Austria was both inevitable and desirable; inevitable, because Austria would never agree to let Prussia act alone; desirable because any Prussian-Austrian settlement of so thorny a problem would leave ample room for picking a quarrel with Austria later whenever he chose.'

(Thomson 1962, p.284)

(iv) 'The origins of the Schleswig-Holstein dispute lay above all in popular German and Danish nationalism. None of these events was of Bismarck's making and he was forced to react in the best way he could.'

(Lemieux 2000, p.28)

(2) How important was Bismarck's role?

(i) Otto Pflanze argues that Bismarck's success was 'one of the most amazing feats in the history of politics' and talks of 'the almost inhuman skills of a wizard of the Wilhelmstrasse' (the place where Bismarck's office was located). For two years, Pflanze claims, Bismarck exploited the Austrian desire for cooperation with Prussia, repeatedly tricking and forcing Vienna into abandoning its vital interests, while he steadily advanced those of Prussia.

(ii) Gall sees Bismarck's first objectives as 'negative' ones. By becoming involved in the Schleswig-Holstein Issue he wished 'to prevent any enhancement of the prestige of the German Confederation'. He was also concerned about dangers on the diplomatic front that might arise from the issue. 'Apart from the very general objective that something must come out of it for Prussia in the end, it was largely negative factors at first that governed Bismarck's actions'. His policy was 'largely dictated by circumstances and by changing conditions - in a word "pragmatic".'

ITEM 2 The Seven Weeks War

When Bismarck came to power in 1862, relations with Austria were already severely strained. Prussia kept Austria out of the Zollverein and, when Austria called a meeting of the German Confederation at Frankfurt in 1863, Bismarck persuaded the King of Prussia not to attend. There was no doubt that Bismarck firmly believed, through the 1850s and into the 1860s, that a confrontation with Austria would have to take place. This did not necessarily mean a war, though Bismarck did not rule that out. He did not, however, plan the path that led from the Schleswig-Holstein involvement to the war in 1866. Rather, circumstances were changing. It is easy to underestimate the strength of Austria and exaggerate that of Prussia in the 1860s. Many contemporaries thought that Austria would defeat Prussia in 1866. However, the balance of military and economic strength had moved in Prussia's favour. When the war came in 1866 it was swift and decisive. Most of the larger states of the German Confederation supported Austria because of their concerns about an over-mighty Prussia - Saxony and Hanover in the North and Bavaria, Württemberg and Baden in the South were the larger states who opposed Prussia (see map in Box 1.1). Austria therefore had more troops - 400,000 to 300,000 Prussian, although Austria had to fight on two fronts because of Italy's entrance into the war. A number of factors account for the speed of Prussia's victory in the Seven Weeks War:

- better organisation and leadership under General von Moltke;
- the speed of Prussian mobilisation and movement into Austria, using the railways
- better weapons, especially breech-loading rifles.

The war was also short because, once the Austrians were defeated, Bismarck insisted, against the wishes of the King and the army chiefs, that there was no point in continuing. Austria was no longer a player in a future united Germany, so there was no point in further antagonising the Austrians or alarming allies, like the French.

Adapted from Breuilly 1996, Breuilly 2001 and Carr 1991.

ITEM 3 Bismarck and the Hohenzollern candidacy

Historians generally agree that Bismarck always thought that a war with France was a possibility. Stiles and Farmer, for example, argue that it seems probable that, from 1866, Bismarck expected an eventual war against France and was prepared for one so long as it could appear to be a defensive war, brought about by French aggression. Such a war would serve to bring the southern German states into the Prussian fold since war was a great unifier. Like Stiles and Farmer, Breuilly sees Bismarck's actions over the Spanish candidacy as 'irons in the fire that could be used or dropped if necessary'. He argues, however, that it is going too far to say that Bismarck supported the Hohenzollern candidacy to bring about war. Lemieux argues that, by demanding guarantees against a future Hohenzollern candidacy in Spain, France was aiming at a diplomatic humiliation of Prussia and that it was only when he was faced with a France eager for war

This painting shows the ceremony at Versailles in 1871 when Wilhelm I of Prussia was declared Kaiser (Emperor) of Germany.

that Bismarck actively worked towards war. The re-writing of the Ems Telegram, he suggests, was intended to provoke the already enraged France into declaring war. Waller disagrees. He argues that Bismarck was intent on a showdown with France after 1866 and that he seized the opportunity of the Hohenzollern candidature eagerly. Waller suggests that it would be foolish to argue that Bismarck wanted to avoid war. Those historians who have argued that he aimed for a diplomatic triumph are wrong. His aim all along was to provoke the French into war.

Adapted from Stiles & Farmer 2001, Breuilly 2001a, Lemieux 2001 and Waller 1998.

Questions

1. a) Using Items 1-3 and your own knowledge, draw a timeline showing the key events on the path to German unification.
   b) 'Without Bismarck there would have been no German unification.' Give arguments for and against this statement.

2. Using Items 1 and 3, describe the historical debate over the role played by Bismarck in the unification of Germany.
3. Why was the Seven Weeks War was an important step on the path to German unification? Use Item 2 in your answer.

2 The German political system

Key issues

1. What was the nature of the Bismarckian system?

2. What was the nature of the Kaiserreich of 1890-1914?

2.1 What was the nature of the Bismarckian system?

Bismarck and the liberal nationalists
Bismarck had been appointed as Chief Minister of Prussia to deal with liberal opposition over the army reforms in 1862 (see Section 1.2 above). Until his success in the struggle with Austria in 1866, he was

widely disliked by German liberals (mainly members of the middle class who believed in constitutional reforms which would give Parliament greater powers). Then his position domestically changed dramatically:

'In Prussia on the same day as the Battle of Konnigratz (3 July 1866) whose outcome was yet unknown, new Landtag elections were held. The liberal opposition was defeated by a surge of Prussian patriotism...Bismarck, basking in military triumph, returned to Berlin and a more compliant Parliament.' (Breuilly 2001, p.151)

Bismarck could have used his success to crush the liberals. Instead he introduced an Indemnity Bill (an 'indemnity' is a legal agreement that penalties should not be paid):

'Instead of using his triumph to destroy the Constitutional Party [ie the liberals who aimed for reforms], the Prime Minister made concessions to it...[He] asked for an "indemnity" [exemption] for...all expenditure incurred illegally by the state from 1862 onwards. The request contained no admission of guilt...What the chamber was given, or allowed to give itself, was the semblance of legality.' (Mann 1996, p.178)

This ended the whole affair of the taxes raised for the army reforms since 1862. The liberals split over whether they should accept the measure. If they supported it, they would be making a wrong into right. If they opposed it, they would remain in opposition and take no part in the shaping of the North German Confederation. The majority voted to accept the Indemnity Bill and formed a new party, the National Liberal Party. This party offered Bismarck enthusiastic support for his foreign policy, collaboration at home and, where necessary, what Mann describes as 'vigilant, loyal opposition'.

The episode of the Indemnity Bill illustrates two important aspects of the relationship between Bismarck and the liberal nationalists as a united German state began to take shape.

1. Bismarck won over many liberals

Bismarck, by his success in war, won over many of the liberal nationalists. They were, in effect, prepared to put their nationalism before their constitutional liberalism. Pflanze believes that this is not surprising:

'The liberal aim was not to overthrow royal authority but to influence its policy.' (Pflanze 1963, p.180)

Also, they feared the masses (peasants and members of the working class) and they were not democrats, factors that Bismarck exploited:

'The liberals were victims of their own limited ends, their lack of genuine popular support and their lust for national power.' (Pflanze 1963, p.326)

Gall (1986) also suggests that the liberals surrendered to Bismarck to pursue their own social and economic interests. Mommsen, however, believes that they were not totally outmanoeuvred by Bismarck:

'The liberals did make considerable efforts to achieve progressive reforms of the political system or at least keep open the possibility of such reforms in the 1860s and 1870s.' (Mommsen 1995, p.7)

2. Bismarck was willing to make concessions

According to Mann, Bismarck's actions after Konnigratz reveal a willingness to make some concessions to constitutional government:

'Bismarck had understood that in his day it was no longer possible to govern completely without a constitution or a Parliament. He needed Parliament all the more urgently because it could

help in assimilating the new provinces, the conquered states.' (Mann 1996, p.178)

He had certainly not become a democrat or a liberal overnight, but neither was he a blind conservative. Breuilly sums up his position:

'Bismarck believed that strong, stable government rested on the support of major social forces. These were never precisely defined but bourgeois [middle-class] liberals were clearly included. Bismarck's anti-liberal measures were not attempts to destroy liberalism but to force it into co-operation with him.' (Breuilly 2001a, p.151)

The North German Confederation's Constitution

Bismarck knew that he could manipulate a constitutional system:

'His experience with the Prussian constitution taught him he had little to fear from nationalists, liberals or those farther to the left. As early as 1851, he had likened a constitution to an empty vessel whose contents are determined by those in power.' (Waller 1997, pp.41-2)

He therefore produced what Waller calls 'a reasonably liberal constitution' for the North German Confederation in 1867 - see Box 1.7. Diehard conservatives were horrified by such measures. Their programme was to maintain the monarchical system 'by purely authoritarian means, using the traditional instruments of power - the Prussian monarchy, the army, the civil service and the higher nobility' (Mommsen 1995, p.24). Instead, Bismarck adopted a

---

BOX 1.7 | **The constitution of the North German Confederation, 1867**

The constitution of the North German Confederation set up in 1867 became that of the new German Empire when that was set up in 1871. The constitution provided a Parliament with two Houses. The Lower House - the Reichstag - was elected by universal male suffrage and had the right to pass an annual budget (though its financial control was limited as it did not have control over the military budget which accounted for c.90% of the confederation's spending). The Upper House (the Bundesrat) was made up of representatives from the governments of member states. The Bundesrat was responsible for government, with power in the hands of the Chancellor. Bismarck was appointed Chancellor by the King of Prussia and could only be dismissed by the King. What Germany did not have was parliamentary government. The Parliament had extensive powers, but it lacked one which was crucial. The Chancellor was not responsible to Parliament, but rather to the Bundesrat and the King. To be enacted, laws had to receive the Chancellor's approval as well as that of both Houses of Parliament.

Adapted from Waller 1997.

flexible policy. By doing so, he gained support from the National Liberals.

Bismarck's aims

It was suggested above that Bismarck realised that he could not simply ignore the growing demand of middle-class liberals to play some part in the political process. Mommsen argues that:

'It was Bismarck's aim to deflect the energies of the liberal movement into safe channels by implementing some of its objectives, albeit by authoritarian means, and thus secure its commitment to the existing system.' (Mommsen 1995, pp.24-25)

The war of 1866 had cleared the way for the creation of a 'little Germany' (Kleindeutsch) in which Prussia, as Bismarck wanted, would be the leading power. The Prussian state came first for Bismarck and if that state could be strengthened through dominating a wider German nation, then Bismarck was happy to adopt some of the German nationalists' programme:

'He thought that the German national movement could be manipulated in the interests of enhancing Prussian power.' (Feuchtwanger 2001, p.16)

Lothar Gall suggests that Bismarck realised from the early 1860s that:

'The nationalist hopes of his liberal opponents could be "instrumentalised" - ie he could adopt the foreign policy aspirations of the liberals (national unification on a "small German" basis).' (quoted in John 1991, p.16)

The 'revolution from above'

Pflanze points out the weakness of the German national movement, suggesting that it lacked a broad popular base. Because of this, Bismarck was able to take over the national movement to carry through his 'revolution from above':

'Bismarck stole the national plank from the liberal platform. He owed his success to the absence of any genuine popular movement in Germany. The common view that German nationalism was a current sweeping down the decade to fulfillment in 1870 is a fiction of nationalistic historians.' (Pflanze 1963, pp.12-13)

The way in which a united German state was created - the so-called 'revolution from above' - has generally been seen to have created many of the problems that were to dog Germany's development in the late 19th and early 20th centuries. What Bismarck created was a 'half-way house, a semi-authoritarian system' which was foisted on the whole of Germany:

'[Bismarck] institutionalised this half-way house in the constitution of the North German Confederation in 1867 and extended it to the German Reich [Empire] in 1871. It was a complicated balance between monarchical and parliamentary power, between federalism and unitary control, which rendered Bismarck himself virtually indispensable as the only man who could master the system.' (Feuchtwanger 2001, p.18)

Lothar Gall suggests, however, that even Bismarck could not really control his creation:

'In the end Bismarck was no more than a sorcerer's apprentice.' (Gall 1986, p.377)

In the story of the sorcerer's apprentice, the apprentice could remember the magic formula to bring a flood, but could not remember the words to call it off.

Bismarck's position after 1871

Historical discussions of the system of government set up in 1871 in the newly united German Empire have usually focused on Bismarck's ideas and aims. The 1871 constitution, it is argued, was very much 'Bismarck's devising, tailored to meet his particular requirements' (Seligmann & McLean 2000, p.15). However, historians have differed over what exactly Bismarck's ideas and aims were. Most would agree that he wanted 'a pre-eminent position in Prussia and the Empire after 1871' (Lerman 2001, p.172). Box 1.8 shows the various elements in the constitution and explores what this meant in practice.

The federal structure

As noted in Box 1.8, the new German state created in 1871 had a federal structure:

'The Reich was declared to be a union of 25 separate states with sovereignty residing collectively in the states themselves. As 22 of the states were monarchies, this entrenched the idea of princely sovereignty into the very heart of the new nation...The constitution ensured that in practice a substantial proportion of government was conducted on the level of the sovereign federal states whose existing constitutions were completely unaffected by the creation of the new Reich.' (Seligmann & McLean 2000, p.16)

Historians agree that this arrangement preserved the conservative rule of the major power among the states, namely Prussia. Seligmann and McLean, for example, point out that:

'[As] federal states held responsibility for all governmental functions not explicitly granted to the centre and were also the agencies through which Reich regulations were implemented at a local level, the nature of their constitutions was of the greatest significance in shaping most people's experience of government. Unfortunately, many of these constitutions were highly authoritarian in nature. This was particularly true for the largest and most populous state in the Reich, namely Prussia...Almost all functions of government were reserved for the King and his ministers.' (Seligmann & McLean 2000, p.16)

BOX 1.8 Bismarck's position after 1871

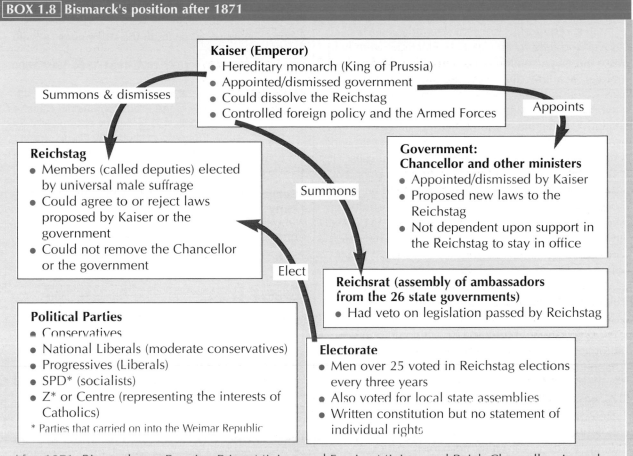

Kaiser (Emperor)
- Hereditary monarch (King of Prussia)
- Appointed/dismissed government
- Could dissolve the Reichstag
- Controlled foreign policy and the Armed Forces

Summons & dismisses

Appoints

Reichstag
- Members (called deputies) elected by universal male suffrage
- Could agree to or reject laws proposed by Kaiser or the government
- Could not remove the Chancellor or the government

Summons

Elect

Government: Chancellor and other ministers
- Appointed/dismissed by Kaiser
- Proposed new laws to the Reichstag
- Not dependent upon support in the Reichstag to stay in office

Reichsrat (assembly of ambassadors from the 26 state governments)
- Had veto on legislation passed by Reichstag

Political Parties
- Conservatives
- National Liberals (moderate conservatives)
- Progressives (Liberals)
- SPD* (socialists)
- Z* or Centre (representing the interests of Catholics)

* Parties that carried on into the Weimar Republic

Electorate
- Men over 25 voted in Reichstag elections every three years
- Also voted for local state assemblies
- Written constitution but no statement of individual rights

After 1871, Bismarck was Prussian Prime Minister and Foreign Minister and Reich Chancellor. As such, he exercised most of the powers theoretically given to the Crown in the constitution, including presiding over the Bundesrat (the Upper House). Bismarck's influence over the Kaiser, Wilhelm I, gave him an immensely strong position which he exploited. Loathing the existence of any rival authority, he ensured that other ministers were little more than senior clerks, carrying out his instructions. There was no form of collective government and no Cabinet. Bismarck was reluctant to confide in his colleagues and distrusted potential rivals. This encouraged him to rely more and more on his son, Herbert, who was Secretary of State at the Foreign Office from 1886. Bismarck's influence was so great that he has sometimes been described as a dictator. But, there were both practical and theoretical limitations on his power, especially in domestic affairs. One constraint was the fact that the new Germany was a federal state (the individual states that had made up the Confederation retained a great deal of independence). The Reichstag was another. Furthermore, Bismarck's long absences from Berlin (he spent much time on his country estates) and his poor health (mainly stomach problems resulting from over-eating and over-drinking) reduced his control of day-to-day decision-making. Most historians today regard him as an opportunist rather than a master-planner. They have also criticised him for his intolerance and bullying. Despite this bullying, he was often thwarted in his efforts to shape the domestic developments of the Reich after 1871.

Adapted from Stiles & Farmer 2001.

Stiles and Farmer, however, argue that the federal nature of the new Reich ensured that non-Prussian interests also had to be taken into account. There were complaints about 'Prussianification', but, in reality, the old Prussia did not survive intact:

'For all the complaints about the "Prussianification" of Germany, the identity of "old Prussia" was significantly diluted by its integration into the Reich. Prussia could no longer be governed without consideration of the wider interests of Germany. Non-Prussians held important posts in government, both in the Reich itself and in Prussia.

It was the new German Reich not Prussia that now engaged the loyalties of most Germans.' (Stiles & Farmer 2001, p.101)

The Reichstag
The Reichstag was a legislative assembly elected by universal male suffrage. It has been described as follows:

'Outwardly...it was one of the most representative popular assemblies to be found anywhere in the world at that time.' (Seligmann & McLean 2000, p.17)

The Reichstag had important legislative functions. All imperial laws, including the budget and the army estimates, required its consent. Deputies (ie MPs) enjoyed the right to free speech. Elections were held every three years (later every five). Universal male suffrage meant the development of mass political parties with popular appeal (see Box 1.9). The outward veneer of liberalism, however, was deceptive. Seligmann and McLean point out that the constitution, upon which the whole legal framework rested, was not a constitution in the normal sense. It was a treaty made between 25 states, an agreement between monarchs which could, in reality, be broken at any time. The threat that the constitution might be suspended or abolished ensured that power remained very much with the Kaiser, the Chancellor and the aristocracy. Furthermore, Stiles and Farmer point out that:

'Most Germans remained deeply respectful of authority, believing that it was right and proper that the Emperor or his Chancellor should rule. There was no widespread conviction that power should be in the hands of the political party which happened to have a majority of seats on the Reichstag. Even members of the more extreme left-wing parties did not expect the Reichstag to exercise such control over government. The most they hoped for was that it would have some influence on government decisions.' (Stiles & Farmer 2001, pp.102-03)

There is some debate over exactly how much influence the Reichstag did exercise. Stiles and Farmer argue that historians have tended to exaggerate the extent to which Bismarck dominated the Reichstag. They argue that there were several occasions in the 1880s when Bismarck seriously considered changing the constitution because he felt that the Reichstag was exerting too much influence.

The Kaiser and the Chancellor
From 1871, the Kaiser was the German Emperor (as well as Prussian King), 'an imperial monarch who headed the political executive and military apparatus, controlled all personnel appointments and enjoyed special powers such as the right to declare war or martial law in an emergency' (Lerman 2001, p.167). He controlled foreign policy, including the right to conclude treaties, the appointment of the Chancellor and all members of the Reich bureaucracy.

The Chancellor was the only minister mentioned in the constitution and was appointed by the Emperor. He presided over the Bundesrat. All imperial decrees and orders had to be countersigned by the Chancellor. He was normally also Chief Minister of Prussia. He was not accountable to the Reichstag and could only be dismissed by the Kaiser. He appointed all government ministers. His only weak point was his dependence on the Kaiser for his

| BOX 1.9 | Political parties 1871-90 |

Party	Number of seats in the Reichstag 1871-90

Party	1871	1874	1877	1878	1881	1884	1887	1890
National Liberals	125	155	128	99	47	51	99	42
	The party of the Protestant middle class. Its main priority was to build a strong German state, though a second aim was to create a liberal constitutional state. Backed Bismarck until 1878.							
Centre Party	58	91	93	94	100	99	98	106
	The Catholic party.							
SPD*	2	9	12	9	12	24	11	35
	Party of the working class with strong ties with the unions.							
German Conservative Party	57	22	40	59	50	78	80	73
	The party of mainly Prussian landowners. Disliked unification. Supported Bismarck after 1878.							
Free Conservatives	37	33	38	57	28	28	41	20
	A party not just of landowners, but of industrialists and the professions. It backed Bismarck throughout.							
The Progressives	47	50	52	39	115	74	32	76
	A liberal party whose priority was to build a liberal constitutional state. Less supportive of Bismarck than the National Liberals.							
National Groups	14	30	30	30	35	32	29	27
	Non-Germans - ie Alsatians, Poles and Danes.							
Guelphs	9	4	10	4	10	11	4	11
	Supporters of the deposed King George.							

*SPD - the Social Democratic Party

Adapted from Stiles & Farmer 2001.

continued appointment. For Bismarck, this was fine as long as Wilhelm I remained alive, but it proved to be his undoing soon after Wilhelm II came to the throne.

The Kulturkampf
In the 1870s, the 'hybrid system' of government inaugurated in 1871 worked reasonably well. The majority party in the Reichstag, the National Liberals, usually worked with Bismarck to secure a number of useful reforms which helped to bring about unity in the new nation - for example:
- the introduction of a national currency and postal and telegraph system
- the creation of the Reichsbank

- the abolition of internal tariffs
- the setting up of a standard legal system.

All of these measures helped to bind together the new empire. The other main area in which Bismarck and the National Liberals worked together was, however, one which was divisive rather than unifying. This was the so-called 'Kulturkampf' (struggle for civilisation or struggle for culture) waged against the Roman Catholic Church in the 1870s:

'During the Kulturkampf a whole variety of legislation was introduced which was designed to undermine the autonomy [freedom] of the Catholic Church in Prussia, to reduce its financial independence and its role in education. The May Laws of 1873 formed the centrepiece of this programme.' (Seligmann & McLean 2000, p.22)

The May Laws were introduced by the Prussian Minister of Religion and Education in May 1873. Stiles and Farmer argue that:

'These aimed to bring the Catholic Church under state control. All candidates for the priesthood now had to attend a secular [non-religious] university before commencing training and all religious appointments became subject to state approval. In 1874, obligatory civil marriage was introduced in Prussia. Clergy could be fined, imprisoned and expelled if they failed to comply with the May Laws. In 1875, the Kulturkampf reached a climax with laws empowering Prussia to suspend subsidies to the Church in dioceses or parishes where the clergy resisted the new legislation and all religious orders, except nursing orders, were dissolved.' (Stiles & Farmer 2001, pp.108-09)

Why was there a struggle with the Catholic Church?

A number of reasons have been put forward by historians for the struggle between the state and the Roman Catholic Church. First, it can be seen as part of a general European clash of ideas. Secular (non-religious), liberal and anti-clerical ideas (support, for example, for a reduction of church power in education) were growing in popularity whilst the Catholic Church was a conservative church opposed to liberal ideas. German liberals urged on the Kulturkampf. Second, the Catholic Centre Party was set up in 1870 and became the second largest party in the Reichstag in 1871, with a wide base and a reforming programme:

'The Centre was unique among German parties in drawing its support from all social strata: aristocracy, middle class and working class...The Centre was also unique among non-socialist parties in its advocacy of social reform.' (Carr 1991, p.125)

Bismarck, historians agree, saw the Centre Party as a political threat:

'Bismarck saw the success of the Centre Party in 1871 as a grave danger to the unity of his new Empire. He thought that the party would encourage civil disobedience among Catholics whenever the policies of the state conflicted with those of the church.' (Stiles & Farmer 2001, p.108)

Carr points out that Catholics were a minority in the new Empire (37% of the population) and were concentrated in southern German states (who had sided with Austria in 1866). Third, the Kulturkampf has been explained by the idea of 'negative integration':

'[Bismarck devised the Kulturkampf as] a manipulative strategy...designed to safeguard the authoritarian system in an age of rapid social and economic change by focusing the attention of ordinary Germans a common enemy, large enough to be credible but not serious enough to threaten the Reich's survival.' (Seligmann & McLean 2000, p.21)

Seligmann and McLean are doubtful about this as an explanation, as is Waller (1997).

The impact of the Kulturkampf

If Bismarck's aim was to dent the Centre Party's electoral success, the Kulturkampf was not a success. Catholics opposed the measures taken against them vigorously and, in the late 1870s, the campaign was dropped. The main reasons why the campaign was dropped are outlined in Box 1.10.

BOX 1.10 Why did the Kulturkampf come to an end?

The major consequence of the Kulturkampf was that the perception of the Catholic minority as a sub-culture within Prussia and the Reich was reinforced. Greater unity among German Catholics and a more highly developed sense of collective identity were the result. The Catholic Centre Party, rather than withering away because of the official onslaught upon it, actually gained greater longevity as a vehicle for Catholic interests as a result. There were also foreign policy reasons for dropping the campaign. In 1879, Germany made an alliance with Catholic Austria. Furthermore, economic problems in the late 1870s prised Bismarck apart from the National Liberals. His break with them in 1879 over free trade (Bismarck came to favour protection whilst the National Liberals were strong supporters of free trade) went hand-in-hand with the dropping of the Kulturkampf. Finally, by the end of the 1870s, the Catholic Church was more conciliatory once a new pope came into office in 1878.

Adapted from Seligmann & McLean 2000.

The 'Great Change' 1878-79

Some historians have identified a 'Great Change' in
Bismarck's domestic policy in the years 1878-79.
According to this view, he switched from working
with the National Liberals in the Reichstag to
cooperating with the conservatives. The result was a
fundamental change in the domestic politics of the
Empire. Other historians, however, believe that the
changes in 1878-79 were far less dramatic or
significant than has been suggested.

What changed?

The first area of change was in economic policy. As
noted above, Bismarck switched to a policy of
protection in 1879 with the passing of the Tariff Law
(the switch was largely in response to pressure from
industrialists and landowners). The National Liberals
were opposed to this move and the party split over
it, with the free traders leaving and joining the
progressives (they formed a new Radical Party in
1884). The second area of change was in the
location of support for Bismarck in the Reichstag.
Between 1871 and 1878, Bismarck generally relied
on support from the National Liberals. After 1878, he
also relied on support from conservatives. In part,
most historians agree, this was a matter of
parliamentary arithmetic. In the election of 1878, the
National Liberals lost 30 seats, meaning that the two
Conservative parties had more seats than the
National Liberals. In addition, the split in the
National Liberal Party in 1879 meant that its left
wing broke away. Those who remained stayed loyal
to Bismarck, but, because he could now rely on the
Conservatives, he was no longer dependent on their
support. The third area of change was the beginning
of Bismarck's campaign against socialism - see
below.

The campaign against the socialists

If the Kulturkampf is an important part of Bismarck's
domestic policy in the early 1870s, his campaign
against socialism played an important part in the late
1870s and 1880s. Stiles and Farmer point out that,
like Catholicism, socialism had an international
appeal (socialists called on workers all over the
world to rise up and overthrow capitalism, replacing
it with a socialist system in which borders between
nation states would be broken down):

'Bismarck was hostile to socialists, regarding them
as anarchic, revolutionary and little better than
criminals. As with Catholicism, he feared the
international appeal of socialist ideology. How
could one be loyal to an international organisation
and to one's own country?' (Stiles & Farmer 2001,
p.112)

The first socialist groups were set up in the 1860s.
There were two wings:

- a moderate wing which aimed to win greater
power for workers by peaceful means

- a radical wing which encouraged the workers to
rise up and overthrow capitalism by force, if
necessary.

In 1875, the two wings united when the Social
Democratic Party (SPD) was set up. This new party
supported the overthrow of capitalism, but it also
supported the 'legal path' to revolution. Stiles and
Farmer claim that Bismarck overestimated the threat
that the SPD posed:

'Socialists were not as strong or as revolutionary as
[Bismarck] feared and as they liked to appear.
However, his fears were rational. Socialism was a
threat to the kind of society Bismarck intended to
maintain. Socialists did preach class warfare.
Moreover, socialist support was growing.' (Stiles &
Farmer 2001, p,112)

In 1876, Bismarck attempted to pass an Anti-Socialist
Law, but the Reichstag rejected it. Then, in 1878,
there were two assassination attempts on the Kaiser.
This provided Bismarck with an opportunity to
dissolve the Reichstag, fight an election campaign on
an anti-socialist platform and then, once the
Reichstag was dominated by conservatives, to pass
the Anti-Socialist Law he wanted:

'Bismarck exploited the crisis atmosphere these
[assassination attempts] created to dissolve the
Reichstag and to fight an election on an anti-
revolutionary platform directed against the SPD
and the left liberals. As a result, a majority in the
Reichstag was secured for an Anti-Socialist Law,
banning the SPD and thus making it difficult for
that party to operate within the Reich.' (Seligmann
& McLean 2000, p.25)

Although some historians have argued that, like the
Kulturkampf, the Anti-Socialist Law can be explained
by the idea of 'negative integration', Seligmann and
McLean deny this, arguing that:

'The real targets of the Anti-Socialist Law were the
left wing of the National Liberals and the
Progressives, not the SPD itself.' (Seligmann &
McLean 2000, pp.25-26)

Whether that is the case or not, the law seems to
have had a similar effect to the Kulturkampf. Support
for the SPD continued to grow - see Box 1.11.

State socialism

Bismarck did not just use negative tactics to
challenge what he saw as the socialist menace. He
also introduced, in the 1880s, a series of welfare
measures for working people, measures which
provided them with significant relief in times of
difficulty. These measures included:

- accident insurance
- medical insurance
- disability insurance
- old age pensions.

By introducing these measures, Germany became a
leader in social welfare, well ahead, for example, of
Britain where such relief was not introduced until

BOX 1.11 The impact of the campaign against socialism

Members of the SPD were not banned from standing for the Reichstag or state governments. After the setback of 1878, the SPD won increasing support. By 1890, it had over a million voters and 35 seats. In fact the Anti-Socialist Law had the same traumatic effect on socialists that the May Laws had on the Catholics. It rallied the faithful and fortified them in their beliefs. In an age when religion was under fire, socialism became a secular religion for thousands of workers outside the influence of the churches. The Centre Party and the SPD both developed social and cultural activities to bind together members. Twelve years of persecution deepened the fortress mentality of the German working class. The party became more radical and class conscious. At a conference in Switzerland in 1880, the party agreed to fight for its goals 'by all means'. The Anti-Socialist Law was enforced rigorously. SPD leaders were arrested and socialist newspapers shut down. The party went underground. It held conferences and published journals as before, but operated from outside Germany. By 1890, it was a well-disciplined and highly organised mass party. A model for those in other European countries. Bismarck's policy failed to bring the socialists to heel. Worst of all, his policy prevented the growing working class from integrating in the new Reich.
Adapted from Carr 1991.

after 1910. Waller argues that:

'The extraordinarily ambitious idea of comprehensive insurance met several needs. The workers would benefit considerably from the security offered by the state and would therefore perhaps be profoundly grateful...The influence of the state and the Chancellor would be enhanced and there would be possibilities for further influence. The determined resistance of the liberals to these proposals would increase their isolation.' (Waller 1997, p.71)

Waller suggests that the liberals would oppose such measures. The reason for this is that liberals supported a 'laissez-faire' approach. 'Laissez-faire' is French for 'leave alone'. Supporters of a laissez-faire approach oppose government intervention. They want a completely free market in which the government leaves them alone. This leaves little scope for social reform.

The fall of Bismarck in 1890

The weakness of the system that Bismarck set up from his personal point of view was that he depended entirely for his position on the Kaiser. In 1888, Kaiser Wilhelm I died. He was succeeded by his son, Friedrich, but Friedrich died three months later from cancer. He was succeeded, in turn, by his son, Wilhelm II:

'[Wilhelm II] was a convinced German nationalist and was totally committed to the belief that he ruled by divine right...After Friedrich's death, Bismarck's position seemed secure again...But a great gulf separated the two, not least age. Treating Wilhelm in a condescending manner, Bismarck assumed he would not involve him much in matters of government. He underestimated the new Kaiser. Wilhelm was determined to rule as well as to reign and resolved to dispense with Bismarck as decently as possible.' (Stiles & Farmer 2001, p.125)

Relations between Bismarck and the new Kaiser deteriorated rapidly in the early months of 1890 and Bismarck finally resigned in March.

MAIN POINTS - Section 2.1

- Although he came from a conservative background, Bismarck was not a blind conservative. He was prepared to make concessions to win the support of liberals. The Indemnity Bill of 1866 and the constitution of the North German Confederation are examples.
- The way in which a united German state was created - the so-called 'revolution from above' which set up a semi-authoritarian political system - created many of the problems in the period 1871-1914.
- Under the terms of the 1871 constitution, Germany was a federal state. Laws had to be passed by the Reichstag. The Kaiser had the power to declare war, to control foreign policy and to appoint the Chancellor. The Chancellor was the only minister mentioned in the constitution, but was not accountable to the Reichstag.
- The 'Kulturkampf' was a 'struggle for culture' waged against the Catholic church in the 1870s. Legislation was passed, curbing the independence of the Catholic Church in Prussia. If the aim was also to reduce support for the Centre Party then it failed.
- Some historians have identified a 'Great Change' in the years 1878-79. Bismarck moved from (1) free trade to protection (2) relying on the Liberals to the Conservatives (3) targeting Catholics to socialists. Other historians, however, believe that the changes were far less significant than has been suggested.
- The Chancellor's reliance on the Kaiser led to Bismarck's downfall once Wilhelm I died and Wilhelm II took over.

Activity 1.2 Germany in 1890

ITEM 1   The downfall of Bismarck

Unlike Bismarck, Wilhelm II was confident that he could win over the working class by a modest extension of the welfare system, including an end to child labour and Sunday working. Bismarck preferred a further attack on socialism. In 1889, he proposed to make the Anti-Socialist Law permanent. Wilhelm wanted the measure watered down. Bismarck refused. But then, in January 1890, the Reichstag rejected the Bill - a sign that Bismarck's power was crumbling - and new elections were called. During the election campaign, Wilhelm produced a proclamation promising new social legislation. The absence of Bismarck's counter-signature caused a sensation. Bismarck had refused to sign. The election in February 1890 was a disaster for Bismarck. His Conservative and National Liberal allies lost 85 seats whilst the Radicals gained 46 seats and the SPD 24. Bismarck was trapped between a Kaiser determined to have his own way and a hostile Reichstag. In March, Bismarck and Wilhelm quarrelled about the right of ministers to advise the Kaiser. Bismarck revived an old order from 1852 which meant that ministers could only approach the Kaiser if they went first to the Chancellor. The Kaiser refused to accept this. Bismarck nearly threw an inkpot at the Kaiser and then annoyed him by showing him a letter written by the Tsar of Russia and critical of Wilhelm's talents. In response Wilhelm sent Bismarck an ultimatum - resign or be dismissed. Three days later, Bismarck, with ill grace, sent a letter of resignation.

This cartoon shows Kaiser Wilhelm II watching as Bismarck, the captain ('pilot'), leaves his ship. The cartoon appeared in Punch magazine on 29 March 1890, with the title 'Dropping the Pilot'.

Adapted from Stiles & Farmer 2001.

ITEM 2   Bismarck's legacy (1)

Most historians, while not necessarily denying that Bismarck's system had some positive aspects, argue that the government structure he created was, from the start, a poisoned chalice for his successors. There are two main reasons for taking this view. First, the system was designed to preserve power for the traditional old forces which Bismarck represented. It did not take into account the changes that Germany was undergoing. This might not have been such a great problem if German society had been stable, but it was not. Following unification, Germany was hit by an agricultural crisis at the same time as it was going through a period of rapid industrialisation. Both developments made a big impact on Germany's economic and social system, creating a momentum for change which heightened existing class differences. By the time Bismarck fell from power, class conflicts had become intense and the nation was divided. Working-class dissent, when combined with the growing power produced by their increasing numbers (due to industrialisation), was leading to demands for political representation of a kind the constitution denied. This demand could not be

Bismarck.

ignored. The second factor was that Bismarck did not consider what would happen after he fell from power. He devised a system that met his needs and he did so bearing his relationship with Wilhelm I closely in mind. He knew that Wilhelm I would allow him complete freedom so long as he followed a mainly conservative agenda designed first and foremost to keep the monarchy in power and to maintain Prussia's place in the world. As these were also Bismarck's aims, he could govern without difficulty. The problem was that the system relied on Chancellor and Kaiser being of like mind. Without that, the system would break down.

Adapted from Seligmann & McLean 2000.

ITEM 3 Bismarck's legacy (2)

Historians are involved in a fierce debate over how best to assess Bismarck's career. In all, there are four separate approaches. First, there is the approach taken by Lothar Gall. He was the historian who described Bismarck as a 'sorcerer's apprentice'. To Gall, Bismarck was not up to his task. Gall doesn't like what Bismarck did and argues that, under him, Germany was out of control. The second approach is that championed by Michael Stürmer. He argues that Bismarck was a clever politician who used the constitution and parliamentary institutions as a cover for his dictatorial government. Wars or the threats of wars were the master's instruments to keep the population cowed or distracted. Stürmer's Bismarck is larger than life. He is very much a manipulator, a sorcerer even, but certainly not the sorcerer's apprentice. The third approach is that of Ernst Engelberg. He sees Bismarck as a unique historical individual and as a conservative statesman, an authentic Prussian. Engelberg argues that, far from being progressive or radical, German liberals were conservative - they merely wanted a constitution granting them some small voice in affairs. This being the case, Bismarck was able to work with them, using them for his own purposes - to extend Prussian power and preserve traditional Prussian customs (ie he had conservative aims). The final approach is that of Bruce Waller. He argues that Bismarck was a liberal moderniser. According to this view, Imperial Germany was, in many ways, 'liberal' and 'modern'. True it was conservative in that the federal structure kept power from the Reichstag, in that the Bundesrat contained representatives opposed to liberal reform and in that the Chancellor was not responsible to Parliament. But the Reichstag was a liberal institution and it did have extensive power. It also had a democratic element - universal male suffrage. Furthermore, each state had a constitution and its own Parliament. As a result, by 1890, Germany had several times the number of people experienced in parliamentary affairs as Britain. Finally, it is common knowledge that Germany's economy was developing very rapidly. What is often forgotten is that the aristocrats were losing out. Their estates were going into middle-class hands and the aristocrats lost influence all round.

Adapted from Waller 1991.

Questions

1. Using Items 1-3 and your own knowledge, evaluate the strengths and weakness of the Bismarckian system.
2. Judging from Item 1, why did Bismarck fall from power in 1890?

3. a) What was Bismarck's legacy? Use Items 2 and 3 in your answer.
   b) Which of the four approaches outlined in Item 3 best describes the approach in Item 2? Explain how you know.

2.2 What was the nature of the Kaiserreich of 1890-1914?

Economic and social change after 1890

Bismarck's fall from power ushered in a new era in Germany. From March 1890, when Bismarck resigned, to November 1918, when Kaiser Wilhelm II was forced to resign in the wake of defeat in the First World War, most historians agree that the Kaiser was an important figure. That is why this period is often described as the 'Kaiserreich'. Katherine Lerman argues that Germany underwent significant economic and social change during the Kaiserreich:

'The transition from the Bismarckian era of unification and national consolidation to the Wilhelmine era, where the political agenda was shaped by the rise of a new kind of popular politics and the desire to secure Germany's place in the world, represented a significant change in the lives of most subjects of the Kaiserreich...The changes in the political landscape from the late

1880s reflected the rapid transformation of Germany's economy and society.' (Lerman 2001, p.199)

The growth of industry and trade 1890-1914

Most historians place great emphasis on the economic strength of Germany in the Wilhelmine period. The conventional view is that:

'Wilhelm II came to the throne of a state whose economy had already successfully completed what economic historians call the "take-off" into sustained economic growth. By 1890, further economic development had led to the predominance of the industrial sector over its agricultural counterpart. And yet, despite the occasional downturn in the trade cycle, for example in 1891 and 1901, the years 1890 to 1914 were to witness another period of economic expansion.' (Layton 1995, p.10)

Layton argues that the large percentage of annual growth in the economy as a whole (c.7-8% per year) was the result of advances not just in older industries like coal, iron and textiles, but even more strikingly in the so-called 'new' industries such as steel, chemicals and electrics. By 1914, he points out, Germany had overtaken Britain (the first country to industrialise and the most advanced) in terms of iron production and was catching up with it in terms of coal production.

The historian William Carr emphasises the expansion of German trade (exports rose in value from £173.25 million in 1872 to £538.51 million in 1914). He argues that:

'It is a significant comment on the changing balance of economic power in Europe that in 1913 the German share of world trade almost equalled that of Britain and was already twice the French share.' (Carr 1991, p.167)

The reasons for such rapid economic growth are examined in Box 1.12.

BOX 1.12 Reasons for rapid economic growth

Rapid economic growth was a consequence of:
- population growth - the sheer number of Germans increased significantly
- the availability and accessibility of raw materials
- the transport system, especially the development of a railway network
- the banking system and investment
- the education system, especially technical education
- state help - for example, the government placed tariffs on imports and passed legislation allowing cartels (ie groups of businesses which worked together to control prices, regulate production, marketing).

Adapted from Carr 1991 and Layton 1995.

It should be noted that many historians see a link between Germany's industrial growth and its military strength. Paul Kennedy, for example, who sees the rise of Great Powers as closely linked to their industrial development, argues that a major factor in Germany's rise to power was 'the sheer speed and extent of Germany's growth in industrial, commercial and military/naval terms' (Kennedy 1989, p.270). He mentions too the striking difference in the level of literacy amongst German army recruits compared with those of its rivals. The figures below show the number of army recruits out of 1,000 who were illiterate:
- Italy - 330
- Austria-Hungary - 220
- France - 68
- Germany - one.

Agriculture

Agriculture in Germany, in contrast to industry, did not fare so well in the period 1890-1914:

'Agriculture was in relative decline vis-à-vis

industry and those landowners who failed to modernise production methods or who did not adapt to changing market conditions were likely to find their financial position under threat.' (Layton 1995, p.14)

Berghahn agrees. He argues as follows:

'That there was still money to be made in agriculture is reflected in the increased use of sophisticated machinery like tractors and steam threshers to achieve productivity gains. But these gains could not overcome a broader structural handicap that inexorably caused agriculture to fall behind industry in the long run: industry was simply more productive.' (Berghahn 2001, p.188)

Berghahn points out that, in the 1880s, the share of agriculture in the GNP (Gross National Product) was 35-40% while industry's share was 30-35%. By 1914, agriculture had fallen back to 25% with industry at 45% and the commercial and service sector at 30%.

Social changes 1890-1914

The social changes that resulted from the economic developments outlined above were of great significance during the period of the Kaiserreich:

'The most pronounced growth and change, and hence social stress came in the period 1890-1910.' (Porter & Armour 1991, p.21)

One cause of this 'stress' was the movement of large numbers of people, mostly from rural to urban areas:

'Whereas, in 1890, 47% of Germans were city dwellers, by 1910 the figure was 60%. In 1871, only eight German towns had more than 100,000 inhabitants; in 1910 there were 48, accounting for 21% of the population.' (Porter & Armour 1991, p.24)

Such changes meant that 'millions of ordinary people were forced to come to terms with fundamental changes in their way of life' (Layton 1995, p.13). Berghahn suggests that the changeover to an industrial society produced 'major social dislocations'. Poverty in rural areas drove people (the young especially) into towns. Here wages were usually better and there was 'a new prosperity and general improvement in material conditions' (Berghahn 2001, p.188).

Lack of social mobility

Layton points out that, while overall there was economic growth, many people remained in poverty:

'Living and working conditions remained dismally poor. For most working people, life was divided between long hours in often unhealthy workplaces and the cold cramped accommodation which represented home.' (Layton 1995, p.15)

In general, historians agree that Germany failed to achieve social mobility (ie very few members of the lower classes rose up into the middle classes):

'German society remained divided along traditional class lines and what mobility there was tended to be within a class rather than movement between different classes.' (Layton 1995, p.14)

This lack of social mobility was, according to Berghahn, particularly true of the working class (who are sometimes called 'blue-collar workers'):

'Most blue-collar workers found a clear line existed between them and the middle classes higher up the scale.' (Berghahn 2001, p.191)

For those who were higher in the social hierarchy, there was also little movement between classes. In spite of the relative decline in agriculture, for example, the landed nobility, particularly the Prussian Junkers, remained powerful, especially in political circles. The rigid class divides in Germany during the period 1890-1914 are explored in Box 1.13.

BOX 1.13 | **Class divisions and attempts to check the growth of the SPD**

Whatever the social differences between members of the aristocracy and the newly wealthy industrialists, there was a great deal of cooperation between the two groups whenever their interests coincided. Furthermore, other middle-class groups, including bureaucrats and academics, small business men and 'white collar' (ie middle-class) office employees, all tended to be conservative both socially and politically. The ruling élite continued to regard the working class (now the majority of German citizens) as a danger to the system. In reality, though, the working class was not a threat. The two main working-class bodies - the SPD and the trade unions' central organisation, the General Commission of Trade Unions, were, in reality, moderate. It is true that the leadership of the SPD continued to talk about a socialist revolution, but increasingly SPD supporters came to believe that a policy of 'gradualism' or 'reformism' was the best way to create a socialist society. The middle classes, however, continued to feel threatened by the 'masses below' and united to confine them permanently to a ghetto - physically in terms of residential patterns and socially by denying them access to channels of upward mobility. The state encouraged this class divide, first by passing anti-socialist legislation and later, from 1890 (when the anti-socialist laws lapsed), by police harassment and vigorous prosecution in the courts. Another means of holding back socialism was by extending the state welfare measures begun under Bismarck. But state welfarism could not prevent the progressive polarisation of national politics prior to 1914. This is indicated by the growing number of SPD deputies in the Reichstag.

Adapted from Layton 1995 and Berghahn 2001.

Political mobilisation after 1890

Trying to work Bismarck's system (see Section 2.1 above) without Bismarck was a problem for his successors. His constitutional structure left only very limited scope for adaptation to changing circumstances. And circumstances were changing fundamentally. Germany was in the midst of a radical and rapid social and economic transformation.

One consequence of this social and economic transformation was the emergence of pressure groups on the conservative right. These groups, along with the organisations of the left discussed in Box 1.13, contributed to a process of political mobilisation:

'As the electorate expanded and became more politicised...the older political process, which had [been in place] during the Bismarck era and depended on a significant proportion of the German population remaining outside the political process, was replaced by a new form of popular politics...Political parties, which had formerly functioned successfully as loose associations of prestigious notables who came together mainly to win elections, were now challenged by demands from new social groups...To survive in the 1890s, political parties had to become better organised.' (Lerman 2001, p.200)

The most prominent standard-bearers of the right were the nationalist organisations such as:

- the Pan-German League (set up in 1891)
- the Navy League (set up in 1898)
- the Imperial League against Social Democracy (set up in 1904)
- the Army League (set up in 1912).

These bodies often held extreme views - they were anti-Semitic (blamed the problems facing Germany on the Jews), anti-democratic, strongly nationalistic and expansionist (they believed that Germany should extend its colonies abroad).

Many historians have made a link between these ideas and those of the Nazis (see Unit 4, Section 1.4 and Unit 6, Section 1.2). There is, however, a debate about the importance of these pressure groups. The membership of the Pan-German League, for example, was not large - at most 25,000 - and there is no evidence that it exerted direct influence on government policy. Despite this, Carr believes that the group did influence government policy indirectly. Eley agrees, arguing that:

'The nationalist pressure groups were a noisy and disruptive presence in German politics and played no small part in radicalising its tone.' (quoted in Seligmann & McLean 2000, p.90)

The Agrarian League

One pressure group that certainly did have some effect on government was the Agrarian League (set up in 1893). It was formed in opposition to attempts by Caprivi, Bismarck's successor, to reduce tariffs on agricultural goods and, by 1900, it had 250,000 members. Although its leadership was drawn mainly from conservative Junker landowners, recent research suggests that it had popular support. Lerman (2001, p.203) argues that the Conservative Party adapted its programme to win the support of the Agrarian League.

Political parties, 1890-1914

Layton points out that, after 1890, the balance of power in the Reichstag shifted significantly (see Box 1.14). The right-wing parties (the Conservatives, Free Conservatives and National Liberals), which usually backed the government, were in decline:

'In 1887, they gained 48% of the popular vote and 55% of the seats in the Reichstag (220); by the time of the last pre-war election of 1912 their share of the vote was down to 26% which in turn gave them 26% of the Reichstag seats (102).' (Layton 1995, p.21)

On the other hand, the parties which were more critical of the government (Left Liberals, Centre Party and SPD) increased their strength, especially the SPD:

'In 1887 the SPD had polled 10.1% of the vote and gained 2.8% of seats (11); in 1912 the figures were 34.8% and 27.7% (110).' (Layton 1995, p.23)

As a result of these changes, governments in the period 1890-1914 found it difficult to gain majority support in the Reichstag for the Bills they produced.

BOX 1.14 Election results 1877-1914

Party	1887	1890	1893	1898	1903	1907	1912
German Conservatives	80	73	72	56	54	60	43
Free Conservatives	41	20	28	23	21	24	14
National Liberals	99	42	53	46	51	54	45
Centre	98	106	96	102	100	105	91
Left Liberals	32	76	48	49	36	49	42
Social Democrats	11	35	44	56	81	43	110
Minorities	33	38	35	34	32	29	33
Right-Wing Splinter Parties	3	7	21	31	22	33	19
Total	397	397	397	397	397	397	397

The system of government under the Kaiser

The Kaiser appointed four Chancellors in the period between Bismarck's resignation in 1890 and the outbreak of war in 1914:

- Caprivi (1890-94)
- Hohenlohe (1894-1900)
- Bülow (1900-09)
- Bethmann-Hollweg (1909-17).

Caprivi (1890-94) and the 'New Course'

Bismarck's replacement, General Leo von Caprivi, has been described as 'more astute and independent-minded than the Kaiser had bargained for' (Layton 1995, p.30) and 'an intelligent, highly principled man with a mind of his own' (Porter & Armour 1991, p.10). His policy, which he called a 'New Course', was an attempt to bring about what Lerman (2001, p.209) describes as 'responsible government'. According to Porter and Armour, his aim was to produce:

- less autocratic control of the government by the Chancellor
- more initiative from ministers
- more cooperation with the Reichstag
- social reform to gain the working class's loyalty to the established order
- lower tariffs which would improve Germany's export trade and enable German industry to expand. (Porter & Armour 1991, p.10)

Although Caprivi had some success in passing social reform through the Reichstag (he passed measures banning work on Sunday and limiting child and female labour in 1891, for example), he largely failed to carry through his programme. According to Lerman:

'[Caprivi] was simultaneously subjected to remorseless monarchical pressure, humiliating parliamentary defeats and damaging attacks.' (Lerman 2001, p.209)

Clark, a recent biographer of the Kaiser, sees the activities of the Kaiser as meddling rather than 'remorseless'. He argues that the Kaiser certainly helped to undermine Caprivi, but he was not completely in control:

'Throughout the early to mid-1890s there was a gap between Wilhelm's wishful absolutist rhetoric and the constrained position he occupied in reality. His freedom to make use of his powers of appointment, for example, was limited. If a Chancellor was determined enough, his orders could be countermanded.' (Clark 2000, pp.71-72)

Other forces hastened the fall of Caprivi - in particular opponents to his tariff reforms - see Box 1.15.

Hohenlohe and the 'policy of concentration'

Hohenlohe was an aged aristocrat whose period as Chancellor saw the rise of a group of ministers 'closely in tune with the Kaiser's wish to embark on what he saw as "personal rule"' (Layton 1995, p.32). These ministers increasingly took over the government, leaving Hohenlohe as a figurehead, until he was finally replaced by the most prominent of the group close to the Kaiser, namely Count Bernhard Bülow, in 1900. Other key figures in the group were:

BOX 1.15 **Caprivi's downfall**

Ever since 1879, Germany had protected both agriculture and industry by imposing tariffs - taxes on imports. However, prompted by wheat shortages which had led to a marked rise in food prices and by the need to stimulate German exports, Caprivi negotiated a series of commercial treaties with Austria-Hungary, Italy, Russia and a number of smaller states. These agreements allowed a reduction of German tariffs on agricultural goods in return for favourable rates for German exports. The result was lower food prices in Germany and greater economic growth with the result that most parties - except the Conservatives - supported this policy. At first, Wilhelm II supported Caprivi on the grounds that kindness would kill socialism. But his advisers, especially those who were landowners, were deeply opposed to tariff reduction (because it made the food they produced cheaper and less profitable). In addition, in 1893, the Agrarian League was set up to lobby against tariff reduction. There was also resentment against Caprivi in military circles because Caprivi reduced the length of conscription from three to two years. Conservative opposition to Caprivi's New Course reinforced Wilhelm's growing doubts and in 1894 matters came to a head. Frightened by a wave of attacks by anarchists throughout Europe and concerned by the gains made by the SPD in the election of 1893, Wilhelm pressed Caprivi to introduce an Anti-Socialist Subversion Bill. Caprivi refused, but his refusal only resulted in an even more extraordinary plan by Wilhelm to set aside the powers of the Reichstag, crush socialism and set up a more authoritarian system centred on the Kaiser himself. This was the final straw for Caprivi. He managed to talk the Kaiser out of taking such a course of action and then he resigned. Caprivi aimed to remove the major causes of discord that had been developing under Bismarck by attempting to create a genuine base of parliamentary support for his government. But the main effect of the New Course was to unleash the forces of the right. He alienated the traditional forces of power and influence. He was abused by the conservative press. And he was the focus of opposition intrigue at court. In the end, he could not rely on the consistent support of the Kaiser.
Adapted from Layton 1995 and Seligmann & McLean 2000.

- Admiral von Tirpitz, Navy Secretary
- Count Posadowsky, Interior Minister
- Dr Joannes von Miquel, the Prussian Finance Minister
- Ernst von Köller, Prussian Minister of the Interior.

Behind the scenes, Philipp Eulenburg exerted a great deal of influence. According to Porter and Armour:
'[Eulenburg was] a personal favourite of the Emperor, who for years fed Willhelm's delusions of "personal rule" with every form of gross flattery.' (Porter & Armour 1991, p.11)
During the period when Hohenlohe was Chancellor

(1894-1900), the group around the Kaiser attempted to implement a 'policy of concentration', the aim being (according to Carr) to encourage members of the middle class to support the Kaiser. Carr notes that:
'Fear of socialism and anarchism...brought landowners and industrialists together again. The alliance of "steel and rye" had broken down in 1892 when Caprivi reduced agricultural tariffs; by the end of the 1890s it was fully restored...It was the emperor's advisers...who devised the new "policy of concentration" to rally the middle classes round the monarchy. Caprivi's social reforms had failed to win over the working class; all it had done was drive the middle classes, the natural supporters of monarchy, into opposition. To redress the balance, Miquel and Köller advocated the defence of middle-class interests plus strong measures against socialism.' (Carr 1991, pp.171-72)

The government introduced two Bills - a Subversion Bill in 1894 and an Anti-Union Bill in 1899 - both of which were designed to clamp down on socialism. Individual German states also took action against socialism. The implications of this are explored in Box 1.16.

BOX 1.16 **The 'policy of concentration'**

The attacks on socialism added up to a highly dangerous and outdated policy calculated to polarise German society into two hostile camps - the forces of law, order and respectability on the one hand, and the forces of radical dissent and non-conformity on the other. Stresses and strains were inevitable in a society where the working class was growing in strength but where the groups which had traditionally held power clung strongly to their privileges. In these circumstances, the adoption of policies deliberately directed against the working class made the situation explosive in the extreme. As it turned out, though, the danger of German society exploding was avoided for the following reasons:
1. The middle classes did not respond as the Kaiser's advisers hoped. The Bills were not passed by the Reichstag. Only the Conservatives supported them.
2. Hohenlohe opposed the policy of concentration and was a moderating force.
3. The socialists acted with caution and great restraint, making sure that they avoided a direct confrontation with the state.

Because the middle classes failed to support the policy of concentration, a state of deadlock existed between government and Reichstag. The government would not introduce legislation acceptable to the majority and the majority refused to accept Bills presented by the government. In the past, governments had usually won. This time, the government gave way.
Adapted from Carr 1991.

The Kaiser and 'personal rule'

It was noted in Section 2.1 above that the main reason why Kaiser Wilhelm engineered Bismarck's downfall was because he wanted to play an active political role himself. He wanted, in other words, 'personal rule':

'It was always Wilhelm's intention to rule rather than to reign. This had been noted by observers as far back as the mid-1880s. However the practical exercise of the powers of the Crown had been so eroded in the Bismarck era that the process of their restoration proved to be a lengthy one. For Wilhelm himself, "personal rule" was perhaps an end in itself...The real architect of personal rule was Philipp Eulenburg...Eulenburg's political instincts proved indispensable to the Kaiser, notably during the years 1894-97 when the struggle between the court and the responsible government was at its height.' (Seligmann & McLean 2000, p.92)

Seligmann and McLean identify two main obstacles that had to be overcome before the Kaiser could achieve 'personal rule':

1. Many ministers still thought of themselves as members of an independent government rather than as servants of the Kaiser. The Kaiser considered engineering a coup on several occasions but, each time, followed Eulenberg's advice and held back (a coup could have led to civil war and the break-up of the Empire).

2. The personality of the Kaiser was a problem. A number of senior politicians had doubts whether he was the right person to lead Germany.

Seligmann and McLean argue that Wilhelm overcame the first obstacle in 1897 by the appointment of Admiral von Tirpitz as State Secretary at the Naval Office (in charge of naval expansion) and Bülow as State Secretary at the Foreign Office (in charge of Weltpolitik - see below). Hohenlohe remained Chancellor until 1900, but he was excluded from decision-making:

'Between 1897 and 1900, Wilhelm II was his own Chancellor. Meetings of the Crown Council no longer involved genuine discussions, but simply decided how best to implement the Kaiser's preferred policies.' (Seligmann & McLean 2000, pp.93-94)

During the period 1897-1900:

- the Kaiser introduced major pieces of legislation including two Naval Bills
- a new policy of 'Sammlung' (rallying together) was introduced - efforts were made to win the loyalty of the middle class.

It is important to note that Wilhelm's power was not absolute, but there had been an important change:

'The Kaiser's power was not absolute in these years. The need to secure majorities in the Prussian Lantag [state Parliament] and Reichstag for legislation still limited his freedom of manoeuvre...However, what had changed as compared with the early years of the reign was that his wishes were no longer thwarted by ministers in the executive. Wilhelm's control over appointments, his direct interventions in policy-making, and his ability to thwart certain courses of action from being adopted by making his opposition known, had all combined to make him the dominant figure within the Prusso-German political system by the end of the century.' (Seligmann & McLean 2000, p.94)

The appointment of Bülow as Chancellor

Bülow replaced Hohenlohe as Chancellor in October 1900. The importance of this appointment is explored in Box 1.17.

BOX 1.17   The appointment of Bülow as Chancellor

Wilhelm himself had identified Bülow as his 'Bismarck'. Eulenburg, in turn, saw Bülow as the individual best suited to act as Chancellor under the Kaiser's 'personal regime'. At first, Bülow was allowed to exercise a degree of autonomy (independence). This was due in part to Wilhelm's lack of interest in domestic affairs, but also to the fact that Bülow was the first Chancellor whom the Kaiser trusted absolutely. In July 1901, Wilhelm told Eulenburg: 'Since I have him, I can sleep peacefully. I leave things to him and know that everything will be alright'. In general terms, the first five years of Bülow's Chancellorship were years of political stability domestically. This was because he sought to avoid trouble. Controversial legislation was avoided as far as possible. But even during this period Bülow was constrained first by the need to gain majorities in the Reichstag and second by the need to retain the support of the Kaiser. These two priorities were often in conflict. In essence, Bülow's standing with the Reichstag was not the key to his position. The Reichstag couldn't remove him. His decisive relationship was with Wilhelm. Everything rested on his ability to preserve the Kaiser's trust and confidence. He was a prisoner in a political system he had helped to create - one where everything turned on the wishes of Wilhelm himself. All high officials, including Bülow himself, had to strive to maintain the Kaiser's favour to retain office. As a result they were forced to compromise and sometimes to pursue courses of action which they saw as ill advised. This political climate went hand in hand with the development of an extravagant and grotesque court culture, wholly at odds with the modern age.

Adapted from Seligmann & McLean 2000.

The impact of Weltpolitik

Layton agrees that there was an important turning point in 1897, not just because the Kaiser made significant appointments, but also because there was a clear change of direction in policy:

'Hohenlohe was no match for the intrigue at court and in government circles and, by 1897, a clique of political figures had emerged which sympathised with the Kaiser's wish to embark on what he saw as "personal rule"...The emergence of this government team has led many historians to view 1897 as an important turning point in German history for it coincided with the drive to achieve world power status for Germany by espousing Weltpolitik - colonial annexations, the creation of economic spheres of influence and the expansion of naval power to complement the strength of the army.' (Layton 1995, p.32)

The Kaiser's support for Weltpolitik ensured that the direction of German foreign policy changed (see Section 3.2 below). It also had implications for domestic policy. For example, some historians have argued that the aim was to rally patriotic support against 'enemies of the state' like the socialists. Also, some historians have argued that such a policy was supposed to overcome the problem of wheeling and dealing with the Reichstag. If that was its aim, however, then it failed. Layton points out that the Bülow government faced two main difficulties:

1. The issue of tariffs which arose again.
2. Military expenditure (especially on the expansion of the navy) which required taxes to be raised.

1. Tariffs

Carr points out that:

'By 1900, the dangerous policy of concentration which had failed to win middle-class support or to retard the growth of socialism, had been abandoned.' (Carr 1991, p.176)

The abandonment of the policy of concentration was followed by a renewed struggle over tariffs. The Conservatives and Agrarian League pressed for high tariffs while the Socialists and Radicals pressed for lower. Layton notes that:

'[Bülow] found government subject to ever increasing pressures, despite the close relationship he enjoyed with the Kaiser. It was not always so easy to maintain a government majority, as was shown most obviously by the political struggle over the renewal of Caprivi's commercial treaties. The Conservatives in conjunction with the Agrarian League had bitterly campaigned against the agreements from the start, whilst the Left Liberals and Social Democrats remained committed to lower tariffs. In the end, the compromise Tariff Law of 1902 restored tariffs to 1892 levels, which was well short of the Conservatives' demands and it was only carried by a combination of the Centre, the National Liberals and Free Conservatives.' (Layton 1995, p.33)

Although a majority in the Reichstag voted for increased tariffs, this was very unpopular with the electorate at large and in the election of 1903 the Socialists won an extra million votes and 26 extra seats. This changed the balance in the Reichstag, ensuring that the government once again found it difficult to gain a majority.

2. Taxation

Layton points out that:

'Weltpolitik generated its own problems too. The budget had moved into deficit as the mounting cost of maintaining the army, expanding the navy and running the empire took effect. If all the "glories" of Weltpolitik were to be continued then substantial tax increases had to be introduced.' (Layton 1995, p.34)

When Bülow introduced Bills which proposed raising taxes, they were defeated in the Reichstag (the Centre joined with the parties of the left to ensure that there was a majority against). As a result, the budget remained in deficit.

Bülow's fall from power

Seligmann and McLean argue that relations between Bülow and the Kaiser came under great strain from the winter of 1905-06:

'Relations between the Chancellor and the Kaiser had come under severe strain, most notably as a result of disagreements between the two men over appointments within the executive. Then there were two serious debacles in foreign policy.' (Seligmann & McLean 2000, p.98)

The 'debacles in foreign policy' were the failure to secure an alliance with Russia in 1905 and the First Moroccan Crisis (see Section 3.2 below). The two debacles greatly weakened Bülow's position and when the *Daily Telegraph* Affair blew up in October 1908, it undermined Bülow's position completely (see Activity 1.3, Item 3):

'The *Daily Telegraph* Affair and Bülow's fall from power mark the effective end of the era of the Kaiser's personal regime. Wilhelm never established the same rapport with Bülow's successor, the gloomy Prussian bureaucrat Theobald von Bethmann Hollweg. Additionally, the Kaiser retreated into a life of lethargy and seemed constitutionally averse to hard work, which reduced his involvement in the governmental process...Instead of leadership at the top, there seemed to be a vacuum. In domestic politics, the conflicts between capital and labour and between political parties in the Reichstag only seemed to intensify in the last years of peace.' (Seligmann & McLean 2000, p.104)

MAIN POINTS - Section 2.2

- Germany was transformed economically and socially during the period 1890-1914. There was rapid economic growth and significant numbers of people moved from the countryside to towns and cities. Class divisions remained fixed, however.
- One consequence of this social and economic transformation was political mobilisation on both the left and the right.
- The balance of power in the Reichstag shifted significantly. Pro-government, right-wing parties declined whilst parties which were more critical of the government grew in strength, especially the SPD. As a result, governments found it difficult to gain majority support in the Reichstag.
- The Kaiser appointed four Chancellors in the period

between Bismarck's resignation in 1890 and the outbreak of war in 1914 - Caprivi (1890-94), Hohenlohe (1894-1900), Bülow (1900-09) and Bethmann-Hollweg (1909-17).
- Caprivi embarked on a policy, which he called a 'New Course'. He resigned after refusing to introduce an Anti-Socialist Bill. He was succeeded by Hohenlohe who soon became a figurehead without any real power.
- It was under Bülow that the Kaiser attempted to impose 'personal rule'. Even in the period 1900-05, however, the Kaiser's power was not absolute. Although the Kaiser looked on Bülow as his Bismarck, at first, he lost faith with him after the *Daily Telegraph* Affair.

Activity 1.3 Who ruled Germany in 1890-1914?

ITEM 1 Who ruled Germany? (1)

Many historians distrust the 'Great Man' theory of history and so are reluctant to accept the views of Röhl and others in emphasising the central role of the Kaiser in Germany between 1890 and 1914. The main arguments are as follows. First, some historians argue that groups like the bureaucracy, the landowners (especially the Prussian Junkers), the army and the judiciary - the traditional, non-elected élites - along with the newly emergent middle-class industrialists filled a power vacuum left after Bismarck's departure. These groups rallied together to defeat the threat posed by socialism and full democracy. Policies of expansion abroad ('Weltpolitik') were adopted to provide a patriotic rallying call to divert the masses away from social and political reform. The Kaiser, in this version of events, is a rather shadowy, peripheral figure. Second, some historians see the major problem of the period as the constitution and its failure to provide a workable system of government. The difficulty of reaching decisions resulted from structural defects rather than the personality of individuals like the Kaiser. Third, some historians have identified tremendous growth in political activity in the Kaiserreich. They argue that the focus should be on what was happening on the ground in Germany, not on what was happening in court. Fourth, Christopher Clark has pointed out that the Kaiser's powers of appointment did not ensure his desired policies were implemented. Even if he could paralyse and demoralise an elderly Chancellor (as he did with Hohenlohe), he still faced the ministers. Even if he could bully the ministers to follow his initiatives, he still faced the quarrelsome Reichstag, not to mention the censure of public opinion. Besides, the appointment of his own people to high positions did not guarantee the expansion of the Kaiser's role in political affairs. For example, Clark believes that for all Bülow's flattering remarks to the Kaiser, he set his own agenda and generally succeeded in imposing his own preferences, while at the same time persuading the Kaiser that he remained personally in control of affairs. And fifth, Clark emphasises that the Kaiser had no consistent domestic political programme and that his interventions in domestic affairs remained haphazard.

This edition of the magazine Simplicissimus came out in March 1906. The cover shows Wilhelm II posing in front of the new German navy.

Adapted from Clark 2000.

ITEM 2 Who ruled Germany? (2)

The arguments in support of the view that the Kaiser was at the centre of affairs in the period 1890 to 1914 are as follows. First, there is no doubt that he had very real constitutional powers. The constitution explicitly granted the Kaiser sovereignty in matters of foreign policy, the right to declare war and conclude peace, control of all personnel appointments in the administration, notably the appointment and dismissal of the Chancellor, the right to dissolve the Reichstag and personal command of the army and navy. Second, Wilhelm II made it clear that he was determined to play a more active role in government than his grandfather (Wilhelm I) had done under the dominant Bismarck. Third, structures were in place to support the Kaiser's intervention. The civil list (money to maintain the Kaiser's court) was huge - 22.2 million marks each year - as were the size of the court and numbers of people involved - a huge and prestigious body, far larger than the Prussian and Reich bureaucracy combined. The Chancellors and main ministers were all appointed by the Kaiser and they were from that hierarchical court society which the monarch could control so readily. They were neither willing nor able to mount any kind of sustained opposition to the will of the

This photograph of Wilhelm II was taken in 1906.

Kaiser and the military men and high aristocrats in his entourage. Fourth, there is clear evidence of the Kaiser's direct involvement in decision-making from his decisive support for naval armaments, through his interest in specific areas of domestic legislation to his frequent interventions in diplomacy and foreign policy. And fifth, the Kaiser had a very close relationship with the military. The army swore loyalty exclusively to the Kaiser. Wilhelm often chose generals in preference to bureaucrats to head offices of state and, unlike ministers, generals had the right of access to the monarch whenever they wished.

Adapted from Röhl 1994 and 1996.

ITEM 3 The *Daily Telegraph* Affair

During a visit to Britain in 1907, Wilhelm II stayed with pro-German Colonel Stuart Wortley. On the basis of a conversation with the Kaiser, Stuart-Wortley wrote an article for the *Daily Telegraph* in the hope of improving Anglo-German relations. It was full of the Kaiser's usual inept comments. He said, for example, that during the Boer War, he had remained neutral even though large numbers of Germans were pro-Boer, that he had personally prevented the formation of an anti-British coalition, and that he had shown Queen Victoria how to win the war. The article was published on 28 October 1908. It was severely criticised abroad, but this criticism was drowned by the uproar in Germany. On 31 October, in an attempt to deflect criticism, Bülow issued a statement accepting responsibility, but shifting the blame to the Foreign Office. He said he had offered to resign, but the Kaiser had refused to let him go. This clumsy manoeuvre only added fuel to the fire. All the major parties, including the Conservatives, attacked the Chancellor. They also criticised the Kaiser for meddling in affairs which were the proper concern of the government. What had actually happened was that Stuart-Wortley had sent the article to the Kaiser and he had passed it on to Bülow. Bülow glanced at it casually and passed it to the Foreign Office. Minor corrections were made there by a junior official (it was assumed that the Chancellor understood the implications and approved of them). When it returned, Bülow passed it unread back to the Kaiser who forwarded it to the *Daily Telegraph*. The whole affair, therefore, was down to Bülow's negligence. The crisis that resulted was serious. There were calls for constitutional reform and serious attacks on Wilhelm's 'personal government'. Under pressure from all parties, Bülow issued a statement making it clear that unless the Kaiser exercised more restraint, Chancellors would have no choice but to resign. Shortly afterwards, Wilhelm promised in writing to respect the constitution. This was enough for the crisis to blow over without constitutional reform. But it was the beginning of the end for Bülow. From that moment on, the Kaiser was determined to be rid of him. The opportunity came in 1909 when Bülow introduced another Finance Bill.

Adapted from Carr 1991.

Questions

1. Judging from Items 1-3 and your own knowledge, who ruled Germany in the period 1890 to 1914?
2. Using Items 1 and 2, give arguments for and against the view that Kaiser was in charge during the period 1890-1914.

3. The *Daily Telegraph* Affair has been described as 'the most serious crisis in the Kaiser's reign before 1914'. Judging from Item 3, what was the crisis all about?

3 Foreign policy 1871-1914

Key issues

1. How successful was Bismarck's foreign policy from 1871?

2. How did foreign policy develop up to 1914?

3.1 How successful was Bismarck's foreign policy from 1871?

Policy objectives

Broad foreign policy objectives

It was noted in Section 1.2 above that German unification was the product of war. In the period 1862-71, the Prussian army was involved in three wars with neighbouring states - Denmark, Austria and France. Yet from 1871, the year of unification, to 1890, the year when Bismarck fell from power, Germany was not involved in any wars against European powers, though it did come close to involvement on several occasions.

In order to understand Bismarck's foreign policy aims, it is important to be aware of the balance of power in Europe in the 1870s. Carr sums this up as follows:

'During the first half of the century, when Germany lay weak and disunited, Austria, France and Russia had been the dominant powers on the continent. After the Franco-Prussian war...the balance of power was deeply disturbed. In the 1870s, France and Austria-Hungary were recovering from defeat; Russia was as interested in Central Asia as in Europe; and Britain was still in [its] isolationist interlude. These circumstances conspired together to assure for Germany, temporarily, a position of relative [strength] in Europe. For the time being [Germany] was...more than a traditional Great Power but less than a world power in the class of Britain and Russia.' (Carr 1991, p.46)

Historians agree that, in terms of foreign policy, Bismarck's main aim was to preserve the status quo of 1871. To do this, it was important to avoid further large-scale war:

'The year 1871 marked a significant change of direction for Bismarck. Bismarck "the Disturber of the Peace" became Bismarck "the Sober, Moderate and Conservative Statesman". Why? In his own words "Germany is a satiated [fully satisfied] power". Hereafter, he was primarily concerned with consolidating the newly unified Germany.' (Bell & Cawood 2000, p.31)

Waller points out that German unification caused great unease in the rest of Europe, with other states wondering who would be the next victim of Bismarck's hitherto aggressive foreign policy:

'[People] wondered where Bismarck would turn to after this, and who would be his next victim. They were not sure whether it would be Holland or Austria. Of the Great Powers, though, only France felt threatened by Germany and they all (including France) tried to come to terms with the new empire.' (Waller 1997, p.48)

Bell and Cawood argue that Bismarck was well aware of other states' unease and it was an important aim to convince them of his peaceful intentions - see Box 1.18.

BOX 1.18   Bismarck and other European powers

Bell and Cawood argue that the essence of Bismarck's foreign policy can be understood from a remark he himself made. He said: 'When we have arrived in a good harbour we should be content, and cultivate and hold what we have won'. In practice, this meant that, whereas before 1870, Prussian foreign policy had been essentially aggressive and warlike, now the Iron Chancellor sought a period of peace - but peace on his terms. Bismarck realised that Germany's military and economic power made it vulnerable. Historically, any Great Power on the verge of European domination found itself the target of a broad European coalition and subsequently the loser of a ruinous war. Bismarck was acutely conscious of this, stating in 1877 his fear that any European conflict might draw Germany in and provide the country's rivals with an opportunity to reverse its recent gains. This explains why the 'nationalist poacher' had to become an 'imperial gamekeeper'. Bismarck had to convince potential rivals in Europe of his peaceful intentions - especially Britain and Russia which were Germany's greatest rivals after France's defeat in 1871. Bismarck found them understandably suspicious of the sincerity of his conversion.

Adapted from Bell & Cawood 2000.

Foreign policy and domestic concerns

It should also be noted that Bismarck's foreign policy aims were not completely divorced from his domestic concerns. Craig (1981), for example, argues that Bismarck realised that war would only make the economic downturn that began in 1873 more intense. There were, in other words, domestic economic reasons for pursuing a peaceful foreign policy. Craig also argues that Bismarck hoped to avoid a 'Europe-wide social revolution' and believed that a period of peace was the best way to achieve this goal. Bismarck's foreign policy, therefore, goes hand in hand with his domestic goal of preserving Prussian traditions. It also fits with his fight against socialism (see Section 2.1 above).

Specific foreign policy objectives

Two specific foreign policy objectives were particularly important. First, Bismarck aimed to keep France isolated. Bell and Cawood point out that the French government remained extremely bitter about the Franco-Prussian war and especially about the loss of Alsace-Lorraine. They argue that:

'French opposition became..."a negative constant" in Bismarck's foreign policy calculations. While Bismarck was confident that the German army could defeat France (or any other continental power) alone, he feared that if France could acquire allies - especially Austria-Hungary or Russia - Germany would be faced with an unwinnable two-front war.' (Bell & Cawood 2000, p.31)

Given that Bismarck was unable to destroy France, Bell and Cawood argue that his strategy was to do everything he could to keep it isolated.

The second specific foreign policy objective was to maintain good relations with both Austria-Hungary and Russia. Bell and Cawood (2000, p.32) argue that this was the most difficult task facing Bismarck throughout the period 1871-90 since 'fundamental Russian interests ran counter to those of Austria-Hungary and Germany'. Carr points out, however, that both Austria-Hungary and Russia had reasons for wanting the friendship of Germany:

'Austria and Russia were both anxious to have the friendship of Germany; Austria because of the growing antagonism with Russia in the Balkans; Russia because [it] did not want to face a hostile coalition of European powers if war broke out in Europe.' (Carr 1991, p.147)

Carr argues that, after disturbing relations with Austria and Russia in the 1860s, Bismarck needed to restore relations with them because of fears of a war on two fronts following an alliance between Russia and France. At the same time, however, Carr points out, Bismarck did not want to be completely dependent on Russia since he did not want to be dragged into Russia's disputes with Britain in Asia. As for Austria-Hungary, friendship was important to Germany, not only because it deprived France of a potential ally, but also because it gave Bismarck a welcome degree of independence in his dealings with Russia.

Relations with Britain

Bell and Cawood argue that Bismarck's failure to build better relations with Britain during the period 1871 and 1890 was a failing. They agree that, it would have been difficult to do more since Britain was following a policy of Splendid Isolation (non-interference in the affairs of mainland Europe). Nonetheless, they argue that Bismarck sowed the seeds of problems that would be faced by his successors.

Key events and developments

1. The Three Emperors' League ('Dreikaiserbund') 1872

It was noted above that one of Bismarck's key objectives was to keep France isolated whilst another was to build close relations with both Austria-Hungary and Russia. The Three Emperors' League (an agreement between Germany, Russia and Austria-Hungary) was an attempt to achieve both of these objectives. According to Stiles and Farmer, the setting up of the League was the result of an initiative from Austria-Hungary. Since the three countries could find little to agree on in concrete terms, the terms of the agreement were vague:

'The emperors identified republicanism and socialism as common enemies and promised to consult on matters of common interest or if a third power disturbed Europe's peace. It was not a cunning plan from Bismarck but it very much suited his purpose.' (Stiles & Farmer 2001, p.116)

Craig agrees that Bismarck was satisfied with this vague agreement:

'He had never been favourably disposed to agreements with binding stipulations, preferring to retain his freedom of action. It was only with reluctance that he turned, six years after this, to the negotiation of a more formal agreement.' (Craig 1978, p.104)

2. The 'War in Sight' Crisis, 1875

France made a much more rapid recovery from the Franco-Prussian war than Bismarck - and most other people - expected. By paying off the compensation demanded by Germany in 1873, they rid themselves of the German army of occupation. Unlike in Germany, where an economic downturn began in 1873, France's economy continued to grow. This and France's growing military strength led to the 'War in Sight' Crisis - see Box 1.19.

3. The Balkans Crisis, 1875-78

As the manufactured crisis with France receded, a far more important test for Bismarck's diplomacy developed in the Balkans. The Turkish Empire in Europe was in a state of crisis (see Box 1.20). Craig argues that:

'Risings against Turkish rule in Bosnia and Bulgaria and armed intervention in these troubles by the Serbs and Montenegrins threatened to embroil all of the Great Powers. Russia was the first to be drawn in this labyrinth, for the plight of its co-religionists under Turkish rule made abstention all

BOX 1.19 The War in Sight Crisis

The German economy was badly shaken by the onset, in 1873, of a depression which was to linger until well past Bismarck's departure from office. France, on the other hand, continued to prosper. A broad economic recovery was in full swing and the army was improving fast. Hoping that warlike noises from Germany would help to impede that recovery, Bismarck encouraged the German press to start talking about a possible new war with France. The climax of this campaign came with an article in the *Berliner Post* in April 1875 which had the headline IS WAR IN SIGHT? The article made it clear that it reflected official views. But, if the idea was to damage France, the article had the opposite effect. It was entirely counter-productive. France received firm diplomatic support from Britain and Russia. Austria-Hungary stood aside, trying to look neutral but hoping that Germany would be taught a lesson. In May 1875 Berlin was isolated whereas a few months earlier it had been Paris that stood alone. The significance of the incident did not escape Bismarck. Up to that point, he had endeavoured to tip the balance of power in his favour in the hope that this would enable him to keep the French in place. Afterwards his approach became more devious and dynamic.

Adapted from Waller 1997.

but impossible. But the Austrians and British were not far behind, the former motivated by suspicion of the Russians and interested in acquiring Bosnia, the latter by concern over the future of the Straits [of Bosporus - the link between the Black Sea and the Aegean] if Russian influence grew in the Balkans.' (Craig 1978, p.110)

Germany was at first less directly concerned. Bismarck said 'the whole of the Balkans is not worth the healthy bones of a single Pomeranian musketeer [ie. German soldier]'. Craig also suggests that:

'Bismarck was not unhappy to see the attention of the Powers diverted to the Near East [ie the Balkans] or to observe the development of serious differences among them.' (Craig 1978, p.110)

But Germany was soon drawn in. Bell and Cawood argue that:

'The terminal decline of the Ottoman Turkish Empire provided a cockpit of Austro-Russian rivalry in the region...Bismarck feared a war...between the two great eastern powers might allow France to escape its diplomatic isolation, because [as Bismarck said] "German foreign policy will always be obliged to join a war if the independence of Austria-Hungary were threatened by a Russian attack".' (Bell & Cawood 2000, p.32)

If Germany fought on the side of Austria, then the feared Franco-Russian alliance might take place, bringing the spectre of the encirclement of Germany. Both Russia and Austria looked to Germany for support in the Balkans, but Bismarck avoided any firm commitment to either power. Stiles and Farmer argue that the atrocities committed by Turkish troops in 1876 were the turning point:

'Turkish atrocities in Bulgaria (some 10,000 Bulgarians were allegedly killed) changed the situation. The atrocities stirred public opinion in both Britain and Russia with important effects. In Britain, Disraeli's government was temporarily prevented from pursuing the traditional British policy of supporting Turkey against Russia. In Russia, the suffering of the Bulgarians and the defeat of Serbian and Montenegrin forces enslaved

BOX 1.20 The Balkans Crisis, 1875-78

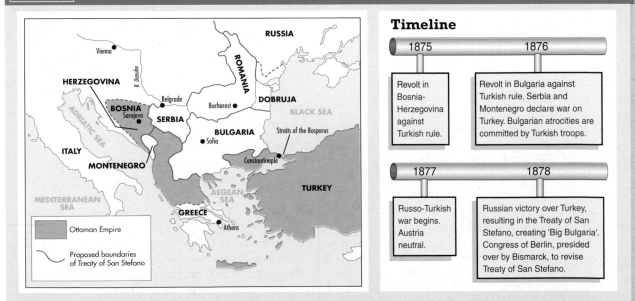

Timeline

1875	1876
Revolt in Bosnia-Herzegovina against Turkish rule.	Revolt in Bulgaria against Turkish rule. Serbia and Montenegro declare war on Turkey. Bulgarian atrocities are committed by Turkish troops.

1877	1878
Russo-Turkish war begins. Austria neutral.	Russian victory over Turkey, resulting in the Treaty of San Stefano, creating 'Big Bulgaria'. Congress of Berlin, presided over by Bismarck, to revise Treaty of San Stefano.

This map shows the Balkans just after the Treaty of San Stefano had been signed in 1878.
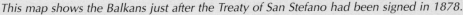

pan-Slavist sentiment to such an extent that the Tsarist government found itself under mounting pressure to intervene.' (Stiles & Farmer 2001, p.117)

In January 1877, the Tsar negotiated a deal with Austria-Hungary. In return for Austro-Hungarian neutrality in a war between Russia and Turkey, Austria would be allowed to take control of Bosnia-Herzogovina. In addition, Russia would not create any new large state in the Balkans following such a war. Then, in April, Russia went to war. The following March, Russia imposed the Treaty of San Stefano on Turkey. Stiles and Farmer argue that:

'This treaty significantly improved Russia's position in the Balkans. European Turkey was to be reduced to small unconnected territories by the creation of a Big Bulgaria. Serbia, Montenegro and Romania were to be fully independent of Turkey. There was no mention of Austria taking Bosnia-Herzogovina.' (Stiles & Farmer 2001, p.117)

The creation of a Big Bulgaria was viewed with horror by Austria-Hungary since it would be a large buffer state controlling Russia's interests in the Balkans. In response, Austria-Hungary mobilised it troops. The San Stefano Treaty was also disliked by Britain. British troops were summoned from India and a fleet was dispatched. Stiles and Farmer point out that.

'Faced with Austro-British hostility and the threat of a major war, which [it] was in no economic or military position to fight, Russia agreed to an international conference to revise the peace terms.' (Stiles & Farmer 2001, p.117)

The Congress of Berlin, 1878

Craig argues that Bismarck knew very well that Germany would be in a very difficult position if other major European states started fighting:

'The Chancellor knew perfectly well that he would be in an awkward, indeed dangerous position if other Powers resorted to hostilities...Both Vienna [Austria-Hungary] and St Petersburg [Russia] would expect German support - the Russians had made it clear that this would be a fair return for their neutrality in 1870 - and neither would forgive either a neutral stance or assistance to its [enemy]. Apart from this, any major war would have incalculable results in the present state of Europe. Bismarck was forced, therefore, to intervene whether he liked it or not.' (Craig 1978, p.111)

A conference of the Great Powers was called at Berlin. It was held in June-July 1878), with Bismarck acting as the 'honest broker'. The result was the Treaty of Berlin - see Box 1.21.

4. The Dual Alliance, 1879 and Triple Alliance, 1882

Waller argues that:

BOX 1.21 | The Congress of Berlin

Much work had been done before the Congress of Berlin met. Russia had agreed to reduce the size of Bulgaria. Britain had agreed to guarantee Turkey's security in return for Cyprus. The Turkish Sultan had agreed to introduce reforms. Britain had agreed to support Austria-Hungary's claims to occupy Bosnia-Herzogovina. Despite this, the Congress was not all plain sailing. Bismarck had to make some important interventions. By the Treaty of Berlin, Big Bulgaria was divided into three. The northern part gained independence. The middle part, Eastern Roumelia was given self-government under Turkish rule. The southern part - Macedonia - returned to Turkey. Russia took part of Romania and gained the valuable port of Batun on the east coast of the Black Sea. Britain gained Cyprus and checked the Russians, as a result regarding the Congress as a success. Russia, by contrast, felt that the

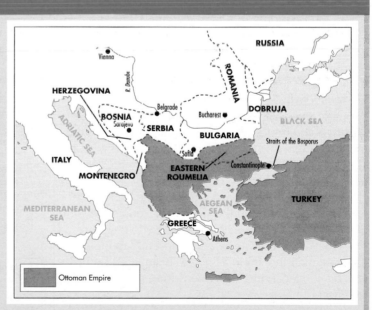

This map shows the Balkans after the Treaty of Berlin was signed.

Congress was a humiliating defeat. Russia had done the fighting and yet Britain and Austria-Hungary had come away with the spoils. For Bismarck, the reaction was mixed. War had been avoided - the primary aim. But, relations with Russia deteriorated. At this point, the Three Emperors' League was truly dead and Germany in danger. Bismarck was now in a potentially dangerous position. There was suddenly the real possibility of a Franco-Russian alliance. It was in this atmosphere of uncertainty about future relations with Russia that led Bismarck to make an important change in his foreign policy in 1879.

Adapted from Stiles & Farmer 2001.

'After the Congress of Berlin in 1878, which attempted a Balkan settlement, a more substantial structure was needed for the original purpose [of isolating France and restraining Austria and Russia], but it also had to control Russian aggression. The core of the second phase of the system was, therefore, a defensive Treaty with Austria, the Dual Alliance of 1879, aimed against Russia.' (Waller 1997, p.57)

Under the terms of the treaty which created the Dual Alliance, each country would help the other if either was attacked by Russia. If Germany or Austria were at war with a state other than Russia, then the other partner would remain neutral. The treaty did not, however, mark an end to Bismarck's attempts to maintain a balance between Austria, Russia and Germany. Instead, according to Craig:

'[Bismarck] was seeking a greater measure of security in an uncertain international climate, and the new alliance enabled him to attain it.' (Craig 1978, p.114)

Seligmann and McLean also see the Dual Alliance as a means of putting pressure on Russia but not cutting links with it:

'As ever, [Bismarck] was conscious of the need for Germany to maintain ties with St. Petersburg as well as Vienna. The Dual Alliance allowed him to pressurise the Russians into agreeing to the renewal of the Dreikaiserbund [Three Emperors' League] in 1881, as the Tsar preferred a new accommodation with Germany and Austria to diplomatic isolation.' (Seligmann & McLean 2000, p.43)

Bismarck himself argued that, of the two powers, Austria was the natural ally. He once wrote in a memorandum: 'With Austria we have more in common than with Russia - German kinship, historical memories, the German language'. But, this memorandum was to the Kaiser who had his doubts about the alliance with Austria. As Bell and Cawood point out, Bismarck also stated:

'I knew that the Russians would come to us once we had nailed down the Austrians.' (quoted in Bell & Cawood 2000, pp.32-33)

The Dual Alliance was extended in 1882 to include Italy, creating the Triple Alliance. Bismarck's purpose was his long-standing one of ensuring the continued isolation of France.

5. The renewal of the Three Emperors' League, 1881

The renewal of the Three Emperors' League (the Dreikaiserbund) in 1881 appeared to mend the damage done to German-Russian relations in 1878-79:

'When, as a result of patient collaboration with Saburov, the Russian ambassador in Berlin, Bismarck achieved a new tripartite alliance in June 1881, which pledged the three partners to neutrality in the event of war between one of their number and a fourth European Power and to mutual consultation in Balkan affairs, he had reason to hope that he could avoid new Austro-Russian confrontations.' (Craig 1978, p.115)

But, relations with Russia remained a problem for Bismarck throughout the 1880s.

6. The Balkans Crisis of 1885-86

It was in the Balkans once again that the next crisis in Austro-Russian relations occurred (in 1885-86):

'Prince Alexander of Bulgaria struck out in an independent line...In September 1885, without consulting his cousin the Russian Tsar, Alexander engineered the union of Eastern Roumalia with Bulgaria.' (Carr 1991, p.156)

Serbia, concerned about Bulgaria's ambitions, attacked Bulgaria and was defeated. Austria, which backed Serbia, threatened military intervention if Bulgaria invaded Serbia:

'The warning stopped the Bulgarian offensive but it strained Austro-Russian relations to breaking point. Bismarck, desperately anxious to remain friends with both powers, had to inform Austria bluntly that Germany could not fight Russia over this issue.' (Carr 1991, p.156)

The implications of the Balkans Crisis of 1885-86 are explored in Box 1.22.

BOX 1.22 The Balkans Crisis of 1885-86

Austria's threat of military action against Bulgaria was enough to ensure that the Bulgarians did not invade Serbia and, therefore, that Serbia did not lose any territory. Then, after negotiations, Austria and Russia finally agreed to a union of East Roumelia and Bulgaria. But this was not the end of the Bulgarian crisis. In August 1886, Prince Alexander was kidnapped by pro-Russian officers. A short time later, he was ordered to abdicate by the Tsar. He did so and retired into obscurity. Bismarck, however, never forgave him for stirring up the Balkans. After Alexander's abdication, the Russians sent a general to take over as Governor of Bulgaria. But, the Bulgarians resisted and, in November 1886, the Tsar broke off diplomatic relations. It seemed that Russia would invade Bulgaria which, in turn, would arouse Austria. Once again Bismarck informed Austria that Germany could not help. In the end, however, Russia didn't invade, though the tension remained for several months. This crisis in Bulgaria in 1885-86 shattered the Three Emperors' Alliance which was due for renewal in 1887. As Austro-Russian relations worsened, Bismarck's fears of France grew. The French Minister of War, General Boulanger, stirred up nationalistic feelings in France. To make matters worse, pro-French ministers in Russia seemed to be exerting great influence over the Tsar. For domestic reasons, Bismarck may have exaggerated the threat of war. However, he was clearly concerned about a Franco-Russian alliance.

Adapted from Carr 1991 and Stiles & Farmer 2001.

7. The renewal of the Triple Alliance

In February 1887, the Triple Alliance was renewed, giving Italy greater status in the alliance than in 1882 and the following month the First Mediterranean Agreement was signed:

'Bismarck persuaded Austria to promise to consult Italy on all matters affecting the Balkans, the Adriatic and the Aegean. In March 1887, with Bismarck's full backing, Britain, Austria and Italy signed the First Mediterranean Agreement, committing themselves to the maintenance of the status quo in the eastern Mediterranean - an action that was clearly anti-Russian.' (Stiles & Farmer 2001, p.123)

8. The Reinsurance Treaty, 1887

The First Mediterranean Agreement was not just anti-Russian, it also confirmed the isolation of France. Still concerned about a Franco-Russian alliance, Bismarck aimed for an agreement with Russia. Hostility between Russia and Austria-Hungary following the Balkans Crisis prevented the Three Emperors' League from being renewed. Instead, Bismarck negotiated the 'Reinsurance Treaty' - an agreement between Germany and Russia alone:

'The treaty, to last for three years, specified that in the case of war both Russia and Germany were to observe neutrality: Germany in the case of a war between Russia and Austria, Russia in the case of war with France.' (Stürmer 2000, p.31)

Carr points out that historians writing in the inter-war period misinterpreted the importance of this treaty:

'Much controversy has surrounded this treaty. Between the world wars, ardent defenders of the old Chancellor hailed it as a masterpiece, the "corner stone" of the "system". This is a gross exaggeration. Bismarck certainly did not attach much importance to it. Herbert Bismarck, close confidant of his father, remarked that "the only value of it was that in an emergency it might keep the Russians off our necks for six or eight weeks longer than otherwise would have been the case".' (Carr 1991, p.158)

The signing of the Reinsurance Treaty illustrates Bismarck's determination to maintain the link with Russia. His view, however, was no longer shared by many in Germany:

'By the end of the 1880s, Bismarck and Wilhelm I seemed to be the only two people in Berlin committed to the Prussian tradition of friendship with Russia. By contrast, the Foreign Office official Friedrich von Holstein believed that dynastic ties [between the Kaiser and the Tsar] were no longer a sufficient guarantee of German-Russian relations and accused Bismarck of "standing in front of the Tsar, cap in hand..." Military figures went even further and urged that a "preventive war" be launched against Russia.' (Seligmann & McLean 2000, p.44)

Bismarck and overseas colonies

In 1881, Bismarck said in public:

'So long as I am Chancellor we shall pursue no colonial policy.' (quoted in Stiles & Farmer, p.121)

Yet in 1884-85, Germany gained a large overseas Empire in Africa. The reasons why Bismarck changed his mind are considered in Box 1.23.

BOX 1.23 Bismarck and Germany's colonies

The early 1880s was the time of the 'Scramble for Africa'. Seizing colonies in Africa was fashionable. Pressure groups - notably the German Colonial Union which was set up in 1882 - sprang up in Germany arguing for colonies on economic grounds and as a sign of national greatness. Within Germany there were concerns about protectionist policies. Companies were complaining of being squeezed out of parts of Africa by foreign rivals. Bismarck hoped that colonies might benefit the German economy by providing new markets and raw materials. Also, by putting pressure on Britain in the colonial field, Bismarck hoped to force it into adopting a more pro-German policy in European affairs. Bismarck also had good political reasons to support German colonialism. The 1884 elections were due and he needed an issue that would weaken the liberals. Colonialism was a convenient stick with which to beat the Radicals and Socialists and to rally support. His ploy worked and in 1884-85 Germany acquired one million square miles of land in Africa.

Adapted from Stiles & Farmer 2001.

Other historians add the following reasons why Bismarck was temporarily converted to colonialism:

1. Bismarck saw benefits for his European diplomatic manoeuvres in playing the colonial card.
2. There was a connection between colonialism and the succession of Crown Prince Frederick - Bismarck used clashes with Britain over colonial mattes to undermine the influence of Frederick's English wife who disliked Bismarck.
3. Bismarck used imperialism to reinforce the conservative power and social structure in Germany by creating an attractive but irrelevant distraction - so-called 'social imperialism'.

Most historians would agree with Mommsen, however, who argues that:

'It was not until the 1890s that imperialist ideas made a serious impact on German public opinion.' (Mommsen 1995, p.80)

MAIN POINTS - Section 3.1

- Historians agree that, in terms of foreign policy, Bismarck's main aim was to preserve the status quo of 1871. To do this, it was important to avoid further large-scale war. This was achieved in the period 1871-90. There were also domestic reasons - eg economic - for avoiding war.
- Two specific foreign policy objectives were particularly important. First, Bismarck aimed to keep France isolated. And second, Bismarck aimed to maintain good relations with both Austria-Hungary and Russia.

- There were eight key developments - (1) The Three Emperors' League, 1872 (2) the War in Sight Crisis, 1875 (3) The Balkans Crisis, 1875-78 (4) the Dual Alliance, 1879 and Triple Alliance, 1882 (5) the renewal of the Three Emperors' League, 1881 (6) the Balkans Crisis, 1885-86 (7) the renewal of the Triple Alliance and (8) the Reinsurance Treaty, 1887.
- In 1881, Bismarck said in public that so long as he was Chancellor, Germany would not pursue a colonial policy. Yet, in 1884-85, Germany gained a large overseas Empire in Africa.

Activity 1.4 How successful was Bismarck's foreign policy?

ITEM 1 Did Bismarck have a plan?

The view that Bismarck's foreign policy was carried out according to a well-laid plan was widely held until the 1950s. Historians such as Langer (who wrote in the 1930s) saw Bismarck as a 'grand chessmaster who dominated the board in the interests of peace. He had a plan for every eventuality'. In 1955, however, the historian A.J.P. Taylor put forward the view that Bismarck 'lived for the moment and responded to its challenge'. Waller believes that the view of Medlicott is nearer the truth, namely 'that Bismarck's approach was a combination of long-range planning and tactics'. Bell and Cawood see Bismarck as 'consistent in his aims but not in his approach to foreign policy. It is not difficult to see him reacting to events as they occurred, often impetuously and without recourse to a grand plan.' Berghahn describes Bismarck's policy as a 'tightrope act'. Even if Bismarck had no plan, his approach to foreign policy after 1871 has often been praised for its success in keeping the peace in Europe. This was achieved not simply by keeping a balance of power in Europe, but by maintaining what has been called a 'balance of tension'. Waller, referring to a memorandum written by Bismarck in 1877 at Kissingen, describes Bismarck's policy as creating a political constellation in which all the powers, except France, needed Germany and were kept from an opposing coalition through their relations with one another. This was not a passive policy of maintaining the status quo, but an active policy of exploiting and guiding the tensions and rivalries between powers in the interests of Germany. It was an active policy because Bismarck relied on the continual balancing of tension. Constant vigilance and effort, employing 'fair means or foul' were needed. The means were too varied and too imaginative to be described by the word 'system' which implies a more static approach. In essence, Bismarck wanted to be the nucleus of European politics.

Adapted from Waller 1997 and Bell & Cawood 2000.

ITEM 2 How successful was Bismarck's foreign policy?

Bismarck's defenders argue that he was responsible for preserving peace in Europe for 20 years. He did not want war himself, it is argued, and he prevented others from going to war by building such an intricate diplomatic web that war became too perilous an undertaking. This is to exaggerate his influence. A factor of equal importance was the desire of other powers to avoid a major war in Europe. The 1880s were a period of colonial expansion which diverted attention from Europe. No-one could deny that Bismarck was a past master in the diplomatic arts. By cleverly exploiting and fostering the rivalries between states, he prevented the formation of any hostile coalition against Germany and assured for his country an assured place at the top table. These are solid achievements. But, equally, it cannot be denied that his policies ended in failure. His bullying tactics, however effective in the short term, were bitterly resented, especially by the Russians, and poisoned international relations in this period. Besides, by the 1880s, public opinion was beginning to influence policy, making it impossible to turn friendships on and off at will. Bismarck could not get France to forget the loss of Alsace-Lorraine. Nor could he keep both Austria-Hungary and Russia as his friends. Public opinion in both countries as well as economic interests widened and deepened their rivalry. It is significant that in his last year or two in office, Bismarck was acutely aware of the failure of his policy. He stood by helplessly as France and Russia moved towards each other and Germany and Russia moved further apart.

Adapted from Carr 1991.

ITEM 3 Bismarck's approach to foreign policy

Bismarck's approach was much more dynamic and imaginative than is usually realised. He made use of formal agreements, but resorted to other strategies as well. There was, first of all, the occasional crude threat of the use of force, as in the War in Sight Crisis of 1875. When allies seemed to be growing too intimate he would generate suspicion between them. So, for instance, the Austrians were frequently reminded of the Russians' unreliability. He was not beyond limited cooperation with his enemies to remind friends of the consequences if Germany broke off its friendship. For example, in the mid-1880s, London was reminded of the need to cooperate with Germany because Germany supported France in opposition to British plans in Egypt. Manipulation of the players on the diplomatic chessboard was a favourite tactic. There was the

This painting shows a scene from the Congress of Berlin in 1878. Bismarck is in the middle of the group of three on the left, talking to the Austrian Emperor Franz Josef. The British Prime Minister, Benjamin Disraeli, is to the right of Bismarck's group.

Mediterranean Agreement of 1887 by means of which he urged Britain, Italy and Austria to block Russia whilst at the same time he was working for an agreement with Russia (ie the Reinsurance Treaty). He could slander a lukewarm friend - the press or other indirect means were used for this. The attacks on Gorchakov, the Russian Foreign Minister, after the Congress of Berlin are a good example - a not unprovoked press campaign was waged against him. Now and then he could also apply direct pressure on an uncooperative government. Austria and Russia, for example, were told on a number of occasions to take care in the Balkans. He also used economic weapons - for example the use of tariffs in the 1880s. If he thought his friends might fall out, he sought to avoid war, but in such a way as to prevent complete reconciliation. This was his guideline during the Balkans Crises. He sometimes played the role of mediator, but was temperamentally unsuited to that role. The essence of Bismarckian diplomacy, however, was the policy of balancing tension.

Adapted from Layton 1995.

Questions

1. What do Items 1-3 tell us about Bismarck's approach to foreign policy?
2. Using Item 1 and your own knowledge, give arguments for and against the idea that Bismarck had a plan.
3. Judging from Items 2 and 3 would you say that Bismarck's foreign policy was a success? Explain your answer.

3.2 Foreign policy under the Kaiserreich, 1890-1914

Why did German foreign policy change after 1890?

A new direction in 1890

Layton argues that, at first sight, German foreign policy after 1890 appeared to be in decline:

'At first sight, it is tempting to view Germany's changed position by 1897 as one of decline - with control having passed to a "second eleven" who had overseen the collapse of Bismarck's diplomatic system and the creation of a set of diplomatic circumstances which set Germany on the path towards 1914.' (Layton 1995, pp.42-43)

Layton, like most historians, agrees that German foreign policy followed a less consistent path after

1890 than it did before. Nevertheless, he argues, the Bismarckian system was already beginning to crack up by 1890 anyway and, besides, changed circumstances necessitated a new direction.

The first sign of a new direction was the decision in 1890 not to renew the Reinsurance Treaty with Russia (see Section 3.1 above for information on the Reinsurance Treaty). Seligmann and McLean argue that this was a major mistake:

'Given the many disastrous foreign policy decisions that were to be made by Germany's leaders in the following 25 years, it is far from easy to decide which should be categorised as the worst ever taken. However, there can be no doubt that the non-renewal of the Reinsurance Treaty must rate as a candidate for this dubious distinction.' (Seligmann & McLean 2000, p.110)

Seligmann and McLean argue that failure to renew

the treaty led directly to an alliance between Russia and France which, in turn, led to the threat of a war on two fronts - exactly what Bismarck had aimed to avoid:

> 'In July 1891, a French naval squadron made a courtesy visit to the Russian port of Kronstadt. Then, in 1892, Russian and French negotiators agreed the terms of a military convention which was ratified as the Dual Alliance in January 1894. In one fell swoop, the nightmare that Bismarck had always striven hard to avoid - that of Germany being surrounded on two sides by a hostile coalition - was not only allowed, but actually encouraged, to come into existence.' (Seligmann & McLean 2000, pp.110-11)

Not all historians agree that the failure to renew the Reinsurance Treaty was such a big mistake. Lerman, for example, argues that:

> 'In 1890, Germany may have "lost control of the system" when Bismarck's successors failed to renew the secret Reinsurance Treaty of 1887 with Russia...However, given the changed conditions in which foreign policy had to be conducted in the 1890s, with the rise of mass politics, the growth of nationalism and the renewed focus on imperial rivalries, some kind of realignment within the European state system was probably inevitable.' (Lerman 2001, p.217)

Lerman, in other words, does not agree that it was a fatal mistake. Nor, unlike some historians, does she blame the 'inexperience' of Bismarck's successors. Layton also makes the point, supported by the views of Lothar Gall, that Bismarck's legacy was not without blemishes, and there were those who from the start saw the Reinsurance Treaty as no more than a temporary expedient with no long-term benefits. Also, as Carr points out, German Foreign Office officials believed that the Reinsurance Treaty was incompatible with the Dual Alliance with Austria. The arguments in support of the view that the failure to renew the Reinsurance Treaty was not a mistake are outlined in Box 1.24.

A 'free-hand' policy

Caprivi and his successors attempted to pursue a 'free-hand' policy in Europe, looking, for example, for a better relationship with Britain (something which Bismarck had largely neglected). One result was a treaty signed in 1890 by which African territory was exchanged between the two countries - Germany acquired Heligoland in exchange for a surrender of German claims to Zanzibar. Layton argues that the aim of this 'free-hand' policy was to ensure that:

> 'Differences amongst other powers combined with friendly German overtures would lead to Germany becoming the decisive voice in Europe. By 1897, Germany had allies in Austria-Hungary and Italy, an improved relationship with France, whilst

BOX 1.24 The failure to renew the Reinsurance Treaty

As early as the beginning of the 1890s, Europe fell into two camps - the German-Austro-Italian and the Franco-Russian. The latter was a reply to the former and not designed to outlast it. Bismarck has been praised for keeping Germany's two flanks apart and for negotiating the Reinsurance Treaty with Russia in 1887. The argument often put is that, unfortunately, his successors did not renew the treaty with the result that the line to Russia was broken and the Tsar looked to France. This, it is claimed, was the start of all future misfortunes. But there is not much to support this line of argument. Even in Bismarck's day, Russia and France were moving towards each other. They were driven in this direction by the Bismarck bloc of central powers - alliances, however peacefully meant, always provoke others. Making a counter-alliance with Russia, as Bismarck did, did not solve the problem. If Germany had a serious alliance it was with Austria-Hungary. Moreover, a piece of paper such as the Reinsurance Treaty achieved little in the best of circumstances. Its existence provided no protection against the real or imagined interests, desires and passions of the Russians. Its disappearance did not prevent Bismarck's successors from seeking new contacts with the Russians and they tried frequently to build ties in the period 1890-1909. If all those efforts failed in the end, what reason is there to suppose that the elaborate secret treaty of 1887 would have survived an emergency? The relationship between the two states was determined not by treaties but by interests and issues. Since Germany's industrial and military strength was far superior to Russia and as a German victory over Russia would completely destroy the balance of power, Russia and France stuck together.

Adapted from Mann 1996.

relations with Russia were slowly recovering ...Britain found itself on far worse terms with Russia and France, than Germany. German foreign policy had moved on from the days of Bismarck and, although the Franco-Russian alliance posed an important constraint upon Germany's strategic and diplomatic freedom of action, the situation was certainly not disastrous. Germany was still the dominant power on the continent.' (Layton 1995, p.43)

The policy of Weltpolitik

The meaning of 'Weltpolitik'

It was Bülow, then Foreign Minister, who first referred to the decision to pursue a policy of Weltpolitik (literally 'world policy') in 1897. As noted in Section 2.2 above, some historians see this as a response to domestic circumstances - as part of the policy of 'social imperialism' pursued by the German government - whilst others see it as a grandiose plan involving both continental and overseas expansion to attain world power status. According to this view, the adoption of a policy of Weltpolitik led inevitably to the outbreak of the First World War in 1914 (see below). As Layton points out, the debate between historians reflects the different ways in which contemporary Germans viewed the term 'Weltpolitik':

'Weltpolitik meant different things to different people. For some, it meant the creation of a larger overseas empire by the acquisition of colonies, in order to aid further the expansion of the German economy. For others, it was simply a policy to assist German business to penetrate and then establish areas of economic influence in as many parts of the world as possible. A third view epitomised by the Pan-German League amounted to nothing less than a racist Lebensraum [living space] policy of creating German settlements both overseas and to the East...The decision to embark on Weltpolitik in 1897 was probably at first no more than a desire broadly felt in Germany that Germany should somehow "catch up". This meant different things to different people.' (Layton 1995, pp.44-46)

Certainly, Weltpolitik meant some form of imperialism and it was also linked with the creation of a large navy (so-called Flottenpolitik). Support for such 'forward policies' came from a variety of sources, from the Kaiser, through government figures like Bülow and Admiral Tirpitz and from pressure groups like the Pan-German League, the Navy League and the German Colonial Society.

Imperialism as part of Weltpolitik

The appointment of Hohenlohe as Chancellor in 1894 marked a revived interest in empire, especially in southern Africa. Here, investment and migration had given Germany a strong interest in the Transvaal Republic. This was also a part of Africa where Germany already had a foothold (in the South-West). In the years 1894-95, Germany involved itself constantly in the affairs of this region, making an effort to appear as the protector of the Boers in the Transvaal against the British. The result was a clash with Britain in 1896 over the Krüger Telegram (see Box 1.25). This was an early illustration of how a 'world policy' could lead to diplomatic problems and it helped to focus attention in Germany on how its role in the world could be strengthened.

Economic imperialism

According to Porter and Armour:

'There was a fundamental tension between economic imperialism, and a type of imperialism

---

BOX 1.25 The Krüger Telegram, 1896

What gave offence to other powers was not so much Germany's desire to be a Great Power, but the Germans' clumsy approach to diplomacy after 1890. German intervention in South Africa in the 1890s is a good example of this. For Britain, vital interests were at stake. So long as the Boer Republics remained independent, Britain could not unite Cape Colony with the Rhodesias. Germany intervened in South Africa for the first time in 1894 when Cecil Rhodes tried to gain control of the railway the Boers had built. German protests obliged Rhodes to abandon his claim. In December 1895, Jameson, an agent of Rhodes, invaded the Transvaal with 800 men in an attempt to seize Johannesburg and overthrow the Boer Republic. The raid was a miserable failure but it incensed the Kaiser who insisted on immediate action. He talked wildly about sending troops to the Transvaal Republic. His advisers persuaded him to settle for what they thought was a less harmful gesture - a congratulatory telegram to Krüger, President of the Transvaal Republic. Anxiety about German investment in the Transvaal and concern for the 15,000 Germans working in the gold mines were of subordinate concern to the Kaiser. He was resentful of British success and hoped to bring pressure to bear. The Krüger Telegram was warmly applauded in Germany. As a diplomatic manoeuvre, however, it was unsuccessful. It did nothing to hinder British plans in South Africa and brought a German-Austrian-Italian axis no nearer. On the contrary, a serious shadow was cast over Anglo-German relations for the first time. The telegram was condemned in Britain as a piece of unwarranted meddling in a purely British concern by a previously friendly monarch and it roused anti-German feeling amongst sections of the British ruling class

Adapted from Carr 1991.

---

peculiarly German - the drive for colonial settlement in Europe, or Lebensraum [living space]. Economic imperialism was by far the more influential in the period 1890-1914...[It] took two main forms. There were those who believed in the necessity of colonies for economic expansion, both as sources of cheap raw materials and of cheap (ie native) labour, and as a secure market for manufacturing goods. Most economic imperialists, however, regarded colonies as [unimportant]. For all economic imperialists, Weltpolitik meant gaining control of the means whereby Germany's economy could continue to expand.' (Porter & Armour 1991, p.40)

So, economic imperialism included the drive to expand the colonial empire first acquired under Bismarck - Germany's 'place in the sun' as Bülow

put it. Some new colonies were acquired:
- Heliogoland from Britain in return for Zanzibar (1890)
- the Chinese treaty port of Kiaochow (1897)
- some Pacific islands - part of Samoa, the Caroline Islands and the Mariana Islands (1899)
- a strip of the French Congo after the Moroccan Crisis of 1911 (see below).

In terms of practical results, these overseas possessions were worth little economically or politically, however. The other aspect of economic imperialism, 'informal imperialism', was more rewarding:

'This took the form of extensive investments in and trade with Latin America, China and, in particular, the counties of south-eastern Europe and the Middle East. Here, if anywhere, the close cooperation of government and business...can be seen in action. The great banks and the Foreign Office worked hand-in-hand to realise the Baghdad railway project which held out the prospect of German access to the Middle East oil fields, and agreements were signed with Turkey for the training of the Turkish army by Prussian officers. German trade treaties took advantage of Austria-Hungary's bad relations with the Balkan states and German finance and manufactured goods flowed into the Balkan economies. The industrialist Hugo Stinnes may have exaggerated in 1911 when he [said] that another three or four years of peace would make Germany "undisputed master of Europe", but the essential insight was correct.' (Porter & Armour 1991, p.44)

The German navy as part of Weltpolitik - Flottenpolitik

If Germany was to achieve world power status, then, in the opinion of many, it would need to have a powerful navy, at least the equal of that of Britain. Seligmann and McLean (2000) suggest five main reasons for building a strong navy - see Box 1.26. The policy of naval expansion was master-minded by Admiral Alfred von Tirpitz, Head of the Reich Naval Office from 1897, and backed by the Navy League. The programme began with the 1898 Naval Law which ordered the building of 19 battleships by 1905. The number was raised to 38 following the passage of a second law in 1900. In addition, further large amounts of money for naval building were obtained by Tirpitz right up to 1912.

The naval policy appears to have been popular, though some historians argue that public opinion was manipulated by the German ruling class. Historians agree that the navy was built to rival that of Britain. But some (eg Porter & Armour 1991 and Seligmann & McLean 2000) argue that it was being built to challenge Britain's supremacy whilst others (eg Mann 1996) argue that it was built as a deterrent against an attack from Britain.

| BOX 1.26 | Five reasons for building a strong navy |

1. There were good economic reasons to build a fleet. Construction would bolster ports and shipping interests and export industries.
2. Failure to build a navy would mean facing decline as a great power.
3. The influential book on naval strategy *The Influence of Sea Power on History* by Admiral Mahan suggested that a large fleet was essential if a state was to gain admission to the ranks of great powers at the end of the 19th century.
4. Building a strong navy would remove the sense of humiliation following the Krüger Telegram debacle of 1896.
5. The Kaiser was strongly in favour of constructing a battle fleet.

Adapted from Seligmann & McLean 2000.

The effects of Weltpolitik on German foreign policy

While it is possible to draw out features of Weltpolitik such as imperialism and the building of a strong navy, it is less easy to see how it worked as a coherent foreign policy. German policy towards Russia and Britain illustrates this vagueness. If it proved impossible to detach Russia from France after their alliance of 1894, it would make sense for Germany to improve relations with Britain. This seemed a likely scenario, with Britain at loggerheads with Russia and France over colonial matters through the 1890s and into the new century. Instead, in spite of their failure to drive a wedge between Russia and France, German politicians like Bülow failed to bring about any agreement with Britain:

'Bülow had never felt that the Russian-French alliance called for a compensatory move in the direction of Britain, since he assumed the tensions between Britain and the two continental powers would keep the door to a German-British rapprochement permanently open.' (Clark 2000, p.139)

Indeed, Weltpolitik had two features that were especially damaging to hopes of better relations with Britain. It led to both colonial and naval rivalry. An early colonial incident was the clash of German and British interests in South Africa (Box 1.25 above). Attempts did follow between 1898 and 1901 to improve Anglo-German relations when Joseph Chamberlain tried to negotiate privately with the German government. This opportunity was missed, however, since Bülow was hopeful of improving relations with Russia and was then involved with Far Eastern problems rather than with Britain. In 1905-06 and again in 1911, Germany became involved in disputes with Britain over colonial matters in Morocco - see Box 1.27. By 1911, Britain had made an agreement with France (the Entente Cordiale signed in 1904) and an agreement with Russia (the

BOX 1.27 | The Moroccan Crises of 1905-06 and 1911

(i) In January 1905, revolution broke out in Russia, distracting the Russian government from foreign affairs. Overnight, the threat of a war on two fronts evaporated. The German government attempted to take advantage. In the past, Germany had not complained of French influence in Morocco. In February 1905, however, the German government decided on a gesture of protest. The Kaiser was asked to visit Tangier during his spring cruise of the Mediterranean. At first the Kaiser was reluctant, but he eventually agreed. During his three-hour visit in March 1905, he was received by the Sultan's uncle and, speaking in a tone similar to the Krüger Telegram, said that Germany considered Morocco to be an independent state and expected it to resist French pressure. This startled other European powers. Confident that European powers would back Moroccan independence, the Germans insisted that an international conference be called. The aim was to humiliate France in public. The French Foreign Minister urged the Cabinet to resist. But the Cabinet was split and he resigned. This was regarded as a great victory for Germany. The Germans continued to press for a conference and reluctantly the French agreed - another German victory. When the Algeciras conference met in January 1906, however, German confidence that France would be isolated turned out to be misplaced. As expected, Moroccan independence was guaranteed. But German proposals on the organisation of the police and state bank were defeated. The Moroccan adventure ended disastrously for Germany since the Anglo-French Entente (an agreement made between the two countries in 1904) emerged stronger than ever and Germany was publicly humiliated by being shown to be isolated, not France.
Adapted from Carr 1991.

(ii) Morocco became the site of a second diplomatic incident in 1911. When the French sent in troops to protect French interests in April 1911, the German Foreign Secretary, Kiderlen was confident that this was the first stage in an attempt to conquer the country - something which was banned by the Algeciras Conference. With the reluctant agreement of the Kaiser and Chancellor, Kiderlen sent a gunboat to the Moroccan port of Agadir, supposedly to protect German interests, but in reality to remind France that Germany must not be ignored on the Moroccan Question. The result was an international crisis. France bitterly resented this move, especially as it was in the middle of negotiations with Germany. Kiderlen made matters worse by suddenly demanding the whole of the French Congo as compensation. The stratagem misfired. The French broke off negotiations and the British backed them. There was a possibility of war, but France reopened negotiations with Germany and a peaceful settlement was reached. Germany recognised the right of France to control Morocco. In return, Germany gained part of the French Congo. This was no victory for Germany, however. The diplomacy had been ham-fisted and the danger of war exposed. And, once more, Britain had come down on the side of France.
Adapted from Carr 1991.

Anglo-Russian Entente, signed in 1907). Most historians agree that Britain made these agreements, in part at least, because it was concerned about Germany's ambitions and because it was alarmed at the growth of the German navy. It is important not to exaggerate British concerns, however. Historians agree that relations between Britain and Germany were complex in the period 1900-14 and there was nothing inevitable about the two states ending up going to war against each other.

It was not just disputes over colonies that soured Anglo-German relations. The decision of the German government to build a large navy was a major cause of the rift that developed between Britain and Germany:

'It was the conscious decision by the German government in 1897 to pursue Weltpolitik and to build a navy to rival that of Britain which turned the latent antagonism between Britain and Germany into active confrontation.' (Seligmann & McLean 2000, p.13)

This does not mean that there was any fear of a direct conflict between the two countries - certainly not before 1911. Furthermore, it is generally agreed that Anglo-German relations improved after the Second Moroccan Crisis.

The Bosnian Crisis 1908-09

Germany's support for Austria-Hungary became of particular importance in 1908-09 when Austro-Hungarian troops took control of Bosnia and Herzegovina (see Box 1.28). Until then, this area had been under Turkish control. The crisis arose because Russia made a deal with Austria-Hungary which, it claimed, the Austro-Hungarians failed to honour. Commenting on the occupation of Bosnia, Henig says:

'This action had been discussed with the Russian foreign minister, Isvolsky, who had given his agreement in exchange for Austria-Hungary using her good offices to secure for Russia greater influence at Constantinople and the right to free passage for Russian ships through the Straits [of the Bosporus] in times of peace and war. However, other powers, especially Britain, were strongly opposed to this second proposition and thus, while Austria-Hungary increased her territories, Russia got nothing.' (Henig 1993, p.19)

BOX 1.28 The Balkans 1908-14

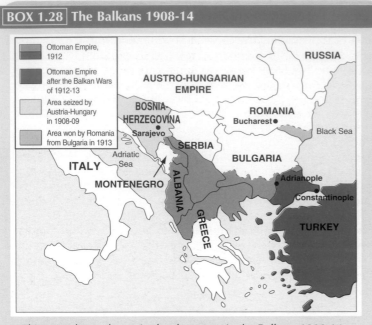

This map shows the main developments in the Balkans 1908-14.

The result was a rapid escalation of tension between Austria-Hungary and Russia and talk of war between the two empires. In January 1909, the German Chief of Staff intervened, making a public declaration to his Austrian counterpart that 'the moment Russia mobilises, Germany will also mobilise'. This was enough to force the Russians to back down. The significance of this event has been described as follows:

'Much of this was bluff: neither the Austrians nor the Russians were militarily or economically in a position to go to war, but the effect was to show both the nature and the limitations of the alliance system because, while the effect of Germany's commitment to Austria was made clear, the Russians had found only lukewarm support in Paris and London for their ambitions at Constantinople.' (Joll 1992, p.57)

According to Martel, Britain and France's failure to provide solid support for Russia was seen in Germany as evidence of weakness and led directly to the Second Moroccan Crisis of 1911 (see Box 1.27 above):

'The Germans regarded the Bosnian Crisis as convincing proof that neither the alliance with France nor the entente with Britain would provide the Russians with any meaningful assistance in the Balkans. Perhaps the Ententes would prove equally useless to France in North Africa where another crisis began to emerge in Morocco.' (Martel 1996, p.71)

What was Germany's role in the origins of the First World War?

Germany's role in the origins of the First World War has been a central issue of historical discussion ever since that war ended. The contemporary view, at the end of the war, was that Germany was responsible for the war. The War Guilt clause of the Treaty of Versailles placed the blame firmly on Germany 'for causing all the loss and damage' on the Allies as a result of 'the war imposed upon them by the aggression of Germany and her allies' (Article 231). In the inter-war years, however, historians came to believe that all the Great Powers had to bear some responsibility for the war and that to blame Germany alone was unjust. This view held sway until, in 1961, a German historian, Fritz Fischer, put the case once again that Germany was the key player in causing the war. He and, later, others like Röhl 'saw Germany's actions in 1914 as the logical consequence of a planned policy of aggression to achieve territory and world power' (Lerman 2001, p.216).

Germany planned the war - the arguments for

There is a variety of views on Germany's responsibility for the First World War. Fischer who, in a sense, revived the idea of the 'war guilt' of Germany believed that 'from the time of the Second Moroccan Crisis (Agadir Crisis) in 1911 the German leadership pursued a consistent policy with the aim of fighting a European war as a means of achieving world-power status for Germany' (quoted in Layton 1995, pp.41-2). Humiliated over Morocco in 1911, Germany was alarmed by the failure of negotiations with Britain in the period 1909-11 and by events in the Balkans (the Balkan Wars of 1912-13 - see Box 1.29 below). It was now clear that in any struggle in Europe, Britain would stand by her entente with France. Also, in the Balkans, Germany's one trustworthy ally, Austria, was threatened by a Russian-backed Serbia. Fischer believes that in this situation Germany began planning war. The evidence he uses comes from a meeting, usually referred to as the 'War Council' (in December 1912). At this meeting, the Kaiser and his top military and naval advisers 'discussed the possibility and desirability of a general European war arising over the Balkans and the need to prepare the public through the press for a war against Russia. The military urged an immediate war, but Tirpitz argued for a delay until June 1914 when the navy would be better prepared' (Lerman 2001, p.224). The significance of this meeting has become the subject of much debate. But, for the Fischer school, the meeting provides conclusive evidence that Germany planned to fight a war, the timing of which would be determined by German military and strategic interests.

BOX 1.29 | The Balkan Wars 1912-13 (see map in Box 1.28 above for the geography of the region)

The outbreak of war between Italy and Turkey in September 1911 ensured that tension mounted in the Balkans. In October 1912, the Balkan states attacked Turkey and, within a few weeks, the Ottoman Empire was in shreds. This was a severe blow to Austria-Hungary since it was commonly believed in Vienna that the Habsburg monarchy would not be able to survive the fall of the Ottomans. The dramatic expansion of Serbia was of particular concern to the Austro-Hungarians since the Serbs looked forward to the liberation of Bosnia in the not too distant future. The Austro-Hungarian Foreign Minister, Berchtold, however, adopted a cautious stance of which the Emperor, Franz Josef, who was the key decision-maker, approved. Tension mounted in the winter of 1912-13 when Montenegro and Serbia seized territory. Berchtold toughened his stance while both Austria and Russia took military measures. War was only avoided because neither Franz Josef nor Berchtold (nor the Russian Foreign Minister, Sazonov) wanted war. Germany also didn't favour war, but informed Austria that, in the event of a Russian attack in support of Serbia, it would come to Austria's assistance. At the Conference of London where the Great Powers set the seal of approval on the territorial changes in the Balkans, Germany and Russia worked together to restrain the hostile parties. But German policy hardened when the Balkan states fell out and went to war in the summer of 1913. The Austrians were concerned by Serb attacks on Northern Albania and consulted Germany before using force. The Kaiser and Jagow, the Foreign Minister, assured Austria that Germany would support it. Fortified by this, Berchtold sent an ultimatum to Serbia ordering its troops out in eight days. The Serbs who were clearly in the wrong and lacked Russian support complied. Berchtold was elated, but a dangerous precedent had been set - where patient diplomacy had failed, an ultimatum backed by force succeeded.

Adapted from Carr 1991.

Germany planned the war - the arguments against

A number of other historians give prominence to the War Council, but they draw back from the idea that war was premeditated and planned from that moment onwards. Seligmann and McLean, for example, agree that the War Council was 'making decisions of a decisive character' but go on to state that

> 'The "War Council" itself is best seen not in terms of a German decision for war, but in terms of a decision against long-term peace...The Kaiser and his military entourage resolved not to preserve peace at any price.' (Seligmann and McLean 2000, p.146)

Mommsen argues that the importance of the meeting has been exaggerated. He points out, for example, that Bethmann-Hollweg, the Chancellor, was not even invited. Clark, on the other hand, argues that the meeting did not bring any significant change in direction. It reveals the extreme attitudes of the military who favoured a 'preventive war', he suggests, but it did not make war inevitable.

Germany planned the war - the middle way

In addition to those historians who believe that war was definitely planned and those who believe that it definitely was not planned, there are historians who take the middle way. This view is outlined by Layton as follows:

> 'To suggest that the evidence proves that the German government was actually planning to unleash a war in the summer of 1914 is to go too far. War plans certainly existed - and the "War Council" meeting of December 1912 is clear evidence of how war was considered to be a viable option. What it also reveals is that from 1912 German leaders were acutely aware in their own minds of how 1914-15 represented the optimal time for war from a German standpoint. These considerations were surely massively influential when the Sarajevo crisis developed.' (Layton 1995, p.48)

MAIN POINTS - Section 3.2

- The first sign of a new direction in foreign policy was the decision in 1890 not to renew the Reinsurance Treaty with Russia. Some historians argue that this was a big mistake. Others disagree.
- Caprivi and his successors attempted to pursue a 'free-hand' policy in Europe. The aim was to ensure that differences amongst other powers, combined with friendly German overtures, would lead to Germany becoming the decisive voice in Europe.
- In 1897, Bülow talked of a policy of 'Weltpolitik'. This meant different things to different people. For some, it meant the creation of a larger overseas empire. For others, it was simply a policy to assist German business. According to a third view, it meant creating German settlements both overseas and to the East.
- Renewed interest in empire under Hohenlohe led to a clash with Britain in southern Africa and the Krüger Telegram (1896). Under Weltpolitik, Germany gained a few (insignificant) colonies and started a naval building programme.
- Key incidents on the path to the First World War include - (1) the Moroccan Crisis of 1905-06 (2) the Bosnian Crisis of 1908-09 (3) the Moroccan Crisis of 1911 (4) the Balkan Wars of 1912-13.
- There is debate over whether Germany planned to go to war against its European rivals in the years 1914-16, or not.

Activity 1.5 Why did Germany go to war in 1914?

ITEM 1 Why did Germany go to war in 1914?

(i)

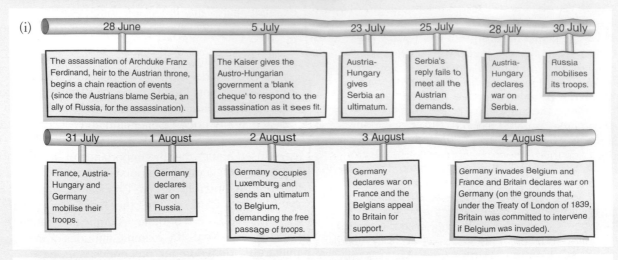

| 28 June | 5 July | 23 July | 25 July | 28 July | 30 July |

The assassination of Archduke Franz Ferdinand, heir to the Austrian throne, begins a chain reaction of events (since the Austrians blame Serbia, an ally of Russia, for the assassination).

The Kaiser gives the Austro-Hungarian government a 'blank cheque' to respond to the assassination as it sees fit.

Austria-Hungary gives Serbia an ultimatum.

Serbia's reply fails to meet all the Austrian demands.

Austria-Hungary declares war on Serbia.

Russia mobilises its troops.

| 31 July | 1 August | 2 August | 3 August | 4 August |

France, Austria-Hungary and Germany mobilise their troops.

Germany declares war on Russia.

Germany occupies Luxemburg and sends an ultimatum to Belgium, demanding the free passage of troops.

Germany declares war on France and the Belgians appeal to Britain for support.

Germany invades Belgium and France and Britain declares war on Germany (on the grounds that, under the Treaty of London of 1839, Britain was committed to intervene if Belgium was invaded).

(ii) Following the assassination of Archduke Franz Ferdinand, the heir to the Austrian throne, Germany's initial reaction was to give full support to Austria-Hungary - the so-called 'blank cheque'. German pressure for swift and decisive action combined with German knowledge of the severity of the ultimatum being being prepared against Serbia suggests that Germany had adopted more than just defensive diplomatic tactics on behalf of its ally. Bethmann-Hollweg seems to have recognised that the situation provided a genuine opportunity to assert Austrian power against Serbia in a localised conflict. This would result, so the argument goes, in a significant diplomatic victory over both Russia and the Entente as a whole. This was risky. Russia might might stand by Serbia and broaden the conflict. In the first four weeks of July the German leaders seem to have been prepared to take that chance, in the belief that Germany would win a continental war. The Austrian ultimatum to Serbia on 23 July brought home the major implications of the crisis. Britain in particular tried to mediate by calling for an international conference. But, significantly, Germany ignored any such proposals and encouraged Austria-Hungary to take military action. It seems that German leaders all agreed on the course of action until 27 July. After this date, however, there were disagreements. The Kaiser returned from holiday on 28 July and proposed that the Austrians should halt in Belgrade and then negotiate with the Serbs. At the same time, Moltke, the Army Chief, pressed Austria to mobilise immediately and Bethmann-Hollweg seems to have been playing an elaborate diplomatic game to make Germany appear to be the innocent party in face of Russian aggression - or, it may have been that he had doubts about the wisdom of the high-risk strategy. On 30 July, Bethmann-Hollweg stated at a meeting that 'things are out of control'. The crisis had gone beyond a point where diplomacy could halt it. Military matters now took precedence. In Germany, this was reflected by the increasing influence of the generals.

Adapted from Layton 1995.

ITEM 2 The Kaiser was to blame

HE WONT BE HUNGRY TILL HE GETS IT

...he bath. It was produced in Britain in 1914.

ITEM 3   Did Germany go to war for domestic reasons?

In the 1970s, the view that Germany went to war in 1914 for domestic reasons gained currency. The argument was that by 1914, Wilhelm II's semi-absolutist regime had been driven into a cul-de-sac as the result of a series of disasters in domestic and foreign policy. The Kaiser's attempt to use patriotism to kill off socialism had failed, as the SPD gains in the 1912 election show. That election result meant Chancellor Bethmann-Hollweg was unable to get measures passed through the Reichstag and the atmosphere of political stalemate made war attractive. This 'domestic encirclement' of the Prussian ruling class was coupled with a sharp deterioration in Germany's international position. By 1911 at the latest, Weltpolitik was universally considered to have failed. Naval competition with Britain ensured relations between the two states remained poor. The attempts to gain concessions from the French in Morocco ended in diplomatic humiliation. The German leadership came to see their future as 'world power or downfall'. The view that Germany went to war in 1914 for domestic reasons no longer seems persuasive, however. Recent research has undermined the gloomy picture of domestic encirclement. It is clear, for example, that Bethmann-Hollweg saw the Conservative Party rather than the SPD as the main threat to effective government. He accused them of wishing to destroy him. So, in one sense the election of 1912 was not a disaster since the results weakened the Conservatives. It had, after all, been the Conservatives in 1909 who had undermined Bülow's Chancellorship by voting against the Reich finance reform and who had humiliated Bethmann-Hollweg during the Reichstag debate which ended the Second Moroccan Crisis. Besides, major pieces of legislation were passed on the eve of the war, such as the Army Bill of 1913 and the imperial tax credit the same year.

Adapted from Seligmann & McLean 2000.

ITEM 4   Who was in charge of German policy in 1914?

One of the problems in assessing Germany's role in the events leading to 1914 is to locate exactly who took the decisions. The Austrian Foreign Minister, Berchthold, stated the problem in 1914 when he asked: 'Who rules in Berlin - Bethmann-Hollweg [the Chancellor] or Moltke [the Army Chief]?'. Moltke and the other army chiefs were prepared to risk a preemptive strike against the Entente powers. They thought that Russia in particular would be militarily better equipped by 1916-17. Bethmann-Hollweg was more cautious, but he too appeared to believe that, in the 1914 crisis, war was an acceptable option. Among other 'candidates' for influence, historians like Röhl have seen the Kaiser as playing a central role in foreign affairs. Röhl quotes with approval the view of the British ambassador in Berlin, Sir Edward Malet, just after Wilhelm II's accession: 'If we were dealing with a country in which the foreign policy was guided by the government and not by the Sovereign, the personal feelings of the monarch would be a matter of small moment, but that is not the case. It is important that the Emperor should be on our side. The Chancellor's position is no longer as strong as it was under Wilhelm I'. The Kaiser's enthusiasm for a strong navy and his tendency to become involved in foreign affairs are undoubted. Mann suggests that the Kaiser often reserved to himself the last word on foreign policy, and more frequently the first and second. He also claims that, with Tirpitz, he firmly prevented all British attempts to limit the naval arms race. The Kaiser is also seen as playing an important role in the events leading to war, from the 'War Council' in 1912 through to the events of 1914. According to this view, it was only with the outbreak of war that the Kaiser lost control. Some historians,

This cartoon was published in the French magazine L'Europe Antiprussienne on 25 December 1914. It shows Kaiser Wilhelm as a butcher, with the ironic caption 'The envoy of God'.

however, argue that the Kaiser's influence before 1914 has been exaggerated. Clark, for example, takes the view that the Kaiser did not have consistent influence in policy-making, even in foreign policy. Neither Bülow nor Bethmann-Hollweg were 'pliant tools' of the Kaiser. Even in regard to the navy, which the Kaiser saw as a pet project, Clark claims that it was Tirpitz, not Wilhelm, who was in control. Clark also believes that the Kaiser's input into the crisis of 1912-14 was generally 'peaceable'.

Adapted from Porter & Armour 1991, Mommsen 1995, Röhl 1994, Mann 1996 and Clark 2000.

Questions

1. 'Given the direction of foreign policy after 1890, it was inevitable that Germany be involved in a war against its European neighbours in the years 1914-16'. Using Items 1-4 and your own knowledge, give arguments for and against this view.

2. Judging from Items 1-3 and your own knowledge, why did Germany go to war in August 1914?

3. a) What does Item 4 tell us about the historical debate over the nature of the Kaiserreich?
   b) Why does it matter historically who made the decisions in Germany in the build-up to the First World War?

References

- **Bell & Cawood (2000)** Bell, D. & Cawood, I., 'Bismarck's foreign policy 1871-90', *Modern History Review*, Vol.11.3, February 2000.

- **Berghahn (2001)** Berghahn, V., 'Demographic growth, industrialisation and social change' in *Breuilly (2001)*.

- **Breuilly (1996)** Breuilly, J., 'The First German Unification', *Modern History Review*, No.3, Feb 1996.

- **Breuilly (2001)** Breuilly, J. (ed.), *19th Century Germany*, Arnold, 2001.

- **Breuilly (2001a)** Breuilly, J., 'Revolution to unification' in *Breuilly (2001)*.

- **Carr (1991)** Carr, W., *A History of Germany: 1815-1990*, Edward Arnold, 1991.

- **Clark (2000)** Clark, C., *Kaiser Wilhelm II*, Longman, 2000.

- **Clark (2001)** Clark, C., 'Germany 1815-48: restoration or pre-March' in *Breuilly (2001)*.

- **Craig (1978)** Craig, G.A., *Germany, 1866-1945*, Oxford University Press, 1978.

- **Feuchtwanger (2001)** Feuchtwanger, E., 'Bismarck, Prussia and German nationalism', *History Review*, No.39, March 2001.

- **Gall (1986)** Gall, L., *Bismarck, The White Revolutionary*, Vol 1, Allen and Unwin, 1986.

- **Goodlad (2000)** Goodlad, G.D., 'The unification of Germany', *Modern History Review*, Vol.12.1, Sept 2000.

- **Henig (1993)** Henig, R., *The Origins of the First World War* (2nd edn), Routledge, 1993.

- **John (1991)** John, M., 'Unification of Germany: the view from below', *Modern History Review*, April 1991.

- **Joll (1992)** Joll, J., *The Origins of the First World War* (2nd edn), Longman, 1992.

- **Kennedy (1989)** Kennedy, P., *The Rise and Fall of the Great Powers*, Fontana, 1989.

- **Kitchen (1996)** Kitchen, M., *Cambridge Illustrated History of Germany*, Cambridge University Press, 1996.

- **Koch (1984)** Koch, H.W., *The Origins of the First World War: Great Power Rivalry and German War Aims (2nd edn.)*, Macmillan 1984.

- **Layton (1995)** Layton, G., *From Bismarck to Hitler: Germany 1890-1933*, Hodder and Stoughton, 1995.

- **Lee (2001)** Lee, R., '"Relative backwardness" and long-run development: economic, demographic and social changes' in *Breuilly (2001)*.

- **Lee (1982)** Lee, S.J., *Aspects of European History: 1789-1980*, Methuen, 1982.

- **Lemieux (2000)** Lemieux, S., 'Bismarck's foreign policy 1862-71: by design or default?', *Modern History Review*, Vol.12.3, Feb 2000.

- **Lerman (2001)** Lerman, K.A., 'Bismarckian Germany and the structure of the German Empire' in *Breuilly (2001)*.

- **Mann (1996)** Mann, G., *The History of Germany since 1789*, Pimlico, 1996.

- **Martel (1996)** Martel, G., *The Origins of the First World War* (2nd edn), Longman, 1996.

- **McKinnon-Bell & Cawood (2001)** McKinnon-Bell, D. & Cawood, I., 'Otto von Bismarck and German unification', *Modern History Review*, Vol.13.2, Nov 2001.

- **Mommsen (1995)** Mommsen, W.J., *Imperial Germany: 1867-1918*, Arnold, 1995.

- **Murphy (1996)** Murphy, D., 'Germany under William II, 1890-1914', *Modern History Review*, Vol.8.2, November 1996.

- **Pflanze (1963)** Pflanze, O., *Bismarck and the Development of Germany*, Vol.1, Princeton University Press, 1963.

- **Röhl (1994)** Röhl, J., *The Kaiser and his Court*, Cambridge University Press, 1994.

- **Röhl (1996)** Röhl, J., 'The Kaiser and his court', *History Review*, No.25, September, 1996.

- **Seligmann & McLean (2000)** Seligmann, M.S. & McLean R.R., *Germany from Reich to Republic: 1871-1918*, Macmillan, 2000.

- **Stiles & Farmer (2001)** Stiles, A. & Farmer, A., *The Unification of Germany 1815-1890*, Hodder and Stoughton, 2001.

- **Stürmer (2000)** Stürmer, M., *The German Empire*, Phoenix Press, 2000.

- **Taylor (1961)** Taylor, A.J.P., *Bismarck*, Grey Arrow, 1961.

- **Thomson (1962)** Thomson, D., *Europe Since Napoleon*, Longman, 1962.

- **Waller (1991)** Waller, B., 'The enigma of Bismarck as imperial Chancellor', *Modern History Review*, Vol.2.2, February 1991.

- **Waller (1997)** Waller, B., *Bismarck*, Blackwell, 1997.

- **Waller (1998)** Waller, B., 'Bismarck', *History Review*, No.30, March 1998.

- **Whaley (2001)** Whaley, J., 'The German Lands before 1815' in *Breuilly (2001)*.

UNIT 2 · Germany 1918-23

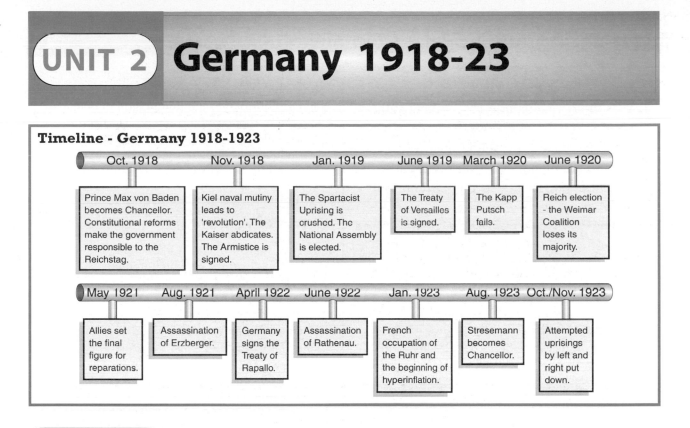

Timeline - Germany 1918-1923

Oct. 1918	Nov. 1918	Jan. 1919	June 1919	March 1920	June 1920
Prince Max von Baden becomes Chancellor. Constitutional reforms make the government responsible to the Reichstag.	Kiel naval mutiny leads to 'revolution'. The Kaiser abdicates. The Armistice is signed.	The Spartacist Uprising is crushed. The National Assembly is elected.	The Treaty of Versailles is signed.	The Kapp Putsch fails.	Reich election - the Weimar Coalition loses its majority.

May 1921	Aug. 1921	April 1922	June 1922	Jan. 1923	Aug. 1923	Oct./Nov. 1923
Allies set the final figure for reparations.	Assassination of Erzberger.	Germany signs the Treaty of Rapallo.	Assassination of Rathenau.	French occupation of the Ruhr and the beginning of hyperinflation.	Stresemann becomes Chancellor.	Attempted uprisings by left and right put down.

Introduction

Failure to win the First World War had severe consequences in Germany. The government deliberately neglected to prepare the German people for defeat and, as a result, defeat hit people harder than would otherwise have been the case. An early casualty was the Kaiser. In November 1918, he was forced to leave Germany for exile. He never returned. The Kaiser's departure ensured that there would be a new system of government in Germany. The question was, what sort of government? Historians agree that, in November and December 1918, there was a revolutionary mood in Germany, but they are divided about whether there was actually a genuine revolution. At first, there was a struggle between those who supported the creation of a democratic republic and those who wanted a socialist republic. This soon led to clashes of which the most serious was that in January 1919 when the Communists (members of the newly formed KPD) tried to seize control of government in the so-called Spartacist Uprising. It was not just the extreme left

that opposed the setting up of the Weimar Republic, however. The new Republic also faced serious opposition from the right. Although the army was prepared to use troops against the extreme left, it was lukewarm about the new Republic and refused to intervene in 1920 when the so-called Kapp Putsch - an attempt to set up a military government - took place. The Kapp Putsch was broken by a general strike and the Republic survived, only to face another major crisis in 1923. Central to events in 1923 is the issue of reparations. Some historians argue that they were the root cause of the crisis, others that they were only a contributory factor. Whichever was the case, there is no doubt that Germany faced a severe economic crisis in 1923 and that groups on both the extreme left and the extreme right tried to take advantage of this crisis to further their own ends. This unit examines the various difficulties faced by Germany in the years 1918-23 and the ways in which the new Republican government responded to them.

UNIT SUMMARY

Part 1 looks at the setting up of the Weimar Republic. It considers whether there was a revolution in Germany at the end of the First World War, whether the Weimar constitution was flawed and what reaction there was to the signing of the Treaty of Versailles.

Part 2 examines the problems that the Weimar Republic faced in the period 1920-23. It focuses on the crises that the German government and people faced between 1920 and 1923.

1 The setting up of the Weimar Republic

Key issues

1. Was there a revolution in Germany at the end of the First World War?

2. Was the Weimar constitution flawed?

3. What were the terms of the Treaty of Versailles and what was the reaction to it?

1.1 Was there a revolution in Germany at the end of the First World War?

The 'revolution from above'

The Germans' last major offensive in the First World War came in March 1918. Initially, they made advances. But, they lacked the troops and supplies to make a decisive breakthrough. The Allies began a counter-offensive in July and on 8 August broke through:

> 'The German lines held until 8 August, a black day for the German army, when the Entente broke through at the Somme with massed tank units, and the Germans fled in panic.' (Kitchen 1996, p.229)

By the end of the September, the German high command had reached the conclusion that the war was lost and an armistice (truce) would have to be sought. Berghahn argues that the decisive meeting was held on 29 September when Germany's Supreme Commander, General Ludendorff, agreed to Admiral Paul von Hintze's arguments that the war was lost and that the military should implement a 'revolution from above' to prevent the monarchy being swept away by a 'revolution from below':

> 'If an armistice were to be signed as soon as possible, there was, in Hintze's view, only one way in which the domestic crisis...could be contained: by involving a broadly based government containing also the parties of the centre of the left. At a crucial meeting on 29 September, Ludendorff, who in previous weeks had been wavering between military optimism and political panic, agreed to Hintze's proposals.' (Berghahn 1987, p.56)

As well as agreeing to implement political reforms, Ludendorff made it very clear that he wanted the members of the military command to distance themselves from the negotiations leading to an armistice. It was, in other words, at this meeting that the steps were first taken to manufacture the 'Stab-in-the-Back' myth. This was the idea that the military leadership was in no way responsible for defeat in the war. Rather, Germany was betrayed (stabbed in the back) by Republican politicians, desperate to bring down the monarchy:

> 'As Ludendorff put it at the meeting of 29 September, as many people as possible were to be held responsible for the humiliation of defeat - with the exception of those who had been instrumental first in unleashing the war and then in conducting it uncompromisingly.' (Berghahn 1987, p.58)

Political reforms in October 1918

The first political fallout from the meeting of 29 September was the appointment of Prince Max von Baden as Chancellor on 3 October. He formed a broad-based government which immediately set about transforming Germany from a monarchy into a parliamentary democracy:

> 'A series of constitutional reforms came into effect which made Germany into a parliamentary democracy: the three-class franchise was abolished in Prussia; the Emperor [ie Kaiser] conceded his powers over the army and navy to the Reichstag [Parliament]; and the Chancellor and government were made accountable to the Reichstag instead of the Kaiser. At the same time, armistice negotiations with the Allies were initiated.' (Layton 1995, p.74)

Whilst there is agreement that these reforms - which were completed by the end of October - amounted to a major structural change in the German political system, there is a debate over the role played by the Reichstag. Some historians, such as Carr, argue that the Reichstag played an important role in forcing change. Others disagree, arguing that the changes were imposed by those with real power - the monarchy and the army - in order to secure better peace terms and to prevent a 'revolution from below' breaking out. Carr's view is that:

> 'While it is fair to say that the first parliamentary government came into being partly by the [orders] of the Supreme Command, it is equally clear that mounting pressure from the Reichstag for political change could not have been resisted for much longer.' (Carr 1991, p.233)

Other historians disagree, on the grounds that the Reichstag had always been ignored in the past. Layton argues, for example, that:

> 'The idea of a Reichstag initiative certainly cannot be ignored, but on balance it would be wrong to read too much into its actions. Over the years, the Reichstag had showed no real inclination to seize the constitutional initiative...The Reichstag adjourned on 5 October [1918] and went into recess [on holiday] until 22 October, when it adjourned again until 9 November. These were hardly the actions of an institution that wished to shape events decisively.' (Layton 1995, p.74)

Popular reaction to news of defeat

For many Germans, news that the government was negotiating for peace was a devastating blow. Box 2.1 examines how people reacted.

BOX 2.1 **Reaction to defeat**

The frank acknowledgment of defeat on 3 October 1918 came as a bombshell to the German public which was completely unprepared for it. To the very last, the great majority had believed the over-optimistic estimates of Germany's position in the war that had been put out by official propaganda. The request for an armistice suddenly and dramatically revealed that the propaganda was false. From that moment on, the German people's only desire was to see the war ended, as quickly as possible and at any price. The peace movement gathered momentum like an avalanche throughout October. It also grew more and more radical. Revolutionary groups which had been small in number and whose activities had been hampered by government police measures received ever-growing support and encouragement from the people. Although public opinion was not primarily anti-monarchical, bigger and bigger sections in the population came to the conclusion that it might be impossible to negotiate a peace settlement if the Kaiser remained in power. The third letter that US President sent to the Kaiser on 23 October - whatever its intent - was interpreted as meaning that, if the Kaiser abdicated, Germany would be offered more lenient peace terms. As a result, the demand for abdication was voiced more and more strongly and openly discussed in the press, despite censorship.

Adapted from Kolb 1988.

The Kiel mutiny

On 28 October, the commanders of the German navy ordered the fleet to put to sea and make a raid on the English Channel. Carr describes the mood at the time:

'The morale of the sailors was perilously low. They resented the arrogance of their officers, the strictness of naval discipline and the disparity in rations between officers and men. The latest order seemed like a lunatic gesture designed to appease fanatical officers and likely to endanger the armistice negotiations.' (Carr 1991, p.236)

As a result, the crews of two ships mutinied. When the naval commanders ordered the arrest of these crews, other sailors demonstrated in Kiel on 3 November and eight were shot dead. This was the cue for a general mutiny. The following day, workers, soldiers and sailors mutinied and began

setting up their own councils. By 8 November, workers', soldiers' and sailors' councils had been set up at all the main cities and ports. It appeared that the 'revolution from below' that the military commanders feared had begun:

'There can be little doubt that a genuinely revolutionary situation prevailed in Germany in early November 1918.' (Layton 1995, pp.74-75)

Whilst most historians agree that there was a 'revolutionary situation' in early 1918, many are keen to point out that many of the people who helped to set up workers' and soldiers' councils were not hoping for a revolution like that which had taken place in Russia in 1917. They were not hoping, in other words, for a socialist revolution in which all the old political structures were broken down and power handed to the workers. Rather, their main aim was the end of the 'old order' and, in particular, the abdication of the Kaiser. Carr argues that the councils that were set up were not revolutionary bodies at all:

'The name ["council"] was an accidental by-product of a revolutionary situation; it certainly did not imply that the councils were seeking to overthrow the existing order of things. Only occasionally did a socialist note creep in, as in Dresden and Leipzig, where the councils promised to socialise the economic system and arm the people to defend the revolution. Most councils were local ad hoc bodies, manned by patriotic Germans anxious to maintain law and order and ensure the smooth running of local services at a time of national crisis. All they had in common was a wish to be rid of the Emperor and see a fully democratic form of government established in Germany.' (Carr 1991, p.237)

The SPD

By 1918, the SPD was a well-established mass party, though it had suffered a split in 1917 - see Box 2.2. It was the only party to have mass working-class support and was, therefore, in a good position to take a lead when the 'revolution from below' broke out. It is important to be clear, however, that, although it supported socialist policies, the SPD did not aim for a revolution like that in Russia where the Communists (Bolsheviks) had overthrown the government by force and imposed socialism without being elected by a majority of the population. The SPD's leaders, Friedrich Ebert and Philip Scheidemann, were both democrats and moderates:

'The SPD, led by Ebert and Scheidemann, represented moderate reformist socialism. Above all, the party upheld democracy and constitutionalism and it rejected [absolutely] anything that might have been equated with Soviet-style communism.' (Layton 1995, p.75)

Feuchtwanger argues that, as events unfolded after

The SPD and USPD

By 1914, the SPD had over one million members and it won the support of 34.8% of the voters in the Reich election that year. Three years later, the party split over the direction of the war effort. The Majority SPD continued to support it, while the Independent SPD (USPD) opposed it. It is important to note that the USPD was not the left wing of the SPD. Rather, the USPD contained those members of the SPD who opposed the war. It had a right and a left wing. Those on the right supported parliamentary democracy. Those on the left supported a Russian-style socialist revolution. The Majority SPD was able to play a major role in determining the course of the revolution in 1918. Under its leaders, Ebert and Scheidemann, the SPD was a constitutionalist party which believed that the working class would come to power via the ballot box. When the Socialists won a majority of votes, then and only then would it be time to introduce socialist reforms. The steady increase in the vote for the SPD, together with the constitutional changes in October 1918, encouraged the SPD to believe that it would be forming a government in the not too distant future. The prospect of bloody revolution appalled and offended the SPD leadership. It had no place in their tidy scheme of things. It would only add to the difficulties facing defeated Germany and might even endanger the unity of the Reich for which German people had fought and died. A deep sense of patriotism and firm belief in Parliament guided them to the conclusion that law and order must be restored as quickly as possible so that the constitutional system of government could be established firmly in the hearts and minds of the people. Nor did the Majority SPD object to the monarchy as such. They only joined in the calls for the Kaiser's abdication because their own supporters were deserting the party in large numbers and joining the USPD. If they were to regain the support of active party workers and prevent civil war, they must place themselves at the head of the popular movement and divert it into constitutional channels.

Adapted from Carr 1991.

the Kiel mutiny, the task facing the SPD was to stay in control of the masses without losing support to the more radical socialists:

'Ebert and his colleagues had to show their followers that they had the measure of the Emperor and his military officers who were blocking the way to an immediate peace.' (Feuchtwanger 1995, pp.14-15)

The abdication of the Kaiser

The 'revolution from below' spread so rapidly that, by 9 November, the Kaiser was forced to abdicate. Kolb argues that the Chancellor, Prince Max von Baden, played an important role that day:

'The wave of revolution reached the national capital on 9 November when several conflicting events took place in Berlin. The Chancellor, Prince Max von Baden, was convinced that the monarchy had a chance of survival only if Wilhelm II and the Crown Prince abdicated without delay; he therefore made frantic efforts from early dawn to persuade the Kaiser at Spa to authorise him to issue a proclamation to that effect. Towards noon, as armies of demonstrators marched through the streets of the capital and the soldiers in barracks joined the movement, Prince Max announced the Kaiser's abdication, although he did not yet have the authority to do so; at the same time, he transferred the office of Chancellor to Friedrich Ebert, Leader of the SPD.' (Kolb 1988, pp.7-8)

It was after Prince Max's announcement and the transfer of power to Ebert that the military High Command informed the Kaiser that he could no longer rely on the Armed Forces for support. Reluctantly, historians agree, the Kaiser then went into exile in the Netherlands. According to Carr, it was events in Bavaria on 8 November that were 'decisive' in forcing the Kaiser's abdication:

'The decisive moment in the German Revolution occurred on 8 November when a republic was proclaimed in Bavaria...The proclamation of the Bavarian Republic was undeniably a revolutionary act. This transformed what had been a rather haphazard movement led by unknown workers and soldiers into a serious political revolution. And it brought home forcibly to Prince Max's Cabinet the gravity of the situation.' (Carr 1991, pp.237-38)

Ebert's position on 9 November

Historians agree that the transfer of power from Prince Max to Ebert was strictly unconstitutional. Feuchtwanger, however, argues that it was important symbolically since it secured the loyalty of the civil service to the new regime:

'When at around 1 pm on Saturday 9 November, Prince Max handed his office over to Ebert, he was acting unconstitutionally in a strict sense, but the element of continuity was sufficient to ensure the loyalty of the imperial bureaucracy to the new masters.' (Feuchtwanger 1995, pp.14-15)

Historians also agree that, whilst Ebert pressed for and supported the abdication of the Kaiser, he hoped to preserve the monarchy. His colleague, Scheidemann, however, made a speech to a crowd from a window in the Reichstag building in which he declared that Germany was now a republic. This angered Ebert, but ensured that any chance of the monarchy surviving was gone. Layton argues that, having failed to preserve the monarchy, Ebert's main concern was that the left would take advantage of the political climate:

'Ebert's main worry was that...the extreme left would gain the upper hand. He saw the growing number of workers' councils as comparable to Russian-style soviets which threatened his chosen path of evolution and legitimacy. He was determined to prevent the descent into civil strife by maintaining law and order and he feared that the return of millions of troops after the armistice agreement, which was eventually signed on 11 November, would create enormous social and political problems.' (Layton 1995, pp.76-77)

To prevent the left gaining the upper hand the SPD leadership supported the setting up of a National Assembly which would be responsible for drawing up a new constitution - see Box 2.3.

BOX 2.3 The SPD leadership's main aim

The primary aim of the Majority Socialist leaders from 9 November onwards was to set up a National Assembly as soon as possible. It was for this body alone, in their view, to take decisions as to the future organisation of state and society. Although the left-wing radicals agitated loudly against the plan for a National Assembly - using the slogan "all power to the councils" - that was not a realistic possibility in November 1918. All political forces of importance were in favour of a National Assembly - the middle class no less solidly than the SPD and trade unions, even the majority of the USPD, most of the workers' councils and - especially important in the early weeks - practically all the soldiers' councils. On 29 November, the Council of People's Commissars (see below) passed a law providing for elections to a National Assembly.

Adapted from Kolb 1988.

The interim government

Since the National Assembly would be set up only once national elections were held, it was necessary to set up an interim government. Feuchtwanger argues that Ebert realised that if a government led by him was to retain popular support, he needed to include USPD members in an all-socialist coalition:

'Without their [ie the USPD's] presence in government, it was unlikely that Ebert and his SPD colleagues could have survived in office at this moment and indeed during the next few weeks. Until now, the SPD leaders had been inclined to continue in coalition with the bourgeois [ie middle-class] parties, but with Ebert rather than Prince Max in the lead. Events were overtaking this possibility.' (Feuchtwanger 1995, p.15)

Rather than a government made up of the SPD and 'bourgeois' parties (ie the middle-class parties which had been in government under the Kaiser), Ebert managed to persuade the USPD to join the SPD:

'The outcome was the formation of a Council of People's Commissars...in which the SPD and USPD held three seats each...The "Russian" flavour of the titles was meant to proclaim the revolutionary credentials of the new government.' (Feuchtwanger 1995, p.15)

The next day, the 10 November, a meeting of representatives from the workers' and soldiers' councils voted to accept the authority of the Council of People's Commissars:

'An Executive Council of the Workers' and Soldiers' Councils of Greater Berlin was established, which in theory was to control the Council of People's Commissars. In practice, it never came anywhere near to exercising such an ambitious function.' (Feuchtwanger 1995, p.16)

The Ebert-Groener Pact

On 10 November, the day after the Kaiser's abdication, the Head of the Armed Forces, General Groener, phoned Ebert and the two men came to an understanding. The Armed Forces would support the new government. In return, the new government would support the steps taken by the Armed Forces to preserve discipline and it would oppose any attempts at revolutionary uprising. Some historians claim that, by making these commitments, Ebert was betraying the revolution. Carr argues, however, that this is to misunderstand Ebert's position:

'This [phone call resulted in] the celebrated Ebert-Groener Pact which left-wing critics denounced bitterly over the years as proof positive that Ebert had betrayed the revolution. Its importance has been exaggerated. From Ebert's point of view, it was not betrayal; Majority Socialists never made any secret of their distaste of revolution; as the government had no reliable forces at its disposal, the understanding with the general staff was an elementary precaution to protect it against violence from the extreme left.' (Carr 1991, p.243)

The Stinnes-Legien Agreement

A series of meetings between prominent trade unionists and employers resulted in the so-called Stinnes-Legien Agreement. This has been described as follows:

'In return for a commitment not to interfere with private ownership and the free market, the unions were guaranteed full legal recognition, workers' committees and the eight-hour working day.' (Layton 1995, p.77)

Layton points out that, like the Ebert-Groener Pact, the Stinnes-Legien Agreement has been criticised by left-wing historians because it involved making a compromise with the forces of conservatism. It was, they argue, another missed opportunity because it allowed free-market capitalism which had existed under the Kaiser to survive his abdication. In the revolutionary atmosphere of November 1919, the workers should have pressed for a socialist system in which industries were nationalised (owned by the state rather than by private individuals).

The clash of 6 December

The transition from Kaiserreich to new republic was, at first, largely peaceful. For the first three weeks, there were no serious clashes, although tension remained high. The first serious clash came on 6 December 1918 when the Spartacists, a left-wing group within the USPD which was soon to break away and form the Communist Party (KPD), held a demonstration. Troops used violence to break this demonstration up. Feuchtwanger (1995, p.24) claims that 16 demonstrators were killed and 12 wounded.

The first National Congress of Workers' and Soldiers' Councils

Historians agree that the first National Congress of Workers' and Soldiers' Councils, which was held between 16 and 20 December 1918, was a significant event. A total of 500 delegates were elected of which c.300 were members of the SPD, c.100 members of the USPD and less than a dozen were Spartacists. At this Congress several key votes were taken:

- the proposal that the German government should be based on the council system was rejected by 344 to 98
- the date of the election to the National Assembly was set at 19 January
- the Congress called on the Council of People's Commissars to nationalise industries - especially the mining industry - beginning straightaway
- the Congress called on the Council of People's Commissars to set up a 'people's militia' in place of the regular army, to abolish all badges of rank in the army and to allow soldiers to elect their own officers.

While the first two votes represented a victory for Ebert and the SPD leadership, the second two made demands which Ebert and the SPD leadership could not or did not want to implement.

The resignation of the USPD

On 29 December 1918, the three USPD members of the Council of People's Commissars resigned. Box 2.4 provides the background to this resignation.

The Spartacist Uprising

On 1 January, the Spartacists finally split with the USPD, setting up the German Communist Party (KPD) under the leadership of Karl Liebknecht and Rosa Luxemburg. Historians agree that neither

BOX 2.4   The resignation of the USPD

On 23 December, the sailors' division, which had come from Kiel to Berlin in November to defend the government, was ordered to leave its quarters in the former royal palace (most members of the division supported the USPD). The disgruntled sailors decided to march on the chancellery and arrest the government. They seized Otto Wels, a commander of the Republican civic guard and barricaded themselves in the palace. Faced with a direct challenge to its authority, Ebert agreed to the use of military force. On 24 December, the regular army attacked the palace. After two hours' fighting, the sailors agreed to leave if they received their back pay (the real cause of the sit-in) and the government sacked Wels. The three USPD members of the Council of People's Commissars were highly critical of Ebert's action, which had gone ahead without their approval. The three were already frustrated by the lack of progress towards socialism. They were also under constant pressure from their left wing which was opposed to collaboration with the SPD and supported the demonstrations organised by the Spartacists. On 29 December, the three ministers resigned from the Council of People's Commissars. The resignations were a huge blunder since, by bowing out of practical politics at this moment of crisis, the USPD ministers destroyed what hope there was of bridging the yawning gulf between the government and the Spartacists. The left was now split into two camps - the Majority SPD driven more and more to the right by the revolutionary language of those on the left and the Spartacists who were small in numbers but bitter about what they regarded as Ebert's betrayal of the revolution.

Adapted from Carr 1991.

Liebknecht nor Luxemburg were responsible for the uprising which broke out in January 1919. Once it had started, however, they felt obliged to support it. Historians also agree that the uprising was a by-product of the resignation of the three USPD ministers from the Council of People's Commissars. Their resignation led to the sacking of other USPD members who were government officials, including Emil Eichhorn, the Berlin Police Chief. Eichhorn's sacking provoked a demonstration which turned into the occupation of the SPD's newspaper offices. The demonstrators formed a revolutionary committee with the intention of overthrowing the government. In response, Ebert agreed to the use of force and put Gustav Noske, one of the new members of the government, in charge:

'Desperate attempts were made to end the occupation of the newspaper building by negotiation, but when they failed, Noske determined to crush the left with a decisive show of force. He accepted the arguments of the generals and officers around him that anything less would damage the morale of the newly recruited forces.' (Feuchtwanger 1995, p.31)

These 'newly recruited forces' were the Freikorps (or 'Free Corps') - volunteer forces recruited by the German High Command because the regular army was in a state of confusion as troops returned from the front and demobilised:

'On 10 January 1919 Free Corps men, led by General von Luttwitz, attacked Communist positions in Berlin. By 13 January the revolt was crushed after savage street fighting in which prisoners were mishandled and summarily shot. The Communist leaders, Liebknecht and Luxemburg, were captured and cruelly murdered on the way to the Moabit prison. The Majority Socialist leaders were shocked by the brutality of their new allies...but were virtually powerless to restrain the fanatics and adventurers who flocked to join the various Free Corps.' (Carr 1991, pp.246-47)

The election of 19 January 1919

The crushing of the Spartacist Uprising allowed the elections to the National Assembly to go ahead as planned. Historians agree that the result of this election was a victory for those parties that supported the setting up of a democratic republic. In particular, the election was a victory for the SPD:

'The SPD maintained its dominant position with about 38% of the vote (165 seats out of 423), while the USPD obtained only 7.6% (22 seats). However, a majority in the National Assembly was held by the bourgeois parties who, aided by unrestricted freedom of the press and the right of public assembly, had conducted an intensive electoral campaign. The strongest middle-class party proved to be the Centre (19.7%; 91 seats), closely followed by the DDP (18.5%; 75 seats). The DNVP [Conservatives, opposed to a democratic republic] obtained just 10.3% of votes (44 seats).' (Kolb 1998, pp.16-17)

As Kolb points out, there was significant continuity between the result in the previous national election in 1914 and the result in January 1919.

Continued violent outbreaks in early 1919

The crushing of the Spartacist Uprising and the result of the elections to the National Assembly ensured that unrest and conflict between government and workers were by no means over. As Carr points out, the brutal crushing of the Spartacist Uprising shocked the left and the election result increased their concerns:

'The election results helped to revive revolutionary sentiment in the spring of 1919 inasmuch as they destroyed hopes on the left of a solid socialist majority. The Weimar Assembly, dominated by the middle classes, was opposed to socialist experiments. The authorities were already attempting to suppress the councils in factories, much to the alarm of the workers. Noske's use of the Free Corps also aroused great bitterness among the workers.' (Carr 1991, p.247)

In February, the KPD organised a series of strikes in defence of workers' councils. In March, the USPD passed a proposal to reject parliamentary democracy and support government by workers' councils. In some towns, there was street fighting and attempts by workers to set up independent socialist republics. Such attempts were short-lived as the government used the Freikorps to crush them. For example.

'The military occupation of Halle [in late February 1919] left 29 dead and 67 wounded.' (Feuchtwanger 1995, p.59)

When, in Berlin, the KPD called for a general strike as the launch pad for the second revolution, the Freikorps were called in, leaving over 1,000 people dead.

The only part of Germany where workers managed to break away from the control of the Reich government was in Bavaria, where an independent socialist republic was set up and remained in power for several months (see Unit 4, Section 1.3). This too, however, was brought down by the Freikorps.

MAIN POINTS - Section 1.1

- On 29 September 1918, General Ludendorff finally agreed that the war was lost. He wanted a 'revolution from above' to preserve the monarchy. The result was the constitutional reforms of October 1918.
- The peace movement gathered momentum throughout October. Then the Kiel mutiny in early November 1918 sparked a 'revolution from below' - a spontaneous wave of workers', soldiers' and sailors' councils.
- The Kaiser reluctantly abdicated on 9 November and Chancellor Baden handed over his office to Friedrich Ebert, Leader of the SPD. The SPD's main aim was to

hold elections for a National Assembly.
- The interim government - the Council of People's Commissars - initially contained members of the SPD and USPD, but the USPD members resigned on 29 December.
- The first clash between soldiers and Spartacists took place on 6 December. The Spartacist Uprising in January 1919 was put down with great brutality.
- The election of 1919 January was a disappointment to the socialist left. It helped stimulate a wave of strikes and clashes between workers and Freikorps in early 1919.

Activity 2.1 Was there a revolution in Germany?

This photo shows sailors meeting at the time of the Kiel mutiny.

ITEM 2 A historian's view (1)

Revolution involves the transfer of power in circumstances outside the normal constitutional process. It results in radical changes to the political - and quite possibly economic and social - infrastructure. The process is usually accelerated by the experience of war and especially military defeat. This happened in Russia in 1917. The usual interpretation is that, like Russia, Germany either underwent two revolutions or a single revolution which developed in two stages. A 'revolution from above' liberalised the constitution in October 1918 and was followed by a 'revolution from below'. This also had two stages. First it laid the foundation of the Weimar Republic in November 1918. Second, it beat off attempts to establish a more radical Communist-style regime in January 1919. The overall result was that Germany was transformed from an authoritarian state into an advanced democracy. But this interpretation can be challenged on the grounds that, whilst a revolutionary situation existed in 1918, it did not actually produce a revolution. Take the 'revolution from above'. The political and constitutional developments of October 1918 were all predictable. There had been constant pressure for such change throughout the Kaiserreich from the Progressives, SPD, National Liberals and Centre Party. What occurred in September 1918 was not a sudden departure but fulfilment of a long-awaited goal. Evolution not revolution. There is a better case to be made that the 'revolution from below' was real. There was undeniably a popular momentum which proved irresistible and which swept away the constitutional compromise provided in October 1918 (ie keep the monarchy but govern by parliamentary democracy). But the setting up of the Council of People's Commissars was not a revolutionary act. Again, the transfer of power was evolutionary - from Max von Baden to Ebert. It was never Ebert's intention to make fundamental changes. The declaration of a republic forced him to go ahead with the Council of People's Commissars rather than a broad-based government including the bourgeois parties (which was his aim). He then did everything possible to prevent the interim government pursuing a radical line. It is difficult to argue that the Social Democrats were even 'reluctant revolutionaries'.

Adapted from Lee 1998.

ITEM 3 A historian's view (2)

Before the 1960s, historians assumed that only two options had been available to Germany at the end of the war - either a Communist dictatorship or a parliamentary republic. Ebert was portrayed as a heroic figure who saved Germany from Communism. From the 1960s, close analysis of the workers' councils movement showed that very few councils fell under the control of the extreme left. The vast majority were led by the SPD, with USPD support. Only after January 1919 did the USPD come to dominate. As a result, it is now generally agreed that the threat from the Communists was greatly exaggerated. This has led to a reassessment of the role played by Ebert and the SPD leadership. Although their sincerity has not been questioned, it has been argued that their reading of the political situation was poor. Blinded by their fear of the left, they were too easily prepared to make compromises with conservative forces when, in fact, there was no need. As a result, they missed the opportunity of creating a solidly based republic built on socialist and democratic principles. By May 1919, after the Freikorps had put down the Communist regime in Bavaria, a degree of stability returned to Germany. There are, however, serious doubts about the nature and real extent of these supposedly revolutionary changes. Undoubtedly, there existed the potential for a revolution at the end of the war as the trauma of defeat shook the faith of the majority of the population in the old order. The Kaiser and other princes were deposed and parliamentary democracy introduced. These were important changes. However, in the end, the 'revolution' did not get much further than the reforms of October 1918. German society was left almost untouched by events and there was no attempt to reform the key institutions. The civil service, judiciary and army all remained intact, as did the structure of the economy.

Adapted from Layton 1995.

ITEM 4 The Spartacist Uprising

This photo shows street fighting in Berlin between government troops and Spartacists during the Spartacist Uprising.

Questions

1. a) Judging from Items 1-4 and your own knowledge, give arguments for and against the view that there was a revolution in Germany at the end of the First World War.
   b) What role did Friedrich Ebert play in the 'revolution'?

2. Look at Items 1 and 4 and explain the significance of (a) the Kiel mutiny and (b) the Spartacist Uprising.

3. Do the authors of Items 2 and 3 believe that there was a revolution in Germany at the end of the First World War? Explain how you know.

1.2 Was the Weimar constitution flawed?

The National Constituent Assembly

The abdication of Kaiser Wilhelm II on 9 November 1919 meant that there was a constitutional vacuum in Germany. The monarchy had fallen and it was unclear what sort of government would be set up in its place. On the same day that the Kaiser abdicated, the Kaiser's last Chancellor, Prince Max von Baden, handed over the Chancellorship to Friedrich Ebert, Leader of the SPD (see Section 1.1 above). Ebert then set up a provisional government. The main task of this provisional government was to organise elections to a new, temporary body - a National Assembly. Members of this assembly would then draw up and agree on a new constitution. According to William Carr, Ebert ordered Hugo Preuss to start work on the new constitution before the elections for the National Constituent Assembly were held:

'In November 1918, Hugo Preuss, a left-wing liberal and and well-known professor of law, had been appointed Secretary of State by Ebert and asked to prepare a draft constitution.' (Carr 1991, p.253)

On 6 February 1919, 18 days after the election to the National Assembly, the members of the assembly met for the first time in the town of Weimar (for the location of Weimar, see the map on p.iv). There is a consensus among historians that they met in Weimar and not the capital Berlin because Berlin was considered to be insecure following the Spartacist Uprising (see Section 1.1 above). Some historians suggest that Weimar was also chosen for its particular qualities:

'The National Assembly elected in January 1919 met in Weimar rather than in turbulent Berlin partly because of Weimar's quiet charm and sheltered setting and partly because its intellectual tradition appealed to the new Germany.' (Haffner 1989, p.137)

What the National Assembly finally agreed on in August 1919 was a document whose aim, according to Mann, was to convert the authoritarian (non-democratic) rule of the past into a system which had tight democratic controls:

'The assumption was that in Germany's recent history it had been the authoritarian state that had failed, not the people; therefore the authoritarian state must be done away with completely and the people must be given complete power. The constitution placed absolute confidence in the people. It wanted to establish...government of the people by the people...The majority was right and must decide. There must be no government without a majority in the Reichstag; no Reichstag majority without a majority in the nation; direct decision by the nation whenever President and Reichstag or Reichstag and people disagreed.' (Mann 1996, p.348)

Feuchtwanger (1995) argues that the new constitution had four main planks:

- Germany was to remain a federal nation - although some decisions would be made centrally, individual states or 'Länder' would still have their own governments and be responsible for many decisions
- Germany was to have a strong President, directly elected for seven-year terms by the people
- national elections to the Reichstag (from which the Chancellor and other members of the government would be chosen) would be conducted using a system of proportional representation
- the rights of German citizens would be clearly laid out for the first time.

Bessel argues that, in reality, these main planks of the new constitution had already been agreed before the assembly met in Weimar. This argument is outlined in Box 2.5.

BOX 2.5   Bessel's argument

The constitutional framework was largely fixed before the Weimar constitution was ratified, or even written. Just two days after the National Assembly convened in Weimar, the Reich government proposed a Bill 'Concerning the Provisional Exercise of Political Power'. Two days later, the Assembly passed it. By doing so, it accepted the essential constitutional outlines of the new Republic. First, the Bill gave the National Assembly the power both to draw up a constitution and to make 'other urgent national laws'. By giving itself the power to make laws, the Assembly became, in effect, the lower House in Parliament - the equivalent to the House of Commons). Second, representatives from the individual Länder helped to devise the Bill and they set themselves up as a second chamber. Third, a Reich President, responsible for conducting government business, was to be elected by the Assembly (the Assembly elected Ebert as President). The President would then be responsible for appointing a Cabinet (Ebert chose Philip Scheidemann, another leading member of the SPD, as Chancellor). And fourth, this Cabinet would require the confidence of the Assembly. While these arrangements were described as 'provisional', in practice, the basic structure of the constitution - with the Reichstag, President and Cabinet - had been decided before the formal discussion of the constitution had begun.

Adapted from Bessel 1997.

A federal nation

There is a consensus amongst historians that the man responsible for drafting the new constitution,

Hugo Preuss, hoped to centralise power in Germany by breaking up Prussia into smaller units and reducing the powers that Prussia and the other Länder enjoyed. In other words, Preuss hoped that, from being a federal nation (a nation where the constitution guarantees certain powers to regional or local governments), Germany would be transformed into a unitary state (a nation where power is concentrated at the centre). Preuss, however, was unable to persuade the Assembly to adopt his proposals:

'These drastic proposals aroused fierce opposition, especially in Bavaria, Württemberg and Baden. In the end, a much revised version of the Preuss draft was adopted in the assembly by 262 votes to 75.' (Carr 1991, p.253)

Although, as a result, Germany remained a federal nation, the Länder did lose some powers:

'The Länder kept their historic form and their administrative institutions. Certain privileges in taxation, rail and postal services and military affairs which had been enjoyed by some of the southern states were abolished. Although some of the powers previously enjoyed by the Land governments were now transformed to that of the Reich, the execution of Germany's laws was still mainly in the hands of officials controlled by the Länder. Police, judges and school teachers were employed by state governments rather than by the authorities in Berlin.' (Nicholls 1979, p.25)

Bessel (1997) points out that, whereas in the past the army had been organised by individual states (notably Prussia and Bavaria), under the new constitution the army, for the first time, came under the control of central government.

A strong President

Under the new constitution, the President was to be elected by the people for seven-year terms. The President was given the power to:

- command the Armed Forces
- appoint and dismiss the Chancellor
- dissolve Parliament and order new elections
- order referendums.

In addition, Article 48 of the constitution gave the President special emergency powers. It allowed the President to use armed force against any Land which failed to abide by the laws of the Reich. In addition:

'[It allowed] the President to restore public law and order in the Reich as a whole, if necessary by armed force. To this end, he could temporarily suspend some of the basic rights guaranteed by the constitution. Any such measures had, however, to be immediately notified to the Reichstag, which could render them invalid by voting against them.' (Feuchtwanger 1995, p.41)

Despite this safeguard, what this article meant in practice was that, in times of emergency, the President could make laws which came into effect regardless of the views of the Reichstag. If the Reichstag objected to a measure, the President could simply dissolve it and call for new elections. Certainly, that is what happened in the period 1930-33 (see Unit 3, Part 2 and Unit 4, Section 3.2).

The electoral system, the government and the Reichstag

Under the new constitution, national elections to the Reichstag were to be conducted using a system of proportional representation. According to Feuchtwanger, Germany was divided into 35 large electoral districts, with parties putting up lists of candidates in these districts (Nicholls 1979 and Carr 1991 claim there were 37 districts). The number of votes cast in a district for a party determined how many candidates from the list were sent to the Reichstag. For every 60,000 votes a party won, one member of that party's list was elected (see Box 2.6). All men and women above the age of 20 were eligible to vote in elections.

Deputies sat in the Reichstag and it was from them that the members of government were chosen. Hereditary political offices were abolished and, apart from the judiciary, key government appointments were made by elected officials. So, the elected President would appoint the Chancellor who, in turn, would appoint the Cabinet from other elected members of the Reichstag. Ministers were accountable to the Reichstag. A vote of no-confidence would bring about the downfall of a government. In normal circumstances, the

---

BOX 2.6 | The electoral system

Parties won one seat in the Reichstag for every 60,000 votes cast in an electoral district. As a result, the total number of seats in the Reichstag varied from election to election because it depended on the total number of people voting. If 60,000 fewer voters voted in one election compared with the previous election, there would be one fewer deputy (MPs) than there had been before the election. Votes which were insufficient to qualify for a seat in one of the 35 electoral districts could ultimately be combined at the national level, provided that a party won a minimum of 30,001 votes in at least one of the electoral districts. If a party won between 30,001 and 60,000 votes in an electoral district, one deputy was elected. A party which won at least one seat could then have the votes for it in districts where it had not won 30,001 votes added up to make a national total, with one deputy being elected for every 60,000 votes. The number of seats won from the national total could not exceed the number won outright in electoral districts, however.

Adapted from Feuchtwanger 1995.

government was responsible for drafting laws. Proposals were put to the Reichstag and deputies decided whether or not to accept them.

The guarantee of basic rights

A special section in the new constitution outlined the basic rights that were to be enjoyed by German citizens - the first time such rights had been guaranteed. These rights are summarised in Box 2.7.

BOX 2.7 | **The basic rights guaranteed by the constitution**

Not only did the Weimar constitution lay down the institutional structures and decision-making processes of the political system, it also included a second section which outlined the rights and obligations of the German people. The statement of new basic rights guaranteed local self-government and the position of the permanent civil service, protected the rights of religious denominations and defined the basic structure of the system of education. It included declarations on the family and the protection of children and young people (it made it clear that illegitimate children were to have the same rights as legitimate, for example). In the field of welfare and the economy, the 'regulation of the economy' was linked to 'principles of justice' and the goal of a 'dignified existence for all people', guaranteeing the 'economic freedom of the individual' (Article 151). On these foundations, a series of specific provisions was built dealing with nationalisation (taking private companies into public ownership), safety measures for workers, welfare insurance (allowing workers to pay into a fund which would then pay them if they fell ill or were injured), labour exchanges (the setting up of job centres), unemployment benefit, freedom of association for trade unions and workers' participation in decision-making in 'economic councils' (groups in which employers and employees were to negotiate over pay and conditions).

Adapted from Peukert 1991.

The Reichsrat

In addition, to the four main planks, the constitution set up a second chamber, the Reichsrat. This was made up of representatives from the Länder (Hiden 1996 notes that Prussia was prevented from monopolising the Reichsrat by a rule which stated that no Land could have more than two-fifths of votes and by an arrangement whereby half of Prussia's votes were given to the Land government - the Landtag - and the other half distributed among Prussia's provinces). Historians agree that the Reichsrat had limited power since it could only offer advice, reject legislation or call for a referendum (see below), it could not propose or amend legislation:

'In practice the powers of the Reichsrat were very limited; it possessed a modified power of veto over legislation which could be removed by a two-thirds majority in the Reichstag. Alternatively, the President could resolve a dispute between the Reichstag and Reichsrat by holding a national referendum.' (Carr 1991, p.255)

Referendums

The Weimar constitution made provision for the holding, in certain circumstances, of referendums or 'plebiscites' as they are also called (in a referendum the electorate is asked to vote 'yes' or 'no' in reply to a specific question). In some circumstances, it was possible for ordinary people to force the government to hold a referendum:

'There was a preliminary process called a "people's request" (Volksbegehren): if a tenth of those entitled to vote supported a properly worked out legislative proposal, by inscribing their names in the appropriate lists, then such a proposal had to be submitted to the Reichstag. If the Reichstag rejected the proposal, then it had to be submitted to a referendum.' (Feuchtwanger 1995, pp.44-45)

Referendums could also be called by the President and by the Reichsrat.

The strengths and weaknesses of the Weimar Republic

Since the downfall of the Weimar Republic came just 14 years after the new constitution was drawn up, it is tempting to argue that the constitution was, in some way, flawed. Certainly, this was often the line taken by historians writing in the past:

'The political system devised at Weimar has, in spite of its theoretical perfection, often been criticised in practice and is held to have contributed to the Republic's downfall.' (Feuchtwanger 1997, p.3)

In recent years, however, historians have begun to question the criticisms of the constitution and to reappraise the factors which led to the Republic's downfall. The debate has focused on four areas of controversy. These are examined below in turn.

1. Proportional representation

The system of proportional representation adopted by the Weimar Republic has been criticised on two main grounds. First, under the British 'first-past-the-post' system in use today (a non-proportional system), it is extremely difficult for small, extremist parties to gain election to Parliament since, to do so, they must win more votes in a constituency than any other party. In a region the size of the electoral regions in Weimar Germany (which would contain many British constituencies) and using the first-past-the-post system, an extremist party might win 30,001 votes, but that would not guarantee it representation in Parliament. It did so under the

Weimar system, however. Any party winning 30,001 votes in a region automatically gained a seat in the Reichstag. As a result, small, extremist parties were able to gain representation in the Reichstag. If a different electoral system had been adopted, it is claimed, the Nazis might not have been able to build mass support and set in motion the electoral bandwagon which began rolling in 1930. And second, the electoral system has been criticised because it made coalition government (ie governments made up of more than one party) inevitable because it was almost impossible for any single party to gain an overall majority:

'Proportional representation, without a threshold, produced a [large number] of parties, encouraged splinter groups and made coalition governments inevitable, with all the internal disagreement which these so often carry.' (Lee 1998, p.6)

Coalition governments, it is argued, are necessarily weaker than single-party governments and they are more prone to collapse. The electoral system, in other words, is blamed for producing weak leadership and bringing political instability.

By no mean all historians accept these criticisms of the Weimar electoral system. Carr, for example, contests the idea that the electoral system paved the way to Hitler's rise to power. He points out that proportional systems have been proved to work in different circumstances and argues that:

'The basic weakness of Weimar lay in the inability of the main parties to coalesce [become united] in defence of the Republic.' (Carr 1991, p.255)

The idea that proportional representation (PR) was destabilising is also challenged by other authors - see Box 2.8.

2. The Reichstag and the presidency

The second area of controversy concerns the relationship between two directly elected institutions - the Reichstag and the presidency:

'The centrepiece of the power structure created by the constitution was the much-debated dual system whereby both the Reichstag and Reich President were elected by direct popular vote.' (Peukert 1991, p.38)

The fact that both the Reichstag and the President were directly elected, it is often argued, resulted in destabilisation:

'The powers of the President have often been seen as amounting to those of an Ersatzkaiser (substitute Emperor) and when set alongside the authority of the Reichstag it seems that the attempt to prevent a monopoly of power by one institution [ie the Reichstag] only succeeded in creating a dualism which was "fundamentally ambiguous".' (Layton 1995, p.85)

Other historians disagree that this 'dualism' - the constitutional uncertainty which arose from the difficulty of being sure whether it was the Reichstag

BOX 2.8 Arguments against the idea that PR was destabilising

(i) The argument that PR was destabilising was particularly popular in the two decades after 1945. The argument was based on the idea that the system encouraged the formation of new parties and splinter parties which, in turn, made it difficult to make and maintain governments. But, it is difficult to see how an alternative voting system based upon a British style "first-past-the-post" could have been more effective. The fundamental problem was the difficulty in creating coalitions and agreeing policies amongst the main parties. The existence of splinter groups was a minor problem. As to the view that PR encouraged the emergence of political extremism after 1929, it now seems clear that the changes in electoral attitudes were just too dramatic to be contained. Indeed, it may well have been the case that a first-past-the-post system would have actually made the Nazis' rise to power easier since, under such a system in July 1932, they might have won two-thirds of seats, enough for them to change the constitution without relying on other parties.
Adapted from Layton 1995.

(ii) Interestingly, the results of the 1919 election were not greatly different from that held in 1912 (when voters voted in single-member constituencies and the electoral system was non-proportional). In 1919, women were allowed to vote for the first time and the voting age was lowered, but these changes did not make much difference. This relatively high degree of continuity in respect to party politics is evidence against the view that PR contributed significantly to the collapse of the Republic.
Adapted from Peukert 1991.

or the President that was the ultimate source of authority in the Republic - was destabilising. Peukert, for example, points out that:

'Since the Republic was destroyed through the active connivance of the second Reich President, Paul von Hindenburg, the dualistic nature of the Weimar constitution has attracted widespread criticism. On the other hand, it can be said that under Ebert the selfsame dual system proved to be a stabilising force during the crises of the post-war years.' (Peukert 1991, p.39)

3. Article 48

The third area of controversy concerns the inclusion of Article 48. This, it has often been argued, provided the President with a tool for bypassing the Reichstag and, as a result, it was a mistake to include it. Craig, for example, argues that the inclusion of Article 48 shows a lack of foresight on the part of the members of the National Constituent Assembly:

'The majority that approved this sweeping grant of power were doubtless thinking of the troubles that had filled the first six months of the Republic's existence and were making sure that the executive had enough power to deal with renewed Communist disorders. They thought that they were making a sensible provision for exceptional conditions and can perhaps be forgiven for their failure to conceive of the exceptional becoming the normal. That failure of imagination, nevertheless, made representative government vulnerable to attack by any extra-parliamentary force that was supported by the President's emergency powers.' (Craig 1981, p.417)

Other historians, however, are less critical of the inclusion of Article 48. Feuchtwanger, for example, argues that it was not the constitution which was at fault, but the way it was used:

'The presidential emergency powers were not in themselves unusual. When Ebert was President, they were used to resolve crises and restore normal parliamentary government, but from 1930 they were deliberately employed to bypass the Reichstag. Thus it was not the political and constitutional arrangements in themselves that were at fault, but the way in which they were used in a country where large sections of the population had little regard for democracy and parliamentary government.' (Feuchtwanger 1997, p.3)

4. Referendums

The fourth area of controversy concerns the constitution's provision that referendums (or 'referenda') should be held in certain circumstances. Some historians argue that this was a weakness because campaigns to hold referendums provided rallying points for those opposed to democracy:

'The constitution allowed for referenda to be held on specific issues. This enabled the enemies of democracy to put their case directly and forcefully before the public. The referendum called by the nationalist, Alfred Hugenburg against the Young Plan in 1929 allowed right-wing nationalists and Nazis to engage in nationwide campaigning to publicise their views. The Nazis were thus able to win seats in the Landtag [Land government] elections in Baden and Thuringia in October 1929 and in municipal [local] elections in the following month.' (Murphy 1997, p.17)

Other historians, however, argue that, on the contrary, there is no evidence that this provision in the constitution was a weakness:

'In practice, referendums were rarely held and were never successful, so the view of earlier historians that plebiscitary elements in the constitution fatally undermined the Republic would not appear to be particularly plausible.' (Peukert 1991, p.40)

Two problems not resolved by the Weimar constitution

Historians agree that there were two problems which were not resolved by the Weimar constitution, namely:

- the problem arising from German culture - the lack of enthusiasm for the values that were required for the constitution to function smoothly
- the problem of 'particularism' - the desire of Länder to have greater independence.

The problem arising from German political culture

Written constitutions alone do not guarantee political stability. As Finer (1979) has pointed out, there also has to be the necessary political will and military support for constitutions to work. A written constitution, in other words, is only as strong as the power-holders in a society wish it to be:

'The constitution could not control the conditions and circumstances in which it had to operate. In this sense, it is just unrealistic to imagine that any piece of paper could have made provision for all the possible consequences arising from Germany's immense problems and its divergent social and political forces.' (Layton 1995, p.86)

In Box 2.9, Brendon suggests that it was the culture - the values held by many Germans - which prevented the constitution from functioning smoothly.

BOX 2.9   German culture

Germany was in many respects a profoundly conservative society. Manners and dress were formal. The hand-shaking ceremony was very formal. Officers and gentlemen clung rigidly to their code. Duelling, though illegal, was still common. Few complained when the police imposed social discipline. There were countless societies for the organisation of culture, leisure and sport. Even hiking was regimented, as the bands of the Wandervögel with their swastika emblems and 'Heil' salutes (both borrowed by Hitler) show. The German bourgeoisie (middle classes) prized order and respected authority. Yet, as though desperate to escape from a demoralising past, many of the new Republicans cast off the old ways. Weimar became a byword for liberalism, modernism and decadence. It was this contrast between the old Germany with its old values and the new Germany with its new values that is at the root of much of the opposition to the Weimar Republic. Although some people entered into what they believed was the spirit of the new constitution, what they did shocked many of those who still held the old values. Another way of putting this is to say that the Weimar constitution never gained legitimacy with part of the German population.

Adapted from Brendon 2000.

The problem of 'particularism'

It was pointed out above that Preuss failed to break up Prussia and impose greater central control on Germany. As a result, the relationship between the Länder and central government was a compromise:

'On the one hand, the constitution was not decentralised enough for those who thought the Länder should have as much [freedom of action] as was compatible with the needs of German unity. On the other hand, it did not establish a single unrivalled source of power in the Reich.' (Nicholls 1979, p.26)

This compromise, it is generally agreed, was responsible for some of the problems faced by the Republic:

'This overlapping of jurisdiction and the additional fact that Reich laws on certain subjects could be effective only if implemented by state regulations made quarrels over competence and open conflict inevitable. The knowledge that the legitimacy of the Republic was widely challenged encouraged its enemies to exploit the ambiguities in the relationship between the separate states and the national government in order to defy the policies of the Reich...The year 1923 was to demonstrate how dangerous this clumsiness, which was perhaps unavoidable, could be.' (Craig 1981, p.419)

The main events in 1923 are examined in Section 3.1 below and in Unit 4, Section 1.6.

MAIN POINTS - Section 1.2

- The new constitution had four main planks - (1) Germany was to remain a federal nation (2) Germany was to have a strong, directly elected President (3) elections to the Reichstag would use a system of proportional representation and (4) the rights of German citizens would be clearly laid out for the first time.
- In addition, to the four main planks, the constitution set up a second chamber, the Reichsrat. This was made up of representatives from the Länder. Provision was also made for the calling of referendums.
- Weimar's system of proportional representation has been criticised for allowing extreme minority groups to gain a foothold in the Reichstag and for ensuring that government was by coalition. Some historians dispute these criticisms.

- Some historians argue that the fact both the President and Reichstag were directly elected was destabilising. Others dispute this.
- Some historians argue that Article 48 provided the President with a tool for bypassing the Reichstag and, as a result, it was a mistake to include it. Others argue that it was not the mechanism that was at fault, but the way it was used.
- Some historians argue that allowing referendums was a mistake. Others dispute this.
- Historians agree that two problems were not resolved by the new constitution - (1) German culture (lack of enthusiasm for values that would allow the constitution to function smoothly) and (2) 'particularism' (the desire of Länder to have greater independence).

Activity 2.2 Was the Weimar constitution flawed?

ITEM 1 Craig's view

The introduction of PR and referendums caused much disruption. PR ensures that all shades of opinion find expression, but it works best in times of peace and in situations where the rules of political engagement are generally accepted. Such an environment did not exist in Germany after the First World War. PR increased the number of parties, making it unlikely that any single party could win a majority. This made coalition government inevitable. It also put the Republic in danger since anti-Republican groups - which otherwise might have died of lack of attention - gained representation. The result was an impression of instability, what appeared to be a continuous game of musical chairs as coalitions were made and unmade and ministries formed and reformed. This, the too frequent dissolution of the Reichstag and the new elections which resulted, reduced people's respect for parliamentary government. So did campaigns for referendums because enemies of the Republic used them to drum up opposition to the system. Article 48 was a mistake - even the old Emperor had never been allowed to set aside the law of the land - and so was the failure to provide for significant reform of the civil service, the judiciary and the educational system. The Republic's business was left in the hands of professional civil servants who favoured a basically anti-democratic approach to politics. Judges openly abused their positions. Some (especially in Bavaria) expressed their monarchist beliefs from the bench and sentenced right-wingers to ludicrously short terms of imprisonment. The constitution gave no protection against such behaviour. Nor did it do anything to defend Germany against more subtle attacks on the new system from the education system. Textbooks were full of aggressive nationalism, praise of the monarchical past and criticism of the Republic. The failure of those who drafted the Weimar constitution to include regulations which prevented or corrected such views was, of all their shortcomings, the most critical. It allowed the post-war generation to be indoctrinated with anti-democratic ideas.

Adapted from Craig 1981.

ITEM 2 The Weimar constitution

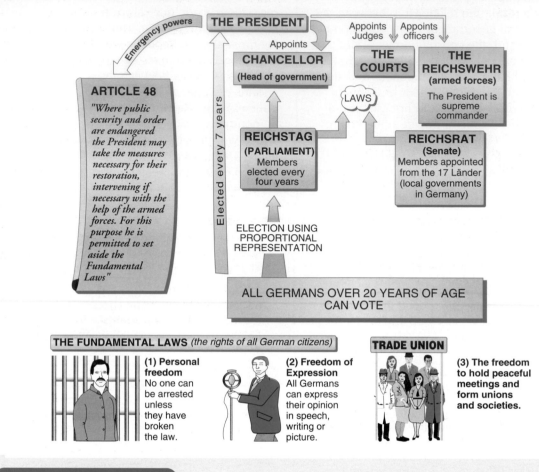

THE FUNDAMENTAL LAWS *(the rights of all German citizens)*

(1) Personal freedom
No one can be arrested unless they have broken the law.

(2) Freedom of Expression
All Germans can express their opinion in speech, writing or picture.

TRADE UNION

(3) The freedom to hold peaceful meetings and form unions and societies.

ITEM 3 Burleigh's view

Since those responsible for drafting the constitution were wary of overwhelming parliamentary powers, the constitution combined an elected presidency with an elected Parliament. The presidency was designed to be a largely honorary figurehead position, filling the vacuum left by Germany's exiled monarch. Article 48 may have been ominously vague, but, at the time, few thought of its potential misuse. Besides, Weimar's constitution can hardly be held responsible alone for the rise to power of a racist, totalitarian dictatorship. The adoption of PR meant that many fringe parties had deputies in the Reichstag. However, detailed computations using alternative electoral models suggest that a Nazi victory might just as well have been accelerated as delayed by voting according to a British-style first-past-the-post system, given the effect on voters of factors unrelated to the electoral system. In other words, the Nazis might have come to power in 1930 rather than three years later. At most, the new voting system might have reduced the bonds between deputy and electors since single-member constituencies were abolished. On the positive side, PR gave a voice to, for example, Catholic or Protestant groups living in areas otherwise dominated by the rival creed. Similarly, critics of referendums, originally designed to provide a democratic outlet between elections, may have exaggerated the damage referendums caused, not least because none of the seven campaigns succeeded.

Adapted from Burleigh 2000.

Questions

1. 'The Weimar constitution was flawed.' Using Items 1-3 and your own knowledge give arguments for and against this statement.
2. a) Compare and contrast the views on the Weimar constitution expressed in Items 1 and 3.
   b) Was the introduction of PR a mistake? Explain your answer.
3. a) Using Item 2 describe the main features of the Weimar constitution.
   b) What does the diagram tell us about the way in which power was supposed to be distributed in the Weimar Republic?

1.3 What were the terms of the Treaty of Versailles and what reaction was there to it?

Wilson's '14 points'

In January 1918, the US President, Woodrow Wilson, issued his '14 points', a framework for discussion once the war was over. Wilson's peace plan was based on the idea that new and democratic states would work together in a League of Nations to prevent future war. These new states would be created using the principle of self-determination. In other words, people who spoke the same language and who shared the same ethnic and historical roots would be allowed to decide their own future. Feuchtwanger points out that two of Wilson's 14 points made it clear that Germany would lose territory:

'Point VIII required the restoration of Alsace-Lorraine to France; point XIII called for an independent Polish state, a demand which was bound to impose territorial sacrifices on Germany.' (Feuchtwanger 1995, pp.46-47)

The armistice

On 11 November 1918, Germany signed an armistice (truce). It is important to note that Germany did not surrender unconditionally, it ceased fighting on the basis that a peace settlement would be made 'between equals':

'Germany had come close to winning the war and German opinion was reluctant to accept the fact of defeat. Germany had not agreed to unconditional surrender, but to an "armistice" and to a promise of "peace between equals" based on the 14 points.' (Lentin 1994, p.33)

In reality, however, Feuchtwanger argues, the armistice laid out many of the elements which would be laid down in the final peace settlement:

'In the West there was to be a return of all German-occupied territories and the permanent [return of] Alsace-Lorraine [to France]. The German areas on the left bank of the River Rhine were to be occupied by the Allies. As a means of pressure, the blockade of German ports was continued and there were to be far-reaching handovers of assets such as gold, foreign currency and railway rolling stock. German forces were to be disarmed and demobilised to a low level. In the East, the treaties of Brest-Litovsk with Russia, and Bucharest with Romania were declared invalid, but German troops were to evacuate their current positions in former Russian territory...only when the Allies demanded it.' (Feuchtwanger 1995, p.47)

The Paris Peace Conference

The peace settlement was worked out in Paris. The Paris Peace Conference first met in January and negotiations continued until June. Although the German Foreign Minister, Count Brockdorff-Rantzau prepared a team of negotiators, the German delegation was excluded from the negotiations. Kolb points out that, between January and May 1919, the German people and government had no idea what, exactly was being decided about their fate:

'Between January and May 1919 no exact information seeped out as to the progress of the discussions among the victors. Consequently, neither the German government nor German public opinion had anything like a clear, realistic idea of the scope of the terms to be imposed on Germany. In the "dreamland of the Armistice period"...people still hoped for lenient, "Wilsonian" peace conditions.' (Kolb 1988, p.30)

Feuchtwanger argues that there were such great divisions between the Allies that it was not realistic for them to include the Germans in their negotiations. Nevertheless, the Germans felt that it was insulting to be ignored.

On 7 May 1919, the Allies broke their silence. The terms of the settlement they proposed were much harsher than the Germans expected. The initial reaction in Germany was one of outrage:

'On 7 May 1919, the German delegation was asked to receive a completed draft of the treaty and invited to make written comments only. On this occasion Brockdorff-Rantzau delivered a speech from a seated position to express his utter contempt for the way the German delegation was being treated. He voiced perfectly the mood of impotent rage and the profound sense of injustice that was sweeping the German nation.' (Feuchtwanger 1995, p.48)

The reasons for this reaction are explored in Box 2.10.

Political developments, May-June 1919

The German delegation handed over its written response on 29 May. Kolb argues that the German delegation's aim was to divide the Allies in the hope of gaining concessions:

'It was Brockdorff-Rantzau's intention, unless the Allies accepted [the German counter-proposals in full], to refuse to sign the treaty in order, as he hoped, to divide the Allies from one another. At the beginning of June, he systematically prepared the German government for this eventuality, which he already regarded as probable. However, the effect of his open resistance was to strengthen Allied solidarity. There [could] no longer be any doubt that the Allies were determined to take military action if Germany refused to sign the treaty.' (Kolb 1988, p.31)

The ultimatum of 16 June

On 16 June, the final text of the treaty was presented

BOX 2.10   Reasons for German discontent

On no other political issue was there such universal agreement within Weimar Germany as in the rejection and condemnation of the Treaty of Versailles. The German case was based on a number of points. First, the treaty was a dictated settlement, allowing for no negotiations and imposed under the threat of further Allied military action. Second, the treaty was considered to be at variance with the 14 points. If borders were to be determined by self-determination, the Germans could not understand, for example, why Germans in what was to become Poland were placed under foreign and not German rule. Besides, the loss of German colonies seemed at variance with Point 5 which talked of 'an impartial adjustment of all colonial claims'. Third, Germany found it impossible to accept the 'War Guilt' clause (the clause which placed responsibility for starting the war on Germany). Most Germans believed the war had been fought for defensive reasons. As a result, Germany should not be made to accept all responsibility and it should certainly not be made to pay compensation (the so-called 'reparations'). And fourth, Germany's treatment by the Allies was viewed as demeaning and unworthy of a Great Power. The clauses limiting the size of the German Armed Forces were considered humiliating. By excluding Germany from the League of Nations, the Allies simply convinced Germans that the League was to be a tool of the Allies.

Adapted from Layton 1995.

to the Germans with an ultimatum - sign within five (later extended to seven) days or face military action. Historians agree that, in principle, all parties in Germany opposed the treaty, but there was the realisation that failure to sign would mean the resumption of war and the probable break-up of Germany. The Cabinet met on the night of the 18-19 June and the Scheidemann government resigned on the morning of 20 June - on the grounds that the treaty was objectionable. A new government was formed under Gustav Bauer (of the SPD). The new government coalition did not contain any members of the DDP, unlike the previous government, since the DDP was not prepared to compromise. Feuchtwanger argues that two factors explain why the new government was inclined to compromise. First, Erzberger, Leader of the Centre Party and a main prop in the new coalition government had been arguing for a less confrontational stance for some time. And second, General Wilhelm Groener, the military commander, made it clear that the German army was not in a position to resist if the Allies attacked.

The final effort to gain concessions

The new government made one last effort to gain concessions. It informed the Allies that it was prepared to accept the treaty on condition that the 'War Guilt' clause was amended:

'On 22 June, the day before the ultimatum was due to expire, the new government declared itself willing to accept the terms with the proviso that it did not acknowledge Germany's responsibility for the war or agree to the condemnation of the Kaiser and the surrender of other individuals for trial. This declaration was approved in the National Assembly by 237 votes to 138. However, the Allied representatives rejected the German conditions and demanded that the treaty be signed without reservation.' (Kolb 1988, p.32)

Carr argues that one reason why the Allies rejected the German conditions was that the German navy sunk the fleet rather than surrendering. This sent out the signal that the Germans were acting in bad faith:

'Unfortunately for the government, news had just arrived in Paris that the Germans had scuttled the fleet at Scapa flow instead of surrendering it as required by the armistice, and that certain captured battle honours due to be returned to France had been deliberately burned by Free Corps men in Berlin. The victorious powers were deeply incensed by this evidence of bad faith and insisted on unconditional acceptance of the treaty.' (Carr 1991, pp.258-59)

It was now clear that the government had a simple choice - accept the treaty or face an Allied military invasion. The government summoned the National Assembly to a meeting and proposed that the treaty be accepted. A majority in the National Assembly voted in support. Significantly, before the vote, the government asked opposition parties - the DNVP, DVP and DDP - to sign up to an agreement that the government was forced to take this step against its will and was acting out of patriotic motives. Although designed to prevent the 'Stab-in-the-Back' myth from gaining credibility, this agreement cut little ice with those who believed that the treaty should never have been signed.

The signing of the treaty

On 23 June, the German government informed the Allies it would sign the treaty unconditionally. On 28 June, the Foreign Minister, Hermann Müller (SPD), and the Justice Minister, Johannes Bell (Centre Party) signed the treaty in the Hall of Mirrors in the Palace of Versailles, just outside Paris.

The provisions of the treaty

It was noted above that the Treaty of Versailles contained the 'War Guilt' clause. By signing the treaty, Germany accepted that it was responsible for starting the First World War and, as a result, it accepted that it should pay the Allies compensation (ie 'reparations'). The treaty did not lay down exactly how much Germany would have to pay in reparations (the Allies could not agree). Feuchtwanger argues that, this aside, the treaty can be divided into four sections:

'The provisions of the treaty fall into four main categories: [permanent removal of territory], occupation of territory subject to time limits and without permanent loss of sovereignty, limitations of forces and armaments and demilitarised zones, and [removal] of economic assets over and above reparation liabilities.' (Feuchtwanger 1995, p.50)

According to Hiden, the treaty ensured that:

'In total, Germany lost some 13% of its territory and over six million subjects.' (Hiden 1996, p.13)

The loss of this territory meant a loss of important resources:

'It was claimed that German territorial losses had deprived the country of 14.6% of its arable land, 74.5% of its iron ore, 68.1% of its zinc ore and 26% of its coal production.' (Feuchtwanger 1995, pp.51-52)

a. Permanent removal of territory

The map in Box 2.11 shows the territory lost by Germany as a result of the Treaty of Versailles. In the West, Germany lost two areas permanently - Alsace-Lorraine (which had been seized during the Franco-Prussian war of 1871) and the area around Eupen and Malmedy which came under Belgian control. In the East, however, the creation of a new Polish state with access to the sea meant that Germany lost Poznania - the area that became known as the 'Polish corridor'. This meant that East Prussia remained part of Germany, even though, geographically, it was now split off from the rest of Germany. It should also be noted that a clause in the treaty prohibited union with Austria, even though the Austrian Provincial Assembly had voted in November 1918 to join the German Reich.

In addition to the areas described above, a number of areas were given the opportunity of breaking away from Germany permanently if they chose to do so. In the North, Northern Schleswig voted to break away from Germany whereas Southern Schleswig did not. In the South-East, Western Upper Silesia voted to remain part of Germany whereas Eastern Upper Silesia did not. In the North-East, Allenstein and Marienwerder voted to remain part of Germany.

Finally, Germany lost all its overseas colonies. The League of Nations took control of them.

b. Occupation of territory by the League of Nations

The map in Box 2.11 also shows the territory occupied by the League of Nations on a temporary basis. In the West, the League occupied the Saar, an important industrial area. In the East, the city of Danzig was made a free city under League of Nations control.

c. Limitations of arms and demilitarised zones

The Treaty of Versailles contained a number of provisions designed to reduce the size and effectiveness of Germany's Armed Forces. These can be summarised as follows:

- conscription was to abolished and the size of the army reduced to 100,000
- the general staff was abolished
- the Armed Forces were not permitted to equip themselves with tanks, big guns or military aircraft
- the German navy was reduced to a maximum of 15,000 personnel, six battleships, six cruisers, 12 destroyers, 12 torpedo boats and no submarines.

BOX 2.11 | Germany's new borders

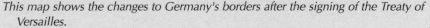

This map shows the changes to Germany's borders after the signing of the Treaty of Versailles.

The main demilitarised zone was the Rhineland. This remained under German control, but fortifications were to be destroyed and no troops were to be barracked in the area:

> 'Allied forces were to occupy the left bank of the Rhine and the 30-mile wide strip on the right bank was to be permanently demilitarised.' (Hiden 1996, p.12)

d. Removal of economic assets

Feuchtwanger points out that the German surrender required, in addition to reparations, the removal of many economic assets:

> 'The surrender was required of many economic assets: merchant marine, patents, overseas investments and property. The Allies were to be granted most-favoured-nation treatment and there was to be a five-year ban on protective tariffs.' (Feuchtwanger 1995, p.52)

These provisions made it harder for Germany to restore its economic fortunes.

The impact of the treaty

Historians agree that the response to the Treaty of Versailles was overwhelmingly negative in Germany. The following passage is typical:

> 'Germans were psychologically traumatised by what they saw as the betrayal of promises held out at the armistice, even though some of their grievances were implicit in the 14 points. What they called their "bleeding frontier" with Poland was felt to be particularly irksome...Particular bitterness was provoked by the clauses relating to war trials and, above all, by the "War Guilt clause". Throughout the 1920s, the open-ended burden of reparations served to keep alive Germany's sense of indignation.' (Lentin 1994, p.33)

Although there was almost universal condemnation of the Treaty of Versailles in Germany, a number of historians have pointed out that, in reality, the treaty was by no means as harsh as it could have been:

> 'It was not nearly so severe as certain sections of Allied opinion had demanded. France had been forced to give way over most of its more extreme demands, such as the creation of an independent Rhineland and the annexation [seizure by force] of the Saar. Thus, much of the contemporary German criticism was emotional rhetoric inflamed by years of nationalist propaganda and the shock of defeat.' (Layton 1995, p.89)

Kolb (1988) claims that it is right to argue that the Treaty of Versailles was both too severe and too lenient. It was too severe in that it caused outrage in Germany and, as a result, revision of the treaty became a primary political aim. On the other hand, it was too lenient in that it did not weaken Germany sufficiently to prevent it from resurrecting its Great Power status. As Layton points out:

> 'Weimar's economic problems certainly cannot be blamed on the imposition of reparations alone, whilst Germany's perceived loss of status in 1919 was illusory, for in some respects it was in a relatively stronger position than in 1914. The great empires of Russia, Austria-Hungary and Turkey had gone, creating a power vacuum in central and eastern Europe which could not be filled by a weak and isolated USSR or by the generally unstable successor states.' (Layton 1995, p.90)

Both Kolb and Layton argue that, if Germany had accepted the treaty and then calmly started to build diplomatic and economic ties, it would have soon become a major player in Europe again. As it was, however, feelings against the treaty ran so high that they fuelled domestic political instability which, in turn, paved the way for Nazism and the blatant defiance of treaty obligations - blatant defiance which eventually led to a second world war.

MAIN POINTS - Section 1.3

- On 11 November 1918, Germany signed an armistice (truce). It did not surrender unconditionally. It ceased fighting on the basis that a peace settlement would be made 'between equals', using Wilson's 14 points.
- The terms of the settlement were made known on 7 May 1919. They were much harsher than the Germans expected. The initial reaction in Germany was one of outrage.
- The German delegation responded on 29 May, hoping to divide the Allies and gain concessions. But, on 16 June, the final text of the treaty was presented to the Germans with an ultimatum - sign within five (later extended to seven) days or face military action.

- On 20 June, the Scheidemann government resigned. On 22 June, the new government announced it would sign if the 'war guilt' clause was dropped. The Allies refused, making it clear they would invade if the treaty wasn't signed. The Germans agreed to sign on 23 June.
- In addition to the war guilt clause which paved the way for reparations, the treaty had four main provisions - (1) the permanent removal of territory (2) the occupation of territory by the League of Nations (3) the limitation of arms and demilitarised zones and (4) the removal of economic assets.
- Historians agree that, while the treaty had a hostile reception in Germany, it was not as harsh as it could have been, allowing Germany to retain the potential to become strong again.

Activity 2.3 The impact of the Treaty of Versailles

(i)

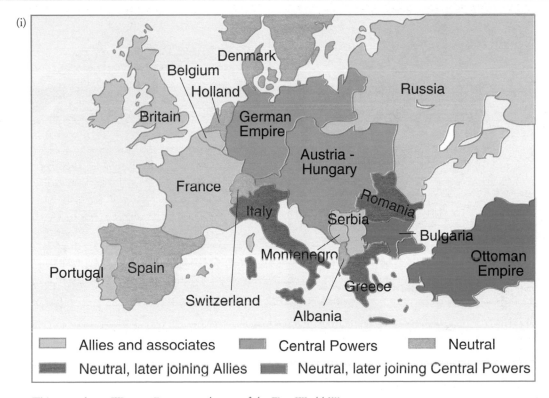

Allies and associates   Central Powers   Neutral

Neutral, later joining Allies   Neutral, later joining Central Powers

This map shows Western Europe on the eve of the First World War.

(ii)

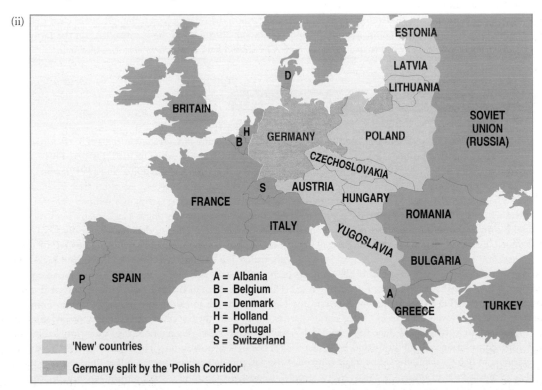

A = Albania
B = Belgium
D = Denmark
H = Holland
P = Portugal
S = Switzerland

'New' countries

Germany split by the 'Polish Corridor'

This map shows Western Europe after the signing of the Treaty of Versailles and the other treaties drawn up after the First World War.

ITEM 2   Two cartoons

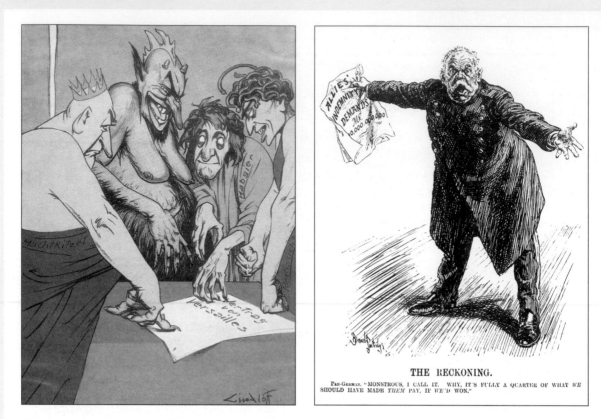

THE RECKONING.

Pan-German. "MONSTROUS, I CALL IT.   WHY, IT'S FULLY A QUARTER OF WHAT *WE* SHOULD HAVE MADE *THEM* PAY, IF *WE'D* WON."

The cartoon on the left was published in Germany after the signing of the Treaty of Versailles. It shows the devil examining the terms of the Treaty of Versailles. He is surrounded by figures who represent revenge, greed and lust for power. The cartoon on the right was published in Britain in April 1919. At that point, the amount to be paid as compensation by Germany (the 'indemnity' mentioned in the cartoon) had not been set, though it was clear that Germany would have to pay some compensation. A caption below the cartoon has the German man in the cartoon saying: 'Monstrous, I call it. Why, it's fully a quarter of what *we* should have made *them* pay, if *we'd* won'.

ITEM 3   The impact of the treaty on Germany (1)

The signing of the Treaty of Versailles cast a long shadow over the political life of Germany in the 1920s. Before the government signed the treaty, it took the precaution of asking its chief opponents - the DNVP, DDP and DVP - to declare that those who signed the treaty were doing so out of motives of patriotism. The DDP and DVP readily agreed. The DNVP was more guarded. The leadership agreed reluctantly, only because it could see no alternative to unconditional surrender. What the DNVP could not do in the months that followed was to accept Germany's military defeat. Deep down, members of the DNVP felt the need for a different explanation of Germany's plight - an explanation which would preserve the army from the stigma of defeat. They found what they were looking for in the 'Stab-in-the-Back' myth. The Weimar Assembly set up a commission to investigate the causes of Germany's defeat. In November 1919, Hindenburg was a witness and he stated: 'An English general has said with justice: the German army was stabbed in the back. No blame is to be attached to the sound core of the army. Its performances call like that of the officer corps for an equal admiration. It is perfectly plain on whom the blame rests'. This was the birth of the Stab-in-the-Back myth and it was accepted without question by the right wing in Germany. The army was not to blame for Germany's defeat. Those responsible were the 'November traitors', the coalition parties - principally the Socialists - who had sabotaged the war effort, engineered a revolution and signed the shameful Versailles dictat. From this time on, the right wing, led by the DNVP, attacked prominent Republicans and poured abuse on democratic institutions. The coalition parties made only feeble attempts to defend themselves. The tragic outcome was that, precisely when the young Republic required maximum support to establish itself in the hearts and minds of people, influential sections of society, anti-democratic by instinct and tradition, failed to be won over to the Republican cause.

Adapted from Carr 1991.

ITEM 4 The impact of the treaty on Germany (2)

How far is it true that the Versailles Treaty wrecked German democracy or that Germany's economy was ruined by reparations or that Germany's security was undermined by restrictions on the Armed Forces? There was little foundation in these claims. German industry, despite losses occurred in the war, soon began to recover its productive capacity. Although the currency suffered a disaster in 1921-23 which was blamed on reparations, other factors were involved. Much more serious than the treaty's economic impact was the political demoralisation which the treaty caused. This was not so important amongst those already inclined to attack the Republic as among the democratic parties which supported it. Nationalists and Communists made it clear from the start that they would not support the Republic. Hitler would have attacked the treaty whatever its terms. The real damage was done to moderates who became disillusioned when they might otherwise have supported the Republic. Two particular issues connected with the peace settlement continued to poison the political atmosphere for many years. The first was the question of war guilt. By trying to prove that Germany did not start the war, the government attacked the whole foundation of the Allied peace plan, arousing the suspicion that it did not intend to abide by it. At home it was believed that Germany could never be prosperous or safe so long as it was still 'shackled' by an unjust peace settlement. The second issue was that of the so-called 'Stab-in-the-Back'. Attempts to deny war guilt had domestic implications. If Germany had not been responsible for the war - as even Republican ministers claimed - then the imperial authorities could not be blamed for what had happened. Rather, the German army had been stabbed in the back. The blame for Germany's defeat lay with politicians at home. Like the war-guilt theory, the Stab-in-the-Back myth became a subject for endless discussion and publicity, with the result that Republican politicians became defensive and found it difficult to counter-attack.

Adapted from Nicholls 1979.

Questions

1. Look at the maps of Europe in Item 1.
   a) Why were most Germans dissatisfied with the borders of the new Europe?
   b) What other grievances did many Germans have with the Treaty of Versailles?
2. a) Describe the different responses to the terms of the Treaty of Versailles in the two cartoons in Item 2 and explain what they tell us about the different mood in each country.
   b) Do you agree that the Germans were treated leniently? Explain your answer.
   c) Why do you think most Germans did not believe that Germany had been treated leniently?
3. Judging from Items 3 and 4 and your own knowledge, what impact did the Treaty of Versailles make on Germany?

2 The consolidation of the Weimar Republic

Key issues

1. What problems did the government face in 1920?
2. Why was there a crisis in 1923 and how did the government deal with it?

2.1 What problems did the government face in 1920?

The range of problems
Historians agree that the period 1920-23 was a time of crisis for the new Weimar Republic. During these years, the continued existence of the Republic was threatened by the extreme left and right within Germany and by pressure from abroad. At the same time, the government inherited an economy under severe strain - strain which led eventually to a full-blown economic crisis. Add to this the difficulty that the government faced in persuading the majority of the population to accept the legitimacy of the new regime and it is easy to see how the historian Detlev Peukert could assert:

'The years 1920-23 were among the most hectic and eventful of the Weimar Republic. There was a headlong succession of dramatic developments in domestic, economic and foreign policy, either combining in their impact or severally constraining the government's ability to act.' (Peukert 1991, p.52)

This section will examine the main problems faced by the Weimar government in 1920. The following section will examine the causes of the crisis of 1923 and how the government dealt with it.

1. The threat from the extreme right
It was noted in Section 1.1 above that, between November 1918 and the summer of 1919, the new government's main concern was with the threat from the extreme left. The government used the Freikorps to put down the Spartacist Uprising in January 1919 and it called on the Freikorps again to put down the

various strikes and rebellions that broke out in the spring of 1919. Although, during this period, there was no significant threat from the extreme right, the formation of the Freikorps was in itself a sign that there was a significant section of the German population which was unhappy with the November 'revolution' and with developments since then. The signing of the Treaty of Versailles in June 1919 (see Section 1.2 above) fuelled the discontent of this section of the population, as did the speech Hindenburg made in November 1919 in which he claimed that the army had been 'stabbed in the back'. By the end of 1919, there was a section of German society which supported the extreme right and completely rejected the new regime. According to Layton, what people on the extreme right wanted was an 'authoritarian-nationalist' regime - government by a single leader whose main aim would be to make Germany a Great Power once again. He sums up the attitude of the extreme right as follows:

'The extreme right was united by its total rejection of the Weimar system and its principles. It sought to destroy the democratic constitution and to establish some kind of authoritarian nationalist regime. Central to this conservative-nationalist opposition was the cultivated belief in the "Stab-in-the-Back" myth. The war, it was argued, had been lost not because of any military defeat suffered by the army, but as a result of the betrayal of unpatriotic forces within Germany. These were the pacifists, the socialists, the democrats, the Jews - a whole range of scapegoats were used by right-wing politicians to take the blame for accepting the armistice.' (Layton 1995, p.100)

The Kapp Putsch, March 1920

It was noted in Section 1.3 above that, under the terms of the Treaty of Versailles, Germany was to reduce the size of its army to 100,000. When the treaty came into effect in January 1920, the government began to take steps to demobilise the army. This involved disbanding the Freikorps - something which, historians agree, provoked the so-called 'Kapp Putsch'. The Kapp Putsch was an attempt by members of the Freikorps to overthrow the Weimar government by force and to set up a new, authoritarian regime under Wolfgang Kapp. The main events are outlined in Box 2.12.

The aftermath of the Kapp Putsch

Although the Kapp Putsch failed, it provided some important lessons for those on the extreme right. It showed, for example, that the army would not necessarily intervene if an attempt was made by the right to overthrow the Weimar Republic by force. It also showed that any attempt to overthrow the government by force required at least some popular backing. These were lessons learned, in particular, by Adolf Hitler. When the political pendulum swung

---

BOX 2.12 The Kapp Putsch

The Kapp Putsch was the work of disgruntled army officers and Freikorps men, angered by the reduction of the army under the Treaty of Versailles. A group of officers led by Freiherr von Lüttwitz, commanding general in Berlin and Wolfgang Kapp, an official from East Prussia and one of the founders of the Patriotic Party, plotted to overthrow the government and hold new elections. Their plot came to a head when the Allied Disarmament Commission insisted on the disbandment of two Freikorps brigades recently returned from the Baltic. When Lüttwitz refused to disband one of the brigades, his arrest was ordered. In response, Lüttwitz and his men marched into Berlin on 13 March 1920. The Kapp Putsch was amateurish in its design and execution and had little chance of ultimate success. What was memorable about it was the ambiguous attitude of the army chiefs. The generals, who had never failed President Ebert when it came to putting down Communists, refused to move against Lüttwitz. General von Seeckt, Head of the General Staff, spoke for most generals when he told Ebert that 'troops do not fire on troops...when the army fires on the army all comradeship within the officer corps has vanished'. Seeckt sympathised with the putschists, though natural caution prevented him from voicing such support openly. Ebert was bitterly disappointed. But, instead of challenging Seeckt and insisting on military action, he and his colleagues withdrew from Berlin to Dresden. A new government was installed in Berlin, but it had little support in the city and even less elsewhere. Before the government left Berlin, the Socialist members called for a general strike. The trade unionists, unlike many generals, did not let the government down. The strike was completely effective. It paralysed the city. All industrial activity ceased. Also, civil servants refused to take orders from Kapp and the Reichsbank refused to recognise his signature. After four days, Kapp and Lüttwitz fled and the Putsch collapsed.
Adapted from Carr 1991.

---

away from the Republic in the autumn of 1923, the Nazis pressed for a second Putsch and eventually took matters into their own hands with the so-called Munich Putsch (see Unit 4, Section 1.6). Two further lessons could be learned from the Kapp Putsch.

First, those responsible for organising similar attempts to gain power could expect to be treated leniently by the judiciary. Berghahn points out that:

'Kapp, though he died while awaiting his trial, would not have had to fear a heavy sentence. Lüttwitz suffered no worse than being sent into retirement on a general's pension...The trial against Adolf Hitler and Ludendorff following their abortive putsch of November 1923 was marked by a similar leniency towards right-wing plotters: Ludendorff was acquitted altogether; Hitler was sentenced to five years, but released after less than 12 months. Leaders of left-wing risings against the Republic were not treated so leniently.' (Berghahn 1987, p.76)

Berghahn records that between 1919 and 1921, 13 murder cases were brought to court in which the defendants were left-wingers. The courts imposed eight death sentences and a total of 176 years in prison. During the same period, 314 murder cases were brought to court in which the defenders were right-wingers. The courts imposed one death sentence and a total of 31 years in prison.

And second, it was not just the ringleaders who treated leniently. So too were those officers who had refused to defend the Republic. The Defence Minister and a number of civil servants were forced to resign, but not the top-ranking officers:

'Noske, a favourite target of left-wing critics was forced to resign in the aftermath of the Putsch and some politically unreliable civil servants were dismissed...Despite widespread criticism on the left of the generals' behaviour during the Putsch, little was done to discipline [disobedient] officers because the government needed the support of the army to suppress fresh disorders.' (Carr 1991, p.264)

Despite the disloyalty he showed at the time of the Kapp Putsch, General von Seeckt was appointed Chief of the Army Command at the end of March 1920. Layton argues that this appointment had long-term significance:

'Amazingly, Seeckt himself was appointed Chief of the Army Command at the end of that very month - an appointment made on the dubious logic that he enjoyed the confidence of his fellow officers and ignoring the fact that his attitude to the Republic was at best luke-warm. Under Seeckt's influence (1920-26) the army was turned into a "state within a state"...with a privileged position which placed it in effect beyond direct democratic accountability. Many within its ranks believed that the army served some higher purpose to the nation as a whole and therefore it had the right to intervene as it saw fit without regard to its obligations to the Republic.' (Layton 1995, p.103)

The Kapp Putsch and Bavaria

One further consequence of the Kapp Putsch was that it triggered the rise to power of the right in Bavaria. A right-wing government came to power at the time of the Kapp Putsch and the right remained in power for the next three years, allowing Bavaria to become the centre of extreme right-wing activity:

'In Bavaria, the Kapp Putsch can be said to have been successful. The Reichswehr [army] commanders in that state obliged the coalition government formed by the Social Democrat Hoffmann to resign; it was replaced by a sharply right-wing government whose object was to make

Bavaria a "focus of order" in the Reich. From 1920 onwards, Bavaria was an [ideal place] for extreme right organisations and leading personalities of militant right-wing radicalism.' (Kolb 1988, p.38)

2. The threat from the extreme left

In addition to the threat from the extreme right, the government of the Weimar Republic continued to face the threat from the extreme left. The difference was that, faced with rebellion from the left, the government could rely on the army to respond positively to any requests for intervention.

The 'civil war' in the Ruhr, 1920

One further consequence of the Kapp Putsch was a significant uprising by left-wingers in the Ruhr. By mid-March, a 'Red Army' of 50,000 troops controlled the region. As usual, the government's response was to send in the army to put the rebellion down. As usual, when it was a matter of combating forces from the left, the army agreed to the government's request. Berghahn describes this as a 'major event' - see Box 2.13

> **BOX 2.13 The 'civil war' in the Ruhr**
>
> In the Ruhr, a 'Red Army' 50,000 strong was formed by socialist workers in protest at the Kapp Putsch. For several weeks this army controlled large parts of the Ruhr, fighting bitterly against the Freikorps troops which the government sent against it. It is a measure of how radical sections of the working class had become and how disappointed they were with the outcome of the November 'Revolution' that a force of this size could be built. The result was nothing short of a civil war in the Ruhr. A major event. And so was the defeat of the Red Army. Once reinforcements and volunteers' units had been brought in, the Red Army was beaten back with a ruthlessness that had also characterised the civil war between the extreme left and the Free Corps the previous year. In April, further disturbances broke out in Saxony and Thuringia. Again, workers' self-defence units carried out attacks on Freikorps and on regular army units. Again, the disturbances were ruthlessly suppressed.
>
> *Adapted from Berghahn 1987.*

Exaggeration of the threat from the extreme left

Although, as Box 2.13 shows, the extreme left did pose some danger to the Weimar government, most historians agree that the Weimar government tended to exaggerate the threat that the left posed and, by so doing, not only alienated still further those on the left, but also encouraged the government to rely on the support of those who were not its natural allies. The Freikorps and Reichswehr were all too willing to use force against the extreme left, but that did not mean that they supported the aims and values of the Weimar government. There is an argument that, by taking the threat from the extreme left too seriously, the Weimar government weakened its position:

'With hindsight, it is clear that the extreme left posed much less of a threat to Weimar than was believed at the time...[The extreme left] frightened many - prompted also by the propaganda of the extreme right - into exaggerated fears. In particular, it drove the parliamentary left and other democrats into increasing reliance on the forces of reaction. However, the reality was not nearly so threatening.' (Layton 1995, p.99)

3. Luke-warm support for the Weimar system

It was pointed out in Section 1.1 above that the election held in January 1919 was a victory for those parties that supported the setting up of a democratic Republic. That election was held to elect the National Assembly. Once the constitution had been drawn up and approved, fresh elections were needed to elect the first Reichstag. These were scheduled for autumn 1920, but, following the Kapp Putsch and uprisings of the extreme left, were brought forward to June. Unlike the election of January 1919, the election of June 1920 was a major setback to those parties that supported the Republic:

'The election was a debacle [disaster] for the parties of the "Weimar coalition". The SPD and DDP suffered heavy losses, while the opposition parties scored huge gains...The coalition thus lost its parliamentary majority at Reich level and was destined never to recover it. In the National Assembly, the coalition had commanded over 78% of the seats (331 out of 423) whereas now the SPD, Centre and DDP together had only 44.6% (205 seats out of 459). As a result, supporters of the Weimar constitution were confronted in the Reichstag by two compact blocs, the "red" [KPD] and the "red, white and black" (the Imperial colours [ie the DNVP and its allies])...The possibility of forming a stable democratic government was in doubt at the outset and was to remain so throughout the Republican period.' (Kolb 1988, p.39)

Already, by the end of June 1920, three different governments had fallen - Scheidemann's in June 1919 over the terms of the Treaty of Versailles, Bauer's in March 1920 over the Kapp Putsch and Müller's as a result of the election result in June 1920. Between the end of June 1920 and the end of November 1923, four further governments rose and fell (see Box 2.14), only that headed by Josef Wirth of the Centre Party remaining in office for more than a year (Wirth's government remained in power from May 1921 to November 1922). As noted in Section 1.2 above, the frequent changes of government and the fragility of the coalitions made it difficult for the new Republic to gain and retain public support - a major problem given the constant attacks from the extreme left and right. Furthermore, structurally

BOX 2.14	Coalition government	
Appointment of Chancellor	Chancellor	Coalition Parties
13.02.1919	Philip Scheidemann (SPD)	SPD, Z, DDP
21.06.1919	Gustav Bauer (SPD)	SPD, Z, DDP (from Oct.)
27.03.1920	Hermann Müller (SPD)	SPD, Z, DDP
25.06.1920	Konstantin Fehrenbach (Z)	DDP, Z, DVP
10.05.1921	Josef Wirth (Z)	SPD, Z, DDP
26.10.1921	Josef Wirth (Z)	SPD, Z, DDP
22.11.1922	Wilhelm Cuno (non-party)	DDP, Z, DVP
13.08.1923	Gustav Stresemann (DVP)	SPD, Z, DDP, DVP
06.10.1923	Gustav Stresemann (DVP)	SPD (to 3 Nov.), Z, DDP, DVP
30.11.1923	Wilhelm Marx (Z)	DDP, Z, BVP, DVP

This table shows the various coalitions which governed Germany in 1919-23.

speaking, Germany was little different in 1920 from how it had been in 1914. As a result, many groups continued to support old values and were suspicious of the new Republic.

4. The economic position in 1920

Historians agree that the German economy was in difficulty at the end of the war. Kolb points out, for example, that:

'Between 1913 and 1919, the national debt had risen from 5,000 million to 144,000 million marks, as the imperial government had not financed the war by rigorous taxation but chiefly by long-term borrowing (war loans) and by increasing the floating debt [ie putting more money into circulation]. Paper money in circulation, including Reichsbank notes, rose from 2,000 million in 1913 to 45,000 million in 1919. The policy of reckless borrowing was continued after 1918.' (Kolb 1988, p.40)

Layton suggests that the Kaiser had been working on the assumption that Germany would win the war and would then be able to impose reparations on the defeated allies, providing Germany with the money it needed to pay back its war loans. But, defeat in the war ruined this plan. The position of the German economy in 1920 is described in Box 2.15. As Box 2.15 suggests, most historians do not accept that the reparations imposed on Germany by the Allies were a root cause of its economic difficulties after the end of the war. There already was high inflation before the final figure for reparations was set in January 1921. Reparations did not cause the economic crisis which developed after 1921, but they did contribute towards it.

BOX 2.15 | The German economy in 1920

The Weimar Republic was saddled, from the very start, with the economic legacy left by the Imperial regime. A lack of capital for investment, a large trade deficit and the difficulties of readjusting a war economy to the requirements of peace were certainly not helped by demands for reparations from the Allies and the loss of important regions as a result of the Treaty of Versailles. However, the main problem was the massive government deficit and the resulting decline of the mark which was reflected in increasing inflation. Between 1913 and 1919 the value of the mark against the dollar fell from 4.20 marks to 14.00 marks and the price of basic goods increased three- to four-fold. Victory, of course, would have allowed the government to pay back its debts by claiming reparations from the Allies. Defeat thwarted this plan. As a result, by 1920, Germany's finances were in a complete mess and the government in a difficult position. Narrowing the gap between government income and expenditure and, by doing so, bringing down inflation and stabilising the currency could only be achieved by increasing taxation and/or reducing public spending. But the idea of increasing taxation or reducing public spending was not very attractive since either option would alienate support for the young Republic, distress the economy and increase unemployment. In 1920, therefore, the government continued its policy of deficit spending in the hope that the economy would stabilise. One consequence was an increase in inflation. Examination of the wholesale prices index shows that prices doubled between 1913 and 1918 and then doubled again between 1918 and 1919. In 1920, prices were fourteen times higher than they were in 1913 and more than four times higher than they were in 1919.

Adapted from Layton 1995.

MAIN POINTS - Section 2.1

- By the end of 1919, there was a section of German society which supported the extreme right and completely rejected the new regime. When the government began to disband the Freikorps in early 1920, a group of right-wingers attempted to overthrow the government in the Kapp Putsch.
- The Kapp Putsch showed that (1) the army would not oppose right-wing coups (2) uprisings required at least some popular backing (3) right-wing rebels could expect to be treated leniently by the judiciary (4) officers who refused to defend the republic would be treated leniently.
- One further consequence of the Kapp Putsch was that the right came to power in Bavaria, ensuring it

became a centre of right-wing extremism.
- The government also faced the threat from the extreme left, but it could rely on the army to intervene against the left - as it did in the Ruhr in March 1920, for example.
- The election of June 1920 was a major setback to those parties that supported the Republic. It resulted in instability, with governments falling in quick succession.
- By 1920, the German economy was in difficulties. The main problem was the massive government deficit and the resulting decline of the mark which was reflected in increasing inflation.

Activity 2.4 Problems facing Germany in 1920

ITEM 1 | Elections 1919-20

(i) Party	National Assembly 19 Jan 1919			6 June 1920		
	Total Votes	%	No. MPs	Total Votes	%	No. MPs
SPD	11,509,100	37.9	165	6,104,400	21.6	102
USPD	2,317,300	7.6	22	5,046,800	17.9	84
KPD	–	–	–	589,500	2.1	4
Centre Party	5,980,200	19.7	91	3,845,000	13.6	64
BVP	–	–	–	1,238,600	4.4	21
DDP	5,641,800	18.6	75	2,333,700	8.3	39
DVP	1,345,600	4.4	19	3,919,400	13.9	65
Wirtschaftspartei	275,100	0.9	4	218,600	0.8	4
DNVP	3,121,500	10.3	44	4,249,100	14.9	71
Other Parties	209,700	0.6	3	651,200	2.5	5

This table shows the results of the Reich elections held in 1919 and 1920.

(ii)

This poster was produced by the DDP for the 1920 Reich election. It says that the DDP is against dictatorship from both left and right.

ITEM 2 A Freikorps recruitment poster

This poster reads 'Comrade! Help me! Against Bolshevism [ie Communism], against the threat of the Poles and against starvation. Register yourself immediately with the German Protection League'. The poster was produced in 1919 by an artist called Wissmann.

Questions

1. a) Judging from Items 1-3 and your own knowledge, what problems did the Weimar Republic face in 1920?
   b) How did the government deal with these problems?
2. Using Items 1 and 3, explain why the Reich election result in June 1920 was significant.
3. Look at Item 2.
   a) Describe the part played by the Freikorps in events in Germany in 1920.
   b) 'The government couldn't live with them or without them'. Is this a fair statement of relations between government and Freikorps in 1920?

ITEM 3 A historian's view

The Kapp Putsch of March 1920 and the uprising in the Ruhr which followed it were symptoms of the political balance at the time. This balance had three main elements:

1. The forces of counter-revolution (ie the extreme right) were too weak and disorganised to topple democracy completely, but they still had to be reckoned with even after the Kapp Putsch had failed.
2. Those parties which supported the Weimar constitution remained in power, but they were forced to manoeuvre within a space bound by the counter-revolutionary right (which had gained in strength) and a working-class left which had become more radical.
3. The workers' and soldiers' council movement had been the vehicle for the revolution in 1919 and for the general strike in 1920, but it was now beaten. Its supporters either withdrew from politics or joined the KPD which now gained the mass support it had previously lacked. This new balance was reflected in the election of June 1920, with the radical parties of both right and left gaining, while the Weimar coalition parties (SPD, Centre, DDP) lost their majority. From this time onwards, the process of forming governments and securing parliamentary backing for legislation became highly unstable. Even though the DVP now threw in its lot with the Republic for the first time, the only possible combinations of parties that could form a government between 1920 and 1930 were:
   (a) centre-left coalition - which would only ever be a minority government.
   (b) centre-right coalition - which would also always be a minority government.
   (c) centre-right plus the SPD - the so-called 'Great Coalition' which took power under Stresemann in 1923.
   (d) centre-right plus DNVP - the so-called 'Bourgeois Coalition'.

The result was that governments either had no clear majority or they were based on such wide and conflict-prone party combinations that it was only a matter of time before they collapsed. This was a reflection of the fact that a majority of voters had become disenchanted with the constitutionalist parties, whilst on the extreme left and right there was utter alienation.

Adapted from Peukert 1991.

2.2 Why was there a crisis in 1923 and how did the government deal with it?

Reparations

Under the terms of the Treaty of Versailles, the final setting of reparations had to be completed by 1 May 1921. In the early months of 1921, there was a constant round of negotiations in an attempt to find a sum which was both acceptable to the Allies and had a realistic chance of being delivered. Feuchtwanger shows the sort of difficulties that had to be overcome:

'A multitude of political and economic pressures frustrated a settlement...German industry feared French domination, French industry feared German competition, the British feared Franco-German control of the European economy and wanted a global sum stated to help in settling the financial markets.' (Feuchtwanger 1995, p.93)

Eventually, on 5 May 1921, the Germans were presented with the so-called 'London ultimatum' (since the ultimatum was issued in London). Germany would have to pay a total of 132 billion gold marks of which 82 billion would be liable in the distant future. The remaining 50 billion gold marks was to be paid off by annual instalments of 2 billion gold marks plus 26% of the value of German exports. Germany was given six days to accept this ultimatum. In response, the Fehrenbach government resigned and was replaced by a government headed by Joseph Wirth of the Centre Party. According to Carr (1991, p.271), Wirth signed the reparations agreement twenty hours before the ultimatum was due to expire. Peukert argues that the burden imposed was not intolerable:

'The actual payments that had to be made were perfectly manageable. Reparations were not, therefore, an intolerable burden, especially since any clear-sighted politician could reckon that after a few years of uninterrupted payment and reduced international tension there was a reasonable chance that the overall size of the debt would be cut down.' (Peukert 1991, p.54)

Peukert goes on to argue that, although this was the case, the importance of reparations should not be underestimated - see Box 2.16.

The 'policy of fulfilment'

The signing of the reparations agreement, historians agree, marked the beginning of the 'policy of fulfilment', a policy associated first with Chancellor Joseph Wirth and his Minister of Reconstruction, Walther Rathenau and then with Gustav Stresemann. Kolb describes the policy of fulfilment as follows:

'The acceptance of the London payments plan by the German government marked the beginning of the 'policy of fulfilment' which was tenaciously

BOX 2.16 The importance of the reparations issue

Although the final sum demanded by the Allies was not unrealistic, the heated disputes over reparations in the 1920s, particularly in the period 1920-24 cannot be dismissed as mere shadow-boxing. Three groups of factors caused the question of reparations to cast a dark shadow over international relations during this period. First, the fact that the overall sum was so high and that the procedures for calculating the payments were so complex was bound to breed fierce German resistance, for obvious psychological reasons. This root and branch hostility to reparations inevitably meant that any attempt to settle for a workable compromise would be condemned as a sell-out. Secondly, the provisions regulating payments - the real burden on Germany - emerged only in the course of bitter exchanges between the parties concerned. More sober negotiations did not take place until after the disastrous confrontation of 1923. Before then, realistic approaches made little headway. And third, above all in 1919-23, nobody had any previous experience of reparations on such a large scale. Some economists who were opposed to reparations - such as the British economist J.M. Keynes - predicted serious consequences for the world economy. And, in fact, reparations did help to make economic recovery after the war more difficult. If Germany was to make payments in cash as well as in kind, it would have to build up its foreign currency reserves. The Western powers, however, had little to gain from a German export drive. Also, since reparation payments were then to be passed on to the USA as repayment for war debts, the reparations did little to stimulate demand in Europe. Reparations, therefore, help to explain why the post-war boom was so short-lived in Europe.

Adapted from Peukert 1991.

opposed by German nationalists. The intention of the policy, which its opponents failed to perceive or regard as valid, was to demonstrate, by complying with the reparations demands to the utmost of Germany's ability, that they were impossible to execute, and thus to compel a revision. It was also hoped to improve Germany's position by gaining time in the "cold war" with France.' (Kolb 1988, p.43)

The idea, therefore, was to do everything possible to fulfil the Allies' demands, but, by doing so, to show that Germany's economy simply could not survive such strain. The Allies would then see that the figure set was unrealistic and be forced to reduce it. This policy lasted for nearly a year - until the Germans signed the Treaty of Rapallo with the Soviet Union on 16 April 1922 (see below) - and was then revived when Stresemann became Chancellor in September 1923. It should be noted that, if the German government had raised the level of taxes or made a concerted effort to reduce public spending, the reparations burden would have been lighter. As it was, the German government had political and economic reasons for not taking such measures. As noted in Box 2.15 above, the government was reluctant to take unpopular economic measures which might 'alienate support for the young Republic'. Furthermore, the policy of fulfilment would have fallen flat if the government showed that Germany could pay reparations without any problem.

The partition of Upper Silesia

In a referendum held in March 1921, nearly 60% of the people of Upper Silesia voted to remain part of Germany while just over 40% voted to join Poland. Kolb describes the consequence as follows:

'At the beginning of May 1921, the Poles launched a rising in which they were aided by the French occupying troops, whereas the British, who wanted the industrial area to go to Germany, allowed the Germans to organise a defensive force.' (Kolb 1988, p.42)

Although the German forces were successful, the Allies, on a recommendation from the League of Nations, decided in October 1921 to partition the area. The industrial area in the East was given to Poland, while Germany was given an area that was larger but less industrially valuable. Feuchtwanger argues that:

'The efforts to make reparations and fulfilment more viable...received a severe setback when the Allied decision to partition Upper Silesia was formally announced. The policy of fulfilment appeared to have been proved to be futile...Upper Silesia entailed the resignation and reconstruction of Wirth's Cabinet.' (Feuchtwanger 1995, p.97)

The struggle intensifies

Although Germany paid its first installment of reparations at the end of May 1921, by the end of 1921, it was clear that its economy was in difficulty:

'In November 1921 a particularly sharp fall [in the value of the mark] occurred when Germany tried to repay a £50 million loan with which she had financed the first installment of reparations. By the end of 1921 it was clear that Germany would soon be in default. In January 1922, the Reparations Commission granted her a moratorium [a postponement] on the January and February installments.' (Carr 1991, p.271)

Germany's economic difficulties coincided with the rise to power in France of Raymond Poincaré. Poincaré was determined to make the Germans pay their dues:

'He pressed French claims to the utmost, insisting rigidly on the letter of the law; Germany had promised to pay but did not want to and must, therefore, be made to pay.' (Carr 1991, pp.271-72)

When, in the summer of 1922, the German government attempted to postpone payment of reparations, the French objected, demanding that Germany make 'pledges' - see Box 2.17.

BOX 2.17   Germany demands a breathing space

On 12 July 1922, the German government asked the Reparations Commission to agree to the suspension of the remaining reparation payments due in that year and it also announced that Germany could not afford to make payments in 1923 and 1924. In November 1922, the German government went some steps further. As a precondition of a stabilisation of its currency, it asked to be released from all obligations under the Treaty of Versailles for three or four years. It also asked for a loan of 500 million gold marks. The French government under Poincaré, however, was determined to assert all its rights under the peace treaty, including taking sanctions against Germany if it failed to keep to the provisions of the Treaty of Versailles. Poincaré's slogan was 'no moratorium without pledges'. His objective was to secure pledges and the insistent German request for a moratorium, therefore, suited him. Britain was opposed to demanding pledges, but was increasingly impatient with Germany's argument that its currency crisis was a crisis of Germany's ability to pay reparations. The British were, therefore, not prepared to take Germany's side unreservedly.

Adapted from Kolb 1988.

The Treaty of Rapallo

One reason why French policy hardened after April 1922 was because Germany signed the Treaty of Rapallo with the Soviet Union. Carr summarises the content, aims and effect of the treaty as follows:

'Diplomatic relations between the two countries were re-established, Russia waived all claim to reparations from Germany and, in return, Germany waived all claims to compensation for expropriated Germany property [ie property seized by the Russians]. On the Russian side, this was a diplomatic manoeuvre to keep the capitalist countries divided; for Germany it was intended to be the beginning of an independent foreign policy. In practice, it was little more than a futile act of defiance which confirmed French suspicion of Germany without obtaining for the latter the advantages of alliance with a strong power.' (Carr 1991, p.272)

Most historians agree that, the signing of the Treaty of Rapallo was an important step on the path to the French occupation of the Ruhr.

The occupation of the Ruhr

When, in December 1922, the Reparations Commission announced that Germany was behind in its deliveries of timber to France, the French government, supported by Belgium and Italy, decided to send a team of engineers take control of industry in the Ruhr. The occupation of the Ruhr began on 11 January 1923:

'A group of engineers were sent with instructions to take charge of the coal syndicate and ensure strict compliance with the delivery programme laid down by the Reparations Commission. The engineers were "protected" by five French and one Belgian division, 60,000 men in all, who occupied the whole area of the Ruhr. In the course of 1923, their numbers were increased to 100,000.' (Kolb 1988, p.46)

Historians agree that, in Germany, there was almost universal outrage at the French occupation of the Ruhr. Many compare the mood in early 1923 to the great feeling of solidarity that existed in 1914 just after the outbreak of war had been announced:

'Germany reacted to the occupation of the Ruhr with an almost unanimous outcry of national indignation. The spirit of August 1914 seemed to return; class [struggle disappeared] for the time being, giving place to a sense of shared, national destiny.' (Kolb 1988, p.46)

Passive resistance

The German government responded to the occupation of the Ruhr by supporting a policy of 'passive resistance'. It ordered everybody living in the Ruhr to refuse to take orders from the invaders and to refuse to work for them. Those going on strike would continue to be paid, by the German government:

'The government embarked on a policy of "passive resistance". It urged workers to go on strike and to refuse to cooperate with the French, in return for the continued payment of their wages.' (Layton 1995, p.94)

The German government also immediately stopped all payment of reparations. By pursuing the policy of passive resistance, historians agree, the German government added further strain to the German economy, transforming the country's economic difficulties into a crisis.

An inflationary decade 1914-24

It is important to note that inflation remained high in Germany throughout the decade 1914-24. Box 2.18 explains why inflation grew during this decade whereas it was virtually unknown before.

Some historians have argued that high inflation was beneficial to the German economy in the period 1918-22 because it ensured that, unlike other parts of Europe, Germany did not suffer from high unemployment and an economic slow-down:

BOX 2.18 | The growth of inflation

Before 1914, inflation was virtually unknown. As a result, people were at a loss, during the war and early post-war period, to know how to respond to the unmistakable decline in the mark's value both at home and compared to foreign currencies. The wholesale price index rose from 1 in 1913 to 2.17 in 1918. By the end of the war, in other words, the mark was worth only half its pre-war value. This was a substantial reduction in the value of money holdings and a drain on the purchasing power of people dependent on fixed incomes. The causes of inflation only became clear gradually. The imperial government had decided against financing the war by imposing special new taxes or even by increasing the taxes of the more wealthy. Instead, it employed two measures which had inflationary consequences. It raised war loans which would be repaid with interest after the 'final victory'. In addition, it increased the volume of money in circulation, gradually abandoning the link between paper money and gold reserves which had been maintained before the war. Shortages of consumer goods and unscrupulous profiteering on armaments also generated price rises which the increased quantity of money caused to rise still higher. The defeat of 1918 shattered any illusions that the government would be able to clear away this mountain of debts and paper money by imposing reparations. Only a radical currency reform could have solved the problem. But this would have meant that those who paid for the war loans and those on fixed incomes would have lost their money and the government didn't want the unpopularity such a dose of austerity would have brought. Also, the government wouldn't have had the funds to pay for much needed post-war reconstruction. As a result, inflation continued to climb.

Adapted from Peukert 1991.

'The German economy compared very favourably with other European economies which went into post-war recession in 1920-21. So, for example, whereas Britain had an unemployment rate of nearly 17% in 1921, Germany had nearly full employment with only 1.8% unemployed and rising wage levels. Such an unusually high level of economic activity at this time also acted as a major stimulus for investment and large sums, especially from the USA, poured into Germany.' (Layton 1995, pp.96-97)

From inflation to hyperinflation

In 1923, high inflation turned into 'hyperinflation' - inflation which is completely out of control. Prices began to rise more and more rapidly. The more money the government printed, the higher prices rose. Money became almost worthless. At one point it cost five million marks to buy a stamp or 80 million marks to buy an egg. One man recalled:

'In 1923...I was advertising chief of a rubber factory. That was during the inflation. I had a monthly salary of 200 billion marks. We were paid twice a day, and then everybody had a half-hour's leave so that he could rush to the stores and buy something before the next quotation on the dollar came out at which time the money would lose half its value.' (quoted in Craig 1981, p.451)

Historians are divided about why this happened. Some argue that it was the occupation of the Ruhr which tipped Germany over the edge:

'Germany, whose currency was already in a precarious state, had to pay out thousands of millions of marks in currency or in kind to the people of the Ruhr district, who were forfeiting their pay on government orders; tax revenue ceased to flow from the Ruhr, as did coal deliveries to the rest of the country, so that the government's entire supply of foreign currency had to be spent on coal from abroad...By April 1923, the government's financial needs had shot up to seven times the normal revenue level...In December 1922, the mark stood at 8,000 to the dollar; in April 1923, the figure was about 20,000 and at the beginning of August one million.' (Kolb 1988, pp.46-47)

Other historians, however, argue that Germany already had hyperinflation before the occupation of the Ruhr and that the occupation, therefore, only intensified a process which was happening anyway.

'The fundamental cause of the German inflation is to be found in the mismanagement of Germany's internal finances from 1914. So although the inflationary spiral did not develop at a uniform rate...the process was undoubtedly cumulative...By the end of 1922 (ie before the French occupation of the Ruhr), hyperinflation had set in. Thereafter the government exerted no control on its financial policy.' (Layton 1995, p.94)

The impact of hyperinflation

As suggested above, during the spring and summer of 1923, Germany's currency became virtually valueless. As a result, many people lost their life's savings and many suffered, but it is important, historians emphasise, to be aware that not everybody lost out. Box 2.19 explores what happened to different people.

The extreme right 1921-23

The failure of the Kapp Putsch in 1920 by no means meant an end to political violence on the right. Kolb argues that:

'The years 1921-22 saw a regrouping and intensified mobilisation of the militant right. The right-wing radicals formed patriotic leagues and numerous secret organisations, mostly illegal successors to the Freikorps which had by this time been officially disbanded.' (Kolb 1988, p.44)

BOX 2.19   The impact of hyperinflation

It has often been claimed that the worst consequence of the hyperinflation was the destruction of the German middle class. The assumption is that a large proportion of the middle class came to vote for the Nazis because of their impoverishment in 1923. Recent research suggests, however, that the impact of hyperinflation was much more mixed than once supposed. It is important to bear in mind that a range of factors, such as region, age and personal circumstances could affect an individual, not just class. The key to understanding who gained and who lost out lies in the nature of an individual's income and how much they were in debt. Clearly, these factors depended to some extent on class, but not entirely. The real winners were those who could pay off their debts, mortgages and loans with inflated and worthless money. This worked to the advantage of groups such as businesspeople, landowners and homeowners (many of whom belonged to the middle class). Some made massive gains by buying real estate from the naive and desperate. The most notorious example was Hugo Stinnes who, by the end of 1923, controlled 20% of all German industry. At the other end were people who relied on savings, those who lost the value of money they had invested and those living on fixed incomes or welfare support - for example, students, the retired and the sick. Their incomes rapidly lost value and many fell into poverty. Between the extremes of profit and loss were to be found the mass of the population. In the countryside, farmers coped reasonably well since food remained in demand and they were less dependent on the money economy to provide themselves with the necessities of life. Shopkeepers and craftspeople also seem to have done good business. It is now generally agreed that workers' standard of living declined in the months of hyperinflation but, for most, did not collapse. Most historians now agree that the main point is that two people from the same social class could be affected in very different ways depending on a host of variables, regardless of what class they belonged to.

Adapted from Layton 1995.

Between 1921 and 1923, the right organised a series of attacks, including the murder of two prominent politicians - Matthias Erzberger in August 1921 and Walther Rathenau in June 1922.

Erzberger's assassination

Erzberger, a leading member of the Centre Party served in government in the early days of the Republic. Under Chancellor Bauer (June 1919 to March 1920), he was Finance Minister. His main 'crime' in the eyes of his right-wing opponents, however, was that he had been one of the signatories of the hated Treaty of Versailles. Erzberger's assassination had an important consequence in Bavaria:

'After the murder, Ebert and the Reich government issued an emergency decree for the protection of the Republic under Article 48 of the constitution. The Bavarian government challenged the validity of this procedure, though condemning the murder of Erzberger. The conflict between Berlin and Munich led to Kahr's fall.' (Feuchtwanger 1995, p.115)

Two years later, in the autumn of 1923, Kahr was to play an important role in the events leading up to the Munich Putsch (see Unit 4, Section 1.6).

Rathenau's assassination

Most historians would agree with Kolb that Rathenau was the 'most eminent' victim of the extreme right. At the time of his assassination, Rathenau was serving as Foreign Minister. Feuchtwanger argues that it is difficult to be sure about the motives for his murder:

'[It is] difficult to be precise about the motives of his killers other than that they wanted to hit a prominent representative of the Republic and of [the policy of] fulfilment, and that they came from exactly the same quarter as the assassins of Erzberger...Blind nihilistic activism drove them on. Rathenau was particularly in their sights as a Jew, doubly hated because he was so German as well and had played so significant a role in German affairs.' (Feuchtwanger 1995, p.116)

Rathenau's murder had important consequences. It was widely criticised abroad and the value of the mark fell as a direct result. It also prompted a response from the German government:

'On 21 July 1921, as a direct result of Rathenau's murder, the Reichstag passed a Law for the Protection of the Republic, valid for five years, which imposed severe penalties for conspiracy to murder and provided a means of prohibiting extremist organisations. The DNVP, BVP and KPD voted against the Bill and Bavaria refused to recognise the new measure...If, contrary to Republican hopes, the law of 21 July did not prove an effective weapon against enemies of the democratic state, this was above all because its application was in the hands of a judiciary which made no secret of its dislike of democracy and its sympathy with the political right.' (Kolb 1988, p.45)

Bavaria's refusal to recognise this law helps to explain why the Nazi Party was able to grow into a significant political force there in the years 1921-23 (see Unit 4, Section 1.5).

Buchrucker's failed Putsch

The occupation of the Ruhr and sense of crisis which resulted from the months of hyperinflation produced a political atmosphere which politicians on the extreme right (as on the extreme left) attempted to exploit. An attempted Putsch under Major Buchrucker in northern Germany in October 1923 was put down by the army (Reichswehr). It was followed a month later by Hitler's Munich Putsch (see Unit 4, Section 1.6).

The extreme left 1921-23

The USPD splits

At a meeting held in Halle in October 1920, members of the USPD voted to join Comintern (an international group of Communist parties under the leadership of the Soviet Union). This vote split the party:

'The minority left the congress and set up a separate party which, after the fusion of the left-wing majority with the KPD two months later, remained as the USPD. In the Reichstag it retained 59 of the 81 USPD members elected in June 1920, while the other 22 joined the KPD, giving it for the first time a sizeable [number of MPs]. The rank and file membership of the USPD divided very differently. Before the split in October 1920, it had risen to nearly 900,000. Around 370,000 joined the KPD while about 340,000 remained with the USPD. The rest retreated from active politics.' (Feuchtwanger 1995, p.103)

As many historians have pointed out, the split in the USPD gave the KPD mass membership and mass support for the first time. It is important to emphasise that the KPD's aim remained to replace the Weimar Republic with a socialist state:

'It wanted...the creation of a one-party socialist state and the major restructuring of Germany's social and economic fabric. Its opposition to the Republic therefore amounted to a wholesale rejection of the system - it was not prepared to be a "loyal opposition" and work within the parliamentary system to bring about its desired changes.' (Layton 1995, p.99)

One consequence of the influx of new members was an attempted uprising in the spring of 1921. Like all attempts at uprising in the period 1919-23, this was quickly suppressed by the army and police - see Box 2.20.

The attempted uprising in 1923

It was noted above that the occupation of the Ruhr and the sense of crisis which resulted from the months of hyperinflation produced a political atmosphere which politicians on both the extreme right and the extreme left attempted to exploit. On 26 September, the crisis became so serious that President Ebert declared a state of emergency under Article 48 of the constitution. This transferred power from local governments to regional military

BOX 2.20   The attempted uprising in Saxony, March 1921

In the spring of 1921, the KPD leadership launched an uprising in the central industrial area of Saxony. The KPD leadership did so in part because it was encouraged to do so by Comintern and in part because it overestimated the increase in the party's strength following the influx of supporters from the USPD. The 'March operation' was supposed to spark a revolution which would result in the overthrow of the Republic. It received some support in other centres of radicalism like Hamburg, but in the Ruhr only around 200,000 workers took part in the general strike called by the KPD. The attempted uprising was put down in a few days by the Prussian police. There was fierce fighting in some places and at least 145 people were killed. The most important consequence of the attempted uprising was to heighten middle-class fears of the 'Red threat'. The defeat caused divisions amongst the KPD leadership - some members of the leadership left the party or were expelled and the 22 MPs split into two groups. As a result, the party was unable to organise any further action for a few months. But the strength of the Communist movement was by no means broken. The KPD was able to keep control of most of its organisations and, from the summer of 1921, its 'united front' tactics made inroads on the membership of the SPD and what was left of the USPD.

Adapted from Kolb 1988 and Feuchtwanger 1995.

commanders. It was this that led to the extreme left's attempted uprising in October 1923:

'In October, the KPD made preparations for revolutionary action based on Central Germany. In Saxony and also in Thuringia, where the SPD and KPD together commanded a majority in the Lantage (state assemblies) these two parties combined to form a government and began to organise proletarian [ie working-class] defence units ("hundreds"). The KPD entered these governments as a tactical manoeuvre under the slogan of a "united front", to gain a basis for a revolutionary uprising.' (Kolb 1988, p.48)

As before, however, mass support for a Communist uprising failed to materialise. A meeting of factory councils on 21 October at which a vote was taken on whether to call a general strike failed to win a majority in favour. An attempted uprising in Hamburg on 23 October was swiftly crushed. That same day, troops were sent into Saxony after the Saxon government had made it clear that it would refuse to obey the local military commander's order that the 'proletarian hundreds' be disbanded. Then,

on 27 October, the Chancellor, Gustav Stresemann issued an ultimatum to the Saxon government demanding the resignation of KPD ministers. When the Prime Minister of Saxony Erich Zeigner (a member of the SPD) refused to act, on 29 October President Ebert replaced him with a Reich commissioner appointed under Article 48. Since a national state of emergency had been declared on 26 September, this was a constitutional act. But it also created a precedent which the Papen government would follow in 1932 and which the Nazis would follow in 1933 (see Unit 3, Section 2.3 and Unit 5, Section 1.2). Ebert's action was successful. The removal of Zeigner was enough to avert the crisis.

The role played by government

It was noted in Section 2.1 above that the election of 1920 dealt a blow to those parties which supported the Weimar Republic because the Weimar coalition now only had minority support in the Reichstag. Between the election in June 1920 and the end of 1923, four different Chancellors held office. As before, therefore, there was a degree of instability. Nevertheless, Lee argues, there was much that was positive about the contribution of the parties supporting the Republic - namely the SPD, DDP, Centre Party and, from 1923 when it agreed to join government for the first time, the DVP:

'Between them the four parties played a crucial role in the formative years of the Republic...[They] ensured the the survival of the Republic in the first ten years of its existence...They overcame the serious threats between 1920 and 1923.' (Lee 1998, p.21)

Lee is particularly complimentary about the role played by President Ebert during 1923. He argues that Ebert's use of Article 48 in 1923 saved the Republic:

'President Ebert made full use of the emergency powers available to him under Article 48 of the constitution to deal with the Kapp and Munich Putsches on the right and the Spartacist, Ruhr and Saxon threats on the left. In the last of these examples, the government declared a state of national emergency. Part of the process involved the transfer of political power to regional military commanders under orders from the Ministry of Defence in Berlin. The Prime Minister of Saxony, Zeigner, was removed from office when he refused to cooperate and the threatened Communist [uprising] was soon mopped up by army detachments and the police. It could therefore be argued that the early history of Article 48 helped to save the Republic, just as its later history was a significant factor in its destruction.' (Lee 1998, p.54)

MAIN POINTS - Section 2.2

- On 5 May 1921, the Germans were presented with the so-called 'London ultimatum'. In response the government resigned. The new government under Wirth signed and pursued a policy of fulfilment. This policy took a blow when the Allies gave part of Silesia to Poland.
- Relations with France deteriorated in 1922, especially after Germany signed the Treaty of Rapallo. The consequence was the occupation of the Ruhr in January 1923.
- The German government responded to the occupation by supporting a policy of 'passive resistance'. It ordered everybody living in the Ruhr to refuse to take orders from the invaders and to refuse to work for them.
- In 1923, high inflation turned into 'hyperinflation' -

inflation which is completely out of control. The more money the government printed, the higher prices rose. Money became almost worthless.
- Historians are divided about why this happened. Some argue that the occupation of the Ruhr tipped Germany over the edge. Others argue that Germany already had hyperinflation by January 1923 and the occupation only intensified a process which was happening anyway.
- Hyperinflation affected people in different ways, but it produced an atmosphere of crisis which members both of the extreme right and the extreme left attempted to exploit.
- Some historians argue that President Ebert's use of Article 48 in 1923 saved the Republic.

Activity 2.5 The crisis of 1923

ITEM 1 Hyperinflation

This photograph shows children playing with bundles of banknotes in 1923. It shows how worthless the German currency had become.

July 1914	4
July 1920	40
July 1921	80
July 1922	500
January 1923	18,000
July 1923	350,000
September 1923	100,000,000
November 1923	4,000,000,000,000

This table shows the number of marks to the dollar.

Two main theories have been used to explain why Germany suffered from hyperinflation in 1923. One is that it was the result of external factors. According to the historian Louis Snyder, 'the entire problem was closely connected with the reparations demanded by the Allies'. This is challenged by Geoff Layton. He argues that 'the reparations issue should be seen as a contributory factor to the inflation, not as a primary cause'. Neither view is quite right. Inflation started before reparations became an issue. The connection with reparations cannot, therefore, be considered the 'entire problem'. Yet reparations were more than merely a 'contributory factor'. It makes sense, therefore, to distinguish between the earlier, creeping inflation which arose because the economy had long-term structural problems and the later hyperinflation which was directly related to the obligation after 1921 to pay reparations. It is no coincidence that inflation became hyperinflation immediately after the announcement, in 1921, that the final amount to be paid in reparations was to be 132 million gold marks. It was then that the government began printing money to meet its demands. The dramatic collapse of the mark came when the French occupied the Ruhr. The French did this because the Germans had failed to pay reparations. So, again, reparations were the key. The second theory is that the German government deliberately provoked the inflationary crisis to avoid paying reparations. There is also a third theory, namely that German inflation was caused by a combination of factors which interacted. The war brought about creeping inflation. The Berlin government accelerated this process by its policy of deficit spending from 1919 on. The clinching factor was that domestic economic collapse would demonstrate to the Allies the injustice of reparations. Once the French invaded, there was little incentive to stop the printing presses.

Adapted from Lee 1998.

ITEM 2 The occupation of the Ruhr

When the French and Belgians occupied the Ruhr in January 1923, the German government, under Chancellor Cuno, was in no position to fight, but it refused to give in to Poincaré's strong-arm tactics. Cuno implemented a policy of 'passive resistance' in the Ruhr. Businesspeople, officials and workers were not to cooperate with the occupying powers. The Reich government would meet the financial losses resulting from resistance. Acts of sabotage were also organised secretly by paramilitary groups that worked with the official army (the Reichswehr). One result was that the Franco-Belgian invasion became a much larger operation than originally planned. Harsh measures were taken against German mine-owners, miners and civil servants. They included jail after court martial and banishment from the occupied zone. Miners were shot down in clashes with French troops. A customs barrier was set up between the Ruhr and the rest of the Reich. The hyperinflation, however, made it impossible for Germany to sustain the policy of passive resistance beyond the autumn of 1923. When the area was first occupied, public opinion ensured that no other policy was possible. The government argued that it would prevent the occupiers gaining any economic benefits and there was a solid basis for this calculation. At first, deliveries of reparations in kind - especially coal - fell off sharply. But they gradually recovered as the French found means of getting deliveries out of the Ruhr. Support for passive resistance was solid among rail employees. The French and Belgians had to bring in their own railway workers to move coal from the pits and even in May 1923 deliveries were only a third of the average monthly reparation deliveries in 1922. There were, therefore, considerable economic pressures on both sides to get back to the negotiating table.

This poster was produced by the German government to encourage the policy of passive resistance in the Ruhr. It shows a German miner being threatened by French soldiers. The caption reads: 'No I will not be forced'.

Adapted from Nicholls 1979 and Feuchtwanger 1995.

ITEM 3 Reasons for the Republic's survival

It is certainly important to recognise that decisive political action was taken in the second half of 1923 to confront the crisis faced by the Weimar Republic. From the end of 1922, things had just been allowed to slide, but Stresemann's appointment as Chancellor meant a new, more vigorous approach. Stresemann called off passive resistance and promised to resume the payment of reparations. He also sharply cut government expenditure and created a new currency - the Rentenmark. The result was an almost miraculous halt to the inflationary cycle, a stable currency and the political basis for international negotiations on Germany's economic plight. The result was the Dawes Plan (see Unit 3, Section 1.3) which tailored reparations to Germany's ability to pay. The acceptance of the Dawes Plan in 1924 can be seen to mark the beginning of a new era in international relations. The crisis was not averted by one man, however. A number of theories have been put forward to explain why the Republic did not collapse. First, it has been argued that popular resentment was channelled more against the French and the Allies than towards Weimar itself. It has also been suggested that, despite the effects of inflation, workers did not suffer to the same extent that they did when there was long-term mass unemployment. Similarly employers tended to show a less hostile attitude to Weimar in its early years than they did in later years. Plus some did very well out of the inflation. It seems, therefore, that, although there was distress and disillusionment in 1923, it had not yet reached critical proportions. Moreover, in 1923, there was no clear political alternative to Weimar. The extreme left had not really recovered from its divisions and suppression in the years 1918-21 and in its isolated position did not enjoy enough support to overthrow Weimar. The extreme right, too, was not yet strong enough - and it was divided and with no clear strategy. The failure of the Kapp Putsch was a clear warning about over-hasty action and was probably the main reason why the army did not take the initiative in 1923.

Adapted from Layton 1995.

Questions

1. a) Judging from Items 1-3 and your own knowledge, why was there a crisis in 1923?
   b) How did the government cope with the crisis?
2. Using Item 1, explain why Germany suffered from hyperinflation in 1923.
3. Why did the Weimar Republic manage to survive the crisis of 1923? Use Items 2 and 3 in your answer.

References

- **Berghahn (1987)** Berghahn, V.R., *Modern Germany: Society, Economy and Politics in the Twentieth Century* (2nd edn), Cambridge University Press, 1987.

- **Bessel (1997)** Bessel, R., 'Germany from war to dictatorship' in *Fulbrook (1997)*.

- **Brendon (2000)** Brendon, P., *The Dark Valley. A Panorama of the 1930s*, John Murray, 2000.

- **Burleigh (2000)** Burleigh, M., *The Third Reich: a New History*, Macmillan, 2000.

- **Carr (1991)** Carr, W., *A History of Germany: 1815-1990*, Edward Arnold, 1991.

- **Craig (1981)** Craig, G.A., *Germany 1866-1945*, Oxford University Press, 1981.

- **Feuchtwanger (1995)** Feuchtwanger, E.J., *From Weimar to Hitler: Germany 1918-33*, Macmillan, 1995.

- **Feuchtwanger (1997)** Feuchtwanger, E.J., 'Why did the Weimar government fail?', *Modern History Review*, Vol.9.1, September 1997.

- **Finer (1979)** Finer, S.E., *Five Constitutions*, Harvester Press, 1979.

- **Fulbrook (1997)** Fulbrook, M. (ed.), *German History since 1800*, Edward Arnold, 1997.

- **Haffner (1989)** Haffner, S., *Germany's Self-Destruction: the Reich from Bismarck to Hitler*, Simon & Schuster, 1989.

- **Hiden (1996)** Hiden, J., *The Weimar Republic*, Longman, 1996.

- **Kitchen (1996)** Kitchen, M., *Cambridge Illustrated History of Germany*, Cambridge University Press, 1996.

- **Kolb (1988)** Kolb, E., *The Weimar Republic*, Unwin Hyman, 1988.

- **Layton (1995)** Layton, G., *From Bismarck to Hitler: Germany 1890-1933*, Hodder & Stoughton, 1995.

- **Lee (1998)** Lee, S.J., *The Weimar Republic*, Routledge, 1998.

- **Lentin (1994)** Lentin, A., '75 years on: the Versailles Peace Settlement and it consequences', *History Review*, No.19, 1994.

- **Mann (1996)** Mann, G., *The History of Germany since 1789*, Pimlico, 1996.

- **Murphy (1997)** Murphy, D., 'The downfall of Weimar and the rise of Hitler', *Modern History Review*, Vol.9.2, November 1997.

- **Nicholls (1979)** Nicholls, A.J., *Weimar and the Rise of Hitler* (2nd edn), Macmillan, 1979.

- **Peukert (1991)** Peukert, D.J.K., *The Weimar Republic*, Penguin, 1991.

UNIT 3 — The Weimar Republic 1924-33

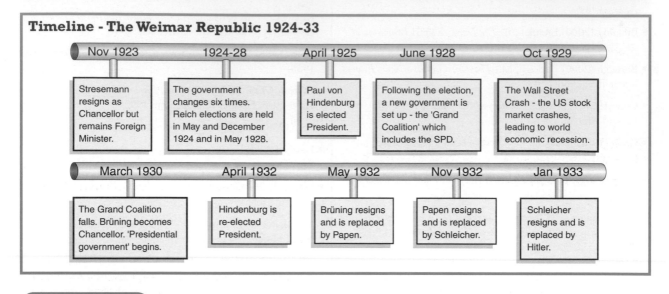

Timeline - The Weimar Republic 1924-33

Nov 1923 — Stresemann resigns as Chancellor but remains Foreign Minister.

1924-28 — The government changes six times. Reich elections are held in May and December 1924 and in May 1928.

April 1925 — Paul von Hindenburg is elected President.

June 1928 — Following the election, a new government is set up - the 'Grand Coalition' which includes the SPD.

Oct 1929 — The Wall Street Crash - the US stock market crashes, leading to world economic recession.

March 1930 — The Grand Coalition falls. Brüning becomes Chancellor. 'Presidential government' begins.

April 1932 — Hindenburg is re-elected President.

May 1932 — Brüning resigns and is replaced by Papen.

Nov 1932 — Papen resigns and is replaced by Schleicher.

Jan 1933 — Schleicher resigns and is replaced by Hitler.

Introduction

The years 1924-29 have traditionally been seen as years of economic and political stability in Germany. This, many historians used to argue, was the 'golden age' of the Weimar Republic, a period in which the Weimar system was able to function normally and the long-term future of the Republic looked rosy. If only the Wall Street Crash of October 1929 had not led to a world economic depression, then the Weimar Republic would have been able to win the hearts and minds of the German people permanently. In recent years, however, such arguments have come under attack. Although there seemed to be greater stability in Germany during the period 1924-29, historians now argue, in fact many of Germany's problems in the period 1929-33 can be traced to developments in the years before the Wall Street Crash. There was, for example, an unhealthy reliance on loans and investment from the USA in the period 1924-29, a reliance which ensured that when the world recession hit, it hit Germany harder than other countries. In addition, although people did not vote for extreme groups in large numbers during the period 1924-29, that does not mean that the majority of people were won over to the Weimar system. The inability of governments to stay in power for more than a few months at a time, for example, gave the impression that there was something wrong with the system. The constant turnover of Chancellors and ministers suggested a lack of direction, inefficiency and a lack of leadership. Many months before the Wall Street Crash, there were signs that the parties of the extreme - the NSDAP and KPD - were reviving. After the Crash the development of an economic and political crisis was rapid.

This unit begins by examining the arguments for and against the view that the period 1924-29 was the Weimar Republic's 'golden age'. It then investigates the economic and political developments which led to the collapse of the Weimar Republic in 1933. Why was the Republic not able to survive the crisis that developed after October 1929?

UNIT SUMMARY

Part 1 examines how stable the Weimar Republic was in the years 1924-29. Is it right to describe these as the 'golden years' of the Weimar Republic?

Part 2 explores why the Weimar Republic was unable to survive the crisis of 1929-33. How did German governments cope with the economic crisis? What political developments led to the downfall of the Republic?

1 The Weimar Republic 1924-29

Key issues

1. Did the Weimar Republic achieve economic stability in the period 1924-29?

2. Did the Weimar Republic achieve political stability in the period 1924-29?

3. What role was played by Gustav Stresemann in the period 1924-29?

1.1 Did the Weimar Republic achieve economic stability in the period 1924-29?

The 'golden twenties'?

The traditional view was that, in Germany, the years 1924-29 were years of political and economic stability, stability that was only shattered when the Wall Street Crash of October 1929 brought economic depression throughout the world and a new crisis in Germany. According to this view, these years were the 'golden twenties', a time when it seemed that the Weimar Republic had ridden the storms of the early years and had a genuine chance of long-term survival. If there had been no Wall Street Crash, the argument went, the Nazis would not have been able to gain power and Germany would have remained a democracy. In recent years, however, such a viewpoint has been questioned. Many historians now argue that the idea that there was political and economic stability in the period 1924-29 is illusory (ie it did not really exist). True, in relative terms, there appeared to be greater stability in 1924-29 than there had been in the period 1918-23 or there would be in the period 1929-33. But, in reality, it was in the period 1924-29 that the seeds for the crisis which developed in 1929-33 were sown. This section examines economic developments in the period 1924-29. The next section examines political developments in the same period.

The traditional view

The economic problems facing Germany in the period 1918-23 culminated in the hyperinflation of 1923 (see Unit 2, Section 2.2). By the end of the year, a new currency had been introduced and the crisis was over. The traditional view is that, economically, the next six years were years of economic growth and prosperity in Germany:

'The usual argument is that the economy of the Weimar Republic went through three main stages - two of which might be seen as "negative " and one as "positive". The first of the "negative periods" (1919-23) was one of inflation, becoming hyperinflation after 1921. The second "negative period" was the Depression from 1929 onwards... Between the two periods there were six years of economic recovery, often seen as the "golden age" of the Weimar Republic, in which the economy went through a boom.' (Lee 1998, p.62)

The evidence in support of this view can be summarised as follows.

Arguments in support of the view that there was economic recovery

There are eight main arguments in support of the view that there was an economic recovery in the period 1924-29.

1. Economic growth

First, the figures show that, looking at the German economy as a whole, there was economic growth in most of the years between 1924 and 1929:

'The economy grew rapidly in 1924, 1925 and 1927, but there was virtually no growth in 1926 and 1928.' (Ferguson 1997, p.262)

2. New production and management techniques

Second, certain sectors of the economy - iron and steel, coal, chemicals and electrical products - introduced new production and management techniques which improved their performance. Carr describes the introduction of these new techniques as 'rationalisation':

'This recovery was due to a burst of rationalisation; the introduction of up-to-date management techniques and more efficient production brought a tremendous increase in productivity; blast furnaces, for example, tripled their output.' (Carr 1991, p.288)

3. Industrial concentration

Third, some historians argue that the German economy benefited from structural changes. In particular, it was in the period 1924-29 that companies merged (so-called 'industrial concentration' - see Box 3.1 below) and set up cartels (a cartel is a group of companies in the same industry or related industries which join together in a single organisation):

'In 1925, the German government estimated that there were about 3,000 cartel arrangements in operation. In the coal and steel industries about 90% of products were affected by such arrangements.' (Feuchtwanger 1995, p.158)

Cartels allowed companies to cooperate rather than compete and they allowed industries to fix prices.

BOX 3.1 Industrial concentration

It was in the period 1924-29 that companies amalgamated into great industrial empires of enterprises engaged in similar or allied productive processes. The best known of these new cartels were I.G. Farben (set up in 1925) and Vereinigte Stahlwerke (set up in 1926). I.G. Farben quickly became the largest concern in Europe, with capital of 900 million marks and interests ranging from rayon (an artificial textile) to dynamite. It also had a virtual monopoly on synthetic dyes and nitrogen production and had extensive interests in the new industries developed by chemical science. Vereinigte Stahlwerke, with capital of 800 million marks, linked together coal, iron and steel interests and controlled between 40% and 50% of total iron and steel production and 36% of coal production. Similar trends were observable in the chemical industry, where Siemens had a virtual monopoly and in shipping and cement, where Wiking Konzern was dominant. Economic power was being concentrated into ever fewer hands - a development of some social and political significance.

Adapted from Carr 1991.

4. Foreign investment high

Fourth, the German economy attracted a great deal of foreign investment which suggests that investors considered it to be a place where there was potential for economic growth. Layton argues that Germany was attractive to foreign investors because interest rates were relatively high:

'By 1928 production levels generally exceeded those of 1913. This was the result of more efficient production techniques, particularly in coal-mining and steel manufacture, and also the large-scale investment of foreign capital into this sector. Foreign investors were attracted to Germany because of its relatively high interest rates.' (Layton 1995, p.111)

5. Wages rising

Fifth, wages rose in real terms throughout the period. If the level of wages in 1913 is 100, Feuchtwanger (1995) calculates that wages rose from 81 in 1925 to 100 in 1928 and 102 in 1929.

6. Welfare state set up

Sixth, it was during the period 1924-29 that the so-called 'Weimar welfare state' was set up. This, it is argued, was only possible because of the degree of economic stability that existed in these years:

'Living standards, which had plummeted during the final stages of hyperinflation, rose considerably. Housing construction, which had virtually come to a halt during the war and had not fully recovered during the period of inflation (when rent controls acted as a great disincentive to build new houses)

rose substantially (with considerable state financial involvement)...Municipal governments undertook impressive public works schemes, which gave their cities new airports, exhibition centres, housing estates and swimming pools. On 16 July 1927, the crowning achievement of the Weimar "welfare state", the "Act on Labour Exchanges and Unemployment Insurance" was enacted, to cover the major area left uncovered by Bismarck's social insurance programmes of the 1880s: by extending unemployment insurance to roughly 17.25 million employees, this scheme embraced more people than did such insurance in any other country.' (Bessel 1997, p.250)

7. Relations between workers and employers good

Seventh, there were fewer industrial disputes than in the period 1919-23. This was largely due to a new system of 'binding arbitration' introduced in October 1923. 'Arbitration' means the settling of a dispute by taking the matter to a third party and then negotiating a settlement. In the case of disputes being settled by 'binding arbitration', the decision made by the third party (the arbitrators) had to be accepted by workers and employers even if one or both parties did not agree with it:

'The Weimar constitution had envisaged a new industrial partnership. Under Article 165, "Workers and employees are called upon to cooperate, on an equal footing, with employers in the regulation of wages and of the conditions of labour"...After 1923, the government played a more active role in this by imposing compulsory [ie "binding"] arbitration over disputes between workers and management, thus reducing the number of strikes.' (Lee 1998, p.63)

Feuchtwanger (1995) claims that 4,000 cases out of a total of 77,000 decided by arbitration were binding.

8. Feel-good factor

And eighth, there is evidence from contemporaries that they believed that they were living through a period of economic prosperity:

'Certainly, for many contemporaries looking back from the standpoint of the end of the 1920s, it seemed as if Germany had made a remarkable recovery.' (Layton 1995, p.110)

Arguments in support of the view that the economic recovery was fragile

Many recent historians who accept that there was a period of economic stability between 1924 and 1929 are keen to make it clear that economic recovery in Germany was not as impressive as it might appear to be at first sight. The following comment is typical:

'The extent of the "boom" has been greatly exaggerated.' (Carr 1991, p.289)

The following arguments have been made in support of this view.

1. Share of world trade down

First, Peukert points out that Germany's share of world trade in 1929 was lower than it had been at the time of the outbreak of the First World War. This suggests that, even by 1929, Germany had not recovered its pre-war economic position:

'It is true that by 1929 Germany had been able to make up some of the economic ground that had been lost during the war and the immediate post-war period, but several crucial indicators remained below pre-war levels.' (Peukert 1991, p.197)

These 'crucial indicators' were as follows:
- between 1926 and 1929, Germany had 11.6% of world industrial production, compared to 14.3% in 1913
- between 1927 and 1929, Germany had 9.1% of world exports compared to 13.2% in 1913
- in 1928 (the best post-war year) the proportion of German exports to national income stood at 17%, compared to 20.2% in 1913.

Box 3.2 shows a comparison of the performance of the German economy with that of other countries.

BOX 3.2 German economic performance compared to that of the world

German industrial production: an international comparison (1913 = 100)

	1920	1925	1929	1932	1938
World	93	121	153	108	183
USA	122	148	181	94	143
Germany	59	95	117	70	149
UK	93	86	100	83	118
France	70	114	143	105	115
USSR	13	70	181	336	857
Italy	95	157	181	123	195
Japan	176	222	324	309	552
Sweden	97	113	151	141	232

This chart shows the performance of the German economy compared to that of other countries in the world between 1920 and 1932. It is based on the assumption that economic performance in 1913 was 100.

Adapted from Feuchtwanger 1995.

---

2. Economic growth variable

Second, economic growth in the period 1924-29 varied from year to year, it was not consistently high. Carr (1991) notes that the USA's economy grew by 70% between 1913 and 1929, while Germany's grew by just 4%. In addition, unemployment remained high throughout the period 1924-29:

'In actual fact, the rapidity of German recovery was deceptive. There was indeed economic growth, but it was far from even and in 1926 production actually declined. The balance of trade was consistently in the red [in other words, more goods were imported than exported]. Unemployment never fell below 1.3 million in this period and even before the shock waves of America's financial crisis began to be felt, it was averaging 1.9 million during 1929.' (Layton 1995, p.111)

3. Over-reliance on foreign investment

Third, reliance on foreign investment disguised the true economic picture and helps to explain why the crisis deepened so quickly after the Wall Street Crash. Nicholls argues that, following the war and the period of inflation, there was a lack of capital (money for investment) in Germany and, as a result, the government relied on foreign loans to pay reparations while industrialists relied on foreign loans to provide investment in new equipment:

'The reparations payments made by Germany were really being financed by foreign loans. In addition, the capital needs of German industry could not find satisfaction in domestic profits or savings...German industrialists were eager to re-equip their factories with new plant, but many of the funds for such enterprises had to be borrowed from abroad. The result was an unhealthy dependence on foreign capital for economic prosperity.' (Nicholls, 1979, p.95)

Carr (1991) points out that expenditure on the Weimar welfare state was very high. The building of schools, hospitals, roads and new housing, he points out, was financed by government subsidies which, in turn, came from foreign loans. The result was that the German economy became overstretched:

'As Werner Abelshauser [a historian writing in 1987] has pointed out, "the Weimar Republic was an overstrained welfare state", and the achievements of the years of "relative stability" became damaging liabilities once the Depression arrived.' (Bessel 1997, p.250)

4. Not all sectors recovering

Fourth, not all sectors of the economy recovered during the period 1924-29. In particular, agriculture failed to recover. In some parts of Germany, agriculture was in recession long before 1929. According to Hiden (1996) the problems faced by many small farmers were due to:
- the lack of land reform (20% of land belonged to 0.7% of farmers and many farms were too small to be profitable)
- the losses of 1923 (many farmers were forced to borrow at high interest rates as a result)

● competition from abroad (which reduced profits).

Feuchtwanger argues that the main problem was that too much was being produced worldwide. Over-production led to a fall in prices which, in turn, meant lower incomes for farmers:

'A worldwide agricultural depression started in the middle 1920s and played a part in aggravating the Great Depression. The war had produced an over-expansion of agricultural capacity, which now caused prices to tumble. The world price of wheat doubled between 1913 and 1920 and then fell back to a third of the 1913 level by 1931. German agriculture was particularly vulnerable, for it produced less of the more marketable refined products, such as dairy products. Experts have calculated that the return on capital [ie profit] was negative in most years after 1925.'
(Feuchtwanger 1995, pp.159-60)

5. Growth of cartels unhealthy

Fifth, some historians argue that the growth of cartels was unhealthy because it stifled competition, making German industry less able to deal with a downturn in the economy:

'The development of cartels cannot be seen automatically as an advantage. These carved up the market between them and arranged prices which were often [harmful] to the consumer. Competition might have driven down prices and [as a result] enlarged the domestic market.'
(Lee 1998, p.64)

According to this argument, greater competition would have benefited both companies and the German people because it would have forced companies to sell more goods to more people at lower prices.

6. Relations between workers and employers poor

Sixth, there is an argument that, although, on the surface, relations between workers and employers seemed to improve in the period 1924-29, in reality they did not:

'Although there were fewer strikes between 1924 and 1929 than in the first years of the Weimar Republic, this does not necessarily mean that there was greater industrial harmony. Expectations among wage-earners were bound to increase, especially [after] the bout of inflation up until 1923...Increased wages did little more than keep pace with the rising cost of living. There was, therefore, plenty of cause for industrial dispute. The number of days lost through strikes was kept down only through government intervention.'
(Lee 1998, pp.64-65)

By the end of this period, Lee argues, such intervention was bitterly resented. In other words, far from being a time when old problems were solved, the period 1924-29 was a time when new problems were brewing. Feuchtwanger argues that matters came to a head when 230,000 workers were locked out of their factories in November 1928 because employers refused to accept arbitration which was supposed to be binding (the workers did not receive wages for weeks during this dispute):

'Employers, initially [unsure] in their attitude to binding arbitration, became gradually more hostile...The great lock-out in the Ruhr iron industry in November 1928, in defiance of a binding award, is, however, clear evidence how determined employers in heavy industry had become to break this aspect of the Weimar [system], if necessary by defying the state itself.'
(Feuchtwanger 1995, p.154)

7. No feel-good factor

And seventh, although some contemporaries believed that they were living through a period of economic prosperity, others did not:

'An argument was insistently advanced by employers in these middle years of the Weimar Republic, particularly by the coal and steel barons of the Ruhr, that the German economy was overstretched and that too much of the national cake was taken up by wages and by social payments and not enough by investment.'
(Feuchtwanger 1995, p.152)

MAIN POINTS - Section 1.1

● According to the traditional view, the years 1924-29 were the 'golden twenties', a time when the Weimar Republic had a genuine chance of long-term survival. If there had been no Wall Street Crash, so the argument goes, the Nazis would not have been able to gain power.

● Many historians now argue that the idea that there was political and economic stability in the period 1924-29 is illusory. In reality, it was in the period 1924-29 that the seeds for the crisis which developed in 1929-33 were sown.

● There are eight main arguments in support of the view that the German economy recovered in the period 1924-29. There was (1) economic growth (2) new production and management techniques (3) industrial concentration (4) high foreign investment (5) rising wages (6) a new welfare state (7) good relations between workers and employers and (8) a feel-good factor.

● There are seven main arguments in support of the view that economic recovery was fragile - (1) share of world trade was down (2) economic growth was variable (3) reliance on foreign loans distorted the true picture (4) not all sectors were recovering (5) the growth of cartels was unhealthy (6) relations between workers and employers were deteriorating and (7) there was no feel-good factor.

Activity 3.1 The German economy, 1924-29

ITEM 1 A historian's view

Germany's economic achievements after 1924 were considerable. Although after the war, the income of the nation had fallen to about half the pre-war level, by 1929 it was back to where it had been or even higher. All the worn-out, antiquated equipment was replaced, together with all the things handed over after the war. Germany had the most modern merchant fleet, the fastest railways and an adequate system of roads. The workers worked well. The inventors, engineers and technicians were good. Industrial planning was magnificent and effective. What was accomplished after 1924 was a tremendous rationalisation, an increase in productivity through mechanisation which went hand-in-hand with further concentration of economic power. The I.G. Farbenindustrie controlled almost the whole of the country's chemical and drugs industry and the Vereinigte Stahlwerke about two-fifths of its iron and steel production. Similar mammoth formations existed for the electrical industry, the production of cement, rubber and so on. The rest was done as in days of old by a variety of cartels - to protect prices, to standardise, to plan production. Concentrated in this manner, industry had even more power over the state than it had before the war. It negotiated as an equal and, at the same time, was part of the power of the state, particularly when the propertied middle classes provided the government, as was almost always the case between 1924 and 1928. One cannot accuse the German industrialists of not taking their job seriously. In a certain sense they regarded themselves as responsible for the nation and for their own workers. But German industry worked for the state and for the export market, not for the rising standard of living of the masses. The director of the coal mine did not like to see his foreman own a car. It was not right for a member of the upper-working class. It was also not right for workers to have a decent home or a motorbike or a fridge. As long as workers could work and live and as long as they were insured against accident, sickness and old age, the employers considered they had done their duty.

Adapted from Mann 1996 (first published in 1968).

ITEM 2 Industrial production 1913-29

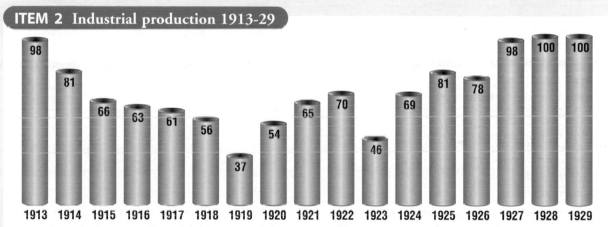

This bar chart shows industrial production in Germany between 1913 and 1929. It is based on the assumption that economic performance in 1928 was 100.

Adapted from Kirk 1995.

ITEM 3 Average annual growth in different sectors

	1913-25	1925-29		1913-25	1925-29
Metal Production	−2.9	5.1	Rubber	7.1	3.4
Pig Iron	−2.9	5.3	Sulphuric Acid	−2.8	8.7
Steel	−3.0	7.3	Soda	−0.1	10.4
Metal Working	2.3	6.7	Nitrates	35.2	11.0
Stone and Earth	0.6	5.9	Artificial Fabrics	15.5	24.2
extractive industries			**Textiles**	−1.7	−0.4
Hard Coal	−2.9	5.3	**Clothing**	−0.1	−2.1
Brown Coal	4.0	9.6	**Leather**	−1.8	−2.4
Chemical	2.4	8.8	**Gas, Water and**	5.8	7.7
Oil Refining	1.9	17.0	**Electricity**		

This table shows the average annual growth in different sectors of the German economy in the period 1913-29.

Adapted from Feuchtwanger 1995.

ITEM 4 Strikes and lock-outs 1913-29

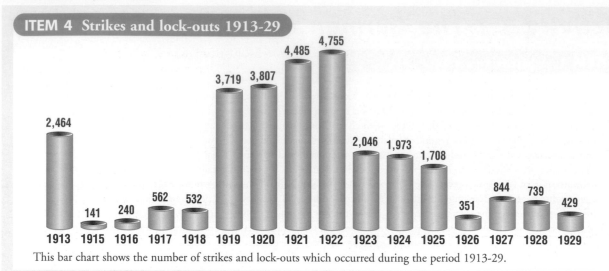

This bar chart shows the number of strikes and lock-outs which occurred during the period 1913-29.

Adapted from Kirk 1995.

ITEM 5 Unemployment 1921-29

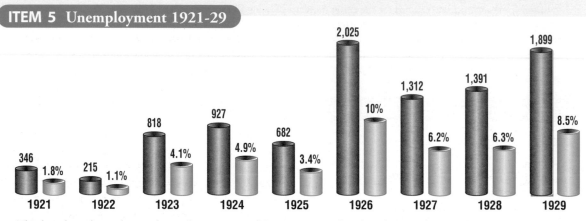

This bar chart shows the number and percentage of Germans unemployed in the period 1921-29.

Adapted from Berghahn 1987.

Questions

1. 'The Weimar Republic experienced six years of economic stability in the period 1924-29'. Using Items 1-5 and your own knowledge, do you agree with this statement? Explain your answer.
2. a) Does the author of Item 1 support or oppose the traditional view of the Weimar Republic in the period 1924-29? Explain how you know.

   b) What arguments might be made against the views expressed in Item 1?
3. a) What do Items 2-5 tell us about the German economy in the period 1924-29?

   b) What other factors need to be taken into account when assessing how stable the economy was in this period?

1.2 Did the Weimar Republic achieve political stability in the period 1924-29?

Evidence of greater political stability

Historians suggest that there are four main reasons for concluding that there was greater political stability in the period 1924-29 than in previous years and that, had the Great Depression not hit Germany in 1929-20, the period 1924-29 would have provided the basis for long-term stability.

1. Election results

First, the results of elections in 1924 and 1928 indicated that the Weimar Republic was gaining the acceptance and support of more and more of the German population (the results of these elections are shown in Box 3.3). Box 3.3 shows that the percentage of votes won by anti-Republican parties - the NSDAP (Nazis) on the right and the KPD (Communists) on the left - was tiny. Even if the percentage won by the DNVP is added to that of the NSDAP and KPD on the grounds that it too was opposed to the Republic (the party's position changed in the late 1920s and it joined a

BOX 3.3 The elections of 1924 and 1928

Party	4 May 1924			7 December 1924			20 May 1928		
	Total votes	%	No. MPs	Total votes	%	No. MPs	Total votes	%	No. MPs
SPD Majority Socialists	6,008,900	20.5	100	7,881,000	26.0	131	9,153,000	29.8	153
KPD Communists	3,693,300	12.6	62	2,709,100	9.0	45	3,264,800	10.6	54
Centre Party	3,914,400	13.4	65	4,118,900	13.6	69	3,712,200	12.1	62
BVP Bavarian People's Party	946,700	3.2	16	1,134,000	3.7	19	945,600	3.0	16
DDP Democrats	1,655,100	5.7	28	1,919,800	6.3	32	1,505,700	4.9	25
DVP People's Party	2,964,400	9.2	45	3,049,100	10.1	51	2,679,700	8.7	45
Wirtschaftspartei Economy Party	692,600	2.4	10	1,005,400	3.3	17	1,397,100	4.5	23
Nationalists DNVP	5,696,500	19.5	95	6,205,800	20.5	103	4,381,600	14.2	73
NSDAP Nazis	1,918,300	6.5	32	907,300	3.0	14	810,100	2.6	12
Other Parties	2,059,700	6.9	19	1,389,700	4.4	12	2,903,500	9.2	28

This table shows the election results in 1924 and 1928. The Wirtschaftspartei (Economy Party) was set up in 1920 by lower-middle-class groups and was close to the BVP in its outlook.
Adapted from Bullock 1991.

government coalition in 1927), more than 61% of people voted for parties which fully supported the Republic in May 1924. This percentage rose to 67.5% in December 1924 and to 72.6% in May 1928, suggesting that more and more people came to support the Republic. Nicholls argues that popular support for the Republic was also suggested by the setting up of the 'Reichsbanner', a Republican defence force, in 1924:

'The Reichsbanner...quickly mushroomed to success. Social Democratic Party locals formed the basis for its growth, but non-socialists were also encouraged to join. Within a year, the Reichsbanner could claim over a million members and had become the most successful paramilitary formation in Germany. Its demonstrations and propaganda reached the remotest parts of the country, teaching the population to celebrate the foundation of their new Republic, honour its flag and constitution.' (Nicholls 1979, pp.91-92)

2. Political violence down

Second, the political violence which had characterised the period 1919-23 subsided and, relatively speaking, the period 1924-29 was peaceful. Although there were some street battles between political rivals, no major political figures were assassinated and there were no attempted coups:

'From 1924, there were no further attempts to overthrow the Republic to compare with the Spartacist uprising (1919), the Kapp Putsch (1919) and the Munich Putsch (1923).' (Lee 1998, p.66)

This suggests that the Weimar Republic had entered a new era of peace.

3. Constitution functioned normally

Third, although there was a very high turnover of governments, laws were passed in the Reichstag following the procedures laid down in the constitution. In other words, this was a period in which the constitution functioned as it was supposed to function.

4. The President strengthened the Republic

And fourth, when Friedrich Ebert died in 1925, presidential elections were held for the first time. Since none of the candidates won more than 50% in the first round, a second round was held, with Field Marshal Paul von Hindenburg entering the race for the first time (as he was allowed to do so under the constitution). Hindenburg won most votes in the second ballot and was duly elected President. Some historians argue that, although Hindenburg did not support the Republic himself, he strengthened it in the period 1924-29. He took great care to act constitutionally and may have improved the standing of the Republic in the eyes of some of those who, up to then, had been suspicious of or opposed to it:

'Hindenburg proved to be absolutely loyal to his constitutional responsibilities and he carried out his presidential duties with absolute correctness. Those nationalists who had hoped that his election might [bring the return of the monarchy or some kind of dictatorship] were to be greatly disappointed. Indeed, it has been argued that, with Hindenburg holding the presidential seals of office, Germany had found its true Ersatzkaiser [Kaiser substitute] and thereby the Republic at last attained respectability.' (Layton 1995, p.117)

Arguments against the view that there was political stability

Although there were some signs that the Weimar Republic was stabilising in the period 1924-29, most historians writing today accept the view of Detlev Peukert who argues that the stability was illusory. This view is outlined in Box 3.4 below. Historians who follow Peukert's line have identified six main reasons for arguing that the seeds of future problems were sown in the period 1924-29.

1. Electoral realignment

Although the election results in 1924 and 1928 can be interpreted as evidence that support for the Weimar Republic was growing, some historians argue that there were trends in these elections that help to explain why a crisis developed after the election in 1928. In particular, as suggested in Box 3.4, Peukert argues that the fall in support for the 'liberal centre' (ie the DDP and DVP) was of great significance. In the elections of 1919 and 1920,

Detlev Peukert entitles his chapter on the period 1924-29 'The illusion of domestic stability'. He suggests that, in describing the period 1924-29 as one of relative stability it is important to emphasise that these years were stable only by contrast with the periods of crisis which came before and after. The period 1924-29, he argues, was marked by a number of smaller crises that revealed the deeper structural tensions in German society. The structural problems created by the Treaty of Versailles and the establishment of the Republic in 1918-19 had not been solved. Nor had the problems arising in the years of inflation. Tensions and frustrations were carried over into the period of so-called 'stabilisation'. As a result, Peukert argues, the problems which arose in the period 1930-33 can be said to have been brewing in the period 1924-29. The Republic had already been heading for the crossroads before the immediate crisis of 1929-30 occurred. Peukert claims that the domestic political picture in the years 1924-29 was extremely varied. There were efforts to create stability and efforts to undermine it. There were attempts to strengthen the legitimacy - the credibility - of the Republic and attempts to destroy it. For Peukert, however, the electoral decline of the liberals was the decisive event of Weimar politics because it undermined the pro-Republican centre from within.

Adapted from Peukert 1991.

these parties had won a combined total of more than 6 million votes (6.99 million in 1919 and 6.25 million in 1920). In the three elections held in 1924 and 1928, this combined total fell (4.62 million in May 1924, 4.97 million in December 1924 and 4.18 million in 1928). Despite the small gain in December 1924, there was a definite trend downwards and this trend continued in the period 1929-33. Peukert argues that:

'The two liberal parties, the DDP and DVP, turned out to be the real "problem children" of the system, steadily losing votes in succeeding elections, then trying to hold their own as small splinter parties and finally succumbing to the advance of the NSDAP. It was during the "stabilisation" period, in fact, and not later that this crucial element in the parliamentary pattern...began to collapse.' (Peukert 1991, p.210)

According to Geary (2000), the Nazis won considerable support in the period 1929-33 from Germans whose bonds of loyalty to a particular political party had been broken (see Unit 4, Sections 2.2 and 3.3). In other words, the party which eventually gained from the decline in support of the 'liberal centre' in the period 1924-29 was the Nazi Party.

2. Coalitions and the turnover of government

It was noted in Unit 2, Section 1.2 that the Weimar electoral system ensured that coalition government - rather than government by a single party - would be the norm since it was highly unlikely that any single party would win an outright majority of the vote. It was also noted that this did not in itself mean that it was inevitable that there would be political instability. Nevertheless, in the period 1924-28, there was an extremely high turnover of governments as coalition after coalition collapsed. Box 3.5 outlines the make-up of the six governments that served between November 1923 and June 1928.

Appointment of Chancellor	Chancellor	Coalition parties	Per cent of Reichstag MPs in coalition parties
30.11.1923	Wilhelm Marx (Z)	DVP, Z, DDP	36.6
03.06.1924	Wilhelm Marx (Z)	DVP, Z, DDP	29.2
15.01.1925	Hans Luther	Z, DDP, DVP, BVP, DNVP	55.6
20.01.1926	Hans Luther	Z, DDP, DVP, BVP	34.7
16.05.1926	Wilhelm Marx (Z)	Z, DDP, DVP, BVP	34.7
29.01.1927	Wilhelm Marx (Z)	Z, DVP, BVP, DNVP	49.1
28.06.1928	Hermann Müller (SPD)	SPD, Z, DVP, BVP, DDP	61.5

This table shows the make-up of the six governments that served between November 1923 and June 1928. Z stands for Centre Party ('Zentrum' in German).

Adapted from Feuchtwanger 1995.

Throughout this period, the SPD remained the largest party in the Reichstag, but it did not serve in government. This made it difficult for the government to gain a majority in the Reichstag. Layton points out that only certain combinations of parties were possible:

'The possible combinations within a coalition were actually very limited. There was never any possibility of a coalition including both the SPD and the DNVP, and the KPD remained completely isolated, so the only possible combinations were: a right-centre coalition of Centre, DVP and DNVP, which tended to agree on domestic issues, but disagree on foreign affairs; a broad coalition of SPD, DDP, DVP and Centre which could agree on foreign policy but had very different domestic agenda; and, finally, a minority government of the political centre, including the DDP, DVP and Centre, but seeking support from the left and right as required. In effect, it was impossible to create a coalition with a parliamentary majority which could also consistently agree on both domestic and foreign policy.' (Layton 1995, p.115)

According to Craig (1987), the only two coalitions with some chance of lasting for a reasonable length of time were the 'Grand Coalition' (a coalition of the SPD, Centre, DDP and DVP) or the 'Bourgeois Coalition' (a coalition of the Centre, DDP, DVP, BVP and DNVP). But, policy differences between the SPD and DVP, and a growing unwillingness to work together, made it increasingly difficult for a Grand Coalition to be formed, whilst the DNVP was reluctant to serve in a government in a system which it disliked (though it did so in 1925-26 and 1927-28).

Consequences of high government turnover

Since it was impossible to form a government with a majority which could agree on both domestic and foreign policy, the turnover of governments was high. This had important and destabilising consequences:

'More and more, parliamentary politics came to resemble an endless Cabinet crisis, with more time and energy expended on the task of filling ministerial chairs than in governing the country. This bored the mass of the voters...But it was a source of deep concern to people who realised that, in certain circumstances, boredom might be transformed by the totalitarian movements into a weapon against the Republic.' (Craig 1987, p.510)

The period 1924-28, in other words, did much to create the conditions in which a sense of disillusion with the political system could lead to support of parties actively opposed to the political system.

3. The behaviour of political parties

It was not just the high turnover of governments that sowed the seeds for the growth of extremism after 1929, it was also the stance taken by the political parties which served in these governments. By 1929, attitudes within the parties had changed, making it more difficult to form a coalition that enjoyed the support of a majority in the Reichstag. Each of the parties involved in government at some time during the period 1924-29 has come in for criticism from historians.

(i) The SPD

Many historians are critical of the stance taken by the SPD in the period 1924-28 (a period in which the party remained out of government, until the Grand Coalition of 1923 was revived in June 1928). Most critics agree that the SPD was burdened by its past and unsure about what attitude to adopt towards the Republic:

'The Socialists, despite their numerical strength, were ill at ease in the Republic. Their spokesmen were still mouthing the slogans of revolutionary Marxism, yet in practice Socialists were reformists, defenders of the Republic and staunch anti-Communists.' (Carr 1991, p.292)

Splits between left and right

The party remained divided between those on the left, who were suspicious of cooperation with the 'bourgeois' parties (ie the DDP, DVP and Centre), and those on the right, who argued that cooperation with those parties was desirable because it would prevent the Republic falling into the hands of extremists who were opposed to the Weimar system. Lee argues that, in the period 1924-29, the party was moving leftwards:

'The SPD were moving further to the left, emphasising their trade union connections and their underlying commitment to expanding the scope of welfare policies. This was enough to keep them out of government between 1924 and 1928.' (Lee 1998, p.67)

Failure to join government

Hiden admits that the SPD faced pressure from the trade unions and from the KPD which competed strongly to win the working-class vote. But, he argues that the SPD's failure to join the government in the period 1924-28 was a serious mistake:

'It can be argued that a better, more effective, if less popular, route to protect the interests for which the SPD stood, and to counter the attractions of the KPD, would have been to remain in government. Within this, the German Socialists should have been able to continue pressing for more attractive and constructive solutions to a range of issues facing Germany in the second half of the 1920s. In opposition, the SPD nonetheless continued to support the political values of the Republic and provided backing for the government of the day as far as it could in a responsible fashion. Many regretted that this was still far from the most satisfactory way to exploit the impressive mass base of the SPD.' (Hiden 1996, p.18)

Ineffective leadership

Craig argues that the party did not make best use of this power because its leadership was ineffective. This failure of leadership, he claims, had serious consequences in the long term:

'The party leadership prided itself on being composed of hard-headed realists. To the country at large they seemed...so uniformly colourless as to be practically indistinguishable from each other and whose realism consisted of carefully avoiding risks and discouraging initiative and imagination ...Instead of making an effort to transform the party into one that could appeal to all classes and rally them to the defence of the Republic, its leaders acted as if they owed responsibility only to the working class. In practice this meant taking their lead from the trade unions and doing nothing that might jeopardise their support, This was to do irreparable harm to the party and the Republic in 1930.' (Craig 1987, pp.501-02)

(ii) The Centre Party

Members of the Centre Party sat in all the Cabinets formed between 1924 and 1929. During this period, however, the Centre Party was also split between its left and right wing - see Box 3.6

BOX 3.6 **The Centre Party in the period 1924-29**

The Centre Party's attempts to build support across different social classes and to extend its appeal beyond its Catholic base not only had limited success (support for the Centre Party remained steady throughout the period 1920-33, the party winning roughly 4 million votes in every election), they also resulted in internal divisions over social and economic policy. In the early years, such differences were put to one side under the clear (but leftish) leadership of Erzberger and Wirth. In the period 1924-29, however, the party moved decisively to the right. The result was that internal splits came increasingly to the surface. In a leadership contest held in 1928, the candidate from the trade union wing was defeated by Ludwig Kaas, the first priest to lead the party. The following year, Heinrich Brüning became chair of the party's parliamentary group. Both Kaas and Brüning were from the right of the party. Both found it more comfortable to build coalitions with conservative or even authoritarian (anti-democratic) political partners than with liberals and social democrats. Their rise to power was a worrying sign for the future of the Centre Party and for Germany itself.
Adapted from Layton 1995.

(iii) The liberal parties

It was noted above that, in terms of electoral support, the period 1924-29 was a time of decline for the DDP and DVP. It was also a time of realignment. Craig (1987) claims that the DDP's poor election performance in 1924, when it won just 25 seats, split the party. The party shifted to the right, becoming 'increasingly critical of parliamentary practice' (p.503). This lurch to the right forced a group on the left of the party to resign. Similarly, the DVP, under the leadership of Gustav Stresemann, came under strain in this period:

'The DVP too was divided between its business and non-commercial supporters and, despite Stresemann's efforts, this remained a continuous source of conflict. It is not really surprising, therefore, that moves to bring about some kind of united liberal party came to nothing and, as a result, the case for German liberalism proved incredibly difficult to present to the electorate with any degree of conviction.' (Layton 1995, p.116)

(iv) The DNVP

In the early years of the Republic, the DNVP

(German Nationalist Party) was deeply hostile to the new political system and it refused to participate in government (the party won a significant number of votes and seats - see Box 3.3 above). In the period 1924-28, however, the party's position changed and twice - in 1925 and 1927 it joined a coalition in government. Poor performance in the election of 1928, however, led to a change of leadership with Alfred Hugenberg, taking control. Under Hugenberg's leadership the party then shifted back to its old position:

'It was little short of tragic that precisely when the more moderate German nationalists were starting to play a constructive political role, the forces of reaction should have triumphed in the party. Their instrument was Alfred Hugenberg, an ambitious and ruthless businessman who became Chairman in 1928...He was deeply hostile to the Republic and all it stood for...This was the end of constructive opposition. Under Hugenberg, moderates were squeezed out of the party and it lapsed once more into blind opposition to the Republic.' (Carr 1991, p.294)

Conclusion

It is clear from this survey of the stance of the parties which made up the coalition governments in the period 1924-29 that there was a realignment in the period 1924-28. The rightward shift in the Centre Party, DDP, DVP and DNVP had important long-term consequences. There was an increasing tendency to be critical of parliamentary democracy and a greater willingness to bypass normal parliamentary procedures (see Section 2.2 below). This played into the hands of the Nazis. So did the SPD's failure to provide strong leadership and stable government. Indeed, it could be argued that the seeds of the Nazis' future success were sown by the developments within political parties which took place in the period 1924-29.

4. Damaging disputes

Some historians argue that the reputation of the Weimar Republic suffered in the period 1924-29 because disputes blew up into serious political rows that, on two occasions, resulted in governments falling - see Box 3.7. Such rows, it is argued, damaged the credibility of the Republic because an unwillingness to compromise too often led a government to fall.

5. Lack of reform of the judiciary and civil service

Several historians argue that the stability of the Weimar Republic was undermined by the failure to replace judges and senior civil servants who had served under the Kaiser with new recruits. Nicholls, for example, argues that the failure to take steps to reform the judiciary, the civil service and the universities (which were a hothouse of anti-Republicanism) ensured that the Weimar Republic

BOX 3.7 Damaging disputes

(i) The flag incident

When the Weimar constitution came into force, the Republic adopted a new flag. The new flag was black, red and gold whilst the old imperial flag had been black, white and red. In early 1926, the government ordered all German diplomatic and consular offices abroad to fly both the Republican flag and the flag of the merchant marine (which was predominantly black, white and red). The government did this to please the new President, Hindenburg (who was well known to be a supporter of the old monarchy). The government's decision caused outrage amongst supporters of the Republic. Following a debate in the Reichstag in May 1926, a motion of no confidence was passed, forcing the Chancellor, Luther, to resign.

(ii) Church and schools

In Article 146, the Weimar constitution took responsibility for education away from the Länder and handed it over to central government. Under Article 174, however, education was to remain under Land control until the Reichstag passed a law putting Article 146 into effect. Such a law had not been passed by the autumn of 1927 and when a law was proposed, it caused so much controversy that the government was eventually forced to resign. The controversy centred on whether primary schools should be 'denominational' - ie on whether or not they should teach religion according to the line set down by a particular church. Article 146 of the constitution laid down that non-denominational schools should be the norm, but that denominational schools should be allowed in areas where the majority of parents wanted them. That would have meant making significant changes since the vast majority of schools in some parts of Germany were denominational. When the government proposed a law which would have put the demands laid down by Article 146 into practice, there was a political row that resulted in the government's resignation. For the majority in all parties this was another ideological issue on which the purity of principle must not be sacrificed. It was this long-standing habit of preferring ideological consistency to compromise which was at the root of the governmental instability of Weimar.

Adapted from Feuchtwanger 1995.

esprit de corps [ie a feeling of support and loyalty] in these years of stability. Collaboration with the existing authorities was necessary because there was no alternative, but enthusiasm was lacking. In Germany's universities many of the students and their professors regarded the Weimar system with contempt. As the 1920s wore on, so projects for the reform of the state to give it a more authoritarian form of government began to be heard...By 1928, the Republic's four years of peace had not produced the impression of stability.' (Nicholls 1979, pp.96-97)

Peukert (1991) points out that, in the 1920s, judges made decisions which were blatantly political. When they sentenced right-wingers accused of political crimes, they made it very clear crimes committed for 'patriotic' reasons should receive mild punishment. Left-wingers, by way of contrast, were given heavy sentences. So, for example, Hitler received a sentence of just five years in prison in 1924 - a light sentence for organising and leading a coup against the state (see Unit 4, Section 2.1), whereas a Communist was sentenced to four weeks in prison just for calling the Weimar Republic a 'robber's republic'.

It was not just in criminal cases that judgements were biased. Judges also have to interpret legislation when test trials are brought before court. Peukert argues that judges made judgements which were, in effect, attacks on the Republic:

'The inevitable result was that the legitimacy [ie credibility] of the Weimar legal system, in the eyes of the population, was severely undermined.' (Peukert 1991, p.224)

A similar argument is made about senior civil servants. They did not actively campaign against the Republic. But, they made it very clear that they disapproved of the Weimar system:

'In their day-to-day dealings and decisions, civil servants let it be known that...the solutions they favoured sprang from social and political ideals other than those for which the Republic stood.' (Peukert 1991, p.225)

6. Constant attacks from the extremes

Although few people joined or voted for the extremist parties in the period 1924-29, these parties produced an enormous amount of anti-Republican propaganda and they were constantly campaigning. This, Hiden argues, did make an impact:

'The painful process towards parliamentary maturity after 1918 must also be judged in the light of extremist efforts on the left and right to discredit the Republican institutions.' (Hiden 1996, p.21)

Lee (1998) argues that, despite the decline in the anti-Republican right's electoral support, the movement became stronger and better positioned in

failed to produce stability in the period 1924-28:

'Nor can it be claimed that other German institutions, such as the civil service and judiciary, developed anything approaching a Republican

the period 1924-29. He argues that this was due to four main developments:

- the NSDAP was reorganised and the party repositioned itself, posing as a mainstream and respectable party which would take the legal path to power (see Unit 4, Section 2.1)
- the DNVP moved to the right after Hugenberg became leader (see above)

- as a result of these two developments, cooperation between the DNVP and the NSDAP became a serious possibility for the first time
- the election of Hindenburg, also a development during the period 1924-29, strengthened the position of the right as he was opposed to the democratic process.

MAIN POINTS - Section 1.2

- Historians suggest that there are four main reasons for concluding that there was greater political stability in the period 1924-29 than in previous years- (1) election results show that the Weimar Republic was gaining support from more people (2) political violence was low (3) the constitution was functioning normally and (4) the election of Hindenburg strengthened the Republic.

- Historians have identified six main reasons for arguing that the seeds of future problems were sown in the period 1924-29. There was (1) electoral realignment (2) a high turnover of governments (3) a problem with the way in which political parties behaved (4) damage done when governments fell over trivial matters (5) no reform of the judiciary or civil service and (6) constant criticism from the extremes.

- There was a realignment of the parties in the period 1924-28. The rightward shift in the Centre Party, DDP, DVP and DNVP had important long-term consequences. So did the SPD's failure to provide strong leadership and stable government.

- The flag incident and controversy over denominational schools discredited the Republic because they led to governments falling over trivial issues.

Activity 3.2 The political system 1924-29

ITEM 1 The Reich elections of 1924-28

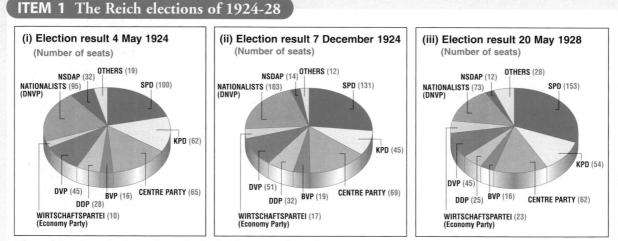

(i) Election result 4 May 1924
(Number of seats)

NSDAP (32) OTHERS (19)
NATIONALISTS (95) (DNVP) SPD (100)
KPD (62)
CENTRE PARTY (65)
DVP (45) BVP (16)
DDP (28)
WIRTSCHAFTSPARTEI (10) (Economy Party)

(ii) Election result 7 December 1924
(Number of seats)

NSDAP (14) OTHERS (12)
NATIONALISTS (103) (DNVP) SPD (131)
KPD (45)
CENTRE PARTY (69)
DVP (51) BVP (19)
DDP (32)
WIRTSCHAFTSPARTEI (17) (Economy Party)

(iii) Election result 20 May 1928
(Number of seats)

NSDAP (12) OTHERS (28)
NATIONALISTS (73) (DNVP) SPD (153)
KPD (54)
CENTRE PARTY (62)
DVP (45) BVP (16)
DDP (25)
WIRTSCHAFTSPARTEI (23) (Economy Party)

These charts show the share of seats in the Reichstag won by each party.

Adapted from Bullock 1991.

ITEM 2 A historian's view (1)

When the Social Democrats emerged once more as the strongest party in the Reichstag in 1928, Hindenburg did not hesitate to offer the chancellorship to their Leader, Hermann Müller, who accepted. This was the normal process. The SPD 'recuperated' in opposition and when it had recuperated sufficiently, it occasionally rejoined the government - not to make great social and economic changes since that was uncalled for at a time when the defeat of the right suggested that, in general, people were satisfied. The parties bargained and bartered as usual and, as usual, the Social Democrats were the losers. During the election campaign the SPD had opposed the building of the small navy allowed under the peace treaty. They argued that the money would be better spent feeding hungry school children. Under pressure from the army, however, the government agreed to build an armoured cruiser. The Chancellor gave in to coalition partners. But his party did not. The result was the absurd sight of the Chancellor voting as MP against a Bill that he himself had introduced as Head of Government. The Bill was pushed through by the combined votes of the right. This incident showed that when the Social Democrats 'governed', they were, at the same time, in opposition, just as, in opposition, they often voted with the government. The result was disappointment and confusion among their supporters.

Adapted from Mann 1996.

ITEM 3 A historian's view (2)

When the Republic celebrated its tenth anniversary in 1929, there seemed reasonable grounds for optimism. Putsches were well in the past. Calls for the restoration of the monarchy had long been abandoned. Prussia felt safe enough in 1928 to lift a speaking ban on Hitler. The DNVP even voted in 1928 for the renewal of a 1922 law which banned the ex-Kaiser from returning to Germany. The formation of a Grand Coalition suggested there was common ground between parties. A closer look at political life quickly destroys such illusions. Superficial prosperity and an improving image abroad masked great political weakness. The existence of a multi-party system was not in itself a cause, nor was coalition government. The difficulty lay in the fundamental disagreements between the main parties. Since the anti-Marxist DNVP refused to work with the (supposedly) Marxist SPD and since the KPD was shunned by all, only four combinations were possible:

- SPD, Centre, DDP - which did not have majority support
- Centre, DNVP, DDP, DVP - which could agree on domestic, but not foreign policy
- SPD, Centre, DDP, DVP, BVP - which agreed on foreign policy but little else
- Centre, DDP, DVP - which also did not have majority support.

As a result, coalitions changed as the emphasis changed, robbing the Republic of stability and encouraging party intrigue in the Reichstag. All-powerful party committees kept an eye on the government and were always ready to sacrifice a Cabinet in return for party advantage. Interference led to some absurd situations. In 1928, for example, the Müller government agreed to build a cruiser, despite the SPD campaign against such a move. In the Reichstag, the party committee criticised SPD ministers for voting for the Bill but, because it wanted to keep the government afloat, instructed them to remain in Cabinet. To confuse matters, the committee then insisted that ministers vote for a motion (which was defeated) calling for a halt to work on the cruiser. Incidents of this kind, trivial in themselves did not improve the credibility of the political system.

Adapted from Carr 1991.

ITEM 4 A historian's view (3)

A Republic governed by Hindenburg, a highly respected member of the monarchy, a man who already in the First World War acted as Emperor in practice if not in name, was something quite different from Ebert and the socialists. It was because of this that the DNVP changed its mind and agreed to join the government. Now the Republic no longer depended on a centre-left coalition. A coalition of centre and right took over and stabilised the country in the years 1925-28. The turning point came in 1928. The 1928 Reich election was a defeat for the ruling centre-right coalition. The German Nationalists lost votes and the SPD scored their greatest victory since 1919. The result was the recreation of the Grand Coalition from the SPD all the way to the right-wing liberals. That was a very weak government because its two wings pulled in different directions. The second development was the election of Hindenburg. In 1925, when he took office, Hindenburg was 77 years old. It was clear that he would not be President for ever. What was to be done? There was no second Hindenburg in sight. The fate of that wonderful compromise worked out in the early Hindenburg years - the near-monarchist republic that the monarchist right was prepared to accept, rested on aged shoulders. The right grew restless. The DNVP had a new, more extreme leadership. Perhaps, they told themselves, Hindenburg's presidency should be seen not as the stabiliser of the Republic, but as the transition to a monarchy.

President Hindenburg

Adapted from Haffner 1989.

Questions

1. a) Using Items 1 and 3, explain why it was difficult to build stable government in Germany in the period 1924-29.
   b) How significant was the fact that there were six different governments between the elections of May 1924 and May 1928?

2. Judging from Items 2-4 and your own knowledge, to what extent did the Weimar Republic achieve political stability in the period 1924-29?

3. a) Judging from Items 2-4, what problems did governments face in the period 1924-29?
   b) Could any of these problems be avoided? Explain your answer.

1.3 What role was played by Gustav Stresemann in the period 1924-29?

Background: Gustav Stresemann 1878-1923

Gustav Stresemann was born in Berlin in 1878. His background is often described as 'modest':

'[Stresemann] was born in Berlin into a modest home. His father had a small business bottling beer and their house doubled as a bar.' (Wright 1989, p.35)

Stresemann studied Economics at Berlin University and then set up a manufacturer's association in Saxony which promoted the interests of small businesses. He was first elected to the Reichstag in 1907 and became its youngest member. He entered the Reichstag as a National Liberal. Wright argues that this was the 'natural' party for him to join:

'Stresemann was an ardent nationalist, a member of the populist Navy League and [a supporter] of colonial Empire. His choice of the National Liberals was therefore a natural one, but some aspects of it made him uncomfortable. Its right wing was under the influence of Ruhr coal-owners who wanted the party to be closely aligned with the Conservatives in domestic as well as foreign policy. Stresemann distrusted the Conservatives [ie the group that became the DNVP].' (Wright 1989, p.36)

The First World War and its aftermath

During the First World War, Stresemann supported those who wanted a 'Seigfriede' - a victory which would allow Germany to dominate Europe and achieve the status of a world power. He also campaigned for unrestricted submarine warfare. Such a stance was not supported by many in his party and, when the party split after the end of the war, Stresemann was not allowed to join the new DDP. As a result, he set up his own party - the DVP:

'In 1919 after the break-up of the National Liberals, he was deliberately excluded from the DDP and was left no real option but to form his own party, the DVP, which at first was hostile to the revolution and the Republic and desired a restoration of the monarchy.' (Layton 1995, p.121)

Stresemann and the Republic

Most historians agree that, although Stresemann was, at heart, a monarchist, he came round to supporting the Republic because he realised that the Republic was the best safeguard against a takeover by the extreme right or left. Although some historians (for example, Nicholls 1979) argue that Stresemann was motivated by a desire to exercise power, most agree that he shifted his position because he was a pragmatist (somebody who responded flexibly to circumstances) and because he had a deep belief in the rule of law. Beghahn's view is typical:

'It was not merely the lure of power-sharing that caused him to change course. With the economic situation steadily worsening and the resistance against Versailles and the Western Allies getting nowhere, the DVP leadership came to recognise that a mindless anti-Republican obstructionism would merely accelerate the plunge into total chaos.' (Berghahn 1987, p.88)

When exactly Stresemann changed his view about the Republic is unclear. Nicholls claims that he had not changed it at the time of the Kapp Putsch in 1920:

'Stresemann and his colleagues in the German People's Party [DVP] were quite favourably impressed with Kapp and seemed ready to negotiate with him.' (Nicholls 1979, p.52)

He argues that the turning point was the assassination of Walther Rathenau in June 1922 (see Unit 2, Section 2.2 for further details on the assassination):

'When Rathenau was murdered, Stresemann took the opportunity to align the DVP more firmly behind the Republican constitution than ever before.' (Nicholls 1979, p.61)

Box 3.8 below considers the implications of Stresemann's initial anti-Republicanism.

Stresemann as Chancellor

Members of the DVP served in the governments headed by Konstantin Fehrenbach (June 1920 to May 1921) and Wilhelm Cuno (November 1922 to August 1923), but Stresemann himself did not serve in government until he was appointed Chancellor in August 1923, following Cuno's resignation. Stresemann then served as Chancellor and Foreign Minister, in a Cabinet which included the Centre Party, DDP and SPD (the so-called 'Great' or 'Grand Coalition') from 13 August to 30 November. He came to power at the time when hyperinflation was at its height and he was still in office when Hitler attempted to overthrow the government on 8-9 November (the so-called Beer Hall Putsch - see Unit 4, Section 1.6). Three important developments took place during Stresemann's Chancellorship (see also Unit 2, Section 2.2):

- the decision was taken to end 'passive resistance'
- steps were taken to combat hyperinflation
- a state of emergency was declared and steps were taken to deal with uprisings organised by both the extreme left and the extreme right.

Most historians are complimentary about Stresemann's Chancellorship. The following passage is typical:

BOX 3.8 Stresemann and the Republic

It was only in the wake of the failed Kapp Putsch and the murders of Erzberger and Rathenau that Stresemann led his party into adopting a more accommodating stance towards the Republic. This transformation has certainly provided plenty of evidence for those critics who have suggested that his support for the Republic was only superficial. But, such a charge is unfair. His career during the war years has tended to overshadow his strong and long-standing opposition to the self-interest of the Conservatives (the group that, in November 1918, set up the DNVP) and his support for moves towards constitutional government in the years before 1914. As Wright (1989) has pointed out, his distrust of Conservatives dates back at least to 1909 when they refused both electoral reform in the state of Prussia and estate duties to help pay for increased spending on defence. The Conservative-Liberal bloc broke down in 1909 and the Chancellor was forced to resign. Stresemann never really forgave the Conservatives for this. He argued later that their selfishness deprived the Chancellor of support at a time when a stable coalition in the Reichstag might have enabled him to restrain the Kaiser and move towards a system of parliamentary government. He also blamed the Conservatives for the huge gains made by the SPD in the election of 1912. After the war, therefore, his distrust of the Conservatives and his belief in constitutional government made it natural for him to want to join the centre ground of politics. Ideally, Stresemann would have liked a parliamentary constitutional monarchy. But that was not to be. By 1922, he had become convinced that the Republic and its constitution provided Germany with its only realistic chance against the dictatorship of either left or right. That was quite simply a realistic pragmatic assessment. It cannot really be claimed that it was a decision motivated by a cynical desire to gain popularity and self-advancement.

Gustav Stresemann

Adapted from Layton 1995.

'Stresemann's "hundred days" as Chancellor marked a real turning point in the Republic's history. He took office when the Republic was at its lowest ebb politically and economically; by the time the Great Coalition collapsed in November 1923, the Republic was well on its way to recovery. Stresemann was one of the few really outstanding political figures in the Weimar period. A statesmanlike figure of immense ability and industry, he was a gifted orator [public speaker] and a dynamic and vigorous personality.' (Carr 1991, p.274)

Stresemann's government fell four weeks after the SPD withdrew its support on 2 November 1923. Although he never served as Chancellor again, Stresemann served as Foreign Minister throughout the period 1924-29.

Main developments in foreign policy, 1924-29

Revision of the Treaty of Versailles and the reduction or abolition of reparations remained at the top of the agenda throughout Stresemann's years as Foreign Minister. During the period 1924-29 (he died of a heart attack in October 1929), he was at the centre of negotiations which led to six major initiatives. These will be examined in turn.

1. The Dawes Plan, January 1924

Stresemann's decision as Chancellor to end 'passive resistance' meant that Germany would resume the payment of reparations. In November 1923, Stresemann asked the Allies' Reparations Committee to investigate Germany's capacity to pay reparations. As a result, two committees were set up:

'In November, the Reparations Committee, in response to a German request, agreed to set up two committees of financial experts, one to deal with the problem of the flight of money from Germany, the other, chaired by the American general, Dawes, to consider ways and means of stabilising the Germany currency and balancing the budget.' (Carr 1991, p.279)

In April 1924, the committee chaired by Charles Dawes published its report which then became known as the 'Dawes Plan'. The Dawes Plan made three main recommendations:

- the amount of reparations to be paid each year should be reduced (and the total be paid back over a longer period)
- Germany's national bank, the Reichsbank should be reorganised
- Germany should receive a large foreign loan.

These recommendations were accepted by the Allies and, after heated debate in the Reichstag, by Germany.

2. The Locarno Pact, October 1925

In the period 1919-23, relations between Germany and France were very cold. Indeed they were so frosty that, in January 1923, the French government even sent in troops to occupy the Ruhr (see Unit 2, Section 2.2). During the period 1924-29, however, relations between the two countries began to improve. The first major step forwards was the signing of agreements in the Italian city of Locarno in October 1925. These agreements - the Rhineland Pact and 'arbitration treaties' - are often described collectively as the 'Locarno Pact'. It was a German initiative which led to Locarno:

'Acting on a hint from his friend the British ambassador, Stresemann [proposed] that the powers directly interested in the Rhineland, that is France, Germany and Belgium, with Britain and Italy acting as guarantors, should solemnly declare their intention never to go to war again over their western frontiers.' (Carr 1991, pp.284-85)

The result was the Rhineland Pact, a binding treaty in which Germany officially recognised for the first time the western border imposed on it by the Allies after the First World War. By recognising this border, the German government accepted the loss of the territory of Alsace-Lorraine and the small amount of territory that had been given to Belgium.

At Locarno, Germany also signed 'arbitration treaties' with Poland and Czechoslovakia guaranteeing the peaceful settlement of future disputes. Significantly, however, Germany did not officially recognise the eastern border imposed on it by the Allies after the First World War. The significance of the Locarno Pact is assessed in Box 3.9.

3. The Treaty of Berlin, April 1926

After the end of the First World War, Germany and the Soviet Union were both outsiders and they both had borders with Poland. These two factors help to explain why the two states signed the Treaty of Rapallo in 1922. This treaty ended all claims that either state might have for compensation arising from the First World War and it set up trade links between the two states. Secret military links were also set up under the treaty. Whilst the signing of the Treaty of Rapallo signalled closer relations between Germany and the Soviet Union, Germany's signing of the Locarno Pact was viewed with suspicion by the Soviet Union:

'The Soviet Union was convinced that Locarno was aimed against it, and indeed France had sought the right to march troops through Germany in the event of war with the Soviets. Stresemann had rejected this suggestion.' (Kitchen 1996, p.241)

BOX 3.9 The Locarno Pact

The Locarno agreements, signed on 16 October 1925, provided the pivot of German foreign policy in the 1920s. The central arrangement concerned the Rhineland. The Rhineland Pact included a guarantee of the status quo of the German-French and German-Belgium borders, a promise not to use force and acceptance that any conflicts should be taken to the League of Nations. Locarno meant that, in effect, France broke away from its East European alliance. If the German western border was guaranteed by Britain and Italy, then France would not be permitted to cross it if Germany became involved in a war with the Poles or Czechs, France's allies in the East. As a result, France switched to a purely defensive strategy. In the wake of Locarno, France built the Maginot line (a series of fortresses designed to counter a German invasion) and made it clear that it no longer considered itself a leading European power with the capacity to guarantee peace in Central and Eastern Europe. Its sole concern was its own security and a desire to learn to live with Germany. France had tried to avoid this by pushing for a guarantee of Germany's eastern border. But this was rejected, not just by Germany but also by Britain and Italy as it was by no means certain that Western powers would be able to guarantee Poland's borders in the event of a war. Also, such a guarantee would have required Soviet agreement, but the Soviet Union was not part of the European power structure and had no intention of guaranteeing Poland's borders against Germany. For Germany, the position after Locarno was that, in the East, it was quietly but effectively working with the Soviet Union to undermine the military provisions of the Treaty of Versailles. In the West, it had something like a new peace with France, England and Italy.

Adapted from Haffner 1989.

Most historians agree that it was to reassure the Soviet Union and to re-establish the warm relationship established by the Rapallo Treaty of 1922 that Germany signed the Berlin Treaty of April 1926:

'Contemporaries hailed the Locarno agreements as a turning point in the post-war period; the past was finally buried now that Germany was again a respectable member of the West European community of nations. The ghost of Rapallo had been laid at last - or so it seemed. In fact, the Locarno Pacts did not keep Germany away from Russia. In April 1926, Germany signed the Treaty of Berlin, which reaffirmed and strengthened the Rapallo agreement. Geography, economic necessity and common prudence obliged [Germany] to be on good terms with Russia.' (Carr 1991, p.286)

4. Germany joins the League of Nations

Under the arbitration treaties signed at Locarno, disputes between Germany and France, Poland and Czechoslovakia were to be resolved by the League of Nations (which was based in Geneva) and, in 1926, steps were taken to permit Germany to join. Historians agree that the actual process of persuading existing members to accept Germany's entry was not straightforward:

'Considerable difficulties emerged in the course of 1926 in actually bringing Germany to Geneva and these threatened, at times, the whole spirit of Locarno. The problem arose from the desire of other countries, particularly Poland, to have their great power status recognised by a permanent seat [on the League's council].' (Feuchtwanger 1995, p.174)

Eventually, these difficulties were overcome and Germany took its permanent seat on the League Council in September 1926. It is important to note that Germany won an important concession on joining the League. As (supposedly) a state which had disarmed, it was permitted not to take any action in the event of a conflict resulting in the taking of sanctions:

'It was clear that what [Stresemann] had in mind was a Soviet attack on Poland, in which case he wanted Germany to be able to maintain strict neutrality. France and Britain did not much like this argument but they accepted it...The importance of this concession for Stresemann was that it was enough to persuade the Soviet Union of its ties with Germany.' (Wright 1989, p.40)

As Box 3.10 shows, historians are divided about Stresemann's attitude towards the League of Nations.

5. The Kellogg-Briand Pact of 1928

In 1928 the French Foreign Minister Aristide Briand made a proposal to the US Secretary of State, Frank Kellogg that the two countries should sign a pact rejecting the use of force to resolve international conflicts:

'At Kellogg's suggestion, a Paris conference in 1928 formally condemned recourse for war and the pact was subsequently signed by 65 states.' (Lenman 2000, p.440)

The pact was signed in August 1928. One of the 65 states to sign was Germany.

6. The Young Plan

The arrangements for the payment of reparations made by the Dawes Plan (see above) were not intended to be a final solution to the problem of reparations. Rather, the Dawes Plan was intended to be a temporary measure:

'The Dawes Plan was never intended to be more than an interim measure until such time as Germany had recovered economically.' (Carr 1991, p.287)

BOX 3.10 | Stresemann's attitude to the League of Nations

(i) Stresemann was no more enthusiastic about the League of Nations than most of his countrymen. But he realised that Germany would be better able to defend its international interests from within the League. When Germany was finally admitted into the League in September 1926, Stresemann used his new platform in Geneva to air the grievances of German minorities under foreign rule - particularly those in Poland.
Adapted from Nicholls 1979.

(ii) Stresemann attached great importance to being in the League. He hoped that it would be a vehicle for change. He pointed out that all the important issues - war guilt, general disarmament, German minorities abroad and so on - were matters for the League of Nations and that a skilful speaker at a meeting of the assembly could make things very uncomfortable for the Allies. To ensure that the question of frontier revision in the East remained on the agenda, Stresemann raised the issue of the treatment of German minorities living under foreign rule whenever possible. Similarly, in the hope of shaming the British and French into a speedy withdrawal from the Rhineland, he continually contrasted the Locarno spirit and the new climate generated by German-French cooperation with the continued presence of foreign soldiers on German soil. Disarmament was another favourite theme at Geneva where he constantly contrasted German disarmament with the failure of others to follow suit. He didn't expect any other state to disarm as a result. Rather, he hoped to embarrass France and gain sympathy for his cause.
Adapted from Carr 1991.

From 1927, the USA began calling for a permanent settlement of the matter and, eventually, in February 1929, a committee of financial experts was set up to draw up a plan. This committee was chaired by an American, Owen Young, who was a Vice-Chair on the Dawes committee. Box 3.11 examines the details of the Young Plan.

Stresemann's aims
Long-term aims

A starting point for an analysis of Stresemann's aims is a private letter that he wrote to the ex-Crown Prince in September 1927. In this letter, Stresemann stated that:

'In my opinion, there are three great tasks that confront German foreign policy in the more immediate future.' (quoted in Layton 1995)

BOX 3.11 | **The Young Plan**

Under the Young Plan, which was finally agreed at a meeting held in August 1929, Germany accepted annual reparation payments averaging two billion marks for 59 years - ie until 1988. The payments would rise from 1.7 billion marks in 1930 to 2.4 billion in 1966. After that, they would go down. In return Germany was to be financially independent. Controls over Germany's railways and banking system were dropped. In future, disputes over payment would be settled at the International Court of Justice at the Hague. Provision was made for one-third of an annual payment to be postponed in case of emergency and another third could be paid in kind. The Young Plan reduced the total reparations bill agreed in 1921 by 75%. Germany's acceptance of the Young Plan paved the way to an early evacuation of foreign troops from the Rhineland (British and French troops had been based there throughout the 1920s - as laid down by the Treaty of Versailles). According to the treaty, troops were scheduled to be withdrawn in 1935. The French refused to consider an early evacuation before the final plan for reparations was in place (the French government used the presence of the troops as a bargaining chip, forcing the German government to accept the final plan for reparations). At two conferences held in August 1929 and January 1930, a date for evacuation was finally settled. It would take place on 30 June 1930.

Adapted from Feuchtwanger 1995.

These 'three great tasks' were as follows:
- finding a solution to the reparations problem which was beneficial for Germany
- the protection of Germans living outside the existing borders of Germany
- the readjustment of Germany's eastern frontiers and union with Austria.

This letter also makes it clear that, because Germany was so weak militarily, its choices were limited. The Germans, he implies, would have to use diplomacy to achieve its aims rather than force.

Historians agree that Stresemann was a 'revisionist'. His long-term aim was to revise the Versailles Treaty in Germany's favour and to restore Germany's position as a 'Great Power':

'His aim was quite simply to make Germany a Great Power once more, freeing her as quickly as possible from the shackles of the Versailles Treaty. He was working for the speedy withdrawal of all foreign troops from German soil, for the recovery of the territory lost to Poland, for the removal of the moral stigma of the war-guilt clause and for Germany's entry into the League of Nations. And although it occupied a secondary place in his thoughts, he did what he could to keep the idea of

the Anschluss [union] with Austria alive.'
(Carr 1991, p.282)

Stresemann's strategy

To achieve these long-term aims, Peukert (1991) argues, Stresemann adopted a strategy which had five elements:

1. He accepted the current balance of power and the treaty obligations, but combined a policy of 'fulfilment' (ie doing what the treaty laid down) with a policy of negotiating piecemeal revisions to the treaty.
2. He worked hard at winning American support (especially economic support) in the hope that this would be beneficial for both the German economy and achieving foreign policy aims.
3. He pursued a policy of 'rapprochement' with the West. In other words, he made concessions to Western countries (notably France) in the hope that they would make concessions to Germany.
4. He was prepared to fix the western borders of Germany provided that there still remained the possibility of revision of the borders in the East.
5. He ensured that the balance between revisionism and rapprochement remained unclear. In other words, he was prepared to make some concessions to other states, but only if he calculated that such concessions would increase the likelihood of revisions to the treaty.

It is in this context that the Dawes Plan, Locarno Pact, Treaty of Berlin, admission to the League of Nations, signing of the Kellogg-Briand Pact and the Young Plan should all be seen. Layton describes Stresemann as a 'moderate revisionist' and the strategy he adopted as 'fulfilment':

'The moderate revisionists recognised that the dangerously weak domestic position of Germany acted as a major constraint in the pursuit of foreign policy. For this reason they believed that Germany must follow a dual policy of economic development at home and reconciliation abroad: only by working with the Allies could Germany hope to [reduce the pain of] the mill-stone of reparations which was holding back the German economy; only by restoring Germany's economic strength could Germany hope to regain an influential voice in international affairs. This policy of moderate revisionism came to be called "fulfilment".' (Layton 1995, p.119)

Box 3.12 examines how this strategy worked in practice.

How new was Stresemann's strategy?

Historians are divided over how much of a departure Stresemann's strategy was from his predecessors. Some argue that it was a continuation of that adopted under Chancellor Wirth:

Stresemann's strategy

Stresemann made commitments where there was little chance of doing anything else and tried to create opportunities where there was room for manoeuvre. He tied Germany down in the West to free it up in the East. He was a tough pragmatist who recognised the need to adapt to changing times. The West was the source of Germany's main difficulties and where the most immediate resolutions were needed. To secure these, Stresemann realised, Germany would have to make concessions. His main aim was to secure direct access to the economic strength and assistance of the USA. The USA would reduce the other Allies' suspicion and improve Germany's position - 'A revision of the Versailles Treaty will not be achieved by the force of arms, but by the forces of the world economic community'. Closely linked to this was the problem of reparations. He was prepared to commit Germany to the Dawes Plan and then to the Young Plan because, in return, Germany would receive American investment. In other words, he was prepared to give an option (which did not really exist) of resisting reparations in exchange for an important concession. The same principle explains the Locarno Pact. He saw it as a major priority to remove the French threat from Germany, but was realistic enough to see that he would have to remove the threat which Germany appeared to pose to France. By guaranteeing Germany's western borders, he agreed to the removal of an option Germany did not have (to regain the territory by force). In exchange, he prevented the French from making use of an option they did have (using force against Germany). Never again would the French be able to occupy the Ruhr.

Adapted from Lee 1998.

'Stresemann did not even believe in the Dawes Plan...The plan was accepted simply in order to secure the foreign loans without which economic recovery was impossible. In September 1925, he told Crown Prince Wilhelm, son of the ex-Emperor, that by 1927 the demands of the plan would strain Germany beyond endurance and that a new conference would be called to relieve her of the burden. Like Wirth before him, Stresemann was pursuing a policy of fulfilment simply in order to prove the impossibility of reparations.' (Carr 1991, p.284)

Other authors, on the other hand, argue that Stresemann's appointment as Foreign Minister meant a new departure. Berghahn (1987), for example, argues that the emphasis on securing support from the USA was new.

Was Stresemann devious and hypocritical?

It has sometimes been argued that Stresemann was devious and hypocritical. In part, this is due to the fact that there was a great deal of opposition to his strategy from right-wingers in Germany. The DNVP (nationalists) were particularly hostile to his approach on the grounds that opposition to the Treaty of Versailles must be absolute. In reality, however, Stresemann's long-term goals were not very different from those of the nationalists. As a result, as Wright points out, Stresemann often used the language of the nationalists:

'Defending himself to nationalist critics at home, he adopted their goals and language, but argued that there was no alternative to his policy given Germany's lack of military power.' (Wright 1989, p.40)

While Stresemann spoke the language of nationalism in Germany, he spoke a very different language in his negotiations with foreign states:

'All of Stresemann's diplomacy, whether agreeing to commitments in the West or freeing up room for manoeuvre in the East involved expressions of peace, reconciliation and good will.' (Lee 1998, p.82)

But, argues Lee, this does not necessarily mean that Stresemann was being devious and hypocritical. Rather he was being diplomatic. The activity which follows considers whether Stresemann's period as Foreign Minister should be regarded as a success or failure.

MAIN POINTS - Section 1.3

- Although Stresemann was, at heart, a monarchist, he came round to supporting the Republic as the best defence against extremism.
- Three important developments took place during Stresemann's Chancellorship in 1923 - (1) the end of 'passive resistance' (2) the combating of hyperinflation and (3) the declaration of a state of emergency to deal with uprisings organised by extremists on left and right.
- Revision of the Versailles Treaty and the reduction or abolition of reparations remained at the top of the agenda throughout Stresemann's years as Foreign Minister. Between 1924-29, he was at the centre of negotiations leading to - (1) the Dawes Plan

(2) the Locarno Pact (3) the Treaty of Berlin (4) joining the League of Nations (5) the Kellogg-Briand Pact and (6) the Young Plan.
- Stresemann's 'three great tasks' were - (1) finding a beneficial solution to the reparations problem (2) protecting Germans living outside the existing borders of Germany and (3) readjusting Germany's eastern frontiers and gaining union with Austria.
- Stresemann adopted a strategy which had five elements - (1) accept the current balance of power (2) win support from the USA (3) rapproachement with the West (4) fix western borders (5) keep the balance between revisionism and rapprochement unclear.

Activity 3.3 Was Stresemann a success or failure?

ITEM 1 Stresemann the bridge-builder

This poster was produced by the DVP during the 1930 Reich election campaign, a year after Stresemann died. It portrays him as a bridge-builder - somebody who built friendly relations between Germany and other states.

ITEM 2 Stresemann's motives

Stresemann's motives in negotiating the Locarno Pact have been the subject of much debate. Naturally, Stresemann presented himself as the champion of greater cooperation in Europe. Documents which came to light after the Second World War, however, show that, at the same time, he was also expressing strongly nationalist views. In addition, there could no longer be any doubt that he knew of the secret military arrangements between Germany and the Soviet Union. There is nothing surprising in this. Stresemann had always been a German nationalist. He made it clear that it was German weakness, not a belief in a peaceful approach, which forced him to make concessions over matters like passive resistance in the Ruhr, reparations or the recognition of Germany's western frontier. So far as Locarno was concerned, Stresemann believed that it would prevent the British and French negotiating an alliance, hasten the removal of Allied troops from the Rhineland and create a better atmosphere in which Germany could rebuild its economic strength. By keeping a free hand in the East and maintaining the Soviet connection, he could still hope for territorial adjustments. This does not mean that he was hypocritical in his attitude towards Western states. It is unlikely that French or British politicians really imagined Stresemann had changed his views. They knew the German Foreign Minister was a tough negotiator, well able to defend the interests of his country.

Adapted from Nicholls 1979.

ITEM 3 The position in 1929

By 1929, Stresemann had constructed an ingenious system, but he was unable to make it work. Germany was both too weak to force its demands on others and also potentially so strong that its recovery was bound to arouse fear and resistance. Stresemann knew that France would not agree to union with Austria. Even had he remained Foreign Minister after 1929, it is not clear how resistance abroad could have been overcome peacefully. Poland was unlikely to agree to frontier revision unless it was forced to do so by war. If Germany were to persuade other states to allow it to rearm and then tried to achieve its aims by force, it would risk isolation and defeat again. How could a framework be found in which Germany could achieve revision without Europe going to war? By the time he died, Stresemann had found no answer to this problem. Indeed, there was a growing feeling in Germany that Stresemann's policy of fulfilment was coming to a dead end. The turning point was Germany's acceptance of the Young Plan. On the surface, agreeing to the Young Plan in return for early evacuation of the Rhineland appeared to be a suitable compromise. But, it inflamed the hostility of the various nationalist groups and united them in opposition. Sensing the coming crisis, a British minister, Robert Vansittart, warned in May 1930 that Germany was 'on the threshold of a new period' in which it 'may be sorely tempted to apply the old methods of diplomacy if [it] finds the new ones...ineffective for changing the status quo to her purpose'.

Adapted from Wright 1989 and Waddington 2001.

ITEM 4 Stresemann - a failure or success?

Gustav Stresemann and his wife, Käthe.

(i) In the longer term, Stresemann achieved very little. By 1929, he himself was disappointed about how much of the Treaty of Versailles remained in place. All he achieved was the rescheduling of reparations payments and the early evacuation of Allied troops from the Rhineland. The evacuation came at a price. In 1928, a German delegation to the League of Nations called for a complete evacuation without ties. But this was rejected by the French. They insisted on making evacuation conditional on Germany accepting the Young Plan. Agreeing to this was a humiliation for Stresemann and he was fiercely criticised by the right. Indeed, the campaign against the Young Plan did much to make Hitler appear respectable for the first time. Nor did Stresemann secure revision of any of the other terms of the treaty. Eastern frontier adjustments had not even been discussed. The Rhineland was still demilitarised. The army was restricted and the ban on an air force remained. Any real progress was made after Stresemann died, largely as a result of a more forceful approach. It is an indication of failure that Stresemann's moderate diplomacy collapsed after 1929.

(ii) The longer-term collapse of a system does not prove it was a failure. In 1923, Germany was isolated and vulnerable in the West. It was unable to pay reparations and unable to convince the Allies that it lacked the means to pay. The government could only stand by as the French invaded. It is true that Germany had made an agreement with the Soviet Union, but this was counterbalanced by the close relations between France and Poland. By the time of Stresemann's death, however, Germany's position had been transformed. The Dawes Plan brought in the USA to support the German economy - Germany received more from the new arrangement than it paid out in reparations. The Locarno Pact ensured that France would never again invade German territory. All that Germany gave up was the option of attacking France, which it was in no position to do. The position in the East was more flexible. Entry into the League of Nations and the signing of the Kellogg-Briand Pact improved Germany's standing in the world. It is difficult to see how the Allies would have agreed to the cancellation of reparations in 1932 unless they had been impressed by Germany's rehabilitation.

Adapted from Lee 1998.

Questions

1. Judging by Items 1-4 and your own knowledge, what was the role played by Gustav Stresemann in the period 1924-29?
2. Why do you think the poster in Item 1 portrays Stresemann as a bridge-builder?

3. Judging from Items 2-4 and your own knowledge, would you describe Stresemann's years as Foreign Minister as a success or failure? Explain your answer.

2 The crisis of 1929-33

Key issues

1. How did German governments cope with the economic crisis of 1929-33?

2. What led to the rise and fall of Heinrich Brüning?

3. What were the aims of Papen and Schleicher in the eight months following Brüning's resignation?

2.1 How did German governments cope with the economic crisis of 1929-33?

Economic factors and the collapse of the Weimar Republic

There is no doubt that the worldwide economic depression which broke out after the Wall Street Crash of October 1929 is somehow linked to the collapse of the Weimar Republic. There is, however, a debate between historians about what exactly this link was. Some historians argue that economic factors were the cause of the collapse of the Republic. According to this view, economic instability - first the period of hyperinflation in the early 1920s and then the period of economic recession after 1929 - caused voters to become so disillusioned with the Weimar system that its collapse became inevitable. In other words, economic developments caused political change.

Other historians deny that this was the case. They argue that:

'The direction was, in fact, the other way round, with political factors causing the violent economic fluctuations of the period.' (Ferguson 1997, p.259)

Classifying historians

Ferguson (1997) first divides historians into two groups:

- those who see the political crisis of 1929-33 as inevitable, given economic developments
- those who believe that the economic crisis was made worse by the actions of the German government.

Ferguson then divides historians into four other groups.

The first two of these groups are divided on whether factors inside Germany or factors outside Germany were more important in explaining why the Weimar Republic collapsed. He argues that:

- some historians believe that the Treaty of Versailles - ie a factor outside Germany's control - was to blame for the crisis faced by Germany (particularly because reparations were imposed and were believed to be a crushing economic blow)
- other historians believe that the causes of Weimar's failure were within Germany itself.

The final two groups both believe that the causes of Weimar's failure were within Germany itself, but they are divided over who was to blame:

- one group argues that the workers were to blame because their excessive power was a source of economic and political weakness
- another group argues that Big Business was to blame because it lost faith in democratic government and campaigned against the Republic.

Nothing inevitable about a Nazi victory

It is important to note that most historians agree that, even if the collapse of the Weimar Republic was inevitable in the early 1930s, it was by no means inevitable that the Nazis would come to power. As James puts it:

'Economic strains at the end of the 1920s eroded democracy and prepared the path for an authoritarian [non-democratic] solution. That does not, however, mean that the specific outcome of Germany's inter-war political crisis - the appointment by Reich President Marshal Paul von Hindenburg of Adolf Hitler as Reich Chancellor on 30 January 1933 - was historically necessary, determined or inevitable...Events played the major role. Germany could have moved towards military dictatorship, the restoration of the monarchy, autocratic rule through the Reich President [or] imitation of Italian Fascism...Only a restoration of 1920s democracy was unlikely.' (James 1990, p.30)

The impact of the Wall Street Crash

Between 24 and 29 October 1929, the USA stock market, which is based in Wall Street, collapsed as the price of shares tumbled down and down. The consequences of this 'Wall Street Crash' were immense. Overnight many people were ruined. Companies closed down in the USA and unemployment rose rapidly. Foreign loans were recalled and investment dried up. This prompted a worldwide economic depression.

It was noted in Section 1.1 above that many historians have argued that economic recovery in Germany was not as impressive in the period 1924-29 as it might appear to be at first sight. Layton argues that two factors, in particular, were 'time bombs' which would be detonated after the Wall Street Crash. Discussing the underlying weakness of the German economy at the end of the 1920s, he suggests:

'At the time, the problems were effectively masked by the massive influx of foreign capital and by the development of an extensive, but costly, social welfare system. Yet both these factors were in their own way "time bombs" waiting to go off.' (Layton 1995, p.113)

Overy argues that, not only were there signs of recession in Germany before the Wall Street Crash, these signs were actually one of the causes of the Crash itself since American investors became concerned that their investments in the German economy would not prove profitable:

'The signs of impending recession in Germany were evident from 1928. Indeed, poor expectations of continued German revival helped to undermine the confidence of American speculators, a cause rather than a consequence of the Great Crash.' (Overy 2001, p.39)

When the Crash occurred, its consequences in Germany were swift and wide-ranging. Box 3.13 provides one historian's account of the impact of the Crash.

The fall of the Grand Coalition

During the first months of the crisis, the Grand Coalition (see Section 1.2 above) remained in power under Chancellor Müller (the Leader of the SPD). The economic downturn, however, put the government under great strain:

'By the end of 1929, there were many alarming signs of impending crisis; mounting unemployment, falling tax receipts and a budget deficit of 1,700 million marks which called for drastic action. On the issue of unemployment benefit the [Grand] Coalition was fatally divided.' (Carr 1991, p.296)

When, in March 1930, a compromise between the coalition partners could not be reached over a proposal to raise unemployment insurance contributions from 3% to 3.5%, Müller asked President Hindenburg to issue a decree under Article

BOX 3.13 The impact of the Wall Street Crash

Almost immediately, the loans and investment dried up and there were demands for their repayment. At the same time, the crisis brought a further decline in the price of food and raw materials. World trade slumped as demand collapsed. German industry could no longer pay its way. Unsupported by loans and with smaller export markets, prices and wages fell whilst the number of bankruptcies increased. During the winter of 1929-30, unemployment rose above 2 million. A year later it had reached 3 million. By September 1932, it stood at 5.1 million. It peaked in early 1933 at 6.1 million. But these figures do not tell the whole story. They do not include those who did not register as unemployed or those whose hours were drastically cut, leaving them with poverty wages. Above all these figures tell us little about the psychological trauma many experienced. The recession affected almost everybody. Huge numbers of manual workers - skilled and unskilled - faced the prospect of indefinite unemployment. They had to feed their families and keep their homes warm on the small amount of money provided by social security benefits. And such problems were not confined to the working class. The Depression also dragged down the middle classes. From small-scale shopkeepers to graduate professionals in law and medicine, people struggled to survive in a world where their goods and services were less and less in demand. For such casualties, the decline in their economic position was accompanied by loss of pride and respectability. In the countryside, the situation was no better than in the towns.

Adapted from Layton 1995.

48 of the constitution. Hindenburg refused and Müller resigned.

Historians agree that the fall of the Grand Coalition was a highly significant moment since, from that point on, no government of the Weimar Republic had a majority in the Reichstag. Instead of passing laws in the Reichstag in the normal way, governments increasingly relied on President Hindenburg to issue decrees under Article 48 of the constitution. There was, in other words, a transfer from parliamentary government to presidential government (see also Section 2.2 below).

Brüning's policy of deflation

The new Chancellor, Heinrich von Brüning, consistently followed a policy of 'deflation'. This involved 'balancing the budget'. In other words, the aim of the policy was to ensure that the amount spent by government (for example, on unemployment benefit and the wages of civil servants) was the same as that received by government in taxes. The problem was that the amount received in taxes went down as unemployment went up. At the same time, the

growth in unemployment led to a greater demand for unemployment benefit (ie it led to a growth in government spending). Brüning's policy has been described as follows:

'Brüning believed that the best way of combating economic collapse was to adopt a policy of deflation. Above all, the budget had to be balanced. If state revenue declined, state expenditure had to be cut. If social security contributions fell because of unemployment, benefits had to be reduced. Civil servants and teachers who...could not be dismissed had their salaries cut. No doubt this was preferable to redundancy, but it was a bitter pill, nonetheless. A petty bureaucrat who had earned 250 marks per month in 1927 saw his income slashed by 58 marks by December 1932.' (Berghahn 1987, pp.115-16)

Brüning attempted to find a majority in the Reichstag to support the deflationary measures he wanted to introduce. When this failed, the measures were introduced in July 1930 in an emergency decree issued under Article 48 of the constitution. The measures which he introduced are described in Box 3.14 (on page 106).

There was one sector of the economy which avoided the deflationary thrust of Brüning's economic strategy, namely agriculture. Agriculture was 'protected' - the government provided farmers with subsidies and maintained tariffs (taxes) on imports of food. As a result, food prices remained higher than they otherwise would have been (Brüning consequently became known as the 'Hunger Chancellor'). Hiden makes it clear that the reason why agriculture was protected was because large landowners had a great deal of political clout (President Hindenburg, in particular, listened sympathetically to their demands):

'The bias of government was all too plain to see from Brüning's protectionist policy towards agriculture...His measures kept the price of bread and cereals abnormally high during a period of ruthless economies and cutbacks in public expenditure.' (Hiden 1996, p.61)

Reparations and the Great Depression

It was noted in Section 1.1 above that it was the Dawes Plan which ensured that US loans and investment flooded into Germany during the period 1924-29. This money was greater than the amount Germany paid to Britain and France in reparations:

'Between 1924 and 1930, some 25.5 billion marks flowed into Germany in the form of loans and investment whereas Germany paid, ultimately, a total of some 22.9 billion marks in reparations.' (Hiden 1996, p.33)

Before the Wall Street Crash, therefore, a circular system developed. The USA loaned or invested money in Germany. This allowed Germany to pay

Brüning's first package of measures was introduced in July 1930. Even though it was only a few weeks since the Grand Coalition had fallen over raising unemployment insurance contributions by just 0.5%, they were raised by a further 1% to 4.5%. Local communities were given the power to raise money by imposing

Heinrich von Brüning

additional drink taxes, including a beer tax. They could also raise money by imposing a poll or head tax. Permanently employed public servants had to pay an emergency contribution and people on higher incomes had to pay higher income tax. The second emergency package was introduced in October 1930. Unemployment insurance contributions were raised from 4.5% to 6.5%. Apart from money raised by contributions, there would be no further money from the government for unemployment benefit. All public employees had their salaries and pensions cut by 6%. Less money was transferred from central government to the Länder. The third emergency decree, issued in June 1931, reduced unemployment benefit by 10-12% and reduced the period for which it was payable. It also reduced payments to those who had run out of unemployment benefit and were receiving 'crisis' payments. A third line of support for the long-term unemployed was the local authorities, but these were now subject to rigorous control. The Länder had the power to force local authorities to balance their budgets. The emergency decree also provided for another reduction of between 4% and 8% in the salaries of public employees.

Adapted from Feuchtwanger 1995.

reparations to Britain and France. Britain and France then used this money to pay off debts to the USA that had been built up during the First World War:

'A sort of circular economic process was under way: Germany paid reparations to England and France who in turn paid war debts to America, who, in order to keep it all moving along, pumped loans into Germany.' (Haffner 1989, p.150)

After the Wall Street Crash, this system collapsed as American loans and investment dried up. Carr argues that Brüning then chose to adopt a deflationary policy in order to show that Germany was incapable of paying reparations, the idea being that this would force the Allies to abandon them:

'Clearly [Brüning] hoped to exploit the economic

crisis to rid Germany of her huge foreign indebtedness and secure the abolition of reparations.' (Carr 1991, p.300)

If that was the aim, then the policy had some success. In July 1931, on the initiative of the American President, Herbert Hoover, the Allies agreed to a moratorium (a temporary halt) on the payment of reparations and war debts and, in June 1932 (when Brüning was no longer Chancellor), reparations were abandoned.

The debate over Brüning's policy of deflation

There is a great deal of historical debate over Brüning's policy of deflation. Some historians argue that, far from helping Germany tackle its economic problems, it made them worse because it ensured that unemployment rose higher than it needed to and more businesses went bankrupt than otherwise might have been the case. Berghahn, for example, goes as far as asserting that:

'If the moratorium on reparations brought some relief, the other results of Brüning's deflation were catastrophic.' (Berghahn 1987, p.116)

Berghahn argues that Brüning's economic policy deepened the recession. Because of the high level of unemployment and restraints on government spending, the amount of money paid out in benefits fell, forcing many people into deep poverty. At the same time, the real income of people who remained in a job fell. Fear of unemployment ensured that trade unions lost their power to negotiate better deals for workers. Profits fell. People became demoralised. Some historians argue that this all fitted in with Brüning's political vision. In his memoirs, Brüning made it clear that he was a monarchist with little sympathy towards the democratic Republic. The argument is that he believed that a dose of deflation would undermine the unions, restore power to the employers and prepare people for the sort of non-democratic rule he supported.

Other historians are less critical. They point out that it is easy to criticise Brüning with hindsight. But, at the time, it was not at all obvious that the recession would be long-lasting. After all, in 1926, Germany had suffered an economic downturn but it had quickly pulled itself around. In 1929 and 1930, there was reason to think that balancing the budget would ensure that the economy was in a healthy state once market forces returned to normal in the near future. It was only after the banking crisis in the summer of 1931 (see below) that the depth of the crisis became clear and, by then, there was little that Brüning could do to prevent unemployment from spiralling up. Box 3.15 summarises this debate.

The banking crisis of 1931

According to Feuchtwanger, the idea that the recession might be a temporary phenomenon (like

The debate over Brüning's policy of deflation

The debate over Brüning's policy of deflation was sparked in the mid-1970s when the historian, Knut Borchardt, claimed that Brüning had no real room for manoeuvre in his economic policy and, as a result, there was no real alternative to deflation. Reflation - trying to revive the economy by borrowing money and spending it on job creation - was just not realistic, he argued, partly because the German economy had structural weaknesses, especially high and uncompetitive wage levels and large governmental debts. But there were also practical restraints. Such an approach would have meant borrowing money from abroad (which would have meant strict preconditions on how it was spent) or printing more money (which would have meant inflation and breaking the terms of the Young Plan). Besides, the true extent of the recession only became clear in the summer of 1931, by which time it was already too late to prevent unemployment rising to 6 million. Leading the opposition to Borchardt has been Carl-Ludwig Holtfrerich who argues that there were very clear policy alternatives, but no real determination to apply them. Although there were weaknesses in the German economy, he argues that it was not doomed to collapse in 1929. Brüning, Holtfrerich argues, adopted the policy of deflation because it suited his own domestic and foreign policy objectives. In terms of foreign policy, he aimed to exploit the Depression to demonstrate to the Allies that the payment of reparations was no longer viable. In terms of domestic policy, he aimed to discredit and decisively weaken the social and economic base upon which the Republic was based.

Adapted from Layton 1995.

that in 1926), gained currency in the first half of 1931 because unemployment began to go down:

'Unemployment, as measured by the official statistics of those registered as unemployed at labour offices, reached a peak of nearly 5 million in February 1931, compared with 3.2 a year earlier. By August, the numbers had dropped by nearly 900,000, compared with a drop of 450,000 in 1930.' (Feuchtwanger 1995, p.238)

This turned out to be a false dawn, however. In March 1931, without consultation with the Allies, the government announced that it was setting up a customs union with Austria. According to Peukert:

'[This] provoked financial counter-reactions from the French which finally set in train the breakdown of the world financial system.' (Peukert 1991, p.256)

On 11 May, Austria's largest bank, the Kreditanstalt,

collapsed. This, together with disappointment with the package of emergency measures announced in June (see Box 3.14) and speculation that Brüning's government was on the verge of collapse led to an outflow of foreign money from German banks. It was on 20 June that President Hoover announced the moratorium on reparations and, as negotiations to win over French support for this began, further foreign money flowed out of Germany. On 13 July 1931, the Danatbank, Germany's largest private bank collapsed and a second large bank admitted being close to collapsing. This, Feuchtwanger suggests, was a turning point:

'These problems were due not only to the collapse of industrial undertakings such as Nordwolle, a big textile firm, but also to the financial difficulties which had engulfed local and municipal authorities. Germany's chronic capital shortage, the difficulties in balancing the Reich budget and the reliance on short-term foreign credits were coming home to roost. There had to be a banking holiday...The future of the capitalist system was in doubt as never before.' (Feuchtwanger 1995, p.248)

Consequences of the banking crisis

The collapse of the Danatbank was part of what Peukert describes as a 'chain reaction' which threatened to force the collapse of the international financial system:

'The immediate casualty of the customs union dispute was the Austrian Kreditanstalt which collapsed in May 1931. The failure of the German Danatbank followed in July, and the collapse of the Bank of England in September 1931 was averted only by Britain's abandonment of the gold standard. In a chain reaction, the international financial system began to break down, nations tried to seal themselves off from world markets, the German financial system became badly crippled and Germany, along with the rest of the world, braced herself for a further, disastrous slump in production.' (Peukert 1991, p.256)

Feuchtwanger (1995) argues that it was only in the period after July 1931 that reflationary measures (such as borrowing money to fund job creation schemes or devaluing the mark to make exports more competitive) were seriously considered for the first time. He suggests, however, that such measures were rejected by Brüning because he believed that, by spending its way out of the downturn in 1926, the Müller government had sowed the roots of the recession which began in 1929. Because he believed this, Feuchtwanger argues, Brüning refused to consider the introduction of any reflationary measures until reparations had been abolished. Reparations, of course, were not abolished until after Brüning had been forced to resign (he was replaced by Papen in May 1932). Feuchtwanger's argument is as follows:

'After the July banking crisis there was an increasing interest in reflationary measures both within the government and bureaucracy, in industry and in the trade unions. It remains true that Brüning himself was very reluctant to take any risks with reflation and preferred to wait until reparations were finally out of the way...In Brüning's view, the budgetary problems he had inherited from the Müller government had themselves been caused by the spending policies adopted in 1926 by Reinhold, the finance minister, to pull out of the recession of 1925-26. They had been aggravated by Köhler's policy of raising civil service pay in 1927.' (Feuchtwanger 1995, p.250)

Overy disagrees with this analysis. He argues that, far from remaining an opponent to reflationary measures, Brüning introduced them secretly. Overy's argument is outlined in Box 3.16.

BOX 3.16 Overy's analysis of Brüning's economic policy 1931-32

Richard Overy points out that many critics of Brüning's economic policy have argued that Germany could have avoided the deep recession which gripped Germany in 1931-32 if the Chancellor had introduced reflationary measures - for example, borrowing money to pay for job creation schemes or devaluing the mark to make exports more competitive. But that, argues Overy, is exactly what Brüning did secretly, with the effect not that the recession was avoided but that it was not as bad as it could have been. Overy produces three pieces of evidence to support this theory. First, he claims that government spending in real terms was a higher proportion of national income in 1931 and 1932 than it was in any year in the 1920s. In other words, the government put extra money into the economy (a reflationary measure). Second, secret permission was given to Germany's national bank, the Reichsbank, to relax the rules about how many banknotes it could print. Allowing the Reichsbank to print more money was also a reflationary measure. And third, the government paid subsidies to export industries. This, Overy claims, had the same effect as devaluation (ie it was a reflationary measure), but it was less dangerous than actual devaluation since devaluation would have been seen as inflationary. Given the hyperinflation of 1923, it was important for Germany to avoid measures which were considered inflationary. The real problem facing Germany, Overy argues, was not Brüning's economic policy, but four other factors, First, the level of foreign demand for German goods was feeble. Second, tariffs (taxes on imports) in foreign countries made it hard for German exporters to sell their goods. Third, foreign countries had little interest in funding a state which was in the process of refusing to pay its debts (ie reparations). And fourth, political pressure at home restricted the government's room for manoeuvre.

Adapted from Overy 2001.

A missed opportunity

Whether Brüning introduced reflationary measures secretly or not, Peukert (who does not believe Brüning did so) points out that the way in which people view a government's economic policy is important and, regardless of what was going on behind the scenes, Brüning was not seen as taking positive steps to end the crisis. As a result, the Brüning government lost a great deal of potential good will:

'By the end of 1931, all manner of proposals for combating the crisis by reflationary measures and work creation schemes had been put forward. It is doubtful whether such programmes would actually have begun to bear fruit during 1932, but they would at least have been symbols of hope for the mass of the population...Indeed, in 1933, the Hitler government was able to [gain advantage from] the civil service's detailed advance preparations for work creation programmes and thus claim undeserved credit for recovery when it came. The Brüning government would have been able to profit from the same good will had it not refused, because of its priorities in foreign policy, to take action to combat the slump until reparations had been finally abolished.' (Peukert 1991, pp.256-57)

Economic developments under Papen

Carr argues that when Brüning did propose to take reflationary measures in May 1932, the result was his downfall and replacement by Franz von Papen (whose background is described in Box 3.17):

'In May, just before he left office, Brüning drew up a plan for modest reflation including proposals for the break-up of some inefficient East Prussian estates and the resettlement of 600,000 unemployed on them. Landowning circles got wind of this and their spokesman, Oldenburg-Januschau, visited Hindenburg...and easily persuaded the disgruntled President that Brüning was an "agrarian bolshevik" bent on socialising agriculture. When Brüning appeared with new emergency decrees the old man refused to sign them.' (Carr 1991, pp.303-04)

Brüning then resigned and Papen was appointed Chancellor.

Although Papen completed the negotiations which led to the cancellation of reparations in July 1932, Berghahn argues that the cancellation of reparations did not lead to the introduction of reflationary measures. Berghahn is even more critical of Papen than he is of Brüning. He describes Papen as a 'reactionary' - an ultra-conservative who supported a return to non-democratic government - and argues that, like Brüning, he adopted a deflationary policy:

'[Papen's] policies can only be called unashamedly reactionary, and he was even more deaf than his predecessor to various alternative economic strategies which were being [suggested] at this time.' (Berghahn 1987, p.116)

Feuchtwanger, on the other hand, argues that the

cancellation of reparations did lead to a marked change of economic approach. He argues that the emergency decree issued on 4 September 1932 put into place a series of measures which was beneficial to industrialists and which marked the beginning of a new approach:

'The reparations restraint on the German government's freedom of manoeuvre in financial matters was now removed. The Papen government could, therefore, contemplate a change...The economic policies of the Papen government marked a real change of course...and most of them continued to be effective until well into the next year, by which time Hitler was in power.'
(Feuchtwanger 1995, pp.292-93)

Amongst the measures introduced by the emergency decree were:

- the granting of tax rebates to employers who took on new staff, a certain amount of tax being returned for each person
- the end of binding (compulsory) arbitration
- a general relaxation of the system of wage agreements.

These measures went down well with employers but were opposed by the parties of the left and the trade unions.

Economic developments under Schleicher

Papen only remained in power until the end of November 1932, when he was replaced as Chancellor by General Kurt von Schleicher (see Box 3.17 and Section 2.2 below for further information on Schleicher). In terms of economic policy, historians agree that Schleicher attempted, but failed, to change direction. His aim was to build bridges with both the Catholic and independent trade unions and with the Nazi labour organisations - what Craig (1981) describes as a 'military-labour alliance'. His attempt to build such a coalition failed, however, and he alienated industrialists, large landowners and the President:

'Schleicher approached the left with a programme of public works, price-fixing, restoration of wage- and relief cuts and land settlement in East Prussia, measures which naturally turned the right wing against him. But he could not overcome the mistrust of the Socialists and Centrists and had finally to return to the presidential palace.'
(Carr 1991, p.307)

By then, Schleicher had lost the confidence of the President and behind-the-scenes negotiations were taking place - negotiations which would result in the resignation of Schleicher and his replacement by Hitler.

BOX 3.17 | Papen and Schleicher

(i) Franz von Papen was born in 1879 into a wealthy aristocratic family. Choosing a career in the army, he served as a military attaché in the First World War. After the war, he left the army for a career in politics. From 1921 to 1932 he belonged to the Centre Party and served in the Prussian Landtag (state Parliament). He failed to gain election to the Reichstag. Throughout his career, Papen supported the anti-parliamentary, anti-Republican right. He clothed both his monarchism and nationalism in pseudo-Christian language which won him little popular understanding or support. However, his aristocratic background, his views, his friendship with Kurt von Schleicher and his close connections with both industry and the army ensured that he

Kurt von Schleicher (left) and Franz von Papen.

was seen as an ideal successor to Brüning in May 1932, despite his lack of experience in government. His appointment was a surprise both in Germany and abroad.
Adapted from Snyder 1976.

(ii) Kurt von Schleicher was born in April 1882 into an old Prussian military family. He joined the Third Foot Guards, Hindenburg's old regiment, in 1903 and then the General Staff in 1913. In 1929, the Minister of Defence, General Wilhelm Groener, appointed Schleicher (now a general) as Chief of Staff in the ministry. In this post, Schleicher engaged increasingly in politics, becoming a major player behind the scenes. By March 1930, Schleicher had come to the conclusion that extremists on the left and right would be encouraged by the weakness of the Reichstag to make a bid for power which would result in civil war and invite a Polish attack in the East. What Germany needed, Schleicher decided, was a period of strong, non-party government. He suggested that Brüning would be ideally suited to be the 'army's Chancellor'. In May 1932, it was Schleicher who engineered Brüning's downfall and Papen's appointment. Finally, in December 1932, Schleicher himself became Chancellor, only to be outmanoeuvred by Hitler and Papen the following month.
Adapted from Carr 1991.

MAIN POINTS - Section 2.1

- Some historians argue that economic factors were the cause of the collapse of the Republic. Others deny that this was the case. They argue that political factors caused the violent economic fluctuations of the period.
- Two economic developments in the period 1924-29 ensured that Germany was hit hard by the economic depression after the Wall Street Crash - (1) its reliance on foreign loans and investment and (2) the building of an extensive, but costly, social welfare system.
- The economic crisis put the Grand Coalition under strain and it collapsed in March 1930. Brüning took over and followed a policy of 'deflation' - trying to ensure that the amount spent by government was the same as that received in taxes. Brüning hoped to show the Allies that Germany could not afford to pay reparations.

- There is a debate about Brüning's policy of deflation. Some historians argue that he had little room for manoeuvre. Others argue that he hoped to undermine support for the Republic so he could impose non-democratic government.
- There is also a debate about Brüning's response to the banking crisis of 1931. Some historians believe he secretly implemented reflationary measures. Others argue that he missed the opportunity to do so and, as a result, lost support.
- Under Papen, reparations were finally abolished. Some historians argue this led to a new economic approach. Others deny this. Historians agree Schleicher tried and failed to build a military-labour alliance.

Activity 3.4 The economic crisis, 1929-33

ITEM 1 Economic statistics 1929-33

(i) Indices of Economic Crisis (1928=100)

	1929	1930	1931	1932	1933
Production:					
Capital goods	103	86	61	46	54
Investment goods	103	84	54	35	45
Employment:					
Employed persons	99	92	80	71	74
Prices and wages:					
Capital goods	102	101	96	86	83
Consumer goods	98	91	80	67	64
Cost of living	102	98	90	80	78
Real wages	101	97	93	87	91

(ii) Av. Growth Rate (%) 1929-32

Metal production	−28.1
Metal working	−20.9
Coal	−31.3
Chemicals	−9.4
Textiles	−6.8
Clothing	−0.9
Leather	−4.0
Utilities	−7.8
Building Industries	−29.9

(iii) Unemployment (1928-1933) in 1,000s and % of working population

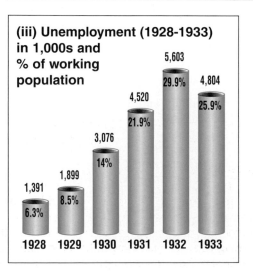

(iv) Index of industrial production 1928-1933 (1928=100)

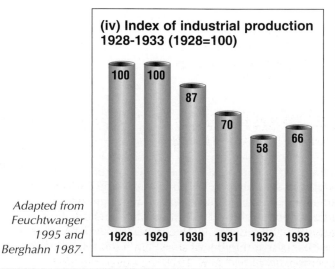

Adapted from Feuchtwanger 1995 and Berghahn 1987.

ITEM 2 The culture of blame

There is no simple link between economic misery and political radicalism. Frequently in history, unemployment has led to political inaction rather than political activism. In Germany at the end of the 1920s, however, economic problems helped to prepare the ground for a large-scale rejection of capitalism. The banking crisis of 1931 accelerated this process. It was not just that anti-capitalist and anti-liberal feelings swelled as a result of the economic depression. The peculiar nature of Germany's highly politicised economy meant that anti-anything sentiment grew. A picture of the world populated by enemies emerged. A failed economy resulted in bitter and unbridgeable political clashes and altered the operation of the political system. When there is economic stagnation, a vicious circle sometimes emerges - political polarisation (ie the growth of extremism), inability to solve economic problems by democratic means, a worsening economic performance and then further political polarisation. Economic and political systems lock themselves in this way into a stalemate. In Weimar Germany, employers believed that they had been obstructed by over-powerful trade unions. Unions believed that the economic downturn was the product of poor decision-making by employers who did not believe in the Republic anyway. The economic crisis led to farmers thinking that they paid high taxes to subsidise unemployed (and idle) workers and bankers who needed state bail-outs when they failed as a result of their own mistaken policies. Workers, on the other hand, thought that their wages were so low because of the limitless greed of German agriculture. This culture of blaming anyone and everyone else dominated political debate.

Adapted from James 1990.

ITEM 3 The impact of the Great Depression

Unemployment started to grow and the effects were deep and bitter. 'In those days', remembers Bruno Hähnel, 'our unemployed would stand in huge queues in front of the the labour exchange every Friday and they would receive 5 marks at the counter. This was a new and different situation - there were many who simply didn't have the means to buy food.' 'It was a hopeless business', recalls Alois Pfaller. 'People walked around with spoons in their pockets because they got a meal for 1 mark [from the charity soup kitchens].' The suffering hit middle-class families, such as Jutta Rüdiger's: 'My father didn't become unemployed but he was told he had to agree to work for a lower salary.' Jutta thought she wouldn't be able to go to university until a kindly uncle stepped in and gave her an allowance. A family experience like the Rüdigers' would not have appeared on any unemployment statistic, yet they suffered and feared further suffering. As German unemployment grew in the early 1930s, the longing for a radical solution to the nation's economic troubles was not confined to the unemployed. It also extended to millions of middle-class families like the Rüdiger's. Social unrest grew along with unemployment. 'You had to sign on every day at the dole office', remembers Alois Pfaller. 'Everybody met there, the Nazi people, the SPD, the Communists - and then the discussions would start and the fights.' Gabriele Winckler gives a young woman's perspective: 'You felt uneasy when you crossed the road, you felt uneasy when you were alone in the woods and so on. The unemployed lay in ditches and played cards.'

Adapted from Rees 1997.

Questions

1. a) Using Item 1 and your own knowledge explain what happened to the German economy in the period 1929-33.
   b) How did German governments cope with the economic problems they faced?
2. Using Items 2 and 3 and your own knowledge, describe the political impact of the economic crisis.

3. a) What does Item 3 tell us about life in Germany in the period 1929-33?
   b) To what extent were German governments to blame for the economic suffering experienced by people during this period?

2.2 What led to the rise and fall of Heinrich Brüning?

The Grand Coalition, 1928-30
It was noted in Section 1.2 above that, in the 1928 Reich election, 72.6% of the population voted for parties which supported the Republic. As in all elections held between 1919 and 1932, the SPD won the biggest number of seats. Unlike between November 1923 and June 1928, however, the SPD served in government as part of the Grand Coalition.

Although outwardly the creation of the Grand Coalition suggested political stability, there were underlying tensions from the start. Hiden (1996) identifies five underlying weaknesses:

1. The 'bourgeois' parties (the DDP, DVP and Centre Party) had lost significant numbers of votes in the 1928 election and, in response, moved to the right (it was after the election that Ludwig Kaas, a right-winger, became leader of the Centre Party, for example - see also Box 3.6 above).

2. There were growing class tensions between the SPD (which was put under pressure by the unions and its left wing to introduce measures beneficial to workers) and the DVP (which was supported by employers and became less inclined to compromise after Stresemann died).

3. The Grand Coalition was built on a 'Cabinet of personalities' - individuals who used their influence with their parties to gain sufficient support to ensure a majority in the Reichstag. The parties did not make formal agreements to support the government.

4. Although not in government, the DNVP (now under Hugenberg - see Section 1.2 above) worked to destabilise the government. Its campaign against the Young Plan (with the Nazis), in particular, gained the media spotlight.

5. Although the extreme parties on the left and right did not receive many votes in 1928, they made gains after the election.

The collapse of the Grand Coalition

The economic downturn, which began to bite while the Grand Coalition was in power, added to the instability and led eventually to the coalition's collapse in March 1930 after a split over unemployment benefit levels (the growing number of unemployed put an increasing strain on the government as it had to spend more and more on unemployment benefit - see also Section 2.1 above). According to Layton, of the five problems outlined above, the second proved the coalition's downfall - ie class interests:

'The SPD, as the representations of the trade unions, wanted to increase contributions [paid into the fund for unemployment benefit] and to maintain the level of welfare payments. The DVP, on the other hand, had strong ties with Big Business. It insisted on reducing benefits in order to cut costs and to balance the budget. In this situation, Müller [Leader of the SPD] resigned as Chancellor and was replaced by Heinrich Brüning, Leader of the Centre Party.' (Layton 1995, p.133)

Feuchtwanger (1995) points out that, although the level of unemployment benefit was the specific issue over which the Grand Coalition fell, support for the Young Plan had been the 'cement' holding the coalition together. It was only two weeks after the Young Plan had been agreed by the Reichstag that the coalition fell.

As noted in Section 2.1 above, the resignation of Müller had significant political consequences. Many historians argue that this was the event which paved the way to the Nazis' rise to power:

'The fall of the Social Democrat Chancellor Hermann Müller and his replacement by Heinrich Brüning of the Zentrum [Centre Party] was the first unnecessary step on the suicidal road of the Weimar Republic...It marked the beginning of the end for the

Weimar Republic.' (Kershaw 1998, pp.322-23)

The significance of Müller's resignation and whether he was in some way to blame for what happened afterwards are explored in Box 3.18.

BOX 3.18 Müller's resignation

(i) The political crisis which ended in Hitler's accession to power in January 1933 started in March 1930 when Heinrich Brüning was appointed Chancellor. Parliamentary government, properly so-called, ended with the fall of Müller. This was the case because when, on 28 March 1930, President Hindenburg appointed Heinrich

Hermann Müller

Brüning as Chancellor, it was made clear that the new Chancellor could rely on the President's emergency powers for the conduct of business, if the Reichstag failed to support him. This was the end of parliamentary government since under the new arrangement ('presidential government', as it was called), the balance of power shifted from the legislature (ie the Reichstag) to the executive (ie ministers and the President) where it had been in 1914.
Adapted from Carr 1991.

(ii) Before the Young Plan legislation was complete, Hindenburg gave the impression that he might allow the Müller government powers under Article 48 to put into place a financial package. As soon as the Young Plan laws had been accepted, however, it was made clear that the President would not grant Müller the use of Article 48, nor was he prepared to dissolve the Reichstag (ie call a new Reich election) at Müller's request. There can be no doubt about the widespread desire on the right, from Hindenburg downwards, to govern without the SPD. The President and his advisers were willing to grant a 'bourgeois' government (ie a government made up of the parties supported by the middle classes) what had just been denied to Müller, namely the use of Article 48 and the dissolution of the Reichstag. Müller's decision to resign is understandable, but, with hindsight, can be seen to have been a mistake of historic proportions. The SPD, still by far the largest party in the Reichstag, never recovered its position and soon its options became desperately narrow. Weimar politics could not function without a degree of cooperation between the SPD and the bulk of the bourgeois parties. This collaboration had now broken down.
Adapted from Feuchtwanger 1995.

Political intrigue

There is a consensus among historians that political intrigue played an important part in the downfall of the Weimar Republic. Most historians focus on the group of advisers around President Hindenburg, a group which included Hindenburg's son, Oskar, and General Kurt von Schleicher (see Box 3.17 above). Feuchtwanger argues that this group worked behind the scenes to engineer the downfall of Müller because its members were determined that there should be a shift to a more authoritarian (non-democratic) form of government. Brüning makes it clear in his memoirs that this was the plan (see Items 1 and 2 in Activity 3.5 below). That Müller's downfall was planned is clear, argues Feuchtwanger, from the fact that Brüning was able to put together his Cabinet so quickly:

'Brüning was able to present his Cabinet within three days of Müller's resignation, which confirmed the impression that it had been planned for some time.' (Feuchtwanger 1995, p.221)

Brüning's government

When Brüning became Chancellor, the parties belonging to his coalition (see Box 3.19) could gather just over 170 votes in the Reichstag. Since this was fewer votes than the combined total of the NSDAP, KPD and SPD (which came to 221 seats), the government needed the support of at least 52 DNVP MPs (the DNVP had 73 seats) if it was to gain a majority. Feuchtwanger argues that, for a few weeks, this was a possibility since not all deputies followed their Leader, Hugenberg, who had decided to oppose the government:

'Only about two-fifths of the DNVP's deputies followed Hugenberg's uncompromising line. This encouraged the hope that Brüning might after all be able to govern with a Reichstag majority and would not have to resort to Article 48, as he had threatened to do. Brüning's assumption of office on 20 March 1930 does not therefore mark the conclusive end of parliamentary government. This was only brought about by the further deepening of the financial crisis during the next few weeks.' (Feuchtwanger 1995, p.223)

When Brüning finally put his proposed financial package before the Reichstag in July 1930, a combination of the DNVP, SPD, KPD and NSDAP defeated it. Brüning immediately issued an emergency decree. The SPD then put forward a motion declaring that the emergency decree was unconstitutional. This motion was passed by 236 to 222 votes. Brüning (with Hindenburg's approval) then dissolved the Reichstag and reissued the emergency decree. Peukert argues that:

'Irrespective of whether this act was itself a breach of [the constitution] in a technical legal sense, it was clearly a fundamental attack on the basic principle that [gave life to] the constitution.' (Peukert 1991, p.258)

The election of September 1930

The election of September 1930 provided the Nazis with the electoral breakthrough they had been waiting for (see Box 3.20). From nowhere, the NSDAP became the second largest party, with 107 seats (see also Unit 4, Section 3.3). The SPD remained the largest party in the Reichstag with 143 seats. The DDP and DVP both lost seats. The DNVP lost almost half its seats. There is some debate over Brüning's decision to press for an election. On the one hand, Peukert argues that the dissolution of the Reichstag was both irresponsible and a deliberate step to replace parliamentary government with presidential government:

'The government was prepared to [dissolve] the Reichstag two years before the expiry of its full term, despite the fact that results in the Länder and local government elections in the preceding months pointed to an alarming surge in support for the National Socialists. The rise of the far left and right has subsequently been blamed on the weakness of Parliament, but this is to put the cart before the horse. Parliament was perfectly capable of effective action and could have continued to provide a clear majority in favour of democracy until 1932. It was

---

BOX 3.19	The composition of Brüning's government

First Brüning administration: 30 March 1930 – 7 October 1931 (presidential Cabinet)

Chancellor	Heinrich Brüning (Centre)
Vice Chancellor	Hermann Dietrich (DDP)
Foreign Minister	Julius Curtius (DVP)
Interior Minister	Josef Wirth (Centre)
Finance Minister	Paul Moldenhauer (DVP)
	Hermann Dietrich (DDP)
Economics	Hermann Dietrich (DDP)
	Ernst Trendelenburg (non-party)
Justice	Viktor Bredt (Business Party)
	Curt Joël (non-party) from Dec 1930
Defence	Wilhelm Groener (non-party)
Food	Martin Schiele (DNVP)
Posts	Georg Schätzel (BVP)
Labour	Adam Stegerwald (Centre)
Transport	Theodor von Guérard (Centre)
Occupied Areas	Gotfried Treviranus (KVP) to 30 September 1930
Without Portfolio	Gotfried Treviranus (KVP) from 1 October 1930

This table shows the composition of Brüning's government in March 1930. In June 1930, the DDP changed its name to the Deutsche Staatspartei (DStP). The KVP was a small party that broke away from the DNVP.

Adapted from Kirk 1995.

BOX 3.20 The elections of 1928 and 1930

Party	20 May 1928			14 September 1930		
	Total votes	%	No. MPs	Total votes	%	No. MPs
SPD Majority Socialists	9,153,000	29.8	153	8,577,700	24.5	143
KPD Communists	3,264,800	10.6	54	4,592,100	13.1	77
Centre Party	3,712,200	12.1	62	4,127,900	11.8	68
BVP Bavarian People's Party	945,600	3.0	16	1,059,100	3.0	19
DDP Democrats	1,505,700	4.9	25	1,322,400	3.8	20
DVP People's Party	2,679,700	8.7	45	1,578,200	4.5	30
Wirtschaftspartei Economy Party	1,397,100	4.5	23	1,362,400	3.9	23
Nationalists DNVP	4,381,600	14.2	73	2,458,300	7.0	41
NSDAP Nazis	810,100	2.6	12	6,409,600	18.3	107
Other Parties	2,903,500	9.2	28	3,724,300	10.5	49

This table shows how many seats parties won in the Reich elections of 1928 and 1930.
Adapted from Bullock 1991.

deliberately sidelined so that presidential rule could be imposed.' (Peukert 1991, pp.258-59)

On the other hand, Hiden suggests that Brüning had little option since the President and those close to him had decided to keep the SPD out of government (Hindenburg would only grant emergency powers to a government which did not include the SPD):

'In dissolving Parliament, Brüning opened the way for the staggering NSDAP electoral successes in the September elections. Those who have criticised his fateful decision and his subsequent reliance on Article 48 to govern by emergency decrees insist that he threw away other chances to secure a working majority...It might well have been asked, however, how long such a compromise would have lasted. Brüning was certainly constrained by the fact that President Hindenburg was only prepared, in the last resort, to back a rightist government with emergency powers.' (Hiden 1996, p.61)

Presidential government

Following the election of September 1930, the government increasingly bypassed the Reichstag and governed by presidential decrees issued under Article 48 of the constitution. Hiden points out that the Reichstag still did sometimes meet and pass Bills as it had done before March 1930, but, more and more, the government simply issued decrees which made proposals law without the approval of the Reichstag:

'Between 1930 and 1932, the Reichstag passed 29 relatively minor Bills, as opposed to 109 emergency decrees that were ratified [ie approved] by the President.' (Hiden 1996, p.67)

Burleigh argues that this change from 'parliamentary government' to 'presidential government' had serious consequences:

'Brüning's two years in power witnessed a steady atrophy [withering away] of parliamentary government. Each year, Parliament sat for fewer days - 94 in 1930, 42 in 1931 and 13 in 1932. The increasing resort to presidential emergency decrees marginalised the [Reichstag] and unelected senior civil servants who drafted these [decrees] gained in importance. Over time, this exceptional form of government, suspended between parliamentary democracy and authoritarianism, came to seem normal. But Brüning grew dangerously dependent on Hindenburg and the unelected group of power brokers which surrounded him.' (Burleigh 2000, p.124)

The SPD's policy of 'toleration'

The success of the extreme left and right in the election of September 1930 put the SPD in what Feuchtwanger (2001, p.109) describes as a 'no-win position'. Kept out of government, the party had to decide whether or not to oppose the government. If it continued to oppose the government, the government had no chance of winning a majority and that could mean the complete collapse of the Weimar system. If it supported the government, however, it risked alienating its own supporters since, given the make-up of the government and the economic crisis, the government was bound to introduce measures which undermined the position of workers. The SPD opted for a policy of 'toleration'. It would reluctantly support the government's issuing of emergency decrees. This ensured that another election (with further gains for the extreme right and left) was avoided in the short term. On the other hand, as Carr points out, by supporting presidential government, the SPD helped to undermine the democratic system that had been in place up to March 1930:

'After an agonising appraisal, the Socialists decided that Brüning was the lesser of two evils and, with their help, he survived a no-confidence motion. Some quarters praised the Socialists for a patriotic and statesmanlike act, others condemned them for betraying the working-class movement...One thing is certain. By tolerating Brüning and his use of [Article] 48, the Socialists enabled presidential government to function with a semblance of Reichstag support for the next two years; in effect Germany reverted to the pre-1914 situation where Chancellors consulted the majority parties from time to time but always retained in their own hands ultimate responsibility for policy.' (Carr 1991, p.300)

Brüning's aims and methods

It was noted in Section 2.1 above that there is some debate over Brüning's aims. Some historians have argued that he introduced presidential government because that was the only way to deal with the economic crisis. Others have argued that he was not interested in preserving the democratic nature of the Weimar Republic. Layton suggests that publication of Brüning's memoirs after his death in 1970 shows decisively that he had no desire to defend the Republic:

'[The memoirs] established beyond any reasonable doubt that [Brüning] was an arch-conservative and monarchist who had little sympathy with the democratic Republic. He stated that his aims in government were decisively to weaken the Reichstag and to re-establish a Bismarckian-type constitution with a more powerful executive which could ignore the power and influence of the political left. To these ends, he was prepared to use the emergency powers of the presidency and to look for backing from the traditional élites of German society.' (Layton 1995, p.134)

Box 3.21 examines Brüning's aims and methods.

The downfall of Brüning

Brüning owed his appointment as Chancellor to President Hindenburg and his close advisers. Historians agree that the same group was responsible for his downfall. In particular, many historians blame Schleicher for Brüning's fall. The following passage is typical:

'The resignation of Brüning in May [1932] was very largely the work of Schleicher. In the course of 1931 Schleicher changed his mind about Brüning, once it was clear that the latter had failed to rally moderate opinion in defence of the presidential system.' (Carr 1991, p.303)

The presidential election of 1932

Events in early 1932 undermined Brüning's position. The main issue was the presidential election which was due in March 1932. First, in January 1932, Brüning attempted to gain all-party support for a plan which would have changed the constitution, extending Hindenburg's term in office without holding an election. This plan, however, was rejected by the DNVP and the Nazis and so the election had to take place. Broszat argues that, although Brüning then campaigned tirelessly on Hindenburg's behalf, his failure to persuade the Reichstag to accept this plan annoyed the President:

'[This] lay at the root of the later "ingratitude" shown by the "old gentleman" to his Chancellor. Hindenburg was deeply angered that Brüning had not succeeded in getting at least Hugenberg...to support his re-election. Instead the President was forced to rely on political forces, above all the Catholics and SPD, about which he had the gravest reservations.' (Broszat 1987, pp.108-09)

In the first round of voting in the presidential election, held on 13 March 1932, Hindenburg narrowly missed an overall majority. As a result, a second round was held on 10 April. On this occasion, Hindenburg won

---

BOX 3.21 Brüning's aims and methods

(i) Governing without Parliament for months on end, Brüning's style of government became increasingly dictatorial. He allied himself with two or three dozen ministers, top civil servants and a few experts. From the peak of the crisis in the summer of 1931, he became more and more intolerant of criticisms voiced by the political parties, pressure groups and the Länder. He was increasingly inclined to place ever greater restrictions on the population, confident that there was no alternative to following the course he had set. As the criticism mounted, he remained unwavering about the wisdom and morality of his policies. This inflexibility was one reason for his downfall in 1932.
Adapted from Broszat 1987.

(ii) Two points are worth stressing. First, whatever his motives and however limited his room for manoeuvre, Brüning's aims were essentially authoritarian. The removal of the Reichstag from the business of government and the restriction of the Länder's freedom of action were not accidental or unfortunate side effects of genuine attempts to preserve Weimar democracy. After the collapse of the Müller government, it was clear that there would be no going back to the political system that existed before March 1930. And second, during his period as Chancellor, Brüning's focus was very much on foreign policy, in particular, the goal of freeing Germany from reparations. For Brüning, harsh emergency measures were not only a way of coping with an economic crisis of huge proportions, nor were his policies only an attempt to use the crisis to achieve constitutional reform. They were also designed to demonstrate to the Allies that the burden of reparations was intolerable and that the burden should be lifted.
Adapted from Bessel 1997.

---

comfortably, though Hitler's 13 million votes were enough for him to claim a moral victory (see Unit 4, Section 3.2). The results of the presidential election are shown in Box 3.22.

The banning of the SA

On 13 April 1932, in response to pressure from the Länder which were due to hold elections on 24 April, an emergency decree was issued banning the NSDAP's paramilitary wing, the SA. This, Kolb argues, was a key factor in explaining the downfall of Brüning's government. By the beginning of May, Schleicher had come to the conclusion that it was necessary to set up a government which would be tolerated by the Nazis and he was able to use the promise of a lifting of the ban as a bargaining chip:

'Undoubtedly, the ban was the principal milestone on the way to Brüning's dismissal, as the NSDAP, backed by other rightist forces, stepped up agitation

BOX 3.22 | The results of the presidential election

Presidential Election, 1932 (votes in millions)

	1st Round (13 March)	2nd Round (10 April)
Adolf Hitler	11.340	13.420
Paul von Hindenburg	18.650	19.360
Ernst Thälmann	4.980	3.710
Others	2.720	0.005

This table shows the result of the two rounds in the presidential election of 1932.
Adapted from Kirk 1995.

against the government...[From the beginning of May], Schleicher conspired with the NSDAP against Groener [Defence Minister] and Brüning, with the object of bringing down the latter's government and replacing it with a presidential regime further to the right and tolerated by the NSDAP.' (Kolb 1988, pp.117-18)

Elections in the Länder, 24 April 1932

On 24 April elections duly took place in the Länder. The results of these elections showed that the NSDAP had made big gains, almost doubling the support they received in September 1930. Feuchtwanger argues that these results undermined Brüning's position:

'Brüning's calculation that his disastrous dissolution of the Reichstag in 1930 had at least given more time for his policies to achieve results was largely proved illusory by these elections. They rammed it home that his government no longer represented the will of the people. They could only confirm Hindenburg, Schleicher and others in their view that it was high time to replace Brüning with a more right-wing government.' (Feuchtwanger 1995, p.271)

Brüning's proposed land reform

The final straw was Brüning's proposal to break up some estates that had fallen into debt in East Prussia and to resettle 600,000 unemployed people on them. This proposal was vigorously opposed by large landowners. Their leading spokesperson, Elard von Oldenburg-Januschau, went to see President Hindenburg and persuaded him not to sign the necessary emergency decree:

'Land-owning circles got wind of this [proposal] and...Oldenburg-Januschau visited Hindenburg at Neudeck and easily persuaded the disgruntled President that Brüning was an "agrarian bolshevik" bent on socialising agriculture. When Brüning appeared with new emergency decrees, the old man refused to sign.' (Carr 1991, pp.303-04)

When Hindenburg refused to sign the emergency decrees, on 30 May, Brüning was forced to resign. Peukert argues that Brüning 'eroded' his own position and was, therefore, to blame for his downfall:

'The more impotent Parliament became, the less need there was for a middleman of his sort. The more deeply his...reforms cut into the bureaucracy, the more he forfeited the loyalty of the officials who had to implement them. As a settlement of the reparations issue drew closer, there was less need for a Brüning figure...And the longer the economic crisis continued, the nearer came the inevitable moment when the man responsible for the unpopular [policies] would be discharged.' (Peukert 1991, p.263)

Brüning's fall a turning point?

Some historians argue that Brüning's fall, rather than his appointment as Chancellor, was a turning point since Brüning had absolutely no intention of allowing the Nazis to play a part in government. Hiden, for example, argues that:

'Whilst there may still be arguments about the significance of Brüning's appointment for the fate of the Republic, many agree that his fall removed the last restraints on the NSDAP in the sense that his successors were preoccupied to a greater or lesser degree with bringing Hitler to the centre of the stage rather than countering his appeal.' (Hiden 1996, p.68)

MAIN POINTS - Section 2.2

- The Grand Coalition had five weaknesses - (1) the bourgeois parties moved to the right (2) there were class tensions between the SPD and DVP (3) it was a 'Cabinet of individuals' (4) the DNVP campaigned against the government (5) the extreme left and right made gains after the 1928 Reich election.
- The Grand Coalition fell in March 1930. Historians agree this was a turning point since it meant the start of 'presidential government' - government by emergency decree without the support of the Reichstag - under Brüning.
- When Brüning's financial package was rejected by the Reichstag, he issued an emergency decree, dissolved the Reichstag and then reissued the decree.

- Some historians argue that this was unconstitutional and irresponsible. Others argue that he had little choice.
- After the election of September 1930, the SPD adopted a policy of 'toleration'. To avoid a further election (and further gains for the extreme left and right), it reluctantly supported the government.
- Brüning's failure to win an extension to Hindenburg's presidency without an election was partly to blame for his downfall (which was engineered by Schleicher). The election results in the Länder in April 1932 were also a factor, but the final straw was a 'mildly reflationary' economic package.

Activity 3.5 Brüning's rise and fall

ITEM 1 A meeting in the spring of 1929

In the spring of 1929, before the economic crash, in a time of seeming calm and
stability, Schleicher invited Brüning to his house. The general then made suggestions
which seemed to invite a coup. The constitution, said Schleicher, must be revised to
clip the wings of the Reichstag and bring back the 'stable conditions' of the
unreformed monarchy of the pre-October 1918 days. Not only should the head of state
have the power to appoint the Chancellor, but he must also have the power to keep him
in office, against the will of the Reichstag, if needs be. This would keep the Reichstag in its
place and prevent it from interfering with policy making, as in the good old days of the
monarchy. This scheme might require frequent dissolutions of the Reichstag, until the

Heinrich von Brüning

parties grew so tired and financially exhausted that they stopped holding elections. And then, in one of those periods
without a Reichstag, the constitution could be changed, bringing into being a purely presidential system in which the
President would play the role of the former Emperor. Brüning was interested. He asked Schleicher how long he thought
all this would take. Schleicher replied that it should be possible to do it in half a year. Schleicher also confided that the
President had a liking to him, the loyal front-line officer whose machine-gun company had fought with distinction to
the very end, and that Hindenburg was considering entrusting him with the task of carrying out such a coup.

Adapted from Haffner 1989.

ITEM 2 Brüning's memoirs, December 1929

After the meal, Schleicher and Meissner (Chief of President Hindenburg's staff) began to make it clear to me that the
President was in no way inclined to leave in office the Müller Cabinet once the Young Plan was settled and that he
expected me not to ignore his pleas. I set out the reasons why I believed the Müller Cabinet must remain in office under
all circumstances until late autumn. Meissner countered by explaining that I would not succeed in convincing the
President of my view. Hermann Müller would be toppled and his successor would get powers under Article 48 in the
event of emergency. I repeated the comments I had made to Schleicher eight months earlier, pointing out that in the
summer of 1929 a talk had taken place on my initiative between Kaas (Leader of the Centre Party) and Hugenberg
(Leader of the DNVP). It had been agreed then that Hugenberg would form a government with the Centre Party in the
autumn of 1930 in the event of the collapse of the Müller Cabinet. Hugenberg had agreed to this, though it would now
be difficult for him to enter a government so soon after the acceptance of the Young Plan (which he had campaigned
against). Groener (the Defence Minister in Müller's Cabinet), Schleicher and Meissner replied by stating that there was no
question of an appointment for Hugenberg, even in the autumn. The President did not want this man. I said that I would
never avoid an unpleasant duty, even if I had no desire in the normal course of events to be a minister. Groener tried to
make it plain to me that he had decisive influence over Hindenburg and that he knew the President would stand behind
me to the last. He asked me to think over the matter and to go out with him alone one Sunday to talk things over calmly.

Adapted from Brüning's memoirs which were published after his death in 1970. The conversation described took place in December 1929.

ITEM 3 Brüning's fall

The immediate causes of Brüning's fall were entirely political. Not having received a mandate from the Reichstag and still
less from the electorate, he was dependent on the good-will of his real supporters - President Hindenburg and the army.
By 1932, Schleicher was disappointed that Brüning had not overcome the opposition of the Nationalists and had to rely
on the SPD for support in the Reichstag. He also wanted to see the SPD removed from their position of power in the
Prussian government. At the same time, Hindenburg - his mind burdened by the constant complaints of his nationalist
friends - was beginning to lose confidence in his Chancellor. The presidential election campaign revealed an extraordinary
reversal of political roles since the previous contest in 1925. Then, it had been the parties of the right which had
supported Hindenburg. The Weimar Coalition parties - DDP, DVP and the Catholic Centre - provided his most serious
opposition. In 1932, however, the vast majority of votes for Hindenburg came from these parties and the SPD.
Hindenburg won, but the result reinforced the charge made by the DNVP that Hindenburg had sold his soul to the anti-
German forces of Marxism and the Pope. Brüning was the man held responsible for having put the President in such a
false position. Following the presidential election, Hindenburg was then disturbed by Brüning's plans for land reform in
East Germany while Schleicher became convinced he could make a deal with the Nazis. The Nazis would support a new
right-wing government in return for new elections and the repeal of a ban on the SA which the Brüning government had
finally imposed after a long period of violence.

Adapted from Nicholls 1979.

1. 'The appointment of Brüning meant the death of the Weimar Republic'. Using Items 1 and 2 and your own knowledge, give arguments for and against this view.
2. a) What do Items 1 and 2 tell us about the nature of politics in Germany in the early 1930s?

b) What do these items tell us about the role played by Schleicher?
3. Using Item 3 and your own knowledge, explain why Brüning was unable to hang on to power in May 1932.

2.3 What were the aims of Papen and Schleicher in the eight months following Brüning's resignation?

The meeting of 8 May 1930

On 8 May 1930, Schleicher met Hitler secretly and the two men made a deal. Schleicher would ensure that the ban on the SA was lifted and that elections were held. In return, the Nazis would support a new government:

'On 8 May 1932 [Schleicher] held discussions with Hitler and arrived at what he called an "agreement": Schleicher undertook that the Brüning government would be dismissed, the ban on the SA lifted, the Reichstag dissolved and a new one elected, while Hitler promised that he would not oppose a nationalist presidential government.' (Kolb 1988, p.120)

Schleicher fulfilled his part of the deal. By the end of the month, Brüning had been dismissed, the ban on the SA was lifted and elections set for 31 July 1932 (the last date possible under Article 25 of the constitution). Despite Hitler's promise, however, the NSDAP remained in opposition to the new government.

Papen's government

Whilst the reality was that Brüning relied on the support of the President (not the Reichstag) to remain in power, the SPD's policy of toleration maintained the fiction that the Reichstag (not the President) was the Chancellor's source of power. Under Papen, however, because the Nazis refused to support the government, there was no attempt to conceal the government's reliance on the President. According to Feuchtwanger, Schleicher's aim was that:

'A purely presidential Cabinet would be formed, free of party ties, in which Schleicher himself as Defence Minister would wield the main influence.' (Feuchtwanger 1995, p.280)

The composition of this Cabinet is outlined in Box 3.23. It had little support in the Reichstag and, crucially, no electoral base:

'Papen enjoyed the confidence of Hindenburg and his entourage...and could properly regard himself as [the] representative of the old élites, employers

BOX 3.23 | The composition of Papen's government

Papen administration: 1 June - 3 December 1932 (presidential Cabinet)

Chancellor	Franz von Papen (non-party) from 3 June 1932
Foreign Minister	Konstantin Freiherr von Neurath (non-party)
Interior Minister	Wilhelm Freiherr von Gayl (DNVP)
Finance Minister	Johann Ludwig Graf Schwerin von Krosigk (non-party)
Economics	Hermann Warmbold (non-party)
Justice	Franz Gürtner (DNVP)
Defence	Kurt von Schleicher (non-party)
Food	Magnus Freiherr von Braun (DNVP)
Posts	Paul Freiherr Wltz von Rübenach (non-party)
Labour	Hugo Schäffer (non-party)
Transport	Paul Freiherr Wltz von Rübenach (non-party)
Eastern aid	Magnus Freiherr von Braun (DNVP)
Without Portfolio	Franz Bracht (non-party)
	Johannes Popitz (non-party) from 29 October 1932

None of the members of Papen's Cabinet were members of the Reichstag. Some were members of the DNVP, but they left the party to emphasise their non-party position. Even more never had any party ties. Four ministers continued to hold the same position under Hitler.

Adapted from Feuchtwanger 1995 and Kirk 1995.

and large landowners. But he lacked the one thing indispensable in modern politics [-] a popular following.' (Peukert 1991, p.264)

As a result, Papen's government was highly unpopular from the start:

'A storm of disapproval greeted this government of "national concentration" which represented the interests of businessmen and landowners so blatantly that contemporaries dubbed it "the Cabinet of Barons". The left was automatically against Papen; the centre bitterly hostile to the man who had ousted Brüning; even the nationalists were annoyed because Papen had been preferred to Hugenberg...Clearly there was no hope of the Reichstag's "tolerating" Papen as it "tolerated" Brüning.' (Carr 1991, p.304)

Papen's aims

Papen made no pretence that he supported the democratic principles which underlay the Weimar constitution. His government supported a non-democratic 'New State', similar to that created by Benito Mussolini and his fascists in Italy. A key feature of Italian fascism was 'corporatism' - the reorganisation of businesses into corporations which did away with trade unions and were controlled by employers:

'[Papen] looked towards the Italian fascist model of "corporatism" to create a "New State": a nationalist, authoritarian and an anti-parliamentarian regime run by conservative élites.' (Layton 1995, p.143)

Feuchtwanger (1995) argues that the Papen government never had a chance of realising such ambitions because it lacked any popular support. Layton argues that his aims 'showed no real grasp of political realities'.

The Prussian coup

Throughout the period 1924 to 1932, Prussia was governed by a coalition of the SPD and Centre Party. In the elections on 24 April 1932, however, the growth in support for the Nazis ensured that the coalition lost its majority. Feuchtwanger argues that the possibility that the SPD/Centre coalition would be replaced by a NSDAP/Centre coalition - which might have given the Nazis control over the Prussian police (which was by far the biggest police force in Germany) - led Brüning to make plans for a possible takeover.

Brüning did not act before his resignation on 30 May, but his successor did. On 20 July 1932, three days after a bloody street fight between Nazis and Communists in Hamburg, Papen declared that there was a state of emergency in Prussia. He suspended the Prussian government and appointed himself Reich Commissioner in charge of Prussian affairs. As Broszat points out:

'It was quite obvious that the constitution had been breached.' (Broszat 1987, p.119)

Despite this, there was no resistance to Papen's action. The elected Prussian government and officials appointed by it simply gave in. There were no protests on the streets and no general strike;

'The question of whether Papen's Prussian coup could or should have been resisted has been hotly debated. In retrospect, it looks like the last occasion when a show of force on behalf of the Republic and of democracy might have been possible. The main weapon would have had to have been a general strike, which had helped to

defeat the Kapp Putsch in 1920. Twelve years later, with a third of the German labour force unemployed, this was a blunt weapon. The word to use it...was never given.' (Feuchtwanger 1995, p.287)

Consequences of the Prussian coup

The consequences of Papen's 'Prussian coup' were severe. In the short term, there was a purge of liberal and SPD supporters:

'Almost everywhere in Prussia Social Democrat or left-liberal police presidents or regional administrators were replaced by conservative civil servants.' (Broszat 1987, p.121)

In the longer term, Papen paved the way to the Nazi dictatorship since, on gaining power, the Nazis followed his example and simply seized control of the remaining Länder (see Unit 5, Section 1.2).

The election of 31 July 1932

The Reich election of 31 July 1932 followed the trend set by the election held in 1930 (see Box 3.24). The Nazis made huge gains while support for the 'bourgeois' parties slumped. The Centre Party and BVP held their ground. On the left, the SPD still gained substantial support, though it lost 600,000 votes to the KPD. Feuchtwanger argues that the gains made by the KPD were important:

'The chief effect of the Communist success now and in the next election was not to increase the real threat of a revolutionary coup, but to increase the fear of it and the exploitation of that fear.' (Feuchtwanger 1995, p.289)

BOX 3.24	The Reich elections of July and November 1932					
	31 July 1932			6 November 1932		
Party	Total votes	%	No. MPs	Total votes	%	No. MPs
SPD Majority Socialists	7,959,700	21.6	133	7,248,000	20.4	121
KPD Communists	5,282,600	14.6	89	5,980,200	16.9	100
Centre Party	4,589,300	12.5	75	4,230,600	11.9	70
BVP Bavarian People's Party	1,192,700	3.2	22	1,094,600	3.1	20
DDP Democrats	371,800	1.0	4	336,500	1.0	2
DVP People's Party	436,000	1.2	7	661,800	1.9	11
Wirtschaftspartei Economy Party	146,900	0.4	2	110,300	0.3	1
Nationalists DNVP	2,177,400	5.9	37	2,959,000	8.8	52
NSDAP Nazis	13,745,800	37.4	230	11,737,000	33.1	196
Other Parties	1,119,300	2.8	9	1,526,100	4.4	11

This table shows the election results in July and November 1932.
Adapted from Kirk 1995.

Key dates - 13 August and 12 September

On 13 August 1932, Papen met Hitler and offered his party seats in the Cabinet and the Vice Chancellorship for Hitler. Hitler refused to accept anything less than the Chancellorship for himself. He repeated this demand to Hindenburg at a meeting later that day and was rebuffed (see also Unit 4, Section 3.2). This meeting was of significance for two reasons.

First, Broszat argues that anger at this rebuttal was behind Hitler's decision to support the KPD motion of no-confidence in the government which was proposed on 12 September at a meeting of the Reichstag. Papen had planned to avoid the vote by dissolving the Reichstag again. But a Nazi, Hermann Göring, had been elected President of the Reichstag on 30 August and he refused to let the Chancellor issue the decree of dissolution before the vote went ahead:

'The desire to take revenge on Papen was behind a move which the Nazis made on September 12...The vote ended with a shattering defeat for Papen. Only 42 deputies supported his Cabinet, with 512 voting against him. There was no more telling proof that the "Cabinet of the Barons" lacked completely in political and social support. With the exception of the DVP and DNVP, all parties were keen to demonstrate this to Papen and therefore voted for the motion.' (Broszat 1987, p.127)

The second reason why the meeting with Hitler on 13 August was important is outlined in Box 3.25.

The Reich election of 6 November 1932

The final stages of the election campaign leading up to the election of 6 November 1932 were dominated by a transport strike in Berlin. To the alarm of many people, this strike was supported by both the Nazis and the KPD:

'The example [of this strike] could be used in support of alarmist arguments about the dangers of a simultaneous uprising from the extremes of right and left. It could also be used in support of the [view] that a decline of the Nazis would principally benefit the Communists and that it had therefore become urgent to bring about the long-delayed "taming" and inclusion of Hitler in the government.' (Feuchtwanger 1995, pp.297-98)

The results of the Reich election of 6 November 1932 did show a reduction in support for the NSDAP. Whilst the Nazis lost 2 million votes, the DNVP gained nearly 800,000 votes and the KPD gained 700,000 votes. Although, research now shows, the KPD's gains came mainly from the SPD, many commentators leapt to the conclusion that they came from the NSDAP. This added to the climate of fear:

'The rise of the KPD vote was simplistically and

BOX 3.25 | Papen's plans after 13 August 1932

After the meeting with Hitler on 13 August 1932, Papen was determined to end parliamentary rule altogether. At the end of August he submitted a plan to Hindenburg which laid down that fresh elections should be postponed for more than the 60 days allowed by Article 25 of the constitution. He accepted that such a postponement would be a breach of the constitution. There was talk of holding a referendum to authorise the long-term dissolution of the Reichstag, but there was recognition that the narrow popular base of the Cabinet would give the government little chance of winning a referendum. Hindenburg appears to have supported Papen's plan and he issued Papen with a decree that he could use at any convenient point to dissolve the Reichstag. Papen made a serious mistake when he failed to attend the first meeting of the new Reichstag on 30 August. At that meeting, the Reichstag voted for the date of the next meeting to be set by the new President of the Reichstag, Hermann Göring. If Papen had attended and dissolved the Reichstag on 30 August, he would have avoided the meeting of the Reichstag on 12 September when Göring allowed the vote of no-confidence to go ahead. As it was, the overwhelming vote of no-confidence ensured that the chance of governing with new elections indefinitely postponed vanished. He was forced to call new elections for 6 November.

Adapted from Broszat 1987 and Feuchtwanger 1995.

falsely seen to be related to the drop in the NSDAP vote and it was feared that this process might go much further.' (Feuchtwanger 1995, p.298)

Papen's resignation

Following the election, Papen tried and failed to persuade the Nazis to join his Cabinet. Having failed, he resigned on 17 November:

'This was purely a tactical manoeuvre for he fully expected Hindenburg to reinstate himself in office as Hitler was still insisting adamantly on being Chancellor in a presidential Cabinet.' (Carr 1991, p.306)

On 19 November, Hindenburg asked Hitler to form a government with a parliamentary majority:

'This was calling Hitler's bluff. Hindenburg knew that it would be impossible, given the certain opposition of the DNVP. The outcome would have been the exposure of Hitler's failure and a weakening of his position. Hitler saw through the tactic straightaway.' (Kershaw 1998, p.393)

Hitler, Kershaw claims, requested a presidential Cabinet with the same powers as that exercised by Papen, but Hindenburg refused. Negotiations continued until the end of the month with neither side giving way:

'On 30 November, [Hitler] rejected as pointless a further invitation to discussions with Hindenburg. The deadlock continued.' (Kershaw 1998, p.395)

Box 3.26 examines the difficulties facing Hindenburg after the November election.

BOX 3.26 | **The difficulties facing Hindenburg**

President Hindenburg

From the time of Brüning's resignation, the aim of the non-Nazi key political players was to find a way of 'taming' Hitler. Ideally, they wanted Hitler to join the Cabinet as Vice Chancellor. This would provide the Cabinet with a popular base but prevent Hitler from directing policy. Hitler was well aware that his hands would be tied and that explains why he resisted all approaches which would mean settling with less than the powers enjoyed by Papen. Following the November election, the crisis was no nearer solution than it had been after the election held in July. The Nazis were still the largest party in the Reichstag and Hitler was still refusing to take any post in a Cabinet except that of Chancellor. Papen could attempt to stay in office, but sooner or later this would require a breach of the constitution. If that happened, there was a serious chance of civil war. The problem would not be substantially different if presidential government continued with another non-Nazi Chancellor. The irony was that the election result and the distribution of seats in the Reichstag were still important even though the Reichstag had, for months, been unable to function and most people agreed that the Weimar parliamentary regime was finished. All the philosophising about a 'New State' could not get round the fact that in 1932 a modern industrial society could not be governed without popular consent.

Adapted from Feuchtwanger 1995.

Schleicher's 'Diagonal Front'

Hitler's refusal to budge from his stance of 'all or nothing' forced Hindenburg to turn again to Papen. But, by the beginning of December, Papen no longer had the support of Schleicher:

'Papen re-emerged from the wings, this time with a new plan. He proposed to declare martial law, dissolve the Reichstag, postpone elections and rule by decree until the constitution had been amended along authoritarian lines and a reflationary programme given time to work. Hindenburg was willing enough to support Papen in this, but Schleicher was not.' (Carr 1991, pp.306-07)

Historians agree that, by the beginning of December, Schleicher had come to the conclusion that the way out of the political crisis was to create a 'Diagonal Front':

'This was an attempt to create a more broadly based government by splitting the Nazis and attracting the socialist wing of the NSDAP and by gaining the support from the trade unions with a programme of public works.' (Layton 1995, p.143)

The key to this plan was Gregor Strasser. At a meeting with Papen and Hindenburg on 1 December, Schleicher claimed that about 60 Nazi deputies would support the government if Strasser was given the post of Vice Chancellor:

'Strasser and one or two of his supporters would be offered places in the government. About 60 Nazi deputies could be won over. Schleicher was confident of gaining the support of the trade unions, the SPD and the bourgeois parties for a package of economic reforms and work creation. This, he claimed, would [avoid] the need for the overturning of the constitution which Papen had again proposed.' (Kershaw 1998, p. 395)

Schleicher becomes Chancellor

On 1 December, Hindenburg rejected Schleicher's plan. But, at a meeting of the Cabinet the following day, Schleicher forced Hindenburg's hand by claiming that Papen's planned breach of the constitution would lead to a crisis with which the army would be unable to cope:

'He informed the Cabinet that Papen's policy would lead to civil war, a general strike and a probably a Polish invasion; to defend Germany against several perils simultaneously was simply beyond the Reichswehr's capacity.' (Carr 1991, p.307)

Historians agree that Papen was Hindenburg's favourite and that it was only with reluctance that he finally decided not to reappoint him Chancellor. However, Schleicher's warning that Papen's plan would lead to civil war was decisive. Schleicher was appointed Chancellor and immediately set about building his 'Diagonal Front'.

Schleicher in power

According to Kershaw, Schleicher held a secret meeting with Gregor Strasser on 3 December 1932:

'At a meeting held in secret in Berlin on 3 December, Schleicher offered Strasser the posts of Vice Chancellor and Minister President in Prussia...That [the meeting] had produced the offer of the Vice Chancellorship to the second man in the party, who had not turned it down, only became clear to Hitler and other leading figures in the party, it seems, when they gathered for discussion...two days later.' (Kershaw 1998, p.399)

At this meeting, there were 'heated exchanges' between Hitler and Strasser. According to Fest (1974, p.354), a second meeting then took place on 7 December, with Hitler accusing Strasser of going behind his back and committing an act of treason. As Kershaw points out, Strasser now had three choices:

- to back Hitler
- to rebel against him and to try to split the party
- to resign.

On 8 December, Strasser took the third option. He wrote a letter to Hitler resigning all offices and then promptly went on holiday.

For Schleicher, this was a major blow since one of the main planks of his strategy had collapsed. He

---

BOX 3.27 The composition of Schleicher's government

Schleicher Cabinet: 3 December 1932 - 30 January 1933 (presidential Cabinet)

Chancellor	Kurt von Schleicher (non-party)
Foreign Minister	Konstantin Freiherr von Neurath (non-party)
Interior Minister	Franz Bracht (non-party)
Finance Minister	Johann Ludwig Graf Schwerin von Krosigk (non-party)
Economics	Hermann Warmbold (non-party)
Justice	Franz Gürtner (DNVP)
Defence	Kurt von Schleicher (non-party)
Food	Magnus Freiherr von Braun (DNVP)
Posts	Paul Freiherr Wltz von Rübenach (non-party)
Labour	Friedrich Syrup (non-party)
Transport	Paul Freiherr Wltz von Rübenach (non-party)
Eastern aid	Günther Gereke (Christliches Landvolk)*
Without Portfolio	Johannes Popitz (non-party)

* A small group that had broken away from the DNVP.

This table shows the composition of Schleicher's government in December 1932.
Adapted from Kirk 1995.

---

was now forced to put together a Cabinet which did not include any members of the NSDAP. The composition of this Cabinet is outlined in Box 3.27. Schleicher was then equally unsuccessful in winning over the left. Furthermore, his attempt to win support from the left lost him the support of conservatives. By Christmas 1932, his plans were in tatters:

'Schleicher approached the left with a programme of public works, price-fixing, restoration of wage- and relief-cuts and land resettlement in East Prussia, measures which naturally turned the right wing against him. But he could not overcome the mistrust of Socialists and Centrists.' (Carr 1991, p.307)

The meeting of 4 January 1933

On 4 January 1933, Hitler travelled to Cologne for what was meant to be a secret meeting with Papen (they were, in fact, photographed arriving at the venue and the photo appeared in a newspaper the following day). Historians agree that the meeting took place on Papen's initiative. Most believe that Papen's motive for meeting with Hitler was, in part at least, to take revenge on Schleicher who, Papen believed, had betrayed him in December 1932 when he refused to back him as Chancellor. The following analysis is typical:

'Papen, it is known, took the initiative. It has rightly been emphasised that his growing activity from mid-December onwards was largely due to wounded ambition and a desire for revenge: he could not forgive his former friend Schleicher for having brought his Chancellorship to an end.' (Kolb 1988, pp.123-24)

According to Broszat, the first part of the meeting dealt with events in the past. Papen blamed Schleicher for Hindenburg's refusal, on August 13 1932, to appoint Hitler as Chancellor. Then, to gain Hitler's confidence, he told him all about Schleicher's part in his own downfall in December. Having made it clear that the President would listen to him sympathetically, Papen then explored the possibility of setting up a Cabinet in which he and Hitler would work closely together. Hitler, Broszat suggests, responded positively, playing down his demands:

'Probably Hitler also repeated what he had assured the Reich President in November: he did not wish to gain total power. All he desired was the Chancellorship. He was quite agreeable to Hindenburg appointing a Foreign Minister and a Reichswehr [Defence] Minister of his own choice.' (Broszat 1987, p.132)

Schleicher's downfall

The three weeks following the meeting between Papen and Hitler were full of secret meetings and frantic negotiations. Broszat (1987) argues that the key events were as follows.

9 January

Papen meets Schleicher and informs him of his meeting with Hitler. On the surface at least, the meeting is friendly. Papen then visits Hindenburg and gives him an account of the meeting. Hindenburg approves of Papen's initiative and encourages him to seek a new coalition with Hitler.

10 January

A Reichstag committee begins to examine charges that government funds had been used fraudulently by large landowners. Later that night, Hitler meets Papen.

11 January

The organisation representing landowners (the Reichlandsbung) lobbies Hindenburg and attacks the Schleicher government. At the meeting, Hindenburg snubs Schleicher by contradicting him in public.

14 January

Schleicher refuses to bring the DNVP into his government (since it would alienate the unions and end his hopes of creating a Diagonal Front).

17 January

Hitler meets Hugenberg, Leader of the DNVP, to discuss a possible coalition. The meeting is frosty. Hitler also meets Papen.

19-20 January

Papen meets Hindenburg and puts the case for a Cabinet headed by Hitler for the first time. He argues that he could ensure there were sufficient safeguards against a Hitler dictatorship. Hindenburg and his son, Oskar, both dislike the idea. Papen persuades Oskar to meet Hitler.

20 January

It is announced that the next meeting of the Reichstag will take place on 31 January.

21 January

The DNVP, which, up to this point, has been seen as supportive of the Schleicher government, makes an attack on the economic policies being pursued.

22 January

Hitler meets Oskar Hindenburg secretly and they talk for two hours. Oskar is impressed.

23 January

Schleicher meets with President Hindenburg. He is forced to admit he has been unable to build a coalition and that he faces a vote of no-confidence on 31 January. Schleicher proposes that the Reichstag be dissolved and elections postponed beyond 60 days (ie the same plan Papen proposed and Schleicher rejected, claiming on 2 December it would lead to civil war). Hindenburg makes it clear that he is not prepared to breach the constitution.

27 January

Hitler meets with Hugenberg, but negotiations break down.

28 January

An old friend of the President, Oldenburg-Januschau, reassures him that the Nazis are not really as bad as they seem. Papen then meets Hindenburg and gets the impression he is considering a Hitler Chancellorship for the first time. Hindenburg meets Schleicher and accepts his resignation. Papen meets Hindenburg again. Hindenburg says it is his duty to appoint Hitler Chancellor with the same powers that Papen had when he was Chancellor.

29 January

Papen negotiates with the Nazis and DNVP, eventually gaining agreement for a Cabinet which includes Hitler as Chancellor, Papen as Vice Chancellor and Hugenberg as Minister for the Economy and Agriculture.

30 January

Hindenburg swears in the members of the new Cabinet. The Cabinet contains three Nazis and nine conservatives.

MAIN POINTS - Section 2.3

- Under Papen, there was no attempt to conceal the government's reliance on the President. The Papen government lacked support in the Reichstag and a popular base. It governed by emergency decree.
- In July 1932, the Reich government took over the Prussian government, Papen appointing himself Reich Commissioner. There was no resistance to this move. The takeover provided a model for the Nazi seizure of power.
- Hitler's meeting with Papen and Hindenburg on 13 August 1932 was important because - (1) a vote of no-confidence went ahead on 12 September and (2) Papen, with Hindenburg's support, decided to govern without the Reichstag, but was forced to hold further elections after the vote of no-confidence.
- Following the election in November 1932, Papen resigned. Negotiations between Hindenburg and Hitler resulted in stalemate. In early December, Schleicher was appointed Chancellor.
- Schleicher's attempt to build a 'Diagonal Front' failed. On 4 January, Papen met Hitler. The three weeks following this meeting were full of secret meetings and frantic negotiations. On 28 January, Schleicher resigned. On 30 January, Hitler became Chancellor.

Activity 3.6 Why did the Weimar Republic fail to survive the crisis of 1929-33?

ITEM 1 Criticisms of single-cause explanations

(i)

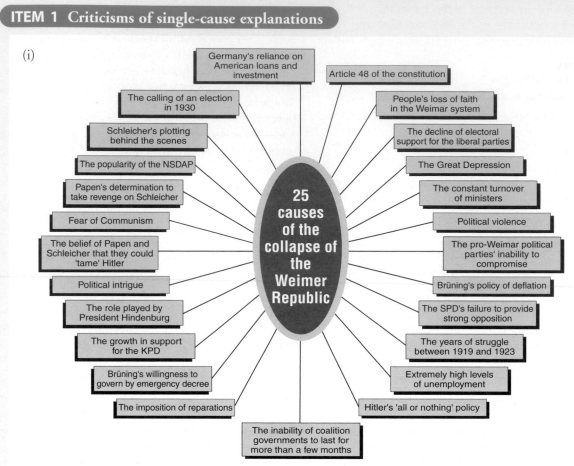

25 causes of the collapse of the Weimer Republic

- Germany's reliance on American loans and investment
- The calling of an election in 1930
- Schleicher's plotting behind the scenes
- The popularity of the NSDAP
- Papen's determination to take revenge on Schleicher
- Fear of Communism
- The belief of Papen and Schleicher that they could 'tame' Hitler
- Political intrigue
- The role played by President Hindenburg
- The growth in support for the KPD
- Brüning's willingness to govern by emergency decree
- The imposition of reparations
- The inability of coalition governments to last for more than a few months
- Article 48 of the constitution
- People's loss of faith in the Weimar system
- The decline of electoral support for the liberal parties
- The Great Depression
- The constant turnover of ministers
- Political violence
- The pro-Weimar political parties' inability to compromise
- Brüning's policy of deflation
- The SPD's failure to provide strong opposition
- The years of struggle between 1919 and 1923
- Extremely high levels of unemployment
- Hitler's 'all or nothing' policy

(ii) Many historians are keen to emphasise that there was no single cause for the collapse of the Weimar Republic. It is, for example, too simplistic to argue that it was just flaws in the Weimar constitution or just the economic downturn following the Wall Street Crash of October 1929 that made the Republic's collapse inevitable. Such explanations share the same defect. They are 'monocausal' - they suggest that a single cause explains what happened. Rather, any account of the collapse of the Weimar Republic should consider long-term problems (such as the legacy of the years of struggle between 1919 and 1923 or the flaws in the constitution) as well as short-term factors.

Adapted from Lee 1998.

ITEM 2 Peukert's explanation

Four separate processes came together to destroy the Weimar Republic. First, the Republic was badly weakened by the economic crisis. This crisis destabilised it, placing a severe strain on it. An economic crisis alone, however, was not sufficient to destroy the Republic, as the previous economic crisis of 1923 proved. Second, in the course of the 1920s, popular support for the Republic underwent a steady decline. This loss of support was already far advanced by 1930 when the international economic crisis set in. The Weimar constitution had become unworkable and unwanted. But this process too was insufficient on its own to bring about the Republic's downfall. A third necessary condition was the determination of the old anti-Republican élites to destroy Weimar's already battered parliamentary and democratic institutions. The appointment of presidential Cabinets in the years 1930-32 finally brought the Republic to an end. A similar move to the right happened elsewhere in Europe, but nowhere else in Europe had both traditional values and new political ideas been so called into question and nowhere else had public life become so politicised and polarised. The result was that the old élites were deprived of the mass support they needed for a return to the old system. Finding themselves with nowhere to go, the old élites eventually decided on an alliance with Hitler. Fourthly, Hitler's movement was not capable of toppling the Republic on its own, despite its dynamism and the level of support for it. By the end of 1932, the movement had peaked and was showing signs of falling back. It was only by forming an agreement with the old élite that Hitler was able to convert the destructive energy of the movement into the seizure of power.

Adapted from Peukert 1991.

ITEM 3 Broszat's views

At first glance, the political intrigue which paved Hitler's way to the
Chancellorship leaves the impression that the collapse of the Weimar Republic
was, above all, the result of the personal ambitions and interests of the
conservative-nationalist élites around Hindenburg. On closer examination,
however, it is possible to see a certain logic which, from Brüning's fall onwards,
was inescapable. When Papen took office and removed the Prussian
government, an irreversible decision had been made to rule through an
authoritarian right-wing regime which was not supported by the Reichstag and
did not take any notice of the left. Schleicher did make an attempt to return to
a better balanced system, but this attempt failed because Big Business, large-
scale agriculture and other conservative-nationalist forces had been strengthened
by the Papen regime. More than in the Brüning era, the aim of these forces was
to exploit the crisis to bring a permanent change to the constitution. Article 48 and
the position of President as 'substitute monarch' provided the constitutional levers

*Kurt von Schleicher (left) and
Franz von Papen.*

to achieve this effect and Hindenburg used these levers well beyond the spirit of the constitution. The special role played
by the army (ie by Schleicher) was also important. But these conservative-nationalist forces were incapable of providing
popular backing and, without that, stabilisation was impossible. Since they had no popular backing the presidential
governments of Papen and Schleicher remained dependent on the support of the NSDAP and this made them vulnerable
to Nazi blackmail. Hindenburg refused to hand power to Hitler for a long time. But when he finally changed his mind, at
the last minute, he was motivated by a desire to restore the popularity of his presidential regime. Schleicher proposed a
risky military dictatorship whereas Papen promised to deliver a government with a broad base, albeit one with Hitler as
Chancellor. Faced with this choice, Hindenburg chose the latter.

Adapted from Broszat 1987.

Questions

1. Judging from Items 1-3 and your own knowledge,
   explain why the Weimar Republic failed to survive
   the crisis of 1929-33.
2. a) Using Item 1, choose the five most important
   causes of the collapse of the Weimar Republic and
   place them in order of importance. Explain why you
   have chosen this order.
   b) Write a paragraph showing how the five causes
   contributed to the collapse of the Weimar Republic.

c) The list in Item 1 is by no means exhaustive.
   Think of other causes and add them to the list.
3. a) The Weimar Republic's collapse could easily have
   been avoided if different people had held the top
   posts'. Using Items 2 and 3 and your own
   knowledge, give arguments for and against this view.
   b) To what extent were Papen and Schleicher
   responsible for the collapse of the Weimar Republic?

References

- **Berghahn (1987)** Berghahn, V.R., *Modern Germany: Society,
  Economy and Politics in the 20th Century* (2nd edn), Cambridge
  University Press, 1987.

- **Bessel (1997)** Bessel, R., 'Germany from war to dictatorship' in
  Fulbrook (1997).

- **Broszat (1987)** Broszat, M., *Hitler and the Collapse of Weimar
  Germany*, Berg, 1987.

- **Bullock (1991)** Bullock, A., *Hitler and Stalin: Parallel Lives*,
  HarperCollins, 1991.

- **Burleigh (2000)** Burleigh, M., *The Third Reich: a New History*,
  Macmillan, 2000.

- **Carr (1991)** Carr, W., *A History of Germany: 1815-1990*,
  Edward Arnold, 1991.

- **Craig (1981)** Craig, G.A., *Germany 1866-1945*, Oxford
  University Press, 1981.

- **Ferguson (1997)** Ferguson, N., 'The German inter-war
  economy: political choice versus economic determinism' in
  Fulbrook (1997).

- **Fest (1974)** Fest, J., *Hitler*, Purnell Book Services Ltd, 1974.

- **Feuchtwanger (1995)** Feuchtwanger, E.J., *From Weimar to
  Hitler: Germany 1918-33*, Macmillan, 1995.

- **Feuchtwanger (2001)** Feuchtwanger, E.J., 'The transition from
  Weimar to the Third Reich' in *Panayi (2001)*.

- **Fulbrook (1997)** Fulbrook, M. (ed.), *German History since
  1800*, Edward Arnold, 1997.

- **Geary (2000)** Geary, D., *Hitler and Nazism* (2nd edn),
  Routledge, 2000.

- **Haffner (1989)** Haffner, S., *Germany's Self-Destruction: the
  Reich from Bismarck to Hitler*, Simon & Schuster, 1989.

- **Hiden (1996)** Hiden, J., *The Weimar Republic*, Longman,
  1996.

- **James (1990)** James, H., 'Economic reasons for the collapse of
  the Weimar Republic' in *Kershaw (1990)*.

- **Kershaw (1990)** Kershaw, I. (ed.), *Weimar: Why did German
  Democracy Fail?*, Weidenfeld and Nicolson, 1990.

References

- **Kershaw (1998)** Kershaw, I., *Hitler 1889-1936: Hubris*, Penguin, 1998.

- **Kirk (1995)** Kirk, T., *The Longman Companion Guide to Nazi Germany*, Longman, 1995.

- **Kitchen (1996)** Kitchen, M., *The Cambridge Illustrated History of Germany*, Cambridge University Press, 1996.

- **Kolb (1988)** Kolb, E., *The Weimar Republic*, Unwin Hyman, 1988.

- **Layton (1995)** Layton, G., *From Bismarck to Hitler: Germany 1890-1933*, Hodder & Stoughton, 1995.

- **Lee (1998)** Lee, S.J., *The Weimar Republic*, Routledge, 1998.

- **Lenman (2000)** Lenman, B.P. (ed.), *Chambers Dictionary of World History*, Chambers, 2000.

- **Mann (1996)** Mann, G., *The History of Germany since 1789*, Pimlico, 1996.

- **Nicholls (1979)** Nicholls, A.J., *Weimar and the Rise of Hitler* (2nd edn), Macmillan, 1979.

- **Overy (2001)** Overy, R., 'The German economy, 1919-1945' in *Panayi (2001)*.

- **Panayi (2001)** Panayi, P. (ed.), *Weimar and Nazi Germany: Continuities and Discontinuities*, Longman, 2001.

- **Peukert (1991)** Peukert, D.J.K., *The Weimar Republic*, Penguin, 1991.

- **Rees (1997)** Rees, L., *The Nazis: a Warning from History*, BBC Publications, 1997.

- **Snyder (1976)** Snyder, L., *Encyclopedia of the Third Reich*, McGraw-Hill (USA), 1976.

- **Waddington (2001)** Waddington, G.T., '"Preaching the gospel of reasonableness": Anglo-German relations, 1919-39' in *Panayi (2001)*.

- **Wright (1989)** Wright, J., 'Stresemann and Weimar', *History Today*, October 1989.

UNIT 4 The Nazis' rise to power

Timeline - The Nazis' rise to power

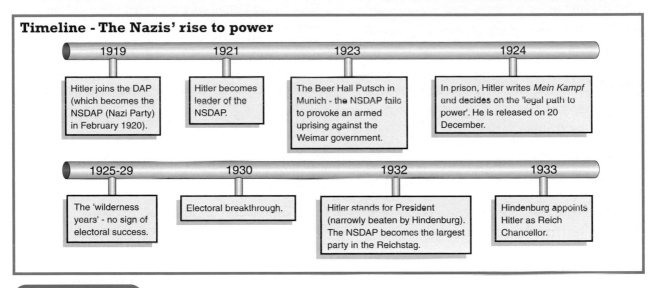

1919 Hitler joins the DAP (which becomes the NSDAP (Nazi Party) in February 1920).

1921 Hitler becomes leader of the NSDAP.

1923 The Beer Hall Putsch in Munich - the NSDAP fails to provoke an armed uprising against the Weimar government.

1924 In prison, Hitler writes *Mein Kampf* and decides on the 'legal path to power'. He is released on 20 December.

1925-29 The 'wilderness years' - no sign of electoral success.

1930 Electoral breakthrough.

1932 Hitler stands for President (narrowly beaten by Hindenburg). The NSDAP becomes the largest party in the Reichstag.

1933 Hindenburg appoints Hitler as Reich Chancellor.

Introduction

The Nazi Party, formally known as the National Socialist German Workers' Party (NSDAP), began life as the German Workers' Party (DAP). Its name was changed in February 1920 when the words 'National Sozial' were added (the 'Na' from 'National' and the 'zi' from 'Sozial' make Nazi). At the time when Adolf Hitler joined the party, in September 1919, it was a tiny organisation, based solely in Munich - one of many extreme right wing splinter groups to grow up at this time. The party's subsequent growth and rise to power falls neatly into three separate phases. The first phase began with Hitler joining the party. It continued for four years as the party developed into a significant force in Bavaria and ended with the 'Beer Hall Putsch' - Hitler's attempt, in November 1923, to persuade the Bavarian government and army to join the Nazis in the violent overthrow of the Weimar government. The Putsch failed. As a result, the second phase began with Hitler's trial for high treason and his subsequent imprisonment. Released after just nine months in December 1924, Hitler became convinced that attempting to seize power by force would not work. In future, the Nazis should work to win power by legal means, through elections. But, although the party was built up into a national organisation during the period 1925-29, it made little electoral progress. As a result, this phase is often described as the 'wilderness years'. The third phase began with the sharp downturn in the economy in 1929, the beginning of the 'Great Depression'. It was then that the fortunes of NSDAP were rapidly transformed. In the Reich election of 1928, the NSDAP remained very much on the fringes. Yet, in an election held just two years later, the party became the second largest in the Reichstag. This breakthrough was followed by further electoral successes in 1932. From July 1932, the NSDAP was the largest party in the Reichstag. A complex series of negotiations then resulted in President Hindenburg appointing Hitler Chancellor at the end of January 1933. This unit examines each of these three phases in turn.

UNIT SUMMARY

Part 1 examines the development of the NSDAP from the formation of the party to the Beer Hall Putsch of November 1923. It explores Hitler's early experiences and his impact on the NSDAP. It provides a profile of the early supporters and an analysis of the Beer Hall Putsch.

Part 2 focuses on the Nazis' wilderness years, the period 1924-29. It looks at the party's aims and tactics and considers who supported it during this period.

Part 3 is concerned with the third and final phase in the rise to power of the NSDAP. What led to the party's massive growth in support and who were the party's supporters and opponents? How did Hitler manage to become Chancellor?

1 Formation of the NSDAP to the Beer Hall Putsch

Key issues

1. What part did Hitler play in the Nazis' rise to power?

2. How did Hitler's early experiences shape his personality?

3. How did Hitler gain power in the NSDAP?

4. What were the Nazis' beliefs and tactics in the period 1919-23?

5. How much support did the NSDAP have in the period 1919-23?

6. What was the Beer Hall Putsch and why did it fail?

1.1 What part did Hitler play in the Nazis' rise to power?

Three schools of thought

Since the Nazis' defeat and the death of Adolf Hitler in 1945, a fierce debate has raged between historians over the part played by Hitler in the Nazis' rise to power and in the Nazi regime that followed. The focus of this debate is very much on Hitler himself. Some historians argue that Hitler was a dominant figure. Others argue that he was not so dominant. Put simply, there are three main schools of thought:

- the intentionalist view
- the structuralist (or functionalist) view
- the Marxist view.

The differences between these three schools of thought are important in terms of the Nazis' rise to power because they have a bearing on the way events are interpreted. If it is assumed that Hitler was a dominant figure who made all the important decisions, it is easy to reach the conclusion that Nazi success owed everything to him. But, if he was not such a dominant figure and he did not make all the important decisions, then other ways of explaining Nazi success need to be found.

1. The intentionalist view

The intentionalist view can be described as the 'great man' view of history. According to this view, history is shaped by the actions of powerful individuals. The focus of historical studies, therefore, should be on the personality and behaviour of these individuals. It is by understanding the personality and behaviour of these individuals that we can understand why events turned out as they did. Intentionalist historians believe that Hitler was a dominant figure:

'Any study which puts Hitler's aims and personality at the centre of analysis is usually described as "Hitlocentric" or "intentionalist". A typical example of this approach was put forward by Hugh Trevor-Roper (Lord Dacre) who portrayed Hitler as "the complete master of Nazi Germany".' (McDonough 1999, p.124)

Intentionalist historians argue that the failure of the Weimar Republic was not inevitable. It was only because certain key individuals behaved as they did that the Weimar Republic fell. Since Hitler was one of these key individuals, indeed since he was the key individual to benefit most from the Weimar Republic's fall, intentionalist historians focus a great deal of attention on the part Hitler played in the downfall of the Weimar Republic.

2. The structuralist (or functionalist) view

Structuralist historians are critical of the intentionalist approach. They argue that Hitler was by no means as dominant a figure as the intentionalists suggest and that it is important to consider factors other than Hitler's personality and actions when explaining the Nazis' rise to power. In particular, structuralists argue that the structure of the Nazi Party and the political, economic, social and military structures of the Weimar Republic need to be considered when explaining the Nazis' rise to power. That is not to say that structuralist historians would deny that Hitler played a key role in bringing the Nazis to power. Rather, they argue that the intentionalists' focus on the actions of key individuals is only part of the full explanation.

3. The Marxist view

Marxists believe that economic forces rather than individuals shape history. As a result, Marxist historians downplay Hitler's role in the Nazis' rise to power. They argue that wealthy capitalists (businesspeople) backed Hitler because they were worried about the threat that German Communists posed to capitalism in general and to their businesses in particular. Hitler, they argue, was a tool (or an agent) of capitalism:

'[Marxist historians] argued that Big Business in Germany had nursed Hitler's career along in order that he should act as its agent in the resurgence of capitalism in Germany and its search for domination over Europe and eventually the world.' (Claydon 2001, p.29)

1.2 How did Hitler's early experiences shape his personality?

Reasons for examining Hitler's early life

Many historians have spent a great deal of time examining Hitler's early years in the hope of discovering information which might help to explain why he came to hold the beliefs he held and why he later acted as he did. The key events in Hitler's early life are summarised in Box 4.1.

One important source of information is Hitler himself. His autobiography *Mein Kampf* (which means 'my struggle') was written in 1924 and makes many references to his early life. Research by historians has shown that much of what Hitler supposedly recalls in *Mein Kampf* is invention or distortion. For example, Hitler gives the impression that he was brought up in a very poor family. In reality, his father, Alois, was a well-paid civil servant and the family was comfortably, if not spectacularly, wealthy. By examining Hitler's early years, therefore, historians are able to dispel some of the myths surrounding it.

There is much debate amongst historians about Hitler's psychological development. Some historians argue that he was 'abnormal':

'Adolf Hitler was not a "normal" person. Hitler's phobias, abnormalities and irrationalities cannot be omitted from any historical account of the Nazi period because they later became public policy.' (Fischer K. 1995, p.79)

Other historians, however, deny this:

'In spite of all the superficial psychoanalysis which has been written about Hitler's childhood, it can be seen it was relatively stable and quite ordinary.

Hitler showed no signs of mental instability or madness and gave no indication he would go on to become a messianic leader.' (McDonough 1999, p.5)

If there is a debate about Hitler's psychological development, there is a consensus that the following experiences made a deep impact on him.

1. The death of Hitler's father

It is generally agreed that Hitler's father, Alois, was a strict authoritarian character and that he and his son often clashed, especially over Adolf's future (from an early age, Adolf wanted to be an artist while his father wanted him to follow in his own footsteps by serving in the civil service). Hitler himself claimed that he never loved his father. He was 13 when his father died in January 1903. Historians agree that Alois' death meant a big change in Hitler's life. The summary in Box 4.2 is typical.

2. Hitler's rejection from the Academy of Fine Arts

In 1907, Hitler persuaded his aunt to give him some money so that he could move to Vienna and apply to join the Academy of Fine Arts (see Kershaw 1998, p.23 - other authors suggest that his mother gave him the money). In September 1907 and again the following year, however, he failed the entrance examination. Historians agree that this was a bitter blow that disillusioned Hitler:

'A young man who pins all his hopes on the

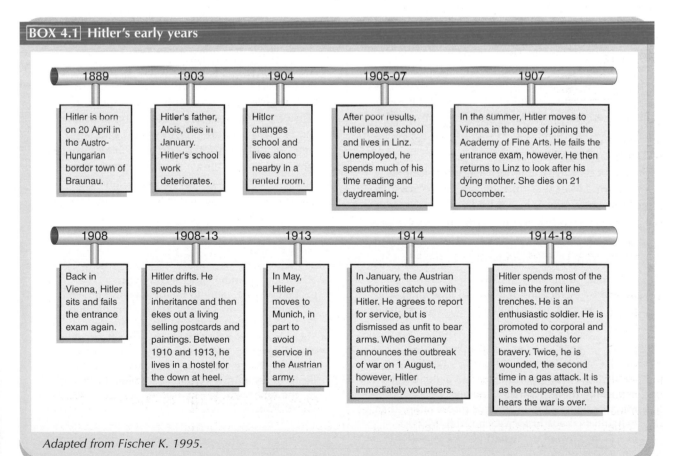

BOX 4.1 Hitler's early years

1889	1903	1904	1905-07	1907
Hitler is born on 20 April in the Austro-Hungarian border town of Braunau.	Hitler's father, Alois, dies in January. Hitler's school work deteriorates.	Hitler changes school and lives alone nearby in a rented room.	After poor results, Hitler leaves school and lives in Linz. Unemployed, he spends much of his time reading and daydreaming.	In the summer, Hitler moves to Vienna in the hope of joining the Academy of Fine Arts. He fails the entrance exam, however. He then returns to Linz to look after his dying mother. She dies on 21 December.

1908	1908-13	1913	1914	1914-18
Back in Vienna, Hitler sits and fails the entrance exam again.	Hitler drifts. He spends his inheritance and then ekes out a living selling postcards and paintings. Between 1910 and 1913, he lives in a hostel for the down at heel.	In May, Hitler moves to Munich, in part to avoid service in the Austrian army.	In January, the Austrian authorities catch up with Hitler. He agrees to report for service, but is dismissed as unfit to bear arms. When Germany announces the outbreak of war on 1 August, however, Hitler immediately volunteers.	Hitler spends most of the time in the front line trenches. He is an enthusiastic soldier. He is promoted to corporal and wins two medals for bravery. Twice, he is wounded, the second time in a gas attack. It is as he recuperates that he hears the war is over.

Adapted from Fischer K. 1995.

BOX 4.2 **Hitler and the death of his father**

It is unlikely that Adolf, now the only 'man in the house' grieved over his father. With his father's death, much of the parental pressure was removed. His mother did her best to persuade Adolf to comply with his father's wishes. But she shied away from conflict and, however concerned she was about his future, was far too ready to give in to Adolf's whims. In any case, his continued poor school performance in itself ruled out any realistic expectation that he would be qualified for a career in the civil service.

Adapted from Kershaw 1998.

fulfilment of artistic greatness, as Adolf Hitler did, is bound to be crushed by failure. When Hitler failed his entrance examination to the Academy of Fine Arts, he was shaken to the depths of his being and his dream of artistic glory, which he had nourished so tenaciously, seemed to dissipate before his eyes.' (Fischer K. 1995, p.83)

3. The death of Hitler's mother

Hitler's mother, Klara, became ill with breast cancer in 1907 and, shortly after being rejected by the Academy of Fine Arts, Hitler went home to Linz to nurse her. After a painful illness, she died in December 1907, leaving Hitler distraught:

'Though he had witnessed many death bed scenes, recalled Dr Bloch [Klara's doctor], "I have never seen anyone so prostate with grief as Adolf Hitler". His mother's death was a "dreadful blow", Hitler wrote in *Mein Kampf*, "particularly for me". He felt alone and bereft at her passing. He had lost the one person for whom he had ever felt close affection and warmth.' (Kershaw 1998, p.24)

4. Down and out in Vienna

There is a consensus amongst historians that, as a young man, Hitler was an idler and a dreamer. He never took a regular job and he lived what is often described as a 'Bohemian lifestyle' (he got up late,

spent much of the time reading and daydreaming, and became obsessed with operas, especially those composed by Richard Wagner). Between 1908 and 1913, Hitler lived in Vienna. He soon spent his inheritance and then fell on hard times. In 1909, he even slept rough for several months, before moving into a hostel for the homeless. For the next four years, Hitler scraped a living selling postcards and paintings, as well as relying on his aunt for financial support. Hitler later claimed that this period in his life was both the hardest and one of the most important in shaping his views. Most historians accept this analysis.

5. Munich 1913-14

In May 1913, Hitler left Vienna for Munich, in part because he had come to detest Vienna and the Austrian state and, in part, because he had avoided service in the Austrian army and he knew that the authorities were on his trail. In Munich, Hitler's pattern of life followed that in the later years in Vienna. He made a poor living from selling hand-painted postcards. In January 1914, however, the Austrian authorities finally caught up with him and he narrowly avoided a hefty fine or even a jail sentence for evading military service. Dismissed as 'unfit to bear arms', he returned to Munich, later describing his time in Munich as the 'happiest' in his life.

6. The outbreak of war

Hitler was in Munich when the First World War broke out in August 1914. Historians agree that this was a major turning point in his life. As soon as war was declared, Hitler volunteered to join the German army. He served as a despatch rider taking messages from the regimental command post to the front and was, historians agree, a competent and enthusiastic soldier. He was wounded twice - part of a shell damaged his thigh in 1916 and a gas attack in 1918 left him temporarily blind - and he won two medals for bravery - the Iron Cross, class one and class two. Hitler's wartime experience is summarised below in Activity 4.1, Item 2.

MAIN POINTS - Section 1.1 - 1.2

- According to the intentionalist view, history is shaped by the actions of powerful individuals and so the historical focus should be on the personality and behaviour of these individuals.
- Structuralist historians argue that Hitler was by no means as dominant a figure as the intentionalists suggest and that it is important to consider factors other than Hitler's personality and actions when explaining the Nazis' rise to power.
- Marxists believe that economic forces rather than individuals shape history. As a result, Marxist historians downplay the part played by Hitler in the Nazis' rise to power.

- Historians examine Hitler's early years (1) to explain why he came to hold the beliefs he held (2) to explain why he later acted as he did and (3) to dispel some of the myths surrounding Hitler.
- There is a consensus that six experiences made a deep impact on Hitler, namely (1) the death of his father (2) his rejection by the Academy (3) the death of his mother (4) the years spent in Vienna (5) the time spent in Munich and (6) the First World War.

Activity 4.1 Hitler's early years

ITEM 1 A historian's account (1)

After the death of Hitler's father, his mother allowed him two and a half years of idleness which he spent daydreaming, occasionally drawing and going to the theatre. At this time, certain personality traits began to emerge - utter self-involvement, a mania for uncontrolled speechifying and the making of grandiose plans, combined with listlessness and an inability to concentrate. The life he led after failing at school was exactly the sort of life that appealed to him. The Hitler myth is that the 17-year-old, forced to earn his living, had to go to Vienna. But, it is simply not true that financial need was responsible for his life in Vienna. The fact is that in 1906 his mother paid for him to go to Vienna where he passed his time sightseeing and going to the theatre, particularly to his beloved Wagner operas. Having failed to gain admission to the Academy of Art, he gave no thought to the possibility of any other profession. He stayed on in Vienna, living the comfortable life of an art student, without telling his ailing mother the truth. After his mother's death, he was still not under immediate financial pressure. There was a substantial inheritance in addition to his orphan's allowance which he continued to collect until he was 23

This picture was drawn by Hitler when he was 11 years old.

under the pretext of being enrolled at the Vienna Academy. Later he also inherited a fairly substantial sum from an aunt. The piteous note struck in *Mein Kampf* is a fake. He was driven to Vienna not by 'need and harsh reality' but by the desire to escape work and the wish to continue the lifestyle of the 'future artist', a pose he was unable to maintain under the watchful eyes of relatives in Linz. The harsh life of the 'common labourer' who had to earn his 'crust of bread' is one of the heart-rending myths of his autobiography.

Adapted from Bracher 1971.

ITEM 2 A historian's account (2)

For Hitler, the war was a godsend. Since his failure in the Academy, he had vegetated, resigned to the fact that he would not become a great artist. Seven years after that failure, the 'nobody in Vienna', now in Munich remained a dropout and nonentity, futilely angry at a world which had rejected him. The war offered him a way out. At the age of 25, it gave him, for the first time, a cause, a commitment, comradeship, an external discipline, regular employment, a sense of belonging. His regiment became home for him. When he was wounded in 1916, his first words to his superior officer were 'It's not so bad, Herr Oberleutnant, eh? I can stay with you, stay with the regiment?'. The prospect of leaving the regiment may have influenced his wish not to be considered for promotion. Hitler was a committed soldier. His superiors held him in high regard.

This photo was taken during the First World War. Hitler is standing on the left, below the cross.

Though his quirkiness singled him out, his comrades respected him and even quite liked him, though he could irritate and puzzle them. They referred to him as 'the artist' and were struck by the fact that he received no mail or parcels after mid-1915, never spoke of family and friends, neither smoked nor drank, showed no interest in visiting brothels and used to sit for hours in the corner brooding or reading. His only real affection seems to have been for his dog, Foxl, a white terrier which had strayed across from enemy lines. Hitler taught it tricks and was distraught late in the war when his unit moved on and the dog could not be found. He didn't feel as strongly about any of the thousands of humans he saw slaughtered. With dogs, as with any human he came into contact with, any relationship was based upon subordination to his mastery. 'I liked [Foxl] so much', he recalled, 'he only obeyed me'.

Adapted from Kershaw 1998.

ITEM 3 Extract from *Mein Kampf*

I owe it to [the time spent in Vienna] that I grew hard and am still capable of being hard. And even more, I exalt it for tearing me away from the hollowness of comfortable life, for drawing the mother's darling out of his soft downy bed...for hurling me, despite all resistance, into a world of misery and poverty, thus making me acquainted with those for whom I was later to fight...To me Vienna, the city which, to so many, is the epitome of innocent pleasure...represents, I am sorry to say, merely the living memory of the saddest period of my life. Even today this city can arouse in me nothing but the most dismal thoughts. For me the name of this city represents five years of hardship and misery. Five years in which I was forced to earn a living, first as a day labourer, then as a small painter. A truly meagre living which never sufficed to appease even my daily hunger. Hunger was then my faithful bodyguard. He never left me for a moment...A visit to the Opera prompted his attentions for days at a time. My life was a continuous struggle with this pitiless friend. And yet during this time I studied as never before. Aside from my architecture and my rare visits to the Opera, paid for in hunger, I had but one pleasure - my books. At that time I read enormously and thoroughly. All the free time my work left me was employed in my studies. In this way I forged in a few years' time the foundations of a knowledge from which I still draw nourishment today. And even more than this. In this period there took shape within me a world picture and a philosophy which became the granite foundation of all my acts. In addition to what I then created, I have had to learn little and I have had to alter nothing.

Extract from Mein Kampf, written by Adolf Hitler in 1924.

Questions

1. Using Items 1-3, explain why it is important to know about Hitler's early years.
2. a) What do Items 1 and 2 tell us about Hitler's personality?
   b) Explain why (i) the years in Vienna and (ii) the First World War were important in shaping Hitler's personality.

c) Given the traits of personality outlined here, what sort of leader would you expect Hitler to be?

3. a) What does Item 3 tell us about Hitler's personality?
   b) What are the difficulties with using this kind of source material? Use Item 1 in your answer.

1.3 How did Hitler gain power in the NSDAP?

Hitler in the months after the war

After recovering from the gas attack, Hitler rejoined his regiment in Munich on 21 November 1918. He did so at a time of great political instability:

'Munich was in a state of unprecedented political crisis. The King of Bavaria was deposed in a socialist revolution. Kurt Eisner, a Jewish Social Democrat, set up the Bavarian People's Republic, but he was assassinated in February 1919 by a renegade army officer. This incident provoked a workers' revolt which led to the creation of a workers' Republic. This did not last long. In April 1919, troops supported by the free corps (Freikorps), consisting of hundreds of patriotic, trigger-happy ex-soldiers crushed the workers' revolt. A moderate Social Democratic government was put back in power, but this was soon replaced by an extreme right-wing nationalist administration led by Gustav von Kahr.' (McDonough 1999, p.9)
Given Hitler's later attacks on socialism (or

'Marxism' as he normally branded it) and his extreme nationalism (ie patriotism), historians might expect to discover that Hitler spent these months plotting against the workers' Republic and then joining the Freikorps to help crush the workers' revolt. But this is not what happened. As Box 4.3 shows, far from fighting against the revolutionaries, Hitler worked for them.

In May 1919, Hitler was picked out to serve as a political instructor. His job had two facets. On the one hand, he was sent to talk to soldiers with 'unreliable' political views to instill in them a sense of loyalty and patriotism. In this, he excelled, discovering that he had a genuine talent for public speaking. On the other hand, he was sent to observe the activity of political organisations and to report back on the views expressed. One of the organisations he was ordered to investigate (in September 1919) was the German Workers' Party (DAP).

Hitler joins the DAP

The DAP was a tiny political party which had been

BOX 4.3 Hitler and the Bavarian workers' revolt

According to the historian Ian Kershaw, during the period of instability in Bavaria in 1919, a time when many soldiers were being discharged, Hitler was desperate to remain in the army. That meant compromising his principles and, to some extent, working with the revolutionaries. After all, the revolutionaries had taken control of the regiment in which he served. Hitler spent much of the time on guard duty. Significantly, he was elected representative of his unit. It is unlikely he would have been elected if he was openly opposed to the revolutionaries. He probably participated in a parade of left-wing workers and soldiers in Munich in April 1919. Almost certainly, he wore the revolutionary red armband worn by other members of the Munich garrison. At the same time, however, there is evidence that Hitler was careful to make it clear to those around him that he preferred the Social Democrats to the Communists and, towards the end, that he sympathised with the counter-revolutionaries (ie the Freikorps). This would explain why, within a week after the crushing of the workers' Republic, Hitler had been appointed to serve on a committee whose job was to investigate the political opinions of other members of his regiment.

Adapted from Kershaw 1998.

set up by Anton Drexler, a toolmaker in 1918. According to Klaus Fischer:

'Drexler was a somewhat slow-witted but well-intentioned do-gooder who wanted to save the German working class from the clutches of international Communism...The new "party" was little more than a beerhall debating society and, for some time, its members had to keep a low profile in order to avoid being shot by the radicals of the left...The defeat of the Communists by the forces of the right, however, enabled the DAP to surface publicly.' (Fischer K. 1995, p.115)

In *Mein Kampf*, Hitler describes the first meeting he attended. There was a lecture and then a discussion. In the course of the discussion, comments were made with which Hitler disagreed. He made a speech, stating his case forcefully. This so impressed Drexler that, when the meeting was over, he gave Hitler a pamphlet he had written and asked him to join the party. Hitler agonised over the offer and a few days later agreed to join. Kershaw, however, argues that:

'Like so much of what Hitler had to say in *Mein Kampf* about his earlier life, his account of entering the party cannot be taken at face value, and was devised, like everything else, to serve the Führer legend that was already being cultivated.' (Kershaw 1998, p.127)

Kershaw argues that what actually happened was that Hitler was ordered by his superior officer to join the party, that he was provided with funds from the army and, unusually, he was allowed to remain in the army (until his discharge in March 1920), on full pay, while working for the DAP full time. This, Kershaw argues, rescued Hitler from a return to a life on the margins of society:

'The path from Pasewalk [the military hospital in which Hitler recuperated at the end of the war] to becoming the main attraction of the DAP had not been determined by any sudden recognition of a "mission" to save Germany...It had been shaped by circumstance, opportunism, good fortune, and, not least, the backing of the army.' (Kershaw 1998, p.128)

It should be noted, however, that, even if Hitler did not join the DAP entirely out of choice, the nature of the party and its low public profile suited him:

'As Hitler frankly acknowledges, this very obscurity was an attraction. It was only in a party which, like himself, was beginning at the bottom that he had any prospect of playing a leading part and imposing his ideas. In the established parties, there was no room for him, he would be a nobody.' (Bullock 1962, p.65)

Hitler and the DAP, 1919-21

The fact that Hitler was able to work for the DAP full time, whilst other members had to fit party work around their jobs gave him an advantage. So did his skill as a public speaker. When he joined the DAP, Hitler was given responsibility for recruitment and propaganda:

'With feverish energy, he began networking among like-minded believers, sending out invitations to meetings, building up lists of potential members and personally soliciting support.' (Fischer K. 1995, p.122)

At a public meeting held in October 1919, he spoke in public for the first time. His speech impressed the 111 people present and 300 marks were raised for the party. Hitler pushed for further public meetings:

'By the seventh meeting, a few weeks later, the attendance had swollen to 400 people. Hitler's star was now in the ascendant.' (Kershaw 1998, p.141)

According to Nazi mythology, Hitler's rise to power within his party was effortless. He transformed a disorganised, amateur splinter group into a professional mass party by sheer force of personality and hard work. Beginning on 24 February 1920 when he wowed a mass meeting for the first time (see Box 4.4), Hitler's ability to sway audiences made him the star of his party and it was only a matter of time before he formalised his position as leader.

In reality, of course, Hitler's rise to power within his party was not as smooth as he later suggested.

BOX 4.4 The meeting on 24 February 1920

The meeting on 24 February was called to announce the DAP's 25-point programme, recently drawn up by Drexler with Hitler's help. Around 2,000 people attended. The meeting was chaired by Hitler, but he was not the principal speaker. That was a Dr Johannes Dingfelder, a man with a high public profile (which Hitler did not yet have). The doctor's speech was dull and then Hitler took the floor. According to *Mein Kampf*, the mood changed as soon as Hitler started speaking. His speech was direct and lively provoking either outrage or raucous support. There were scuffles and heckling, but Hitler carried on speaking to mounting applause until, at last, he had swayed the audience into ecstatic support for the new programme. The legend, Kershaw argues, was designed to portray the beginnings of the Führer figure, Germany's coming great leader and saviour. Towering over the weak early leaders of the party and certain of himself, his greatness was apparent even in the first few months after joining the party. This personal triumph is not borne out in press reports of the meeting (Hitler is hardly mentioned). But, as Bullock points out, for him the experience was decisive. This was the moment when the decision to devote himself to politics first bore fruit. From now on, he set to work to develop the gift of arousing the emotions of a mass meeting, making it the foundation of his career.

Adapted from Kershaw 1998 and Bullock 1991.

But, the number of people attending meetings called by the NSDAP continued to rise throughout 1920 and the first half of 1921 and Hitler's public profile, in Munich at least, grew correspondingly (the party changed its name after the meeting in February, adding the words 'National Socialist' to the title - the term 'Nazi comes from the NA in 'NAtional' and the ZI in 'SoZIal'):

'It was largely owing to Hitler's public profile that the party membership increased sharply from 190 in January 1920 to 2,000 by the end of the year and 3,300 by August 1921. He was rapidly making himself indispensable to the movement.' (Kershaw 1998, p.149)

As Propaganda Chief, Hitler did not just rely on public speeches, he also worked behind the scenes gaining contacts and raising money. Although the party was frequently short of money in its early years, in December 1920, it raised sufficient funds to buy a newspaper, the *Völkischer Beobachter (People's Observer)*, to transmit the party's views and news to a wider public.

Hitler's resignation, July 1921

Despite this growth, the NSDAP remained one of many small groups on the political right in Bavaria. In addition, some of the original leadership of the DAP disapproved of Hitler's efforts to win mass support. In July 1921, differences within the NSDAP leadership came to a head. While Hitler was in Berlin, members of the leadership began negotiating a merger between the NSDAP and a similar group headed by a Dr Otto Dickel (the merger would have resulted in the Party HQ moving from Munich to Berlin). Hearing about this, Hitler first attempted to dissuade the negotiators from negotiating and, when this failed, wrote a letter to the committee resigning from the party. The committee - in particular Drexler - realised that the loss of Hitler might be a fatal blow for the party and approached Hitler in the hope that he would reconsider. Hitler's reply was that the following conditions would have to be met:

- he would be given 'the post of chairman with dictatorial powers'
- the party HQ would be fixed in Munich
- the party programme would remain fixed
- there would be no more attempts at merger.

The committee gave in to Hitler's demands. Hitler rejoined on 26 July, and a party congress held on 29 July voted to change the party's constitution accordingly.

Whether or not Hitler had been planning to seize control of the party is debatable. Some historians (for example, Bracher 1971) argue that his resignation was part of a well laid plan, while others (for example, Kershaw 1998) argue that he was simply responding to events as they happened. This difference in interpretation is important since it says much about what kind of a person different historians think Hitler was. Some see him as a rational schemer, sure of his goals and coldly prepared to gamble to achieve them. Others see him as a man governed by his emotions, reacting on impulse, thinking only of what would be best for himself.

Structure and organisation of the NSDAP in 1921-23

Before Hitler's resignation, the NSDAP had worked on vaguely democratic principles. Key decisions were made by a majority vote of the executive committee. Once Hitler's conditions for rejoining the party had been met, however, ultimate power rested in his hands. In August 1921, the structure of the NSDAP was reorganised:

'The new executive branch of the party now consisted of a three-man action committee dominated by Hitler. All policy matters originated with this group, while the details of party organisation were turned over to six sub-committees: propaganda, finance, youth organisation, sports, investigation and mediation. Hitler made sure that his personal loyalists were appointed to leadership posts in these subcommittees.' (Fischer K. 1995, p.129)

The sports sub-committee was of particular significance since it was that which became responsible for organising the NSDAP's paramilitary wing - the Storm Troops or 'SA' as it was called from October 1921 (see below).

The Führerprinzip

Some historians argue that, as soon as he gained control of the NSDAP in July 1921, Hitler began to impose the 'leadership principle' or 'Führerprinzip' - the idea of absolute loyalty to the Leader (the Führer - ie Hitler) and complete acceptance of whatever decisions he made:

'Hitler's coup secured formal recognition of his dominant position and at the same time established the "leadership principle" (Führerprinzip) as the central organisational pattern of the party. The principle, once accepted, not only gave Hitler the right to make arbitrary decisions, but substituted for the hierarchical structure of the civil service and the army, with its strict regard for rules, precedent and procedure, the concept of personal and unconditional loyalty to the Führer. The whole Nazi movement (and eventually the Nazi state as well) followed the same principle.' (Bullock 1991, p.84)

Kershaw, however, argues that Hitler did not attempt to impose the Führerprinzip at first. It was, he claims, only after Mussolini's March on Rome in October 1922 (see Box 4.5) that Hitler started to develop a leadership cult:

'There had been no trace of a leadership cult in the first years of the Nazi Party. The word "leader" ("Führer") had no special meaning attached to it. Nor had Hitler endeavoured to build up a personality cult around himself. But Mussolini's triumph obviously made a big impression on him. It gave him a role model...His followers portrayed him, in fact, as Germany's "heroic" leader before he came to see himself in that light. Not that he did anything to discourage the new way he was being portrayed from autumn 1922 onwards.' (Kershaw 1998, pp.182-83)

The SA

Under the terms of the Treaty of Versailles, Germany was supposed to discharge most of its troops and disarm. In practice, however, a whole host of paramilitary organisations remained in existence in Bavaria in 1919-23. The Citizens' Defence Force, for example, was an openly paramilitary organisation set up after the downfall of the workers' Republic in 1919 to protect Bavaria against attacks from left-wingers. Kershaw (1998) claims that, in 1920, it had nearly half a million members and over 2 million weapons.

BOX 4.5 Mussolini and the March on Rome

Benito Mussolini was born in Romagna, North Italy, the son of a blacksmith and a schoolteacher. As a young man, he was a member of the Italian Socialist Party (PSI), but, in 1915, was expelled from the PSI for supporting Italy's entry into the war. Mussolini served in the war and was wounded. Then, in March 1919, he chaired the meeting in Milan which gave birth to the Fascist movement, a movement which soon spread to other cities and towns. In 1921, Mussolini abandoned revolution and prepared Fascism for a parliamentary struggle, setting up the National Fascist Party. In 1921, the Fascists won 35 seats in Parliament. The party's strategy was to distance itself from other parties and to refuse to cooperate with them. When, in the summer of 1922, law and order broke down, Mussolini at first resisted calls to try to seize power. In October 1922, however, he organised the 'March on Rome'. According to Fascist mythology, Mussolini's blackshirts gathered and marched on Rome, gloriously seizing power against all the odds. In reality, around 20,000 poorly armed Fascists marched in four columns to the outskirts of Rome and then went home. The army could easily have crushed the marchers, if it had been ordered to do so. The next day, the King, Victor Emmanuel III, invited Mussolini to form a government. Mussolini bluffed his way into power without a shot being fired.

Adapted from De Grand 1982 and Brendon 2000.

Like many other political organisations, from the start, the DAP relied on force:

'The beginnings of the SA...reach back to the start of 1920, when the DAP set out to stage bigger meetings in the Munich beerhalls and, as was the practice in other parties, needed a squad of bouncers...to deal with any disturbances. This was turned in November 1920 into the party's "Gym and Sport Section"...Following Hitler's "seizure of power" within the party in July 1921, it was reshaped and given a pivotal role.' (Kershaw 1998, pp.172-73)

In the spring of 1921, pressure from the Berlin government forced the Citizen's Defence Force and other openly paramilitary organisations to dissolve. Many of their members ended up in the SA, largely due to the efforts of Captain Ernst Röhm, a key figure during the period 1919-23. In addition to recruiting thousands of ex-soldiers and members of other paramilitary groups into the SA, Röhm provided Hitler with a continued link with the army and it was he who, together with Dietrich Eckart, purchased the NSDAP's newspaper *Völkische Beobachter* at the end of 1920, Eckart becoming the editor. Fischer argues that the ambitions of Röhm and other commanders for the SA were different from those of Hitler:

'Those who commanded [the SA] saw in it a germ cell for a revitalised German army of the future; they intended it to serve not just as a defensive organisation designed to keep control at political meetings but as an instrument to gain political control.' (Fischer K. 1995, p.143)

Hitler, he argues, did not see the SA in this way.

Rather, he saw it as a propaganda tool. To Hitler, the SA's role was to stifle any opposition at meetings, allowing him to speak without interruption, and, by engaging in violence, to bring the party publicity:

'Unlike Röhm, who saw [the SA] as a catalyst for a new radical army, Hitler viewed it as a propaganda weapon, subservient to the political branch of the party and answerable to his command.' (Fischer K. 1995, p.144)

MAIN POINTS - Section 1.3

- Hitler may have collaborated with the workers who revolted in Bavaria.
- In September 1919, Hitler joined the DAP and he helped to draw up its programme four months later.
- By the summer of 1921, Hitler had proved himself indispensable to the NSDAP. When he resigned, the executive committee asked him to reconsider. Hitler only agreed to rejoin the party if he was given the position of sole Leader with dictatorial powers.
- Once he was Leader, Hitler reorganised the party to ensure he had control. Some historians argue that it was then that the idea of 'Führerprinzip' became established. Others argue that it was later.
- Hitler and Röhm differed over the role of the SA.

Activity 4.2 Hitler and propaganda

ITEM 1 Swastikas and symbolism

Hitler placed great emphasis on the need for symbols and myths in party organisation. As early as August 1920, he approved of the swastika as the party's main symbol. The swastika was frequently used by nationalist groups in Germany, though the final Nazi design with black swastika in a white circle on a red background was unique to that party. Although he did not originate the use of many symbols, he was very interested in them. He would spend hours thumbing through art magazines to find the right eagle for the standard rubber stamp of the party. About the same time that the swastika became the official party symbol, he commissioned a jeweller to design the party's official badge. Red party armbands also displaying the swastika came into being shortly afterwards and Hitler insisted that all party members wear them during duty hours. By the end of 1922, Hitler had also designed NSDAP 'standards' - poles with an eagle at the top, a swastika in a circle below and a square party shield below that. The party shield was red, with another swastika in a white circle and the slogan 'Germany awaken'. The greeting 'Heil Hitler'

This photo shows members of the Nazi Party carrying standards decorated with the Swastika.

was not officially used in the early 1920s, though some individual members addressed each other in this way even before 1923. Hitler was willing to learn and borrow even from institutions he hated such as the Communist Party or Catholic Church. The Communists taught him the importance of rank and file discipline, commitment to ideals and the drive towards revolution. The Catholic Church taught him the secret of psychic control - the art of binding members of a group in the mysteries of communal fellowship. In all matters of party organisation, Hitler insisted on the strictest military discipline. He agonised over the minutest detail of ceremony. Such scrupulous attention to detail, together with an intense effort regarding propaganda and public spectacles led to a steady increase in party membership.

Adapted from Fischer K. 1995.

ITEM 2 Hitler the propagandist

There was nothing new, different, original or distinctive about the ideas Hitler was peddling in the Munich beerhalls. What Hitler did was advertise unoriginal ideas in an original way. Others could say the same thing but make no impact at all (Drexler and the other members of the executive committee fitted into this category). As it was to be throughout his career, presentation was what mattered. He consciously learnt how to make an impression through speaking and his success taught him that he was able to mobilise the masses. For him, this was, from the outset, the main route to scoring political goals. According to Heinrich Hoffman, Hitler's photographer, when asked to give a short speech at a wedding in the early 1920s, Hitler refused. 'I must have a crowd when I speak', he explained. 'In a small intimate circle, I never know what to say. I should only disappoint you all and that is a thing I should hate to do. As a speaker at a family gathering or funeral, I am no use at all'. Hitler's unease in dealing with individuals contrasted greatly with his self-confident mastery in exploiting the emotions of an audience listening to a major speech. The satisfaction gained from the wild applause of cheering crowds must have offered compensation for the emptiness of his personal relations. More than that, it was a sign that he was a success, after three decades in which, apart from the pride he took in his war record, he had no achievements of note to set against his outsized ego. Drexler offered the chairmanship of the party to Hitler several times before July 1921, but Hitler refused it. The party chairmanship meant organisational responsibility. Organisation he could leave to others. Mobilising the masses was what he was good at and wanted to do.

Adapted from Kershaw 1998.

ITEM 3 Hitler speaks

This painting shows Hitler speaking in a beer cellar in 1921.

Questions

1. 'It was as a propagandist that Hitler made his mark in these early years'. Explain this statement using Items 1-3

2. a) What do Items 1 and 2 tell us about (i) Hitler's personality and (ii) the nature of the Nazi Party in the early 1920s?
   b) Judging from these items, what qualities did Hitler bring to the leadership of the Nazi Party?

3. Using Item 2, explain why Hitler's discovery that he had talent at public speaking was a turning point in his life.

4. a) What does Item 3 tell us about the Nazi Party in the early 1920s?
   b) What are the difficulties of using pictures like this as source material?

1.4 What were the Nazis' beliefs and tactics in the period 1919-23?

The 25-point programme

It was noted in Section 1.3 above that the DAP (as it was then called) organised a public meeting in February 1920 to announce the party's 25-point programme. This programme, most historians agree, was drawn up by Drexler and Hitler. Kershaw, for example, notes that:

'The 25 points of the programme - which would in the course of time be declared "unalterable" and be in practice ignored - had been worked out and drafted over the previous weeks by Drexler and Hitler.' (Kershaw 1998, p.144)

It was after this meeting that the DAP added the words 'National Socialist' to its name (making it the NSDAP). This was a reflection of the ideas lying behind the 25-point programme:

'Certainly, the 25-point programme, formulated in 1920, contained principles which could be seen as both nationalist and socialist.' (Lee 1998, p.3)

In addition to a focus on principles that can be described as 'nationalist' and 'socialist' (what this actually meant will be explored below), Nazi thinking at this time was characterised by:

- a hatred of Jews (anti-Semitism)
- a hatred of Communism (anti-Communism)
- a hatred of democracy (a belief in authoritarianism).

Each of these elements of Nazi thinking at this time is explored below.

Nationalism

The Nazis were fervent nationalists. They believed that all Germans had a shared ethnicity, culture and set of beliefs and that they all shared a glorious past. It followed from this that all Germans should be able to live together in one nation, namely a Greater Germany - a Germany whose borders had been expanded to accommodate all Germans:

'Hitler advocated the pan-German [all-German] vision of a Reich which would include all ethnic Germans: he wanted *ein Volk, ein Reich* (one people, one empire).' (Geary 2000, p.5)

Article 1 of the 25-point programme called for 'the union of all Germans in a united Germany'. Such ideas were not new or original. They had a long tradition. Groups had been calling for a Greater Germany long before the First World War broke out:

'With the proclamation of the German Empire in January 1871, German power again became the potentially decisive factor on the European continent after a hiatus [gap] of many hundreds of years. However, the Prusso-German Reich left many millions of Germans outside its boundaries (notably in the multi-national Habsburg Empire)...The German national question remained acute and even intensified as the Habsburg Empire drifted into crisis in the early 1900s.' (Fischer K. 1995, pp.32-33)

After the war, the 'German national question' re-emerged. The post-war settlement meant that many more people who were German-speaking and who considered themselves to be German found themselves living outside the borders of Germany. Post-war Poland and the new state of Czechoslovakia had particularly large German minorities, for example. The Nazis believed that not only should the territory taken away from Germany after the end of the First World War be restored, but also that Germany should occupy new territory. From the start, therefore, the Nazis called for a programme of territorial expansion. What the German people needed, the Nazis argued, was 'Lebensraum' (living space). The implications of this are outlined in Box 4.6.

BOX 4.6 Lebensraum

The Nazis believed that the German people were being forced to live in a territorial area that was overcrowded and could not meet the needs of the German people. Such circumstances bred moral and political decay. What the people needed was Lebensraum (living space). In turn, this raised the question: where was such living space to be found? At first, the Nazis were vague about this. The earliest pronouncements on this subject suggest that they believed that Lebensraum would be found by the occupation of colonies outside Europe. But, Hitler came to reject such a solution. Colonies could not be easily defended and could be cut off from the fatherland by naval action, as had happened between 1914 and 1918. Increasingly, Hitler came to believe that Lebensraum would have to be found in the east of Europe and in Russia in particular, where foodstuffs and raw materials were abundant.

Adapted from Nicholls 1979 and Geary 2000.

The Nazis' nationalism was closely bound up with their racialism (see the section on anti-Semitism below). They believed that Germans were racially distinct and racially superior to other people. As a result, they envisaged a Greater Germany in which only Germans would have full rights as citizens. Other races would be denied full citizen rights, especially Jews (the Nazis claimed that Jews were racially different from other people).

Socialism

It might seem odd that a political party on the extreme right would describe itself as 'socialist'. After all, the term 'socialism' is sometimes used as a substitute for the term 'Marxism' (which the Nazis despised). When 'socialism' is used in that sense, it suggests support for class struggle and for greater power and equality for members of the working class. But 'socialism' in the Nazi sense did not mean this, as Fischer points out:

'Although for some, the terms "nationalism" and "socialism" stood for incompatible goals, for Hitler they were little more than symbolic or even mystical slogans...Socialism in Hitler's mind was not to be taken in its "degenerate" Marxist sense of class struggle and proletarian [working-class] equality, but [as] class harmony, hard work, obedience and service to the state...[Hitler's socialism] was driven by nationalism...Germans must be taught that they work not just for their own selfish ends but for the good of the nation; and by working for the collective, Germans should be secure in the knowledge that the state, in turn, works on their behalf.' (Fischer K. 1995, pp.125-26)

That the Nazis chose to use the term 'socialism' was, in part, an attempt to encourage members of the working class and lower middle class to join the party and, in part, a reflection of the anti-capitalist stance the party took in its early days:

'In the early days, the NSDAP had to seek its adherents mainly among those who suffered from a sense of dispossession, not only the working and lower middle classes, but the many déclassé members of the middle class [ie those members of the middle class whose status had dropped because they had fallen on hard times]. Therefore the anti-capitalist elements in Nazi ideology figured quite prominently in Hitler's speeches and propaganda.' (Feuchtwanger 1995, p.111)

Most historians agree that the 'socialist' pledges in the Nazi programme were included to ensure that the party appealed to the widest spectrum of support possible. They also agree that, when it became politically desirable to drop the socialist element of the programme, the Nazis were quick to do so:

'In the early 1920s, NSDAP agitation and propaganda centred on three predominant issues: anti-Semitism, overt nationalism and anti-capitalism. The first two became clarion cries of the Nazi Party until the very end of its regime. In contrast, the strong anti-capitalist language was deemed counterproductive in the medium to longer term and was gradually discarded, its supporters silenced and, once in power, abandoned.' (McGowan 2001, p.252)

Anti-Semitism

Historical research has shown that anti-Semitism - hatred of Jews - was widespread in Europe in the late 19th and early 20th century and it was nothing unusual for an extreme right-wing party to express anti-Semitic views. Indeed, the Nazi Party was one of many anti-Semitic parties to spring up in Germany after the First World War.

Anti-Semitism was central to Nazism. All the leading Nazis were strongly anti-Semitic, none more so than Hitler. Fischer argues that:

'Anti-Semitism was the oxygen of Hitler's political life.' (Fischer K. 1995, p.89)

Although it is not clear whether Hitler was an anti-Semite as a boy, many historians agree that he was strongly hostile to Jews by the time he left Vienna. Kershaw, however, argues that Hitler's anti-Semitism only came to the fore in 1919. Referring to Hitler at the time when the 25-point programme was announced he writes:

'The all-devouring manic obsession with the Jews to which all else is subordinated - not observable before 1919, never absent thereafter - courses through almost every Hitler speech at this time. Behind all evil that had befallen or was threatening Germany stood the figure of the Jew. In speech after speech he lashed the Jews in the most vicious and barbaric language imaginable.' (Kershaw 1998, p.151)

As noted above, the Nazis' views on race were closely bound up with their views on a Greater Germany. The connections are drawn in Box 4.7.

BOX 4.7 The Nazis' views on race

The Nazis viewed life as a struggle for existence between the strong and pure races and the weak and mixed ones. Wars were a key part of this struggle since they determined that only the strongest and purest races would dominate. The Nazis divided the world into three racial groups:

- Aryans - the race which creates culture
- bearers of culture - races which are incapable of creating culture themselves, but which are able to copy from Aryans
- inferior peoples - races which are unable to create culture or to copy from Aryans, being capable only of destroying culture.

The ideal for the Nazis was the creation of a pure Aryan race of Germans who did not weaken their blood by having children with people of other races. This pure Aryan race would, of course, live in Greater Germany - the Germany whose borders had been expanded to accommodate all Germans. Standing in the way of this ideal were the Jews. The Jews, Nazis claimed, were not a religious group but a united race. This race was stateless (Israel was not founded until 1948) and the Jews undermined the ethnic unity of every state they lived in. Anti-Semitism had two functions in Nazi ideology. It provided a simple explanation for all the problems and divisions in German society and suggested that a full solution to those ills could be achieved only by eliminating Jews from German society.

Adapted from McDonough 1999.

The 25-point programme was anti-Semitic. Three articles in particular were directed against Jews:

- Article 4 which made it clear that Jews were to be denied full German citizenship
- Article 8 which demanded an end to non-German immigration
- Article 23 which demanded that non-Germans be excluded from any influence within the media.

Anti-Communism

The Bolshevik (Communist) success in engineering a revolution in 1917 and taking power in Russia had repercussions throughout Europe. Inspired by the Bolsheviks' success, Communist groups attempted to manufacture their own revolutions in many European states. Germany was no exception (see Unit 2). Although the Spartacists (German Communists) failed to seize power in 1919, German Communists continued to enjoy a significant degree of support throughout the 1920s. Consequently, anti-Communism became an important element in the programmes of many right-wing groups, including that of the Nazis.

Some historians have argued that Hitler's hatred of Jews developed out of fear of Communism (see, for example, Nolte 1987). Nolte's argument is that horror stories of atrocities committed by Russian Communists during the revolution and in the civil war which broke out after it profoundly influenced Hitler. Hitler, so the argument goes, came to believe that Jews were responsible for the Russian revolution and the violence that followed it and, as a result, he became profoundly hostile towards the Jews. His hatred of Communism led to his anti-Semitism. According to Kershaw, however, Hitler's hatred of Jews developed long before his hatred of Communism. In other words, it was not his hatred of Communism which inspired his anti-Semitism since he was already anti-Semitic when he first came to develop a hatred of Communism. Kershaw argues that it was only in the second half of 1920 that Hitler began to develop an extreme hatred of Communism. That, he argues, is why there is no reference to Marxism or Communism in the 25-point programme of February 1920:

'Hitler admitted in August 1920 that he knew little of the real situation in Russia. But - perhaps influenced above all by Alfred Rosenberg [a leading Nazi], who came from the Baltic and experienced the Russian Revolution at first hand, but probably soaking up images of the horror of the Russian civil war which were filtering through to the German press - he plainly became preoccupied with Bolshevik Russia in the second half of the year...These images appear to have provided the catalyst to the merger of anti-Semitism and anti-Marxism in his "world view" -

an identity which, once forged, never disappeared.' (Kershaw 1998, pp.152-53)

Whether Hitler's hatred of Communism led to his anti-Semitism or vice versa, the Nazi Party had become staunchly anti-Marxist by 1923. Indeed, by then, anti-Marxism was a central part of the Nazis' political platform and it remained so until the party won power. It is important to note, however, that this hatred of Marxism was completely tied up with hatred of Jews:

'Hitler had a burning, indeed obsessive and passionate, hatred of Marxism. It runs through all his writings and speeches. But whenever Hitler spoke of Marxists, he implied that they were all "Jews" or "controlled by Jews". To a very great extent. Hitler's anti-Marxism was interwoven with his anti-Semitism.' (McDonough 1999, p.14)

Authoritarianism

Section 1.3 above describes Hitler's rise to power within the Nazi Party and his imposition of the Führerprinzip. By 1923, the Nazi Party was a profoundly undemocratic party whose members rejected democracy outright. Nazis did not believe that decisions should be made by debating and then accepting the majority rule. Rather, they accepted that decisions should be dictated to people by strong leaders. They believed, in other words, in authoritarianism. Geary describes the Nazi viewpoint as follows:

'Democratic politics brought out the divisions within a nation rather than unity and would not prove strong enough to resist the threat of Communism. What was needed, therefore, was a strong leader, a *Führer*, who would recognise and express the popular will and unite the nation behind him in a "people's community" (*Völksgemeinschaft*) in which old conflicts would be forgotten.' (Geary 2000, p.8)

The 'people's community' (Völksgemeinschaft)

The idea of building a 'people's community' or 'Völksgemeinschaft' is central to the Nazi project since it is the end goal, the ultimate aim of the movement. What the Nazis hoped to produce was a radical and complete transformation of German society. They hoped to set up a racially pure German state which would work on authoritarian lines. Such a society would be completely free of class struggle, religious conflict and political conflict. Instead, the nation would be united behind their Leader in the struggle to rebuild Germany's glorious past:

'The idea of creating a folk community was a very popular and nostalgic idea among all sections of the German nationalist right. It denoted a return to a primitive form of rural society based on "blood and soil" and it romanticised Germany's medieval past...The type of government for such a folk community would be an authoritarian one, with no majority decisions...one in which everything was decided by "one man" and an "élite of leaders". The leader (Führer) would give orders downwards which were expected to be obeyed. The individual in such a society was expected to follow these orders without question or discussion...Hitler defined the folk community as a classless society in which individuals would find their own natural level through hard work, willpower and effort.' (McDonough 1999, pp.13-14)

Central to the idea of a Völksgemeinschaft were the following principles:

- principle that the common good must come before the good of the individual
- the principle of racial purity - only pure German citizens would be allowed to live in the Völksgemeinschaft (including Germans who, at the time, were living in other European states)
- the principle of struggle - the idea that the German people would commit all their energy to rebuilding Germany's glorious past.

To build a Völksgemeinschaft, the current political and social structures would have to be torn down. There would, in other words, have to be a revolution.

Authoritarianism and opposition to the Weimar Republic

The Nazi belief in authoritarianism went hand in hand with deep opposition to the Weimar government. From the outset, the Nazis' long-term aim was the overthrow of the Weimar Republic and its replacement with a dictatorship. The Nazi Party, therefore, was a revolutionary party. It aimed for a revolution, a complete change in the system of government. Until 1924, the party refused to recognise the Weimar system of government. As a result, before 1924, no Nazi candidates were put up to stand in elections. The party aimed to win power by gaining popular support and by the use of force.

Authoritarianism and historical debate

It is partly because the Nazi Party was organised along authoritarian lines that the historical debate between intentionalists and functionalists (as structuralists are also called) has arisen (see Section 1.1 above). Because of the Führerprinzip, it sometimes difficult to separate Hitler's personal beliefs from those held by Nazi members in general. Intentionalist historians focus on Hitler, speculating on his psychological state and motivations. The following passage is typical:

'Two fundamental attitudes dominated Hitler's political career. The first was his hatred of the Jews...The second and more important motivating force in his life was a desire to achieve and exercise power over others. He always firmly believed that it was necessary and morally justifiable for the strong to rule - and even destroy - the weak. Although he was to owe his success to the way in which he aroused mass support, he spoke of the masses with open contempt...They had to be bullied, cajoled and deceived by strong-willed leaders if they were to be politically effective. For this reason the techniques of mass manipulation fascinated Hitler.' (Nicholls 1979, p.70)

Structuralists, on the other hand, tend to emphasise the lack of originality in the ideas supported by the Nazis and to examine in detail the roots of these ideas. They argue that such ideas had a long tradition in Germany and that, whereas they had previously been confined to the fringes, the peculiar circumstances in the inter-war period allowed them to gain a credibility they had not previously enjoyed. Activity 4.3 examines ways in which the Nazis tried to put their ideas into practice in the period 1919-23.

MAIN POINTS - Section 1.4

- Nazis believed that all ethnic Germans should live together in a Greater Germany (ie they were nationalists).
- Nazis believed that Germans should live in a classless society where people worked for the good of the state not thermselves (the Nazi version of 'socialism').
- The Nazi ideal was to create a pure Aryan race of Germans who did not weaken their blood by having children with weaker races. Standing in the way of this ideal were the Jews. Hatred of Jews (anti-Semitism) was central to Nazism.

- Whether Hitler's hatred of Communism led to his anti-Semitism or vice versa, the Nazi Party was staunchly anti-Marxist (ie anti-Communist).
- The Nazis did not believe in democracy. They believed that decisions should be dictated to people by strong leaders (ie they were authoritarians).
- The idea of building a 'people's community' or Völksgemeinschaft is central to the Nazi project. In order to build such a community, it would be necessary to overthrow the Weimar Republic and replace it with a dictatorship.

Activity 4.3 Nazi tactics 1919-23

ITEM 1 The SA

(i) The SA, paramilitary in both organisation and appearance, had military ranks, wore uniforms and marched in formation. A good indication of the nature of the organisation is provided by the pledge that every stormtrooper had to make on joining. It reads as follows: 'As a member of the storm troop of the NSDAP, I pledge myself by its flag to be always ready to stake life and limb in the struggle for the aims of the movement, to give absolute military obedience to my military superiors and leaders, to bear myself honourably in and out of service and to be always companionable towards other comrades'. The SA protected Nazi meetings from disruption, assisted in propaganda activities and disrupted the meetings of other parties. Political violence, whatever its outcome, gave Hitler and his party publicity.

Members of the SA in Munich in the 1920s

Adapted from Noakes & Pridham 1983.

(ii) The meeting, which was well attended, came to a premature end owing to an attack planned by the Nationalist Socialists. Nazi youths had early on taken the seats near the speaker's platform, and numerous Nazis were distributed as well throughout the hall. When Hitler, the Nazi Leader, appeared in the hall, he was greeted by his followers with generous applause. His arrival was the cue for the violence that followed...Hitler's followers, bent on making it a National Socialist meeting, occupied the platform. But a large section of the meeting protested and demanded that Ballerstedt should speak. He had pushed his way through to the platform, but could not begin because the National Socialists were all the time shouting 'Hitler'. The uproar became even worse when someone tried to prevent the fight which was feared by switching off the electricity. When the lights came on again, Ballerstedt declared that anybody who tried to disturb the meeting would be charged with breach of the peace. After this the young people on the platform, many of them hardly in their teens, surrounded him, beat him up and pushed him down the platform steps...Three members of the state police appeared in the hall. A detective declared the meeting dissolved. A fairly strong group of state police then cleared the hall.

On 14 September 1921, a meeting of the Bavarian League was held in Munich, with the League's Leader, Otto Ballerstedt, as the main speaker. The account above appeared in the Munchner Neueste Nachrichten on 15 September 1921.

ITEM 2 Nazi tactics in the early 1920s (1)

To get Bavarian politicians and the Bavarian public to take him seriously, Hitler had to create a presence, to make a name for himself. He was greatly helped in his search for publicity when, in December 1920, a number of his backers put up the money to buy the newspaper *Völkischer Beobachter*, which was then turned into the party's own newspaper. Hitler's main vehicle for publicity, however, was the mass meeting, with its giant posters and party banners, the Heil Hitler salute, the military style parades, the solemn dedication of party flags and standards, the tension built up in advance, the martial music, the entry of picked squads marching in ranks and dipping their flags in salute and, finally, the delayed entry of the Führer. The size of audiences

Hitler watches the SA and other paramilitary troups march past during a ceremony to mark the laying of a war memorial foundation stone in Munich on 4 November 1923.

frequently reached 2-3,000. On one occasion in February 1921, 6,500 packed into the huge tent of Munich's Krone Circus to cheer wildly when Hitler spoke on 'Future or Ruin' and attacked the Allies' claim for reparations. At a meeting held in November 1921, Hitler found himself confronted with a large body of socialists from nearby factories, intent on breaking up the meeting. Only 50 members of the SA were present to defend him. In the riot which broke out half way through the speech, these members of the SA took heavy punishment, but they won the battle. Later, in *Mein Kampf*, Hitler idealised the incident, describing it as a heroic event in which the SA had their 'baptism of fire'.

Adapted from Bullock 1991.

ITEM 3 Nazi tactics in the early 1920s (2)

Following the incident with Ballerstedt, Hitler (see Item 1 ii) was imprisoned for a month. Apart from this short interlude, he did not let up with his agitation. Brushes with the police were common. There were 30 bans on publications, placards and other Nazi publicity in 1921. Hitler remained dissatisfied with the coverage - even negative coverage - he received in the press. Nevertheless, the actions of the NSDAP and its Leader ensured that they remained in the public eye. In the first half of 1922, open attacks on opponents became the order of the day. Rubber truncheons and knuckle-dusters were the main weapons, but pistols and even home-made bombs were used. Meanwhile Hitler made speech after speech abusing the Weimar and Bavarian governments. German President Ebert was booed, whistled at, insulted and spat upon by Nazi demonstrators when he visited Munich in the summer of 1922. When Hitler was threatened with expulsion from Bavaria, he made political capital out of it by pointing to his war record. It was at a joint rally held in August 1922 that the SA first appeared in public as a paramilitary formation under its own banners. There were, however, just 800 members of the SA compared to 30,000 belonging to the other organisations attending the rally. Hitler's most notable propaganda success in 1922 was his party's participation in the so-called 'German Day' in Coburg in October. Hitler scraped together what funds the NSDAP had to hire a special train - a novel propaganda stunt - and took 800 stormtroopers to Coburg. On their arrival they were met by a crowd of both supporters and opponents. Hitler ordered the stormtroopers to ignore police instructions banning a march and they unfurled banners and marched in formation through the town. Opponents lining the street hurled abuse and the Nazis, in turn, leapt out of formation to beat their tormentors with sticks and truncheons. A furious battle erupted. But after ten minutes in which the SA had police support, the stormtroopers triumphantly claimed the streets as theirs. For Hitler, the propaganda victory was what counted.

Adapted from Kershaw 1998.

Questions

1. a) Using Items 1-3, describe the tactics used by the Nazis in the period 1919-23.
   b) What do you think the Nazis were trying to achieve by using these tactics?
2. a) What does Item 1 tell us about the nature of the NSDAP in the period 1919-23?

b) Explain how the structure and organisation of the party reflected Nazi views.

3. 'The formation of the SA was a crucial development in the history of the Nazi Party'. Explain this statement using Items 2 and 3.

1.5 How much support did the NSDAP have in the period 1919-23?

Growth in support

When Hitler joined the DAP in September 1919, it was a tiny organisation:

'The DAP had less than 40 members.' (McDonough 1999, p.10)

A year later, membership had grown to over 1,000 and, four years later on the eve of the Munich Putsch in November 1923 (a 'putsch' is an attempt to seize power), party membership had grown significantly, to over 55,000:

'The membership rose from about 1,100 in June 1920 to 6,000 in early 1922, and about 20,000 in early 1923, after the German Socialist Party dissolved itself and voted to join the NSDAP (on Hitler's terms), giving it for the first time a membership outside Bavaria. The crisis year saw a further big increase, reaching 55,000 at the time of the November Putsch. This figure, however, has to be compared with a total German electorate of 38 million.' (Bullock 1991, p.87)

The growth in membership of the NSDAP is described by Michael Kater (1983) as 'remarkable'. That an extreme party like the NSDAP could persuade so many people to support it is a reflection both of the instability of the Weimar Republic in its early years and of the sense of political crisis which was developing in Germany during this period. The surge in membership in 1923, for example, can be explained as a reaction to the feeling of disillusion and outrage which many people experienced after an economic crisis developed following French troops' occupation of the Ruhr in January 1923:

'The crisis, without which Hitler would have been nothing, was deepening by the day. In its wake, the Nazi movement was expanding rapidly. Some 35,000 were to join between February and November 1923, giving a strength of around 55,000 on the eve of the Putsch.' (Kershaw 1998, p.190)

See Unit 2, Section 2.2 for information on the occupation of the Ruhr and see the maps on page iv for the location of the Ruhr.

Who joined the Nazi Party?

Michael Kater's study of the background of members and leaders of the NSDAP (Kater 1983) shows that, even in the early years, people from all social classes joined the party. Members of the middle class and upper class, however, were over-represented (ie there was a greater percentage of people from these classes in the the party than the percentage of members of these classes in the population as whole). The sort of people who joined the party in this period were as follows:

'Beleaguered members of the lower middle classes, of course, but also demobilised and declassed military men, alienated students and intellectuals, upper-middle-class professionals or business owners who had ben frightened by the prospect of Communism, and failed outsiders without marketable skills or with deviant tendencies.' (Fischer K. 1995, p.131)

Lower-middle-class Nazis

Kater's analysis of the occupations of those who joined the Nazi Party in the period 1919-23 shows that the party appealed to merchants, artisans and low-ranking civil servants. Although 65% of the population of Bavaria in the period 1919-23 was made up of farmers, it was only in 1922 that farmers began to join the NSDAP. Kater offers a number of explanations for this. First, he points out that the NSDAP was, at first, confined to a city (Munich) and suggests that farmers needed time to gain trust in a movement based in a big city. Second, he notes that Hitler began referring to farmers in his speeches in July 1922 and that this encouraged them to join. And third, he argues that many farmers had ties with the Bavarian People's Party and needed time and good reason to break links with that organisation. Kater argues that, when farmers began to join the NSDAP, this helped to solidify the lower-middle class character of the party.

Upper-middle-class and upper-class Nazis

Kater also shows that, from the start, the Nazi Party gained some support from upper-middle-class and upper-class Bavarians. In particular, university students (many of whom had been officers in the army during the First World War) and academics were attracted to the party. In addition, a number of wealthy business owners joined the party and supported it financially. Kater points out that high-ranking civil servants were very reluctant to join the party.

Working-class Nazis

Although the NSDAP tried to present itself as a workers' party, members of the working class were under-represented both at grass-roots level and higher up the party hierarchy (ie there was a smaller percentage of people from this class in the party than the percentage of workers in the population as whole). Kater argues that this was because the Nazis' anti-Semitism - the argument that Germany's problems were the fault of the Jews - did not appeal to many workers. Other parties which aimed to appeal to the workers (the SPD and Communist Party, KPD), Kater suggests, argued that problems in Germany were the result of the division of society into exploiters (the middle and upper classes) and the exploited (the working class), but the Nazis argued that rather than blaming the exploiters, workers should blame the Jews (see Box 4.8). This, Kater argues, did not make sense to most workers because they did not feel that they were in danger from the Jews.

BOX 4.8 The working class and Nazism, 1919-23

Left-wing parties argued that workers could only improve their lives by economic means such as going on strike. The Nazis, by contrast, resisted the idea of an economic division of society into exploiters and exploited. In place of such an economically based class struggle, they visualised a contest that would be determined by biology (ie by race). Pure-blooded "Aryan" Germans, they argued, were being abused by the racially "alien" Jews. Racist anti-Semitism, therefore, was at the basis of the Nazi definition of a 'worker', a definition that was echoed in the 25-point programme of 1920. In principle, the worker was anybody who was of unadulterated German blood and who toiled, with brain or hand, to make a living. The natural enemy of the worker was not the captain of industry or the heavy industrialist tycoon, but the Jewish banker or petty dealer who was thought to live unproductively by collecting interest on money lent to honest German folk. These planks in the Nazi platform, which did nothing to further workers' claims against capitalists (ie members of the middle and upper classes) were ill received by many. In actuality, the average worker was in no danger from Jews. Workers simply did not understand the links made by the Nazis between Jews, capitalism and undue profits. Many Jews were union leaders and union leaders were generally trusted. Workers rarely read Jewish-controlled newspapers and, if they did, it was beyond their capabilities to determine in what sense they were 'Jewish' and why, because of that, they were 'bad'. The closer workers felt to leftist parties, the less time they had for racism and anti-Semitism. As for issues dearest to the workers' hearts, the Nazi Party's position did it more harm than good. On the question of strikes, the Nazi leaders tended towards non-involvement. At a time when workers were constantly ready to strike, this was not a popular stance. On this issue, as others, it was far better for workers to remain with the parties of the left.

Adapted from Kater 1983.

Even though the Nazi Party did not have wide appeal to workers, some workers did join the NSDAP in its early years. Kater argues that these, mainly skilled rather than unskilled, workers were disenchanted with the left-wing parties and saw the NSDAP as a right-wing alternative to them:

'They were men of nationalist leanings with peculiar, ingrown prejudices against Jews; they were disenchanted...with Marxist ideology and practice as seen in the leftist parties...Above all, a goodly number of them must have harboured hopes of upward social mobility that were not typical of their class.' (Kater 1983, p.23)

Most historians agree that the fact that people from all social classes joined the party is important. This was not the case with most other parties:

'Unlike all other parties, with the exception of the Catholic Centre Party, the membership at this early date [1919-23] was spread across all classes and subgroups.' (Bullock 1991, p.87)

The ability of the party to appeal to people from all classes helps to explain its broad appeal later.

The NSDAP's regional support

It is important to bear in mind that, throughout the period 1919-23, the NSDAP remained very much a Bavarian party (see map on p.iv for the location of Bavaria) and, for most of this period, its support was concentrated in Munich:

'In April 1920 the first branch of the party outside Munich was founded at Rosenheim; by the end of the year, the party had established branches in ten provincial areas outside Munich and one locale outside Bavaria (Mannheim).' (Fischer K. 1995, p.127)

Despite this, Hitler did make efforts in the period 1919-23 to broaden the Nazis' base. He travelled frequently to Berlin and other regions to make speeches and to raise funds:

'Although he owed his growing prestige to the loyalty of his Munich organisation, Hitler did not confine his activities to Bavaria. He travelled widely in Germany and other German-speaking regions to address meetings and contact sympathisers. He was by no means a provincially-minded politician when matters reached crisis point in 1923.' (Nicholls 1979, p.72)

Despite Hitler's efforts, however, there was little sign of the Nazi Party becoming a national force before 1923. The vast majority of members continued to be concentrated in Bavaria.

MAIN POINTS - Section 1.5

- The membership of the NSDAP grew from under 40 in September 1919 to c.1,000 in September 1920 to over 55,000 in November 1923.
- Members of the working class were under-represented in the party while members of the middle and upper classes were over-represented.
- Although workers were under-repesented in the party, some did join or support it, ensuring that support for the NSDAP was spread across all classes - something not achieved by other parties.
- In the period 1919-23, the NSDAP was not a national party. Its support was concentrated in Bavaria.

Activity 4.4 Who supported the NSDAP in 1919-23?

ITEM 1 Membership of the NSDAP, 1919-23

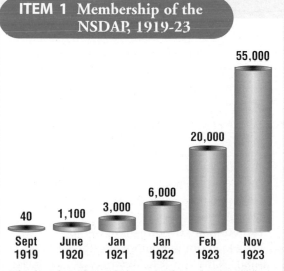

This bar chart shows the growth of membership of the NSDAP between 1919 and 1923.

Adapted from Kershaw 1998.

ITEM 2 Membership of the Nazi Party

The NSDAP's propaganda pursued a catch-all strategy promising something for everyone. Each social group was addressed separately and offered some specific gains in order to lure its members into the clutches of the party - jobs for the unemployed, guaranteed incomes and the writing off of mortgages for the farmers, shelter from market pressures for shopkeepers, artisans and small business owners, security for the elderly, career prospects for the young, orders for industry and so on. Admittedly the NSDAP's membership was not an exact mirror of German society, but it covered a wide spectrum, ranging from the bottom to the top. More than half of members came from the middle class. Compared with the overall population, workers were significantly under-represented while clerks were significantly over-represented. Farmers, artisans, professionals, low-ranking bureaucrats, small businessmen, university graduates and Protestants all had high quotas among NSDAP members, while workers, aristocrats, Catholics and women had low quotas.

Adapted from Berghoff 2001.

ITEM 3 The occupation of Nazi Party members, 1919-23

Working Class	%	Lower-middle Class	%	Upper-middle & Upper Classes	%
Unskilled workers	20.6	Master craftsmen	3.4	Managers	1.2
Skilled (craft) workers	6.0	Non-academic professionals	5.6	Higher civil servants	1.7
Other skilled workers	1.9	Lower employees	11.8	Academic professionals	6.5
		Lower civil servants	9.9	Students	10.4
		Merchants	19.2	Entrepreneurs	0.5
		Farmers	1.1		
Subtotal (45.1)	28.6	Subtotal (34.5)	51.0	Subtotal (21.4)	20.4

This table shows the percentage of people in Munich who joined the Nazi Party between January 1920 and August 1921 by occupation. The figures in brackets shows the percentage of people in Germany as a whole who did these jobs at the time of the census in 1925.

Adapted from Kater 1983.

ITEM 4 Motives for joining the NSDAP

If workers had difficulty in understanding the Nazis' anti-Semitism, the members of the lower-middle class did not. Indeed, anti-Jewish propaganda seemed to be tailor-made for them. To the small shopkeeper and artisan, the Jews were responsible for the system of factories and chain stores that threatened their livelihood. The farmers too could look back on a firm tradition of rural anti-Semitism in the 1880s and 1890s. Many farmers were taken in by the stereotype of the Jewish cattle dealer or the Jewish Marxist in the city. The reasons for students' attraction to the NSDAP are obvious. Still emotionally attached to the old system of monarchy, they embraced Nazism with the enthusiasm of which only disillusioned youth is capable. Besides, the NSDAP's anti-Semitism blended smoothly with the tradition of Jew-baiting that had been common in universities before the First World War. They were particularly keen to take action and many joined the SA. It was at the end of 1922 that Rudolf Hess, a student himself, set up an SA student battalion as part of the SA regiment in Munich. Other representatives of the upper-middle and upper classes joined the NSDAP not so much for its activist appeal as for its illiberal attitudes which were distinctly opposed to the new Republic. Although the party did little to encourage academics and well-educated professionals to join the NSDAP, this subgroup was heavily over-represented. As with students, more came from large cities, particularly Munich, rather than from small towns or the countryside. Their motives for joining are less obvious. One reason is that Nazism had an appeal which was grounded in hatred for what were regarded as the vulgarities of socialism. Many, including Ernst Hanfstaengl (Head of a famous Munich publishing house and member of Hitler's inner circle), delighted in the unsophisticated behaviour of Hitler and his cronies and thought it fashionable to identify themselves with such earthy ways.

Adapted from Kater 1983.

Questions

1. What do Items 1 and 3 tell us about the nature of NSDAP membership in the period 1919-23.
2. Item 2 describes Nazi membership in 1930. How accurate is it as a description of membership in 1923? Explain your answer.
3. Using Item 4 explain the Nazis' appeal to members of the middle and upper class.

1.6 What was the Beer Hall Putsch and why did it fail?

The main players

In order to make sense of the complex factors which led to the Beer Hall Putsch of 8-9 November 1923, it is necessary to understand who the main players were, how they were related and what their aims were. As Bullock (1962) points out, there were four main players:

1. Hitler and his allies.
2. The three men at the head of the Bavarian government.
3. The Weimar government in Berlin.
4. The Head of the Reichswehr (the German army), Hans von Seeckt, who was also based in Berlin.

It should be noted that the Beer Hall Putsch is also sometimes known as the 'Munich Putsch'.

Hitler and his allies

It was noted in Section 1.4 above that the Nazis' long-term aim was the overthrow of the Weimar Republic and its replacement with a dictatorship. In 1923, Hitler became convinced that circumstances provided just the sort of political atmosphere where there was a real chance of achieving this goal. Hitler, therefore, supported a March on Berlin (like Mussolini's March on Rome - see Box 4.5) and the seizure of power. The problem Hitler faced, however, was that this March on Berlin only had a realistic chance of success if it was supported by the Bavarian government and the members of the Reichswehr in Bavaria. If these two organisations resisted such a march, it had no chance of success. There is some debate about the nature of Hitler's aims at this point. Alan Bullock argues that Hitler may have been aiming to install General Ludendorff (see Box 4.9) in power rather than seizing power himself. Referring to September 1923, Bullock argues:

'The question of who was to be the dictator was left open. General Ludendorff...assumed that he would be; whether Hitler yet saw himself in this role, as more than the "drummer", is not clear.' (Bullock 1991, p.98)

BOX 4.9 | General Ludendorff

General Erich von Ludendorff was commanding officer, virtual dictator of Germany and the chief driving force of the war effort between 1916 and 1918. At the end of the war, he briefly fled from Germany, to escape the extreme left, and lived in Sweden. In Sweden, he wrote his memoirs entirely from memory in just three months. He then returned to Berlin in February 1919, after the Spartacists had been defeated, hoping to further his political ambitions. In many quarters, he was celebrated as a war hero. In 1920, his radical nationalism, hatred of the new Republic and his support for the 'stab-in-the-back' legend brought him a part in the Kapp Putsch (see Unit 2, Section 2.1). When the Kapp Putsch failed, he moved out of harm's way to Munich where he was regarded by many as the symbolic leader of the radical nationalist right. By 1923, he was connected with all the strands of nationalist paramilitary politics in Bavaria, though he did not control any of them. Many historians note that it is ironic that such a high-ranking army officer should have come into close contact with and later been eclipsed by Hitler, given that Hitler had only reached the rank of corporal.

Adapted from Fischer K. 1995 and Kershaw 1998.

The three men at the head of the Bavarian government

It is important to be aware of the federal structure of the Weimar Republic (see Unit 2, Section 1.2). The Bavarian government had a great deal of autonomy (freedom to do what it liked) and relations between the Weimar government and Bavarian government were often tense in the period 1919-23. At the time of the Beer Hall Putsch, three men controlled the Bavarian government - Gustav von Kahr (Head of Government), Otto von Lossow (the general in charge of the Reichswehr in Bavaria) and Hans von Seisser (Head of the Bavarian police force). Like the Nazis, these three men's long-term aim was the overthrow of the Weimar government. According to Klaus Fischer (1995):

1. Kahr was a monarchist who wanted either to replace the Weimar government with a government headed by a new Kaiser or to set up an independent Bavaria with a monarch at its head. He was appointed Head of Government on 26 September 1923 and granted dictatorial powers.
2. Lossow (like Hitler) wanted a dictatorship.
3. Seisser had similar views to those held by Kahr.

The three men are known as the 'triumvirate' since, despite differences on occasion, they worked closely together. Fischer sums up their approach as follows:

'Seisser and the other triumvirs had too much to lose by staking their careers on a risky venture; they would commit themselves only if the odds were overwhelming. When this did not happen, they preferred to sit on the fence, waiting to support the winner.' (Fischer K. 1995, p.151)

Another factor to bear in mind is that these men had much in common with Hitler but they were by no means trustworthy allies:

'[Hitler] could never overcome the distrust of the other players, who were glad enough of the support he could bring (the party grew by 35,000, the SA by 15,000 between February and November 1923), but who had no intention of accepting him on equal terms, still less of letting him take control.' (Bullock 1991, p.97)

The Weimar government

Whilst the Weimar government faced the danger of a left-wing uprising in other parts of Germany, it was all too aware that Bavaria posed the threat of a right-wing uprising. The political and economic crisis that grew throughout 1923 led to a change of government in August 1923, with Gustav Stresemann replacing Wilhelm Cuno as Chancellor. It was the aim of Stresemann and the President, Friedrich Ebert, to maintain peace. To do this, they relied on the support of the Reichswehr.

The Head of the Reichswehr, Hans von Seeckt

The views of the Head of the Reichswehr, Hans von

Seeckt, were crucial, not least because, on 26 September, a state of emergency was declared and, under Article 48 of the constitution, he had responsibility for crushing any attempted uprising against the state. Whilst there was no doubt that Seeckt would order the army to put down any attempted uprising organised by the left, there was some doubt about how he would react to an uprising organised by the right:

'Some of his actions in the six months preceding the coup [ie the Beer Hall Putsch] were sufficiently ambiguous to arouse suspicions that he was toying with the idea of throwing in his lot with the anti-Republican forces on the right.' (Fischer K. 1995, p.152)

Despite this, Fischer argues, Seeckt consistently supported the principle that the army should be above politics and, by 1923, was prepared to use the army against any groups which attempted to organise an armed uprising, whether they were on the left or right:

'By 1923 Seeckt had reached the conclusion that the [Weimar] Republic, despite its democratic drawbacks, was no longer a threat to the army. Accordingly, he decided to oppose anyone who threatened the Republic with armed insurrection.' (Fischer K. 1995, p.152)

It should be noted that, although Seeckt was Head of the Reichswehr and, therefore, Lossow's commanding officer, there were occasions in 1923 when Lossow ignored Seeckt's orders without Seeckt taking action in response.

What led to the Munich Putsch?

The year 1923 opened with the French occupation of the Ruhr (see Unit 2, Section 2.2) and the beginnings of a serious economic crisis:

'On 2 January 1923 one dollar cost 7,260 marks; on 11 January it had risen to 10,450 marks and on 31 January to 49,000 marks.' (Feuchtwanger 1995, p.119)

From the outset, the Nazis attempted to take political advantage of these developments.

As early as January 1923, there were rumours that Hitler was planning a putsch - see Box 4.10. Two further developments of note in the first half of the year also need to be mentioned.

The Working Union of Patriotic Fighting Associations

First, in February 1923, the NSDAP reversed its previous policy and formed an alliance with other right-wing paramilitary forces. According to Kershaw, the setting up of the 'Working Union of Patriotic Fighting Associations' was largely the work of Röhm. Fischer on the other hand, claims that Hitler was responsible:

'In February, Hitler formed that fatal alliance with other right-wing paramilitary forces that would

> **BOX 4.10** The first Reich Party Rally
>
> When the Bavarian government discovered that the Nazis were planning to hold the first Reich Party Rally in Munich on 27-29 January 1923, it declared a state of emergency, convinced that Hitler would use the occasion to attempt a putsch. The rally was, at first, banned. But the intervention of Kahr (who was not appointed Head of the Bavarian government until 26 September 1923) and Lossow was decisive. Lossow summoned Hitler to him and when Hitler guaranteed the peaceful conduct of the rally and promised on his "word of honour" that no putsch would be attempted, Lossow promised his support. Hitler gave similar assurances to Kahr with the same result. They then used their influence and Hitler was allowed to go ahead with 12 mass meetings (all of which he addressed on the same evening) and a parade on 28 January in front of 6,000 SA troops. Had the party had fewer friends in high places and had the government held firm, this would have been a blow to Hitler's prestige. As it was, thanks to the Bavarian authorities, he could celebrate another propaganda victory.
>
> *Adapted from Kershaw 1998.*

also wreck his career.' (Fischer K. 1995, p.145) Whether or not Hitler wanted this alliance, he did not (Kershaw suggests that he could not) oppose it. One consequence was that the NSDAP gained greater contact with the Reichswehr. SA troops, like others in the alliance, were trained by the Bavarian Reichswehr:

'The formations were trained by the Bavarian Reichswehr - not for the incorporation in any defence against further inroads by the French and Belgians (the threat of which was by this time [February] plainly receding), but evidently for the eventuality of conflict with Berlin.' (Kershaw 1998, p.194)

In addition, Hitler gained contact with high-ranking members of the Reichswehr (including a rather unsuccessful meeting in March with Seeckt).

By the spring of 1923, Kershaw argues, Hitler's position was strong, but shaky:

'He was now a player for big stakes. But he could not control the moves of other, more powerful, players with their own agendas. His constant agitation could mobilise support for a time. But it could not be held at fever pitch indefinitely. It demanded action.' (Kershaw 1998, p.195)

Hitler was, in other words, under pressure to take decisive action. As the year went on, this pressure increased. The existence of this growing pressure is an important factor in explaining why Hitler finally did take action in November.

The May Day fiasco

Before that, in May, however, it is clear that the pressure was already beginning to tell. The second development of note in the first half of 1923 was what can be described as the 'May Day fiasco'. This is described in Box 4.11. Following the May Day fiasco, Hitler left Munich to take stock. It was in the weeks that followed that the economic crisis intensified as hyperinflation took hold. Returning to Munich, Hitler attempted to make political capital out of this. Throughout the summer, he made impassioned speeches to packed halls. But, it was only in September that the crisis came to a head.

The crisis comes to a head

On 26 September, the Weimar government announced that the policy of 'passive resistance' was to end. The Bavarian government's response was immediate. A state of emergency was declared and Kahr was placed in charge of government with dictatorial powers. One of Kahr's first acts was to ban 14 meetings organised by the NSDAP. Kershaw claims that:

'Hitler was in a frenzy of rage. He felt bypassed by the manoeuvre to bring in Kahr and certain that [he] was not the man to lead a national revolution. Alongside attacks on the Reich government for betraying the national resistance [to France], Hitler now turned his fire on Kahr.' (Kershaw 1998, p.202)

There is a consensus amongst historians that the end of passive resistance produced a political atmosphere in Bavaria that made an attack on the Weimar government seem inevitable. In October, the triumvirate seriously considered a March on Berlin. On 24 October, Kahr even publicly stated that he supported such a course of action. But, two developments made the triumvirate think again. First, earlier in October an attempted left-wing uprising had broken out in West Germany. By the end of October, the Reichswehr had the situation under control and, as a result, the triumvirate could not claim with any justification that it was marching on Berlin because the Weimar government had lost control. And second, a meeting between Seisser and Seeckt in Berlin on 3 November made the triumvirate think again:

'The Reichswehr chief made plain at the meeting on 3 November that he would not move against the legal government in Berlin. With that, any plans of the triumvirate were effectively scuppered.' (Kershaw 1998, p.204)

At a meeting held on 6 November, Kahr revealed that the triumvirate was no longer committed to an immediate March on Berlin. It was this meeting which sparked Hitler's decision to take matters into his own hands. The result was the Beer Hall Putsch.

What was the Beer Hall Putsch?

The Beer Hall Putsch was an abortive attempt by Hitler to kick-start a national revolution which

---

BOX 4.11 | The May Day fiasco

In their accounts of the May Day fiasco, the historians Ian Kershaw and Alan Bullock differ over details. A summary of each account is provided below. It is important to be aware that, in Munich, May Day was a special day for both the left (since it was the workers' special day) and the right (since it was the day when "liberation" from the Bavarian People's Republic was celebrated).

Bullock's account

Hitler planned a large-scale demonstration on 1 May aimed at preventing or breaking up left-wing demonstrations. When the Bavarian government agreed to a mass meeting and parade, but banned street processions, Hitler ignored the ban. In defiance of Lossow's orders, SA men went to barracks and took weapons which were stored there but belonged to the 'patriotic leagues'. They then gathered for a parade, convinced there would be a putsch. Hitler arrived wearing a helmet and his medals. Lossow insisted that Röhm, who was still a regular soldier, return the weapons and sent an escort of troops and police to ensure his orders were obeyed. Hitler had no choice but to comply (because he could not risk taking action without the support of the Bavarian Reichswehr) and ordered the weapons to be returned. Although he made a speech trying to explain it away, everybody realised this was an important reverse.

Adapted from Bullock 1991.

Kershaw's account

On the afternoon of 30 April, at a meeting with paramilitary leaders, Lossow, worried about a right-wing putsch, refused to hand over weapons. Hitler accused Lossow of betrayal, but could do nothing. Next morning there was a gathering of c.2,000 paramilitaries (c.1,300 SA) in the barracks area north of the city, away from the left's May Day demonstration. They carried out tame exercises with weapons distributed from Röhm's arsenal. Then, after standing around, holding their rifles and facing the police, the men handed back their weapons at 2 pm and dispersed. This was a severe embarrassment for the Nazis. The lesson was that the Nazis were powerless without the Reichswehr's support.

Adapted from Kershaw 1998.

---

would result in the overthrow of the Weimar government and the imposition of a dictatorship. The plan was to take control of Munich on the night of 8 November and then to march on Berlin, gathering support on the way. To have any chance of success, Hitler needed the support of the Bavarian police force and army. This, of course, meant that he needed the support of the triumvirate. Knowing that the triumvirate would be attending a meeting in the Bürgerbraü Beer Cellar on the night of 8 November, the plan was to take control of the meeting by force, to persuade the triumvirate to join the revolution and then to begin the March on Berlin. Things, however, did not go according to plan. The triumvirs promised their support, but then disappeared. When the rebels marched to the centre of Munich the following day, the police fired on them. The revolution was over before it had really begun. The activity which follows compares the different accounts of events given by leading historians.

MAIN POINTS - Section 1.6

- There were four main players in the Beer Hall Putsch - (1) the Nazis (2) the three men at the head of the Bavarian government (3) the Weimar government in Berlin and (4) the Head of the Reichswehr, Seeckt.
- There is some debate about whether Hitler aimed to seize power for himself or for Ludendorff in November 1923.
- The triumvirate at the head of the Bavarian government were not trustworthy allies of the Nazis (Lossow showed this in May 1923 when he refused to hand over weapons, and Kahr did so in September when he banned Nazi meetings).

- To counter a right-wing uprising the Weimar government relied on the Reichswehr. Seeckt made it clear that he was prepared to use the army against such an uprising.
- The economic crisis in Germany in 1923 provided the conditions in which Hitler became convinced that an uprising had a good chance of success.
- Although the triumvirate seriously considered a March on Berlin in October 1923, they made it plain on 6 November that they would not act. The Beer Hall Putsch was an attempt to force them into action.

Activity 4.5 The Beer Hall Putsch

ITEM 1 Alan Bullock's account

On the night of 8 November, the triumvirate were all present at a meeting held in the Bürgerbraü Beer Cellar, around 2,000 people in attendance. Shortly after the meeting began, Hitler burst in and stormed the platform, gun in hand, shouting that the national revolution had begun. After pushing the triumvirs into a sideroom, he returned to the platform to announce that a provisional government had been formed. With Ludendorff's help, he got the three triumvirs back on the platform where they promised loyalty and shook hands with Hitler. They then made excuses and disappeared into the night while Hitler was otherwise occupied. When it came to decisive action and the use of force, Hitler proved singularly ineffective.

Nothing had been properly planned and when he realised that the triumvirs were taking measures to make sure the putsch failed, he suffered a nervous collapse. He remained shut up in the Beer Hall, isolated from the crowd, unable to make up his mind whether to risk further action. Ludendorff persuaded him to lead a march through Munich. At noon next day, this march began, with Hitler and Ludendorff leading a column of several thousand supporters. When a police cordon opened fire, the ranks broke and 14 demonstrators and three police officers were killed. While Ludendorff marched through the cordon, Hitler, after being pulled to the ground and dislocating his arm, scrambled to his feet and fled. He was arrested two days later.

This photo shows weapons being distributed to Nazi supporters during the Beer Hall Putsch.

Adapted from Bullock 1991.

ITEM 2 Brendon's account

On the evening of 8 November, the triumvirs were attending a meeting in the Bürgerbräu Beer Cellar. It attracted a large, fashionable crowd. Shortly after 8 pm, Hitler, wearing a trench coat over ill-fitting evening dress arrived in his new red Mercedes. He and a group of Nazis pushed their way through a police cordon. He then sat in the hallway sipping a litre of beer which cost a billion marks. Half an hour later, in the middle of a dull speech by Kahr, lorry loads of stormtroopers surrounded the hall. As their leaders burst through the doors, Hitler cast aside his beer mug and fought his way through the throng, firing a shot into the ceiling. From the rostrum, he bellowed: 'The National Revolution has begun'. Hitler herded the triumvirate into a side-chamber at gun point. Here, after a long argument, he obtained their reluctant support. He was

This photo shows a truckload of Nazis in the centre of Munich during the Beer Hall Putsch. A Nazi banner is being attached to the City Hall. The city centre is crowded

assisted by Ludendorff. Hitler also won over the Beer Hall crowd which had earlier heckled him. But after an uneasy show of unity, Hitler made the mistake of allowing the triumvirate to slip away with the departing crowd. They immediately went back on their promises because they had been extracted by force and began to organise resistance to Hitler. The next morning Hitler resolved on a final desperate gamble. At the head of a column of some 2,000 stormtroopers the Nazi leaders marched towards the centre of Munich. At the Odeonsplatz, they met a cordon of police. Who fired the first shot was never established, but within moments the street was raked with gunfire. Hitler fell to the ground - either from an old soldier's reflex or pulled down by his dying comrade, Erwin von Scheubner-Richter, with whom he had linked arms. Fifteen other Nazis and four policemen were killed. Göring and others were wounded. Only Ludendorff marched straight through the police lines and was arrested. The Nazis scattered. Two days later, Hitler was picked up by the police.

Adapted from Brendon 2000.

ITEM 3 Ian Kershaw's account

At around 8.30 pm, Hitler and two bodyguards advanced through the hall. Unable to make himself heard, Hitler took out his pistol and shot through the ceiling. He then announced that a national revolution had begun and that the hall was surrounded. He requested the triumvirs to accompany him into a side room. After hesitating, they did so. After ten minutes, Hitler returned to the main hall. By the time he had finished his speech, the mood in the hall had swung completely in his favour. He returned to the side room and, after nearly an hour, returned with Ludendorff (who had meanwhile arrived) and the triumvirate. The triumvirs spoke and then shook hands with Hitler. It appeared to be his night. From this point, however, things began to go wrong. Outside, neither the army nor the police had joined forces with the Nazis. Hearing reports of the difficulties, Hitler made his first mistake. He decided to go in person to intervene. Ludendorff was left in charge and, believing the word of officers and gentlemen, allowed the triumvirate to depart. They immediately took steps to ensure the putsch would fail. On returning to find that Ludendorff had let the triumvirate depart, Hitler realised that the

This photo shows Nazis marching through Munich on the morning of 9 November 1923, shortly before the police fired on them.

cause was lost. He then spent hours debating about what to do. It was only in the course of the morning that he and Ludendorff came up with the idea of a march through Munich. Around noon, c.2,000 men set out. At the Odeonsplatz they met a police cordon. Shots rang out. The evidence suggests that the first shot came from the Nazis. When the firing ceased, 14 Nazis and four policemen lay dead. One of the dead was Erwin von Scheubner-Richter who had linked arms with Hitler. Hitler either took evasive action or was wrenched to the ground. In any event, he dislocated his left shoulder. Some Nazis were arrested on the spot. Hitler was arrested two days later.

Adapted from Kershaw 1998.

Questions

1. Using Items 1-3 and your own knowledge explain why the Beer Hall Putsch failed.
2. a) Each of the accounts in Items 1-3 provides different details. Read through the three accounts and then write your own account of what happened.
   b) Make a list of the details in the three accounts which differ.
   c) Why do you think the details differ so much?
3. a) Judging from Items 1-3 and your own knowledge, what do you think Hitler was aiming to achieve on 8 November 1923?
   b) Why do you think he took this action at this time?

2 The Nazis 1924-29

Key issues

1. What were the aims and tactics of the Nazis in the period 1925-29?
2. Who supported the Nazis in the period 1925-29?

2.1 What were the aims and tactics of the Nazis in the period 1925-29?

The Hitler trial

There is some doubt about when exactly the trial of Hitler and other Nazis arrested following the Beer Hall Putsch began. Snyder (1976) and Fischer K. (1995) say that it opened on 24 February, whereas Bullock (1991) and Kershaw (1998) claim that it started two days later. Whatever the date, there is a consensus that Hitler immediately took the initiative and transformed the trial into a propaganda triumph. Taking advantage of the fact that the trial was public and that the judges were sympathetic to his cause, in his opening speech Hitler made no attempt to deny the charge of high treason. Rather, he pursued two lines of defence. First, he accused the chief prosecution witnesses (Kahr, Lossow and Seisser) of being as guilty as he was, since they too had been planning a putsch. And second, he argued that: 'There is no such thing as high treason against the traitors of 1918'. At the end of the speech there was loud applause:

'His conclusion, "I consider myself not a traitor, but a German who wanted the best for the German people", was greeted with loud applause in the crowded court room.' (Bullock 1991, p.150)

In the days that followed, the judges allowed Hitler to make long speeches. These were then reported in the national press. The result was that Hitler's message was heard by many people throughout Germany for the first time:

'Each day the country listened with increasing excitement as the Nazi leader converted the trial into a triumph for himself and his party. His plan was simple: instead of apologising or admitting his guilt, he took the initiative and in long, impassioned speeches presented his case to the German people...Newspapers which had never mentioned Hitler before now devoted columns to him. Millions of Germans were electrified by the man of action who was playing a hero's role in the courtroom at Munich.' (Snyder 1976, pp.237-38)

The ten defendants (see Box 4.12) were sentenced on 1 April. Four, including Hitler, received five-year prison terms. Five were given 15-month prison terms. Ludendorff was discharged altogether. As Fischer points out:

'[Hitler] had won a moral victory, while the democratic Republic had received a stunning rebuke. In right-wing Bavaria, a plot against the government had merited only a slap on the wrist.' (Fischer K. 1995, p.162)

BOX 4.12 **The defendants at the Munich trial**

This photo shows nine of the ten defendants posing after the Munich trial. From left to right, they are Pernet, Weber, Frick, Kriebel, Ludendorff, Hitler, Brückner, Röhm and Wagner. The tenth defendant, Pöhner, is absent.

Hitler's prison term

Hitler served just nine months of his sentence before being granted parole. He spent these nine months in the fortress of Landsberg in conditions which, historians agree, were more like those in a holiday camp than in a labour camp:

> 'They had an easy and comfortable life. They ate well, had as many visitors as they wished and spent much of their time out of doors in the garden...The prison staff treated Hitler with respect as no ordinary prisoner...He had a large correspondence in addition to visitors and as many newspapers and books as he wished.' (Bullock 1991, p.155)

The spell in prison gave Hitler time to ponder the future. Kershaw argues that it was during this time that Hitler came to two important conclusions. First, he came to the conclusion that the strategy adopted between 1919 and 1923 - namely, of working to overthrow the Weimar Republic and to seize power by force - was not feasible any longer. In the future, the Nazis should work to win power by legal means, through elections. Having won power legally, the party could then set about the dismantling of the Weimar Republic. And second, before the spell in prison, there was some doubt about whether Hitler saw himself as a genuine candidate to be dictator or whether he saw himself as a 'drummer' - drumming up support for somebody else (possibly Ludendorff) to be dictator. By the end of the spell in prison, however, Kershaw claims that Hitler no longer had any doubts that he himself was the strong leader that Germany needed:

> 'Hitler's experience was to lead to the last, and not least, of the lessons he would draw from his "apprenticeship years": that to be the 'drummer' was not enough; and that to be more than that meant he needed not only complete mastery in his own movement, but, above all, greater freedom from...competing groups on the right, from paramilitary groups he could not control, from the bourgeois [middle-class] politicians and army figures who had smoothed his political rise, used him and then dropped him when it suited them.' (Kershaw 1998, p.218)

Mein Kampf

It was in prison that Hitler began 'writing' Mein Kampf (actually, he dictated it and his secretary wrote it down). The first volume was published in July 1925 and the second in December 1926. Kershaw argues that the process of writing this book was important:

> 'The process of writing the first volume of his book cemented and rounded off his "world view". It also reinforced his unbounded, narcissistic [self-obsessed] self-belief. It gave him absolute conviction in his own near-messianic [Christ-like] qualities and mission, the feeling of certainty that he was destined to become the "Great Leader" the nation awaited...By the time he left Landsberg, the transition - in his own mind as in that of his followers from "drummer" to "leader" was complete.' (Kershaw 1998, p.224)

Mein Kampf did not sell in huge quantities before the Nazis came to power. Kershaw claims that the first volume had sold 23,000 copies by the end of 1929 and the second volume 13,000 copies. From 1930, however, sales rose rapidly (1.5 million copies were sold in 1933), making Hitler a rich man. It was not just for money that Hitler wrote the book, however. Fischer argues that he wrote it for two main reasons:

> 'Hitler wrote Mein Kampf to fabricate a certain image of his life and to articulate a consistent racial view of the world. His autobiographical impressions are primarily aimed at creating the mythology of a common man who rose from humble yet respectable circumstances and reluctantly abandoned his artistic career in favour of saving Germany from its enemies...Of greater importance is the author's effort to articulate a coherent Weltanschauung [world view] for the Nazi Party.' (Fischer K. 1995, pp.165-66)

The main themes in Mein Kampf are outlined in Box 4.13.

The NSDAP at the time of Hitler's release

By the time that Hitler was released from prison on 20 December 1924, the NSDAP was in disarray. Officially, the party was banned. Unofficially, it continued to exist under the temporary leadership of Alfred Rosenberg (Hitler's choice). Most historians agree that Rosenberg lacked leadership qualities (which is why Hitler chose him) and that 1924 was a year in which support for the Nazi movement drained away - not least because various factions within the movement fell out over the direction the movement should take. One dispute was over the question of whether the Nazis should fight for seats in local and national elections. Those Nazis who agreed that they should fight for seats joined forces with other nationalist groups in the so-called 'Völkischer Block' which put up candidates and campaigned in the Bavarian state election held on 6 April (the Block won 17% of the vote) and in the Reichstag election held on 4 May (the Block won 6.5% of the vote and 32 seats). Whilst these results were promising, they could not be sustained. There was further falling out between factions - particularly over whether the NSDAP should merge with another nationalist group, the DVFP - and, in a second Reichstag election held on 7 December, the level of Nazi support fell sharply (the party won just 3% of the vote and just four seats). Kershaw argues that this played into Hitler's hands:

BOX 4.13 | Mein Kampf

Mein Kampf is extremely important because it outlines Hitler's view of Germany under his leadership, the fundamental principles of his world view and his key foreign policy objectives. Race is a dominant theme in the book. Hitler viewed life as a struggle for existence between the strong and pure races and the weak and mixed ones. War was a key part of this struggle, in which the strongest and purest races would dominate. The type of society Hitler wanted to create was a popular folk community (Völksgemeinschaft - see Section 1.4 above). Anti-Semitism had two functions in the book. It provided a simple explanation for all the divisions and problems in German society, and suggested that a full solution to those ills could only be achieved by eliminating Jews from German society and then from the country most dominated by 'Jewish bolshevism' - the Soviet Union. The greatest amount of space in the book is devoted to foreign policy aims. The first aim was to abolish the Treaty of Versailles as a first stage in the resurgence of German militarism. The central aim, however, was to gain Lebensraum (living space) in eastern Europe. This implied a war against the Soviet Union. Success in this would provide enough living space to create a Greater German Reich of 250 million racially pure Germans, self-sufficient in food and raw materials, a dominant European superpower. The great difficulty for historians is to decide whether Hitler's ideas were a blueprint for action or a dream.

Adapted from McDonough 1999.

'It was a disastrous result. But it pleased Hitler. In his absence, Völkisch [nationalist] politics had collapsed, but his own claims to leadership had, in the process, been strengthened. The election result also had the advantage of encouraging the Bavarian government to regard the danger from the extreme right as past.' (Kershaw 1998, p.234) Less than two weeks later Hitler was released from prison. His first priority was to persuade the Bavarian government to lift the ban on the NSDAP, a goal which he achieved on 16 February 1925, following a meeting with Bavarian President Heinrich Held in January. The NSDAP was then relaunched as an independent party under his leadership at a meeting held in the Bürgerbräukeller in Munich on 27 February (a meeting which resulted in Hitler being banned from speaking in public in most of Germany for the next two years).

Hitler consolidates his position 1925-27

It is generally agreed that one lesson that Hitler learned from the failed Beer Hall Putsch was that the NSDAP would only achieve its goals if it adopted the 'legal path to revolution'. In other words, the party should no longer work towards an armed uprising. Instead, it should attempt to win power by winning votes:

'[Hitler] realised that his tactics of seizing power by a military coup in cooperation with fraternal paramilitary groups had been a fatal blunder. From now on the mission of the party was to work within the democratic system, using the methods of democracy to destroy democracy. Strict legality was to be the order of the day.' (Fischer K. 1995, p.192)

To put this plan into practice, Fischer argues, Hitler focused on three areas in the period 1925-27:

- removing people who had become a liability to the movement
- building up a strong core of loyalists in Munich and the South
- neutralising opposition within the party.

The result was that, by the end of 1927, Hitler was secure in his position of undisputed leader of the nationalist right.

Removing rivals

Two key rivals were removed within a few months of Hitler's release. First, Hitler persuaded Ludendorff to stand for the position of Reich President, following the death of Friedrich Ebert on 28 February 1925. Kershaw argues that this was a deliberate ploy to discredit Ludendorff. If so, it was a ploy which worked:

'His derisory showing, 1.1% of the vote, proved conclusively that Ludendorff had no future in politics.' (Feuchtwanger 1995, p.195)

And second, in April 1925, Hitler summoned Röhm to a meeting and forced his resignation. Since his release from prison in April 1924, Röhm had been attempting to rebuild the SA into a paramilitary force like that which had existed at the time of the Beer Hall Putsch. But Hitler opposed this. He wanted the SA to play its old role of protecting party members and training activists (see Box 4.15 below). Röhm travelled to Bolivia before being recalled in 1930 by Hitler.

Building a loyal band of supporters

It was in the period after his release from prison that the Führerprinzip (see Section 1.3 above) became firmly established:

'The establishment of the Führer cult was decisive for the development of the Nazi movement. Without it, as 1924 had shown, it would have been torn apart by factionalism. With it, the still precarious unity could be preserved by calling on loyalty to Hitler as a prime duty.' (Kershaw 1998, pp.295-96)

Feuchtwanger argues that building the Führer cult was related to changes in structure and organisation of the party - see Box 4.14.

BOX 4.14 The Führer cult and party organisation

Hitler was determined to maintain his independence, deliberately disregarding all other nationalist groups. In order to do this, he had to build the party entirely around his own myth as the Führer who had suffered martyrdom in 1923, but who would eventually lead Germans to their glorious destiny. In 1925 only people whose relationship with reality was disturbed were likely to swallow such a claim. Hitler, therefore, aimed to build up a following of fanatically dedicated believers, even if it was small. He imposed tight control from party headquarters in Munich. Here a number of grey bureaucrats ran the party on Hitler's behalf and relieved him from the day-to-day drudgery. The system of Gauleiters (regional party bosses) was set up. The term 'Gau' (plural 'Gaue') comes from an old Germanic custom of dividing land and people into specific regions. The Nazi Party began to use the term extensively after 1925 to refer to its highest political units. Between 1925 and 1928, these Gaue developed spontaneously and did not correspond to existing state or electoral boundaries. It was only after the poor showing in the 1928 election that they were reorganised to fit electoral boundaries. It was the Gauleiters who made up the leadership of the Nazi Party. They were appointed by Hitler, had personal ties of loyalty to Hitler and could only be dismissed by him. They were given considerable freedom within their regions. In return, they were expected to fulfil certain obligations - such as recruiting members, raising funds and spreading the Nazi message. As Hitler's personal agents, the Gauleiters did much to perpetuate the Führer cult.

Adapted from Feuchtwanger 1995 and Fischer K. 1995.

Neutralising opposition within the party

Hitler did not just neutralise opposition within the party by removing rivals. Some potential dissidents (for example, Joseph Goebbels) were converted into loyal supporters, whilst others (for example, the Strasser brothers, Gregor and Otto) were persuaded to follow Hitler's lead. It was noted above that there was a struggle between different factions within the party while Hitler was in prison. In part, this was a struggle between regions - the Nazis in the south against the Nazis in the north. In part, it was a struggle over Nazi policy and ideas. After Hitler was released from prison, this struggle continued. In March 1925, Hitler sent Gregor Strasser to organise the NSDAP in the north. According to Kershaw, Strasser was a 'superb organiser':

'Most of the local branches in the north had to be created from scratch. By the end of 1925, these numbered 262, compared with only 71 on the eve of the putsch.' (Kershaw 1998, p.270)

During the course of 1925, however, Strasser and other Nazis in the north (notably Goebbels) began to push for a greater emphasis on the party's 'socialism'. Referring to the Strasser brothers and Goebbels, Feuchtwanger argues:

'Their distinguishing mark was that they took revolutionary socialism seriously and saw themselves replacing the false prophets of Marxist socialism with a truly German socialism among the working class.' (Feuchtwanger 1995, p.196)

The meeting at Bamberg, February 1926

In November, Strasser drew up a new party programme which drew on this approach and circulated it. This prompted Hitler (who realised that the programme could be seen as a challenge to his authority) to call a meeting of leading Nazis from both the south and the north. This meeting, held in the town of Bamberg (just north of Nuremberg) on 14 February 1926, resulted in Hitler strengthening his position and Strasser retreating. But, although Hitler made it clear that he did not support Strasser's programme (afterwards Strasser agreed to collect all copies of his draft programme and to destroy them), he was careful not to alienate Strasser altogether. At the Bamberg meeting, he made a point of going over to Strasser and putting his arm round his shoulders. Shortly afterwards, in September 1926 he appointed Strasser as his Party Propaganda Leader. Similarly, he made a point of inviting Goebbels to visit him in Munich and, as a result of this visit, won Goebbel's absolute loyalty. In December 1926, Goebbels was appointed Gauleiter of Berlin. As well as neutralising potential rivals within the party, Hitler took steps to tame the SA. Having forced Röhm to resign, Hitler appointed Franz Pfeffer von Salomon Head of the SA and wrote him a letter explaining what role he wanted the organisation to play (see Box 4.15).

Nazi strategy 1928-29

Between September 1926 when Gregor Strasser became Party Propaganda Leader and late 1927, the Nazis' strategic focus was on the urban working class - the so-called 'urban plan'. Strasser aimed to build a mass party by converting workers disillusioned with the left to Nazism. This strategy, however, had little success:

'Even to outside observers, it was plain by autumn 1927 that this strategy was not paying worthwhile dividends and was at the same time in danger of alienating the lower-middle-class support of the NSDAP.' (Kershaw 1998, p.300)

Fischer suggests that the urban plan did not work for two main reasons. First, Hitler refused to allow the setting up of Nazi unions. And second, workers tended to regard the NSDAP as a party for the

BOX 4.15 **The SA after Röhm's resignation**

The training of the SA must be carried out not on a military basis, but in accordance with the needs of the party. When members undergo physical training, the main emphasis must not be on military drill, but rather on sports activities. The organisation as well as the uniform and equipment of the SA must not be carried out on the model of the old army. The SA must not meet in secret, but should march in the open. Individual SA members must be taught to see their mission not as the removal of criminals but as helping to build a new National Socialist racialist state. By doing this, the struggle against the state will be raised above the level of petty acts of revenge and conspiracy to the greatness of an ideological war of extermination against Marxism. What we need is not a hundred or two daring conspirators, but hundreds of thousands of fanatical fighters for our cause. We must not work in secret but in huge marches. The path cannot be cleared for the movement by dagger, poison or pistol, but only by conquering the street. We have to teach Marxism that National Socialism is the future master of the streets, just as it will, one day, be master of the state.

Part of a letter written by Hitler to Captain Pfeffer von Salomon on 1 November 1926 (Adapted from Noakes & Pridham 1996).

middle classes. Aware of the lack of progress and informed of opportunities in rural areas, Kershaw argues that Hitler took four steps to refocus the party before the May 1928 Reichstag election:

- in November 1927, he held a meeting with Gauleiters at which he announced that the lower-middle class should be targeted rather than the working class
- in December 1927 he spoke, for the first time, to an audience made up of peasants
- in January 1928, he removed Gregor Strasser from the post of Party Propaganda Leader (he became Reich Organisation Leader) and took over the post himself, seconding Heinrich Himmler to do the leg work

- in April 1928, he 'corrected' point 17 of the 25-point programme, making it clear that the Nazis would not take over land owned by private individuals unless it was owned by Jews (a correction designed to reassure the middle classes).

These steps were not enough to prevent the Nazis performing poorly in the May 1928 Reichstag election, but an analysis of the election result confirmed that the Nazis did better in rural areas than in urban areas. As a result:

'Hitler and the Reichsleitung (Reich directorate) decided to shift the party's electoral focus from urban areas, where it had performed very poorly to rural districts, where it had gained steady support across the board...The *Völkischer Beobachter* (31 May 1928) pointed out...that with a smaller expenditure of energy, money and time much better results could be achieved in the rural areas than in the big cities. Moreover, mass meetings were likely to have a far greater impact in rural areas, where they represented a real novelty and were talked about for weeks afterwards.' (Fischer K. 1995, p.204)

In August 1928 Hitler called the party leadership to Munich. At this meeting:

'Hitler called for a switch in priorities from the cities to the countryside, and a redrawing of the boundaries of the districts (Gaue) into which the party was divided. The rural electorate was spread out, not concentrated as in the cities, requiring much more effort to reach, in effect a year-round electioneering campaign.' (Bullock 1991, p.177)

It should be noted that, although Hitler called for a change in priorities, he did not officially criticise or abandon the urban plan. As Fischer points out:

'It was to his political advantage to maintain the illusion that the NSDAP was a working-class party.' (Fischer, K. 1995, p.204)

The NSDAP's change in priorities coincided with the beginning of an economic downturn. As discontent grew as a result of this economic downturn, the Nazis' appeal grew. By the end of 1928, the party had turned the corner. The 'wilderness years' were over.

MAIN POINTS - Section 2.1

- **Hitler transformed his trial into a propaganda triumph, gaining national attention for the first time.**
- **Hitler served just nine months of his sentence. He wrote *Mein Kampf* in prison. In prison, he came to the conclusion that the NSDAP must take the legal path to power.**
- **On Hitler's release the NSDAP was in disarray. Hitler consolidated his position by (1) removing rivals (2) building a loyal band of supporters and**

- **(3) neutralising opposition within the party.**
- **Rivalry between Nazis culminated in the Bamberg meeting of 14 February 1926. This ended the attempt by the Strasser brothers and Goebbels to challenge Hitler's programme.**
- **The 'urban plan' was in operation between September 1926 and late 1927. When it did not work, Hitler changed tactics, aiming at support in the countryside.**

Activity 4.6 The wilderness years

ITEM 1 Rebuilding the party (1)

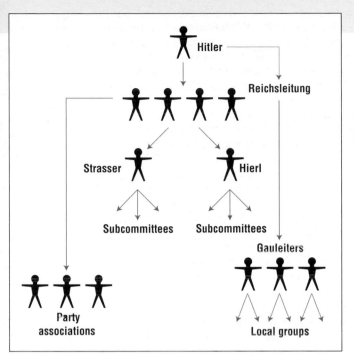

In the years 1928-29, Hitler not only reorganised the Gaue, bringing them into line with the electoral districts of the Republic, he also expanded the party structure and modelled it on the institutions of the German government. A new committee was formed at the top of the party - the Reichsleitung (members of this committee were called 'Reichsleiter'). Below the Reichsleitung, the party was divided into two branches. One was responsible for organising elections (headed by Gregor Strasser). The other was responsible for developing the structures which the party would use to take control of the state once it won power (headed by Konstantin Hierl). Both these branches were then subdivided. Unsurprisingly, there was a vertical chain of command. At the top was Hitler and the Reichsleitung, followed by the Gaue. The locals were at the bottom of the pyramid. Each level was subordinate to the one above. Hitler communicated only general directives down the chain. In the day-to-day operations, the Reichsleitung communicated directly with the Gaue, expecting the local Gauleiter to implement policies in their areas and holding them accountable by way of monthly reports and periodic audits. Hitler was reluctant to deal in day-to-day decision making and, besides, getting to see Hitler was difficult. Those running party business in Munich often had to wait for days before they could sort some matter out with him. For leading figures in the movement, too, he could prove inaccessible for weeks at a time. Bullock argues that this was not just a reflection of his personal preferences. It was essential to his concept of leadership that he should not become involved in activities himself, but should devolve the detailed work of administration to an impersonal bureaucratic machine. As well as changes at the top of the party hierarchy, it was in the period 1928-29 that new party associations began to be set up for particular groups - such as young people (the Hitler Youth), students (the National Socialist German Student League), teachers (the National Socialist Teachers' League) and many other professions.

Adapted from Fischer K. 1995.

ITEM 2 Rebuilding the party (2)

The 'wilderness years' of 1924-29 laid the platform for the later triumphant rise of Hitler and the Nazi Party. During this period, Hitler became the undisputed leader of the radical right and the NSDAP was transformed into a 'leader party' of a unique kind. By 1929, Hitler was no conventional Party Chair, nor even a leader among others. He was now 'the Leader', with complete mastery over his movement. In addition, by 1929, the organisation of the party had changed significantly. Between 1924 and 1929 the party spread (however thinly) around the country. By 1929, it was in a strong position to exploit the new crises which descended on Germany that year. One reason was that, although Nazi voters were few in number, the activist core was relatively large. Thirdly, although disputes between factions simmered below the surface, the NSDAP was a far more united force by 1929 than it had been in 1923. And, by 1929, its rivals on the extreme right had disappeared or been absorbed. These developments were strongly influenced by Hitler's changed leadership position. The Hitler cult caught hold amongst the party faithful in ways scarcely imaginable before 1923 and was well on the way to elevating Leader above party. But, Hitler's own contribution should not be exaggerated. What is remarkable is not how much, but how little Hitler had to do to transform the NSDAP. His crude scheme remained what it had been in 1919 - mobilise the masses, take over the state, destroy internal enemies, prepare for external conquest. His sole recipe was, as always, use ceaseless propaganda to convert the masses and wait for events to turn in his favour. His certainty that they would do so impressed his followers. It made him appear to be a visionary. It was his followers who encouraged the Führer myth. And the important restructuring of the party was largely the work of Gregor Strasser.

Adapted from Kershaw 1998.

ITEM 3 The Bamberg meeting

Hitler invited Strasser, Goebbels and the other northern dissidents to a meeting at Bamberg on 14 February 1926 - not to discuss the possibility of a compromise, but to re-establish his complete dictatorial control. The conference was a vintage Hitler production, designed to teach the poor cousins from the north where the real power actually resided. Bamberg was chosen with good reason, as it was a Nazi stronghold. Furthermore, holding the meeting there would mean that the northerners would be outnumbered. When they arrived, the northerners were impressed by the fact that the local Nazis had managed to sign up a significant proportion of the electorate, when they could barely manage to rope in 20 or 30 members in a group in the most populous parts of the north. Hitler spoke to them for several hours in a very cutting and uncompromising tone. He bluntly deflated their hopes and made it unmistakably clear that party unity required undisputed leadership and centralised control. Although the dissidents did not completely cave in that day - in fact they toyed with challenging Hitler's rigid party line for a week - they were too divided to resist Hitler's will. Strasser had already convinced himself that, if he left, he would probably have been unable to take many members with him. Then, on 10 March, he was badly injured in a car crash. This deprived him of whatever energy he had left for the fight. In the meantime, Goebbels went through a rapid conversion. Hitler had a keen eye for disciples and saw certain qualities in Goebbels he could use. He invited Goebbels to Munich and wined and dined him, generously letting Goebbels use his car and speak at the Bürgerbräu Beer Cellar. Goebbels was completely won over.

Gregor Strasser (the man in the raincoat) and Joseph Goebbels (on Strasser's right) watching the SA parade past Hitler, Braunschweig, 18 October 1931.

Adapted from Fischer K. 1995

ITEM 4 Rebuilding the party (3)

The Nazis differed from other parties by holding meetings before, during and between elections, often selecting particular regions for saturation coverage. These meetings were a means of reinforcing solidarity among isolated activists. There was no such thing as passive membership. Many Nazi activists lost their jobs because their political commitments took over their lives. Meetings were a vital source of income, too, with entry charges and collections. The Nazis also differed from other parties on the right by their use of violence. Significantly, though, they rarely acted violently against representatives of the state. They relied on 'passive aggression' - provoking opponents to attack them. In that way, they avoided the charge of causing a breakdown in law and order. The SA provided

This photo shows Hitler saluting members of the SA as they march past during the Nuremberg Rally of 1927.

young men with an opportunity to let off steam in the service of an ideology and in uniform. The uniform transformed young men, otherwise utterly unremarkable in their daily workclothes, into aggressive authority figures. En masse, the SA gave the Nazis a visible presence that was difficult to ignore. Major engagements involving Hitler began to assume a separate style. Care was taken with the venue, which was decorated with flowers and Nazi symbols. SA men were forbidden to drink alcohol or smoke and stood ready to pounce on hecklers. There was a long wait. Anthems, hymns and stage lighting generated effect. Hitler swept in accompanied by drums, fanfares and salutes. The first party rally was held in Weimar in 1926 because Hitler was not banned from speaking there. From 1927, they migrated to Nuremberg. The rallies were a combination of open-air festival, military display and solemn occasion. The climax was the consecration of SA banners, a matter of touching the bloodstained banner of 9 November 1923 to the flags of the new formation.

Adapted from Burleigh 2000.

2.2 Who supported the Nazis in the period 1925-29?

Growth in support

When Hitler left prison in December 1924, membership of the Nazi Party had more than halved. At the time of the party's relaunch in February 1925, just 27,000 members and 607 local branches remained (Fischer C. 1995, p.71). Growth over the next two years was slow. Orlow (1971) claims, for example, that membership had grown to just 35,000 by July 1926 and that it stagnated in many areas in 1926-27. The turning point came after the Reichstag election of May 1928. By October 1928, membership had risen to 100,000 and, by the end of the year to 109,000. By December 1929, membership was at 178,000 and in October 1930 at 300,000 (figures from Kershaw 1998 and Fischer C. 1995). A number of reasons have been suggested to explain the Nazis' resurgence after May 1928. These include the following:

1. On the surface at least, the party was united behind Hitler, making it more attractive than it had been in 1924-26.
2. The reorganisation of the party structure made it more efficient and, therefore, better at recruiting.
3. The move away from the urban plan and the attempt to capture rural support paid dividends.
4. The position of other right-wing parties deteriorated in this period, giving the Nazi Party the opportunity to attract new support.
5. The economic climate was deteriorating in 1928, with some sectors (such as farmers) suffering more than others and, as a result, more inclined to join a party opposed to the government.
6. The Nazi Party was careful to present itself as a party hostile to the Weimar Republic, something that appealed to people who became embittered with the system.

Most historians agree that economic conditions were the key to the Nazi resurgence. The Nazis' so-called 'wilderness years' coincided with a period of relative economic stability, a period often described as Weimar's 'Golden Years' (see Unit 3, Part 1). But Kershaw points out that, despite the appearance of stability, these years were not as golden as they seemed. There were problems lurking beneath the surface. Discussing the period 1924-29, he argues that:

'Germany had been throughout a society profoundly divided...Social grievances remained acute. Relatively high levels of unemployment - over two million were out of work in 1926 - radicalised many workers, a good number of them young. Small shopkeepers and producers felt threatened and angered by department stores and consumer cooperatives. Along with many craftsmen, feeling their traditional status and livelihood undermined by modern mass-production...they had no affection for Weimar democracy, even in its best years. Farmers...were up in arms at the collapse of agricultural prices.' (Kershaw 1998, p.306)

It was discontent like this that the Nazi Party, with its consistent anti-Weimar stance, was able to exploit.

When did the Nazi revival begin?

It is often asserted that the economic meltdown in the years 1929-31 was crucial in the Nazis' rise to power (see, for example, McDonough 1998). But, it is important to note that the rapid growth in support for the Nazi Party began before 1929. Particularly important was the development of a crisis in agriculture in the period 1926-28. This, combined with the Nazis' realisation that they were more likely to gain success if they switched their focus from urban to rural areas, is an important factor in explaining the Nazi resurgence:

'Agricultural prices, which had begun to stabilise after the early 1920s, were already falling by 1927 and collapsed in the depression of 1929-33. The result was a crisis of indebtedness for farmers whose alienation was already forming in the 1926-28 period. The agrarian crisis fuelled a campaign of rural violence against tax collectors and local government and led to the first significant gains of the NSDAP in the agricultural areas of Schleswig-Holstein and Lower Saxony in 1928.' (Geary 2000, p.20)

It should be noted that, although the party grew in the period 1924-29, its poor performance in the three Reichstag elections (two in 1924 and one in 1928 - see Box 4.16) indicates that it remained very much a fringe party. Most historians would agree with Fischer who, referring to the summer of 1929, claims:

'Hitler could hardly have imagined that millions would soon flock to the banner of the Nazi Party, which was still small and politically insignificant.' (Fischer K. 1995, p.211)

BOX 4.16 Membership and votes won 1924-30

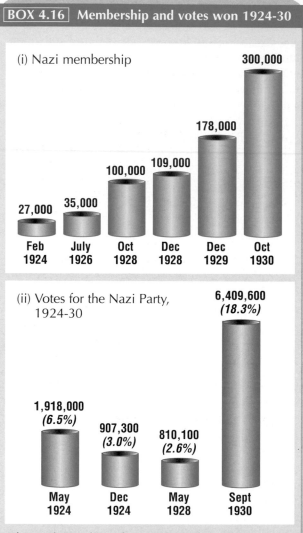

These charts show the number of party members and the number of votes for the NSDAP in Reich elections during the period 1924-1930.
Adapted from Fischer C. 1995 and Kershaw 1998.

Who joined the Nazi Party?

Michael Kater's study of the background of members and leaders of the NSDAP (Kater 1983) shows that, as in the period 1919-23, people from all social classes joined the party in the period 1924-29. Also as before, Kater argues, members of the middle class and upper class were over-represented while members of the working class were under-represented. Kater makes two further points about membership in this period. First, he points out that there was a great deal of turnover in the period 1924-29 and that this has important implications:

'Many would-be Nazi Party members joined the NSDAP for trial purposes only; they stayed for a few months or a few years and then dropped out. Many joined and rejoined several times...During certain phases of the Weimar Republic, the overall dropout rate amounted to as much as 50% of the total membership. This tells the student of Nazism a good deal about the provisional character of the Nazi Party in these years.' (Kater 1983, p.34)

And second, Kater's study of the social background of Nazi leaders comes to the conclusion that the social background of the leaders mirrored that of the membership.

Lower-middle-class Nazis

Kater's analysis of the occupations of those who joined the Nazi Party in the period 1924-29 shows that, as in 1919-23, the party appealed to merchants, artisans and low-ranking civil servants. In addition, there is evidence that small retailers and people who owned small businesses were particularly prone to join the Nazi Party. Kater explains this by pointing out that, although there was, overall, economic security in the period 1924-29, there were pressures on small businesses:

'In spite of the undeniable prosperity experienced by the majority of small businessmen between 1924 and 1929, a sizeable minority encountered serious difficulties. There were simply too many retailers in business after 1924 and so the less competitive were faced with reduced incomes. Additionally, female help was becoming increasingly difficult to get because of the lure of better-paying jobs in the more efficient chain-stores and cooperatives.' (Kater 1983, p.39)

Kater also shows that, although small farmers did not join the Nazi Party in any great number before 1927, the beginning of the agricultural crisis mentioned at the beginning of this section, combined with the change in focus from urban to rural centres, was sufficient to ensure that they flocked into the party in 1928. By 1929, they were over-represented in the party.

Upper-middle-class and upper-class Nazis

Kater shows that, as in the period 1919-23, the Nazi Party gained some support from members of the upper-middle class and upper class. As before, university students were particularly likely to join and intellectuals were over-represented in the party (although they did not join in as large proportions as in 1919-23). Kater is careful to make it clear, however, that, although the Nazis had some links with Big Business, these were by no means as important as historians used to think was the case (Kater's view on this matter is now standard). It used to be argued that the Nazis needed donations from Big Business to keep the party afloat financially. It has now been established, however, that, although donations were welcome, the main reason why the party stayed financially afloat was because it raised money from its own members and supporters (see, for example, Burleigh 2000, p.110).

Working-class Nazis

Kater argues that, despite the NSDAP's efforts to recruit workers in the period 1924-29, the working class remained under-represented:

'In spite of its leaders' efforts, the Nazi Party achieved little overall success among the blue-collar [ie working-class] population of the Reich until the Reichstag elections of September 1930.' (Kater 1983, p.35)

Box 4.17 shows, for example, that the number of working-class recruits to the Nazi Party remained under 43% throughout the period 1925-29. The census held in 1925 showed that in the population of Germany as a whole, 53.7% of men belonged to the working class (very few women joined the Nazi Party in this period - see below). Box 4.17 also shows that the number of new workers joining the NSDAP peaked in 1926-27. Kater argues that those workers who joined the party in the period 1925-29 came largely from small towns or rural areas rather than from the big cities. He argues that the Nazis found it hard to recruit members in big cities because workers there were loyal to the parties of the left (the KPD and SPD). One important reason for this was that the KPD and SPD supported the formation of trade unions and the use of strike action

(the Nazis generally did not support strike action). Attempts to set up Nazi unions were unsuccessful until the National Socialist Shop Organisation (NSBO) was set up in 1929. Once the NSBO was set up, it failed to attract substantial support from the workers at first:

'The NSBO gained ground only gradually, especially in the urban centres of the Ruhr and it seems to have attracted a much higher percentage of white-collar [ie middle-class] workers than would be expected of a union with genuine proletarian [ie working-class] interests.' (Kater 1983, p.37)

It is Kater's view that members of the working class who were disillusioned with the Weimar Republic were far more likely to join the KPD in the period 1924-29 than the NSDAP. In 1927, more than 80% of members of the KPD belonged to the working class.

Criticisms of Kater's approach

While later studies do not disagree with Kater that members of the lower-middle class were over-represented in the Nazi Party, some historians (notably Fischer C. 1995 and Falter 1996) have argued that, regardless of this, there were such great variations within each social class that to talk in terms of class is all but meaningless.

'The range of living and working conditions concealed behind the collective term "worker" was huge. Thus the East Prussian...labourer who was paid largely in kind and received an hourly cash payment of 10 pfennig or less belonged to this group as much as the factory-employed craftsman

BOX 4.17 Social class of people who joined the NSDAP 1925-29

Class	Occupation	1925	1926	1927	1928	1929
Working class	1. Unskilled workers	12.7	17.8	19.1	18.7	18.7
	2. Skilled (craft) workers	19.5	23.6	23.5	19.7	20.0
	3. Other skilled workers	-	-	-	-	-
Subtotal		**32.2**	**41.4**	**42.6**	**38.4**	**38.7**
Lower-middle class	4. Master craftsmen	11.3	13.7	13.5	11.4	11.6
	5. Non-academic professionals	-	-	-	-	-
	6. Lower employees	21.4	18.1	19.1	17.2	14.6
	7. Lower civil servants	11.4	5.2	5.0	4.9	5.5
	8. Merchants	11.3	8.5	8.3	8.1	11.1
	9. Farmers	3.6	6.1	5.2	13.3	12.0
Subtotal		**59.0**	**51.6**	**51.1**	**54.9**	**54.8**
Upper-middle & upper classes	10. Managers	-	-	-	-	-
	11. Higher civil servants	1.7	0.5	0.4	0.7	0.7
	12. Academic professionals	4.7	3.4	3.1	2.9	2.1
	13. Students	2.0	2.8	2.4	2.7	2.5
	14. Entrepreneurs	0.4	0.3	0.4	0.4	1.2
Subtotal		**8.8**	**7.0**	**6.3**	**6.7**	**6.5**

This table shows the social class of people joining the NSDAP in 1925-29. The figures are percentages. *Adapted from Kater 1983.*

or the highly specialised skilled worker who might earn ten times as much in the industrialised conurbations [big cities].' (Falter 1996, p.10)

To describe the the the NSDAP as a 'lower-middle-class party', Falter argues, is misleading. In 1925, 40% of members of the NSDAP were from the working class (compared to 53.7% in the population as a whole). While this does mean that the working class was under-represented, it also means that there was a large body of workers within the party. Given the problem of accounting for the variations within each social class outlined above, Falter argues that it is better to avoid describing the NSDAP in class terms. The fact that membership cut across class boundaries and included people from a wide range of occupations suggests that it would be more accurate to describe the party as a 'people's party':

'It possessed the character of a people's party or national party more than any other large Weimar party.' (Falter 1996, p.40)

Membership of the SA

Research carried out by Conan Fischer (see Box 4.18) has shown that, while workers were under-represented in the Nazi Party, they were over-represented in the SA. This over-representation was more striking in the period after 1932, but it existed in the period 1925-29. A second striking characteristic about membership of the SA is the young age of many of those who joined. Geary (2000) claims that the average age of recruits to the SA in the period 1925-32 varied between 17 and 22. A third characteristic is that many of those who joined were unemployed. Summing up his findings, Fischer concludes that:

'The SA's members were recruited largely from among the younger, male unemployed population of Germany. Most were workers.' (Fischer, C. 1995, p.169)

Age, gender, region and religion

Historians do not just examine membership in terms of social class. They have examined membership of the NSDAP in terms of other factors such as age, gender, region and religion. Their findings can be summarised as follows:

- the NSDAP was a youthful party - the average age of those joining between 1925 and 1932 was just under 29 (Falter 1996)
- very few women joined the NSDAP (c.10% of members were women in 1919-23 and the percentage dropped from c.8% in 1925 to c.4% in 1929 - Kater 1983)
- although many areas had very small percentages of female members, some had higher percentages (for example, the town of Barmen in the Ruhr had 13.3% female members in 1925 - Kater 1983)
- women were banned from leadership positions

in the party in 1921 (Kater 1983)
- membership varied considerably in both numbers and composition according to region - in the western Ruhr, for example, over 50% of members were working class in the period February 1925 to December 1932 while in the area around Hanover, just 37.1% were working class (Mühlberger 1995)
- Protestants were more likely to join the Nazi Party than Catholics (Geary 2000).

Just as membership of the party had been analysed in terms of age, gender, region and religion, so too has support for the party. Geary (2000) argues that 'virtually all commentators' agree that the Nazis gained more support:

- in Protestant areas rather than in Catholic areas
- in rural areas rather than in urban areas
- in small towns rather than in big cities
- from white-collar (middle-class) workers in the public sector rather than from white-collar workers in the private sector.

BOX 4.18 Membership of the SA		
Class	**Occupation**	**Feb 1925 to Jan 1933**
Workers	Agricultural	2.9
	Unskilled	15.4
	Skilled	35.4
	Public sector	0.9
	Apprentices	1.5
	Servants	0.4
Subtotal		**56.5**
Lower-middle & middle classes	Master artisans	1.3
	Non-graduate professions	3.3
	Salaried staff	8.8
	Civil servants	2.7
	Soldiers	0.0
	Salesmen/merchants	10.4
	Farmers	4.3
	Family helpers	2.1
Subtotal		**32.9**
Upper-middle & upper classes	Senior salaried staff	0.2
	Senior civil servants	0.1
	Military officers	0.0
	University students	4.1
	Graduate professions	1.2
	Entrepreneurs	0.2
Subtotal		**5.8**
Unclear	Schoolboys/students	1.9
	Retired	0.4
	Others/no info	2.0
Subtotal		**4.3**

This table shows the social class of members of the SA in the period February 1925 to January 1933.

Adapted from Fischer C. 1995.

Geary makes two further claims. First, he asserts that, until 1930, hardly any women voted for the NSDAP. And second, he argues that the local context is particularly important in determining whether people supported the Nazis:

'[Support] came primarily from areas without strong political, social, ideological or cultural loyalties. In Catholic, as in social-democratic Germany [ie in areas where there was a tradition of supporting the SPD], voters' loyalty to their traditional representatives was reinforced by a dense network of social and cultural organisations (trade unions, sports clubs, choral societies, educational associations and so on), as well as - in the Catholic case - by the pulpit.' (Geary 2000, p.24)

MAIN POINTS - Section 2.2

- Membership of the NSDAP grew slowly between the relaunch of the party in February 1925 and May 1928. Then it began to rise rapidly.
- Six reasons have been suggested to explain the onset of rapid growth - (1) the NSDAP was united behind Hitler (2) the party was more efficient (3) targeting rural areas was successful (4) other right-wing parties were losing ground (5) the economic climate was deteriorating and (6) the anti-Weimar stance appealed.
- The social profile of Nazi membership was the same as that before 1923. Workers were under-represented but some did join. The middle and upper classes were over-represented.
- Some historians have argued that analysis of Nazi membership in terms of class has led to the misleading conclusion that the NSDAP was a party of the lower-middle class. The fact that membership cut across classes suggests that it was a 'people's party'.
- Research shows that membership of the NSDAP in the period 1924-29 - (1) was youthful (2) was mainly male (3) varied in size and composition from region to region and (4) was mainly Protestant.

Activity 4.7 Who supported the Nazis 1924-30?

ITEM 1 Nazi membership in different towns

Class		Occupation	Hamburg Mar 1925	Langerfeld Nov 1925	Brunswick 1925-26	Starnberg July 1927	Königsberg 1928	Königsberg Jun 1929
Working class	1.	Unskilled workers	17.9	27.0	13.3	14.8	5.6	2.5
	2.	Skilled (craft) workers	13.8	27.0	13.9	21.1	22.7	21.4
	3.	Other skilled workers	1.9	2.7	2.3	11.1	4.7	3.8
Subtotal			**33.6**	**56.8**	**29.5**	**47.0**	**33.0**	**27.7**
Lower-middle	4.	Master craftsmen	7.9	16.2	8.0	12.2	13.1	12.4
class	5.	Non-academic professionals	0	2.7	2.3	0	3.9	1.7
	6.	Lower employees	14.2	0	19.5	7.4	14.2	20.0
	7.	Lower civil servants	8.5	5.4	11.7	11.1	5.6	6.7
	8.	Merchants	30.2	13.5	15.6	0	14.2	18.3
	9.	Farmers	0	0	7.8	0	4.3	0.8
Subtotal			**60.8**	**37.8**	**64.9**	**30.7**	**55.3**	**59.9**
Upper-middle	10.	Managers	0.9	0	1.6	0	0	0.4
& upper	11.	Higher civil servants	0.9	0	0	14.8	0.9	0.8
classes	12.	Academic professionals	3.8	2.7	2.3	3.7	1.3	2.1
	13.	Students	0	2.7	0.8	0	7.8	7.9
	14.	Entrepreneurs	0	0	0.8	3.7	1.7	1.3
Subtotal			**5.6**	**5.4**	**5.5**	**22.2**	**11.7**	**12.5**

This table shows the social composition of the Nazi electorate in various towns between 1925 and 1929. The figures are percentages.

Adapted from Kater 1983.

ITEM 2 The social composition of the Nazi electorate

		Census 1925	Election May 1928	Election Sept 1930
Religion	Catholics		30	20
	Others		70	80
Community size	0-5,000	42	39	41
	5,000-20,000	13	14	13
	20,000-100,000	14	16	15
	Above 100,000	31	31	31
Class	Workers	45.1	40	40
	Lower-middle	34.5	37	39
	Upper-middle & upper	21.4	22	21

The left hand column in this table (with the heading 'Census 1925') provides information about the German population as a whole (the figures are in percentages and derived from the census taken in 1925). The two other columns provide information about the people who voted for the NSDAP in 1928 and 1930. The figures are also percentages.

Adapted from Fischer C. 1995.

ITEM 3 Women in the Nazi Party

In the 1930s, a Social Democrat called Carl Mierendorff remarked that women played 'no significant role' in the Nazi Party. Usually the conspicuous absence of women from the NSDAP has been explained by reference to the Nazi leaders' misogyny (hatred of women) and a corresponding desire by women not to be involved in the NSDAP. The Nazi leaders shared a belief in male supremacy. Their sexist and militaristic attitude is well illustrated in *Mein Kampf* where Hitler makes it clear that he believes that women were essentially breeding material for future warriors and that their place is to be in the home, by the hearth and with the children. He also makes it clear that, in his view, a wife was inferior to her husband and should obey him without question. As early as January 1921, women were excluded from leadership positions in the party. As late as August 1927, during a party rally in Nuremberg, although girls and women were allowed to join the SA parade in Nazi uniform, they were prevented from passing by the grandstand to salute the Führer. When the NSDAP was relaunched in 1925, women once again joined up. Although the numbers varied from place to place, hardly anywhere exceeded the levels of the 1919-23 period. It seems likely that 1928-29 marked a low point in women's involvement in the party and that, from then on, they again turned to the party in greater strength. Throughout the period 1919-29, the average age of female members was slightly older than that of men. One explanation is that there was a surplus of marriageable women in the early 1920s. According to the census of 1925, this surplus first appeared among women aged 30-34. For women aged 35-80 there were two unmarried women to every unmarried man. Older unmarried women, it seems, were more likely to consider Nazi membership than unmarried men of the same age.

Adapted from Kater 1983.

ITEM 4 Voting behaviour

The Nazis were more successful in Protestant than Catholic Germany because they were successful where they did not have to cope with pre-existing loyalties. Germany's Catholic community had been strongly represented over decades by the Centre Party (or the BVP in Bavaria). Loyalty to the party was reinforced by Catholic leisure organisations and by the pulpit, from which Nazism was sometimes denounced as being godless. On the other hand, Nazi success in Protestant rural and middle-class Germany resulted from the fact that political loyalties were either weak or non-existent. For example, peasants in Schleswig-Holstein and Lower Saxony had already deserted the DNVP while the lower-middle class in the towns had abandoned the political parties they had traditionally supported. On the other hand, the Social Democrats in Leipzig and Dresden beat off the Nazi challenge precisely because a high percentage of SPD voters in these towns were also members of the party and because there existed a dense network of Social Democratic leisure and cultural organisations. There were two other important factors in voting behaviour - age and gender. The youthful image of the NSDAP (and the SA) has some foundation. But, youth politics were not uniform. They divided to some extent according to social class, religious belief and gender. The young unemployed were more likely to turn to the Communists than the Nazis, for example. It is also true that the Nazis enjoyed remarkable success with elderly voters. Women voted less frequently than men, especially in rural areas. It is true that the female vote divided along lines of class, religion and region, but it still remained distinctive. By 1930, 3.5 million women voted for the SPD. But very few women voted for the KPD. Women were more likely to vote for parties close to the churches (DNVP if Protestant, Centre Party if Catholic). Until 1930, they were unlikely to vote Nazi, but this then changed.

Adapted from Geary 2000.

Questions

1. Using Items 1-3 and your own knowledge, describe what sort of people joined the Nazi Party in the period 1924-29.
2. According to Items 1 and 2, what characteristics would the typical member of the Nazi Party have in the period 1924-29?
3. Judging from Item 3, why do you think so few women joined the Nazi Party in the period 1924-29?
4. What does Item 4 tell us about the factors determining whether people would vote Nazi in the period 1924-29?

3 The Nazis and the crisis of 1929-33

Key issues

1. What led to the massive growth in support of the Nazi Party in the period 1929-31?
2. How did Hitler manage to become Chancellor in 1933?
3. Who supported the Nazis after September 1930?
4. Who opposed the Nazis?

3.1 What led to the massive growth in support of the Nazi Party in the period 1929-31?

The Reich election of September 1930

There is a consensus among historians that the Reich election of September 1930 was a turning point in Nazi fortunes. Overnight, the Nazis' position changed from being that of a party on the fringes to being the second largest party in the Reichstag. The Nazi vote rose from 810,100 in 1928 to 6.4 million in 1930 and the number of seats rose from 12 to 107. As Fischer points out, this transformation in electoral fortunes produced a bandwagon effect:

'The September election produced an immediate bandwagon effect on the Nazi movement. As Joachim Fest [a historian] observed, it even became chic to join the party, particularly after one of the Kaiser's sons, Prince August Wilhelm ("Auwi"), became a member.' (Fischer K. 1995, p.228)

Throughout 1931, this bandwagon continued to roll. Party membership grew considerably, as did membership of the SA (Klaus Fischer claims that party membership had risen to 800,000 by the end of 1931 and that the SA numbered 225,000 while other historians quote lower figures - for example, Bullock 1991 claims that party membership had only risen to 450,000 by the end of 1931). Publicity stunts and the constant flow of propaganda ensured that the momentum continued to flow.

The economic downturn

Historians agree that the massive growth in support of the Nazi Party in the period 1929-31 was related, in some way, to the economic downturn that took place during this period (the economic problems that Germany faced in the period 1929-31 are examined in detail in Unit 3, Section 2.1). Many historians argue that the Wall Street Crash of October 1929 was the key event because the Crash resulted in a worldwide economic depression. The standard view is as follows:

'The onset of the 1929 world economic depression immeasurably radicalised the political climate in Germany.' (Burleigh 2000, p.124)

As was pointed out in Section 2.2 above, however, the economic downturn in Germany began many months before the Wall Street Crash. An agricultural crisis began to develop as early as 1926 (encouraging the Nazis to target rural areas) and industrial unrest and unemployment began growing in the year before the Wall Street Crash occurred:

'By the time Hitler spoke in the Sportpalast [on 16 November 1928], the first dark clouds were already gathering over Germany's economy. The mounting crisis in agriculture was leading to widespread indebtedness, bankruptcies, forced sales of land and enormous bitterness in the farming community. In the biggest industrial belt, Ruhr industrialists refused to accept an arbitration award and locked out the whole workforce of the iron and steel industry, leaving 230,000 workers without jobs or wages for weeks. Meanwhile, unemployment was sharply on the rise, reaching almost 3 million by January 1929.' (Kershaw 1998, p.305)

Why did support for the NSDAP grow?

While there is no doubt that the worldwide economic depression that followed the Wall Street Crash affected Germany deeply and was somehow related to the growing support for the Nazis, it is important to note that Nazi support had been growing rapidly in the year prior to the Crash. The shockwaves which followed the Crash, in other words, intensified a process which had already begun. Furthermore, it should not be assumed that there is a simple link between the economic downturn and the growth in support for the Nazis. As Kater points out, it was not necessarily those directly affected by the downturn who joined the NSDAP:

'In one occupational group, the lower clerks, it was the younger clerks, those least affected by the Depression, who were attracted to the NSDAP. And, among workers, it was those living in country areas where dislocations were least likely to occur who joined the NSDAP in greatest strength.' (Kater 1983, p.156)

Kater argues that factors other than the economic climate may have played a part in persuading people to support the NSDAP during this period. He suggests that people may have come to support the NSDAP because they were:

- anti-Semitic
- scared of, or hated, Marxism
- militarists (they believed that society should be organised on military lines)
- activists (they wanted action not just words)
- psychologically traumatised by the First World War and Germany's defeat
- converted in the same way that they might have been converted to a religion.

Nevertheless, even if the link between experience of economic hardship and the massive growth in support for the Nazis was not direct (or was not the only explanation for the growth in support), there were a number of ways in which economic hardship - or the fear of economic hardship - was translated into growth of support for the Nazi Party after 1928. First, many people - whether directly affected by the economic downturn or afraid that they would be affected by it - blamed the Weimar government for failing to take steps to prevent or alleviate the economic hardship that Germany as a whole was suffering. Since the Nazi Party was consistently and openly hostile to the Weimar government, its message began to appeal to those who were becoming disillusioned with the government. Second, it was not just the government that was blamed for the economic hardship. Many people began to blame the political system as a whole. Again, since the Nazis were opposed to the system as a whole, this benefited them (just as it benefited the KPD which was also opposed to the system as a whole). Third, some people began to argue that the economic hardship was the result of a failure to provide strong leadership. Since strong leadership was what the Nazis promised, their message began to appeal. Fourth, the economic downturn coincided with a rise in support for the KPD. This scared many people (whether affected by the downturn themselves or not) and encouraged them

to support the party they believed would best prevent a Communist takeover. And fifth, according to Klaus Fischer, the Wall Street Crash brought about a state of panic:

'The stock market crash provided the psychological impetus for a panic mentality...The economic shockwaves reached Germany in a matter of weeks because American loans had, in large part, propped up the sluggish German economy. The result was a deep depression, comparable in economic scope to that in the United States, but far more serious in its political implications.' (Fischer K. 1995, p.216)

In times of panic, so the argument goes, people look for extreme solutions and an extreme solution is what the NSDAP offered.

Nazi policy

Kershaw argues that, in order to understand the Nazis' policy in the period 1925-31, it is necessary to understand that Hitler was a man with a long-term mission and that, because of this, the Nazis were flexible, not rigid, in their approach. What mattered was winning power because that was the only way for the mission to be accomplished. If that meant changing tactics, tactics would have to be changed. But, Kershaw emphasises, that does not mean that the Nazis were prepared to say or do anything to gain power. The party always adopted policies and produced propaganda that remained true to its fundamental principles. Box 4.19 explores how these fundamental principles affected the way in which the party developed policy.

Kershaw points out that Hitler said time and again that he was uninterested in day-to-day issues. In his speeches he always focused on his long-term aims:

'What he offered, over and over again, was the same vision of a long-term goal, to be striven after with missionary zeal and total commitment. Political struggle, eventual attainment of power, destruction of the enemy and build-up of the nation's might were stepping stones to the goal. But how it was to be then attained was left open. Hitler himself had no concrete notion. He just had the certainty of the fanatical "conviction politician" that it would be attained.' (Kershaw 1998, p.290)

Dual appeal

Since Hitler adopted this approach, the Nazi Party had a flexibility that other parties lacked. The lack of detail was a strength. By constantly looking forward to the future - to a time when the Weimar Republic no longer existed - the Nazis avoided the need to propose detailed policies which addressed the needs of the time. In the 'wilderness years', this was a problem. The NSDAP's vision lacked appeal. But in the changed economic circumstances of 1929-31 people began to take notice. David Welch agrees with Ian Kershaw that the vagueness of the Nazi

BOX 4.19 Hitler's world view

The 'idea' Hitler stood for was not a matter of short-term objectives. It was a 'mission', a 'vision' of long-term future goals and of his own part in the accomplishment of them. Certainly, these goals - national salvation through 'removal' of the Jews and the gaining of 'living space' in the east - did not amount to short-term practical policy guidelines. But taken together with the idea of the 'heroic' leader, they did add up to a dynamic 'world view'. This world view gave Hitler his drive. He spoke repeatedly of his 'mission'. He saw this in religious terms. The hand of 'Providence' was in his work. His fight against the Jews was 'the work of the Lord'. He saw his life's work as a crusade. It would be a serious mistake to underestimate the driving-force of Hitler's few central ideas. He wasn't by any means an 'unprincipled opportunist', as Alan Bullock has argued. Since Hitler's world view consisted of a few basic but unchangeable principles, it was compatible with short-term tactical adjustments. And it had the advantage of accommodating and reconciling a variety of otherwise conflicting positions on particular issues raised by subordinate Nazi leaders. Within the framework of his world view, Hitler was flexible, even indifferent, towards issues which could obsess his followers. Historians have often argued that Nazi ideology (the set of ideas supported by the Nazis) was just a cloak for the ambition to gain power. But this misinterprets the driving force of Hitler's own basic ideas, few and crude as they were. And it is to misunderstand the ways those basic ideas came to function in the Nazi Party and then, after 1933, in the Nazi state. What mattered for Hitler was indeed the road to power. He was prepared to sacrifice most principles for that. But some principles (and those were, for him, the ones that counted) were not only unchangeable, they formed the essence of what he understood by power itself. Opportunism was always itself shaped by the core ideas.

Adapted from Kershaw 1998.

vision was a strength. He notes that, in the period 1929-31, the Nazis managed to win over both the 'old' middle class (which he describes as 'small retailers, self-employed artisans, peasant farmers, pensioners and those on fixed incomes) and the 'new' middle class (which he describes as 'white collar, non-manual employees' - ie clerks and low-ranking civil servants). The Nazis won over these groups, Welch argues, because it had a 'dual appeal'. The vagueness of the vision allowed people to reach different conclusions about what the Nazis stood for. Some people thought they were reactionary (ie they would restore the sort of values that had existed in Germany before the First World War) while others saw them as revolutionary (ie they would produce a new type of society):

> 'Some looked to the Nazis as the saviour of old style capitalism that would restore the old status quo. For such groups, the Nazis represented a "reactionary" force, restoring former status and values. While others, particularly among younger, white-collar workers, saw National Socialism as a "revolutionary" movement bent on destroying archaic [ie very old] social hierarchies and replacing them with a new social order. The secret of their success was this "dual appeal".' (Welch 1995, p.58)

Nazi propaganda

The way in which the Nazis communicated their vision was via propaganda (see Box 4.20):

> 'The skilful exploitation of propaganda techniques has been cited by historians of widely different political persuasions and approaches as having played a crucial role in mobilising support for the Nazis. In this context, attention has, by and large, been focused on the dynamics of the Nazi Party, its parades, its symbols, the uniforms and banners, the bands, the marching columns of the SA etc which "captured the imagination" of the masses. In the light of such consensus, it would appear that one of the most important factors contributing to the Nazis' rise to power was the cumulative effect of their propaganda.' (Welch 1993, p.55)

But this view of Nazi propaganda, Welch argues, is misleading. The idea that the Nazis 'conquered the masses' or 'brainwashed' people into supporting the Nazi Party is a distortion for two reasons. First, such an idea suggests that people were somehow duped into supporting the Nazis when, in fact, they were not. The Nazis' message genuinely appealed to many people and they supported the party because they believed it was in their best interests to do so. And second, by claiming that propaganda 'brainwashed' people, the implication is that blame lay with the Nazis and not with the other politicians and political parties in the Weimar system. A counter argument, however, is that the other politicians and political parties were to blame for the Nazis' rise to power because they did not provide a viable alternative to the Nazis.

Preaching to the converted

Welch argues that, despite Hitler's claims about the power of propaganda, propaganda is not necessarily a mechanism for converting a non-believer into believer. Many non-believers, he points out, were never converted to the Nazi cause and no amount of propaganda would have converted them. To be effective, propaganda must appeal to an audience which is at least mildly sympathetic towards the ideas being expressed:

BOX 4.20 Hitler and propaganda

In *Mein Kampf*, Hitler was quite explicit about how he would achieve his great vision. He would 'nationalise' the masses, making them fanatical supporters through unrelenting propaganda until, at last, shaped into a superbly organised fighting force, they would carry out their sacred racial mission. Hitler's main weapon was propaganda. Without propaganda, he believed, it is impossible to reach the hearts of the people and fill them with a sense of purpose and mission. Effective propaganda, he argued, did not rest on logic, but on faith and emotions. The masses crave certainty. In order to reach their hearts, it is necessary to teach them a fanatically one-sided set of beliefs since, once the masses have found a political faith, it is very difficult to undermine it. So, the success of the movement, Hitler believed, relied on mass manipulation. As a result, Hitler made no distinction between education and propaganda (it is important to note, however, that he saw propaganda as a means to an end not as an end in itself. The end of politics is, of course, power). Since propaganda aims at persuasion rather than instruction, Hitler claimed, it is far more effective to appeal to the emotions. This can be done most effectively through the spoken word and in settings where masses of people can be reached. Hitler believed that crowds are more impressionable than individuals. They are prone to believe the unbelievable. In fact, they swallow the big lie more easily than the small lie. In the end, people are persuaded only when the last vestiges of doubt are removed from their minds. This cannot be achieved by presenting both sides of an argument, but rather by insisting that only one side is the absolute truth. In politics, Hitler claimed, there are no shades of grey.

Adapted from Fischer K. 1995.

'Propaganda is as much about confirming as converting public opinion. Propaganda, if it is to be effective, must in a sense preach to those who are already partially converted. Writing before the Second World War, Aldous Huxley observed: "Propaganda gives force and direction to the successive movements of popular feeling and desire; but it does not do much to create these movements. The propagandist is a man who canalises an existing stream. In a land where there is no water, he digs in vain".' (Welch 1995, p.55)

So, according to Welch, it would be wrong to say that Nazi propaganda produced the massive growth of support for the Nazis in the period 1929-31. Rather, the economic downturn produced an environment in which disillusion with the Weimar system and fear of Communism grew. As this disillusion and fear grew, Nazi propaganda, which had previously fallen on deaf ears, began to strike a chord with some groups in German society. The propaganda encouraged people to support the Nazis. It did not make them do so.

Party organisation and membership

The reorganisation of the party structure in 1925-29 (see Activity 4.6, Item 1) ensured that it was able to cope with rapid growth in the period 1929-31:

'By 1929, the organisation of the party, which had been built up to accompany its nationwide expansion (however thinly spread at first) bore little comparison to the hand-to-mouth administration of the pre-Putsch party, and placed it in a far stronger position to exploit the new crises that descended on Germany from the autumn of that year.' (Kershaw 1998, p.259)

It is difficult to be sure exactly how many people were members of the Nazi Party at any one time because turnover was high. Nevertheless, Conan Fischer (1995) calculates that membership rose from 178,000 in December 1929 to 300,000 by the autumn of 1930. The Nazis' electoral success in September 1930 then provided another boost and membership continued to grow, reaching more than 500,000 by the time that Hitler became Chancellor in January 1933. Allen (1984) shows that even in areas where the Nazis made no impact before 1929, small cells of Nazis existed and these small cells became the launch pad for the growth of Nazism on a local level. In Northeim, a small town in North Germany, for example, in the election of May 1928, the Nazis won 123 votes - just 2.3% of the total vote. A year later, the local Nazi Party had just five members. Although, Allen shows, the economic downturn only affected workers in the area and did not really hit the middle classes, it created an atmosphere of fear amongst them - especially fear of Communism - and support for the Nazi Party began to grow rapidly. By January 1930, the local party had 58 members and in the election held in September 1930, the Nazis won 1,742 votes - 28% of the total vote. This growth in support, Allen argues, was largely due to Nazi campaigning. The Nazis were much more active than other right-wing parties in the area and their activism encouraged people to support them. What happened in Northeim happened in towns throughout Germany during this period.

Electoral realignment

Thomas Childers argues that the roots of Nazi success in 1929-31 lie in an 'electoral realignment' which had begun taking place in the early 1920s. He argues that the economic downturn and hyperinflation of 1922-23 resulted in many members of the middle classes in Germany abandoning their traditional middle-class political parties. At first, they moved to 'special interest alternatives':

'The period following the inflation and stabilisation crises witnessed a phenomenal growth of special interest or single-issue parties that flourished under the Republic's system of proportional representation. In the elections of 1919 and 1920, these small parties had accounted for only 3% of the vote. By May 1924, however, they represented over 10% of the German electorate. Significantly, that percentage did not decline during the period of relative political and economic stability in the mid-1920s.' (Childers 1983, p.125)

Members of the middle classes, Childers argues, voted for these special interest parties because they were disillusioned with the traditional liberal and conservative parties. When, in turn, the economic downturn began to bite, these voters began to become disillusioned with the special interest parties, eventually transferring their loyalty to the Nazis. Central to Childers' argument is the idea that party loyalty had already become unstuck during the Weimar Republic's 'Golden Years' and that this helps to explain why the Nazis gained so much support after the economic climate began to deteriorate.

The Nazis enter the mainstream

There is a consensus among historians that it was the campaign against the Young Plan, agreed in June 1929 (see Unit 3, Section 1.3 for details on the Young Plan) that first provided the Nazis with a significant platform in national politics. Alfred Hugenberg, Leader of the DNVP (German National People's Party) and media tycoon, invited the Nazis to join his campaign to win the holding of a plebiscite - a referendum. When the Nazis agreed to join this campaign, they were provided with a huge amount of free publicity:

'Cranking up his media resources - newspapers, wire services, UFA (Universum-Film Aktiengesellshchaft [Universal-Film Joint-Stock Company] newsreels - he unleashed a campaign of such...intensity that even Hitler was impressed by it. In fact, Hitler was delighted to be associated with this campaign because it gave the Nazi Party a national forum free of charge.' (Fischer K. 1995, p.212)

In addition to publicity, Kershaw (1998) points out, the campaign gave the Nazis access to Big Business and a degree of respectability that it had never enjoyed in the past. Furthermore, the campaign resulted in humiliation for Hugenberg - something which benefited the Nazis as the DNVP were close rivals electorally:

'When the plebiscite finally took place, on 22 December 1929, only 5.8 million - 13.8% of the electorate - voted for it. The campaign had proved a failure - but not for Hitler. He and his party had benefited from the massive exposure freely afforded him in the Hugenberg press. And he had been recognised as an equal partner by those in high places, with good contacts to sources of funding and influence.' (Kershaw 1998, p.310)

Hitler's new high profile helped the bandwagon, which was beginning to roll, to gather pace.

MAIN POINTS - Section 3.1

- The breakthrough for the Nazis came with the Reich election of September 1930 when their vote increased from 810,100 in 1928 to 6.4 million and the NSDAP became the second largest party in the Reichstag.
- Historians argue that the massive rise in support for the Nazis was due to - (1) experience of and fear of the economic downturn (2) Nazi policy, which was particularly flexible (3) Nazi propaganda, which attracted people already inclined to listen to Nazi ideas (4) party organisation, which encouraged activism and (5) electoral realignment in the 1920s, which had left a political vacuum.
- It was the campaign against the Young Plan of June 1929 that first provided the Nazis with a significant platform in national politics.

Activity 4.8 Growth of support for the Nazi Party

ITEM 1 National elections 1928 and 1930

Party	Election May 1928			Election Sept 1930		
	Total votes	%	No. MPs	Total votes	%	No. MPs
NSDAP	810,100	2.6	12	6,409,600	18.3	107
DNVP	4,381,600	14.2	73	2,458,300	7.0	41
DVP	2,679,700	8.7	45	1,578,200	4.5	30
BVP	945,600	3.0	16	1,059,100	3.0	19
Centre Party	3,712,200	12.1	62	4,127,900	11.8	68
SPD	9,153,800	10.6	153	8,577,700	24.5	143
KPD	3,264,800	10.6	54	4,592,100	13.1	77

This table shows the results of national elections held in Germany in 1928 and 1930.

Part of the explanation for the change in the Nazis' fortunes in the Reich election of September 1930 was a dramatic increase in the turnout - 82% of those eligible to vote, 35 million against the 31 million of 1928. The other main source of the increased Nazi vote was among former voters from the 'bourgeois' parties - the DNVP, the DVP (right-wing liberals) and the DDP (progressive liberals). Their share of the vote halved between 1928 and 1930 and halved again in July 1932. By contrast, the Catholic Centre Party held its own and, while the SPD's vote was eroded, the KPD was the only other party, apart from the NSDAP, to raise its percentage. If the vote for the two working-class parties is combined, it holds remarkably steady during the years of the Great Depression. As always, the Nazis did better in Protestant areas than it did in Catholic areas. The Nazi emphasis on traditional family life seems to have appealed to women for the first time. Regionally, there was variation. The Nazis did best in Protestant and agricultural areas in the north and east. They did less well in urban and industrial areas. Nevertheless, Nazi support came from all classes. In 1930, more so in 1932, they drew on support from across a wider spectrum of the electorate than any of the other parties. In 1930, the Nazis attracted support from workers who did not belong to unions and who were engaged in handicrafts and small-scale manufacturing. That election also marks the beginning of the Nazis' success in attracting support from the professions. They made great play out of their appeal to youth. But, with a population in which well over half belonged to the working class and the Nazis unable to challenge the KPD and SPD's grip, much of their support came from the middle classes.

Adapted from Bullock 1991.

ITEM 2 Regional and local elections

The NSDAP won 5% of the vote in the election held in Saxony on 12 May 1929. The following month, the party gained 4% in the Mecklenburg elections - double what it had achieved the previous year in the national election. Its two elected members then held the balance of power. Towards the end of June, Coburg in Northern Bavaria became the first town in Germany to elect a Nazi-run town council. By October, the NSDAP's share of the vote had reached 7% in the Baden state elections. This was still before the Wall Street Crash brought in the Great Depression. Less than two months after the Crash, on 8 December, the Nazis trebled their vote of 1928 in an election in Thuringia, breaking the 10% barrier for the first time. They won six seats (out of 53) and held the balance of power. Invited to join an anti-Marxist coalition, Hitler agreed to allow the successful candidates to join the Thuringian state government. He demanded that the Nazis be given two ministries - the Ministry of the Interior and the Ministry of Education. His demand was accepted. When, five months later, elections were held in rural Oldenburg, the NSDAP won 37.2% of the vote and became, for the first time, the largest party in a state Parliament. In Saxony, on 22 June 1930, the NSDAP received 14.4% of the vote, becoming the second largest party there. Then, in Hessen in November 1930, a remarkable poll gave the Nazis 37.1% of the vote, making it, with 27 seats, the largest party in a state Parliament where it had previously been unrepresented. The Nazi success was largely due to the decline of the bourgeois (traditional middle-class) parties, a process soon to be replayed at national level. The combined vote of the DVP and DNVP fell from 21.4% in 1929 to 13.5% in 1930.

Note: The location of the states mentioned in this item can be found on the maps on page iv.

Adapted from Feuchtwanger 1995.

ITEM 3 The Nazis in Northeim

To most Northeimers, the NSDAP was first and foremost an anti-Marxist party. When Northeimers thought of Marxism, they were not likely to think of the KPD, who in 1928 had received only 28 of the 5,372 votes cast in the town. The 'Marxist' party in Northeim was the SPD, the dominant political force there. In the 1928 Reich election, they won almost 45% of votes - more than the next three parties combined. That the SPD was a non-revolutionary party did not matter. The socialists carried a red flag and sang the *Internationale* (the Marxists' song). They were associated with all that went wrong in 1918. They represented the unwashed workers and the unemployed. To oppose these supporters of equality was of great importance in an environment of economic depression. The SPD planned a rally for 27 April 1930. This was what the Nazis were waiting for. Three days later, they announced they would also hold a rally that day. This was too much for the police. Because of previous outbreaks of violence, Prussia had banned open air meetings and processions for a three-month period which had just ended on 30 March. In the week when the rallies were announced, there were two violent clashes. The police banned the rallies. The Nazis announced their rally would go ahead in a village two miles north of Northeim. Over 2,000 attended and 800 stormtroopers marched. Afterwards, three truckloads of stormtroopers passed through Northeim scattering leaflets.

Party	No. Votes 1928	No. Votes 1930
NSDAP	123	1,742
DNVP	475	320
DHP	455	271
Staats-partei	505	246
DVP	834	788
Centre Party	170	184
SPD	2,210	2,246
KPD	28	115
Others	572	275

The table above shows the number of people in Northeim voting for each party in the 1928 and 1930 Reich elections. The DHP was the Hanoverian Party, a conservative party which supported independence for the areas around Northeim. The Staats-partei was also a conservative party which supported orderly middle-class parliamentary rule.

Skilfully, therefore, the Nazis not only blocked the SPD, they dominated the press and 'powerfully impressed' Northeimers with their size and determination. The second idea of Nazism that the Northeimers recognised clearly in these early days was its support of extreme patriotism and militarism. This gave the Nazi Party a foot in the door of respectability. The extent to which Northeim accepted these values was shown by the visit of Field Marshal von Mackensen in May 1930. Arriving by special train, he was greeted by 1,000 people at the station and crowds lined his route as he rode through the town.

Adapted from Allen 1984.

Questions

1. Using Item 1, explain why the Reich election of September 1930 has been described as a turning point in Nazi fortunes.
2. Judging from Items 1 and 2 and your own knowledge, why do you think support for the Nazis began to grow so rapidly?
3. What does Item 3 tell us about why support for the Nazis began to grow so rapidly in the period 1929-31?

3.2 How did Hitler manage to become Chancellor in 1933?

The legal path to revolution

It was noted in Section 2.1 above that, by the time Hitler left prison in 1924, he had become convinced that the Nazis should pursue a 'legal path to revolution'. Although this consistently remained Nazi policy, right up to 30 January 1933 (the day on which Hitler was appointed Chancellor), there was constantly pressure on Hitler, especially from the SA, to seize power by force. As Bullock points out, Hitler had a difficult balancing act to perform:

'Hitler had to hold the balance between "illegality" - which, it allowed to get out of hand, put at risk his credibility as a possible partner in the eyes of the army leaders and the group round the President - and "legality" which, if pressed too hard, could disillusion the large number who had joined the party and the SA in the belief that force, not majority votes, should settle national issues.' (Bullock 1991, p.254)

Bullock argues that Hitler managed to keep the balance by 'creating an aura of uncertainty'. On the one hand, he never condemned violence carried out by the SA, for example, and often encouraged the use of strong-arm tactics. On the other hand, whenever possible, he also took steps to persuade members of the 'Establishment' (senior politicians, army officers and people surrounding the President) that he could be trusted.

The trial at Leipzig, September 1930

One such step on the road to winning over the Establishment came just after the Reich election of 14 September 1930. On 23 September, a trial began in Leipzig of three army officers accused of 'preparing to commit High Treason' by spreading Nazi propaganda. Hitler was called as a witness for the defence and used the opportunity to make clear, under oath, that he was committed to the legal path to revolution:

'Hitler emphasised that his movement would take power by legal means and that the Reichswehr - again becoming a "great German people's army" - would be the "basis for the German future". He declared that he had never wanted to pursue his ideals by illegal measures...But he assured the presiding judge: "if our movement is victorious in its legal struggle, then there will be a German State Court and November 1918 will find its atonement [ie revenge], and heads will roll".' (Kershaw 1998, pp.337-38)

According to Bullock, Hitler's comments, made under oath, helped to reassure at least some members of the Establishment that the Nazis would not resort to force:

'When General Jodl, Hitler's Chief of Staff during the war, was interrogated at the Nuremberg Trials after the war, he told the Tribunal that he had not been reassured until Hitler swore under oath in the court that he opposed any interference with the army. This explicit statement was designed to open the way to the subsequent negotiations with the Reichswehr leaders.' (Bullock 1991, p.256)

Obstacles blocking the legal path to revolution

If the Nazis had ever won more than 50% of the vote in a Reich election, then their path into government would have been smooth. The President would have had no choice but to make Hitler Chancellor. This, however, did not happen. Although the growth in electoral support for the Nazis was phenomenal, it peaked at the Reich election of July 1932, when the Nazis won 37.4% of the vote. In the Reich election held four months later in November, support for the Nazis actually fell (to 33.1%). Despite this, the Nazis managed to gain power using legal means in January 1933. They did so by overcoming two main obstacles:

- President Hindenburg's distrust of Hitler (Hindenburg had the power to appoint the Chancellor)
- the distrust and opposition of other right-wing politicians (since the Nazis never won an overall

majority of seats, they could only win power if they were prepared to cooperate, to some extent, with other right-wing politicians).

It is important to note, therefore, that, although the massive growth of support for the Nazis ensured that the party came to the verge of power, it was not inevitable that the party would actually gain power:

'Hitler needed not only confidence but patience. He could build up the pressure from outside, but as long as he held to his tactics of legality, he had to wait for those on the inside to take the initiative in bringing him into negotiations. This waiting game was a severe test of the party's and of Hitler's own faith in his predestined success, the core of the Führer myth. But there were four objective factors outside his control which were yet capable of being turned to his advantage.' (Bullock 1991, pp.257-58)

These 'four objective factors' are summarised in Box 4.21

The decline of parliamentary government

Box 4.21 suggests that one factor which worked to Hitler's advantage was 'the substitution of presidential for parliamentary government'. By 'parliamentary government' Bullock means the making of law in the normal way under the Weimar constitution. This was the system in operation until the resignation of the SPD Chancellor, Hermann Müller in March 1930. Put simply, the government drew up proposals for laws and these proposals were put before the Reichstag, only becoming law if a majority in the Reichstag voted for them. After Heinrich Brüning (of the Centre Party) took over in March 1930, however, the government began to bypass the Reichstag. Under 'presidential government', emergency decrees were drawn up by government and then issued by the President under Article 48 of the constitution, whether the Reichstag supported them or not. 'Presidential government' is examined in more detail in Unit, 3 Section 2.2.

Advantages to the Nazis

The breakdown of normal parliamentary democracy was advantageous to the Nazis for four main reasons. First, it increased the sense of crisis in Germany (the country was, after all, governed as if in a state of emergency). This drew people away from the 'traditional' parties (which were seen as having failed) and to the Nazis (who, as outsiders, offered a way out of the crisis). Second, the breakdown of normal parliamentary democracy helped to convince people that the Weimar system was flawed and should be replaced. Again, this played into the Nazis' hands since this was the message the Nazis had always tried to put across. Third, the three years of governing without Parliament before the Nazis came to power prepared at least part of the German population for the

(see Section 1.4 above) - was of great significance. During the period 1930-33, the Nazis gained support from all social classes (see Section 3.3 below). Fischer finds it curious that middle-class Nazis were prepared to mingle in the same party with their class enemies - working-class Nazis. Other parties were unable to gather supporters which cut across class barriers. The reason why the NSDAP was able to gain support across the classes, he argues, is because the NSDAP appealed to all Germans regardless of class and because the Nazi leadership made it clear that its aim was to build a new society in which class conflict would be ended. This emphasis on classlessness, Fischer argues, had a particular appeal to members of the middle classes, many of whom were weary of the class struggle and sought an escape from it:

> 'It might be that the National Socialists attracted their middle-class constituency not because they promised to rally it against the workers, but because they strove to short-circuit the language of class politics altogether through their advocacy of the national ethnic community [ie the Völksgemeinschaft]...It does indeed appear that many middle-class Nazis did not seek to regroup around the banner of special interest politics or class warfare, instead seeking an escape from them. Not only were they weary of such struggle, but feared the consequences if it continued unchecked and ended in a Social Democratic, or worse still a Communist, victory. By integrating people from all walks of life, the Nazis offered these middle-class followers the prospect of a political and social truce once the "classless" National Socialist movement had overthrown Weimar and remoulded society in its own image.' (Fischer C. 1995, pp.101-02)

The NSDAP - a unified party

It was not just the party's message which explains its appeal in the period 1930-33. On three occasions in the period 1930-33, Hitler's authority was challenged by members of the NSDAP but, on each occasion, he took decisive steps to eliminate the threat to party unity and ended up in a stronger position than he had been in before. These demonstrations of strong leadership helped to project the idea that Hitler was a man of action and decision - qualities needed by a potential Chancellor.

The clash with Otto Strasser

First, between April and July 1930, Hitler clashed with Otto Strasser, brother of Gregor, with the result that on 4 July, Strasser and a few of his colleagues left the party. According to Kershaw, the clash erupted when Strasser published an article in support of a strike when Hitler had specifically ordered party members to oppose the strike. This

---

BOX 4.21 Four objective factors beyond Hitler's control

The first factor which was beyond Hitler's control was the economic depression in 1931-32. Unemployment in Germany grew to over 6 million, a higher percentage of the workforce than any other industrialised country. This helped the Nazis to maintain their momentum. The second factor was the intensification of the political crisis which accompanied the Depression. The increased vote for the extreme right and left and the rise in political violence was one form of this. Another was the end of the temporary stabilisation of the Weimar Republic. The economic crisis became a political crisis as all the ills from which Germany was suffering were blamed on the 'system'. The third factor which worked in Hitler's favour was a change in the policy of the Reichswehr. Throughout the period 1919-33, the army was a state within a state, loyal not to the government of the day or the Republic, but to what officers believed to be the interests and values of 'eternal Germany'. The architect of this unique position was General Hans von Seeckt, Commander in Chief between 1920 and 1926. He successfully protected the army's independence by claiming that politics must have no place in the army, whilst playing an important role in politics himself (in the crisis of 1923, he was given full executive powers to preserve the state). The election of Hindenburg as President in 1925 and the retirement of Seeckt in 1926 meant a change in attitude. The aim of the army was to build (in secret) a new model army. To this end, senior officers worked with the politicians to find the political stability and support the army needed to carry out a rearmament programme. The army's search for stability was a major factor in making possible Hitler's admission to office. In 1931, that was still a long way off, but the army's change in attitude had a powerful effect in contributing the substitution of presidential for parliamentary government (see below) - the fourth factor which worked to Hitler's advantage.

Adapted from Bullock 1991.

---

authoritarian style of rule that the Nazis wanted to implement. And fourth, the system of government which developed provided Hitler with an opening. If he could persuade the President to appoint him as Chancellor, he would be able to use the President's emergency powers to keep the Nazis in power permanently.

Conan Fischer's thesis

In attempting to explain why the NSDAP was able to gain such broad support in the period 1930-33, Conan Fischer argues that the Nazis' emphasis on the building of a classless state - a Völksgemeinschaft

challenge to the Führer's authority then developed into a debate over the direction of the party, similar to that which Hitler had diffused in 1925 (see Section 2.1 above). Strasser's resignation from the party ensured that Hitler's authority remained intact.

The Stennes rebellion

Second, Hitler put down a rebellion in the SA, organised by Walther Stennes, SA leader in Berlin. Details are provided in Box 4.22.

BOX 4.22 Stennes' rebellion

(i) With the influx of thousands of new SA members (who joined for the money as much as for the ideas) dissatisfaction resulted in open mutiny in the spring of 1930. The rebellion centred on the Berlin SA Leader Walter Stennes. He demanded independence from Berlin's Gauleiter, Joseph Goebbels, and better pay, announcing a general strike until his demands were met. The situation in Berlin deteriorated to such an extent that Goebbels had to call on Hitler to restore order. Knowing that a mutinous SA could seriously undermine Nazi prospects in the September election, Hitler hurried to Berlin and, by his presence, managed to restore order. On 2 September, he replaced Pfeffer (the man who had replaced Röhm as Head of the SA) and took personal charge of the SA, shortly afterwards recalling Röhm to be in charge of day-to-day operations. Although the crisis was temporarily settled, Stennes continued to be a source of friction and had to be removed in April 1931.
Adapted from Fischer K. 1995.

(ii) The Berlin SA mutinied just before the election of September 1930. The principal grievance was over pay, but there was a strong feeling that they were undervalued. Hitler rushed to Berlin, pleaded with the rank and file, promised better pay and announced that he would become SA Supreme Commander in place of Pfeffer. As soon as he could after the election, he recalled Röhm and allowed Himmler to expand the SS (the SS started out as Hitler's personal bodyguard and developed into an élite army corps). The grumbling at Hitler's commitment to the legal path to revolution, however, continued. At the end of March 1931, the government issued a decree ordering political rallies to be approved by the police a day in advance. Hitler ordered the party to obey the law. This was too much for Walter Stennes. He denounced Hitler, drove out the party's political leadership in Berlin and placed both party and SA under his command. Hitler again placed his personal prestige on the line and dismissed Stennes. Stennes' revolt failed as only a handful of people followed him.
Adapted from Bullock 1991.

Gregor Strasser's resignation

And third, on 8 December 1932, Gregor Strasser, one of the top Nazis, resigned from the party. For some time, historians agree, Strasser had been critical of Hitler's policy (Hitler refused to join the government unless he was offered the post of Chancellor) and, on 3 December, the Chancellor, Kurt von Schleicher, secretly offered Strasser the post of Vice Chancellor. Although Strasser eventually chose not to accept the post, the fact that it was offered behind Hitler's back was enough to ensure that matters came to a head. At a meeting held on 5 December, Hitler made it clear that he was not prepared to change his approach. This, it seems, was the final straw for Strasser. He wrote a letter of resignation and then left Germany for a holiday in Italy. His departure, historians agree, was a big blow to Hitler. Kershaw even claims that:

'There was a real concern that the movement would fall apart.' (Kershaw 1998, p.401)

But, this concern proved to be unfounded. Although the Nazi leadership worried that others might follow Strasser out of the party, they did not:

'Although the immediate impact of Strasser's resignation was devastating on some rank and file members, the Nazi Party had become so strongly oriented around Hitler that Strasser's defection was quickly neutralised...Schleicher [the Chancellor who had offered Strasser the post of Vice President] had expected that at least 60 Reichstag deputies [MPs] would follow Strasser's defection, but none did.' (Fischer K. 1995, p.252)

The resignation of Gregor Strasser may even, therefore, have strengthened Hitler's position for three reasons. First, it dashed Schleicher's hope of splitting the Nazi Party (he hoped that others would defect with Strasser, but they did not). Strasser's defection proved that Hitler's policy of holding out for the position of Chancellor had the confidence of the rest of the party. Second, the loyalty of Nazis at all levels in the party reaffirmed Hitler's supremacy in the movement. And third, Schleicher's inability to persuade Strasser to join the government as Vice Chancellor made his job of building a government more difficult. Indeed, it made it so difficult that, by the end of the month, he was forced to resign, allowing Hitler to gain the prize he had been holding out for.

The presidential election of 1932

On 22 February 1932, the Nazis announced that Hitler would stand in the presidential election due in March. When the announcement was made, Hitler was technically not qualified for office because he was not a German citizen (he had lost his Austrian citizenship in 1925 and was, officially, stateless). On 26 February, however, the newly elected Nazi state government in Brunswick made Hitler a German citizen by appointing him to a minor post in the civil service. Kershaw argues that Hitler had little choice but to stand, even though there was little chance of beating the sitting President, Hindenburg, who was standing for re-election:

'In the event of presidential elections, [Hitler] could scarcely refrain from standing. Not to stand would be incomprehensible, and a massive disappointment to his millions of supporters. They might turn away from a leader who shied away from the challenge.' (Kershaw 1998, p.361)

Once the decision had been taken, the Nazis launched an election campaign unlike any previous one:

'Goebbels finally succeeded in finding the money needed to plan a campaign the like of which Germany, or for that matter any other European country, had never seen before...No radio or television was available, but the walls of every town in Germany were plastered with Nazi posters and films of Hitler and Goebbels were made and shown everywhere (an innovation in 1932). As in 1930, but with bigger and better-organised forces, the Hitler-Goebbels strategy was to cover every district in Germany in a saturation campaign.' (Bullock 1991, p.268)

The result was a rise in the Nazi vote from 6.4 million in September 1930 to 11.5 million in March 1932 (see Box 4.23). This was not enough to beat Hindenburg, but it was enough to force a re-run on 10 April. Once again, the Nazi campaign was distinctive:

'In view of the violent intensity of the last campaign, the government limited actual campaigning to only one week (3-10 April), making it difficult for Hitler to marshal the full force of his movement. However, Hitler managed to use the short time available to him in a very effective and clever manner: he chartered a plane and...began his famous "flights over Germany", visiting 21 cities in a week.' (Fischer K. 1995, p.237)

The result of the re-run was victory to Hindenburg. But Hitler increased his vote by 2 million. Kershaw argues that this was enough for Hitler to be more than satisfied:

'This time there was no disappointment in the Nazi camp...[Hitler] had done much more than save face. Well over 13 million, 2 million more than in the first round had voted for him. The Führer cult, the manufactured commodity of Nazi propaganda and once the property of a tiny collection of fanatics, was now on the way to being sold to a third of the German population.' (Kershaw 1998, p.363)

The Reich elections of 1932

It was noted above that, although the growth in

BOX 4.23 The presidential election of 1932

	First Round (13 March)	Second Round (10 April)
Adolf Hitler	11.340	13.420
Paul von Hindenburg	18.650	19.360
Ernst Thälmann	4.980	3.710
Winter	0.110	
Theodor Duesterberg	2.560	
Splinter votes	0.005	0.005

This table shows the result of the two rounds in the presidential election of 1932. The figures are in millions.
Adapted from Kirk 1995.

---

electoral support for the Nazis was phenomenal, it peaked at the Reich election of July 1932. The votes and seats won by the Nazis in the two elections held in 1932 are shown in Box 4.24. Analysing the result of the July election, Kershaw argues that:

'Compared with the Reichstag elections of 1930, let alone 1928, [the Nazis'] advance was indeed astonishing. But from a more short-term perspective, the outcome of the July election could even be regarded as disappointing. They had scarcely improved on the support they had won in the second presidential election.' (Kershaw 1998, p.370)

Hitler refuses to join the Cabinet

Although, from July, Hitler was the leader of the largest party in the Reichstag, the Nazis had no overall majority. Following negotiations at the beginning of August, Hitler was offered the post of Vice Chancellor in a Cabinet led by Franz von Papen (the current Chancellor). Hitler rejected the offer and the Nazis in the Reichstag remained in opposition to the government. When, at a rare meeting of the Reichstag on 12 September 1932, the Nazis supported a motion proposed by the KPD and defeated the government by 512 votes to 42, the Chancellor, Papen, with the backing of Hindenburg called a further general election, to be held in November. Fischer argues that Hitler's 'all or nothing' tactic and the violence in which the SA engaged, together with the lack of funds and electoral exhaustion, made the chance of further Nazi gains unlikely:

'There were, in fact, several encouraging signs that the Nazis had not only peaked in popularity but had overstepped the line of public decency to such an extent that many Germans were beginning to wonder whether they should ever be entrusted with political power.' (Fisher K. 1995, p.248)

Kershaw's analysis of the November 1932 election

Kershaw makes the following points about the Nazis' reduction in support:

BOX 4.24 | Nazi votes and seats, Reich election 1932

Party	Election July 1932			Election Nov 1932		
	Total votes	%	No. MPs	Total votes	%	No. MPs
NSDAP	13,745,800	37.4	230	11,737,000	33.1	196
DNVP	2,177,400	5.9	37	2,959,000	8.8	52
DVP	436,000	1.2	7	661,800	1.9	11
BVP	1,192,700	3.2	22	1,094,600	3.1	20
Centre Party	4,589,300	12.5	75	4,230,600	11.9	70
SPD	7,959,700	21.6	133	7,248,000	20.4	121
KPD	5,282,600	14.6	89	5,980,200	16.9	100

This table shows the results of the two Reich elections held in 1932.
Adapted from Kirk 1995 and Bullock 1991.

- turnout was lower (in part because of electoral exhaustion - this was the fourth major election of 1932) and many of those who failed to turn out had voted Nazi in July
- the Nazis appear to have lost votes to all other parties, particularly to the DNVP (a 'more respectable' nationalist party)
- the middle classes were beginning to desert the NSDAP
- lack of funding was a big handicap (funding four major campaigns in one year was a huge burden)
- Hitler's refusal to join the Cabinet in August may have been a factor since people may have become reluctant to vote for Hitler once he had rejected the opportunity of joining the government
- some Protestant voters had become alienated because Hitler had entered negotiations with the Centre Party in August (negotiations which failed to result in a firm agreement)
- the election campaign had focused on attacking Papen's conservatism and this had put off some middle-class supporters, as had the decision to support the strike of transport workers in Berlin in the days just before the election (the Nazis were worried that they would not win votes from workers if they did not support the strike).

Manoeuvres behind the scenes

Historians often comment on how ironic it is that it was after an election in which the NSDAP had lost support that Hitler finally gained power. That he did so was largely due to manoeuvres behind the scenes - manoeuvres which owed something to the personal relations between the people involved. It was noted above that, to gain power, the Nazis had to win over both President Hindenburg and other conservative politicians. But, historians agree, Hindenburg did not

like Hitler. Kershaw describes, for example, the meeting between Hindenburg and Hitler in August 1932 in which Hitler refused to serve as anything other than Chancellor:

'The Reich President firmly refused. He could not answer, he said, before God, his conscience and the Fatherland if he handed over the entire power of the government to a single party and one which was so intolerant towards those with different views. He was also worried about unrest at home and the likely impact abroad.' (Kershaw 1998, p.373)

With reference to the same meeting, Bullock notes that Hindenburg looked down on Hitler as a social inferior:

'The President had no wish to exchange the aristocratic von Papen for the uncouth Hitler, whom he disliked.' (Bullock 1991, p.276)

Between August and December 1932, Hitler's refusal to join the government unless he was given the post of Chancellor resulted in stalemate. So what changed Hindenburg's mind?

What changed Hindenburg's mind?

To answer this question, most historians focus on the personal struggle between Kurt von Schleicher and Franz von Papen (see also Unit 3, Section 2.3). Papen is generally characterised as Hindenburg's favourite, Schleicher as an unprincipled schemer. Following the election in November 1932, Papen remained Chancellor, so the argument goes, but Schleicher succeeded in ousting him and becoming Chancellor himself. This was bitterly resented by Papen who - in order to take revenge on Schleicher - approached Hitler and made a deal with him. Hitler could be Chancellor if he accepted Papen as Vice Chancellor and a Cabinet made up mainly of non-Nazis. After a great deal of negotiating, all parties accepted the deal. Papen then presented the deal to

Hindenburg and persuaded him of its advantages (he argued that it would bring political stability and that the non-Nazi members of the Cabinet would be able to keep the Nazis in check). Hindenburg withdrew his support from Schleicher, forcing him to resign. Two days later Hitler became Chancellor.

Who was to blame?

In his explanation of how Hitler became Chancellor, Klaus Fischer places the blame largely on the shoulders of Schleicher. Schleicher, he argues, was a major influence behind the scenes and it is through his actions that Hitler finally gained power. His viewpoint is summarised in Box 4.25. Other historians agree that Schleicher was an important influence behind the scenes, but they do not place such a burden of blame on his shoulders as Klaus Fischer does. Bullock, for example, agrees with Fischer that Papen's motivation for making a deal with the Nazis was to take revenge on Schleicher, but he suggests that Papen, not Schleicher, was to blame for Hitler's acquisition of power. He points out that it was Papen who initiated the negotiations with Hitler and it was he who persuaded Hindenburg that it was safe to allow Hitler to become Chancellor because he and the other non-Nazis in the Cabinet would be able to 'tame' him:

'Papen had only himself to blame for one the most egregious [shocking] mistakes in 20th century history.' (Bullock 1991, p.284)

Kershaw, on the other hand, argues that Hindenburg was to blame. In a meeting with Hindenburg on 19 January 1933, Schleicher requested the President to allow him to dissolve the Reichstag and hold fresh elections. But Hindenburg refused to do so:

'There was no inevitability about Hitler's accession to power. Had Hindenburg been prepared to grant to Schleicher the dissolution that he had so readily allowed Papen...a Hitler Chancellorship might have been avoided. With the corner turning of the economic depression and with the Nazi movement facing potential break-up if power were not soon [gained], the future... would have been very different.' (Kershaw 1998, p.424)

BOX 4.25 | Kurt von Schleicher

Schleicher first began to wield influence behind the scenes when the Head of the Reichswehr, General von Seeckt, resigned in 1926. By 1930, Schleicher had become one of the most powerful people in Germany. Unfortunately, he did not use his power for constructive purposes. He increasingly saw himself as the king-maker behind the throne, making and breaking friends and enemies alike. Working behind the scenes, Schleicher torpedoed the Müller government in 1930 by persuading Hindenburg to withdraw his support. When this did not produce the stability he wanted, in early 1932 he plotted to bring down Brüning (who resigned in May 1932). It was Schleicher who chose Brüning's successor, namely Papen. Following the election in November 1932, he then plotted against Papen. Schleicher tried to persuade Hindenburg that he would be able to build a Grand Coalition that would cut across the political spectrum, uniting moderate elements in the army, the bourgeois parties, the SPD, the unions and even moderates in the NSDAP. He felt sure he could split the Nazis by involving Strasser in his new government. First, Hindenburg asked Papen to form a government, but when members of his Cabinet (worked on by Schleicher) refused to participate on the grounds that Papen's policies would result in civil war, Papen resigned. On 2 December, Schleicher became Chancellor. In revenge, Papen made a deal with the Nazis. By mid-January, Schleicher's position had deteriorated. He had failed to split the Nazis and lost the support of the DNVP. At the same time, his agricultural policies had been condemned as 'Communistic' - which greatly alarmed Hindenburg. Papen's assurance to Hindenburg that Hitler could be tamed if allowed to serve as Chancellor in a Cabinet with Papen as Vice Chancellor fell on sympathetic ears. As a result, Hindenburg withdrew his support from Schleicher, leaving the path clear for Hitler to take over as Chancellor.

Adapted from Fischer K. 1995.

MAIN POINTS - Section 3.2

- Hitler used the Leipzig trial of September 1930 to reassure the Establishment that he would not attempt to use force to gain power.
- The Nazis won power by overcoming two main obstacles - (1) President Hindenburg's distrust of Hitler and (2) the distrust and opposition of other right-wing politicians.
- There were also four factors beyond Hitler's control - (1) the economic downturn (2) the intensification of the political crisis which developed as a result of the downturn (3) the Reichswehr adoption of a new policy and (4) the substitution of presidential for

parliamentary government.
- The classlessness of the NSDAP's appeal and Hitler's decisive steps to eliminate threats to party unity help explain the growth in support for the NSDAP.
- The presidential elections in 1932 and the election of July 1932 were successes for the Nazis. But the party lost ground in the election in November.
- Relations between Hitler, Papen, Schleicher and Hindenburg played an important part in the behind-the-scenes negotiations which led to Hitler being appointed Chancellor in January 1933.

Activity 4.9 How did Hitler become Chancellor?

ITEM 1 The meeting of 4 Jauary 1933

On 16 December 1932, Papen made a speech in Berlin criticising Schleicher's tactics with the Nazis. He suggested that the way forwards was not to split or destroy the Nazis, but to involve them responsibly in government. After the meeting, Papen was approached by Kurt von Schröder, a banker, who proposed to act as a go-between. A meeting between Papen and Hitler - later described by the historian Karl Dietrich Bracher as 'the hour of the birth of the Third Reich' - was arranged at Schröder's home in Cologne and took place on 4 January 1933. It is not certain what was discussed at the meeting since Papen and Schröder gave different versions at the Nuremberg war trials in 1946. On the one hand, Papen claimed that it was not his aim to undermine Schleicher. On the contrary, he argued, his aim was to strengthen his position by persuading Hitler to join Schleicher's Cabinet as Vice Chancellor. This high-minded but self-serving account cannot be trusted. Why would Papen arrange a secret meeting and negotiate behind Schleicher's back if his aim was not to outfox the

Franz von Papen (right) during the time when he served as Chancellor.

man who had brought about his downfall from power. Schröder, on the other hand, made it clear that Papen was angry with Schleicher and expected Schleicher's government to fall within a short time if he could do a deal with Hitler. According to Schröder, Papen proposed a new government headed by Hitler and with himself as Vice Chancellor. Of course, this is exactly what happened later in the month and it is highly likely that Papen was already toying with this strategy. This also fits with other evidence suggesting that Papen's scheming was part of a campaign of revenge against Schleicher. The likelihood is that Papen was prepared to bring the Nazis into the political limelight to use them as an instrument to further his own ambitions.

Adapted from Fischer K. 1995.

ITEM 2 Winning over Hindenburg

The following factors were involved in winning over the President. First, Schleicher's economic policy was opposed by Big Business on the grounds that it was inflationary and too favourable to workers. People representing Big Business pressed their views vigorously with the President. Second, Hindenburg had never really forgiven Schleicher for forcing Papen's resignation. He wanted Papen back in government. And third, Schleicher failed to achieve his objective of gaining a mass base for his government. He had no alternative to offer, other than another election, action against the Nazis and a dictatorship through Article 48. This was not far from the policy he had prevented Papen from carrying out and the President did not see why he should allow Schleicher to do what Papen had been prevented from doing. Hindenburg's refusal to allow Schleicher to dissolve the Reichstag and call another election forced his resignation on 28 January. Yet, despite his growing disenchantment with Schleicher, Hindenburg was still not happy about the idea of Hitler as Chancellor. As late as 26 January, he said to high-ranking officers: 'Surely, you would not credit me with appointing this Austrian corporal Chancellor?'. Hindenburg was finally persuaded by the

Hindenburg and Hitler in January 1933.

structure of the proposed government and by the fact that it promised to secure a parliamentary majority which would relieve him of the responsibility of governing. The fact that the Ministry of Defence would be given to Blomberg, a general acceptable to Hindenburg, was important (Hindenburg didn't realise that Blomberg was a Nazi sympathiser). Eventually, Hindenburg became convinced that, as Papen put it, Hitler would be 'framed' within the Cabinet by conservatives who would be able to control the policies which Hitler would 'sell' to the country through his party and propaganda machine.

Adapted from Noakes & Pridham 1996.

ITEM 3 Burleigh's view

Hitler's final ascent to the German Chancellorship was due to his own political skills, the decisions made by his immediate predecessors and President Hindenburg's decision to pursue this fateful option. It was fateful because the Nazis had frequently announced their contempt for the rule of law and by 1932 were promising to imprison Communist and Socialist opponents in concentration camps. When Hitler met Papen on 4 January, he stated that his aim was 'the removal of all Social Democrats, Communists and Jews from leading positions in Germany and the restoration of order in public life'. This did not stop Papen from making a deal. The Nazis used the melodramatic term 'seizure of power' to describe what was actually a complex process of bargaining and intrigue in which they were not always the main actors and the outcome was never certain. Papen's role was important. He was determined to return to power - whether as a front-seat or a back-seat driver - and to do this he needed to demonstrate that he had the support of a major party, something which his recent administration had lacked. At the same time, a Nazi Party which had recently suffered an electoral setback saw the opportunity Papen was presenting. One weapon Papen had against Schleicher was his sheer proximity to the President, who had never forgiven the general for forcing him to dismiss Papen. While his official residence was being refurbished, Hindenburg moved to the Chancellory. Schleicher and Hindenburg may have shared office space, but Schleicher went home at night, leaving Papen to pay informal visits from his apartment which was separated from the Chancellery only by a garden behind the building. Papen turned Hindenburg's dislike of Schleicher into hostility. At the same time, he persuaded him that Hitler could be contained.

Adapted from Burleigh 2000.

Questions

1. Using Items 1-3 and your own knowledge explain how Hitler managed to become Chancellor in January 1933.
2. Look at Items 1 and 3
   a) Why do you think the meeting of 4 January 1933 has been described as 'the hour of the birth of the Third Reich'.

   b) 'Papen was to blame for Hitler's elevation to power'. Give arguments for and against this view.
3. Judging from Items 2 and 3, why do you think Hindenburg finally agreed to appoint Hitler as Chancellor?

3.3 Who supported the Nazis after September 1930?

Growth in support for the Nazi Party

If the Reich election of September 1930 was the breakthrough for the Nazi Party, the figures showing the party's electoral support in 1932 in Boxes 4.23 and 4.24 (see Section 3.2 above) show that, from then on, the party had genuine mass backing right up to the point when Hitler was appointed Chancellor. When the breakthrough came in September 1930, the NSDAP won 6.4 million votes. Two years later, in the election of July 1932, the party more than doubled this figure, winning over 7 million more votes. In the presidential elections of 1932, Hitler won first 5 million and then 7 million more votes than in September 1930. Even when the vote for the Nazis fell in November 1932, they still won 11.7 million votes, more than 5 million more than in September 1930. So, who were these new supporters and where did they come from? This section will first examine the composition of the NSDAP. It will then consider who voted for the party.

Who joined the Nazi Party in 1930-33?

Michael Kater's study of the background of members and leaders of the NSDAP (Kater 1983) shows that, as in earlier phases, people from all social classes joined the party in the period 1930-33. Also as before, Kater argues, members of the middle class and upper class were over-represented while members of the working class were under-represented. Kater makes a number of further points about membership in this period.

First, although the NSDAP remained a more youthful party than any other (except the KPD), the average age of members began to increase after 1930:

'The average age of party joiners jumped from somewhat over 30 in 1930 to almost 32 in 1932.' (Kater 1983, p.141)

Kater explains this rise by claiming that the number of older upper-middle-class joiners increased after 1930. His main emphasis, however, is on the continued youthful nature of the party. The age of the party may have increased slightly in the period 1930-33, but it remained much lower than the other parties (except the KPD). One theory is that:

'The NSDAP, an overtly radical party, was able to absorb many of those youthful elements in German society that were thirsting for action and were disappointed by the complacency of the staid established parties. Among these, the SPD were the most staid.' (Kater 1983, p.142)

Second, the number of women joining the NSDAP increased after the election of September 1930. The percentage of women in the party grew from 5.9% of the party membership in the period 1925 to September 1930 to 7.8% in January 1933. Kater offers the following reasons for the rise after September 1930:

- the Nazis made an effort to win the votes of women and this encouraged more to join the party
- women activists in the party worked hard at increasing female membership
- more and more upper-middle-class women joined, providing role models which attracted women from all social backgrounds to the party.

Third, Kater points out that it was only in the period 1930-33 that the Nazis succeeded in building a truly mass movement. In terms of social class during this period, he argues that the proportion of workers in the party increased (though they remained under-represented) while the proportion of members of the lower-middle class decreased (though they remained over-represented). It should be noted that the criticisms of the analysis of Nazi membership by social class mentioned in Section 2.2 above are just as relevant to the period 1930-33 as they were to earlier periods.

Working-class Nazis, 1930-33

Kater points out that, although many members of the working class stayed with the 'Marxist' parties (the SDP and KPD) or switched from the SDP to the KPD, it was in the period 1930-33 that more members of the working class abandoned these parties for the NSDAP than ever before. In many cases, he argues, groups of workers who belonged to the KPD and met at a particular venue made the decision to switch en masse to the NSDAP. Kater explains this phenomenon as follows:

'This switching process resulted on the one hand from the KPD's long-standing failure to bring about, by parliamentary means, any lasting improvement in the [lives of members] of the working class. On the other hand, it can be traced to a gradual fusing in the early 1930s of the public image of the two radical camps: the Nazis, like the Communists, had perfected the dubious art of street fighting, especially in the large industrial areas.' (Kater 1983, pp.53-54)

Box 4.26 shows that, in some places, Nazis and Communists lived side by side.

The Nazis did not only gain working-class support from the KPD. Members of the SPD also came over

BOX 4.26   Nazis and Communists

This photo was taken in the early 1930s. It shows a tenement block in a poor district in Berlin. The slogan on the wall means 'food first, rent later'. The swastikas of the NSDAP are flying next to the hammer and sickle of the KPD.

to the NSDAP. Allen (1984), for example, shows that the bulk of members of the working class who joined the NSDAP in Northeim in the period 1930-33 were former members of the SDP. Kater argues that there were three main reasons why workers switched allegiance in the period 1930-33:

- Nazi propaganda was more effective than it had been before since the emphasis switched from planning for the distant future to making concrete suggestions about how to solve immediate problems
- the party provided welfare for the unemployed - for example, they set up soup kitchens
- the party supported strikes (membership of the Nazi union, the NSBO grew from 39,000 in December 1931 to 400,000 in January 1933).

Lower-middle-class Nazis, 1930-33

In his study of the rise of Nazism in Northeim, William Allen (1984) argues that fear of economic hardship rather than experience of it explains why members of the lower-middle class supported the NSDAP in the period 1930-33. Kater (1983) points out that the rate at which members of the lower-middle class joined the NSDAP in the period after September 1930 was not so fast as it had been in the previous two years. Furthermore, although the overall numbers rose, the proportion of farmers, merchants, low-ranking civil servants and white collar workers who joined the party was lower than in the period May 1928 to September 1930. Nevertheless, an indication of how widespread support for the NSDAP became amongst the lower-middle class in the period 1930-33 is suggested by Kater's claim that 10% of all civil servants (teachers and police officers as well as administrators) had joined the NSDAP by January 1933. This figure probably underestimates the real level of support since civil servants were banned from joining the party in some parts of Germany.

Upper-middle-class and upper-class Nazis

Kater argues that it was amongst the upper-middle class and upper class that support for the NSDAP grew most impressively during the period September 1930 to January 1933. In 1933, the upper-middle and upper class made up just 2.78% of the population. Yet, in Germany as a whole in the period 1930-32, 9.2% of people joining the NSDAP came from these classes. Many of these new members came from cities and small towns (15.5% of new members in cities and 9.9% of new members in small towns came from these classes). Even in the countryside the percentage of new members was well above the average (6.6% of new members). This suggests that it was becoming 'respectable' to join the NSDAP. Kater claims that, in particular, the NSDAP made significant gains amongst four groups within the upper-middle and upper classes:

- large farmers
- Protestant clergymen
- professionals and intellectuals
- high-ranking civil servants.

He argues that support from Big Business was never as strong as some historians have claimed and that it was only after the fall of Papen in December 1932 that significant numbers of industrialists backed Hitler's candidacy for the Chancellorship. Box 4.27 provides a summary of the changes in the composition of the party as a whole that took place after the Reich election of September 1930.

Who voted for the Nazis?

Traditionally, the answer to the question 'who voted for the Nazis?' was 'basically, the middle class':

'Few historians would claim that the Nazi movement was monolithically [ie only] middle class, for the presence of working-class voters and activists has always been acknowledged. However, their numbers have been regarded as too small to affect the prevailing middle-class explanatory model.' (Fischer C. 1995, p.99)

Since 1970, however, this answer has been modified in three ways.

BOX 4.27 | Party composition after September 1930

There was a massive increase in the number of members of the NSDAP following the Reich election of September 1930. The party recruited from all sections of society, though it did not do so evenly. The vast majority of members were men. It was a youthful party - only the KPD had an average age as young as the NSDAP. The Protestant middle classes were, as among voters, over-represented. But a significant proportion belonged to the working class (the SA and the Hitler Youth had a larger proportion of workers than the party itself). The breakthrough in September 1930 meant that, for the first time, 'respectable' local citizens felt ready to join the party. Teachers, civil servants, even members of the Protestant clergy joined and, by doing so, changed the party's social standing. In Franconia, for example, the NSDAP already had the appearance by 1930 of a 'civil service' party. After September 1930 success bred success. But the structure of the party's support changed. Many of the recent converts were not the fanatics of earlier years, prepared to sacrifice everything for their beliefs. Turnover in membership was considerable and support was dependent on success.

Adapted from Kershaw 1998.

Middle-class support

First, as the following passage shows, Thomas Childers broadly accepts that the middle class was the Nazis' main bank of support:

'By the summer of 1932, the NSDAP had succeeded where the traditional parties of the bourgeois [middle-class] centre and right had repeatedly failed, becoming the long-sought party of middle-class concentration. The miseries of the Depression radicalised voters, contributing directly and powerfully to the rise of National Socialism after 1928. Yet, the dramatic Nazi victories during the Depression era are hardly conceivable without the erosion of traditional loyalties within the middle-class electorate that had been underway since...the mid-1920s.' (Childers 1983, p.262)

Childers argues that the Nazis appealed both to the 'old' middle class (merchants artisans and farmers) and to the 'new' middle class (clerks, low-ranking civil servants and pensioners). These people, he claims, abandoned the parties they had traditionally supported and switched to the NSDAP. Childers goes on, however, to qualify the view that the NSDAP targeted and relied on middle-class support alone. He points out that the Nazis won votes from the upper classes and working class as well as from the middle classes and that young people and women voted Nazi as well as old people and men. The NSDAP, he concludes, became a 'people's party', albeit one which remained highly unstable:

'Even at the height of its popularity in the polls, the NSDAP's position as a people's party was tenuous [ie shaky] at best. If the party's support was a mile wide, it was at critical points an inch deep. The NSDAP had managed to build a remarkably diverse constituency, overcoming regional divisions, linking town and country, spanning the social divides and shrinking the gaps between [religions]. Yet the basis of that extraordinary electoral alliance was dissatisfaction, resentment and fear. As a result, the Nazi constituency, even at the pinnacle of the party's popularity remained highly unstable.' (Childers 1983, pp.268-69)

Working-class support

Second, a study by Max Kele (1972) argues that the NSDAP set out to win and did manage to win substantial support from the working class. As a result, he argued, it is inaccurate to suggest that it was only members of the middle class who voted for the NSDAP. Further research has confirmed that the NSDAP did indeed win substantial support from the working class:

'It appears that some 40% of voters and party members and some 60% of SA members were working class, leading to the typification of Nazism as a popular or people's movement instead of a class movement.' (Fischer, C. 1995, p.99)

Fischer goes on to point out that, by July 1932, the NSDAP's working-class electorate was larger in absolute terms than that of either the KPD or SPD. Geary (2000) points out, however, that levels of working-class support varied widely from place to place. It was higher in rural areas and small towns than in large cities, for example, and could vary from district to district within a town or city. Research has found that:

'Roughly one in four workers voted Nazi in July 1932 and that 40% of the NSDAP's vote came from the working class.' (Geary 2000, p.26)

Support from the wealthy

And third, a detailed study by Richard Hamilton (1982) of the way in which people voted in a number of German cities shows that the more prosperous the area was, the better the Nazis did in elections. In lower-middle-class areas, the Nazis did not do as well as in upper-middle- and upper-class areas. Referring to Hamburg (see Box 4.28), for example, he reaches the conclusion that:

'With only a single exception, National Socialist support exceeded the city-wide average in all districts from Harvestehude to Eilbeck in all seven elections [from 1924 to July 1932]. These best-off districts gave the NSDAP above average

BOX 4.28 Support for the NSDAP in Hamburg by district

District	MAY 1924	DEC 1924	MAY 1928	SEPT 1930	JULY 1932	NOV 1932
Harvestehude	**7.0**	**2.9**	**2.7**	**22.0**	**40.9**	**30.6**
Hohenfelde	**8.8**	**3.5**	**3.6**	**29.7**	**47.9**	**38.0**
Eilbeck	**8.6**	**3.6**	**3.3**	**25.4**	**43.1**	**35.7**
Langenhorn	3.1	1.1	1.1	12.5	25.5	20.5
St Georg	5.6	2.1	2.6	18.9	31.7	26.1
Neustadt	4.4	1.6	2.5	16.8	27.0	21.5

This table shows the percentage of the vote the NSDAP won in districts in Hamburg between 1924 and 1932. Figures in bold show that the result was above the city-wide average. Harvestehude, Hohenfelde and Eilbeck were prosperous areas. Langenhorn, St Georg and Neustadt were not.
Adapted from Hamilton 1982.

support...In the key election, that of July 1932, the percentages of the well-off districts were over 40. That must be contrasted with the city-wide figure of 33.3%. Hohenfelde, a very affluent upper-middle-class area leads all the rest with the National Socialist vote there amounting to 47.9% of the total.' (Hamilton 1982, p.110)

In other words, the NSDAP won the votes of the upper-middle and upper class rather than the lower-middle-class. This fits with the idea often put forward that, by the early 1930s, the ruling élite (and those who shared their values) had come to the conclusion that the Weimar Republic had failed and should be abandoned.

Female Nazi voters

It was noted above that the number of women joining the Nazi Party grew in the period 1930-33. The same is true of the number of women voting Nazi:

'Until 1930, [women] were unlikely to vote Nazi; but this then changed. The gap between male and female voting in this regard narrowed quite markedly between 1930 and July 1932 when 6.5 million women cast their votes for the Nazis. The probability is that these were women with few previous political ties.' (Geary 2000, p.29)

Geary points out that a substantial number of the women who voted Nazi in July 1932 belonged to the working class. Referring to the new women Nazi voters, he suggests that:

'The probability is that these were women with few previous political ties. Where they came from the working class, they were likely to be non-

unionised textile operatives or domestic workers.'
(Geary 2000, p.29)

Backlash against the 'new woman'

Gellately argues that, for many of these women, the decision to vote Nazi was, in part at least, a backlash against the idea of the 'new woman' - women who were independent, free-thinking and liberated - which had been fashionable in Germany in the 1920s. Many women, he argues, rejected the feminist values of 'new women' and accepted that it was their role to stay at home looking after the family (ie they accepted the anti-feminist position):

'Conservative, Catholic, and even liberal women by and large shared the point of view advocated by the Nazis as to a "naturally" determined sexual division of labour and that it was important to reconstruct a "community of people" in which they would be involved primarily as wives and mothers and "not be forced to compete with men for scarce jobs and political influence".' (Gellately 2001, p.10)

The Nazis' anti-feminism appealed

Childers notes that the Nazis' opponents responded to the NSDAP's anti-feminism by claiming that, if the Nazis came into power, they would throw thousands of women out of their jobs. The Nazis denied this vigorously and, at the same time, argued that the Weimar system had deprived millions of women of their 'right' to stay at home and bring up a family:

'The NSDAP was reluctantly prepared to accept single women in the labour market but intimated that job opportunities for married women would be curbed or even eliminated. While reassuring some working women, this position, repeated throughout the campaigns of 1932 certainly did little to diminish [ie reduce] the party's already established anti-feminist reputation - and this, in fact, may have been precisely the point.' (Childers 1983, pp.239-40)

Women followed the lead of men

There may be a further reason why more women voted Nazi after 1930 - namely, because more men did. Jill Stephenson claims that:

'Married women overwhelmingly voted in the same way as their husbands, while daughters, sisters and other female adherents often tended to vote in the same way as the [male] head of the household.' (Stephenson 1983, p.36)

Stephenson points out that Catholic areas were an exception to this rule. In Catholic areas, more women than men voted for the Centre Party. In other words, the women did not vote for the same party as their husband or male head of household. This was also the case in the (non-Catholic) Ruhr and Upper Silesia. In these areas, more men voted KPD and more women Centre.

Voting by age, region and religion

The points made in Section 2.2 above remain valid for the period 1930-33. According to Geary (2000), the Nazis continued to do better in:

- Protestant areas rather than Catholic areas (in July 1932 the Nazis won almost double the amount of votes in Protestant areas compared to Catholic areas)
- rural areas rather than urban areas
- small towns rather than big cities (in July 1932 the Nazis scored 10% less than the national average in big cities).

The NSDAP continued to attract the support of the young and to have substantial support amongst pensioners. The general patterns may have remained the same but, obviously, the huge rise in support brought in new types of supporters. In the rural areas for example:

'[The NSDAP] made its first gains in 1928 in Schleswig Holstein and Lower Saxony. By July 1932, the scale of its support in such areas indicates that this came not solely from small peasant farmers but from other sections of rural society too, such as some large landowners and many rural labourers.' (Geary 2000, p.24)

Support from 'respectable' people

The Nazis' use of force should not be underestimated. Röhm's return in 1931 resulted in the reorganisation of the SA along paramilitary lines. Street fighting against the Communists became common in the big cities. Following the lifting of a ban imposed between April and June 1932, this fighting became so intense that there were serious fears of civil war:

'The lifting of the ban on the SA and SS eventually took place, after some delay, on 16 June. It was already by then being openly flouted. It ushered in a summer of political violence throughout Germany such as had never been seen before. The latent civil war that had existed throughout the Weimar Republic was threatening to become actual civil war. Armed clashes and street fighting between the SA and Communists were daily occurrences.' (Kershaw 1998, p.368)

Murder at Potempa

In August 1932, there was a particularly brutal attack which resulted in five SA men standing trial:

'Probably the most revolting incident that revealed what many Nazi stormtroopers were really like came on August 10 when five SA men broke into the home of a Communist in the village of Potempa in Upper Silesia and literally trampled him to death in plain sight of his horrified mother.' (Fischer K. 1995, p.248)

The trial gained a great deal of publicity and, when the five murderers were sentenced to death, the Nazi leadership took steps to turn the men into

BOX 4.29 'Respectable' people's support for the Nazis

The Nazis' enthusiastic use of political violence distinguished them from the 'bourgeois' (ie the middle-class) parties. But Nazism's primary focus on 'Reds' and secondary focus on Jews or Poles did not reduce its appeal to respectable citizens. Unlike Communist violence, which challenged the state head-on, Nazi violence was rarely directed against the police. Many Nazi sympathisers were also members of church committees, of business, dining or sporting clubs and they indirectly domesticated an extremist party more effectively than any propaganda could. In Marburg, for example, a university town of just below 30,000 people, the 194 mainly student Nazi Party members before January 1933 had cross-affiliations with 375 non-political voluntary organisations. It is often said that word of mouth is the best form of advertising. Here were people well placed to speak about Nazism favourably. The Nazi members' conventional social commitments neutralised any negative impressions given by their membership of a party with an extremist agenda. Often when a particularly respected member of the community joined the NSDAP, others followed. For example, in Northeim, a gentle bookshop owner with an excellent reputation locally became the town's first Nazi, leading fellow citizens to remark: 'if he's in it, it must be all right'. A similar naturalisation of National Socialism took place in rural areas where village élites - local landowners, larger farmers, pastors and school teachers - lent authority and respectability to the NSDAP. Nazi word of mouth was accompanied by Nazi infiltration of interest groups and the creation of parallel organisations - like the organisations for lawyers and doctors or for grammar school pupils and university students. This reflected the party's totalitarian ambitions in the sense that the Nazis believed that no area in life was to remain unpolitical. Nazism developed its own self-help network, a society in miniature.

Adapted from Burleigh 2000.

martyrs. Hitler even sent a telegram giving them his backing:

> 'The head of Germany's largest political party was publicly expressing solidarity with convicted murderers.' (Kershaw 1998, p.382)

Despite this level of violence, however, and despite Hitler's willingness to support Nazis who committed acts of violence many 'respectable' people joined or supported the NSDAP, as Box 4.29 shows.

Why did 'respectable' people support the NSDAP?

How could it be that Nazis gained an aura of respectability at the time when its use of violence was so blatant? Kershaw argues that, in part, it was the very use of violence that gave the party respectability. People who feared a Communist uprising did not believe that the Nazis were to blame for starting the violence. Rather, they believed that the Communists were to blame and that all the Nazis were trying to do was to restore order. In other words, to these people, Nazi violence was seen as serving the interest of the nation:

> 'Nazi violence, it might be thought, ought to have put off the "respectable" bourgeois [ie middle-class] following it was increasingly attracting. But since such Nazi supporters saw the threat as lying on the left, the anti-Communist thuggery [claiming] to serve the interests of the nation alienated remarkably few voters.' (Kershaw 1998, p.368)

MAIN POINTS - Section 3.3

- As in earlier phases, people from all social classes joined the NSDAP in the period 1930-33. Also as before, the working class was under-represented and the middle and upper classes over-represented.
- Differences with earlier phases were - (1) members were on average older (2) more women joined (3) the proportion of workers joining rose (4) the rate at which members of the lower-middle class joined was not as fast in the previous phase.
- Traditionally it has been argued that it was mainly members of the middle class who voted Nazi. Since 1970, this view has been modified in three ways - (1) Childers argues that the Nazis won votes from all classes, becoming a genuine 'people's party' (2) Kele argues that the NSDAP won substantial support from the working class and (3) Hamilton argues that the Nazis won substantial support from the upper-middle and upper class.
- A substantial number of women voted for the Nazis in the period 1930-33. The NSDAP continued to do better in - (1) Protestant areas (2) rural areas and (3) small towns.
- Despite Nazi violence, the Nazis were supported by many 'respectable' people - probably because they believed the Nazis were responding to Communist attacks and their aim was to restore order.

Activity 4.10 Who supported the Nazis after September 1930?

ITEM 1 Germany 1930-32

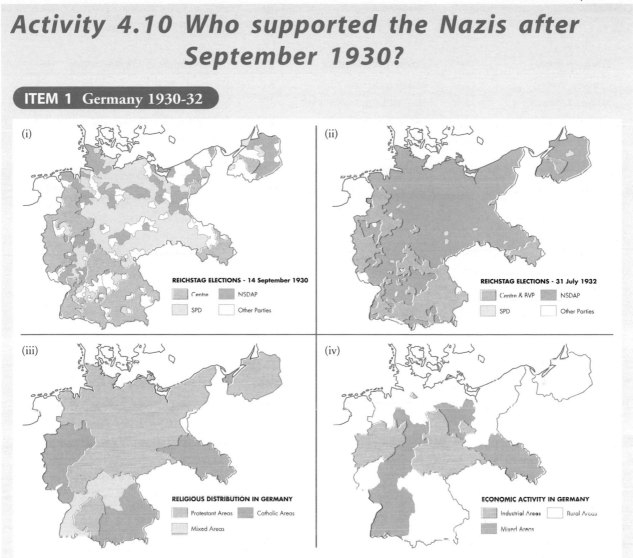

Maps (i) and (ii) show the support for various parties in the elections of September 1930 and July 1932. Map (iii) shows the distribution of Protestants and Catholics in Germany. Map (iv) shows industrial and rural areas in Germany.

ITEM 2 Working-class support for the Nazis

The Nazis were able to attract significant sections of the German working-class electorate - particularly in rural Germany and in small provincial towns rather than in big cities and in areas of artisan or cottage industry rather than in heavy-industrial districts. Substantial numbers of working-class women voted Nazi in July 1932, as did agricultural workers (rural labourers were the people most likely to vote for Hitler), workers for whom employment in industry was a secondary activity and commuters who worked in the towns but lived in the countryside. Significantly, all these groups had a lack of tradition of joining trade unions and/or the SPD or KPD. The sheer size of these previously under-organised groups of workers should not be underestimated. In the early 1930s, agriculture still employed over one-fifth of the labour force, and one-third of those employed in industry and handicrafts were self-employed or worked in firms with fewer than five employees. More than half of those registered as 'workers' in the census of 1925 lived in small towns or villages. As a result, the Nazis had the potential to win support from workers who were not in the SPD or KPD (since support for those parties was concentrated in the cities). The NSDAP also won over another group of workers with an unusual political tradition. These were workers who voted National Liberal before the First World War and DNVP after it. They tended to live in company housing provided by big employers, to be members of company unions and to be tied to their firms by company insurance schemes and pension benefits. In addition, some Nazi votes came from workers in the utilities (gas, water, electricity), the postal services and transport. The NSDAP (and the KPD) benefited from the fact that it was SPD-run state governments which cut wages or laid off workers during the Depression. Despite all this, workers (who made up 54% of the workforce) remained under-represented in both the membership and electorate of the NSDAP.

Adapted from Geary 2000.

ITEM 3 The social profile of the NSDAP in 1933

Working class	%	Lower-middle class	%	Upper-middle & Upper classes	%
Unskilled workers	12.6	Master craftsmen	8.9	Managers	2.3
Skilled (craft) workers	15.4	Non-academic professionals	4.2	Higher civil servants	2.8
Other skilled workers	2.7	Lower employees	10.6	Academic professionals	3.0
		Lower civil servants	11.7	Students	1.7
		Merchants	12.8	Entrepreneurs	2.4
		Farmers	8.9		
Subtotal	**(54.56) 30.7**	**Subtotal**	**(42.65) 57.1**	**Subtotal**	**(2.78) 12.2**

This table shows the social profile of those people who joned the NSDAP in 1933. The figures in brackets show the percentage of Germans doing these jobs in 1933 in the population as a whole.

Adapted from Kater 1983.

ITEM 4 Nazi support in Berlin

The highest levels of support for the NSDAP in Berlin came from the upper-class and upper-middle-class districts - notably Zehlendorf, Schöneberg and Wilmersdorf (see table, right). In fact, the figures for these districts probably underestimate the extent to which the traditional Prussian upper classes offered support for the NSDAP since some workers, Centre Party supporters and Jews lived in these districts. As a result, it can be estimated that actual support for the NSDAP among the upper classes was over 60% in 1932. The closest approximation that can be made to identifying the lower-middle class is the mixed districts - for example, Treptow, Pankow and Reinickendorf. The voting patterns in these districts are not especially distinctive - the levels of support for the NSDAP were average to that in the city as a whole or just above average. Had the lower-middle class played the decisive role so often claimed for it, the level of support should have been well above average.
Furthermore, the population in these mixed areas were relatively late converts, unlike the upper-class districts where Nazi support was above average from 1924 on. The working-class districts - such as Neukölln, Wedding and Friedrichshain - provided strong support for the parties of the left throughout the period in question. There was, however, a fair-sized minority in those districts who had originally supported the conservative or Liberal parties. The losses suffered by such parties in these areas were considerable. Some of these votes went left and some right. At the same time, it should be noted that support for the NSDAP was not miniscule in these districts. It ran between a fifth and a quarter of the total. Put another way, almost half of Berlin's NSDAP vote came from the nine working-class districts of the city.

District	MAY 1924	DEC 1924	MAY 1928	SEPT 1930	JULY 1932	NOV 1932
Zehlendorf	9.8	4.2	1.8	17.7	36.4	29.4
Schöneberg	5.8	2.3	2.1	19.9	35.7	31.7
Wilmersdorf	6.7	2.5	2.1	18.8	35.1	29.3
Treptow	3.1	1.1	1.0	12.5	27.8	25.8
Pankow	4.0	1.3	1.3	**15.3**	**32.4**	29.8
Reinickendorf	4.0	1.4	1.3	13.8	**28.9**	**27.0**
Neukölln	3.0	1.3	1.1	11.1	23.9	22.2
Wedding	2.4	0.9	0.8	9.0	19.3	18.0
Friedrichshain	3.3	1.3	1.2	11.6	21.6	20.0

This table shows the percentage of the vote the NSDAP won in districts in Berlin between 1924 and 1932. Figures in bold show that the result was above the city-wide average.

Adapted from Hamilton 1982.

Questions

1. Using the information in Items 1-4 and your own knowledge, explain who supported the Nazis in the period between September 1930 and January 1933.

2. What does Item 1 tell us about the nature of support for the Nazis?

3. 'Without the solid support of the lower-middle class, the NSDAP would not have come to power'. Discuss this statement using Items 2-4 and your own knowledge.

4. What are the problems with generalising from the findings outlined in Item 4?

3.4 Who opposed the Nazis?

The opposition in outline

It is important to emphasise that, even in the Reich election of July 1932 - the NSDAP's electoral high point before gaining power - just 37.4% of the electorate voted for the Nazis. In other words, a large majority of the electorate - 62.6% - did not. Furthermore, in the Reich election of November 1932, this figure rose to 66.9%. Even after Hitler became Chancellor and the NSDAP had the apparatus of government at its disposal, a majority of the German people (56.1%) still voted (in March 1933) for parties other than the Nazi Party.

Of course, the attitudes of those not voting for the Nazis varied. Some people and some political parties were bitterly opposed to the NSDAP while others looked on the NSDAP more kindly. It was noted in the previous section that the NSDAP did best in Protestant rural areas and small towns. Conversely, although there was opposition (sometimes bitter opposition) to the Nazis in Protestant rural areas and small towns, opposition was more widespread in Catholic areas and in large cities. It was also noted in the previous section that the NSDAP genuinely became a 'people's party', attracting support from all social classes. Conversely, there were people in all social classes who remained opposed to the NSDAP. This section will examine who these people were and why they responded as they did.

Working-class opposition

Even in the period 1930-33 when support for the NSDAP was growing considerably, members of the working class remained under-represented in the NSDAP (see Section 3.3 above). In particular, the NSDAP found it hard to make any headway in heavily industrialised areas and in big cities - places where the majority of workers belonged to trade unions and had a tradition of supporting either the SPD or KPD:

'Workers were far less likely than middle-class elements to be members of the NSDAP or vote for the party...The massive rise in the NSDAP vote between 1930 and 1932 left the combined SPD/KPD vote more or less solid, again suggesting that previously organised workers were more immune to Nazi propaganda than many other groups in German society.' (Geary 2000, pp.25-26)

Geary also argues that it is wrong to suggest that the Nazis won support from people who became unemployed as a result of the economic downturn. Unemployed manual workers were far more likely to support the KPD than the NSDAP:

'In the Ruhr town of Herne, the NSDAP did least well in areas of high unemployment, often scoring under 13% of the vote, even in July 1932. In such areas, the KPD enjoyed enormous success

(between 60% and 70% of the vote). In the Reich more generally the unemployed were overwhelmingly concentrated in the large industrial cities, precisely where the Nazis polled less well.' (Geary 2000, p.27)

Conan Fischer (1995) argues that one reason why workers and unemployed workers remained 'immune to Nazi propaganda' was that loyalty to party (the SPD/KPD) had already been established. These workers understood and spoke the language of class struggle - the language used by the SPD and KPD. This taught them to dislike and to be highly suspicious of the 'bourgeoisie' (the middle classes) who were often described as 'class enemies'. The NSDAP, by way of contrast, refused to use the language of class struggle and Nazis promised that they would build a classless society. Furthermore, many members of the bourgeoisie joined and supported the NSDAP. Whilst the emphasis on classlessness helped to broaden the NSDAP's appeal with some sections of the population, it failed to appeal to workers with the background described above.

The SPD

In terms of votes won and seats in the Reichstag, the SPD remained the largest party in opposition to the NSDAP in the period 1930-33. Since that was the case, the strategy the SPD adopted to counter the challenge posed by the rapid rise in support of the NSDAP was of great significance. Most historians agree, however, that the party failed to provide opposition which was sufficiently robust. A typical analysis is given in Box 4.30.

The KPD

On the one hand, the KPD and NSDAP were deadly rivals. The vast majority of acts of violence in the period 1930-33 involved Nazis fighting against Communists:

'The level of violence was frightening. In the second half of June [1932], after the lifting of the SA ban, there were 17 politically motivated murders. During July, there were a further 86 killings, mainly Nazis and Communists. The number of those seriously injured rose into the hundreds. Four were killed and 34 injured in a single clash on 10 July in Ohlau in Silesia. In the worst incident, the Altona "Blood Sunday" of 17 July, 17 people were killed and 64 injured as shooting broke out during an SA parade seen as a direct provocation by the town's Communists.' (Kershaw 1998, p.368)

It could be argued, therefore, that the KPD was the most active and fiercest opponent of the Nazis. On the other hand, the KPD and NSDAP were united in the aim of overthrowing the Weimar Republic and sometimes cooperated. For example, in the meeting of the Reichstag held on 12 September 1932, a Communist motion of no-confidence in Papen's

BOX 4.30 The SPD's opposition strategy

In the election of September 1930, the SPD lost 5% of the vote, though it remained the largest party in the Reichstag. The Nazis' gain of 15% of the vote presented it with a dilemma. Every time the SPD voted against Brüning, his legislation would be defeated and the President would use his powers to call a new election. The only beneficiary of this would be the Nazis. As a result, the SPD adopted a policy of 'toleration'. They would support Brüning both to keep the Nazis out of office in the short term and, in the hope that, once the economic crisis was overcome, the threat posed by the Nazis would fade. The success of 'toleration' was limited. While the presidential Cabinets did keep the Nazis at bay for a while, the SPD looked increasingly immobile. SPD officials found it hard to explain to the rank and file why the party supported legislation which put burdens on workers. Also whilst some in the SPD leadership supported greater activism, the majority did not. When, in July 1932, Brüning's successor, Papen, toppled the Prussian government, replacing it with a Reich Commissar (see Unit 3, Section 2.3), the SPD challenged the move in court, but did nothing else. This was a missed opportunity. On the day of the so-called 'Prussian coup', organised workers waited for the signal from their leaders for a general strike. But the signal never came. The leaders were afraid of a bloody civil war and knew that, given the economic downturn, prospects of a strike succeeding were not good. Nevertheless, would it not have been better to have risked open confrontation in July 1932 rather than to have passively accepted its total destruction at the hand of the Nazis in the spring of 1933? Nine months later, the rank and file were too disillusioned and demoralised to be mobilised again.

Adapted from Berger 2001.

government was steered through by the Nazi, Hermann Göring who was President of the Reichstag (and, therefore, chaired meetings). MPs from both parties voted in support of the motion. Similarly, the two parties both supported the Berlin transport strike which broke out in November 1932, just before the Reich election:

'The final stages of the election campaign were overshadowed by a strike of transport workers in Berlin. It was notable for the fact that it was called against the advice of the official trade union representation and that the Communist RGO [trade union] and Nazi NSBO collaborated in promoting it.' (Feuchtwanger 1995, p.297)

Members of the middle and upper classes

Although the middle and upper classes were over-represented in the NSDAP and there is good evidence that many in these classes supported the Nazis, there were many members of these classes who opposed Nazism. Michael Kater (1983) shows that some groups were more susceptible than others to support the NSDAP. Conversely, some groups were more susceptible to oppose the Nazis than others. For example, many teachers in universities (academics) were opposed to Nazism, not least because the Nazis were often scathing about the benefits of studying.

Catholics

It was noted in Sections 2.2 and 3.3 above that the Nazis gained greater support in Protestant areas than in Catholic areas. Catholics, in other words, were more likely to oppose Nazism than Protestants were. Geary argues that this was because the Catholic Church created bonds of loyalty which made people less willing to change their political affiliation (many Catholics supported the Centre Party, which had been set up in 1870 to protect the interests of Catholics, or its equivalent in Bavaria - the Bavarian People's Party or BVP):

'The NSDAP was most successful where it did not have to cope with strong pre-existing ideological or organisational loyalties. Where these did exist, as in Social Democratic and Communist strongholds, it did less well. The same applied to Germany's Roman Catholic community, strongly represented over decades by the Centre Party (or BVP in Bavaria). Loyalty to the party was reinforced by a plethora of Catholic leisure organisations and by the pulpit, from which the NSDAP was sometimes denounced as godless.' (Geary 2000, p.28)

Burleigh points out that the Centre Party vote was strongest in small rural areas, especially where Catholic communities were surrounded by Protestants. He describes the relations between the Catholic leadership and the NSDAP as 'ambivalent'. On the one hand, he points out that some Catholic priests (not many) supported the Nazis and that some Catholics approved of the Nazis' anti-Semitism. On the other hand, he makes it clear that the Church disapproved of the Nazis' paganism (the flag waving, torchlit processions, party symbols and party rituals, some of which were borrowed from the Catholic Church itself) and that:

'Roman Catholic priests in Germany were [instructed] to shun National Socialism and the Nazis did not get from the clergy the endorsement they often enjoyed in Protestant areas.' (Burleigh 2000, p.70)

Conan Fischer gives an indication of the extent of Catholic opposition to the Nazis when he notes:

'In July 1932, some 38% of registered Protestant voters supported the Nazis, but just 16% of registered Catholic voters.' (Fischer 1995, p.99)

Box 4.31 shows that Catholic opposition to the Nazis

BOX 4.31 **Catholic and Nazis in Northeim, 1933**

The smooth relations between the Nazis and Northeim's Protestant Church were not paralleled by the party's relationship with the town's Catholic Church. The priest was a firm supporter of the Centre Party and was attacked by the Nazis as a result. In March 1933 editorials were written against him in the Nazi newspaper on two occasions because he encouraged parishioners to vote for the Centre Party. The situation worsened in July 1933 when the Catholic Young Men's Society was dissolved and its property and flags were seized by the SA. Other Catholic clubs were not disturbed, but the NSDAP could still count on the enmity of the Catholic priest. Since only c.6% of the population were Catholic, this was a negligible factor.

Adapted from Allen 1984.

continued to be expressed in the predominantly Protestant town of Northeim even in the months after the Nazis had come to power.

Women

It was noted in Section 3.3 above that significantly fewer women voted for the NSDAP than men in the period 1924-30. Childers argues that women were reluctant to support the NSDAP during this period because other parties promoted policies aimed at equal rights with men and better living and working conditions for women while the NSDAP promoted an 'anti-feminist' line. In addition, women tended to vote for political parties which were linked to churches. Childers suggests that the Nazis' 'hazy' view on religion put off many women. He concludes:

'Although National Socialism's hazy attitude on religious issues undoubtedly reduced the party's appeal to many women, its unregenerate anti-feminism certainly detracted from its appeal to others.' (Childers 1983, p.174)

At first sight, this argument might seem to contradict, Gellately's argument (outlined in Section 3.3) that the Nazis' anti-feminist stance appealed to women after 1930 and explains why more women voted for the party in the period 1930-33. But, Stephenson (1983) suggests that anti-feminism had a greater appeal in the Depression than before it. In other words, it was in a period of massive unemployment that many women came to agree with the Nazis that it would be better if women stayed at home to look after the family rather than taking jobs that could be done by men. In overall terms, voting figures show that women's opposition to the NSDAP was reduced after 1930. But, there was one group which remained resolutely opposed to the Nazis right up to January 1933 - Catholic women. Geary (2000) argues that an important reason why support for the Centre Party remained stable in the period 1930 to 1933 was because women remained loyal to it.

Minorities

The Nazis did not just blame the problems faced by German society on the Jews. They blamed other minorities - particularly Gypsies and Slavs (people from Eastern Europe - for example, immigrants from Poland - see Unit 6, Section 2.2):

'Nazi ideology revolved around the concept of a superior German Aryan race under threat from other inferior groups both inside and outside German borders. These essentially fell into three categories in the form of Jews, Gypsies and Slavs, the last of which consisted of national groupings ...These groups became the central racial victims of Nazi ideology. By 1919, all constituted minorities within the German national state, founded in 1871, although both Jews and Gypsies had existed as minorities for centuries before that time.' (Panayi 2001, p.218)

Panayi claims that:

- the Jewish population in 1925 totalled 564,000, less than 1% of the population
- nearly 75% of Jews made their living from trade, commerce, banking and the professions (especially the law and medicine) compared to just 25% of the non-Jewish population
- nearly 75% of Jews lived in large cities and 31% of all Jews lived in Berlin
- by 1926 only c.26,000 Gypsies lived in Germany
- in 1925, around 200,000 Polish speakers lived in Prussia, together with c.400,000 who spoke both Polish and German
- around 500,000 Poles lived in the Weimar Republic as a whole
- the 1925 census revealed that 70,908 Sorbs (a Slavic group who came from Czechoslovakia and spoke their own language, Wendish) were living in Germany
- in 1928, 236,870 foreign workers (from Russia, Italy, the Netherlands, Belgium and Switzerland) worked in the Weimar Republic
- most foreign workers had short-term annual work permits
- the Depression meant a decline in foreign worker recruitment and it fell to 10,866 in 1932.

Since they were the targets of Nazi abuse, unsurprisingly, these minority groups all opposed the Nazis.

Big Business

It has recently been argued that opposition to the Nazis came from a rather surprising source - Big Business. This is surprising because, according to the Marxist view (see Section 1.1 above), Big Business did not just support the Nazis financially, key industrialists actually levered the Nazis into power in 1933 because they had become convinced that a

Nazi government was the best tool with which to defend themselves against a Communist revolution. In other words, to Marxist historians, Big Business, was an important supporter of Nazism, not an opponent. Research since 1980, however, has shown that this line of argument needs modification. First of all, a consensus has now emerged amongst historians that the NSDAP did not receive significant financial donations from Big Business. The party stayed financially afloat mainly because it raised money from its own members and supporters (see, for example, Kershaw 1998, pp.299-300). Although there were some donations from major industrialists - for example the well-known donation of 100,000 marks from the Ruhr industrialist Emil Kirdorf in 1927 - Michael Kater (1983) has shown that, until late in December 1932, donations and support for the NSDAP came from small businesses rather than Big

Business. Until the fall of Papen in December 1932, Kater argues, Big Business supported the 'bourgeois' parties rather than the NSDAP. In other words, Big Business remained opposed to a Nazi government right up to the month before Hitler came into power.

The Establishment

Finally, the account of the Nazis' rise to power in Section 3.2 above shows that, right up to late January 1933, the Nazis' had to fight against opposition from within the 'Establishment' (ie senior politicians, army officers and people surrounding the President). Hitler remained an outsider right up until his appointment as Chancellor and there was a great deal of suspicion within the Establishment about his intentions. It was only by breaking down in particular President Hindenburg's opposition to his appointment as Chancellor that Hitler was able to gain power.

MAIN POINTS - Section 3.4

- Even at its electoral high point in July 1932, 62.6% of people did not vote for the Nazis.
- Although there was some opposition to the Nazis in Protestant areas, there was more in Catholic areas. Although the NSDAP had support from all social classes, there were people in all social classes who opposed the party.
- Working-class opposition was strongest in heavily industrialised areas and big cities - places where the majority of workers were unionised and had a tradition of supporting the SPD or KPD.
- Most historians agree that the SPD failed to provide

opposition to the Nazis which was sufficiently robust. Although the KPD and NSDAP were bitter rivals and fought against each other, they both wanted to overthrow the Weimar Republic and sometimes cooperated.
- Other opposition to the NSDAP came from - (1) some members of the middle and upper classes (2) many Catholics (3) some women, especially Catholic women (4) minorities - Jews, Gypsies and Slavs (5) Big Business - until the fall of Papen in December 1932 and (6) the Establishment - right up to January 1933.

Activity 4.11 The KPD and the Nazis

ITEM 1 The KPD

Unemployed Germans turned in large numbers to the KPD. Party membership trebled between 1928 and 1932, its share of the vote rising from just over 10% to 17%. While the Communists won disproportionate gains in precisely those areas with high unemployment - such as inner-city Berlin, Saxony and Thuringia - and began to pick up rural support too, the Nazis did correspondingly badly. But the growth in Communist support was in several respects illusory. There was a high turnover of membership. Since self-evidently the unemployed were not in factories, the KPD could not use the tactic of going on strike. Instead, it opted for demonstrations on the streets and extended its grip on working-class areas by propaganda and the use of political violence. Shops were robbed during cashless 'proletarian shopping trips'. Shopkeepers who refused to pay protection money were closed down by boycotts. The Nazis' and Communists' paramilitary wings were set on collision course. They lived in close quarters and aimed to appeal to the same constituencies. In Berlin, the atmosphere was heated by Goebbels' talk of Communist 'assaults' against 'Red' Berlin's working-class quarters. There were brawls at meetings, organised assaults on rival hang-outs and headquarters and tit-for-tat provocations and assassinations. Although they had no problem with murderous violence, the Communists suffered a disadvantage. Since unemployed members could not afford beer, the Nazis persuaded landlords to cater exclusively to them. In this way, the SA gained control of a pub on Richardstrasse in Berlin in 1930. The Communists organised a rent strike to eject the publican. When this seemed to be failing, a decoy demonstration lured the police away. They then blocked the police-station exit and formed a crowd in front of the pub. Four or five gunmen fired about twenty rounds into the building, wounding four people as well as the publican, who died three hours later. Often the KPD targeted the police. In August 1931, for example, three police officers were murdered in Berlin. Whilst it was the Depression which brought the big rise in support for the KPD, this rise scared the middle classes, driving them into the arms of the Nazis. It also extended Nazi support to a sizeable proportion of the working classes.

Adapted from Burleigh 2000.

ITEM 2 Election poster from 1930

This poster was produced by the KPD. The caption reads 'Betrayed by the Socialists. Vote Communist'. The KPD argued that, by collaborating with the bourgeois parties and supporting the Weimar Republic, the SPD was responsible for many of the problems that faced Germany. Following instructions from the Bolshevik government in Russia, in the late 1920s and early 1930s, the KPD targeted the SPD as its main enemy, not the NSDAP.

ITEM 3 Oral accounts

(i) For some young people in the late 1920s, such as Alois Pfaller, the Nazis' anti-Semitism proved a barrier to joining the party. 'That was something very strange', he recalled during the making of a television documentary in 1997. 'This extreme anti-Semitism, the Jews being held responsible for everything. I knew Jews and I had friends with whom I used to spend time and I absolutely didn't understand what difference there was supposed to be - we're all humans. I have always stood up for justice - what is just and reasonable, that was my problem, and always fighting injustice, that was my problem and not somehow persecuting other races or other people.' Alois Pfaller turned his back on the SA, but, still looking for a radical solution to the country's problems, he joined the KPD.

(ii) When Eugene Leviné heard the news that Hitler was Chancellor, he was less concerned because he was Jewish than because he was a Communist. He remembered during the making of the television documentary that 'there were quite a few stormtroopers who had Jewish girlfriends and, therefore, a lot of Germans thought "oh well, it's not going to be so bad - they have Jewish girlfriends they can't hate us all".' He also had personal reasons to suppose that the Nazis were capable of exercising their anti-Semitism with a degree of restraint. 'At one of the schools I was in, there was a Nazi and he said to me, "You really should be one of us". I said, "Look I can't, I'm a Jew", and he would say, "We really don't mean you, decent chaps like you will be perfectly all right in the new Germany".' As for the KPD, their attitude to the news of Hitler's Chancellorship was scarcely a call to world revolution. 'It all happened so fast in those days after one had seen it coming gradually', recalled Eugene Leviné. 'The Communist Party line, to which I still belonged, was that it didn't matter if Hitler gets to power. That's good. He'll soon have proved himself incompetent and then it's our turn. For some extraordinary reason they didn't realise that he was going to change the law once he came into power'.

Adapted from Rees 1997.

Questions

1. What do Items 1-3 tell us about the nature of opposition to the Nazis?
2. 'The KPD failed to provide effective opposition to the NSDAP'. Explain this statement using Items 1-3 and your own knowledge.
3. a) What do Items 1 and 2 tell us about KPD tactics?
   b) Assess the effectiveness of such tactics.
4. a) What does Item 3 tell us about people's motives for joining the KPD?
   b) Why should evidence like this be used carefully by historians?

References

- **Allen (1984)** Allen, W.S., *The Nazi Seizure of Power: the Experience of a Single German Town 1922-1945* (2nd edn), Pelican, 1984.

- **Berger (2001)** Berger, S., 'The SPD' in *Panayi (2001)*.

- **Berghoff (2001)** Berghoff, H., 'Did Hitler create a new society? Continuity and change in German social history before and after 1933' in *Panayi (2001)*.

- **Bracher (1971)** Bracher, K.D., *The German Dictatorship: the Origins, Structure and Consequences of National Socialism*, Penguin, 1971.

- **Brendon (2000)** Brendon, P., *The Dark Valley: a Panorama of the 1930s*, Jonathan Cape, 2000.

- **Bullock (1962)** Bullock, A., *Hitler: a Study in Tyranny*, Pelican, 1962.

- **Bullock (1991)** Bullock, A., *Hitler and Stalin: Parallel Lives*, HarperCollins, 1991.

- **Burleigh (2000)** Burleigh, M., *The Third Reich: a New History*, Macmillan, 2000.

- **Childers (1983)** Childers, T., *The Nazi Voter: the Social Foundations of Fascism in Germany, 1919-33*, The University of North Carolina Press, 1983.

- **Claydon (2001)** Claydon, J., 'Interpretations of Nazi Germany', *History Review*, No.39, March 2001.

- **De Grand (1982)** De Grand, A., *Italian Fascism: its Origins and Development*, University of Nebraska Press, 1982.

- **Falter (1996)** Falter, J., 'How likely were workers likely to vote for the NSDAP?' in *Fischer, C. (1996)*.

- **Feuchtwanger (1995)** Feuchtwanger, E.J., *From Weimar to Hitler: Germany 1918-33*, Macmillan, 1995.

- **Fischer, C. (1995)** Fischer, C., *The Rise of the Nazis*, Manchester University Press, 1995.

- **Fischer, C. (1996)** Fischer, C. (ed.), The Rise of Nationalism and the Working Classes in Weimar Germany, Berghahn Books, 1996.

- **Fischer, K. (1995)** Fischer, K.P., *Nazi Germany: a New History*, Constable and Company, 1995.

- **Geary (2000)** Geary, D., *Hitler and Nazism* (2nd edn), Routledge, 2000.

- **Gellately (2001)** Gellately, R., *Backing Hitler*, Oxford University Press, 2001.

- **Hamilton (1982)** Hamilton, R., *Who Voted for Hitler?*, Princeton University Press, 1982.

- **Kater (1983)** Kater, M.H., *The Nazi Party: Social Profile of Members and Leaders, 1919-45*, Blackwell, 1983.

- **Kele (1972)** Kele, M.H., *Nazis and Workers. National Socialist Appeals to German Labour 1919-1933*, Macmillan, 1972

- **Kershaw (1998)** Kershaw, I., *Hitler 1889-1936: Hubris*, Penguin, 1998.

- **Kirk (1995)** Kirk, T., *The Longman Companion Guide to Nazi Germany*, Longman, 1995.

- **Lee (1998)** Lee, S., *Hitler and Nazi Germany*, Routledge, 1998.

- **McDonough (1999)** McDonough, F., *Hitler and Nazi Germany*, Cambridge University Press, 1999.

- **McGowan (2001)**, McGowan, L., 'The extreme right' in *Panayi (2001)*.

- **Mühlberger (1996)** Mühlberger, D., 'A "workers' party" or a "party without workers"' in *Fischer, C. (1996)*.

- **Nicholls (1979)** Nicholls, A.J., *Weimar and the Rise of Hitler* (2nd edn), Macmillan, 1979.

- **Noakes & Pridham (1996)** Noakes, J. & Pridham, G., *Nazism 1919-45: Volume 1: the Rise to Power: a Documentary Reader*, University of Exeter Press, 1996.

- **Nolte (1987)** Nolte, E., 'Zwischen Geschischtlegende und Revisionismus' and 'Vergangenheit, die nicht vergehen will', *'Historikerstreit'. Die Dokumentation der Kontroverse um die Einzigartigkeit, der nationalsozialistischen Judenvernichtung*, Munich, 1987, pp.13-47.

- **Orlow (1971)** Orlow, D., *The History of the Nazi Party, Volume 1, 1919-33*, David and Charles, 1971.

- **Panayi (2001)** Panayi, P. (ed.), *Weimar and Nazi Germany: Continuities and Discontinuities*, Longman, 2001.

- **Rees (1997)** Rees, L., *The Nazis: a Warning from History*, BBC Publications, 1997.

- **Snyder (1976)** Snyder, L., *Encyclopedia of the Third Reich*, McGraw-Hill (USA), 1976.

- **Stachura (1983)** Stachura, P.D. (ed.), *The Nazi Machtergreifung*, Allen & Unwin, 1983.

- **Stephenson (1983)** Stephenson, J., 'National Socialism and women before 1933' in *Stachura (1983)*.

- **Welch (1995)** Welch, D., 'Hitler: who voted for him', *History Review*, No.22, September 1995.

UNIT 5 · The Nazis in power

Timeline - The Nazis in power

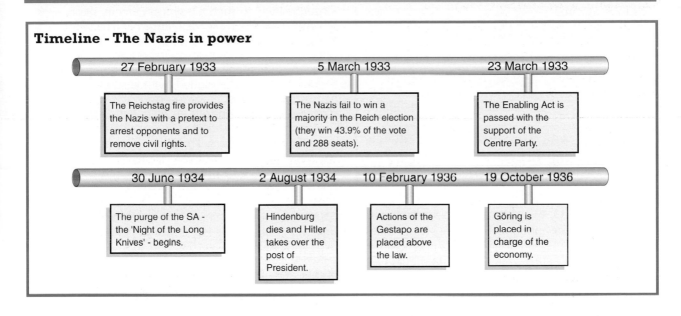

27 February 1933
The Reichstag fire provides the Nazis with a pretext to arrest opponents and to remove civil rights.

5 March 1933
The Nazis fail to win a majority in the Reich election (they win 43.9% of the vote and 288 seats).

23 March 1933
The Enabling Act is passed with the support of the Centre Party.

30 June 1934
The purge of the SA - the 'Night of the Long Knives' - begins.

2 August 1934
Hindenburg dies and Hitler takes over the post of President.

10 February 1936
Actions of the Gestapo are placed above the law.

19 October 1936
Göring is placed in charge of the economy.

Introduction

Hitler's appointment as Chancellor in January 1933 by no means guaranteed long-term Nazi rule. Hitler was just one of three Nazis in a Cabinet of 12 and his conservative colleagues were confident that they would be able to use him for their own ends and then discard him. But in the 20 months between January 1933 and August 1934, the Nazis engineered a 'legal revolution' which removed all serious opposition and cemented Hitler into a position in which he could wield absolute power. The first part of this chapter focuses on these 20 months, in particular on the Reichstag fire and the 'Night of the Long Knives'. Perhaps the most notable characteristic of these 20 months was the brutality that the Nazis were prepared to use in their pursuit of power. Although the fiction was maintained that they were gaining power by 'legal' means, there was a great deal of violence on the ground - a 'revolution from below', as Hitler characterised it.

By the summer of 1934, however, this revolution from below was threatening to alienate two key groups whose support Hitler needed to have, namely the Armed Forces and Big Business. Historians agree that it was largely to please these groups that Hitler went ahead with the 'Night of the Long Knives' - a bloody purge of the leadership of the SA and of other political rivals and enemies. The fact that Hitler's popularity remained high after this act of murder says a great deal about the political atmosphere in Germany at the time. President Hindenburg's death, a month after the 'Night of the Long Knives' then provided Hitler with the security he had previously lacked. The second part of the chapter explores what kind of dictatorship emerged once Hitler was securely in power. It focuses on two areas - the way in which Hitler's dictatorship worked and the way in which the Nazis dealt with people who opposed them.

UNIT SUMMARY

Part 1 examines the Nazis' consolidation of power. It considers the significance of the Reichstag fire, analyses the 'legal revolution' and discusses how the 'Night of the Long Knives' and the death of Hindenburg affected Hitler's position.

Part 2 looks at the Nazi political system. The first section focuses on the way in which the political system worked. The second section examines the way in which the Nazis responded to political opposition in the period 1935-39.

1 The consolidation of power: 1933-34

Key issues

1. What was the significance of the Reichstag fire?

2. What was the 'legal revolution'?

3. What was the significance of the 'Night of the Long Knives' and the death of Hindenburg?

1.1 What was the significance of the Reichstag fire?

The Nazis stir up anti-Marxist hysteria

On 1 February 1933, two days after his appointment as Chancellor, Hitler announced to the Cabinet that President Hindenburg had agreed that a new Reich election should be held and that it would be held on 5 March. That evening, Hitler made a radio broadcast to the nation. This broadcast set the tone of the election campaign. In passage after passage, Hitler blamed Germany's ills on 'the Marxists' (ie the SPD, KPD and trade unions). The following passage is typical:

'Fourteen years of Marxism have undermined Germany. One year of Bolshevism [ie Communist rule] would destroy her. If Germany is to experience political and economic revival, a decisive act is required: We must overcome the demoralisation of Germany by the Communists.' (quoted in Bullock 1991, p.342)

Central to Nazi propaganda in the weeks that followed this broadcast was the idea that a Communist uprising was imminent. This idea, in turn, was used to justify the steps that the Nazis took against their political opponents.

The first of these steps was taken on 4 February when a decree was issued under Article 48 of the constitution giving state governments (Landtage) the power to ban newspapers and public meetings. This allowed Nazi-controlled states to intimidate their political opponents. Such intimidation soon became particularly evident in Prussia, Germany's largest state (Land). It was noted in Unit 3, Section 2.2 that, in July 1932, Papen toppled the Prussian government, replacing it with a Reich Commissar. When Hitler was appointed Chancellor, Papen took the post of Reich Commissar whilst Göring (one of the two Nazis in the Cabinet apart from Hitler) was put in charge of the Prussian Ministry of the Interior. This meant that Göring was in charge of the Prussian police force. Although Papen was supposedly Göring's superior, Göring simply ignored him:

BOX 5.1 | State-organised violence in February 1933

Unsurprisingly in such a political climate, the violence unleashed by Nazi terror bands against their opponents and against Jewish victims was uncontrolled. Communists suffered from particular savagery. Individuals were brutally beaten, tortured, seriously wounded, or killed, with absolutely no action taken against those responsible. Communist meetings and demonstrations were banned in Prussia and in other states under Nazi control, as were their newspapers. The SPD's newspapers were also banned or restrictions placed on reporting. This reign of terror was an outbreak of hatred and revenge which had been boiling up for some time. It was the 'day' long promised to the Nazi rank and file. Rudolf Diels, head of the Prussian Gestapo (the Nazis' secret police, set up by Göring in Prussia in 1933 and soon a national network) later wrote that: 'The uprising of the Berlin SA electrified the remotest parts of the country. Around many big cities in which the authority of the police had been transferred to the local SA leaders, revolutionary activities took place. In Silesia, the Rhineland, Westphalia and the Ruhr, unauthorised arrests...forcible entry into public buildings, smashing up of homes and nightly raids had begun before the Reichstag fire at the end of February'. During this first orgy of state violence, Hitler played the moderate. He gave the Cabinet the impression that radical elements in the movement were disobeying his orders, but that he would bring them under control. He asked for patience. Hitler had no need to involve himself in the violence. He could safely leave it in the hands of Göring and others. The terror wave in Prussia was the first sign that state-imposed constraints on inhumanity were now suddenly lifted. But the brutality and violence did not damage Hitler's reputation. Many who had been critical at first came to believe during February that Hitler was the 'right man'. A slight upturn in the economy helped. But the fervent anti-Marxism of much of the population was much more important. Pumped up by Nazi propaganda, fear of a Communist rising was in the air.

Adapted from Bullock 1991 and Kershaw 1998.

'Göring completely bypassed his weak nominal superior, Franz von Papen, and ruthlessly Nazified the Prussian police force. He retired 14 Prussian police presidents, fired numerous subordinate officials and appointed SS-Oberführer Kurt Dalugue...as "Commissioner for Special Duty", assigned to purge the police of political opponents.' (Fischer 1995, pp.270-71)

Having gained control of the police force, Göring then made his intentions clear by issuing an order, on 17 February, which encouraged the police to use violence when dealing with 'Communist terrorist acts':

'Communist terrorist acts are to be proceeded against with all severity and weapons must be used ruthlessly when necessary. Police officers who in the execution of their duty use their firearms will be supported by us without regard for the effect of their shots. On the other hand, officers who fail from a false sense of consideration may expect disciplinary proceedings.' (quoted in Noakes & Pridham 1996, p.136)

Five days later, Göring issued a second order. The Prussian police force was to be reinforced by the recruitment of volunteers from the SA and the SS (the SS began as Hitler's personal bodyguard and developed into an élite army corps). This, Göring claimed, was necessary to combat 'the growing excesses of the radical left, especially in the Communist camp'. According to Bullock, a total of 50,000 joined, wearing a white armband over their SA or SS uniform. The consequences of the steps taken by Göring are described in Box 5.1 above.

The Reichstag fire

It was in the context described above that the Reichstag (the German Parliament building) was gutted by fire on 27 February 1933, a deliberate act of arson. At the subsequent trial, it was established that:

- the fire was started at around 9 pm
- by about 9.15 the local fire station had been alerted
- within ten minutes firemen were attempting to tackle fires which were breaking out in several parts of the building
- just before 9.30 a huge explosion occurred, engulfing the great chamber in flames.

A young Dutchman, Marinus van der Lubbe (see Box 5.2), was discovered in the building and was immediately arrested for starting the blaze. Although Lubbe confessed to arson, claiming that he alone was responsible for the fire, the true extent of his involvement is still uncertain. At the time, the Nazis claimed that the fire was a Communist plot. Four Communists - the Chair of the Communist Parliamentary Group, Ernst Torgler and three Bulgarian Communists - were also arrested. But, at the end of the trial held between September and December 1933, all four were acquitted and only Lubbe convicted. Kershaw notes that many people at the time refused to believe that the fire was a Communist plot:

'The view that the Nazis, with most to gain, had set fire to the Reichstag themselves was immediately given wide currency among diplomats and foreign journalists, and in liberal circles in Germany.' (Kershaw 1998, pp.731-32)

BOX 5.2 Marinus van der Lubbe

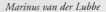

(i) Marinus van der Lubbe was a dim-witted, slobbering young man. At his trial, he was brought to the courtroom in chains. When his interrogation began, he stood with head forward, his mouth open, his tangled hair falling over his forehead. It was almost impossible to to

Marinus van der Lubbe

obtain a coherent account of his former life. Born in the Netherlands in January 1919, he had become a labourer. In 1927, an apprentice to a builder, he had received in his eyes a splash of lime which had permanently damaged his sight. He drifted from the Netherlands in 1931, wandering through Austria, Yugoslavia and Hungary. He also left the Communist Party in 1931, though he still believed in Communism. At the end of the trial he was sentenced to death. He went shambling, with sunken head to the guillotine. He was executed on 10 January 1934. *Adapted from Snyder 1976.*

(ii) Marinus van der Lubbe came from a Dutch working-class family and had once belonged to a Communist Party youth organisation in the Netherlands, though he left it in 1931. He arrived in Berlin on 18 February 1933. He was 24 years old, intelligent, a solitary individual, unconnected with any political group. Nevertheless, he possessed a strong sense of injustice at the miseries suffered by members of the working class. His aim was to make a lone and spectacular act of defiant protest against the Nazi government in the hope this would rouse the working class into struggle against the government. Three attempts at arson on 25 February in different buildings in Berlin failed. Two days later he succeeded. *Adapted from Kershaw 1998.*

(iii) 'My action was inspired by political motives. I have always followed German politics with keen interest...I was a member of the Communist Party until 1929. I did not like the way Communist leaders lord it over the workers instead of letting the workers decide themselves. I decided to go to Germany to see for myself...Something had to be done in protest. Since the workers would do nothing, I had to do something by myself. I considered arson a suitable method. I did not wish to harm private people, but something that belonged to the system itself...I acted alone...Nobody helped me, nor did I meet a single person in the Reichstag'. *Part of Lubbe's statement to the police, given on 3 March 1933.*

Some historians (for example, Fischer 1995) still agree with this theory. It has been argued, for example, that the fire was too big to have been the work of one man and that the timing of the fire - just six days before the election - was simply too convenient for the Nazis (in a mock retrial held by Communists in Paris in 1934, various pieces of evidence were put forward to 'prove' the Nazis' responsibility, but historians have since questioned the validity of such 'evidence'). Kershaw claims that most historians now accept the verdict of a German investigation completed in 1962, namely that the fire was indeed started by Lubbe working alone. He suggests that the consequences of the fire were more important than who started it, though he admits that the line taken on who started it does have some importance:

'The question of authorship was nevertheless of significance since it revolved around the question of whether the Nazis were following through carefully laid plans to [set up] totalitarian rule or whether they were improvising reactions to events they had not expected.' (Kershaw 1998, p.732)

In other words, how far did the Nazis plan and mastermind their rise to power and how far did they seize opportunities as they arose? Assuming that the Nazis were not responsible for the Reichstag fire, then the fire provides a good example of the Nazis' opportunism. It certainly provided them with a perfect excuse to take further steps to dismantle the Weimar constitution and to eliminate political opposition.

The Nazis' immediate reaction

On the night of the Reichstag fire, Hitler and Göring went rapidly to the scene and quickly came to the conclusion that the fire was part of a Jewish-inspired Communist plot to seize power. Eyewitness accounts suggest that Hitler reacted with a mixture of outrage and excitement, realising immediately how he could turn the event into a propaganda coup. Sefton Delmer, an English reporter, describes in his book *Trail Sinister* how he accompanied Hitler, Göring and Papen as they inspected the burned-out building:

'Hitler was moved to prophesy: "God grant that this be the work of the Communists. You are now witnessing the beginning of a great new epoch in German history, Herr Delmer. This fire is the beginning". Just then he tripped over a hosepipe. "You see this building?", he said, recovering his balance. "You see how it is aflame" - and he swept his hand around. "If the Communists got hold of Europe and had control of it for but six months. What am I saying! Two months. The whole continent would be aflame like this building". [To Papen:] "This is a God-given signal, Herr Vice-Chancellor! If this fire, as I believe, is the work of

the Communists, then we must crush out this murderous pest with an iron fist!".' (Delmer 1961, pp.188-89)

When police chief Rudolf Diels tried to tell Hitler that the fire had been started by a single person, Hitler angrily insisted that it was a carefully prepared plot. In his account, Diels notes:

'Hitler shouted uncontrollably, as I had never seen him do before: "There will be no mercy now. Anyone who stands in our way will be cut down. The German people will not tolerate leniency. The Communist MPs must be hanged this very night. Everybody in league with them must be arrested. There will no longer be any leniency for Social Democrats either".' (quoted in Bullock 1991, p.345)

Having decided the line to take, the Nazis wasted no time. Göring took action at once:

'Losing no time, Göring ordered the arrest of all Communist deputies [MPs] and leading officials, the closing of the party's offices and a ban on all their publications, as well as a 14 day ban on the SPD press. As many as 4,000 arrests were made.' (Bullock 1991, p.345)

The arrest of the Communist MPs was particularly important since it changed the parliamentary arithmetic in the Reichstag.

The consequences of the Reichstag fire

By the morning after the fire, Wilhelm Frick, Nazi Reich Minister of the Interior, had drafted a decree 'For the Protection of People and State', a decree which was then signed by President Hindenburg. This decree was of the utmost importance since it became the basic foundation on which Nazi rule rested. At a stroke, the 'Reichstag Fire Decree', as it is sometimes known, removed the civil rights that the Weimar constitution had guaranteed:

'The decree empowered the government to take "all necessary measures to restore order and public security". It placed severe limitations on personal freedom, the right of free expression, the freedom of the press, and the freedom of assembly; it permitted the authorities to spy on people's private communications through the post, telegraph and telephone; it allowed the police to conduct search and seizure operations in private homes, and it enabled the police to arrest people and put them in...custody without charging them with a specific offence. From that point on, therefore, the Nazi police enjoyed extraordinary and largely unlimited powers.' (Johnson 2000, p.87)

The Nazis were careful to make it clear that the decree was a temporary measure, designed to last for the duration of the crisis. According to Bullock (1991), this ensured that the non-Nazi members of the Cabinet did not object to it. The decree, however, was never repealed. It remained in force throughout the Nazis' years in power.

The election campaign

With the Reichstag Fire Decree in place, the SA and SS were free to arrest, beat up, torture and even murder hundreds of Communists and Socialists, as well as other anti-Nazis. Communist election posters were torn down and replaced with Nazi ones, while Nazi propaganda spread the story of the Communist plot. Nevertheless, Hitler stopped short of banning the KPD. If this was a ploy to ensure a split in the left-wing vote at the forthcoming election, then it was a success:

> 'By arresting the KPD deputies [MPs] but not formally banning the party, and even allowing a KPD list in the elections, Hitler had secured the best of both worlds. The KPD attracted nearly 5 million votes which might otherwise have gone to other parties, but as all the Communist seats in the Reichstag...remained vacant following the earlier arrests, the Nazis had an absolute majority.' (Bullock 1991, p.347)

The tone of propaganda put out by the NSDAP after the Reichstag fire is shown in Box 5.3.

The election of March 1933

It is difficult to be sure how much influence the Reichstag fire had on the result of the election on 5 March 1933. In the remaining week of the election campaign, Nazi propaganda claimed that the fire was proof that there was a vast Communist conspiracy and that drastic measures were needed to counter an imminent Communist uprising. This may have convinced some floating voters who had not been fully convinced by Nazi propaganda before the fire. Certainly, turnout was very high (at 88%) which suggests that there was a great deal of interest in the issues at stake and the Nazi vote rose (by 5.5 million). Of course, turnout might have been high and the Nazi vote might well have been up without the fire. But, most historians agree that the fire was of benefit to the Nazis electorally. Bullock claims, for example, that:

> 'The threat of a Communist rising was taken seriously by ordinary Germans and the confidential reports by police and other official agencies on the state of public opinion confirm that the drastic efforts taken by the government encountered little criticism, were widely welcomed and gave Hitler's popularity a new boost on the eve of the election.' (Bullock 1991, p.346)

As for the Nazis' opponents, it should be emphasised that it was the fire which provided the pretext for the passing of the decree 'For the Protection of People and State'. The issuing of this decree allowed the Nazis to use the week before the election taking action against their opponents:

> 'Coming shortly before the March 5 election, the decree allowed the Nazis to marshal the whole

BOX 5.3 Newspaper report

A few days ago, Germany was shocked by the news of arson in the Reichstag. Fires were started in more than twenty places in the building, which was almost totally destroyed. The leading conspirator is the Head of the KPD deputies, Torgler. The press also revealed another unsettling report. Secret passages were discovered in the basement of the Communist Party Headquarters. Materials promoting civil war were found, including detailed plans to murder individuals and groups of citizens. The bloody uprising was intended to spread throughout Germany in the near future. Murder and arson were to occur in cities and villages. These reports have had a strong effect throughout Germany. Formerly indifferent citizens who had been reluctant to accept the huge danger of Bolshevism now look in horror towards Berlin. The burning Reichstag building has brought every German to his senses. But the German people do not know the true origin of this terrible uprising, this murderous arson. They will fight in vain against this poison, this disease, if they fail to recognize the villains who concoct the poison and spread the disease. The truth is that both the parties that want civil war, that hate the Fatherland - the KPD and SPD - were founded by Jews and Jews still lead both of them. The leaders and rabble rousers of the 1918 November Revolution were all Jews. The Marxist movement is in reality a Jewish movement. Its goal is to make the confused, roused masses into an enormous army of Jewish slaves. This army would be used to reach the goal of Jewish world domination.

Part of an article which appeared in Issue 10 of a magazine called 'Der Stürmer'. Issue 10 was published shortly after the Reichstag Fire. 'Der Stürmer' was edited by the Nazi, Julius Streicher.

force of law against their political opponents. The political campaign, which culminated in a rousing speech (the "Day of the Awakening of the Nation") by Adolf Hitler on March 4 in Königsberg, was the most frenetic and violent to date. Political opponents were rounded up, their headquarters ransacked and their meetings disrupted; hair-raising accounts of "Red blood baths" served as pretexts for mass arrests as SA and SS auxiliaries rounded up numerous left-wing opponents.' (Fischer 1995, p.272)

Historians agree that, considering the strong-arm tactics and the widespread fear of a Communist uprising, it is surprising that the Communists did as well as they did in the election of 5 March and that the Nazis still failed to win an outright majority in the Reichstag.

Conclusion

Hitler would probably have crushed resistance to Nazism even without the Reichstag fire, but less easily, and not so quickly. As it was, the fire provided the Nazis with the pretext to pass the decree 'For the Protection of People and State' which provided the foundation of the police state that subsequently emerged. In addition, by describing the fire as proof of a Communist plot, the Nazis added momentum to their electoral campaign. As many historians have pointed out, it is little wonder that Hitler described the fire as 'a beacon from heaven'.

MAIN POINTS - Section 1.1

- In the weeks before the Reichstag fire, Nazi propaganda claimed that a Communist uprising was imminent. In Prussia, Göring encouraged the police to use violence against Communists.

- The Reichstag was set on fire on 27 February. Most historians believe that Marinus van der Lubbe started the fire, acting on his own. A few believe that the Nazis started it or that Nazis helped to spread the fire.

- The fire had three main consequences - (1) it led to the issuing of the Reichstag Fire Decree (2) it led to the arrest of all Communist MPs and (3) it provided impetus to the Nazis' electoral campaign.

- Despite the Nazis' use of strong-arm tactics and the widespread fear of a Communist uprising, the Nazis still failed to win a majority of votes in the election held on 5 March 1933.

Activity 5.1 The significance of the Reichstag fire

ITEM 1 A historian's account (i)

Whether Lubbe, a half-crazed Dutch Communist was solely responsible for the Reichstag fire or, more likely, was used by the Nazis to divert attention from their own involvement remains unproven. A major investigation in 1962 concluded that Lubbe acted alone, but 18 years later the West Berlin authorities acquitted him of the crime. Whether the Nazis were involved or not, it is undeniable that the incident occurred at exactly the right time for them. At once they claimed that the fire was a signal for a Communist uprising - something they knew to be a remote possibility. On the strength of this, Hitler obtained the President's agreement to a decree suspending most civil and political liberties - a purely 'temporary' measure which remained in force for 12 years. The Nazi dictatorship had begun. In the early days of March, the left-wing press was muzzled, hundreds of Communists and Socialists were arrested, meetings broken up and hundreds wounded and many killed in street clashes while the Reichswehr and police stood by helplessly. When the country voted, the Nazi vote grew significantly, but they won fewer votes than they hoped to win. Centre and Socialists had stood firm under unprecedented intimidation and even the Communists lost only 1 million votes. Still, the Nazis had won 43.9% and with the help of

The Reichstag burning on the night of 27-28 February 1930.

the DNVP's 52 seats now had an absolute majority in the Reichstag. The Nazi success in the poll was due in large measure to the willingness of more people to come out and vote than in previous elections. Broadly speaking, the middle classes who were drifting away from the Nazis in the autumn of 1932 were stampeded back again by the fear of a Communist uprising. Whatever doubts people had about the origins of the fire, it had rid Germany of 'Marxism' and, as the Nazis grew more powerful, many people made peace with the new order of things.

Adapted from Carr 1991.

ITEM 2 A historian's account (ii)

The crucial event on the path to dictatorship was the Reichstag fire. Hitler, with Papen's agreement, used this act of arson as a pretext to persuade President Hindenburg to sign an emergency decree granting him almost unlimited powers. The constitution was more or less suspended. All basic rights were taken away. Arbitrary arrests became the order of the day. All this had been well prepared and took effect immediately on 28 February. A new feature was introduced into German political life - legalised state terror. At first, this was used selectively. The first victims were Communists and other left-wing political figures. In the first weeks, terror was not yet widespread, but it had crucial consequences. The 81 Communist MPs elected a week after the fire were no longer in a position to take their seats in the newly elected Reichstag when it met three weeks later. They had either been sent to the new concentration camps which were springing up or they had gone underground or emigrated. In effect, therefore, the election was null and void. The result did not please the Nazis. The NSDAP and DNVP together won only a slim majority of 52%. But once the Communist MPs had gone, the NSDAP had an absolute majority and together with the non-Socialist parties, they even had the two-thirds majority they needed for the ultimate revision of the constitution.

Adapted from Haffner 1989.

ITEM 3 The election result, March 1933

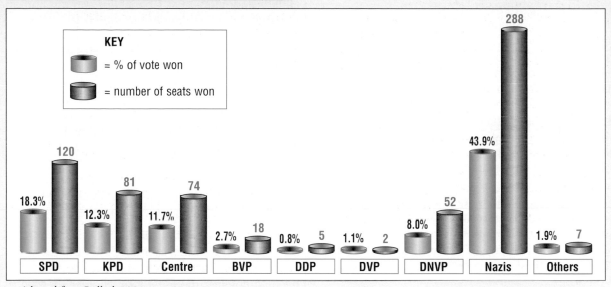

KEY
= % of vote won
= number of seats won

	% of vote	seats
SPD	18.3%	120
KPD	12.3%	81
Centre	11.7%	74
BVP	2.7%	18
DDP	0.8%	5
DVP	1.1%	2
DNVP	8.0%	52
Nazis	43.9%	288
Others	1.9%	7

Adapted from Bullock 1991.

ITEM 4 A historian's account (iii)

Whoever was responsible for the Reichstag fire, the Nazis exploited their opportunity to the full. Yet it appears that the measures which followed were not carefully planned, but were rather spontaneous and largely irrational responses to an imagined threat of a Communist uprising. The arrests of Communists, for example, were carried out on the basis of lists drawn up by the political police before 1933 and were not as successful as later claimed. In fact the Nazis had hoped to postpone the elimination of Communists until after the election when they would be in a stronger position to deal with them. But their fear of an uprising prompted them to take immediate action, resulting not just in these arrests but also the most important single legislative act of the Third Reich - the Decree of the Reich President for the Protection of People and State. The origins of this decree are not clear. It appears the original idea came from a member of the DNVP, Ludwig Grauert, a top official in the Prussian Ministry of the Interior. Hitler accepted the idea and put it on the agenda for the Cabinet meeting scheduled for the morning of 28 February. Before the meeting, however, the Reich Minister of the Interior, Frick, redrafted the measure. Under the Weimar constitution, the powers of the Reich Minister of the Interior were limited because state governments (Landtage) had direct authority over the police.

The Reichstag after the fire had been put out.

Frick decided to use this opportunity to strengthen his control over the states (Länder), basing this new decree on the Prussian decree of July 1932 which had transferred control of the Prussian government to a Reich Commissioner. Article 2 enabled Frick to take control of any state and, unlike the Prussian decree, the Reich government, not the President, would decide when Article 2 should be applied. This provided the legal basis for the regime of terror which was to follow.

Adapted from Noakes & Pridham 1996.

Questions

1. Using Items 1-4, explain the significance of the Reichstag fire.
2. Using Items 1 and 3, write an analysis of the Reich election of March 1933 (it may be helpful to refer to the previous elections in 1932 - the results can be found in Unit 4, Box 4.26).
3. Look at Items 1, 2 and 4.
a) What are the points of agreement in the three accounts?
b) On what points do the accounts differ?
c) With what parts of each account might other historians disagree?

1.2 What was the legal revolution?

The term 'legal revolution'

The term 'legal revolution' is often used to describe the transformation of Germany in 1933-34. The term is paradoxical (self-contradictory). The two words 'legal' and 'revolution' appear to contradict each other since most revolutions use force to overthrow the constitution and are, therefore, illegal. In 1933-34, however, the Nazis did not rely simply on force to overthrow the constitution. They attempted to give the impression that the dictatorship they built rested on a legal foundation. The steps they took did not necessarily break the letter of the constitution, though they did break its spirit and, cumulatively, changed it beyond recognition. Since this was the case and since the threat of violence was ever-present, it could be argued that it would be more accurate to talk of a 'pretend' or 'pseudo-legal' revolution.

Most historians agree that the legal revolution began on 30 January 1933 the day when Hitler became Chancellor and was over by 2 August 1934 - the day when Hitler abolished the presidency:

'The rapidity of the transformation that swept over Germany between Hitler's takeover of power on 30 January 1933 and its crucial consolidation and extension at the beginning of August 1934, after Reich President Hindenburg's death...was astounding for contemporaries and is scarcely less astonishing in retrospect. It was brought about by a combination of legal measures, terror, manipulation - and willing collaboration.' (Kershaw 1998, p.435)

Historians such as Bracher (1971) and Bullock (1991) argue that the key events occurred in the early months. It was noted in Unit 4 (Section 2.1) that it was in prison in 1924 that Hitler came to the conclusion that the NSDAP should give up the idea of winning power by force and, instead, follow the legal path to power. The legal revolution was culmination of this strategy.

Hitler's aims

The debate as to how far Hitler had a plan, and about his role in the Nazi rise to power (see Unit 4, Section 1.1) applies as much to the legal revolution as to other periods. It has already been suggested that Hitler's use of the Reichstag fire demonstrated his opportunism (see Section 1.1 above). According to Noakes and Pridham:

'Hitler had no blueprint or timetable for the take-over of power. It took the form of a complex and dynamic process involving both initiatives from above as well as pressures from below, some of which were orchestrated but many of which were spontaneous and uncoordinated.' (Noakes & Pridham 1996, pp.123-24)

Phase 1 - January to March 1933

The first phase in the legal revolution began with Hitler's appointment as Chancellor and ran until the passage of the Enabling Act in March 1933 (see below). Most of the main developments in the period up to the election on 5 March 1933 - most notably the issuing of the Reichstag Fire Decree which removed civil rights - have already been discussed in Section 1.1 above. It was noted there that the election result was disappointing for the Nazis because it failed to give them the two-thirds majority they needed in the Reichstag to make constitutional changes. Nevertheless, the result was enough to trigger the seizure of power in the state governments (Länder), a process which had begun in Hamburg before the election took place.

Seizure of power in the Länder

By 9 March 1933, just four days after the election, Nazi seizure of power in the Länder had largely been completed, though it took another six months for the last traces of state autonomy to be destroyed. The way in which the Nazis took control of the Länder is described in Box 5.4.

BOX 5.4 **The Nazis seize control of the Länder**

The election was the trigger to the real seizure of power that took place in those Länder not already under Nazi control. Hitler needed to do little. Party activists needed no encouragement to undertake 'spontaneous' actions. The pattern in each state was similar - pressure on the non-Nazi state governments to place a Nazi in charge of police; threatening demonstrations by the SA and SS; the symbolic raising of the swastika banner on town halls; the surrender of elected governments with little or no resistance; the appointment of a Reich Commissioner to restore order. The same process was repeated in state after state. The weakening of Prussia by the Papen coup (the overthrow of the elected Prussian government and its replacement by a Reich Commissioner in July 1932 - see Unit 3, Section 2.2) and the takeover of Prussia by the Nazis in February 1933 provided the platform and the model for the extension of control to the other Länder. These now passed more or less into Nazi hands. Despite the semblance of legality (for example the appointment of Reich Commissioners - who were all Nazis), the Reich's seizure of the Länder's powers was a plain breach of the Weimar constitution. The use of force and pressure from the Nazis - political blackmail - had been solely responsible for creating the 'unrest' that required the restoration of 'order'. The terms of the Reichstag Fire Decree provided no justification since there was plainly no need for defence from 'Communist acts of violence endangering the state'. The only such acts were committed by the Nazis themselves.

Adapted from Kershaw 1998.

As Kershaw suggests in Box 5.4, unofficial Nazi paramilitary violence was the essential counterbalance to Hitler's policy of legality. Bracher (1971) cites the case of Bavaria, whose Reichstag deputies were reassured by Hitler that no Reich Commissioner would take over there. Hitler did add, however, that pressure from below might force the Reich to intervene. Conveniently enough for the Nazis, it soon did. Bavaria was then punished for resisting. The takeover was especially brutal, with opponents tortured and murdered, or thrown into temporary prisons and concentration camps (it was in March 1933 that Dachau concentration camp was first opened). Bracher argues that this interplay of a stage-managed revolution from above and a manipulated revolution from below was vital to the seizure of power.

'Day of Potsdam'

Since the Reichstag building had been burned down, deputies could not meet there. Instead, the opening ceremony (the first meeting following the election) was scheduled for 21 March and held in Potsdam. The Nazis ensured that the 'Day of Potsdam' was a day of pomp and ceremony which symbolically demonstrated the unity of the old order and the new. During the ceremony, Hitler, in civilian clothes rather than uniform, bowed with apparent respect to President Hindenburg and shook his hand. The day did much to persuade people that the Nazis stood for stability as well as change:

'The "Day of Potsdam" was an imposing spectacle ...designed to lull Germans into the belief that the Nazis were merely carrying out the best features of Germany's conservative past...When Hitler and Hindenburg entered the church, the former dressed in a frock coat, the latter in his resplendent Field Marshal's uniform, the spectators got precisely the impression Hitler wanted to create: the old Prussian military tradition, embodying old-fashioned German values of honour, loyalty and love of country was now linking up with a new dynamic Germany that was symbolised by the simple, front-line soldier Adolf Hitler.' (Fischer K. 1995, pp.275-76)

The Enabling Act

Under the Weimar constitution, proposals for laws had to be approved by a majority in the Reichstag. Treaties with foreign states had to be approved by a majority in the Reichstag. Constitutional amendments could only be made if approved by a two-thirds majority in the Reichstag. All these democratic checks were designed to limit the power of the government.

According to Kershaw (1998), Hitler had made plans to pass an 'Enabling Act' as early as November 1932. His aim on becoming Chancellor was to hold an election which gave the NSDAP a two-thirds majority in the Reichstag and then to pass a law (the Enabling Act) which changed the constitution, abolishing all the democratic checks described above and transferring all such powers to the government. The problem was that the Nazis did not win a two-thirds majority in the election held on 5 March 1933. They won 288 seats out of a total of 647. They could rely on the support of the 52 DNVP deputies, but that only gave them 340 votes, a long way short of the 432 needed. They then bent the rules by ruling that all deputies were to be counted as being present unless officially excused (to ensure that a boycott by opponents did not prevent them receiving enough votes) and by deducting the KPD deputies from the total:

'To ensure the two-thirds majority, Frick had worked out that if the Communist deputies were simply deducted from the total membership of the Reichstag, only 378, not 432, votes would be needed. Göring added that, if necessary, some Social Democrats could be ejected from the Chamber. That is how little the Nazis' "legal revolution" had to do with legality.' (Kershaw 1998, p.466)

Under the new arrangement, the Nazis and DNVP combined were still short of the two-thirds majority, but this would be secured if they could persuade the Centre Party's 74 deputies to support the proposed legislation.

In the build-up to the Reichstag meeting of 23 March at which the Enabling Act was passed, the Nazis negotiated with the Centre Party. According to Klaus Fischer, their bargaining chip was the Reichstag Fire Decree which had removed civil rights - see Box 5.5.

The meeting of 23 March

The Reichstag meeting of 23 March was held in an atmosphere of great intimidation. SA and SS troops lined the walls, shouting abuse at the non-Nazi deputies and cheering loudly when Hitler spoke. Hitler delivered a long speech full of promises which were soon broken. SPD Leader Otto Wels then made a brave speech against the proposed Bill, despite the threatening chants of the SA and SS troops. Bullock claims that Hitler reacted furiously to this speech:

'Brushing aside von Papen who tried to restrain him, [Hitler] launched into an abusive tirade, shouting that it was only on account of justice and for psychological reasons that he was appealing to the Reichstag "to grant us what in any case we could have taken". As for the Social Democrats: "I can only tell you: I do not want you to vote for it. Germany shall be free, but not through you!" A prolonged ovation and shouts of "Heil" greeted Hitler's outburst, to be repeated when the result - 441 to 94 in favour - was announced.' (Bullock 1991, pp.352-53)

BOX 5.5 Hitler wins over the Centre Party

Even with the support of the DNVP, Hitler still did not have enough votes to pass the Bill by a two-thirds majority. So, he persuaded the Centre Party to vote for the Bill by agreeing to its demand that he repeal the Reichstag Fire Decree. By abolishing basic rights (including the freedom of worship which was very important to the Centre Party's Catholic constituency), the Reichstag Fire Decree had gone further than the proposed Enabling Law. The Centre Party leaders reasoned that they could probably not block the passage of the Enabling Bill one way or the other. They hoped that, if they supported Hitler, he would treat the Centre Party with respect and support Catholic interests in Germany by restoring the basic rights that had been suspended. Hitler agreed verbally to the Centre Party's demands and promised to send the party a written document confirming this. On 23 March, this document had not arrived. Only when Frick, the Nazi Minister of the Interior, assured the Leader of the Centre Party, Ludwig Kaas, that the letter was on its way did the party agree to vote for the Bill. Needless to say, no letter ever arrived and nor would Hitler give the Centre Party or Catholic Church special treatment. The Centre Party's decision to support the Enabling Bill showed that it cared more for the freedom of the Catholic Church than it did for the freedom of German Catholics.

Adapted from Fischer K. 1995.

The passing of the Enabling Act allowed the Nazis to bypass the Reichstag. It gave the government the power to:
- alter the constitution
- make laws
- agree treaties with foreign states.

It also allowed the Chancellor to draft legislation. The Act was (supposedly) a temporary measure, limited to four years.

Phase 2 - 23 March 1933 to 30 June 1934

Gleichschaltung - the beginning of Nazification

The passing of the Enabling Act ended the first phase of the legal revolution since it provided the foundation stone of the dictatorship established by the Nazis:

'In purely legal terms the Weimar constitution was never dissolved, but in practice the Enabling Act provided the basis for creating the arbitrary dictatorship which evolved during 1933.' (Layton 2000, p.43)

The passing of the Enabling Act did not mean that the legal revolution was over. In the next phase - from March 1933 to June 1934 - a process began which was termed 'Gleichschaltung'. According to Klaus Fischer, the term 'Gleichschaltung' comes from the German word 'Gleichrichter' which means

'a device which allows an electrical current to flow in only one direction'. The idea was that, like the electrical current, policy would flow in one direction - from the Führer through the government and party to the people. For this to happen, all institutions needed to be Nazified. Fischer argues:

'Gleichschaltung proceeded along two related paths: synchronisation of all government institutions and mass mobilisation of all citizens for the National Socialist cause. The first approach involved the eradication of all political opponents and parties and the second the creation of mass organisations for mass control.' (Fischer K. 1995, p.278)

It is important to note that the process of 'coordination' (Gleichschaltung) was not just imposed on the German people by the Nazi leadership. This did happen to some extent, but, at the same time, it was a voluntary process - a 'revolution from below':

'To some extent Gleichschaltung was generated by the power and freedom now enjoyed by the mass ranks of the SA at the local level - in effect a 'revolution from below'. But it was also directed by the Nazi leadership from the political centre in Berlin - in effect a 'revolution from above'. Together these two political impulses attempted to "coordinate" as many aspects of German life as possible along Nazi lines.' (Layton 2000, p.43)

This explains why the term 'Gleichschaltung' is sometimes translated as 'coordination'.

The end of federalism

It was noted above that Länder came under Nazi control in the days following the March election. For a few weeks, the apparatus of state government (Cabinet and assembly) remained in place, but then the Nazis began a process which would result in Germany's federal structure being dismantled. This process is described in Box 5.6.

The smashing of the unions

Trade unions, with their close ties to the SPD, were a potential source of opposition to Nazi rule and they did not escape the process of coordination (Gleichschaltung). Layton argues that, like many other groups in Germany, trade union leaders mistakenly believed that they would be able to survive by cooperating with the Nazis:

'Like so many others, trade union leaders deceived themselves into believing that they could work with the Nazis and thereby preserve a degree of independence and at least the structure of trade unionism.' (Layton 2000, p.44)

Kershaw shows that, in the weeks following the March election, the trade union confederation - the ADGB - had declared its loyalty to the Nazi regime and begun expelling anti-Nazis and other radicals. There appeared to be a chance that this approach

The dismantling of Germany's federal structure

In line with the policy of preserving the impression that the Nazis were acting constitutionally, the Enabling Law guaranteed the continued existence of the Reichsrat, the federal body which represented the Länder in the Reichstag (see Unit 2, Section 1.2). By the time that the Enabling Law was passed all the Länder were under Nazi control and there was, as a result, no difficulty in passing the Enabling Law in the Reichsrat. Eight days later, on 31 March, the Nazis issued the Law for the Coordination (Gleichschaltung) of the Länder. This transferred power from the Land assemblies to the Land governments, empowering the governments to make laws and reorganise their organisations independently of the Land assemblies. A week later, a law with the same title set up 'Reich Governors' whose job was to ensure that the policies of Land governments stayed in line with those of the Reich Chancellor (ie Hitler). This was a hasty measure which appears to have been designed to limit independent action by the party Gauleiters and SA leaders who had taken control of the Länder. The constitutional process was finally taken to its logical conclusion by a third law with the same title issued on 30 January 1934. This ended the Bismarckian federal settlement by abolishing Land assemblies, transferring the sovereign rights of the Länder to central government and making Land governments as well as Reich Governors subordinate to central government. Since this went beyond the bounds of the Enabling Law, Hitler called a meeting of the Reichstag and the Reichstag - which, by then, only contained Nazis - passed an 'improved' Enabling Act which allowed the Reichsrat to be abolished 'legally'. All this elaborate constitutional scene shifting was designed not only to remove obstacles to the will of central government but also to secure the cooperation of the civil service and the smooth working of the government machine.

Adapted from Bullock 1991.

would be successful when the Nazis announced that 1 May would be a national holiday - a 'Day of National Labour'. Then, the very next day, the SS forcibly shut down all the unions, arrested their leaders, and confiscated their assets:

'Within an hour, the "action" was finished. The largest democratic trade union movement in the world had been destroyed.' (Kershaw 1998, p.476)

A new Nazi trade union - the DAF (German Workers Union), headed by Robert Ley - was set up, largely as a means of control. Workers were obliged to join it. Such decisive action won the approval of many employers.

The end of party politics

Apart from the unions, the other obvious source of political opposition to the Nazis came from the political parties. In June 1933, steps were taken to ensure that this potential threat was neutralised:

'The KPD, although never formally banned, had already been effectively suppressed. Its leaders were in prison, concentration camp or exile, its papers had been closed down, its offices occupied and assets seized. Henceforth it could function only from abroad or underground. The SPD was able to operate legally a little longer, but the move of part of its leadership to a base abroad in Prague provided the excuse to prohibit its activities in Germany and seize its assets as "an organisation hostile to the German state and people" (22 June).' (Bullock 1991, p.354)

Under pressure from the Nazis, other parties then had little choice but to dissolve themselves shortly after this. Between 22 June and 5 July, party after party chose to dismantle itself. On 14 July, the Nazis passed a law preventing the formation of parties and making the NSDAP the sole legal party. In November 1933, an 'election' was held in which only Nazi candidates were allowed to stand. Turnout was high (95.2%) and the NSDAP won 39,638,800 votes.

Fischer points out that other laws passed on 14 July gave the government the right to:
- confiscate the property of organisations
- remove the citizenship of individuals without saying why
- control rural settlement
- hold plebiscites (referendums) to discover public opinion on policies.

Significantly, another law, the Law for the Prevention of Progeny with Hereditary Diseases legalised compulsory sterilisation on 14 July. This was the first step on the road to the euthanasia programme which resulted in the death of over 100,000 people who had 'lives not worth living'. Fischer concludes that:

'After July 14 there remained only a parliamentary shell in the form of a coordinated Reichstag that, obediently doing the bidding of Adolf Hitler, would pass any law, no matter how outlandish or unjust.' (Fischer K. 1995, p.282)

The beginning of the persecution of the Jews

One consequence of the process of coordination (Gleichschaltung) was a steadily increasing institutionalised discrimination against Jews. On 1 April a national boycott of Jewish shops took place. Many Nazis had wanted a longer, or permanent, boycott, but in the face of international disapproval and threatened sanctions Hitler eventually settled for a one-day action. Many Germans ignored the boycott, but gradually violence against Jews became routine. Nothing was done by the government to prevent such violence. On the contrary, the government began to pass legislation which began to exclude Jews from professional and social life. On 7 April 1933 the Law for the Restoration of the Civil Service included an 'Aryan paragraph' which

banned Jews from working for the civil service
(President Hindenburg insisted that those who had
served in the First World War should be exempted).
Other laws passed in April:

- banned Jews from the legal profession
- banned Jewish doctors from treating National
  Insurance Scheme patients
- limited the number of Jewish children in
  schools.

The coordination of local groups and the professions

It was pointed out above the the process of
coordination (Gleichschaltung) was not just imposed
from above, but was also a voluntary process that
took place at the grass roots. Kershaw argues that
the Nazis' seizure of power at national level started
a bandwagon rolling at local level. Town councils
expelled 'Marxist' councillors and many councillors
elected as representatives of other parties switched
to the NSDAP. Teachers and civil servants flocked to
join the NSDAP. As Box 5.7 shows, all sorts of clubs
and societies were taken over by Nazis and
'Nazified'.

Klaus Fischer notes that the Nazis made special
efforts to 'coordinate' the legal profession. Although
there was some resistance, many judges and lawyers
embraced Nazism with enthusiasm:

'How far legal Gleichschlatung had gone may be
illustrated by the oath taken at a mass meeting
held in front of the Supreme Court building in
Leipzig in October 1933. On that day, 10,000
lawyers, with their arms raised in the Hitler salute,
publicly swore "by the soul of the German people"
that they would "strive as German jurists to follow
the course of our Führer to the end of our days".'
(Fischer K. 1995, p.283)

The same was true of students and university
teachers. In universities all over Germany on 10
May 1933, students and university teachers
organised a burning of books considered
unacceptable to the Nazi regime. Libraries were
stripped of the offending books and huge bonfires
blazed through the night. As Kershaw points out, this
gesture was symbolic - a sign of the mood sweeping
through the country.

Resistance to the process of coordination (Gleichschlatung)

Although there was a great deal of voluntary
coordination, it would be a mistake to think that
Germany was completely transformed overnight.
There were important sectors in German society that
remained relatively untouched by the Nazis'
national rising:

'By mid-1933, the process of Gleichschlatung was
well advanced in many spheres of public life in
Germany, although it was certainly far from
complete. In particular, it had failed to make any
impression on the role and influence of the

BOX 5.7 Voluntary 'coordination' at a local level

Coordination - ie Nazification - extended deep
into the fabric of every town and village. Few of
the huge range of clubs and societies that formed
the social network of every town in the country
were left untouched. A report from a tiny
community with a population of 675 people in
Upper Franconia gives an idea of what was
happening. It reads: 'The Veteran's Association
was coordinated on 6.8.33, on 7.8.33 the Singing
Association in Theisenort. With the Shooting Club
in Theisenort this was not necessary since the
board and committee are up to 80% party
members'. A few months earlier, members of the
'Small Garden Association' in Hanover were told
that 'also in the area of small gardens the true
national community now has to emerge in
accordance with the will of the government of the
national rising' (the Nazi leadership described
their seizure of power as a 'national rising').
Business and professional organisations, sports
clubs, choral societies, shooting clubs, patriotic
associations and most other forms of organised
activity were taken under (or pressured to put
themselves under) Nazi control in the first months
of the Third Reich. One person who lived in
Northeim at the time commented that: 'There was
no more social life. You couldn't even have a
Bowling Club that wasn't coordinated'. The same
was true of Germany's cultural life. Goebbels
took up with great energy his task of ensuring that
the press, radio, film production, theatre, music,
the visual arts, literature and all other forms of
cultural activity were reorganised. The aim he
said in his first speech as Propaganda Minister
was 'to work on people until they have given in
to us' and 'to unite the nation behind the ideal of
the national revolution'. One of the most striking
features of the coordination of culture was how
willing intellectuals, writers, artists, performers
and publicists were to jump on the bandwagon.
Adapted from Kershaw 1998.

Christian churches, the Army and Big Business.
This was mainly due to Hitler's determination to
regulate the "revolution from above" and to avoid
[annoying] such powerful vested interests.' (Layton
2000, p.45)

The Nazis did try to infiltrate the Protestant Church
during the months after March 1933. According to
Burleigh (2000), in May 1933 Hitler appointed
Ludwig Müller as Reich Bishop and ordered him to
set up a unified pro-Nazi Protestant Church. Müller
failed to heal the splits within the Protestant Church,
however, and one wing of the Church - the
Confessional Church led by Martin Niemöller -
actively and successfully campaigned against the
Nazification of the Church. As for the Catholic
Church, a deal was struck in July 1933 when Hitler
signed a concordat (agreement) with the Vatican in

Rome (the Catholic Church's headquarters):

'The concordat was regarded by world opinion as a great diplomatic victory for Hitler. In return for the assurance from Rome that it would not meddle in German politics, the Führer granted Catholics freedom to practice their religion. He made the agreement for several reasons: to undermine the strength of the Catholic Centre Party in German politics, to cut the influence of the Catholic [trade] unions and to win public recognition for his new regime.' (Snyder 1976, p.58)

Phase 3 - June to August 1934

The final phase of the legal revolution began with the 'Night of the Long Knives' on 30 June 1934. This phase is examined in Section 1.3 below.

MAIN POINTS - Section 1.2

- The legal revolution consolidated Hitler's power and transformed German society. It destroyed the independence of the Länder and produced a one-party state.
- The first phase in the legal revolution began with Hitler's appointment as Chancellor and ran until the passage of the Enabling Act on 23 March 1933.
- The Enabling Law (passed with the support of the DNVP and Centre Party) allowed the Nazis to bypass the Reichstag. It gave the government the power to - (1) alter the constitution (2) make laws (3) agree treaties with foreign states. It also allowed the Chancellor to draft legislation.

- In the second phase of the legal revolution, a process of 'coordination' (Gleichschaltung) began. This had two characteristics - the Nazification of the political process and the winning of mass support for the Nazi way of life.
- Coordination required the removal of political opponents. To this end, the unions were smashed, all parties but the NSDAP were dissolved, local leisure groups and professional bodies were taken over by the Nazis, Jews were barred from certain jobs.
- There was some resistance to coordination, notably in the Protestant Church and no attempt was made to coordinate the army or Big Business.

Activity 5.2 The legal revolution

ITEM 1 Timeline - the key events

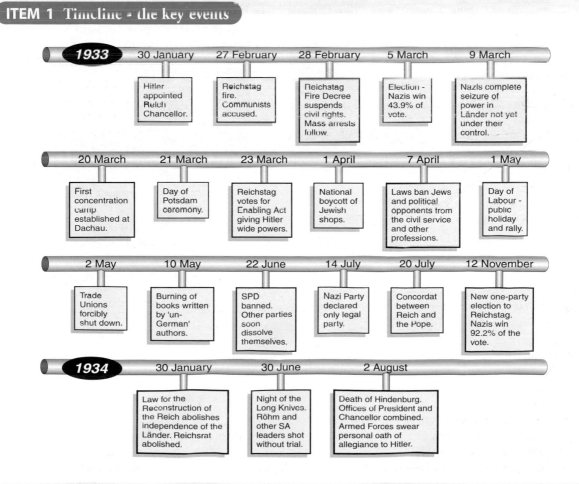

ITEM 2 Historians' views

(i) The degree of violence and intimidation exercised by the Nazi organisations has sometimes been underestimated in accounts which stress the pseudo-legality of the steps that the Nazis took. The maintenance of an appearance of legality was undoubtedly an important element in Hitler's strategy. But, it was only one element and it was not always the one most evident at the time. In reality, the seizure of power was anything but peaceful. It was true that there was no fighting on the streets because the left offered no resistance. During March 1933, however, 'a revolution from below' began. Local Nazi organisations took it upon themselves to interfere with the administration of local government, with the course of justice and with commercial life. The importance of Hitler's pseudo-legal strategy was that it was a contrast to the violence on the ground. With some justice, Hitler could argue that he was simply taking the use of emergency powers a stage further than his three predecessors. This was reassuring for the civil servants and employers faced with the 'revolution from below'. The fact that Hitler was keeping to the law was an incentive to cooperate with the regime in the hope that this would encourage the 'moderate' Hitler to keep the local militants in check.
Adapted from Noakes & Pridham 1996.

(ii) The Enabling Act was of great psychological importance. Many sober-minded officials and soldiers brought up in the strict law-abiding atmosphere of the pre-war period were repelled by the rowdy street hooligans in uniform. The Act, which seemingly put the legality of the regime beyond doubt, enabled these Germans to suppress their anxieties and fears and to serve their new masters as faithfully as the old. The continued presence of Hindenburg at the head of affairs and the fact that non-Nazis remained in the Cabinet was also reassuring. Hitler, the view commonly was, should be given his chance to put Germany's house in order and end the state of near civil war which had threatened Germany for two years. It was significant that, when the SPD was dissolved on 22 June 1933, the middle-class parties hastened to dissolve themselves. The Reichstag still remained in being but ceased to be a place for democratic discussion. The one-party state had arrived and the 'National Revolution' began.
Adapted from Carr 1991.

ITEM 3 'Day of Potsdam'

Hitler and Hindenburg on the Day of Potsdam.

Today and here, the marriage took place, if not for ever then at least for a time, between the masses led by Hitler and the Spirit of Potsdam, Prussian values, represented by Hindenburg. How marvelously it's been staged by that master producer Goebbels. The procession of Hindenburg, the government, and the MPs goes from Berlin to Potsdam past a solid line of cheering millions. The whole of Berlin seems to be on the streets. Government and MPs walk from St Nicholas Church to the Garrison Church together. The radio announcer almost weeps with emotion. Then Hitler speaks. It cannot be denied. He has grown in stature. A true statesman seems to be developing. The government's declaration is marked by notable moderation. Not a word of hatred for the opposition, not a word of racial ideology, no threat aimed at home or abroad. Hindenburg lays wreaths on the graves of the Prussian kings. The old Field Marshal shakes hands with the World War corporal. The corporal makes a deep bow. Cannons thunder over Potsdam - over Germany. Nobody can escape the emotion of the moment. Father too is deeply impressed. Mother has tears in her eyes.

Adapted from an account written by Erich Ebermeyer. Ebermeyer and his family were liberals who were generally unsympathetic to the Nazis. This account is quoted in Noakes & Pridham 1996.

ITEM 4 Hitler the dictator

THE RED PERIL.

This cartoon was published on 8 March 1933, three days after the German election. It shows President Hindenburg and Chancellor Hitler as Roman senators. In ancient Rome, senior senators were appointed to the special post of dictator at times when there was a state of emergency. In the background the Reichstag building burns. Hindenburg says to Hitler: 'This is a heaven-sent opportunity, my lad. If you can't be a dictator now, you never will be'.

Questions

1. The following four factors all played a part in establishing Nazi power: (i) self promotion and propaganda (ii) violent intimidation (iii) Hitler's opportunism (iv) genuine support for the regime. Using Items 1-3 and your own knowledge, place the factors in order of importance and explain why you have chosen this order.
2. Look at Items 1 and 2.
   a) Pick out four key events. Explain their importance and why they occurred.
   b) Using Item 2 explain why it was important for the Nazis to give the impression they were acting legally.
3. What does Item 3, tell us about (a) Nazi tactics and (b) the public's mood in March 1933?
4. The cartoon in Item 4 predicts that Hitler will become dictator. Explain how he managed to do this.

1.3 What was the significance of the 'Night of the Long Knives' and the death of Hindenburg?

Threats to Hitler after 14 July 1933

Historians have identified four main groups with the potential to challenge Hitler's position of supremacy after the declaration of the one-party state on 14 July 1933:

- the army, particularly the traditionalists in its leadership
- President Hindenburg - old but still influential, with at least the theoretical power to bring down the government
- the group of Conservative politicians surrounding Franz von Papen
- the SA under Ernst Röhm.

Kershaw shows that the threat posed by these four groups was of particular concern to Hitler in the second half of 1933 and first half of 1934 for two main reasons - because of the age and deteriorating health of Hindenburg and because of tensions between the SA and the army. He suggests that if Hindenburg had died before the 'Night of the Long Knives' (30 June 1934), it was by no means inevitable that Hitler would have become Head of State:

'President Hindenburg was old and frail. The issue of the succession would loom within the foreseeable future. Hindenburg...was the figurehead behind which stood still powerful forces with somewhat [uncertain] loyalties towards the new state. Most important among them was the army [Reichswehr], of which as Head of State Hindenburg was supreme commander. The Reichswehr leadership was intensely and increasingly alarmed by...the SA. Failure on Hitler's part to solve the problem of the SA could conceivably lead to army leaders favouring...a restoration of the monarchy and a...military dictatorship. Such a development would have met with favour among sections, not just of the military old guard, but of some national-conservative groups...The office of the Vice Chancellor, Papen, gradually emerged as the focal point of hopes of blunting the edge of the Nazi revolution.' (Kershaw 1998, p.500)

The other significant player in this competition for power was the SS, under the leadership of Heinrich Himmler. By mid-1933 it was developing into an élite paramilitary organisation (see Box 5.8).

The SA in 1933

After the election of 5 March 1933, the SA played a vital role in taking over the state governments. Röhm personally took charge of the takeover in Bavaria. The SA also supervised the boycott of Jewish shops on 1 April, as well as mounting numerous 'actions' against both Jews and left-wingers. In the early days, while Papen and others complained about the SA's unruliness, Hitler 'marvelled at [its] tremendous discipline' (Broszat 1981, p.79). However, there had long been tensions between the SA and the Nazi Party. Röhm saw the SA's function as military. Hitler saw it as political. Hitler had even dismissed Röhm over this difference in approach (in 1925), only recalling him in 1931 (see Unit 4, Sections 2.1 and 3.2). In the summer of 1933, the old tensions resurfaced. Carr argues that members of the SA felt let down:

'Having put the Führer in power, the SA men expected a privileged status with well-paid posts to compensate them for long years in the wilderness. They were quickly disillusioned. Hitler had no intention of disrupting the economic and commercial life of Germany; on the contrary, he forbade the party to interfere with the work of economic experts whose services were indispensable if Germany was to solve the problem of unemployment...Röhm concluded...that the Führer no longer shared the objectives of the SA.' (Carr 1991, p.314)

On the other hand, from Hitler's point of view, the SA had done its job and was now becoming a liability:

'Hitler's unruly party army, the SA, had outlived its purpose. That had been to win power. Everything had been [based on scoring] that single goal. What would follow the winning of power, what would be the purpose and function of the SA in the new

BOX 5.8 | The SS

The SS (short for 'Schutzstaffel', meaning 'élite guard') was set up in 1925 as Hitler's black-shirted personal bodyguard. From 1929, it was transformed and expanded by its leader, Heinrich Himmler (see right), eventually becoming the mass army on which Nazi power ultimately rested. The name was universally abbreviated to SS and written as a lightning flash. The SS was also known as the 'Black Order'. Members of the SS served as a political police and were later responsible for administering concentration camps and extermination camps. When Hitler became Chancellor in 1933, the members of the SS (like the SA) were authorised to act as auxiliary police officers. After the 'Night of the Long Knives' (see below), the SS emerged as the chief police arm of the

Leading members of the SS. Himmler is second from the left in the front row. Heydrich is second from the right.

Nazi Party. The SS's job was to find, fight and destroy all open and secret enemies of the Führer and the National Socialist movement and to organise a 'racial resurrection'.

Adapted from Snyder 1976.

state, what benefits would flow for ordinary stormtroopers had not been [made clear]. Now, months after the "seizure of power", the SA's politics of hooliganism were a force of disruption for the state.' (Kershaw 1998, p.499)

Röhm's aims

As noted in Section 1.2 above, the SA's thuggish violence (the so-called 'revolution from below') complemented and supported Hitler's pseudo-legal tactics. The SA, though, resented Hitler's tactic of legality:

'It downgraded their own role and appeared to taint National Socialism with the self-seeking venal [corrupt] attitudes which they associated with party politics' (Fischer C. 1995, p.42)

The SA's Leader, Ernst Röhm, was an old 'brother-in-arms' of Hitler (see Unit 4), but he had a different outlook to the Führer. According to Carr:

'Röhm had expected to come to power not by the back door but on the barricades in classic revolutionary fashion. A "National Revolution" of the kind symbolised by Hitler's meeting with Hindenburg in [Potsdam] was totally inadequate; what Germany needed was a "National Socialist Revolution" to destroy the power of the...upper classes and [reduce] unemployment by adopting those socialist measures to which the party was at least nominally committed.' (Carr 1991, p.315)

In the summer of 1933, therefore, Röhm and other SA leaders began openly to call for a 'second revolution' which would overthrow the traditional power structure of army, industry and Prussian aristocracy and replace it with what Kershaw calls an 'SA state':

'Röhm's ambitions...amounted to little less than the creation of an "SA state", with extensive powers in the police, in military matters and in the civil administration.' (Kershaw 1998, p.502)

Central to Röhm's plans was the reform of the army. By the summer of 1933, the SA was huge - Kershaw says it had c.4.5 million members. Carr argues that Röhm aimed to merge the SA with the Reichswehr:

'Of central importance in the quarrel between Röhm and Hitler was the question of army reform...Röhm was bitterly critical of Hitler's failure to deal with this "stronghold of reaction" and pressed upon Hitler his plan for the amalgamation of Reichswehr and SA to create a people's militia, a truly revolutionary army under Röhm as Minister for War.' (Carr 1991, p.315)

Röhm's behaviour

Röhm did not pursue his aims in secret. He openly and publicly made appeals for a 'second revolution' and he attempted to put pressure on Hitler by organising large parades and demonstrations:

'Now that Hitler had become Chancellor, Röhm took no more trouble than he had in the 1920s to guard his mouth or disguise his scorn for Hitler's compromises with the established order. His appointment to Hitler's Cabinet and Hitler's cordial letter of thanks at the end of the year only strengthened his belief that "Adolf" secretly agreed with him. He not only continued to be free in his criticisms of the regime and its policies, but carried out a...series of parades, inspections and demonstrations throughout Germany and began to secure additional supplies of arms partly from abroad.' (Bullock 1991, p.378)

Hitler's response

If Röhm and his SA wanted a 'second revolution', Hitler was equally determined that there would be no such thing. This, however, presented him with a dilemma. This dilemma is examined in Box 5.9.

Why didn't Hitler side with Röhm?

Most historians accept that Hitler's central long-term aim was to secure Lebensraum (living space) for Germany through war. To achieve this aim, he needed the support of the Reichswehr leadership:

'The truth was that Hitler had decided to throw in his lot with the regular army because he realised that, without the organisational talents of the conservative generals, his long-range military plans could never be fulfilled.' (Fischer K. 1995, p. 286)

In addition Hitler knew that the 'bullying arrogance and rowdy disturbances of the power-crazed SA...was deeply offensive to the sense of public order and morality of middle-class Germans,' whose support he also required (Kershaw 1987, p. 85). The same point can be made about the upper classes - especially the big industrialists. If Hitler was to fight wars, he needed to rebuild Germany's Armed Forces and this could only be done if the German economy boomed. As a result, Hitler needed the support of employers - especially big employers - and he could not afford to alienate traditional conservatives:

'Conservatives feared the...anti-establishment attitudes of rebellious storm troopers. Hugenberg told Hitler in June 1933 that he would not return to government service until the National Socialists reined in their "left wing". While Hitler was quite happy to be rid of Hugenberg, he had to deal with growing conservative hostility to those aspects of Nazi rule that threatened the interests of traditional élites.' (Stackelberg 1999, p.114)

To gain and retain the support of these key interest groups - the army, the middle classes and Big Business, Hitler would have to take action against the SA. As Box 5.9 makes clear, however, it was unclear for a year what this action would be.

Steps taken before June 1934

Although Box 5.9 suggests that 'Hitler did little to resolve the tensions which continued to build', a number of important steps were taken before the 'decisive action' of 30 June 1924. These are outlined in Box 5.10.

Hitler meets Röhm, 4 June 1934

In June 1934, matters came to a head. On 4 June 1934 Hitler had a five-hour private discussion with Röhm. Klaus Fischer claims that this meeting produced two surprises:

'Hitler probably warned Röhm to scale down SA actions but otherwise gave the SA chief no inkling about the exact role of the SA in the Nazi state. This meeting, however, produced two surprises.

BOX 5.9 The dilemma facing Hitler

The elimination of the SA or at least the reduction in power was no easy matter. It was a huge organisation - far bigger than the party itself. It contained many of the most enthusiastic 'old fighters'. It had been the backbone of the violent activism which had forced the pace since Hitler became Chancellor. Röhm's ambitions had never been the same as Hitler's and the SA had never fully accepted that it was subordinate to the political wing of the party. Whatever crises had arisen in the past, Hitler had always managed to retain the SA's loyalty. To challenge the SA's leadership, however, was to risk losing that loyalty. It could not be done easily or approached lightly. Faced with the dilemma about what to do about the SA, for months Hitler did little to resolve the tensions which continued to build. Characteristically, he acted finally when there was no longer a choice - but then with utter ruthlessness. The pressure from the Reichswehr leadership and from Göring, Himmler and his deputy, Heydrich played decisive roles in bringing the matter to a head in the summer of 1934. Then, within a matter of five weeks, the destruction of the SA leadership (and of other leading opponents) in the 'Night of the Long Knives' and the rapid takeover by Hitler of the headship of state on Hindenburg's death (under a law agreed by the Cabinet while he was alive) amounted to a decisive phase in the securing of total power.

Adapted from Kershaw 1998.

Röhm declared himself willing to undergo a "personal-illness vacation"...at Bad Wiessee and to send the whole SA on a kind of vacation or leave of absence during the month of July.' (Fischer K. 1995, p.287)

Despite this, tensions mounted. Kershaw argues that, by this time, there was growing discontent with the regime:

'At the level of the ordinary mass of the population, the excited...mood of "national renewal" that had swept the country during the breathless upheavals of 1933 had given way to widespread discontent and criticism as disillusionment and material disappointment took over.' (Kershaw 1998, p.507)

Papen's speech, 17 June

While this may have encouraged Hitler to take action, Kershaw argues that it was the action of the conservative group around Papen which was decisive. At the beginning of June, President Hindenburg told Papen, 'Things are going badly, Papen. Try to straighten them out' (Fest 1973, p.457). Papen's response was to deliver a speech at the University of Marburg on 17 June in which he made a stinging attack on the government. Kershaw

BOX 5.10 | Steps taken between July 1933 and June 1934

The first step that Hitler took to counter the threat posed by Röhm was to make a speech on 6 July 1933 in which he declared that the revolution was over. This brought an important change in approach as other Nazi leaders followed Hitler's line. Despite repeating this message at a meeting of Reich Governors held in September 1933 and promising action, however, Hitler took no further action until January 1934. This suggests that he was unsure how to proceed. In early January 1934, however, Hitler summoned Rudolf Diels, Head of the Prussian Gestapo, and ordered him to collect evidence which could later be used against the SA leadership. This suggests that, at this point, Hitler still hoped to avoid a confrontation, but he realised that he needed to be prepared. The next key development came on 1 February 1934 when Röhm sent a memorandum to Blomberg, the Minister of Defence and Head of the Armed Forces. This memorandum (which has not survived) probably demanded that the SA should be placed in charge of national defence. Certainly, it provoked a hostile response from the Reichswehr. The army began to lobby Hitler and, to win his support, introduced the NSDAP's emblem into the army and accepted the 'Aryan paragraph' for officers, leading to the prompt dismissal of some 70 officers. On 28 February, Hitler made a speech which rejected Röhm's plans for the SA. Röhm was forced to sign an agreement, but, when Hitler left, was overheard saying that he would ignore it. In February, Hitler met the British minister Anthony Eden twice and told him that he would reduce the size of the SA by two-thirds and would never allow a second army to be built. Then, in April, Hitler met the top military leaders on board a cruiser and made a gentleman's agreement. In return for the military's support for his dictatorship, Hitler would quash Röhm's plans and guarantee the military's independence. By May, Göring and Himmler (who had been helping Diels with his investigation) had produced 'evidence' that the SA were plotting a coup and the Reichswehr made weapons and transport available to the SS for use in an assault on the SA.

Adapted from Bullock 1991, Fischer 1995 and Kershaw 1998.

played for time. He could not afford Papen to resign as Hindenburg might use the resignation as the cue to dissolve the government. Hitler, therefore, asked Papen to delay making a final decision before the two of them had been to see President Hindenburg. Papen agreed. On 21 June, Hitler then went to see Hindenburg alone (using the excuse that he needed to discuss a meeting he had recently had with Mussolini). On the way to this meeting, he met Blomberg, the Defence Minister and Head of the Army, who told him that, unless Hitler took decisive action, the President would declare martial law and put power in the hands of the Reichswehr. Hindenburg himself then told Hitler to deal with the 'revolutionary troublemakers'. On 27 June, Blomberg and his deputy, Reichenau presented Hitler with 'evidence' that Röhm had issued an order for the SA to arm itself. Bullock adds that, during June, Göring and Himmler built up 'evidence' that an SA uprising was imminent:

> 'Göring and Himmler put together "evidence" of a conspiracy aimed at overthrowing the present regime by force and merging the army, the SA and the SS under a single command to be held by Röhm. Hitler himself was to remain as Chancellor, with von Schleicher (who was alleged to be a central figure in the conspiracy) as Vice Chancellor.' (Bullock 1991, pp.380-81)

Bullock argues that Göring and Himmler made plans to prevent this 'conspiracy' taking place and that, when these plans were put before Hitler on 26 June, he agreed to them (Bullock suggests that Hitler may genuinely have believed that there was a conspiracy). Other historians (for example, Kershaw) suggest that events unfolded in a more haphazard way than Bullock implies and that Hitler acted on the spur of the moment rather than following a pre-arranged plan.

Operation Hummingbird: the purge

On 28 June Hitler went to a wedding in Essen, perhaps 'to lull the supposed conspirators into a sense of false security' (Fischer K. 1995, p. 290). Most historians agree that it was on that day that Hitler finally made up his mind to act and started to make secret preparations for action. The next day, the arrangements were finalised and, in the early morning of 20 June, action was finally taken. Box 5.11 gives two historians' accounts of what happened.

Reactions to and consequences of the 'Night of the Long Knives'

Although there was a great deal of outrage abroad, historians agree that Hitler's extraordinarily brutal action gained general approval in Germany. Feuchtwanger (2000, p.122) says that, far from repulsing the German population, the murders

describes the speech as the 'decisive trigger' for what happened at the end of the month since the speech could be seen as the beginning of a campaign to persuade Hindenburg to dismiss Hitler.

Pressure builds on Hitler

Kershaw claims that events then unfolded as follows. Immediately after the speech, Goebbels, the Minister of Propaganda, prevented the press from mentioning it (with partial success). This, in turn, led Papen to call a meeting with Hitler on 19 June in which he threatened to resign as Vice Chancellor. Hitler

BOX 5.11 | The purge

(i) At 2 a.m. on Saturday 30 June, Hitler arrived in Munich and was informed that the SA had attempted a putsch there. This was a lie, but it threw Hitler into a frenzy. When the two top local SA leaders arrived, he ripped off their insignia of rank and screamed: 'You are arrested and will be shot'. He then travelled to the hotel in Bad Wiessee where Röhm and the SA leaders were staying, accompanied by senior Nazis, police and SS officers. The entourage arrived at the hotel at about 6.30 am and most of the guests were still asleep. The SA leaders were arrested and taken to Stadelheim prison, where six were executed immediately. Arriving back in Munich, Goebbels phoned Göring with the codeword 'Kolibri' (Hummingbird). This set in motion the murder of SA leaders and other 'enemies' of the party. The official death toll was 77, but it is generally agreed that the true figure was at least double this. Röhm was shot on 2 July after refusing to commit suicide. Although this purge is often described as the 'Night of the Long Knives', the killing lasted most of the weekend.
Adapted from Fischer K. 1995.

(ii) On 30 June 1934, Hitler arrived unexpectedly at the hotel in Bad Wiessee where Röhm had summoned SA leaders to meet him. SS officers burst into the rooms where the SA officers were sleeping and arrested them, including Röhm. They were then taken under guard to Munich. There and in Berlin, where Göring and Himmler directed operations, executions without any pretence of trial went on throughout the weekend. At the same time as Röhm and the SA commanders were killed, a number of figures from the past were routed out and murdered. Among them were Gregor Strasser (Hitler's former right-hand man - see Unit 4), former Chancellor Schleicher, von Kahr (who betrayed Hitler in 1923 - see Unit 4, Section 1.6) and Edgar Jung (who had written Papen's speech of 17 June).
Adapted from Bullock 1991.

brought 'a great collective sigh of relief' because people realised that the threat from the SA was at an end. The murders were particularly welcomed by the army. On 1 July, Defence Minister Blomberg in a statement to the army, praised Hitler's actions, adding that the gratitude of the Armed Forces would be marked by 'devotion and loyalty' (Kershaw 1998, p. 517). Hindenburg sent a telegram of congratulation and thanks - although there is doubt about whether he wrote it himself. On 3 July, Hitler justified his actions to ministers:

'Anticipating any questions about the lawlessness

of his actions, he likened his actions to those of a captain of a ship putting down a mutiny, where immediate action to smash the revolt was necessary and a formal trial impossible.'
(Kershaw 1998, p.517)

The Cabinet then passed a law confirming that the actions taken had been lawful. Hitler did not make a public statement on events for ten days. Then, on 13 July, he made a passionate speech in the Reichstag, justifying his actions. Kershaw suggests that he might have remained silent for ten days because he was worried how the mass of people would respond. If so, he had little cause to worry. As Bullock notes:

'The reports from all over Germany...showed not only an almost total absence of criticism of the Führer, but admiration for the forcefulness with which he had acted. There seems to have been little doubt that there had actually been a plot and the [hatred] of the SA was reflected in the general satisfaction that the Führer had put them down so decisively.' (Bullock 1991, p.382)

Historians suggest that the purge had five main consequences. These are outlined in Box 5.12.

BOX 5.12 | The consequences of the purge

First, the purge ended the threat that the SA would become a serious alternative power base. New leaders were put in place, it was restructured and its size was reduced by 40% within a year, transforming it into little more than a military sports and training body. Second, by murdering a number of conservatives (for example, Papen's speech writer, Jung), Hitler effectively ended the opposition that had been building from that quarter. Third, the purge bound the army more closely to Hitler. The leaders of the Reichswehr did not allow themselves to be disturbed by the murder of two of their senior colleagues, Schleicher and Bredow. They repaid the debt they thought they owed Hitler by smoothing his succession to Hindenburg at the beginning of August 1934 and by themselves suggesting the wording of the oath that tied the Armed Forces to their new supreme commander. Fourth, the fall of the SA led to the rise of the SS. And fifth, the discovery that there were circumstances in which the German people would accept summary executions was an important step on the road to the Holocaust. It set a legal precedent that forced the courts to sanction the regime or at least prevented them from making any moves against the murderers. The Nazis may have passed a law that legalised the murders, but the 'lawful state of National Socialism' was quite clearly a state of injustice, arbitrary rule, and government by crime.
Adapted from Bracher 1971, Kershaw 1998 and Feuchtwanger 2000.

Machtan's thesis

In October 2001, Lothar Machtan's controversial book *The Hidden Hitler* was published in English for the first time. This book argues that one of the reasons that Hitler was so careful to keep details about his private life out of the public sphere was that he was a homosexual. Far from being a side issue, Machtan argues, Hitler's sexuality is of central importance. In particular, it helps to explain why Hitler acted as he did at the end of June 1934. According to Machtan, the 'Night of the Long Knives' was not just an attempt to resolve the conflict between the Reichswehr and the SA. Nor was it simply a means to cement Hitler's position in power. It was also an exercise designed to kill or intimidate all those people who knew or suspected that Hitler was a homosexual. This explains, Machtan argues, why many of the people on the death list were targeted and why the SS used the 'state of emergency' to confiscate and destroy documents:

> '[The Night of the Long Knives] was a carefully planned campaign against people who knew or were suspected of knowing too much about Hitler. The violent imposition of a state of emergency was intended to enable the authorities to gain possession, at a stroke, of documents considered dangerous by Hitler and his regime...Hitler's motive for taking action against "Röhm and associates" was fear of exposure and blackmail. What additionally confirms this is that the mountains of confiscated documents were not to be used in trials of any kind but handed over to Himmler's Gestapo and thus to Hitler himself. The elimination of witnesses and evidence - that was the real purpose of this act of terrorism.' (Machtan 2001, p.17)

The death of Hindenburg

Just a month after the 'Night of the Long Knives', on 2 August 1934, President Hindenburg died, aged 87. Kershaw claims Hitler was well prepared:

> 'On 1 August, while Hindenburg was still alive, Hitler had all his ministers put their names to a law determining that, on Hindenburg's death, the office of Reich President would be combined with that of the Reich Chancellor.' (Kershaw 1998, p.524)

According to Klaus Fischer (1995, p.293) it was just one hour after Hindenburg died the following day that it was announced that Hitler had become Head of State and supreme commander. Symbolically, the title Reich President was dropped (to underline the break with past, suggests Bullock). As noted above, the army leadership immediately volunteered to swear an oath of loyalty. Bullock notes that civil servants also swore the oath and that the oath was to Hitler the person, not to the constitution:

> 'Instead of an oath to the constitution, all officers, soldiers and civil servants, including Reich ministers, were required to swear "before God" a personal oath to "Adolf Hitler, the Führer of the German Reich and German people".' (Bullock 1991, p.384)

As Fischer points out, these oaths revealed the 'unlimited nature of Hitler's dictatorship'. Absolute power had now been grasped.

The plebiscite of 19 August 1934

On 19 August, a plebiscite (referendum) was held, inviting voters to approve the union of the offices of Head of State and Head of Government. Bracher (1971, p.307) describes this as 'the final farce of the pseudo-legal revolution'. Despite coercion, vote-rigging and propaganda, the 'Yes' vote was far from unanimous. In some areas, especially in Berlin, it was well below the pro-Nazi vote in November 1933, showing a decline in Nazi popularity. Nonetheless, the Nazi propaganda machine was able to present it as another resounding success. As Kershaw (1998, p.526) points out, it showed that Hitler had the backing of the vast majority of the population.

MAIN POINTS - Section 1.3

- In July 1933 there were four main groups with the potential to challenge Hitler's position of supremacy: (1) the army (2) President Hindenburg (3) conservatives around Papen and (4) the SA.
- The SA had helped the Nazis come to power but, from the summer of 1933, SA violence and Röhm's demands threatened to alienate business and the middle classes. When Röhm began calling for a 'second revolution' Hitler made it clear he was opposed.
- Hitler made some preparations to curb the SA but did not act until June 1934. The speech made by Papen on 17 June may have been the trigger. Then,

between 30 June and 2 July at least 77 people and probably more than a hundred were murdered by SS officers on Hitler's orders - the 'Night of the Long Knives'.
- The 'Night of the Long Knives' had five main consequences: (1) the SA and (2) the conservatives were no longer a threat (3) the army felt indebted to Hitler (4) the SS gained importance and (5) it was an important step on the road to the Holocaust.
- When, a month later, Hindenburg died, Hitler became Head of State and supreme commander. The army and civil servants volunteered to swear an oath of allegiance to Hitler personally.

Activity 5.3 The 'Night of the Long Knives'

ITEM 1 Hitler speaking to the Reich Governors, 6 July 1933

More revolutions have succeeded in their first assault and then, once successful, have been brought to a standstill and held there. Revolution is not a permanent state, it must not develop into a lasting state. This revolution must be guided into the secure bed of evolution. To achieve this, the most important part is played by the education of the people. Circumstances must be improved and people must be educated to understand what it means to live in a National Socialist state. A businessman must not, therefore, be dismissed if he is a good businessman even if he is not yet a good National Socialist. The task of National Socialism is to safeguard the development of our people. But we must not keep looking round to see what next to revolutionise.

Adapted from Noakes & Pridham 1996.

ITEM 2 Röhm on Hitler

Adolf is rotten. He's betraying all of us. His old comrades aren't good enough for him. So he brings in these East Prussian generals. They're the ones he pals around with now. Adolf knows perfectly well what I want. I've told him often enough. Not a second pot of the Kaiser's army, made with the same old grounds. Are we a revolution or aren't we? Something new has to be brought in, understand? A new discipline. A new principle of organisation. The generals are old fogies. They'll never have a new idea. But Adolf is and always will be a civilian, an 'artist', a dreamer. 'Just leave me be', he thinks. Right now all he wants to do is sit up in the mountains and play God. And guys like us have to cool our heels, when we're burning for action, the chance to do something really new and great, something that will turn the world upside down. It's a chance in a lifetime. But Hitler keeps putting me off. He wants to let things drift. Keeps counting on a miracle. That's Adolf for you. He wants to inherit a ready-made army all set to go. He wants to have it knocked together by 'experts'. When I hear that word I blow my top. He'll make it National Socialist later on, he says.

Ernst Röhm

Part of an article written by Röhm in 1933. Adapted from Fischer K. 1995.

ITEM 3 Papen speaks

No nation that would survive before history can afford a permanent uprising from below. At some stage the movement must come to an end. At some point there must emerge a firm social structure held together by a legal system secure against pressure and by a state power that is unchallenged. A ceaseless dynamic creates nothing. Germany cannot be allowed to become a train hurtling into the blue with no one knowing where it will stop. History flows of its own accord, it does not need to be constantly driven forward. If, therefore, a second wave of new life is to sweep through the German revolution, then it must do so not as social revolution, but at the creative completion of work already done.

Part of the speech made by Papen at the University of Marburg on 17 June 1934, quoted in Noakes & Pridham 1996.

ITEM 4 A British cartoon

This cartoon makes a joke out of the Hitler salute. It shows members of the SA with both hands up in surrender as Hitler and Göring confront them with pistols (Goebbels is on his knees between them). Corpses lie in the bottom left and the regular army stands menacingly in the top right.

Questions

1. Read Items 1-3 and then summarise the different attitudes they contain towards revolution and the state. Explain how these differences created tensions.
2. Items 1 and 3 are extracts from speeches made in the build-up to the 'Night of the Long Knives'. Explain why these speeches were important.
3. a) What does Item 2 tell us about the character and ambitions of Ernst Röhm?
   b) Explain why Hitler finally decided that he had to kill him.
4. Using Item 4 and your own knowledge, explain the significance of the 'Night of the Long Knives'.

2 The Nazi political system

Key issues

1. How did the Nazi political system work?
2. How did the Nazis respond to political opposition in the period 1935-39?

2.1 How did the Nazi political system work?

Social Darwinism

In order to understand how the Nazi political system worked, it is necessary to understand the term 'Social Darwinism'. This has been defined as:

'The application of biological evolution to human society, often summarised in the phrase "the survival of the fittest".' (King 1997, p.24)

Clive King points out that the phrase 'survival of the fittest' was actually coined by Herbert Spencer, not by Charles Darwin. He argues that it was Spencer, rather than Darwin, who devised the ideas that later became known as 'Social Darwinism'. Spencer believed the 'laws of nature' meant that life was a struggle in which the strong rose to the top whilst the weak fell to the bottom. Since this was the natural order of things, people should not interfere as that would prevent progress being made:

'As a 19th century liberal, Spencer believed in progress, which he saw as the result of individual endeavour. This meant placing few restrictions on those who had the will to succeed and doing little to protect those who did not. Life was a struggle, a constant battle for survival. Nothing but harm could be done by helping the weak to survive against the laws of nature.' (King 1997, p.24)

The phrase 'laws of nature' is important. King argues that Spencer believed that he had discovered a scientific explanation of the way the world works and that these 'laws' were absolutely fixed.

On an international level, therefore, Social Darwinists see the relations between nations in terms of struggle. Nations compete against each other to gain control of limited resources. Sometimes this leads to wars which the stronger nations win and the weaker lose. Equally, on a national level, there is a constant struggle between groups and individuals within society. The stronger groups and individuals are successful - they gain power and wealth - while the weaker groups are a kind of natural wastage. King notes that, in versions of Social Darwinism current in the early 20th century, the issue of race became important. There was concern that the 'weaker' elements in society were racially inferior and that it was, therefore, necessary to breed out this inferiority:

'Increasingly the fear was that the unfittest elements would survive and thus imperil the "efficiency" of the nation. These fears fuelled the development of eugenics, which sought to improve the physical and mental quality of a population, either through the enhanced procreation of the fittest elements or by eradicating the weaker.' (King 1997, p.25)

Social Darwinism is central to explaining both Nazi ideology (see Unit 4, Section 1.4 and Unit 6, Section 1.2) and the Nazi system of government. *Mein Kampf* shows that Hitler saw the world in Social Darwinist terms:

'In *Mein Kampf*, Hitler [wrote]: "Men dispossess one another and, one perceives at the end of it all, it is always the stronger who triumphs. The stronger asserts his will. It is the law of nature".' (Welch 1998, p.52)

It is, therefore, no surprise that, once he gained power, the system of government Hitler built was built on Social Darwinist lines.

The Führerprinzip

It was noted in Unit 4, Section 1.3 that, as soon as he gained control of the NSDAP in July 1921, Hitler began to impose the 'leadership principle' or 'Führerprinzip' - the idea of absolute loyalty to the Leader and complete acceptance of whatever decisions he made. This remained the basis of government once the seizure of power was complete in the summer of 1934:

'In theory, his power was unlimited. Nazi Germany was a one-party state and Hitler was undisputed leader of that party.' (Layton 2000, p.99)

Although, in theory, Hitler's power was unlimited, historians agree that it would be wrong to describe the Nazi regime as centralised and highly efficient. On the contrary, most historians now accept the view of Hitler's Press Chief Otto Dietrich who claimed in a recent interview that:

'In the 12 years of his rule in Germany, Hitler produced the biggest confusion in government that has ever existed in a civilized state.' (Rees 1997, p.57)

The system that developed once Hitler had established himself in power is outlined in Box 5.13.

The nature of the Nazi political system - a 'dual state'?

Some historians have argued that the Third Reich was a 'dual state'. The old pre-Nazi conservative élite did not disappear overnight. It remained in place. Fischer argues, for example, that the Nazis were able to make hardly any changes at the top of the civil service. Top civil servants continued to work as they had done before the Nazis came to power, implementing the policies devised by their ministers. Until 1938, not all ministers were Nazis - Schacht remained Economic Minister until 1936 and Blomberg (War Minister) and Neurath (Foreign Minister) remained in post until 1938. The old state structures remained separate from Nazi Party structures. But, because Germany became a one-party state, Nazi Party structures competed for power:

'In the early years, Nazi Germany was really a "dual state", consisting of representatives from the old conservative establishment and a new leadership group drawn from the Nazi Party. It was a situation in which traditional groups sought to preserve independence and power, while activists in the Nazi governing group demanded greater party control in all spheres of society. This tension and conflict went on throughout the period 1933-45, with the Nazi élite gradually gaining the upper hand.' (McDonough 1999, p.30)

How useful is the term 'dual state'?

Klaus Fischer, however, has reservations about using the term 'dual state'. He is concerned that it is misleading, though he does think it might have its uses:

'The label "dual state" is misleading and perhaps even a contradiction in terms. There was only one state and Hitler controlled it. [The term], however, is useful if it is applied to the functions of government because these often resided in the hands of officials who not only belonged to the

BOX 5.13 Decision-making under the Nazis

In a dictatorship - a state where the Führerprinzip was meant to be in place - it might seem logical to imagine that government and administration functioned easily. Hitler, the Führer, gave the orders and these were then transmitted downwards and enacted by the relevant authorities. There is no doubt that, when Hitler wanted something, he got his way. Equally, some of the most momentous decisions made in the Third Reich, especially in foreign policy and military matters, were made by Hitler and no-one else. However, there is now a body of research which suggests that the processes of German decision-making between 1934 and 1945 were much more complicated, even, at least in some cases, chaotic. In the first place, when the Nazis came to power, they did not fuse together the institutions of the party with the existing government institutions. As a result, the old bureaucracy remained side-by-side with the NSDAP. Second, Hitler was prone to set up institutions which were independent of both the NSDAP and the state bureaucracy and whose power then expanded massively. Third, Hitler allowed some institutions to grow into personal power bases, owing allegiance only to the Führer, their powers limited by no set of rules. The obvious example is the SS. Under Himmler, it grew into a huge and powerful organisation after 1934. It is crucial to realise that the different organs of party and state and the independent organisations set up by Hitler did not stand in any hierarchical relationship to one another. There was no rational bureaucratic chain of command, nor were areas of responsibility clearly defined or demarcated. All certainly owed allegiance to Hitler, but, for the most part, they followed their own ambitions and interests. As a result, decision-making often began in an uncoordinated way and was not the simple result of directives from a central administration.

Adapted from Geary 2000.

party but also held positions and administered offices of a similar nature in both party and state.' (Fischer K. 1995, p.310)

Fischer gives the following examples:

- Goebbels was a 'Reichsleiter' (a member of the Reichsleitung - the committee at the top of the Nazi Party) and Chief of Propaganda in the NSDAP as well as being Minister for Propaganda
- Walther Darré was a Reichsleiter and head of the NSDAP's Office for Rural Affairs as well as being Reich Food Minister and Reich Agricultural Leader
- Hans Frank was a Reichsleiter and Head of

Legal Affairs in the NSDAP as well as being Reich Minister of Justice

- Himmler was a Reichsleiter and Head of the SS as well as being Chief of the German Police within the Ministry of the Interior (he eventually became Minister of the Interior).

Fischer also points out that the situation was complicated because Hitler set up special organisations to deal with specific problems. These organisations were independent of party and state:

'Dr Fritz Todt, for example, was appointed as General Inspector for German Roads and charged with building a new network of interstate highways (Autobahnen), but his position was not housed in the Ministry of Transport; instead it was attached directly to the Reich Chancellery [the body which liaised between the various Reich ministries] and Hitler.' (Fischer 1995, p.310)

Fischer also gives the example of Konstantin Hierl who was appointed as Director of Labour Service in charge of setting up a scheme requiring all men aged between 18 and 25 to do six months community work. Although, in theory, Hierl was based in the Ministry of Labour, in practice his organisation was independent.

'Polycracy' and 'totalitarianism'

Broszat (1981) suggests that, rather than describing the Third Reich as a 'dual state', it would be more accurate to describe it as a 'polycracy'. A polycracy is a state which has many competing centres of power. Again, however, Fischer has reservations about using this term. He argues that the key to understanding the way in which the Nazi political system worked is the term 'totalitarianism'. His arguments are outlined in Box 5.14.

Hitler's leadership style

As far as day-to-day administration was concerned, Hitler was very much a 'hands off' decision-maker. He would have the final say on a matter if it was brought to his attention and, in certain circumstances, he would take the initiative, but, on the whole, he relied on his subordinates to take and implement decisions. He spent much of the time at his mountain retreat in southern Germany (the Berghof) or engaged in pet projects (he was particularly interested in grandiose architectural plans). Historians agree that he disliked reading reports or undertaking administrative tasks. His lifestyle has been described as follows:

'[Hitler] would stay in bed until after 11 am, then he read the newspapers before a leisurely breakfast. He would only begin meeting government and party advisers at midday...Lunch at the Berghof would not begin until 2 pm and often continued, usually with minister and party officials present, until 4 pm. Hitler would then go off for a short walk...When he returned, there

---

BOX 5.14 | The nature of the Third Reich

Like the term 'dual state', the term 'polycracy' is useful because it captures a significant reality of how the Nazi state often functioned in practice. But the term does not capture the essence of the Nazi system or its habitual style. The Nazi state was a highly bureaucratised system whose ultimate aim was the total control of its citizens' lives. In practice, this aim was not met because the competing power bases within the state ensured that it was not as efficient as it needed to be to achieve such an aim. But the style adopted in varying degrees both by the party and the state was 'totalitarian'. A totalitarian state is one which has six key features - (1) an official ideology which every citizen was expected to support (2) a single mass party closely interwoven with the state and typically led by one man (3) complete control of the Armed Forces (4) complete control of mass communication (5) terroristic police control and (6) complete control of the economy. By 1939, Nazi Germany had all six features. A political system had been built whose aim was to destroy individualism and to exploit people for their usefulness to the state.

Adapted from Fischer 1995 and Lewis 1994.

would be coffee and usually chocolate cake. This was followed by a nap or reading a book...There would be dinner at 9 pm...This was nearly always followed by a viewing of the latest German or Hollywood film...After the film was over, Hitler would return to his favourite armchair and give a long (and very boring) monologue...which could go on well into the early hours.' (McDonough 1999, p.29)

Kershaw points out that it became increasingly difficult for those involved in government to gain direct access to Hitler. Only Göring, Himmler and Goebbels could count on getting a brief private audience. Those in his immediate circle often prevented others (including Cabinet ministers and top party officials) from gaining access to him. Those who did gain access were at pains to flatter and agree with him. As a result, Hitler became increasingly detached from reality and inclined to believe in the myth of his own god-like stature and special destiny (Kershaw 1998, pp.485-86).

'Working towards' the Führer

The Hitler cult, which had been developing during the Nazis' rise to power (see Unit 4, Section 2.1) reached new heights after the death of Hindenburg. Kershaw speaks of the 'near-deification of Hitler' and argues that, since there was no stream of commands from the centre, decision-makers took the initiative by making decisions which, they believed, fitted with what Hitler would desire:

'Possibilities of questioning, let alone opposing, measures which Hitler was known to favour were becoming as good as non-existent...Hitler's authority now opened doors to radical action previously closed, lifted constraints, and removed barriers on measures that before 30 January 1933 had seemed barely conceivable. Without direct transmission of orders, initiatives imagined to be in tune with Hitler's aims could be undertaken - and have good chances of success.' (Kershaw 1998, p.486)

As a result of Hitler's inaccessibility and his reluctance to give policy directives - or even to read documents - a process developed which has come to be known as 'working towards the Führer'. This process is examined in Box 5.15.

The legislative process

As the discussion above implies, the old methods of law-making were not used after 1934. Formal institutions such as the Reichstag and Cabinet were not abolished, they were simply bypassed:

'As a collective group, the Cabinet did not coordinate policy or discuss major policy decisions. Hitler had no interest in calling Cabinet meetings, preferring instead to deal with each Cabinet minister separately. Cabinet government gradually disappeared in Nazi Germany. In 1933, as Hitler consolidated his rule, there were 72 Cabinet meetings, but by 1936, this had dwindled to six. In 1938, the Cabinet met once and it never met on a formal basis again.' (McDonough 1999, pp.30-31)

Although Hitler did not call meetings of the Cabinet, the individual ministries which had existed before the Nazi seizure of power continued to function. Hitler left his ministers to draw up proposals for laws. Such proposals circulated around the ministries going back and forth until agreement was reached between the various interested parties. The proposals would then be presented to Hitler:

'In the absence of Cabinet discussions which might have determined priorities, a flood of legislation, emanating independently from each ministry had to be formulated by a cumbersome and grossly inefficient process whereby drafts were circulated and recirculated among ministers until some agreement was reached. Only at that stage would Hitler, if he approved after its contents were briefly summarised for him, sign the Bill (usually scarcely bothering to read it) and turn it into law.' (Kershaw 1998, p.533)

The Reich Chancellery

Klaus Fischer argues that, before the outbreak of the Second World War, a key role in law-making was played by Hans Lammers, the Head of the Reich Chancellery, because he was the link between the ministries and the Führer. It should be noted that the Reich Chancellery was just one of five separate offices

---

BOX 5.15 | Working towards the Führer

The phrase 'working towards the Führer' comes from a speech by Werner Willikens, State Secretary in the Ministry of Food, on 21 February 1934. Willikens said: 'Everyone who has the opportunity to observe it knows that the Führer can hardly dictate from above everything he intends to realize sooner or later. On the contrary, up to now everyone with a post in the new Germany has worked best when he has, so to speak, worked towards the Führer...In fact, it is the duty of everybody to try to work towards the Führer along the lines he would wish. Anyone who makes mistakes will notice it soon enough. But anyone who really works towards the Führer along his lines and towards his goal will certainly both now and in the future one day have the finest reward in the form of the sudden legal confirmation of his work.' 'Working towards the Führer' suggests a strange kind of political structure. Not one in which those in power issue orders, but one in which those at the lower end of the hierarchy initiate policies themselves within what they take to be the spirit of the regime and carry on implementing them until corrected. Perhaps the nearest example in British history is when Henry II is supposed to have asked: 'Who will rid me of this turbulent priest?' and the barons rushed to Canterbury to murder Thomas à Becket. No direct order was given, but the barons sensed what would please the king. 'Working towards the Führer' gives the lie to the excuse offered by so many Nazis that they were just 'acting under orders'. Often, they were, in fact, creating their own orders within the spirit of what they believed was required of them. Nor does the idea excuse Hitler from blame. The reason Nazis acted as they did was because they were making a judgement about what Hitler wanted of them and, more often than not, Hitler later confirmed that he approved of their actions, sometimes by issuing decrees putting such action on a 'legal' basis.
Adapted from Rees 1997.

---

that supported Hitler. The others were:
- the Führer's Chancellery headed by Bouhler
- the Presidential Chancellery headed by Meissner
- Hitler's personal adjutant and staff headed by Brückner
- the office of the Führer's deputy headed by Bormann.

Fischer describes Lammers' job as follows:

'Hitler picked him essentially to serve as his secretarial rubber stamp, preparing proposed laws, handling personnel matters relating to ministerial bureaucracy, serving as a liaison between the various ministries and basically informing him of ongoing state business.' (Fischer 1995, p.312)

Welch, however, points out that Lammers only managed to see Hitler regularly until 1935. In the following years, unlike Göring, Goebbels and Himmler who would automatically gain access to Hitler, Lammers' requests for meetings were often rejected. Welch argues that, as far as the law-making process was concerned, formal structures were unimportant. What mattered was gaining access to Hitler. Welch's arguments are outlined in Box 5.16.

BOX 5.16 | **The importance of gaining access to Hitler**

Lammers was the Head of the Reich Chancellery and, therefore, the only formal link between Hitler and his ministers. Until 1935, he managed to see Hitler on a regular basis. But he had no right of access to the Führer and Hitler often rejected requests for meetings. As Hitler disliked paperwork, attending committees or chairing Cabinet meetings, the most usual form of contact was through face-to-face contact with ministers and subordinates, of which few records were kept. In the absence of agendas and minutes of meetings, Hitler's 'directives' (which were often short and abrupt) became extremely important. The key to gaining and maintaining power was to convince people that you were operating with the blessing of the Führer. To do this, you had to gain access to Hitler. Not surprisingly, a power vacuum developed between the top level of political power (those with easy access to Hitler) and the lower Reich ministers who did not belong to this privileged group. The fragmentary and complex nature of the administrative structure is further illustrated by the role (or lack of it) of the Reich Chancellery. The Führerprinzip meant that the Cabinet was never the final source of authority. Although the influence of the Reich Chancellery briefly increased as it replaced the Cabinet, it had no formal role in the policy-making process and Lammers' power was strictly limited. As a result, the decision-making process was uncoordinated and, since there were no clear-cut channels of command, Hitler remained unchallenged. He preferred instead to allow his trusty henchmen (Göring, Goebbels, Himmler, Bormann) to compete against each other for power and influence.

Adapted from Welch 2001.

Cumulative radicalisation

The process of 'working towards the Führer' paved the way for what Hans Mommsen has called 'cumulative radicalisation'. Nazi Party officials competed for Hitler's favour and had to work out for themselves what he wanted, based on his pronouncements. Moreover, they found that, on the whole, he favoured radical solutions to problems, provided they could be put into practice without creating too much popular dissent. If a policy seemed to be successful, it would, as Willikens says, receive 'legal confirmation' from Hitler. The more Nazis experimented with radical policies and the more they realised Hitler approved of them, the more radical policies became. There was, therefore, a cumulative effect.

A system based on Social Darwinian principles

The system that emerged can be explained in Social Darwinian terms. The competition between party, state and independent organisations mentioned above ensured that there was competition and rivalry between individuals in these organisations. The strong (those whose initiatives best gained Hitler's approval) survived and prospered while the weak (those whose initiatives did not gain Hitler's approval) soon found themselves out of power. Welch argues that:

'This extraordinary state of affairs whereby the more powerful Nazi "warlords" were left free to build up their rival empires and even to feud with each other reflected Hitler's racial belief in the survival of the fittest...Hitler's Social Darwinism led him to conclude that, if he allowed the law of the jungle to prevail in his own government, the strongest would emerge and he could then support the victor. Hitler was, therefore, encouraging conflict by creating new institutions in a struggle for the survival of the fittest.' (Welch 1998, p.52)

For Hitler, this system of 'divide and rule' had a further great advantage. It protected him from criticism since, by remaining aloof, he could allow others to take the blame for policies that were unpopular.

Development of the system over time

According to Layton (1995), there were three stages in the development of the Nazi political system once the seizure of power was complete. In the first stage - between 1934 and 1936 - the Nazis were reliant on the support of the army and Big Business. Layton points out that the 'Night of the Long Knives' was, in large part, an attempt to reassure the army and Big Business. He argues that, in the two years which followed, care was taken not to alienate these groups. It was in the second phase - between 1936 and 1938 - that the Nazis took steps to reduce the power and status of the army and Big Business. In October 1936, Hitler put Göring in control of the economy (see Unit 6, Section 3.2) and, in 1938, scandals involving senior members of the military allowed the Nazis to gain a grip over the army. Significantly, it was during the period 1936-38, that the SS began to grow into a formidable force. By the end of 1938, Layton argues, the army and Big Business had been 'reduced to the role of junior partners'. From 1939, the SS was the dominant force. Layton points out that some historians have even described Germany in the period 1939-45 as an 'SS state' (see also Unit 6, Section 3.1).

Historians' views on Hitler's role in the Third Reich

Although historians agree that the Nazi political system was 'chaotic', there is a serious debate over the following question. Was Hitler a masterful schemer who encouraged administrative chaos to enhance his own power, or was he a weak dictator, and at best a good opportunist? It was noted in Unit 4, Section 1.1 that there is considerable disagreement between 'intentionalist' historians and 'structuralist' historians. This disagreement is particularly marked over the question of whether Hitler was a 'strong' or a 'weak' dictator.

The intentionalist view

Intentionalist historians such as Bracher (1971) share a belief that Hitler had a broad 'programme' - a set of policy objectives - which he continued to pursue from the 1920s right up to the last days of his life. They see the political system which developed after 1933 as the result of Hitler's clever scheming rather than his inefficiency. They argue that Hitler knew what he was doing and made the most of his opportunities:

'The so-called intentionalist approach continues to uphold the absolutely vital role of Hitler in the development of the Third Reich. Consequently the prevailing chaos is seen as the result of a deliberate policy of divide and rule on the part of Hitler - in effect an attempt (and obviously successful) to maintain his own political authority by encouraging division and confusion in both the structure and personnel of government.' (Layton 2000, p.101)

The structuralist view

Whereas intentionalists see Hitler as a 'strong' dictator - a Leader who knew what he was doing and who was fully in charge of events - structuralists suggest that Hitler was a 'weak' dictator. Historians such as Broszat (1981) do not agree that Hitler was fully in control. They argue that rather than implementing a plan worked out years before, Hitler responded to the circumstances in which he found himself. The political system which developed was chaotic not because

Hitler wanted it to be so, but because he did not have the power to streamline the system even if he wanted to do so. Structures - such as the structure of the economy, the political structures that remained in place after the seizure of power and the structure of the NSDAP - ensured that Hitler's room for manoeuvre was limited. Kershaw sums up the structuralist view as follows:

'In Broszat's view…the administrative chaos was not consciously devised, but nor was it pure chance. Rather, it was the inevitable result of the form of authority exerted by Hitler, of his unwillingness and inability to regulate systematically the relationship between party and state and to create an ordered system of authoritarian government.' (Kershaw 2000, p.75)

For the structuralists, Hitler was an approver of policies rather than an initiator of them. Some structuralists have argued that, far from being decisive, Hitler found it difficult to make decisions. The structuralist historian Hans Mommsen argues that it is because of this that Hitler can be described as a 'weak dictator':

'[Hitler was] unwilling to take decisions, frequently uncertain, exclusively concerned with upholding his prestige and personal authority, influenced in the strongest fashion by his current entourage, in some aspects a weak dictator.' (Mommsen quoted in Kershaw 2000, p.70)

Synthesis

Although these issues are still strongly debated, in recent years Ian Kershaw has argued for a middle way. He writes:

'Hitler's "intentions" are indispensable to explaining the course of development in the Third Reich. But they are by no means an adequate explanation in themselves. The conditions in which Hitler's "will" could be implemented as government "policy" were only in small measure fashioned by Hitler himself, and, moreover, made the ultimate failure of his aims and the destruction of the Third Reich almost inevitable.' (Kershaw 2000, p.91)

MAIN POINTS - Section 2.1

- In order to understand how the Nazi political system worked, it is necessary to understand the term 'Social Darwinism'. This is often summarised in the phrase 'the survival of the fittest'.
- Although, in theory, Hitler's power was unlimited, historians agree that it would be wrong to describe the Nazi regime as centralised and highly efficient. Most historians now accept the view that the system was inefficient and even chaotic with many different power centres competing for Hitler's attention and approval.
- The Nazi political system has been described as a 'dual state' (because party and state structures existed side by side), a 'polycracy' (because there were many centres of power) and a 'totalitarian'

state (a state whose aim was to destroy individualism and to exploit people for their usefulness to the state).
- Hitler's leadership style ensured that he was not involved in day-to-day decision-making. As a result, party and state officials 'worked towards' the Führer. The legislative process was informal and legislation gradually became more radical.
- There is a debate between historians over whether Hitler was a weak dictator. Intentionalists argue that he was guided by a long-term programme and that he remained in control. Structuralists argue that his power was limited and he was indecisive, reacting to events rather than controlling them.

Activity 5.4 The Nazi political system

LOWER RANKING PARTY OFFICIALS, CIVIL SERVANTS & OFFICERS

MINISTERS, TOP OFFICERS & TOP PARTY OFFICIALS

HITLER'S CLOSEST ADVISERS

ADOLF HITLER

HITLER'S CLOSEST ADVISERS

MINISTERS, TOP OFFICERS & TOP PARTY OFFICIALS

LOWER RANKING PARTY OFFICIALS, CIVIL SERVANTS & OFFICERS

Some historians argue that Hitler designed the competition between the various agencies of state and party in order to 'divide and rule'. There can be no doubt that the ability to play off bureaucrats against Gauleiter or Göring against Himmler did give Hitler exceptional power. But the real explanation for the fragmented, multi-institutional decision-making in the Third Reich is to be found elsewhere - in the nature of the Nazi seizure of power and the roots of Hitler's position as Führer. The Nazis did not come to power by overthrowing old élites in a revolution, but by joining forces with them. As a result, Hitler had to tread warily, at least early on in the regime, in his dealings with Big Business and the army. Both these groups had considerable influence, as witnessed by the 'Night of the Long Knives'. A second cause of the complexity of power relationships within Germany after 1933 was related to the nature of the NSDAP. The party had been created for the sole purpose of propaganda and the winning of elections. It did not have the organisational structures to administer a state. That explains the continued existence of bureaucratic institutions that had existed under Weimar. The structure of the NSDAP was such that there was already considerable rivalry and competition for Hitler's support within the party before the seizure of power. This rivalry and competition for Hitler's support became more marked in the Third Reich. Because Hitler rarely took the initiative, policy began to be made in a piecemeal fashion from 'below'. Hitler was often indecisive. Issues were often shelved and Hitler was particularly loath to intervene when he knew the result would be unpopular with the public. The absence of clear lines of authority and Hitler's own behaviour left a space in which personal conflicts and institutional rivalries flourished.

Adapted from Geary 1993.

ITEM 3 Policy-making (1)

(i) Sterilisation

Without direct transmission of orders, initiatives imagined to be in tune with Hitler's aims could be undertaken and have a good chance of success. An example was the Law for Prevention of Progeny with Hereditary Diseases which was passed on 14 July 1933. It provided for the compulsory sterilisation of anyone with a hereditary disease. Within months of Hitler becoming Chancellor, the newly appointed Special Commissioner for Medical Affairs in the Prussian government, Dr Leonardo Conti (a Nazi) appointed a previous outsider, Dr Arthur Gütt to an influential post in the medical department of the Reich Ministry of the Interior. Gütt, already a Nazi District Leader in 1923 then surrounded himself with a committee of 'experts' on population and race. In early July, this committee came up with a proposal for the compulsory sterilisation of those suffering from a range of illnesses. Hitler had nothing to do with the preparation of the law, but it was prepared in the knowledge that it was in line with his sentiments. At this stage the Cabinet still had some involvement in law-making and Vice Chancellor Papen protested that such a law would alienate the Catholics. He tried to make the sterilisation voluntary rather than compulsory. Hitler, however, overruled his objections.

This photograph is a still from *I Accuse*, a film made by the Nazis to promote euthanasia. In the film, Hanna (left), the wife of Professor Heyt (right), develops multiple sclerosis. She and her husband agree that it is best for her to die. Heyt gives her an overdose and is then accused of murder. At the trial, the arguments in favour of euthanasia are rehearsed and the professor is acquitted.

(ii) The Children's Euthanasia Programme

The Children's Euthanasia Programme was a more extreme expression of Hitler's desire to promote German supremacy by eliminating the sick and the weak. At the end of 1938, the father of a severely handicapped child wrote to Hitler asking for the child to be 'put down'. Officials in the Chancellery of the Führer (one of the five offices supporting Hitler) selected it as one of the few petitions to go before Hitler, knowing that it was in accord with sentiments expressed in Hitler speeches. Hitler passed the decision on to one of his personal doctors, Dr Karl Brandt. The result was the setting up of the Reich Committee for the Scientific Registration of Serious Hereditary and Congenital Diseases. Reports were sent in by doctors and midwives asking what to do in cases of serious deformities. The reports were then scored by three doctors with a red plus sign or a blue minus sign. Children marked with a red plus sign were killed by lethal injection.

Adapted from Kershaw 1998 and Fischer K. 1995.

ITEM 4 Policy-making (2)

Hitler's impulsive agreement to suggestions from subordinate leaders sometimes proved embarrassing. When, in October 1934, Robert Ley obtained Hitler's signature on a decree which would have strengthened the hand of the Labour Front at the expense of employers and Reich ministries, this led to difficulties. Neither the Ministry of Labour nor the Ministry of Economics had been properly consulted. Rudolf Hess, Hitler's Deputy, also protested (as well as being Head of the Labour Front, Ley had been put in charge of the NSDAP's organisational matters and was, therefore, a rival to Hess who was theoretically in charge of the party). Since Hitler could not afford to come into conflict with the Minister of Economics, Schact, he backed down under pressure. To save face, the decree was not repealed. It was simply ignored. A few months later, the reverse happened. Hitler backed down to pressure from the party after initially agreeing to a proposal from a minister. On this occasion, Labour Minister, Seldte, won Hitler's support for a proposal to replace regional wage structures for building workers with a single structure for the whole Reich. This led to loud protests from local Gauleiter about the impact of the wage reductions in some areas on workers' morale. Hitler gave in to the pressure. Again, to save face, the earlier decision wasn't reversed. Hitler simply ordered further deliberations for an indefinite period. The matter was shelved and then forgotten.

Adapted from Kershaw 1998.

Questions

1. a) What do Items 1-4 tell us about the nature of the Nazi political system?
   b) How does an understanding of Social Darwinism help us to understand the Nazi political system?

2. Judging from Item 2 would you say that Dick Geary is an intentionalist or a structuralist historian? Explain your answer.

3. What do Items 3 and 4 tell us about (a) the way policies were made in the Third Reich and (b) Hitler's role in policy-making?

2.2 How did the Nazis respond to opposition between 1935-39?

What opposition was there?

The Enabling Act (March 1933) gave Hitler dictatorial powers. The trade unions were forcibly dissolved on 2 May 1933. From July 1933, Germany became a one-party state (see Section 1.2 above). Finally, after the 'Night of the Long Knives' (June 1934) the SA was broken as a political force (see Section 1.3 above). During the 'legal revolution' there was widespread intimidation, imprisonment and even the murder of left-wing political opponents of the Nazi regime. The first concentration camps were set up as early as March 1933 (see Box 5.17). Gellately (2001) estimates that in 1933 as a whole, over 100,000 people spent time in a concentration camp and that, of these, around 500 to 600 people were killed.

Remarkably, the Nazis retained wide support throughout the period in which the 'legal revolution' took place. As a result, by the end of 1934, the regime felt secure. Accordingly arrests declined and many prisoners were freed, leaving only 3,000 in the camps. As Gellately puts it:

'It made perfect sense to close the camps, because by 1934-35 the country was positively inclined towards Hitler's dictatorship. Organized opposition was silent or as good as dead. The surprise was that, for all Hitler's popularity and the social consensus that supported the new regime, the camps did not disappear.' (Gellately 2001, p. 61)

Hitler's Gleichschaltung (coordination) of German society (see Section 1.2 above) eliminated almost all institutions that could have provided a framework for organised opposition. Only the churches and the army retained the capacity to oppose the regime. Even the mildest forms of protest were illegal and punishable by imprisonment or death. The efforts of the Gestapo (political police), aided by informers, ensured that individual efforts at opposition were doomed almost from the start.

Resistance and Resistenz

Owing to the near-impossibility of effective opposition, there has been much debate over what can be regarded as resistance to the regime. German historians have been especially anxious to make the most of what little resistance there was. In relation to this, Ian Kershaw (2000) has identified two analytical approaches:

- fundamentalist
- societal.

The fundamentalist approach

The fundamentalist approach focuses on active anti-Nazi political activism. Most of this came from small 'élite' groups whose positions of power gave them

---

BOX 5.17 | The first concentration camps

The first concentration camps were hardly 'camps' at all. They were temporary places the Nazis used to hold their political enemies once Hitler became Chancellor. These camps were set up as a result of local initiatives not in response to central directives. In the beginning nobody seems to have thought that the camps would become a permanent part of the dictatorship. They were set up in buildings like old military barracks and castles or were merely special sections in a workhouse or prison. Accused people were picked up, sent for a stint in the camp and released. They were then replaced by new prisoners. Whilst the official figures suggest that c.100,000 people spent time in concentration camps in 1933, this figure does not include the substantial number who were taken to a camp, beaten by the SA and then let go. The estimates of such illegal arrests for Prussia alone suggests that this happened to 30,000 people in the period up to the end of April 1933. In Berlin there were more than 100 temporary torture chambers in working-class districts where Communists and Socialists lived. The majority of those who spent time in concentration camps in 1933 had connections with the KPD. After 1933, Communists continued to be over-represented in the camps. A list from 10 April 1934, for example, shows that, of the 2,405 people in concentration camps in Bavaria, 1,531 (62.5%) were accused of engaging in Communist activities. Another 222 (9.1%) were in for 'High Treason' and another 33 (1.3%) for lesser forms of treason. A further 98 were accused of engaging in 'Marxist activities' and may therefore also have been Communists. The only other politicals mentioned were 24 members of the SPD who made up just 1% of prisoners.

Adapted from Gellately 2001.

---

some hope of overcoming the government or at least of defeating it on some issues. These groups were mainly located either within the army or in the churches. Secret Communist and Socialist organisations still existed, but there was little they could do other than keep their ideas alive in small groups and supply information to their parties in exile.

The societal approach

The societal approach is much broader than the fundamentalist approach. It examines any behaviour falling short of the total support for the regime that the Nazis hoped to secure. A good example is Martin Broszat's Bavaria Project which was launched to investigate the subject in 1973. This project investigated resistance to the Nazi regime made by organised groups, but it also gave weight to forms of 'civil disobedience', such as:

'[The] refusal to give the "Heil Hitler" greeting; insistence on hanging out the church flag instead of the swastika banner; objections by peasants to farm legislation; public criticism of anti-church measures by Catholic priests; continued trafficking with Jewish cattle-dealers; or fraternizing with foreign workers.'(Kershaw 2000, p.193)

According to Kershaw, these were often piecemeal acts of dissent:

'[They sprang out of] social resentment, economic misery, blind protest, fury at Nazi treatment of family and friends, religious conservatism, as well as principled struggle for a better social and political order.' (Kershaw 2000, p.194)

For this kind of behaviour, Broszat coined the term 'Resistenz' (not to be confused with more active and deliberate 'resistance'). Swiss historian Walter Hofer has criticised this approach on the grounds that it reduces planned and morally courageous acts of fundamental resistance to the same level as more or less accidental or selfishly motivated acts of dissent. He also claims that such minor acts of dissent had little or no effect on the regime.

Criminalising anti-social behaviour

Kershaw points out that much of what the Nazis saw as political opposition would have been seen as normal behaviour in other societies and such behaviour did not necessarily spring from political motives. Such forms of behaviour include:

- telling jokes about the Führer
- keeping in touch with ex-party comrades
- spreading rumours
- listening to foreign radio broadcasts.

People who did any of these things in Nazi Germany were committing a criminal offence. The rebellious behaviour of young people was also criminalised (see Box 5.18). Young people who listened and danced to jazz, smoked and drank under-age or went on unsupervised hikes and bike rides were committing criminal offences and could be punished. As a result, Nazi laws politicised this sort of behaviour. It could be argued, however, that since the Nazi regime aimed at total control of the hearts and minds of the German people, non-conformist behaviour did represent a political threat since it undermined a feeling of consensus. Nazi laws recognised this by criminalising what it regarded as anti-social behaviour.

Worker resistance

Although many workers came to support the Nazi regime, many remained at least passively resistant. The majority of Socialists and Communists imprisoned after March 1933 were workers or unemployed. The historian Detlev Peukert argues that workers played an important part in providing resistance to the Nazi regime. He claims that

BOX 5.18 Youth protest

Most young people in Germany from 1933 to 1945 were loyal members either of the Hitler Youth (for boys) or German Girls' League. These organisations attempted to control every aspect of the leisure time of German youth and encouraged unhesitating support for Hitler and the Nazi regime. In March 1939 it became compulsory for all young people to join. In the late 1930s, however, groups of predominantly working-class youths rebelled. In order to stress their free-spirited individuality, these groups called themselves 'Edelweiss Pirates'. Most Edelweiss Pirates were boys aged 12 to 18, though some girls joined too. They wore distinctive clothes. They had longer hair than normal. Most had left the Hitler Youth or never joined it. One of their main slogans was 'Eternal war on the Hitler Youth', a slogan they often painted on walls as graffiti. They operated in small gangs, congregating on street corners. To break free of Nazi discipline, they went on long hikes, carrying rucksacks. Once they had pitched their tents, they would sing parodies of Hitler Youth songs and tell each other jokes about the sexual activities of the Hitler Youth. The response of the Nazi authorities to the Edelweiss Pirates was by no means uniform. In some areas, their activities were regarded by the local police force as childish pranks. During the war, however, there was a crack down. In December 1942, nearly 800 were arrested. In November 1944, the leaders of the Cologne Edelweiss Pirates were hanged publicly as a deterrent.

Adapted from McDonough 2001.

despite, intimidation and the threat of being sent to the camps:

'Tens of thousands of members of the banned workers' parties joined the organised resistance, especially in the early years of the Third Reich (till 1935-36).' (Peukert 1982, p.117)

He adds that in addition to organised worker resistance, there were stubborn refusals to co-operate, from absenteeism, go-slows and acts of sabotage to strikes. He goes so far as to say that resistance by workers formed the 'most significant component' of the German resistance movement. Tim Mason is another historian who emphasises worker resistance. He argues that labour shortages from 1936 onwards enabled workers to exert pressure on employers for higher wages, and that their successes seriously hindered the Nazi regime's ability to choose when, and on what terms, to fight the war for which it was preparing. On the other hand, as Kershaw points out:

'[Strikes were] small in scale and politically ineffective.' (Kershaw 2000, p.201)

Peukert accepts that this was the case, but argues that this was because they would inevitably lead to intervention by the Gestapo, rather than because workers had no complaints about their conditions or widely supported the regime. Gestapo involvement led rapidly to ringleaders being imprisoned in concentration camps or executed for treason.

The churches

The Christian churches, both Catholic and Protestant, were centres of resistance because they offered people an alternative source of authority and a focus for group action. Their main weakness lay in their divisions.

The Protestant Church

Some Protestant groups wholeheartedly supported the Nazi regime and Hitler tried to make them the basis of a new all-German Church. Resistance was led by Martin Niemöller's 'Confessional Church' :

'The Nazi regime responded to the resistance activities of the Confessing Church by placing its supporters under surveillance. In many cases, pastors were removed from their parishes by the Gestapo and incarcerated in concentration camps. In July 1937, Niemöller was placed in "protective custody" in a concentration camp where he was to remain until his release in 1945. In addition, in March that year, 800 pastors who supported the Confessing Church had also been detained in concentration camps.' (McDonough 2001, p.32)

McDonough argues that the struggle with the Protestant Church was embarrassing to the Nazis and, in 1937, Hitler made a deal. He allowed the (non-Nazi) Church authorities to remain in control of the Church, in return for the Church's loyalty to the regime. As a result, the Church remained independent, but open resistance to the Nazi regime ended. McDonough also points out that the Protestant Church's main concern was to preserve its independence. It did not object to Nazi rule in principle - see Box 5.19.

The Catholic Church

The Catholic Church was in one respect in a stronger position than the Protestant Church since its centre was outside of Germany, in Rome. Initially it pursued a policy of appeasement towards the Nazi regime in order to preserve its freedoms and privileges. It agreed a Concordat with the regime in July 1933. This was supposed to guarantee non-interference in Catholic institutions in return for priests not preaching against the regime. The Nazis, however, failed to keep their side of the bargain:

'The Nazi regime frequently violated the terms of the Concordat by suppressing the religious activities of Catholic schools, by banning Catholic youth organisations and by closing down Catholic newspapers.' (McDonough 2001, p.33)

| BOX 5.19 | The Protestant Church and Nazism |

Opposition to Nazi attacks on the Protestant Church did not imply that the Church disapproved of Hitler's foreign policy or Germany's rearmament. Also hardly any members of the Protestant clergy spoke out against the persecution of the Jews. Even the Confessing Church stressed that it was fighting to preserve its independence not trying to oppose the regime's domestic or foreign policy or calling for its overthrow. Indeed, Martin Niemöller was an enthusiastic supporter of the Nazi regime at first. He even offered to fight for Germany in the Second World War. The only leading Protestant pastor actively involved in resistance was Dietrich Bonhöffer, who joined the Confessing Church in 1935. He helped build up overseas contacts for the resistance and was critical of the Nazi regime. By 1940, he had been banned from preaching and publishing on Church affairs. In 1943, he was arrested by the Gestapo. In April 1945, he was executed.

Adapted from McDonough 2001.

When Cardinal Faulhaber met Hitler to complain in 1936, the two could not agree on the subjects of racial laws and sterilisation for those suffering from genetic diseases. It appears that the meeting did not improve relations. Nazi harassment of Catholic priests continued unabated, leading to a statement by the Pope in March 1937, entitled *With Burning Anxiety*, condemning the attacks. The Nazis responded with a smear campaign in the press against priests, monks and nuns. Hundreds were arrested on trumped-up charges, from embezzlement to sexual aberrations, and sent to concentration camps.

Extent of resistance

Kershaw notes the many acts of courage carried out by priests and pastors, both Protestant and Catholic. According to estimates around one in three Catholic priests suffered reprisals during the Third Reich. About 400 Catholic priests and 35 Evangelical pastors were imprisoned in a Priests' Block at Dachau alone. However, Kershaw agrees with most other historians when he adds:

'As institutions, nevertheless, the Churches offered something less than fundamental resistance to Nazism.' (Kershaw 2000, p.211)

The police

Himmler became Chief of the Gestapo in 1934 and Chief of the German Police on 17 June 1936. His drive to strengthen and centralise the police was in keeping with Hitler's vision. Himmler was nominally subordinate to Frick as Minister of the Interior. In practice, however, Himmler was answerable only to Hitler. Klaus Fischer states:

'By the late 1930s, Frick had been reduced to a pliant ministerial rubber stamp for Hitler and Himmler.' (Fischer K. 1995, p.323)

As head of the SS, Himmler was in charge of an increasingly vast empire of repression - see Box 5.20.

Klaus Fischer defines the function of the SD as follows:

'[The function of the SD is] to arrest the enemies of National Socialism and ideally arrest them before they had done anything wrong.' (Fischer K. 1995, p.664)

The SD's function, therefore overlapped with that of the Gestapo:

'The primary mission of the Gestapo was to identify enemies of the state, put them into "protective custody"...use any methods deemed necessary to extract information, and consign such enemies to prison or concentration camps.' (Fischer K. 1995, p.642)

Himmler's deputy, Reinhard Heydrich, combined the two institutions in 1939.

The changing role of the police

It was noted above that, by the end of 1934, the regime felt secure and the number of arrests and inmates in concentration camps began to fall. In June 1935, however, the first step was taken to reverse this trend:

'Himmler won Hitler's support for the retention of camps at a meeting on 20 June 1935 and, at the same time got agreement that by 1 April 1936 the camps and guards would be funded under the federal budget, which was important to the future of the camps.' (Gellately 2001, p.61)

Two further steps followed. At Nuremberg on 11 September 1935, Hitler announced a new 'struggle against the internal enemies of the nation'. These 'enemies' were described as 'Jewish Marxism and the parliamentary democracy associated with it'; 'the politically and morally depraved Catholic Centre Party' and 'certain elements of an unteachable, dumb and reactionary bourgeoisie (ie. members of the middle class)' - all three quotes are cited in Gellately 2001, p.39. Then, on 18 October 1935, Himmler met with Hitler again and the two agreed a new, broader definition of 'enemies'. Now, these were to include 'asocials' - people whose behaviour was regarded as not conforming to that required by the Nazis.

Preventive policing

From the summer of 1935, the trend was increasingly towards 'preventive' policing. This meant arresting and imprisoning anyone thought likely to commit a crime (see Box 5.21). As a result, not only ordinary 'habitual criminals', but also anyone whose political loyalty was in doubt might be arrested, especially if they were Jewish. Gellately notes that the number of people in concentration camps began to rise again. He also makes it clear that Hitler knew what was going on:

'That Hitler was aware of what was going on can be seen from the note of a conversation he had with Himmler, the gist of which was communicated to the Minister of Justice on 6 November 1935. Justice officials continued to be concerned about the death of prisoners in the camps. Hitler's response was that they should pay them no attention.' (Gellately 2001, p.62)

The Gestapo

A Prussian law of 10 February 1936 placed the

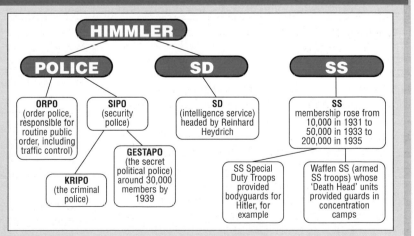

BOX 5.20 | Himmler's empire

The SS had been formed in 1925 as an élite bodyguard for Hitler, but it remained a relatively minor section of the SA until Himmler became its leader in 1929. By 1933, the SS numbered 52,000 and it had established a reputation for blind obedience and total commitment. In the course of 1933-34, Himmler gained control of all the police forces in the Länder, including the Gestapo in Prussia (Göring set up the Gestapo - the Prussian political police force - in April 1933). The part played by the SS in the 'Night of the Long Knives' resulted in it becoming an independent organisation within the party. In 1936, all police powers were unified under Himmler's control as Chief of the German Police. Himmler controlled a massive police apparatus which was answerable only to Hitler. The SS-police-SD system assumed responsibility for all security matters.

Adapted from Layton 2000.

BOX 5.21 Preventive policing

The preventive police mission of a political police is to search out the enemies of state, to watch them and at the right moment to destroy them. In order to fulfil this mission the political police must be free to use every means required to achieve the necessary goal. In the National Socialist leader state it is the case that those institutions called upon to protect the state and the people who carry out the will of the state possess as of right the complete authority required to fulfil their task, an authority that derives solely from the new conception of the state and one that requires no special legal legitimisation.

Statement made in 1936 by Werner Best, a lawyer and a key figure behind the setting up of the new Gestapo system.

Gestapo above the law:

'According to this law, virtually any actions taken by the Gestapo were no longer subject to court review, not even in the event of wrongful arrest and nobody could sue for damages. In other words, if the Gestapo was above the law even earlier, by early 1936 that situation was formalised.' (Gellately 2001, p.40)

The Gestapo's legal expert Werner Best stated that the new police regarded attempts to maintain any political theory other than National Socialism as 'a symptom of sickness, which threatens the healthy unity of the indivisible Volk ["Volk" is German for "people"] organism', and that such attempts would be 'eliminated'. He explained that in order for the Gestapo to fulfil its 'preventive police mission' it had to be completely free to use whatever means it thought fit.

An important trend

Gellately identifies a gradual blurring of the distinction between political and other crimes during the pre-war period. This trend is also noted by Noakes and Pridham (2000, p.279). On the one hand Nazi ideology tended to see all crimes as crimes against the German people and, therefore, against the state. On the other hand, it suited the regime's propaganda to identify political prisoners as 'common criminals' rather than allowing them higher status.

An important controversy

An important controversy, dealt with more fully in Unit 6, Section 2.1, is the question of how far ordinary people helped the Gestapo by informing on neighbours and work colleagues. Gellately, as the title of his book *Backing Hitler* suggests, argues that there was a broad consensus of support for the regime. In addition, people often informed for selfish reasons such as material gain or revenge. Daniel Goldhagen, in *Hitler's Willing Executioners* (1996), argues that widespread and deep-rooted anti-Semitism played a

large part in ensuring this support for the regime and compliance with the Gestapo in upholding race laws and combating the threat of Communism (which many people saw as a Jewish conspiracy).

The changing role of the courts

In March 1933, Special Courts were created to deal with cases that arose under the Reichstag Fire Decree (see Section 1.1 above), including cases of 'malicious gossip' (a law introduced in December 1934 made public criticism either of the government or of the Nazi Party a crime). The number of these courts grew until, by 1941, there were 63 of them. A 'People's Court' was established in Berlin in 1934 to try cases of treason, however minor - see Box 5.22. It made frequent use of the death penalty. The Special Courts used speeded-up procedures, giving the accused few rights.

BOX 5.22 The People's Court

The loyal cooperation of the already right-wing judiciary meant that the Nazis could afford to leave the justice system essentially unchanged. However the greatly increased caseloads meant that some innovation was required. The People's Court was set up in April 1934 to deal with cases of treason. The courtroom was decorated with three large swastika banners and busts of Frederick the Great and Hitler. Bright lights blazed for the benefit of film cameras. At a long table sat two professional judges and five others selected from party officials, the SS, and the Armed Forces. The two professional judges could outvote the others. At the centre of the table sat Roland Freisler, the presiding officer. From his position of power, Freisler shouted abuse at the defendants, denouncing them for treason and threatening dire punishments. The public was not allowed to view the proceedings (unless excerpts were shown on film). There was no right to appeal. The People's Court eventually sent more than 5,000 people to their death. Nevertheless, as time went on, the work of the People's Court and that of the other Special Courts was taken over more and more by the Gestapo. A clash between the People's Court and Gestapo came in 1937 when a judge in the People's Court objected when the Gestapo arrived in court to arrest a woman. The judge told the Gestapo officers that the People's Court was sovereign and they had no business there. In the short term, the judge got his way. But two days later, the Gestapo arrested the woman. On 21 April 1937, the Minister of Justice informed the President of the People's Court that the judge was out of line.

Adapted from Snyder 1976, Stackelberg 1999 and Gellately 2001.

Hitler and the judiciary

By 1 January 1935, the administration of justice was uniform across Germany since the state Justice

Ministries had all been brought under central control. But, the regular courts administered by these Justice Ministries were soon in danger of losing authority since:

'Hitler consistently favoured police prerogatives over the regular court system.' (Gellately 2001, p.7)

Hitler felt free to intervene personally to reverse or alter court decisions, and he was happy for his police to enjoy similar powers. In November 1935, Hitler personally intervened, ruling that there would be no legal representation for those in 'protective custody'. From 1936, the Gestapo began to 'correct' court decisions, rearresting and imprisoning those found not guilty for lack of evidence or given 'lenient' sentences. A principle of Nazi lawyer Hans Frank was often quoted:

'Law is what serves the people and unlawful is what hurts it.' (quoted in Gellately 2001, p.42)

The Gestapo and the courts

The Gestapo frequently bypassed the courts altogether, simply placing suspects under 'preventive custody' in concentration camps. They were meant to apply every three months to keep a person in custody. However, since the application was to be made to their own Berlin headquarters, this restraint was meaningless. Moreover, when the Minister of the Interior, Frick, attempted to establish minimal guidelines for the use of protective custody, in effect all power was still left with the Gestapo.

Gestapo 'corrections' inclined judges to be more severe and to convict on flimsy evidence, in order to avoid having their authority further undermined. Noakes and Pridham also make the point that since the Nazis did not systematically overhaul the legal system, they relied on judges interpreting the law according to Nazi principles and they introduced various restraints on them to ensure that this happened. (Noakes & Pridham 2000, p.278)

The concentration camps

The threat overshadowing even the smallest act of defiance was the concentration camp. These were brutally run by SS guards. The Nazi propaganda machine wanted their image to act as a sufficient deterrent to potential dissenters. Yet, at first at least,

it also wanted to present them as places of strict but healthy rehabilitation through work. The idea was that inmates would be educated into social responsibility, so that they could eventually become useful members of society. Of course this aim was applied to 'Aryans' rather than to Jews. In 1939, Himmler described concentration camps as follows:

'Concentration camp is certainly, like any regime which involves the deprivation of personal liberty, a tough and strict measure. Hard productive labour, a regular life, exceptional cleanliness in matters of daily life and personal hygiene, excellent food, strict but fair treatment, instruction in learning how to work again and how to learn the necessary crafts - these are the methods of education.'

Theodor Eicke, appointed Inspector of Concentration Camps and SS Guards in 1934, systematised camp brutality, prescribing precise punishments for each infringement of the rules. In March 1936, Hitler agreed to a longer-term plan for the camps devised by Eicke. Naturally, Himmler was in favour, since it extended his own SS empire. In January 1937, he justified the increasing numbers in the camps, now up to 8,000. He explained that, with growing international tension, it was necessary to rearrest Communists. He also said that 'asocials' belonged in the camps. This reflects a gradual change in the propaganda image of the camps. Official photographs now began to present them not just as places of healthy rehabilitation, but as dumping-grounds for the socially and racially inferior. As Himmler put it in January 1937:

'There is no more lively demonstration of the laws of heredity and race than such a concentration camp. There are those with hydrocephalus, cross-eyed, deformed, half-Jews, and a whole series of racially inferior types. The whole lot is there together.' (Gellately 2001, p.65)

Gellately argues that both Hitler and Himmler saw the need for the camps in the light of a coming war. Such a war would need to be fought against both the foreign enemy and also on the home front, against the enemy within the state. By the outbreak of the Second World War in September 1939, camp prisoner numbers had risen to 25,000 (Noakes & Pridham 2000, p.326).

MAIN POINTS - Section 2.2

- By 1935 there was a broad consensus of support for Hitler, and little organised resistance.
- Martin Broszat and others have emphasised the importance of minor acts of dissent (Resistenz) as well as more determined resistance.
- The attitude of the regime politicised what other societies regard as normal nonconformist behaviour.
- There was some worker resistance, mostly in the form of uncooperative behaviour, but sometimes strikes.

- Some churches opposed some of the regime's policies, and many clergy were imprisoned, but there was no concerted church opposition.
- The Gestapo increasingly used 'preventive policing' and bypassed the courts.
- Opponents of the regime were sent to brutal concentration camps. Prisoner numbers steadily rose from 1935.

Activity 5.5 The Nazis and political opposition 1935-39

ITEM 1 A dissenter

This photo shows shipyard workers giving the Hitler salute at the launching of the training ship *Horst Wessel* in Hamburg in 1936. One man (circled) stands with his arms folded, refusing to salute. By refusing to salute, he was breaking the law and risked being sent to a concentration camp.

ITEM 2 Prisoners at Dachau

The photograph on the cover of this magazine shows concentration camp prisoners at Dachau in 1936.

ITEM 3 Regulations on punishment

NOTICE

All internees are subject to the following regulations from the time of their imprisonment to the hour of their release. Authority for ordering punishment lies in the hand of the camp commander. Tolerance means weakness. In light of this, punishment will be handed out whenever the interests of the fatherland warrant it.

The following are punishable with two weeks solitary confinement:
* Anyone changing his quarters without permission.
* Anyone hiding forbidden articles.
* Anyone entering or leaving barracks, shelters or other buildings by other than authorised entrances.
* Anyone smoking in shelters, toilets and places which are fire hazards.

The following are punishable with two weeks solitary confinement and twenty five strokes to be administered before and after serving the sentence:
* Anyone leaving or entering the internment camp without an escort or who joins an outgoing work party without proper authority.
* Anyone making critical remarks in letters or other documents about Nazi leaders, the state or government.
* Anyone keeping forbidden articles, tools or weapons.

In accordance with the law on revolutionaries, the following offenders, considered as agitators, will be hanged. Anyone who, for the purpose of agitating, does the following: discusses politics, carries on controversial talks and meetings, forms cliques, loiters around with others; who for the purpose of supplying the propaganda of the opposition with atrocity stories, collects true or false information about the concentration camp; receives such information, buries it, talks about it to others, smuggles it out of the camp into the hands of foreign visitors or others by clandestine or other means, passes it on in writing or by word of mouth to released prisoners who are placed over them.

These regulations were issued by the Commandant of Dachau Concentration Camp, Theodor Eicke, on 1 October 1933 and extended to all concentration camps in October 1934.

Adapted from Noakes & Pridham 2000.

ITEM 4 The Gestapo and 'opposition'

In popular myth, the Gestapo was an all-seeing, all-powerful instrument of terror which oppressed an unwilling population. But this is far from the truth. In Würzberg in south east Germany, 18,000 Gestapo files survived the war. These files show that there were only 28 Gestapo officers in Lower Franconia (the Land in which Würzberg is located). Twenty-two were assigned to Würzberg, with almost half of these engaged in administrative work. The idea that the Gestapo was constantly spying on the population is a myth. These Gestapo officers relied on ordinary Germans to supply information. Only 10% of political crimes committed between 1933 and 1945 were discovered by the Gestapo. Another 10% of cases were passed on by local police. So, 80% of crimes were discovered by ordinary citizens. The files are full of accusations made by ordinary people about their neighbours. For example Ilse Sonja Totzke's Gestapo file reveals that she was denounced first by a distant relative who complained she was too friendly to Jews. Totzke was put under surveillance by the Gestapo. But the surveillance took an odd form. The Gestapo asked neighbours to keep an eye on her. There follows in the file a mass of contradictory evidence. Sometimes she gave the 'German Greeting' (Heil Hitler). Sometimes she did not. Overall, she made it clear that she would not stop being friendly to Jews (something which, at this point, was not a crime). Although she had committed no crime, the Gestapo brought her in for questioning and bluntly warned her about her attitude. The denunciations kept coming in and, on 28 October 1941, Totzke was summoned again and it was made clear that if she kept her contacts with Jews, she would be sent to a concentration camp. When she was next summoned to the Gestapo, she tried to escape to Switzerland, but was handed back and sent to a concentration camp where she probably died.

Adapted from Rees 1997.

Questions

1. Judging from Items 1-4 and your own knowledge, how did the Nazis respond to opposition in the period 1935-39?

2. What do Items 1 and 4 tell us about the nature of opposition in the period 1936-39?

3. a) What do Items 2 and 3 tell us about the way in which concentration camps were run in the period 1935-39?

    b) Who would you expect to find in concentration camps? Explain your answer.

References

- **Bracher (1971)** Bracher, K.D., *The German Dictatorship: the Origins, Structure and Consequences of National Socialism*, Penguin, 1971.

- **Broszat (1981)** Broszat, M., *The Hitler State*, Longman, 1981.

- **Bullock (1991)** Bullock, A., *Hitler and Stalin: Parallel Lives*, HarperCollins, 1991.

- **Burleigh (2000)** Burleigh, M., *The Third Reich: a New History*, Macmillan, 2000.

- **Carr (1991)** Carr, W., *A History of Germany 1815-1990*, Edward Arnold, 1991.

- **Fischer, K. (1995)** Fischer, K.P., *Nazi Germany: a New History*, Constable and Company, 1995.

- **Geary (2000)** Geary, D., *Hitler and Nazism* (2nd edn), Routledge, 2000.

- **Gellately (2001)** Gellately, R., *Backing Hitler*, Oxford University Press, 2001.

- **Goldhagen (1996)** Goldhagen, D., *Hitler's Willing Executioners: Ordinary Germans and the Holocaust*, Little, Brown and Company, 1996.

- **Haffner (1989)** Haffner, S., *Germany's Self-Destruction: the Reich from Bismarck to Hitler*, Simon & Schuster, 1989.

- **Johnson (2000)** Johnson, E., *The Nazi Terror*, John Murray, 2000.

- **Kershaw (1998)** Kershaw, I., *Hitler 1889-1936: Nemesis*, Penguin, 1998.

- **Kershaw (2000)** Kershaw, I., *The Nazi Dictatorship* (4th edn), Arnold, 2000.

- **King (1997)** King, C., 'Social Darwinism', *Modern History Review*, Vol.9.1, September 1997.

- **Layton (2000)** Layton, G., *Germany: the Third Reich 1933-45* (2nd edn), Hodder and Stoughton, 2000.

- **Lewis (1984)** Lewis, P., 'Concepts: totalitarianism', *History Review*, No.18, March 1994.

- **Machtan (2001)** Machtan, L., 'Hitler, Röhm and the Night of the Long Knives' in *History Today Supplement*, November 2001.

- **McDonough (2001)** McDonough, F., *Opposition and Resistance in Nazi Germany*, Cambridge University Press, 2001.

- **Noakes & Pridham (1996)** Noakes, J. & Pridham, G. (eds), *Nazism 1919-45: Volume 1: the Rise to Power: a Documentary Reader*, University of Exeter Press, 1996.

- **Noakes & Pridham (2000)** Noakes, J. & Pridham, G. (eds), *Nazism 1919-45: Volume 2:State, Economy and Society 1933-39* (2nd edn), University of Exeter Press, 2000.

- **Peukert (1987)** Peukert, D., *Inside Nazi Germany: Conformity, Opposition and Racism in Everyday Life*, Penguin, 1987.

- **Rees (1997)** Rees, L., *The Nazis: a Warning from History*, BBC Publications, 1997.

- **Snyder (1976)** Snyder, L., *Encyclopedia of the Third Reich*, McGraw-Hill (USA), 1976.

- **Stackelberg (1999)** Stackelberg, R., *Hitler's Germany: Origins, Interpretations, Legacies*, Routledge, 1999.

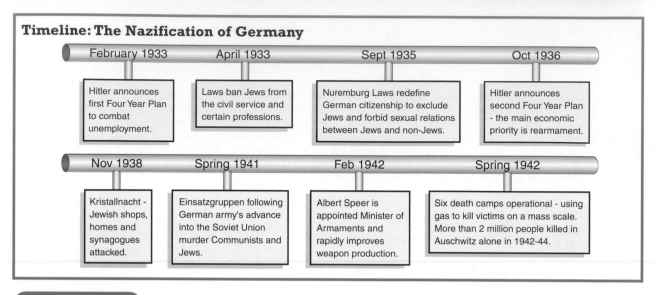

UNIT 6 · The Nazification of Germany

Timeline: The Nazification of Germany

February 1933	April 1933	Sept 1935	Oct 1936
Hitler announces first Four Year Plan to combat unemployment.	Laws ban Jews from the civil service and certain professions.	Nuremburg Laws redefine German citizenship to exclude Jews and forbid sexual relations between Jews and non-Jews.	Hitler announces second Four Year Plan - the main economic priority is rearmament.

Nov 1938	Spring 1941	Feb 1942	Spring 1942
Kristallnacht - Jewish shops, homes and synagogues attacked.	Einsatzgruppen following German army's advance into the Soviet Union murder Communists and Jews.	Albert Speer is appointed Minister of Armaments and rapidly improves weapon production.	Six death camps operational - using gas to kill victims on a mass scale. More than 2 million people killed in Auschwitz alone in 1942-44.

Introduction

Previous units have examined the Nazis' rise to power and their consolidation of power once they had taken office. This unit examines the impact that Nazi rule made on German society in the 12 years of the Third Reich. It begins by examining the nature and impact of Nazi propaganda. For 12 years, Germans lived in a country whose media and cultural life were closely controlled by the state. The first part of the unit examines the ways in which the Nazi regime put across their message and what exactly that message was. It also considers whether the Nazi regime was genuinely popular or whether the propaganda fell on deaf ears. By its very nature, of course, propaganda attempts to conceal. What Nazi propaganda concealed was an ugly reality in which terror and persecution played an important role. The second part of the unit shows that there was a gradual escalation of terror and persecution before the outbreak of the Second World War and then a rapid acceleration once war had broken out. The shocking result was that, by 1945, the Nazi regime was responsible, within its own borders, for the deaths of over 6 million people, most of them Jews but many from other minorities too. The Holocaust was one of the most shocking episodes in history and, consequently, takes a central place in this unit. The final part of the unit looks at the ways in which the Nazi regime affected the position of women in Germany, the impact it made on Germany's class structure and the way in which the Nazis managed the economy. It is important to draw strands together. There is, for example, no doubt that economic recovery ensured that the Nazis retained at least a degree of popularity. At the same time, it was economic recovery which provided Germany with the means to rearm and pursue an aggressive foreign policy. This aggressive foreign policy led to the outbreak of the Second World War. It was under the cover of the Second World War that all the large-scale Nazi atrocities occurred. All this raises the question of blame. Is it enough to blame Hitler and his henchmen or should the blame be spread more widely? Different historians have answered this question in different ways.

UNIT SUMMARY

Part 1 looks at the nature and impact of Nazi propaganda. How did the government put across its message? What were the messages that the regime wanted to put across? To what extent did the German people believe and accept what they were told?

Part 2 examines the extent to which Nazi Germany can be described as a 'police state'. It then analyses the steps which led to the murder of over 6 million Jews and people from other minority groups in the Holocaust.

Part 3 considers whether the Nazi regime made a significant impact on the role played by women in Germany and on Germany's class structure. It then explores the ways in which the Nazis managed the German economy.

1 Indoctrination

Key issues

1. What were the different forms of Nazi propaganda and indoctrination?

2. What sort of messages was the propaganda attempting to convey?

3. How popular were the Nazis in the period 1934-45?

1.1 What were the different forms of Nazi propaganda and indoctrination?

The importance of propaganda

It is widely agreed that propaganda was vital to the Nazi seizure of power. Hitler wrote two chapters on it in *Mein Kampf*. He believed in the popular idea, disputed by historians, that Germany lost World War One because it had failed to use propaganda as effectively as the British. He also believed that propaganda was essential to the establishment of a political regime:

'In every really great world-shaking movement, propaganda will first have to spread the idea of this movement.' (Hitler 1925, p.531).

Significantly, too, he wrote:

'If propaganda has imbued a whole people with an idea, the organisation can draw the consequences with a handful of men. Propaganda and organisation, in other words, supporters and members, thus stand in a certain mutual relation. The better the propaganda has worked, the smaller the organisation can be.' (Hitler 1925, p.530)

Summing up Hitler's attitude, Klaus Fischer writes:

'The chief strategy in Hitler's arsenal of gaining, maintaining, and expanding power was propaganda. Without propaganda, it is impossible to reach the heart of the people and imbue them with a sense of purpose or mission. Effective propaganda, Hitler believed, did not rest on logic or reason but rather on faith and emotions.' (Fischer K. 1995, p.172)

Most historians agree that propaganda played an important part in maintaining public support for the Nazi regime.

Goebbels' views on propaganda

Naturally, one of Hitler's first acts after gaining power was to create, on 13 March 1933, a Ministry of Popular Enlightenment and Propaganda (RMVP: *Reichsministerium fur Volksaufklarung und Propaganda*). The man he placed at its head, Joseph Goebbels, was to become extremely influential.

Goebbels, whom Klaus Fischer calls 'one of the true creative geniuses of the Third Reich', shared most of Hitler's views on propaganda. Goebbels argued that:

- propaganda should appeal to the widest possible number of people, and to the masses rather than to intellectuals
- it should contain a few simple ideas, hammered home by repetition
- it should generate strong emotions such as love and hate, because emotion is stronger than knowledge
- where appropriate it should use pictures and slogans to make an impact
- it should aim to generate blind faith and commitment.

Hitler spoke of the masses as 'feminine' in nature - essentially receptive and lacking in individual initiative and, therefore, open to manipulation by propaganda. He despised the gullibility of the masses, yet he and the rest of the regime were also very anti-intellectual, regarding critical habits of mind as 'Jewish' and un-German. Although he believed the masses lacked initiative, Hitler appreciated that people were able to identify their own interests, and, as a result, he tailored his public addresses according to the composition of his audience. When the particular medium made it possible, Goebbels made similar adjustments in propaganda, shaping it according to the interest group that was being targeted. Conan Fischer writes that, according to some historians, Nazi propaganda cynically 'promised everything and anything to virtually anyone' (Fischer C. 1995, p.31).

Hitler and Goebbels disagreed on one point. Hitler felt that propaganda was less important once a movement had become established in the public's mind. Goebbels, on the other hand, thought that it needed to be sustained in order for the movement to flourish. It should be noted, however, that Goebbels' own ambitions were hardly likely to encourage him to play down the task on which his personal role depended.

Cultural immersion

Historians who identified Nazism as 'totalitarian', such as Hannah Arendt and Carl Friedrich in the 1950s, and Karl Bracher in the 1970s, saw the German population as being 'atomised' and 'mobilised' by terror and propaganda. To them, the defining feature of the regime was its determination to dominate every aspect of the individual's life. Certainly, the Nazi attitude to propaganda seems to bear this out. In accordance with this, Goebbels persuaded Hitler that his brief should be to ensure that the whole of German cultural life - including the arts and not just what we would now call 'the media' - expressed Nazi values. In June 1933 Hitler even said that Goebbels was responsible for the 'spiritual direction of the nation' (Welch 1993, p.23). The comprehensive nature of Goebbels' organisation - the RMVP - is explored in Box 6.1.

BOX 6.1 The structure of the RMVP

The comprehensive nature of Goebbels' organisation can be seen in the areas allocated to its seven departments. Each department concentrated on instilling Nazi values in the areas allocated to it:

Department 1 Legislation and legal issues; finance.
Department 2 Coordination of popular enlightenment and propaganda; regional agencies; German Academy of Politics; official ceremonies and demonstrations; national emblems; race; Treaty of Versailles; opposing ideologies; youth organisations; health and sport; Eastern and border issues; national travel.
Department 3 Broadcasting.
Department 4 National and foreign press; journalism; press archives; news; National Association of German Press.
Department 5 Film industry; film censorship; newsreels.
Department 6 Theatre.
Department 7 Music, fine arts, people's culture.
Adapted from Welch 1993.

Television

It was now possible for Goebbels to reach a mass audience through broadcasting. Television had recently been invented, but it was unreliable and expensive, and few Germans possessed a set. Goebbels experimented with it, but he never developed its use to any great extent (some historians have seen this as a mistake). Surviving television footage shows that very little money was spent on it. Views of big public spectacles, such as a parade or a visit from Hitler, are filmed from far back in the crowd. The 'ringside seats' went to those covering the event for radio or cinema newsreels.

Radio

Radio was hugely important to the regime. Goebbels saw it as a means of creating uniformity and a sense of national community (Völksgemeinschaft). He told German Radio Controllers:

'We make no bones about the fact that the radio belongs to us and to no one else.' (Noakes & Pridham 2000, p.191)

However, the Nazis had to overcome Germany's federal tradition. When they came to power, there were nine autonomous regional radio stations. Goebbels persuaded Hitler to issue a decree, backed up by personal letters to the Reich Governors, placing radio under the central control of the RMVP. Regional stations became branches of the RRG (Reichsrundfunkgesellschaft: Reich Radio Company). Membership of the RRG became compulsory for anyone working in broadcasting - even radio salespeople.

Goebbels also launched a campaign to ensure that every German home had at least one radio set. He persuaded manufacturers to produce cheap sets. The heavily subsidised Völksempfanger ('People's Radio') sold at 35 marks, payable by instalments; a better set sold for 75 marks. Interestingly, only the cheaper set was deliberately limited in its reception range so that owners could not listen to foreign broadcasts - an activity that became illegal during the war. An early poster campaign announced that 'The whole of Germany listens to the Führer with the People's Radio', and by the outbreak of the Second World War, 70% of homes had a set. Those without one were encouraged to listen to the Führer's addresses on a neighbour's set.

Community listening

Community listening was also encouraged and, in fact, became almost compulsory. Whenever an important political announcement or speech was to be made, especially if it was to be made by Hitler himself, local Nazi Party officials would rig up speakers in factories, schools and public places - even restaurants. Sirens would sound and ordinary activity would cease for the duration of the 'community reception'.

Radio as effective propaganda

The propaganda effectiveness of radio was shown soon after the Nazis came to power. In advance of the League of Nations' plebiscite to decide whether the Saar area should be returned to Germany, Goebbels organised a campaign of broadcasts aimed at its population. When the referendum was held in January 1935, there was a massive vote in favour of returning to Germany (over 90% of the population voted in favour). Klaus Fischer argues that:

'The political benefits of radio became apparent during the course of 1934 when the Nazis transmitted regular weekly broadcasts to the Saar...Although the Saar would have returned to Germany in any case, the remarkably high vote of over 90% may well have been in part the result of this campaign.' (Fischer K 1995, p.371)

Only two disappointments marred Goebbels' success with radio before the outbreak of the Second World War. The first was that people became bored with political broadcasts. As a result, a variety of programmes had to be produced to avoid this. The second was that Hitler - such an emotive speaker at rallies - turned out to be hopeless in a studio without an audience. Once this became apparent, he was only recorded in public.

Radio in the Second World War

Radio became especially important during the war, with the regime anxious to ensure that Germans heard only the Nazi version of events (see Box 6.2). A network was set up to jam foreign radio stations. There were also propaganda broadcasts aimed at undermining Allied morale, including those by the notorious William Joyce - known in Britain as 'Lord Haw-Haw' because of his aristocratic English accent.

BOX 6.2 | **The extraordinary radio measures of 1939**

The idea of forbidding Germans from listening to foreign radio was initially floated by the staff of Hitler's deputy, Rudolf Hess in mid-August 1939. Hitler was soon convinced and ordered Goebbels, the minister responsible, to work out the details. Although some senior figures voiced reservations, Hitler signed the decree suggested by Goebbels on the day it was presented to him - 1 September 1939. Goebbels' measures addressed Hitler's deep concerns about the negative effects of enemy radio propaganda on the German people. The 'extraordinary radio measures' decree stated that 'in modern war the enemy fights not just with military weapons but also with methods intended to influence and undermine the morale of the people. One of these methods is the radio.' Clearly, the decree argued 'every word that the enemy sends our way is obviously untrue and is designed to hurt the German people'. It followed that every upright citizen would not wish to listen to foreign broadcasts. For those who lacked that sense of responsibility, the new measure made listening into a serious crime, and even threatened the death penalty. As early as 1937, there had been proposals that listening to Communist radio broadcasts from Moscow should be made illegal. Even though nothing came of these proposals, when anybody was accused of listening to Communist broadcasts, the Gestapo treated it as a crime, especially if that person had a Communist past.

Adapted from Gellately 2001.

The press

Goebbels, himself regarded by some historians as a writer of some talent, described the press as a piano on which the regime could play to influence the public in whatever way it decided. Hitler was often dismissive of the press, but still regarded it as being significant as a propaganda tool.

Noakes and Pridham (2000) identify three main developments regarding the press once the Nazis gained power:

1. Individuals employed to work in the press began to be vetted for 'racial purity' and political correctness.
2. The Nazi publishing house, the Eher Verlag, gradually gained control of most of the press.
3. Press content was closely controlled through party press conferences and briefings. Offending editors risked arrest and the banning of their publication.

The 'coordination' of the press and publishing houses

The 'Reichstag Fire Decree' (28 February 1933 - see Unit 5, Section 1.1) allowed Hitler to suspend the left-wing press in the run-up to the election of March 1933. Catholic papers and other middle-class daily papers followed. A few prestigious liberal papers were permitted to publish for a while, largely to create a good impression internationally. Like other institutions anxious to survive in some form, the Publishers' Association coordinated itself (see Unit 5, Section 1.2 above for explanation of the term 'coordination'). First it replaced politically unacceptable members. Then it appointed Max Amann - a Nazi and personal friend of Hitler - as its Chair under the new title of 'The Association of German Newspaper Publishers'. On 15 November 1933, Amann was also appointed President of the newly created Reich Press Chamber. Membership of the Chamber was compulsory for those in publishing, and membership was denied to anyone deemed to be 'politically unreliable'.

Similarly, the Reich Association of the German Press appointed Nazi Press Chief Otto Dietrich as its head. On 30 April 1933, membership of the Association became compulsory for those working in the press. Moreover, membership was open only to those who passed screening for 'racial and political reliability'. By 1935, 1,300 'Jewish and Marxist' journalists had been forced out of their jobs.

Growth in Nazi press ownership

Also of major importance was the growing Nazi press ownership. This is outlined in Box 6.3.

Goebbels and the press

Goebbels told the press what he expected of them:
'We want to have a press which cooperates with the government just as the government wants to cooperate with the press…We do not want a state of daily warfare, a state of continual bans, rather we wish government and press to work together with mutual trust. You need not be afraid of making statements with obvious bias. There is nothing unbiased in the world. Everything unbiased is sexless and thus worthless.' (Noakes & Pridham 2001, p.199)

Nor would Goebbels be content with passive compliance. He wanted journalists who would 'take a stand for the new Reich and its Führer, not

BOX 6.3 The growth in Nazi press ownership

In early 1933, the Nazis owned only 59 daily newspapers with a combined circulation of 782,000. By the end of 1933, they owned 86 daily papers, with a circulation of 3,182,000. Then, in 1934, they acquired a large Jewish publishing firm, Ullstein. In April 1935, Max Amann and his deputy Rolf Reinhardt announced that newspapers would be shut down or bought out if:

- they had Jewish or politically unsound connections
- they were owned by a corporation, society or foundation
- they were aimed at a specific religious, vocational or special interest group.

Using these criteria, between 500 and 600 newspapers were closed over the next 18 months. In addition, on 1 October 1935, the public display and sale of all Jewish papers was banned. By 1939, Nazi control of the press had grown still further. The Nazis controlled 66% of the press. By 1944, this figure had increased to 82%. Many papers, however, retained their old names, so the public was unaware of the change in ownership. Uniformity was further promoted by the fusion of the two main news agencies into a single new official agency, the Deutsches Nachrichtenburo (DNB). This new agency provided more than half of the information available to the press, and newspapers were often instructed to print the agency's news stories word-for-word as supplied.

Adapted from Welch 1993.

because they have to, but because they wish to do so' (Welch 1993, p.37). As a result, journalists were largely self-censoring. They knew that if they failed to support the regime they would, at the very least, lose their jobs. Nevertheless Goebbels felt it necessary to hold frequent press conferences and briefings, and to issue directives telling journalists what stories to cover and how to cover them. In addition, a new 'Editors' Law' made editors, rather than publishers, responsible for the content of their newspaper and, therefore, liable to arrest if the newspaper offended against Nazi ideology or the official interpretation of events.

Having achieved uniformity in the press, Goebbels was worried about it becoming boring since this would make it ineffective as propaganda. He tried to prevent this by launching occasional press campaigns, for example supporting the 'Winter Help' scheme by which households were encouraged to have an Eintopf - One-Pot Meal - once a week and to give the money saved to collections for impoverished fellow Germans. This was backed up by poster campaigns, especially during the war. However, Goebbels was never happy about the dullness his policies had achieved. He wrote in his diary:

'No decent journalist with any feeling of honour in his bones can stand the way he is handled by the press department of the Reich government…Any man who still has a residue of honour will be very careful not to become a journalist.'

The film industry

It is clear from his writing and speeches that Goebbels was a firm believer in the power of film. He believed that propaganda was most powerful when least expected. Film could easily conceal its propaganda message because it was associated with recreation and relaxation. However, in 1932, the industry was suffering from the combined effects of the Depression and the invention of the 'talkies'. Films were now even more expensive to make, just at a time when the public could least afford to go to the cinema. As a result, the industry was ripe for a takeover. Cinema owners were coordinated in March 1933, when Nazi members of the German Cinema Owners' Association succeeded in having their leader, Engl, elected to the board. When the rest of the board resigned over a dispute with another organisation, Engl and the Nazi Party were left in charge. Other parts of the industry were soon absorbed in the official Nazi union, the DAF.

Goebbels created the RFK (Reichsfilmkammer) on 14 July 1933, to coordinate and control the film industry. Its structure and function remained largely unchanged after incorporation into the RKK (Reich Chamber of Culture - see below). Since the industry as a whole feared Nazi restrictions, the FKB (Filmkreditbank) was formed, partly to allay their fears, but also to give the regime economic control of the industry. By 1936, the FKB was financing 73% of all German feature films. Film projects were closely vetted for suitability, and credit could be refused at pre-production stage if a film was not actively pro-Nazi. Films were subject to a system of 'distinctions'. These had to be earned in order for the film to be shown. Further distinctions would earn tax deductions. In addition there was a system of 'positive' script censorship. It was not enough for a film to avoid criticising the Nazis. Active support was required, even in light entertainment films.

At first Goebbels was reluctant to nationalise the film industry, partly because this might damage its contacts with foreign distributors, and partly because one of the biggest film companies was owned by Alfred Hugenberg, who was Minister of Economics in the new government. But moves towards nationalisation were eventually begun, and the process was completed in 1942.

Active propaganda films were made, such as *Eternal Forest*, which portrays a mystical idea of the German master race and its origins in the mists of time, and Leni Riefenstahl's famous *Triumph of the Will*. However, fictional feature films were more successful in box office terms - see Box 6.4.

Propaganda and the film industry

Most of the feature films made in the early years of the Third Reich were no different from the nationalist productions of the Weimar era. In their first wave, propaganda films were unsuccessful and Leni Riefenstahl's films of the 1934 Reich Party Congress (*Triumph of the Will*) and her films of the 1936 Olympic Games (*Festival of the Peoples* and *Festival of Beauty*) were, even then, unlike anything else. Reasonably entertaining historical biopics like *The Old and the Young King* (1935) and *Bismarck* (1940) were more likely to awaken the desired associations in the minds of audiences. Nazi indoctrinators miscalculated with anti-Semitic films like *Jud Süss* and *The Eternal Jew* (a 'documentary') and a film like I *Accuse* (1941) which supported the case for euthanasia was hardly the best way to avoid unrest amongst the population, considering the news which was leaking out about the killing of the mentally ill. Far better suited to strengthen the will to carry on during the second half of the Second World War were light, entertaining old films. Film fanatics like Goebbels - and Hitler - seemed to understand this. In any case, blatant propaganda films always only represented a fraction of the annual production of around 100 films.

Adapted from Frei 1993.

Newsreels

Of equal importance were the newsreels shown before a feature film. These were a popular source of information and entertainment until the war started to go badly for Germany. Then, with the regime increasingly distorting the news, audiences started to hang around outside the cinema in order to miss the newsreel. Goebbels dealt with this by ordering cinemas to be closed during the newsreel. Anyone not already inside would miss the feature as well.

Art, literature and music

Both Hitler and Goebbels saw the arts as existing to serve the state. As Hitler put it, 'The artist cannot stand aloof from his people' (quoted in Welch 1993, p.27). According to Nazi ideology, to view the arts as a means of individual expression, of challenging mainstream perceptions, or of creating beauty for its own sake, was decadent and, therefore, against Nazi values. The arts, therefore, were part of the propaganda machine. It was in this spirit that the Reich Chamber of Culture - the RKK - was set up on 22 September 1933. This was a coup for Goebbels in his bitter rivalry with the hardline ideologist Alfred Rosenberg. Rosenberg set up the 'Combat League for German Culture' and the ironically named 'Reich Association for the Encouragement of German Literature'. The RKK was the main agent of coordination, allowing Goebbels' Ministry of Propaganda to exert control over almost all of German culture. No artist was allowed to work without a work permit, and work permits were denied to anyone racially or ideologically unacceptable.

Formal censorship was rarely necessary, since artists who had not fled or been imprisoned exercised self-censorship for fear of losing their work permit. Even music was subject to the same restrictions. In particular, the Reich Music Chamber was gradually purged of Jewish influence: 'The battle was waged on two fronts: against individuals and against tunes' (Friedlander 1997, p.132). The ludicrous nature of this campaign emerges in Friedlander's account:

'Goebbels' Herculean task was bedeviled by the all but insuperable [impossible] difficulty of identifying the racial origins of all composers and librettists [writers of lyrics], and by the dilemma created by well-known pieces tainted with some Jewish connection.' (Friedlander 1997, p.133)

Literature was similarly afflicted by the obligation to reflect Nazi values - see Box 6.5. Many writers fled abroad. There was some early resistance to Nazi coordination in the Prussian Academy of Arts. In 1933, Heinrich Mann, Head of its literature section, and Käthe Kollwitz, a member of the arts section, signed and circulated a petition calling on the Communist and Socialist parties to unite to save the country from 'sinking into barbarism' (Fischer K. 1995, p.365). But Bernhard Rust, the Nazi Commissioner for Culture in Prussia, threatened the academy with closure and silenced the dissidents.

The burning of the books

On 10 May 1933, there took place an appalling event in the history of German culture - the 'burning of the books'. In a 'cleansing action' organised by the German Student Union, a nationwide synchronised burning of thousands of books deemed 'un-German' took place. Books from libraries, shops and homes were thrown onto the street, collected and burned. Particularly likely to go up in smoke were books by Jewish authors.

Adapted from Fischer K. 1995.

BOX 6.6 | The Nuremburg rallies

This photo gives an impression of the huge scale of the Nuremburg rallies.

Rallies, parades and displays

Throughout the life of the Nazi Party, massed public demonstrations of its power and discipline played a large part in its appeal. Before Hitler struck his decisive blow against the power of the SA in 1934, the SA's parades, and even their running of soup kitchens, acted as powerful Nazi propaganda. Zeman, author of *Nazi Propaganda* (1973), regards the SA as perhaps a more powerful propaganda weapon than even Hitler's words (see Fischer C. 1995). Richard Bessel, in *Political Violence and the Rise of Nazism*, says that the spreading of propaganda by the SA was propaganda in itself.

Mass rallies

After the SS had taken the SA's place in the power structure, parades continued to be important. Mass rallies at which Hitler or other Nazis spoke were perhaps even more important in creating a sense of the regime's power and of Germany's emotional unity. The larger events, including all those at which Hitler himself spoke, were stage-managed by Goebbels. The Day of Potsdam (see Unit 5, Section 1.2) was an early example. There was an emphasis on pageantry, and choreographed torch-lit processions, with much use of the Nazi flag. Conan Fischer writes that the flag, used so widely on these occasions, was itself a brilliant invention: red for blood and socialism, black and white for the pre-Weimar empire. There is also the dynamic image of

the swastika itself, derived from an ancient symbol for the revolving sun.

When Hitler spoke, he would always arrive late, allowing time for the crowd to reach a fever-pitch of anticipation. He would begin quietly and become increasingly impassioned, rousing the crowd to a frenzy of nationalist enthusiasm. Some senior deputies, such as Goebbels, earned their own reputation as speakers. Throughout Germany, according to Conan Fischer, care and professionalism went into Nazi speech-giving. Even local speakers needed a certificate to speak regionally, and regional speakers needed one to speak nationally. Certificates were earned by passing formal exams in technique and ideology.

The effect was often enhanced, as at the Nuremberg rallies, by the architectural setting. Hitler's chief architect, Albert Speer, was responsible for developing a pseudo-classical monumental style of architecture that satisfied Hitler's tastes and Nazi ideology. A central aim was to emphasise the insignificance of the individual compared with the might of the nation. Box 6.6 shows the huge scale of Nazi rallies.

Youth indoctrination

Hitler regarded the indoctrination of youth as being essential to the long-term success of the Nazi regime, even referring to older people as 'a lost generation' (Bullock 1991, p.361). The Nazis set out to achieve this through two means: the education system and youth groups.

Education

Alan Bullock writes that:

'Characteristically, there was more rivalry than coordination between the different agencies concerned to indoctrinate the younger generations with Nazi beliefs.' (Bullock 1991, p.361)

The Minister of Education, Bernhard Rust, issued a directive (18 December 1934) stating:

'The principal task of the school is the education of youth in the service of nationhood and state in the National Socialist spirit.'

Although he frequently came into conflict with Hess, Bormann, Ley and Goebbels over the policies to achieve this, all five Nazis were broadly agreed on the overall aim.

As with the press, broadcasting and the film industry, the first step was coordination of the profession. Purging of politically unreliable individuals was facilitated by the Law for the Re-establishment of a Professional Civil Service issued on 7 April 1933 (teachers were civil servants). Klaus Fischer (1995) notes that, in Prussia, 15% of male head teachers were sacked and 32% of female head teachers. Throughout Germany, 60% of College of Education lecturers lost their jobs. Teachers were also subject to a professional organisation, the National Socialist Teachers' League (NSLB), which, like the DAF for workers, was largely a means of control rather than of improving conditions.

The organisation of education was centralised, so that regions had to carry out the policies of the Reich Ministry of Education. Further uniformity was ensured in 1937 when the number of different types of secondary schools was reduced from nearly 70 to three. Finally, the leader principle - the Führerprinzip (see Unit 4, Section 1.3) was applied. In effect, each head teacher became a little Führer. Other teachers lost the right to take part in decision-making.

Within the classroom, indoctrination became paramount. This was achieved both by direct teaching of subjects such as 'racial science', and indirectly through the way in which textbooks presented other subjects. One example is the setting of maths problems based on how much money the state would save if it no longer had to provide for the mentally ill. There was also a new emphasis on PE and competitive sport, encouraging physical fitness and discipline.

Youth movements

When Hitler came to power, Germany already had a wide range of youth groups. These were gradually co-ordinated, with the Catholic ones succumbing last. In their place came the HJ (Hitler Jugend - Hitler Youth) for boys, and the BDM (Bund Deutsche Madel - League of German Maidens) for girls. The movement's youthful leader was Baldur von Schirach, who in July 1933 was officially made 'Youth Leader of the German Reich'. He organised the coordination of existing groups, helped by a directive to teachers to pressurise pupils to join the HJ. Further pressure to join came when state-controlled jobs and apprenticeships increasingly became open only to members of the HJ. Moreover, in July 1936 Schirach forged an agreement with the Reich Sports Leader that gave the HJ a monopoly over sports activities up to the age of 14, later extended to 18.

Schirach's power reached its zenith when, on 1 December 1936, Hitler granted him independence of the Reich Ministry of the Interior. After this date, the HJ was subordinate only to Hitler himself.

Members of the HJ and BDM were expected to spend much of their spare time in tightly organised group activities that allowed them no waking time to themselves. Lisa Pine writes:

'The Nazi regime claimed that youth autonomy and the principle of self-leadership were central to its youth groups, but in practice, as in all Nazi formations, individual independence was not valued. Members were bound to a community of peers, and above and beyond that, to the community of the nation.' (Pine 1999, p.25)

Through these activities, members were indoctrinated in Nazi ideology. At the same time, boys were prepared to be blindly obedient soldiers, and girls to be dutiful wives and mothers.

MAIN POINTS - Section 1.1

- Hitler and Goebbels saw propaganda as vital to Nazi success. Most historians agree that it was.
- Hitler and Goebbels agreed that propaganda had to reach the widest possible audience, and appeal to the emotions and faith rather than the intellect, with a few simple points being repeated.
- The RMVP, under Goebbels, was the principal Nazi propaganda institution, although it had to compete with other bodies such as Rosenberg's Combat League for German Culture.
- The RMVP controlled all cultural life - broadcasting, the press, film, the arts and public events. It did this by vetting and purging individuals in the respective professions, taking over corporations and professional organisations, and censorship.
- Youth was controlled and indoctrinated through education and by the HJ and BDM. The youth movement aimed at indoctrination through group activities, including the preparation of boys for war and girls for motherhood.
- The education system was controlled by the vetting of the profession, centralisation and restructuring. Its aim became indoctrination.

Activity 6.1 Nazi propaganda

ITEM 1 A Nazi rally - an eyewitness account

More than 100,000 people had paid to squeeze inside, while another 100,000 packed a nearby race track where loudspeakers had been set up to carry Hitler's words. And, at home, millions were waiting by the radio. Around the stadium, banners were silhouetted against the darkening sky. Row under row, the seats stepped down to the centre field. Opposite them reared the dramatic speaking stand, its bold, cubical masses hung with giant swastikas. Draperies, also with swastikas, made a simple and thrilling background. Picked men were drawn up in close ranks below the stand. Twelve huge SA bands played military marches with beautiful precision and terrifying power. Behind the bands, on the field itself, solid squares of uniformed men stood in strict military order. Suddenly, a word was tossed from man to man. Hitler is coming! Hitler is here! A blare of trumpets split the air and 100,000 people leaped to their feet. All eyes were turned towards the stand, awaiting the approach of the Führer. There was a low rumble of excitement and then, releasing its pent-up emotion, the crowd burst into a tremendous ovation, the 'Heil' swelling until they were like the roar of a mighty waterfall.

Eyewitness account of a Nazi rally, written by Karl Ludecke in 1937.

ITEM 2 Goebbels outlines his views

(i) We have set up a Ministry for Enlightenment and Propaganda (RMVP). These two titles have different meanings. Popular enlightenment is something passive. But propaganda is something active. We cannot be satisfied with just telling the people what we want and enlightening them as to how we are doing it. We must rather replace this enlightenment with an active government propaganda, a propaganda which aims at winning people over. I view the first task of the RMVP as being to achieve coordination between the government and the whole people. It is not enough for people to be more or less reconciled to our regime, to be persuaded to adopt a neutral attitude towards us. Rather, we want to work on people until they have completely given in to us. The most important tasks of this ministry must be the following. First, all propaganda ventures and all institutions of public information belonging to the Reich and the states must be centralised. Second, we must modernise. We must not allow technology to run ahead of the state. And third, the leaders of today must be modern princes of the people. They must be able to understand the people but need not follow them slavishly. It is their duty to tell the masses what they want and to put their message across in such a way that it is understood.

Extract from a speech made by Goebbels on 15 March 1933. He was speaking at a press conference.

(ii) We make no bones about the fact that the radio belongs to us and no-one else. And we will place the radio at the service of our ideology and [the speaker bangs on the lectern] no other ideology will find expression here. The radio must subordinate itself to the goals which the government has set itself. First principle - at all costs avoid being boring. I put that before everything. So do not think that you have the task of creating the correct attitudes, of indulging in patriotism, of blasting out military music and filling the airwaves with patriotic verse. No this is not what this new orientation is about. Rather you must help bring forth a nationalist art and culture which is truly appropriate to the pace of modern life and the mood of the time. The correct attitudes must be put across but that does not mean they must be boring.

Extract from a speech made by Goebbels on 25 March 1933. He was speaking to Controllers of German radio.

Adapted from Noakes & Pridham 2000.

ITEM 3 The Führer speaks

The caption on this propaganda poster produced in 1936 reads: 'The whole of Germany listens to the Führer on the People's Radio'.

ITEM 4 Pledging loyalty to the Führer

This photograph shows girls pledging their loyalty to the Führer at a League of German Maidens (BDM) summer camp in 1940. The historian Lisa Pine argues that one of the BDM's aims was for the Nazi state to replace parents as the source of authority. At summer camps like this, girls were taught to accept Nazi values unquestioningly.

Questions

1. a) Using Items 1-4 and your own knowledge, explain how the Nazis attempted to indoctrinate people.
   b) What does this tell us about the nature of the Nazi regime?
2. a) Using Items 1-3 and your own knowledge, describe the role of the Ministry of Enlightenment and Propaganda (the RMVP).

b) How did the RMVP help the Nazis to remain in power?
3. a) What does Item 2 tell us about the role Goebbels intended propaganda to play in the Nazi regime?
   b) How did Goebbels and the other Nazi leaders put these ideas into practice?

1.2 What messages did Nazi propaganda and indoctrination convey?

Ideology and motivation

Some historians see Nazi propaganda merely as a cynical means of gaining and retaining power. Others, like Karl Bracher (1971), have argued that the ideology propaganda conveyed was a genuine motivating force for leading Nazis as well as for the people as a whole. Ian Kershaw comments on this debate as follows:

'Perhaps the most significant shift in perspective, compared with the position in the early or mid-1980s is the seriousness with which Nazi racial ideology is now viewed as a key motivating force for action. Given the ragbag nature of Nazism's assemblage of phobias and prejudices, it has always proved tempting to see ideology as no more than an amalgam of ideas at the service of propaganda and mobilisation. In some ways, this

has become almost reversed: propaganda and mobilisation are now seen to have served a racial ideology of central importance to the "cumulative radicalisation" of the regime.' (Kershaw 2000, pp.263-64)

Although much of Nazi ideology is based on prejudices and unthinking assumptions, it does have a kind of internal logic. In other words, its main themes do connect in a more or less logical way. These themes can be summarised as follows:

- the Völksgemeinschaft - the national community uniting all Germans
- the virtues of stable family life
- the Führerprinzip - the leader principle, stating that this (and any) community worked best if led by a strong individual
- Social Darwinism - the survival of the fittest, both on the individual and international level, with Germans as the master race
- Strength through Work - campaigns designed to maximise workers' productivity
- Lebensraum - the need and right of Germany to

carve out 'living space' for its people by seizing it from 'inferior' neighbouring peoples (especially Slavs and Russians)

- anti-Bolshevism - Communism was seen as a major threat to civilisation
- anti-Semitism - Jews were seen as inferior and yet a major threat.

1. Völksgemeinschaft

The idea of a unified German national community evolved in the 19th century. It must be remembered that in the mid-19th century, Germany, like Italy, was a loose collection of independent states. Even when the Nazis came to power, German unity was still a relatively new and exciting concept, with a romantic appeal. Conan Fischer characterises this concept of unity as follows:

'It presumed that all Germans shared a common ethnicity, culture and set of values which stemmed from a glorious (part-mythologised) history.'
(Fischer C. 1995, pp.31-32)

Fischer says that during the First World War the Frontsgemeinschaft (Front-line community) gave a modern relevance to the Völksgemeinschaft, and that this was also a major force after the war. This gave rise to paramilitary groups, including the SA, and to politicians being anxious to represent their parties as Völkisch (People's) parties, and even changing their names accordingly.

Box 6.7 shows that Völksgemeinschaft became the bedrock of Nazi ideology from which all its other ideological beliefs followed.

The *Eternal Forest*

The Nazi propaganda film *Eternal Forest* played on this romantic and mythical idea of German origins. This reaching back in time is significant in three ways:

1. Industrialisation drew many people from their traditional communities to cities where they felt no sense of belonging. It also introduced class conflict. Volkisch ideology argued that people's resulting feelings of alienation from society could be replaced by identification with the nation.
2. Nazi propaganda praised rural life, idealising 'peasant values' as healthier than those found in cities.
3. The ideology looks back to a time when Germans, supposedly, were racially pure - and had not been 'corrupted' by Jews.

2. The virtues of stable family life

Propaganda and school indoctrination promoted the ideal of the stable family unit (the poster on the cover of this book is a good example). The family was the means of continuing the all-important German bloodstock and preserving morality. As a result, it was a focus for propaganda. For example, listening to the Führer's speeches on the radio was meant to be a family activity. In addition, 'traditional' values were encouraged. Men were meant to be in charge and to protect their family. A woman's role was to serve and nurture her family, and to have plenty of children. Women were even given medals for producing five or more children. Klaus Fischer writes:

'The Nazis looked upon the family primarily as a reproductive unit furnishing future soldiers for the Reich. Of course, such blatantly crude ideas were rarely publicized. Nazi art evoked the traditional image of the clean-cut sheltering family whose members relate to each other in loving support and perform their assigned roles without question. Thousands of posters or picture postcards idealized

---

BOX 6.7 Völksgemeinschaft as the bedrock of Nazi ideology

The primary goal of Nazi propaganda was to restructure German society in a very radical way so that loyalties between members of the same social class, between members of the same religion and between members of the same groups or organisations would be replaced by a new heightened national awareness. This involved building up a new system of beliefs which had a kind of religious dimension. The idea was that believing in a 'national' or 'people's' community (ie in Völksgemeinschaft) would displace or override people's other beliefs. The desire for unity which is at the root of the concept of Völksgemeinschaft drew its strength from an idealised past rather than from the present. In addition to

A propaganda photo showing Hitler (right), Goebbels (to his left) and other leading Nazis eating a 'One-Pot' meal.

propaganda which conveyed the general idea of Völksgemeinschaft, there were campaigns that were partly intended to address practical problems, but which were equally important in their reinforcement of national consciousness. These included families eating the Eintopf (One-Pot meal) once a month (see Section 1.1 above). This was presented as 'a sacrifice for the community', echoing the slogan 'Don't give - sacrifice!'. This ideal of sacrifice was also promoted in school textbooks.

Adapted from Welch 1993.

the image of well-groomed blond children who are lovingly supported by their protective Aryan parents.' (Fischer K. 1995, p.354)

Propaganda also aimed to preserve order within the family. Lisa Pine (1997) describes how many children's books promoted 'the natural order'. In one fable, for example, a husband and wife swap roles. The husband takes over the cooking, and the wife goes and works in the fields. The result is disaster, and so the husband tells his wife that it is better 'not to reverse the order of nature'.

3. The Führerprinzip

The leader principle went hand in hand with the Völksgemeinschaft, producing the slogan 'One people, one homeland, one Führer'. According to Bracher it is based on 'the belief that the German people were essentially incapable of self-government' and that strong non-democratic leadership provided 'a superior command structure girded [ready] for battle' (Bracher 1971, p.423). He adds that it is founded on the traditional German (especially Prussian) respect for authority. Hindenburg was a pseudo-emperor and in effect Hitler was his successor.

Nazi propaganda presented Hitler as the sole representative and voice of the German people. As the embodiment of the people's will, he was a godlike figure. The 'Hitler myth' was the result of propaganda which cultivated a faith in Hitler as the unwavering protector and leader of his people. Rallies, posters, radio coverage and documentary films helped to create this image. In addition, as shown in Unit 5, Section 2.1, Hitler's distance from policy-making helped to deflect any criticism from himself onto the Nazi Party. As a result, he enjoyed a popular support which far exceeded that for the Nazi Party as a whole.

This 'leader principle' was also applied to businesses, schools and colleges. Any existing democratic process was replaced by authoritarian rule by leaders who were supposed to embody the will of the entire institution.

4. Social Darwinism

The origins and meaning of the term 'Social Darwinism' are described in Unit 5, Section 2.1. According to Nazi ideology, the struggle for survival, and for supremacy, were an absolute fact of human society and political life. Moreover, this struggle was justified by observation of nature. One Nazi propaganda film shows two stag beetles fighting, with one eventually killing the other. A white coated 'scientist' points out to his young female assistant that this is simply a law of nature, and that it applies equally to human society.

It follows that, even before 1939, Hitler strove to create a sense of the nation as a battle unit fighting the injustice of the Treaty of Versailles and Germany's internal enemies. These enemies were perceived as Jews, Communists, and anyone who failed to give enthusiastic support to Nazism. Within Germany, the Nazis saw 'Aryans' (the 'typical' German racial type, tall, with blond hair and blue eyes) as superior to non-Aryans - especially Jews. Internationally, they saw Germany as destined to rule Europe, and even the world. Nazi rallies and the films and postcards commemorating them emphasised Germany's greatness and majesty, founded on a glorious past yet forging ahead into a brave new future.

A master race

Propaganda conveyed the message that, as members of the master race, Germans had a duty to become fit and healthy. So, documentary films showed young men and women developing healthy bodies by outdoor physical exercise and sport, with the emphasis on regimented group exercise rather than individual achievement (see Box 6.8). There were also propaganda campaigns against smoking and excessive drinking.

BOX 6.8 Regimented group exercise

This photograph shows college students exercising in Berlin in 1935.

The need for physical fitness and toughness was particularly instilled into young men, along with a belief in German superiority. Hitler writes:

'This self-confidence must be inculcated in the young national comrade from childhood on. His whole education and training must be so ordered as to give him the conviction that he is absolutely superior to others. Through his physical strength and dexterity, he must recover his faith in the invincibility of his whole people. (Hitler 1925, p.374)

In schools this belief in German-Aryan superiority was reinforced through the curriculum. Racial 'science' became an essential part of biology, and history lessons focused on the glorious triumphs of Germany's past.

Those who were a drain on the nation's health

Conversely, Nazi ideology saw those who were chronically ill, mentally deficient or criminal as a drain on the health and strength of the nation. Gellately notes that, in 1936, there was a new propaganda emphasis on portraying concentration camp inmates as degenerates who might be beyond hope, and that this can be seen as a preparation for extermination (Gellately 2001, p.63). In other areas, the propagandists had to tread more carefully. They could not risk public disapproval by putting up posters advocating euthanasia for the mentally ill, but they could encourage school textbooks that set maths exercises based on the expense of running mental institutions.

5. Strength through Work

Members of the national community also had a duty to work for the benefit of the community. This explains why propaganda extolled the virtues of work, especially physical work. Aware that support for the Nazi Party was weakest among the industrial working class, much propaganda was aimed at this group. A great deal such propaganda was based on the idea of the 'Betreibsgemeinschaft', or 'factory community', a Völksgemeinschaft in miniature, with the factory boss taking the place of Hitler as the leader to whom the workers should give unquestioning loyalty. Campaigns focused on pride and patriotism, and on the ennobling nature of work.

There were strict limits on pay increases, so the Nazi union DAF had to offer other incentives to workers. Two new organisations were particularly important:

- Beauty of Labour
- Strength through Joy.

Beauty of Labour

Beauty of Labour ran propaganda campaigns such as 'Fight against noise', 'Good ventilation in the workplace' and 'Clean people in a clean plant'. These campaigns offered practical benefits, promoted the idea of community, and attempted to persuade workers that the regime cared about their welfare.

Strength through Joy (Kraft durch Freude - KdF)

The aim of Strength through Joy was to promote leisure activities in the hope of gaining maximum productivity from the workers. Posters showed workers having good clean fun, visiting resorts and going on cruises. Few workers were actually able to go on cruises, but the idea that it was possible may have improved morale. In another scheme, workers were encouraged to pay five marks a week into a savings scheme towards buying a Volkswagen (People's car). Many never actually got the car, but the dream may have given them hope.

6. Lebensraum

Lebensraum (living space) was both a foreign policy objective and a propaganda principle (see also Unit 4, Section 1.4). Karl Bracher identifies it as one of Hitler's two core beliefs, the other being his racism (Bracher 1971, p.316). Certainly both are prominent in *Mein Kampf*, Hitler arguing that Germany needed to increase its size to match its population and its importance. Given Hitler's belief in the German people's destiny as the master race, it is not surprising that he claimed a right to expand Germany's borders by enslaving or eliminating surrounding populations. His particular targets lay to the East - Czechoslovakia and Poland, whose people Hitler regarded as inferior, and the Soviet Union, which he believed was both inferior and controlled by Jewish Bolsheviks (Communists) who were aiming at world domination.

The German pursuit of Lebensraum began with regaining the territories taken from Germany and reallocated in 1918. There were still German-speaking populations in the Polish part of Upper Silesia, the Sudetenland (part of Czechoslovakia) and the Saar (part of France), as well as Russia, Lithuania, the Ukraine, Hungary and Romania. Most Austrians were German-speakers. In addition, the Rhineland had been designated a neutral zone in which Germany was not permitted to mount defences. Radio, press and poster campaigns preceded the Saar plebiscite (see Section 1.1 above), the remilitarisation of the Rhineland in 1936, the Anschluss (union) with Austria in 1938, and the invasions of Czechoslovakia and Poland in 1939.

After 1939, propaganda portrayed Slavs (people who lived in Poland and Czechoslovakia) as 'untermenschen', sub-humans whose territory should be controlled by Germany. From 1941, similar propaganda portrayed the Russians in a similar light, but with special emphasis on their bestial cruelty. This was intended to spur on German troops and to justify Operation Barbarossa (the invasion of the Soviet Union). By launching Operation Barbarossa, Hitler broke the mutual non-aggression pact with Stalin. As the German invasion advanced, propaganda was aimed at the conquered populations, encouraging them to cooperate. An example of this kind of propaganda is shown in Box 6.9.

Was Lebensraum a serious objective?

One issue here is how far Lebensraum was a serious objective rather than mere propaganda. Martyn Housden notes that:

'After the war, Martin Broszat argued that Hitler's writings and statements did not constitute a programme which directly determined his actions. Rather they provided a series of appealing propaganda images which helped give shape to

BOX 6.9 Propaganda following Operation Barbarossa

ВИННИЦА

This poster was designed by the Nazis during the Second World War. The caption is in Russian and the poster was displayed in parts of the Ukraine under Nazi rule. The man in the background is both Jewish and Communist. The women are Ukrainians, inspecting a mass grave after an atrocity committed by the Red Army. The aim was to convince Ukrainians that the Soviet government (which was supposedly controlled by Jews) was the real enemy, not the Nazi government.

the Nazi movement and which rallied the support of the nation. Party members could put their differences to one side and dedicate themselves to complete support for an organisation oriented towards a far-sighted vision of territorial conquest; other Germans could feel enthusiasm for winning an extensive empire.' (Housden 2000, p.51)
According to Broszat, therefore, the Lebensraum propaganda was a means of rallying and maintaining support. It was not serious policy proposal. Housden himself disagrees with this conclusion. He argues that the idea of Lebensraum was fundamental to Hitler's outlook and that it was more than just a propaganda image. He argues that:

'For all the difficulties in interpreting what Hitler meant by Lebensraum, one thing stands out - the sincerity of his belief in the value of imperial conquest...Never once did those around Hitler become disillusioned and suggest that he was being cynical or dishonest. There is hardly a justification for us to disagree. Hitler's idea of living space was not just a propaganda image. It was the germ of a serious policy proposal.'
(Housden 2000, p.54)

7. Anti-Bolshevism

The Bolsheviks were a faction in pre-1917 Russia that developed into the Communist Party. Even before Operation Barbarossa was launched against the Soviet Union in 1941, Nazi propaganda was fiercely opposed to Bolshevism, or Communism in any form, which it saw as essentially Jewish. The Communist call to the workers of the world to unite ran directly counter to German nationalism, and to notions of Social Darwinism. Nazis saw Communism as a plot to prevent the survival of the fittest, in fact to undermine human evolution. The anti-Bolshevik propaganda took on a new ferocity once Germany was at war with the Soviet Union.

8. Anti-Semitism

Anti-Jewish propaganda probably accounted for more than any other kind, from the 1920s onwards. Many historians, such as Daniel Goldhagen, think that anti-Semitism was the only ideological belief to which Hitler sincerely and consistently adhered. Bracher writes that it was essential to Nazism because a totalitarian system needs an 'absolute enemy' for mobilisation of political and social forces and as a distraction from its problems - and that the Jews were this enemy (Bracher 1971, p.316).

The propaganda message

The essential propaganda message was that the Jews were:

- inferior to Aryans physically and morally
- to be despised because they had no homeland
- parasites who took jobs from true Germans
- dirty and lazy
- conspiring to destroy Germany
- natural-born criminals and liars
- a sexually voracious threat to Aryan honour and racial purity
- the leaders of an international Communist plot
- as international capitalists, responsible for poverty and injustice.

Propaganda and anti-Semitism

Several contradictions can readily be seen in this list. Jews were inferior and yet a dangerous enemy. They were job stealers but lazy. They were both Communists and capitalists. Nevertheless, all these claims were made in various forms of propaganda. Newspapers such as Julius Streicher's notorious *Der Stürmer* were full of irrational anti-Semitic propaganda. The example below was printed shortly after the Reichstag Fire in 1932:

'It is not hard to discover the true cause of worldwide Marxist-Bolshevist criminality. It is as clear as daylight. One need only open one's eyes to see it. The truth is that both the parties that want civil war, that hate the Fatherland and that acknowledge only an "Internationale", were founded by Jews. The Jew Karl Marx gave his name to the movement and wrote its manifesto. The Jews La Salle, Kautsky, Bernstein, Hilferding, Moses, Rosa Luxemburg, Liebknecht, Munzenberg and others still lead the Socialist and Communist parties. The leaders and rabble rousers of the 1918 November Revolution were all Jews…The Marxist movement is, in reality, a Jewish movement. Its goal is to make the confused, roused masses into an enormous army of Jewish slaves. This army would be used to reach the goal of Jewish world domination.'

Government posters, newspaper cartoons and even school textbooks portray the Jew as ugly, grasping, fat and greedy, and physically defective. Films such as *Jud Suss (Suss the Jew)* and *Der ewige Jude (The Eternal Jew)*, both made in 1940, portray a similar image. The latter, a documentary, emphasises the fact that the Jew is 'an eternal wanderer', having no homeland, which in Nazi ideology justifies contempt rather than pity (in reality the Jews were expelled from their homeland by the Romans).

MAIN POINTS - Section 1.2

- Some historians see Nazi propaganda merely as a cynical means of gaining and retaining power. Others, argue that the ideology it conveyed was a motivating force.
- Nazi propaganda promoted eight main goals - (1) a Völksgemeinschaft (2) stable family life (3) the Führerprinzip (4) Social Darwinism (5) Strength through Work (6) the need for Lebensraum (7) anti-Communism and (8) anti-Semitism
- The primary goal of Nazi propaganda was to restructure German society so that old loyalties were replaced by a new heightened national awareness. The idea was that believing in a 'national' or 'people's' community (a Völksgemeinschaft) would override people's other beliefs.

- The Führerprinzip went hand in hand with the Völksgemeinschaft, producing the slogan 'One people, one homeland, one Führer'.
- Racist Nazi propaganda reflected the belief in Social Darwinism - the idea that Germans were a master race and others - especially Jews, Slavs and Communists were inferior.
- Propaganda was designed with practical ends in mind. The Strength through Work campaigns for example were designed to increase productivity at work.
- There is a debate over whether propaganda promoting Lebensraum was designed to encourage enthusiasm for the government or to promote a serious policy objective.

Activity 6.2 Propaganda messages

ITEM 1 The Führer

Ein Volk, ein Reich, ein Führer!

This poster has the caption 'one people, one state, one Leader'.

ITEM 2 Propaganda aimed at children

Mein Führer!

(Das Kind spricht:)

Ich kenne dich wohl und habe dich lieb
       wie Vater und Mutter.
Ich will dir immer gehorsam sein
       wie Vater und Mutter.
Und wenn ich groß bin, helfe ich dir
       wie Vater und Mutter,
Und freuen sollst du dich an mir
       wie Vater und Mutter!

A page from a Nazi textbook produced in 1935, a first reader. The girl says: 'My Leader. I know you well and love you like Father and Mother. I shall always obey you like Father and Mother. And when I grow up, I will help you like Father and Mother. And you will be proud of me like Father and Mother'.

ITEM 3 Strength through Joy

The man in charge of the German Labour Front (DAF), the organisation set up to take over the function of trade unions, was Robert Ley. In his view, the Nazi triumph over trade unionism signalled the end of class struggle in Germany and the creation of a Völksgemeinschaft. Whilst there was a great deal of working-class cynicism about the DAF, its recreational branch, the Strength through Joy (KdF) programme, achieved genuine popularity. Activities organised by the KdF ranged from concerts, theatre, exhibitions, sport and hiking to folk dancing and adult education. But by far the most popular activity on the KdF programme was tourism. By 1938, a special KdF office was organising holidays and travel for c.10.3 million Germans. The age of mass tourism had arrived. Workers seized the opportunity to travel - until then a middle-class privilege. To the Nazis, mass tourism promised two great benefits. First, it was thought that those who benefited from holidays organised by the state would be more likely to be reconciled to the aims of the state. And second, tourism presented new opportunities to promote national integration. Excursions within Germany allowed participants to acquaint themselves with the features and customs of unfamiliar regions. Meanwhile, journeys into other parts of the world - for example on the famed KdF cruise ships - gave travellers from different parts of the country an opportunity to get to know each other better. Popular though these holidays were, the ulterior motive was evident in the very title. A DAF spokesman said: 'We did not send out workers on holidays or on ships or build them huge seaside resorts because it was fun for us or for the individual who can make use of these facilities. We did it only to preserve the working capacity of the individual and to have him return to his workplace strengthened and refocused'.

Adapted from Monteath 2000.

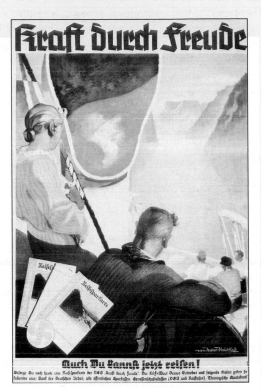

This poster was produced for the Strength through Joy programme. It advertises the cruises organised by Strength through Joy. Although these cruises were presented as being models of classlessness, the majority of people allowed to go on them came from the middle classes.

Questions

1. a) What message is being conveyed by each of the three pictures in Items 1-3?
   b) Explain how these messages fit in with Nazi ideology.

2. Using Items 1 and 3, explain how the ideas of Völksgemeinschaft and Führerprinzip are linked.

3. Using Items 2 and 3, suggest reasons why the Nazis chose to produce propaganda like this.

1.3 How popular were the Nazis in the period 1934-45?

A controversial question

The question of the Nazis' popularity with ordinary Germans is a controversial one. After the war, most Germans were reluctant to admit to having supported the Nazis. Even nations that had fought against Germany found it easier to contemplate post-war cooperation with its new governments if they could blame Hitler and other top Nazis rather than Germans as a whole. Historians tended to echo this. As Detlev Peukert says:

'The uniform readiness of the Germans...to keep doing their "duty" to the end, as soldiers or as workers on the "home front", was generally explained by historians in one of two ways: in terms of seduction theory, or of a supervision theory.' (Peukert 1987, p.67)

In other words, the theory was that most Germans were either seduced by effective propaganda or forced to conform by the terror of the Gestapo.

It is generally agreed that fear of the Gestapo and of the concentration camps played an important role, but both Robert Gellately (2001) and Laurence Rees (1997) have shown that the Gestapo depended heavily on denunciations from the public. Eric Johnson also mentions this dependence, referring to research by Hermann Weber, and refutes the idea that Germans were cowed into submission by the threat of terror:

'Many, probably most, still believed that the police and the laws were there to protect them. Nazi terror posed no real threat to most ordinary Germans...Most ordinary Germans had an experience during the years of the Third Reich wholly unlike that of the Nazi regime's targeted enemies.' (Johnson 2000, pp.253-54)

If this is true, does the lack of coordinated opposition to the Nazis mean, that, in reality, the Nazi regime was genuinely popular? One problem with answering this question lies with the sources. The problem is outlined in Box 6.10.

BOX 6.10 **The problem with sources**

There are four main sources for assessing the Nazis' popularity. Each has its own problems for historians:

1. Nazi reports, compiled by the SD (secret police), the Gestapo and party agencies.
These could hardly be expected to be unbiased. On the other hand, the regime did value accurate information on public opinion, on which it could base propaganda.

2. Reports from agents of SOPADE, the SPD (Social Democratic Party) in exile.
Again, we have to question the impartiality of these reports, though many speak of Hitler's popularity and quote positive assessments of him.

3. Plebiscites and elections.
After 1933, figures from plebiscites and elections cannot be relied on since voting was rigged and results misrepresented. One can only speculate that anything less than a 100% vote for Hitler (eg 89.9% in favour of him heading both state and government in 1934) suggests a significant opposition.

4. Post-war surveys.
Several studies have sought information from Germans who lived through the Nazi era. These are interesting, but they rely on people's subjective memories, and on what they now want to believe - or want others to believe - about their past attitude to Nazism.

Popular appeal

According to David Welch, historians have begun to challenge the view that Nazi propaganda was 'the war that Hitler won' (Welch 1993, p.5). Welch points out that there are two popular misconceptions about propaganda:

1. Propaganda always aims to change views and persuade. Actually, it more often reinforces or channels existing views.
2. Propaganda always consists of lies. It usually contains some truths and half-truths.

Applying this to Nazi Germany, he argues that propaganda was important but also that:

'Nazi policies and propaganda reflected (many of) the aspirations of large sections of the population.' (Welch 1993, p.9)

Many people were prepared to desert traditional allegiances because they saw the Nazi Party as serving their interests. The propaganda simply reinforced this view.

In addition, several historians, including Welch, have claimed that the Völksgemeinschaft ideal and the Führer myth (see below) were effective as propaganda because they tapped into existing feelings. Noakes and Pridham write:

'A crucial element in popular consent to the regime was the fact that Nazism embodied, albeit in an extreme form, many of the basic attitudes of a very large section of the German people. Apart from the obvious nationalism and militarism, people also approved of its cultural conservatism, its hostility to modern movements in the arts.' (Noakes & Pridham 2001, p.380)

They go on to say that conservative Germans approved of the regime's hostility towards 'sexual licence' as well as towards Jews, gypsies, homosexuals, tramps and the 'work-shy'.

Völksgemeinschaft and the Führer myth

As mentioned in Section 1.2 above, the notion of the national community went hand in hand with a belief in Hitler. He was seen as the embodiment of the will of the German people, the man whose iron determination would free Germany from the continuing humiliation of the Versailles Settlement and make it once again a triumphant world power. An important factor in the regime's popularity was the Führer myth. Vital to this was the separation of Hitler from the party as a whole. Whereas an extreme 'structuralist' historian such as Hans Mommsen might see this as evidence of Hitler not being fully in charge, a greater number of historians veer towards 'intentionalism' on this question, seeing this separation as part of a plan - whether masterminded by Hitler or by Goebbels.

This separation meant that people could complain about the party and about specific policies without rejecting Hitler. It was often assumed that if only Hitler knew about a particular injustice, he would set it right. Peukert writes:

'The Führer myth made it possible for people to give voice to everyday "grumbles" and yet consent to the overall dispensation. This basic consent, articulated primarily in the Führer myth, comprised approval of personal, authoritarian control, enthusiastic support for the posture of "decisive action" and the imposition of order through terror, and uncritical applause for both the real and the specious propaganda achievements of the system.' (Peukert 1987, p.73)

One result of the Führer myth was that Hitler was often seen in religious terms, as a kind of Messiah - see Box 6.11.

However, as Peukert also says, the Führer myth

depended on foreign policy successes being wholly attributed to Hitler. As a result, Hitler became even more popular after the plebiscite which returned the Saar area to Germany in January 1935, with his remilitarisation of the Rhineland in 1936 (against the terms of the Treaty of Versailles), and with Anschluss with Austria in 1938. A SOPADE report notes:

'There is no mistaking the enormous personal gains in credibility and prestige that Hitler has made, mainly perhaps among workers. The fact that Austria was subjugated by force has had little or no effect so far on the way the event is being judged.' (quoted in Peukert 1987, p.69)

It follows that when the war started to go badly for Germany, Hitler's popularity declined. There was less desire to hear him on the radio, and so he made fewer appearances. Peukert says:

'For most Germans, the Führer myth was dead before he took his own life.' (Peukert 1987, p.75)

Welch says that according to the SD, loyalty to Hitler began to wane after Stalingrad (February 1943) and Hitler's refusal to address the public at this time. It only secured a short-lived revival after the 1944 bomb attempt on Hitler's life (Welch 1993, p.87).

Jewish policy

Saul Friedlander is another historian who notes that Hitler's personal popularity enabled people to grumble about the party or conditions without blaming Hitler (Friedlander 1997, Chapter 4). Significantly, he adds that sympathy with Hitler meant buying into his anti-Semitism. Other historians have argued that Nazi popularity was partly due to the regime's anti-Semitism, which reflected that of the population. The most extreme proponent of this view is Daniel Goldhagen (1997). But Friedlander adds:

'Some groups of the population not only rejected anti-Jewish violence and hesitated to sever their economic ties with Jews, but even at times showed signs of sympathy for the victims.' (Friedlander 1997, p.118)

According to Israeli historian David Bankier, most Germans approved of the Nuremberg Laws (1935 - see Section 2.2 below) because they approved of segregation and thought laws would help maintain public order by preventing unofficial violence against the Jews. Friedlander reaches the following conclusion:

'To sum up, the vast majority of the population approved of the Nuremberg laws because they identified with the racialist policy and because a permanent framework of discrimination had been created that would end the reign of terror and set precise limits to anti-Semitic activities.' (Friedlander 1997, p.163)

Who did the Nazis appeal to?

At least up until the war, Nazi popularity benefited from the regime's policies on law and order and its economic successes. Hitler was perceived as a 'firm hand' not afraid to clamp down on crime and socially deviant behaviour. Ironically, on one notable occasion when Hitler was seen to be personally involved in keeping order - the 'Night of the Long Knives' in 1934 (see Unit 5, Section 1.3) - he was widely applauded for organising mass murder. Propaganda helped to persuade people that concentration camps were necessary and beneficial, either turning 'asocials' into good Germans through work and discipline or at least isolating them from the rest of society.

The Nazis were also popular on account of their economic achievements, especially for ending inflation and unemployment (see Section 3.2 below and Box 6.12).

How popular were the Nazis with the workers?

Welch notes that Tim Mason argues that Nazi propaganda was an unmitigated failure among industrial workers, an argument built on Ian Kershaw's claim that the ideal of Völksgemeinschaft had little effect on behaviour in largely Catholic Bavaria. Against this, however, Welch argues that, while propaganda did not eliminate social barriers, it did achieve a heightened sense of national awareness, which led to social stability (Welch 1993, p.58).

Welch says that the SOPADE reports show a mixed response from the workers. The provision of sports and other facilities by Strength through Joy had some impact on working-class perception of the party, but some workers were disgruntled that they had to build their own swimming pools in their spare time, without pay. In addition, the fact that wage increases were only made possible by overtime had a negative effect on morale (Welch 1993, p.58). On the other hand, whilst in 1933 over a third of the working population was unemployed, by the outbreak of the Second World War the regime had achieved nearly full employment - though a large proportion of this was due to military production.

Conan Fischer (1995, p. 62) claims that studies show that the Nazis did have a large working-class following, and that the majority verdict is that they had wide class appeal. He also says that some works suggest that they especially appealed to women. Falter (1996), however has shown that women were slightly less likely to vote Nazi. Some women must have objected to Nazi attempts to deprive them of all social roles other than that of wife and mother, but there is little evidence of the regime being less popular with women than with men.

What age groups did the Nazi regime appeal to?

Interestingly, while the Nazis appealed to middle-aged conservatives, they were even more popular with young people. They liked the Nazi regime's contempt for intellect and its slogan 'Youth must be led by youth'. Völksgemeinschaft offered an alternative to the Weimar establishment, and young people often rebelled against their parents by preferring HJ (Hitler Jugend - Hitler Youth) and the BDM (Bund Deutsche Madel - League of German Maidens) to Sunday School. For young men, the regime offered employment, and promotion to positions of responsibility. Noakes and Pridham identify youth appeal as a major factor in the high level of consent achieved by the regime (Noakes & Pridham 2000, p.185). By the late 1930s, there were various youth groups opposed to Nazi regimentation - such as the Edelweiss Pirates, but youth propaganda was generally effective.

The overall pattern of support

The overall pattern of support for the Nazi regime in one particular city is explored in Box 6.13

BOX 6.13 Support in one German city - Cologne

Historian Eric Johnson and sociologist Karl-Heinz Reuband conducted a survey of 300 Cologne residents in 1993. Cologne had a relatively low support for the Nazi regime. But 55% of those who replied said they believed in Nazism at the time (and possibly those who did not reply were Nazis!). There was more support reported by educated people, and by men. Over half (53%) said they had listened to foreign broadcasts (which was illegal); 27% had told anti-Nazi jokes (subject to severe penalties, especially during the war); 9% had helped victims of the regime; and 4% had been in outlawed youth groups.
Adapted from Johnson 2000.

Depoliticising

A noticeable development in the current historical debate over the popularity of the Nazi regime has been a recognition of how the regime achieved passive consent by making people withdraw from public life, and by encouraging them to leave politics to party members. It is now widely agreed that this 'depoliticising' was an important factor in consent to Nazi policies:

'As National Socialism penetrated traditional social milieux and institutional structures, partly breaking them up, partly taking them over, so it drove their former members into the private domain. Views that had become politically taboo or criminal could be maintained only within the family circle or among close friends, if at all. Even politically-minded people withdrew into privacy in face of the constant pressure to conform.' (Peukert 1986, p.77)

Noakes and Pridham give a slightly different emphasis:

'On the one hand, [the Nazi regime] attempted to organise, control, and mobilise [Germans] by requiring repeated gestures of conformity...On the other hand, it aimed to depoliticise them by turning them into passive consumers who listened to undemanding radio programmes, interspersed with the occasional patriotic but not overtly Nazi one, followed the fashions, and aspired to purchase the ultimate consumer durable, the new Volkswagen.' (Noakes & Pridham 2000, p.185)

Welch reaches a similar conclusion:

'By turning large sections of the population into passive consumers, the Nazi technique of organisation and atomisation led to a gradual process of depoliticisation which effectively achieved the desired consent.' (Welch 1993, p.65)

MAIN POINTS - Section 1.3

- The question of the Nazis' popularity is controversial. After the war, people found it easier contemplate post-war cooperation if they could blame Hitler and other top Nazis rather than Germans as a whole.
- It is difficult to assess how popular the Nazi regime was because the source material presents problems.
- Since propaganda (1) often reinforces or channels existing views and (2) contains some truths and half-truths, the argument that the Germans were conned into supporting the regime does not stand.
- Some historians believe that Nazi ideology - Völkgemeinschaft, the Führer myth and anti-Semitism

- had widespread appeal. Economic prosperity also added to the regime's appeal.
- The regime was not popular with all sections of the population. Some historians claim that it was particularly unpopular with workers. Conversely, it seems to have been particularly popular with the young.
- Recently, there has been a recognition of how the regime achieved passive consent by 'depoliticising' them - making people withdraw from public life, and by encouraging them to leave politics to party members.

Activity 6.3 How popular was the Nazi regime?

ITEM 1 Contemporary accounts

(i) Hitler is still outside the line of fire of criticism, generally speaking at least, but the messianic belief in him has more or less died out. People do not criticise him, whereas, for example, Goebbels is almost universally loathed even among the Nazis. As far as the economic future is concerned, everyone is feeling uncertain, although the large numbers of people who have got work through rearmament regard this work creation as a great feat. In general, one can say that almost everybody blames the previous system for failing to get the unemployed, and particularly youth, off the streets. The reduction in unemployment, rearmament, and the drive it shows in its foreign policy are the big points in favour of Hitler's policy and, on the basis of his own observations, he personally believes that only a tenth of the population does not recognize these facts.

These comments were made by a part-Jewish teacher to an SPD contact in 1936 (quoted in Noakes & Pridham 2000).

(ii) There can be no doubt that the Nazis have succeeded in persuading the masses to leave politics to the men at the top. The Nazis try, as they say, to turn everybody into committed National Socialists. They will never succeed in that. People tend rather to turn inwardly away from Nazism. But they are ensuring that people are no longer interested in anything.

These comments were made by a SPD agent in Westphalia in 1936 (quoted in Noakes & Pridham 2000).

(iii) And the world? The best thing is to shut your eyes to it and to stop hearing and seeing all the dreadful fuss and bother that is getting more and more confusing and difficult to sort out. No-one has any idea where it is all going. Most people have completely stopped even asking, and are just sticking to the tiring daily business of shopping and thinking about food. The emptiness inside one is getting more and more noticeable.

This is an extract from a wartime diary written in Germany (quoted in Peukert 1987).

ITEM 2 Historians' views

(i) Welch points out that protest could and did take place - over such controversial humanitarian issues as in the 'euthanasia question'. This, he argues undermines the argument put forward by some 'apologists' (ie those who defend the idea that the majority of the German population was not to blame for the actions of the Nazi regime). Their argument is based on the idea that terror and repression alone deterred any dissent. Welch accepts that dictatorship gradually corrupts the moral fibre of its citizens and that resistance became increasingly difficult as the authority of the Nazi state became more firmly established. Nevertheless, he believes that it is important and legitimate to ask why there was so little resistance, particularly at the beginning.

Adapted from Welch 1993.

(ii) Hitler aimed for an authoritarian and leader-oriented system, but one that had popular backing and his regime was deeply concerned, one might say, even paranoid about popular opinion. Germans were expected not just to adjust to the new regime but to be engaged. In their successful cultivation of popular opinion, the Nazis did not need to use widespread terror against the population. Many Germans went along, not because they were mindless robots, but because they convinced themselves of Hitler's advantages and of the 'positive' sides of the new dictatorship. There was a tendency to excuse Hitler if things went wrong and to blame such problems on the 'little Hitlers' - the leaders below the Führer. Even the most educated Germans found reasons for supporting the system and were less regimented or forced to conform than is often assumed. Many Germans supported the crackdown on 'criminals' and were pleased to see them go to concentration camps. As the camps were created, they were widely publicised and even the local populations living near the camps were generally in favour of them. Most people had no direct confrontation with the Gestapo or the camps. While they read about the People's Court, few attended its sessions. In other words, they had second-hand knowledge based on what they saw in films, heard on the radio or found out by word of mouth.

Adapted from Gellately 2001.

ITEM 3 Propaganda

HER ZU UNS!

Hinein in die Hitler-Jugend

This is a recruiting poster for the Hitler Youth. The caption reads: 'Join us! Be part of the Hitler Youth'.

Questions

1. 'The Nazi regime was genuinely popular with the mass of the German population'. Using Items 1-3 and your own knowledge, give arguments for and against this view.
2. a) Judging from Item 1, how did the Nazis gain consent for their regime?
   b) What are the problems with dealing with this sort of source material?
3. Using Item 2 and your own knowledge explain why there was so little resistance to the Nazi regime.
4. How would you expect most German people to respond to the poster in Item 3? Explain your answer.

2 Terror and persecution

Key issues

1. To what extent was Nazi Germany a police state?
2. What measures were taken against minorities before 1939?
3. What measures led to the Holocaust?

2.1 To what extent was Nazi Germany a police state?

Key questions and interpretations

Most definitions of 'police state' refer to a totalitarian state in which citizens are controlled or closely supervised by a political police force. In a 'totalitarian' state a single party, typically led by one man, has complete control over mass communications, the Armed Forces and the economy, and demands total support from the people (for a more detailed discussion of Germany as a totalitarian state, see Unit 5, Section 2.1).

A question, therefore, is: How far were the German people controlled by the police? This question, in turn, relates closely to that asked in Unit 6, Section 1.3, namely: How popular were the Nazis? The more popular we perceive the Nazis to

be, the less we will see the German people being forced into obeying the regime against their will. A secondary question implied by this is: How far was society genuinely Nazified by propaganda and reorganisation? In other words, were ordinary Germans persuaded or pushed?

Immediately after the war, historians in countries that had fought against Germany tended to see Nazism as a product of the German 'national character'. A.J.P. Taylor (1964) is one example. German historians, on the other hand, were more likely to see it as the product of the Versailles settlement and the Depression. Neil Gregor points out that, by the 1950s, a new image was emerging, both in West Germany and elsewhere - that of a repressive totalitarian regime which used propaganda to dupe its population and terror to cow people into submission. Gregor sums up this view as follows:

'The Nazi leadership had been guilty of committing appalling crimes; the mass of the German population had been innocent' (Gregor 2001, p.10)

This unit focuses on a third view which began to emerge in the early 1980s and to which historians increasingly subscribe. According to this view, while the Nazi leadership deserve much of the blame, they received a great deal of help from ordinary Germans.

The Nazis' police force (see also Unit 5, Section 2.2)

Historians agree that Hitler had little respect for the law, although he frequently used it to achieve his ends when it suited him - as in the legal revolution of 1933, exploiting the traditional German respect for legality (see Unit 5, Section 1.2). He declared himself to be the ultimate source of German law, and Nazi lawyers such as Werner Best produced pseudo-legal justifications for this principle of 'Führer law'. However, to enforce his will, Hitler turned not to the courts, but to the SS and its leader, Heinrich Himmler, who was unwaveringly loyal to the Führer - see Box 6.14.

BOX 6.14 Himmler and the SS

Himmler's SS was rewarded for its role in the 'Night of the Long Knives' in 1934 (see Unit 5, Section 1.3 above) by being given the status of an independent organisation within the Nazi Party. During 1933-34, Himmler gained control of all the regional police forces, including that of Prussia, whose police had until then been controlled by Göring. Himmler's power was consolidated on 17 June 1936 when Hitler issued a decree which merged the police and the SS and made Himmler Chief of German Police. The removal of the police from the control of the Reich Ministry of the Interior was contested by its head, Frick, who insisted on Himmler's title being amended to 'Reichsführer SS and Chief of German Police within the Reich Ministry of the Interior'. In theory, therefore, Chief of German Police Himmler was responsible to Frick. This was made meaningless, however, by the fact that as Head of the SS Himmler answered only to Hitler. Besides, Hitler persistently favoured Himmler over Frick and eventually, in August 1943, Himmler took over the Ministry of the Interior. Alan Bullock makes the point that to call Nazi Germany a police state is misleading, since what Hitler and Himmler aimed to achieve by the 1936 decree was to remove the police (who were traditionally the instrument for the enforcement of the law) from control by the state. By merging the police with the SS, the organisation which more than any other was identified as the instrument of the Führer's arbitrary authority to act outside the law, Hitler ensured that the police would be controlled by him personally and not by the state as a whole.
Adapted from Bullock 1991.

Police powers

Even before 1936, the Reichstag Fire Decree (see Unit 5, Section 1.1) had given the Gestapo sweeping powers - which it exercised throughout the duration of the regime. Most importantly, the Gestapo could take suspects into 'protective custody' and hold them indefinitely without any right to trial or appeal.

Increasingly, members of the Gestapo became a law unto themselves, independent of the courts. They often used torture - officially sanctioned by Hitler during the war. If a court acquitted someone whom the Gestapo considered to be guilty, or gave a sentence they considered too short, they could rearrest the accused either immediately or on release and hold them in custody or send them to a concentration camp. Moreover, this was all with Hitler's backing.

In addition, as discussed in Unit 5, Section 2.2, an increasing emphasis was placed on 'preventive policing', which meant imprisoning someone considered likely to commit a crime without waiting for them to commit it. Kershaw says that the police were encouraged to see themselves as a force fighting internal enemies of the state. In practice, this meant Jews, Communists, Freemasons, Jehovah's Witnesses, homosexuals, Gypsies and the 'work-shy', as well as ordinary criminals. (Kershaw 1991, p.83).

Punishable offences

Two other factors that might justify calling Nazi Germany a police state were the increasing number of activities that became offences and the harshness of the penalties for them. Concentration camps (see Unit 5, Section 2.2) had barbaric regimes and the death penalty was introduced for a wide range of crimes. In the wake of the Reichstag fire (1933) one of these was arson. The penalty was retrospectively - and therefore illegally - applied to the man accused of starting the fire, Marius van der Lubbe (see Unit 5, Section 1.1).

A second decree announced on the same day as the Reichstag Fire Decree, 'Against Treason to the German Nation and against Treasonable Activities' enlarged the concept of treason, giving wider scope for arrests. The Malicious Practices Act of 21 March 1933 banned critical or offensive remarks about the state or its leaders - which included jokes. This was essentially a law against freedom of speech - even private speech. It was especially significant, as we will see later, because it opened the door to a huge number of denunciations.

As noted in Unit 5, Section 2.2, many ordinary Germans were in effect turned into political criminals by laws that banned what in other countries were normal activities. During the war, the law, and the Gestapo's arbitrary application of it, became even harsher. Otherwise law-abiding people were even executed for telling jokes about Hitler or listening to foreign radio (see below).

Persuasion and terror

There is a debate about the extent to which the Nazis used persuasion and the extent to which they relied on terror - see Box 6.15.

BOX 6.15 | The debate over persuasion and terror

Eric Johnson argues that most Germans did not live in fear of a knock on the door from the Gestapo. Alan Bullock, in common with many historians, points out that many Germans were impressed by the regime's apparent achievements, such as ending unemployment and curbing inflation, and that propaganda made the most of these successes. He adds that failure to attend national celebrations, such as that for Hitler's birthday, or at least to hang out a swastika flag, was noted by the Block Warden (the Nazi in charge of the neighbourhood), and might lead to a person being marked as 'politically unreliable'. This could lead to the person not being promoted at work, to dismissal, or to arrest. The same applied to a failure to contribute to the supposedly voluntary Winter Help or Days of National Solidarity collections. But, for most Germans, terror was always a veiled possibility rather than something witnessed at first hand. Bullock asserts that, during the mid-1930s, the implicit threat of it was more important than its use. Julian Reed-Purvis agrees. He argues that the Gestapo revelled in its reputation for utter ruthlessness. This reputation was largely a creation of propaganda designed to hide the Gestapo's structural and bureaucratic weaknesses. A more sinister note is sounded by Detlev Peukert, who says that many Germans approved of terror as a means of ensuring social conformity. He argues that, even if such attitudes fell short of a demand for the death penalty or the gas chamber (though these demands were common enough), they prove the existence of popular consent to a specific form of terror, namely dealing with non-standard behaviour, or non-standard categories of person, by bundling the individuals concerned into camps and subjecting them to drill even if not to annihilation.

Adapted from Johnson 2000, Bullock 1991, Reed-Purvis 1999 and Peukert 1987.

Denunciations

Julian Reed-Purvis points out that, as late as the 1990s, historians were still giving the idea that there was a member of the Nazis' secret police on every street corner during the period 1933-45. He quotes historian William Carr who wrote in 1991 that:

'No one was immune from the surveillance of some branch of the ubiquitous secret police.' (quoted in Reed-Purvis 1999, p.5)

In recent years, however, this view has been strongly challenged, especially by Robert Gellately in his book *Backing Hitler* (2001). Gellately conducted extensive research into surviving Gestapo records - which were kept with a care and precision surprising for an organisation best known for its brutality. His work reveals just how few Gestapo agents there

were and just how much they depended on the support of ordinary Germans who voluntarily denounced their neighbours, colleagues and family. There were so many denunciations that the regime became concerned about the Gestapo's increased workload. Hitler himself was worried about denunciations undermining the sense of national unity.

Persecution of the Jews

Gellately studied records relating to denunciations of Jews and non-Jews for breaking race laws. He found that in one of the few areas where records survived, Lower Franconia (see map on p.iv), even before there were official race laws, Nazis and non-Nazis had begun to inform the authorities about Jews whom they suspected of having sexual relations with non-Jews. Lower Franconia, Gellately points out, had given relatively weak support to the new Nazi regime, and was not especially known for anti-Semitism.

The table in Box 6.16 shows how the Lower Franconian Gestapo received their initial information about cases of 'race defilement', 'befriending Jews' and criticising anti-Semitic policies. The majority of cases began with reports from ordinary Germans. If we assume that most of the 'Source not known' cases were also based on such reports, the total of cases based on denunciations from ordinary non-Nazi Party members of the public is close to 70%. Gellately points out that on this evidence the Gestapo was 'primarily reactive', only actively tracking down one case out of 210. Gellately concludes that:

'Without the active collaboration of the general population it would have been next to impossible for the Gestapo to enforce these kinds of racial policies.' (Gellately 2001, p.135)

BOX 6.16 | Gestapo case files from Lower Franconia 1933-45

Sources of information	Number of cases	%
1. Reports from the population	123	59
2. Information from other control organisations	8	4
3. Observations by Gestapo and Agents	1	0
4. Information via communal or state authorities	0	0
5. Statements at interrogations	26	12
6. Information from businesses	1	0
7. Information via Nazi Party, Nazi organisations, or Party members	27	13
8. Source not known	24	12
TOTAL	**210**	**100**

This table shows the number of cases (and percentage of cases) dealt with by the Gestapo in Lower Franconia in the period 1933-45.

He adds that a study by Sarah Gordon on the region of Düsseldorf found similar levels of denunciations. Ian Kershaw reaches similar conclusions (Kershaw 1991, p.84).

The motivation of denouncers

Gellately also comments on why people informed. He refers to another study, by historian Richard Mann, of 825 Gestapo cases in Düsseldorf. Mann identified only 26% of cases as beginning with a denunciation. However, he found that only about 25% of these seemed to have been motivated by loyalty to the regime, patriotism or hatred of 'national enemies'. Most had 'primarily selfish motives', such as annoyance with a neighbour, business rivalry or a family dispute (Gellately 2001, pp.136-37). Gellately explains what was going on as follows:

'First of all, denouncers took advantage of the state's means of coercion for selfish purposes, and in that respect citizens in Nazi Germany were not entirely unlike those in other "totalitarian" regimes. They rendered a service to the state by providing information and the state rendered a service to them by settling a conflict or removing one of the parties involved. In all of these systems, citizens lost many of the "traditional" means for resolving conflicts, but they soon adopted and came to rely on direct access to the means of coercion.' (Gellately 2001, pp.137-38)

He also argues that, although the motives of most informants were selfish, their awareness of what would probably happen to those denounced - especially Jews - suggests a degree of support for the system and a growing social consensus (pp.139-40).

Laurence Rees acknowledges the predominantly selfish motives of denouncers, but also makes another point: He argues that:

'Denunciations became a way in which Germans could make their voices heard in a system that had turned away from democracy' (Rees 1997, p.66)

In other words, denunciations allowed politically disempowered individuals to seize a little power for themselves.

Foreign radio

One of the richest sources of denunciations was a by-product of Goebbels' propaganda campaign, namely, his encouragement of widespread radio ownership. Despite the fact that many radio sets were designed to be too weak to receive foreign stations, most people at some point listened to foreign radio in an attempt to find out what was really going on. This was especially true during the Second World War. Listening to foreign radio broadcasts became illegal on the day that Germany invaded Poland, namely 1 September 1939. Gellately notes that:

'By September 1941, in keeping with the further radicalisation of the terror that set in after the beginning of the war against the USSR, there was a first newspaper report of two death penalties for listening to foreign radio.' (Gellately 2001, p.186)

In a study of selected cases, Gellately (2001, p.188) found that, despite the seriousness of the consequences, 73% of such cases began with information provided by members of the public. He also quotes a study carried out in northern Germany by historian Gerhard Paul, who found that 84% of accusations came from denunciations, including anonymous letters.

A surprising finding in Gellately's work was that the proportion of Gestapo cases arising from denunciations was actually higher for non-racial crimes than for racial ones. He adds that this finding is backed up by other studies. Another interesting finding was that men were far more likely to be denouncers than were women (Gellately 2001, pp.188 & 197).

Who and where were the Gestapo?

It seems, then, that the Gestapo had no shortage of informants. This was fortunate for them since another finding that undermines their traditional image is that there was a shortage of Gestapo officers. Far from being 'everywhere', there were so few of them relative to the population that they had no choice but to rely on denunciations. As pointed out in Unit 5, Section 2.2, in Lower Franconia there were only 28 Gestapo officers and 22 were assigned to the town of Würzburg, with almost half of these being administrators. Reed-Purvis writes:

'The Gestapo, outside the big cities, was understaffed and struggled to cope with the steady increase in its workload. The town of Northeim had one officer stationed there, and most German towns of 10,000 people never saw a Gestapo officer. The usual roll call at Würzburg was 21 officers.' (Reed-Purvis 1999, p.6)

Both Rees and Reed-Purvis refute another myth about the Gestapo, namely that they were all fanatical Nazis. Reed-Purvis says that in Würzburg, only two of the 21 had been Nazi Party members before 1933, while in Saarbrucken in 1935, only 10% were SS members, and 50% Nazi Party members. Reed-Purvis concludes:

'The degree of Nazification in the Gestapo was similar to that in German society generally...The secret police were no more Nazified than the rest of German society.' (Reed-Purvis 1999, pp.6-7)

Rees adds that:

'What actually happened was that most of the police remained in their posts when the Nazi regime began, but they did not have to carry on as usual; they were now off the leash. Under the Nazis, the German police could act in ways which, for many of them, must have been liberating - disregarding the rights of suspects and pursuing what in their view was a strong law and order policy.' (Rees 1997, p.70)

Conclusion

While the threat of Gestapo brutality and of the concentration camps did prevent opposition to the regime and help to ensure conformity, the evidence now strongly suggests that most Germans at least passively accepted the regime, and many actively supported it. At the very least, they were prepared to use it for their own ends. Nazi Germany was a police state in that the government successfully used control of the media, propaganda and the threat of the Gestapo to keep people in line. However, it was not a police state in the sense of the majority of people being forced to do things to which they were completely opposed.

MAIN POINTS - Section 2.1

- Historians have moved from seeing the Nazi regime as (1) the product of the German 'national character' to (2) a regime in which the Nazi leadership was guilty and the people innocent to (3) a regime in which there was wide support for the government.
- The police were merged with the SS under Himmler. The joint organisation became independent from the Ministry of the Interior. The Gestapo increasingly became a law unto itself, acting without restraint and overriding rulings by the Courts.
- Previously ordinary activities such as gossip and listening to foreign radio were made illegal, often punishable by death.
- The threat of terror did much to keep people in line.
- There were relatively few Gestapo officers, and they relied on willingly supplied denunciations by the public.

Activity 6.4 Was Nazi Germany a police state?

ITEM 1 Würzburg, 1943

A colleague heard Railway Inspector Max Heinrich (born 1896) and his colleague Hans Vogel (born 1891) make negative remarks about the situation in which Germany found itself. Word of the treasonous remarks was reported to local Nazi Party headquarters by a party member and another railway employee, Friedrich Henning (born 1909). Henning was asked by the Nazi Party to listen attentively to the remarks of Heinrich and Vogel and to take exact note of times and places in order to help build a case against them. Over almost a three-month period, Henning kept track of what was said, much of it 'defeatist' remarks based on listening to foreign radio. All the while, he engaged the two in conversation but did not object to anything, in case he alerted the suspects to his real opinion. By mid-September he had enough evidence and passed it over to the Gestapo. They sent the case to the People's Court in Berlin which sentenced Heinrich to death. The execution took place on 26 September 1944. Vogel's crimes were considered somewhat less serious and he escaped with a heavy prison sentence, and survived the war.

Adapted from Gellately 2001.

ITEM 2 Letter from Himmler to Heydrich, 26 January 1942

All the ringleaders, and I mean ringleaders both male and female, and teachers with enemy views who are encouraging the swing youth [groups of young people who liked Jazz music and refused to conform - like the Edelweiss pirates - see Unit 5, Box 5.19], are to be assigned to a concentration camp. There the youth should first be given thrashings and then put through the severest drill and set to work. I think that any sort of labour camp or youth camp would be inappropriate for these youths and worthless girls. The girls should be put to work weaving and do land work in the summer. The spell these people should spend in concentration camp must be a fairly long one, two to three years. It must be made clear that they will never he allowed to go back to their studies. We must investigate how much encouragement they have had from their parents. If they have encouraged them, then they should also be put in a KL [concentration camp] and their property confiscated.

On 10 November 1944, 13 Edelweiss Pirates were hanged by the Gestapo in Cologne. As the war went on, punishments became more and more severe.

This letter is quoted in Peukert 1987. It was written from Himmler to Heydrich on 26 January 1942.

ITEM 3 Reports of people listening to forbidden radio broadcasts in three German towns, 1939-44

Sources of information	Number of cases	%	Sources of information	Number of cases	%
1. Reports from the population	164	73	5. Information from businesses	1	0
2. Observations by Gestapo	6	3	6. Information via Nazi Party	17	7
3. Information from other control organisations	8	4	7. Source not known	23	10
4. Statements at interrogations	7	3			

This table shows the source of reports of people listening to forbidden radio broadcasts in Düsseldorf, Würzburg and Neustadt during the Second World War.

Adapted from Gellately 2001.

Questions

1. Using Items 1-3 and your own knowledge, give arguments for and against the view that Nazi Germany was a police state.
2. What do Items 1 and 2 tell us about the way in which Nazi Germany was policed?
3. What does Item 3 tell us about the nature of the Nazi regime?

2.2 What measures were taken against minorities before the outbreak of war?

Those outside the Völksgemeinschaft

As explained in Section 1.2 above, a major feature of Nazi ideology was the concept of Völksgemeinschaft - the national community of Germans. Some social groups, however, were seen as genetic or moral threats to the German Volk (people). These groups were excluded from the national community and scapegoated. The Jews were perceived as the greatest threat, but other minorities were also excluded:

- Gypsies (both the Sinti and the Roma)
- homosexuals (especially male, but also female)
- 'asocials' - any Aryans who failed to fit into the national community
- those with hereditary illnesses or abnormalities.

Hitler and other Nazi ideologists believed in 'eugenics' - the idea that a race of people could be improved by selective breeding. According to the Nazi view, Germany's racial and moral degeneration had contributed to it losing the First World War. The Nazis wanted to produce a 'pure' and strong Aryan Germany, fit to rule over other nations. In this, they were not entirely at odds with several other countries of the period. The USA, for example, had already carried out sterilisation of criminals on eugenic grounds.

Excluding the Jews

European Jews had been the victims of prejudice for centuries. This prejudice was based on:

- the idea that Jews were supposedly responsible for having Christ killed
- the idea that Jews were different in appearance, customs and religion from other Europeans
- the fact that many Jews were successful as financiers and lawyers, and in other professions.

In Germany, Jews were widely resented on the grounds that they enjoyed privileges non-Jews did not enjoy. This was due, in large part, to the fact that Jews had become concentrated in certain trades and professions. In 1933, there were about 500,000 Jews in Germany - less than 1% of the population. Yet, they made up 16% of lawyers, 10% of doctors and 5% of writers and editors (Layton 2000, p.70). In addition they dominated the garment industry. As a result, for both racial and economic reasons, the Nazis sought to exclude them.

Few historians doubt that Hitler was genuinely anti-Semitic. *Mein Kampf* and his speeches provide abundant evidence of this. In his January 1933 election campaign, however, Hitler played his anti-Semitism down and some historians have argued that, in the 1930s, his anti-Jewish measures were largely introduced in response to pressure from below:

'During the pre-war years...it seems clear that Hitler took no specific initiative in the "Jewish question" and responded to rather than instigated the confused and often conflicting lines of "policy" which emerged.' (Kershaw 2000, p.105)

Other historians, like Saul Friedlander, while accepting that there were pressures from below, warn against underestimating Hitler's role (see

Friedlander 1997, p.3). Whether Hitler was the main architect or not, there is clear evidence of a gradual acceleration in action against Jews (and the other minorities targeted by the Nazis). Box 6.17 shows this.

Boycotts

One way for the Jews to be excluded economically was through boycotts. The first major anti-Jewish measure was a national boycott of Jewish shops and businesses on 1 April 1933. Even in remote villages, committees organised boycotts of Jewish shopkeepers, lawyers and doctors. Stormtroopers stood guard outside their premises to intimidate would-be customers and clients. Those who would not be deterred were insulted, threatened and photographed so that they could be identified in the press. Shop windows were daubed with anti-Semitic slogans. Owing to international pressure, the official boycott lasted only one day, but:

> 'It gave the signal for the beginning of officially sanctioned and remorselessly pursued exclusion of the Jews from the economy.' (Abraham Barkai, quoted in Burleigh 1996, p.90)

Similar scenes occurred from that 1 April 1933 on, often coupled with attacks and humiliation.

In keeping with the view that Hitler tended to respond rather than initiate anti-Semitic policy, both Barkai (see above) and Ian Kershaw see the 1 April boycott as an attempt by the Nazi Party leadership to appease its radicals, take control and halt 'wild' individual actions by the SA (Kershaw 2000, p.105). The early reactions of non-Jews to boycotts indicate limited resistance to the Nazi regime. Saul

Friedlander writes that people still dealt with Jews when it was to their advantage. Jewish shops were often cheaper and better stocked and Jewish cattle dealers paid in cash and sold on credit. People would travel to the next town in order to use Jewish shops without being recognised (Friedlander 1997, p.126).

Anti-Jewish legislation

Most historians agree that Hitler was aware that the public would be more likely to follow him if his persecution of minorities was gradual and cloaked in legality. This explains the large number of individual laws were passed during the period 1933-39. The overall aim was to deprive the Jews of their livelihood, property, citizenship and dignity, and to prevent them from mixing with Aryans. Jews started to be dismissed from professional positions as soon as Hitler came to power. On 7 April the Law for the Restoration of the Professional Civil Service officially excluded Jews from the civil service. This was extended to university lecturers on 6 May. Numerous similar laws eroded Jews' employment rights. They were banned from being lay assessors, jurors or commercial judges (7 April), patent lawyers or state insurance panel physicians (22 April), and dentists (2 June). A law of 25 April 'against the overcrowding of German schools' limited the number of school places for Jewish children. Non-Aryans and anyone married to them were banned from all government posts (28 September). Jews were banned from all cultural and entertainment enterprises (29 September). In early October the National Press Law prevented Jews from working in the press.

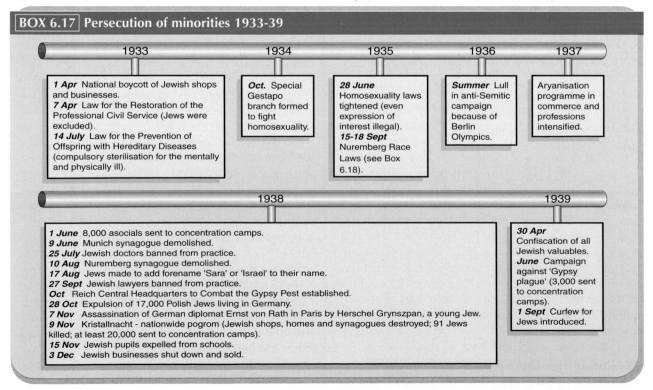

BOX 6.17 | Persecution of minorities 1933-39

1933	1934	1935	1936	1937
1 Apr National boycott of Jewish shops and businesses. **7 Apr** Law for the Restoration of the Professional Civil Service (Jews were excluded). **14 July** Law for the Prevention of Offspring with Hereditary Diseases (compulsory sterilisation for the mentally and physically ill).	**Oct.** Special Gestapo branch formed to fight homosexuality.	**28 June** Homosexuality laws tightened (even expression of interest illegal). **15-18 Sept** Nuremberg Race Laws (see Box 6.18).	**Summer** Lull in anti-Semitic campaign because of Berlin Olympics.	Aryanisation programme in commerce and professions intensified.

1938	1939
1 June 8,000 asocials sent to concentration camps. **9 June** Munich synagogue demolished. **25 July** Jewish doctors banned from practice. **10 Aug** Nuremberg synagogue demolished. **17 Aug** Jews made to add forename 'Sara' or 'Israel' to their name. **27 Sept** Jewish lawyers banned from practice. **Oct** Reich Central Headquarters to Combat the Gypsy Pest established. **28 Oct** Expulsion of 17,000 Polish Jews living in Germany. **7 Nov** Assassination of German diplomat Ernst von Rath in Paris by Herschel Grynzpan, a young Jew. **9 Nov** Kristallnacht - nationwide pogrom (Jewish shops, homes and synagogues destroyed; 91 Jews killed; at least 20,000 sent to concentration camps). **15 Nov** Jewish pupils expelled from schools. **3 Dec** Jewish businesses shut down and sold.	**30 Apr** Confiscation of all Jewish valuables. **June** Campaign against 'Gypsy plague' (3,000 sent to concentration camps). **1 Sept** Curfew for Jews introduced.

The Nuremberg Laws

In 1934 there was a lull. However, persecution at street level increased in 1935. SOPADE reports suggest that there were many local initiatives in which towns simply denied entry to Jews or banned them from using public amenities such as swimming pools. Hitler Youth, SA units and Nazi Party radicals played their part in organising anti-Jewish violence and boycotts, backed by Nazi propaganda. By mid-May shops were being openly attacked in Munich. By July, Jews were suffering attacks on the streets of Berlin, unaided by passers-by. However, the disorder reached a level at which the Nazi leadership became concerned about negative public opinion, reports in the foreign press, and the economy. At the same time Hitler and his colleagues had to satisfy party activists. The result was the Nuremberg Laws of 15-18 September - see Box 6.18. The Nuremberg Laws ruled that:

1. Jews were now subjects, not citizens, and therefore entitled only to limited state protection.
2. Marriages and sexual relations between Jews and Aryans were banned. Jews could not employ female German citizens under the age of 45.
3. Couples wanting to marry had to undergo medical examinations in order to gain permission to do so. The examination included an inquiry into hereditary conditions and racial background.
4. Less dramatically, the swastika became the official German flag; Jews were banned from flying it.

Historians debate whether these laws were as haphazard as they seemed. They reflected contemporary Nazi radical demands, but they were so quickly produced that they had to be supplemented by further decrees. A decree of 14 November defined who exactly was 'a Jew' - anyone who had at least three Jewish grandparents, or who had two but was married to a Jew or belonged to the Jewish religion when the law was passed or who later joined it. Half-Jews (Mischlinge), with two Jewish grandparents, were still discriminated against, but less so than full Jews. A decree of 21 December closed loopholes previously allowing some Jews to be professors, teachers, doctors, lawyers and notaries.

It seems that even non-Nazi Germans approved:

> 'The vast majority of the population approved of the Nuremberg Laws because they identified with the racialist policy and because a permanent framework of discrimination had been created that would end the reign of terror and set precise limits to the anti-Semitic activities.' (Friedlander 1997, p.164)

Kristallnacht

Robert Gellately comments on the inconsistency and lack of clarity in Nazi policy on Jews in the 1930s, even after 1935. In 1938, however, this began to change. On 26 April 1938 a decree ruled that Jews (and anyone married to a Jew) had to register all

---

BOX 6.18 | Drafting the Nuremberg Laws

The key year concerning racial 'hygiene' (ie the attempt to ensure that the German race remained 'pure') was 1935. That was the year when the three Nuremberg Laws were passed:

1. The Reich Citizenship Act - 'A citizen of the Reich is that subject only who is of German or kindred blood'.
2. The Law for the Protection of German Blood and German Honour (marriages or sexual relations between Jews and Aryans forbidden).
3. The Law for the Protection of the Genetic Health of the German People (couples obliged to undergo medical examination to qualify to marry).

Two out of the three laws came about when Hitler made a last-minute decision to include 'something dramatic' in the annual Nazi Party Congress because he felt that the planned programme was too thin and lacking in impact. This followed a year of relative calm on racial issues, especially anti-Semitism. The first draft of a law to ban mixed marriages (ie marriages between Aryans and Jews) was hastily thrown together on 13 September and rejected by Hitler on the same day. Next day the three drafters - Bernard Lösener, Head of the Jewish Office in the Ministry of the Interior and two colleagues from the ministry - met again and penned several versions, differing in toughness. About midnight Hitler asked them for a law excluding Jews from citizenship - which they quickly produced on the back of a menu. Early in the morning of 15 September, Hitler accepted the mildest version of the marriage law and then crossed out the sentence 'These laws are applicable to full Jews only'. This was kept in only for the official news agency DNB, probably for the benefit of the foreign press. The three racial laws represented the deepest wishes of the Nazi leadership. They expressed, above all, the paranoid thinking of a group of racists obsessed with people of 'inferior blood'.

Adapted from Fischer K. 1995 and Friedlander 1997.

---

their possessions. Gellately sees this as 'a transition from haphazard practices'. Between April and November alone more than 4,000 Jewish businesses were confiscated by the government (Gellately 2001, p.124). This suggests that there was a certain method, rather than mere opportunism, in what happened next in November 1938:

> 'On 7 November 1938, a German diplomat, Ernst von Rath, was assassinated in Paris. The assassin was 17-year-old Herschel Grynszpan, whose parents had been among the 17,000 Polish Jews forcibly ejected from Germany on 28 October. At the time, Goebbels had fallen from grace with Hitler for having an extramarital affair. Goebbels seized on the assassination as a means of gaining favour with his Führer by whipping up a new

wave of anti-Semitic violence. On 9 November the Nazis celebrated the anniversary of the Beer Hall Putsch. Goebbels' diary states: "I put the matter before the Führer. He decides: let the demonstration carry on. Pull back the police. The Jews should for once be made to feel the full fury of the people...Straightaway, I give directions along those lines to police and party".' (Kershaw 2000, p.109)

Klaus Fischer also notes Hitler's approval, pointing out that Hitler was keen that the 'SA should be allowed to have a fling' (Fischer K. 1995, p.392), which they did. All over Germany on the night of 9-10 November 1938, Jewish business premises, homes and synagogues were burned down or sacked. Jews were beaten up, close to a hundred were killed (91 is Kershaw's figure) and between 20,000 and 30,000 were sent to concentration camps. The name Kristallnacht means 'Night of broken glass', referring to the shards of glass from Jewish shop windows. Significantly, in public Hitler kept quiet about the pogrom ('pogrom' is a Russian word meaning 'organised massacre of Jews' - Kristallnacht was a typical example of a pogrom), even when addressing press leaders the next day (Kershaw 1991, p.150).

Kershaw considers that, in propaganda terms, Kristallnacht was a failure (Kershaw 2000, p.110). However, it was an important step on the way to excluding Jews from the economy and depriving them of their livelihood. Where insurance money was paid out for damaged Jewish premises, either this money was confiscated or the premises were seized after repairs had been done. Surviving Jewish businesses were liquidated or transferred to the state. Half of remaining Jewish property went to the state and Göring imposed a collective fine on the Jews of one billion marks for the assassination and for 'causing' Kristallnacht (Barkai in Burleigh 1996, p.95). Most historians agree that Kristallnacht was a turning point, an important step along the road which led to the Holocaust.

Emigration

Before Kristallnacht, the Nazi leadership had taken steps to encourage German Jews to emigrate:

'In August 1933, the Jewish Agency for Palestine, which sponsored Jewish immigration to the region, concluded a series of agreements with the German Economic Ministry. Under the terms of the so-called "Haavara Agreements", if German Jews left for Palestine, they would pay money into a Jewish trust company. Once in Palestine, the immigrant would get half the money back, in Palestine pounds; the other half would be used by the Jewish Agency to buy German goods, thus benefiting the German economy. Normally Jews who emigrated from Nazi Germany could not take their savings with them, but in the interests of financial gain and of ridding themselves of German Jews, the Nazis were

prepared to bend the rules.' (Neville 1999, p.25) After Kristallnacht, the government stepped up what Klaus Fischer calls 'phase two' - forced emigration. By the time of Kristallnacht, about 150,000 Jews had already emigrated. In addition, following the Anschluss - union with Austria - forced emigration had begun in Austria (Austria had a large Jewish population). A key player was Adolf Eichmann (see Box 6.19). He was responsible for arranging the forced emigration of over 100,000 Austrian Jews between the Anschluss and outbreak of the Second World War (Neville 1999, p.36). Another 150,000 German Jews were deported before the war. Fleeing Jews had to pay a substantial 'tax on flight from the Reich', as giving 'gifts' to officials.

BOX 6.19 | **Adolf Eichmann**

Adolf Eichmann (1906-62) joined the SS in 1933. In 1938, he oversaw the forced emigration of over 100,000 Austrian Jews. For this achievement he was transferred to similar duties in Berlin in 1939 where he helped to deport 150,000 German Jews. He headed the Jewish deportation section of the Reich Main Security Office. When Jewish policy became more radical, Eichmann rounded up over three million Jews in German-controlled territories and sent them to extermination camps. As a low-profile 'bureaucratic murderer', he was overlooked after the war and escaped to Argentina. However, he was kidnapped by Israeli agents, tried, and executed in 1962.
Adapted from Snyder 1976.

Other racial groups

The other main racial group was composed of the Gypsies, or Sinti and Roma as they differentiate themselves. They had long been discriminated against because they were considered to be racial outsiders and because settled people looked on their travelling lifestyle with suspicion. They did not play such a major role in the economy as the Jews, but they were accused of crime, laziness and a lack of hygiene. Many local authorities in 1935 and 1936 demanded that they all be sent to Dachau. At first, police enforced existing laws and a limited number were sent to concentration camps. Then, between 1935 and 1939, special Gypsy camps were set up in major cities. These were not quite concentration camps, but life in them was regimented and restricted.

In October 1938 the government set up a 'Reich Central Headquarters to Combat the Gypsy Pest' under the Kripo (the criminal police - see Unit 5, Box 5.18). The Kripo applied their existing powers to deal with 'asocials' and the 'work-shy'. Numbers of Gypsies sent to concentration camps were still relatively small, but the Nazis registered and closely supervised them. As with the Jews, steps taken against Gypsies accelerated as time went on. One of the decrees supplementing the Nuremberg Laws on 14 November 1935 extended the marriage law to Gypsies and black people. It hardly needed to be applied to the latter group, since the only black people in Germany were the 500 or so Rheinlandbastarde, children of German mothers and black French occupation troops. These had been registered and then sterilised soon after Hitler had come to power (see Fischer K. 1995, p.387).

By March 1939, most Gypsies were forced to undergo racial examinations, and in July the Kripo were told that, in the event of war, they would be sent to concentration camps. The campaign against Gypsies was stepped up first in Austria in 1938 and then in Germany in June 1939, when the Kripo were ordered to arrest 2,000 men and 1,000 women and send them to concentration camps. This, as it turned out, was just the start of things to come.

Homosexuals

Most Nazis viewed homosexuality as a severe deviation from the Aryan ideal. It didn't conform to German family values, and it certainly wasn't going to increase the birth rate. There was something of a homosexual culture in the SA, and its leader Ernst Röhm was homosexual. Hitler had at one time defended Röhm's private life as his own business, and blamed his sexual orientation on life in the tropics (see also Unit 5, Section 1.3). But the alleged sexual deviance of the SA leadership was much reported as a further justification of Hitler's actions in the 'Night of the Long Knives'.

Police persecution of homosexuals was stepped up in 1933, with existing laws enforced with new vigour. Homosexual pornography was also targeted. Lesbians were less of a target. An accusation of lesbianism was a convenient excuse to get rid of politically troublesome women, but there was no campaign against lesbians in general. In October 1934, a special branch of the Gestapo was created to fight homosexuality and the law was tightened in June 1935. There were actions against homosexuals in the summer of 1936 and homosexuals were registered. In an effort to discredit the Catholic Church, many priests were accused of sexual deviation. Many investigations for homosexuality were the result of denunciations, and men investigated were put under such pressure that some committed suicide in their cells (Gellately 2001, p.115).

Himmler was particularly anti-homosexual and reportedly said that any SS man found to be homosexual would be 'sent on my instruction to a concentration camp and shot while attempting to escape' (Fischer K. 1995, p.388). Gellately claims that convictions for homosexuality increased each year of the Third Reich. Klaus Fischer (1995) estimates that close to 15,000 were sent to concentration camps between 1933 and 1945.

Asocials

Another targeted minority group was conveniently elastic in definition. The term 'asocial' was applied to all those people who failed to fit in to the national community but were not in any readily identifiable racial or sexual group. These included habitual criminals, the 'work-shy' (defined by Himmler as anyone fit for work who turned down two jobs or left one for no good reason), vagrants, beggars, alcoholics, prostitutes and promiscuous women. The last two categories were associated with spreading venereal disease, a particular horror of a regime obsessed with racial purity. Despite this, the regime later set up brothels for foreign workers to cut down the risk of them 'polluting' Aryan women.

There was a round-up of beggars in September 1933, and Himmler ordered numerous arrest sweeps, periodically filling up Dachau concentration camp. He mounted a 'special action' on 9 March 1937 aiming to arrest 2,000 'work-shy' (it was assumed by now that anyone without a job had only themselves to blame). The police enthusiastically arrested 2,752 people (Gellately 2001, p.96). Gellately makes the point that Himmler benefited from incarcerating asocials. Once in a camp they could be put to work making profits for the SS. Even before the war, thousands were incarcerated:

> 'Concentration camps increasingly confined social outsiders. By the end of October 1938, for instance, if we take the camp at Buchenwald as an example, its 10,188 prisoners included 1,007 "professional criminals" and 4,341 picked up as "asocials".' (Gellately 2001, p.99)

The mentally and physically ill

On 14 July 1933 the Nazis passed the Law for the Prevention of Progeny with Hereditary Diseases. This introduced compulsory sterilisation for anyone who, in the opinion of a genetic health court, suffered from one of a number of specified diseases:

- congenital feeble-mindedness
- schizophrenia
- manic-depressive insanity
- hereditary epilepsy
- Huntingdon's disease
- hereditary blindness
- deafness
- serious physical deformities
- chronic alcoholism (Fischer K. 1995, p.384).

It can easily be seen that some of these are so vague as to enable the authorities to use the law as they saw fit. By the outbreak of war, Fischer claims that 400,000 had been sterilised.

The law reflected Nazi ideas about eugenics and the necessity of strengthening the German gene pool. In addition, the chronically ill were seen as a drain on the economy, reducing the nation's ability to fight a war. Michael Burleigh notes that these eugenicist ideas stemmed from medical men, rather than just

Nazi officials. The administrators were thorough. Once an individual had been sterilised, the genetic courts would sometimes investigate the whole family and recommend further sterilisations. In an even more sinister development, school children would be told to draw their family tree, to enable the courts to identify abnormalities (Burleigh 2000, p.50). Burleigh is amongst the historians who trace a progression from sterilisation to the 'euthanasia' programme begun just before the war, and from here to the Holocaust itself.

MAIN POINTS - Section 2.2

- The Nazis aimed to exclude Jews, Gypsies, homosexuals and asocials from German society. There was a gradual acceleration of measures taken against these groups.
- Jews were excluded by boycotts, legislation, confiscation and deportation. The Nuremberg Laws of 1935 removed Jewish citizenship and banned Aryan-Jewish marriages.
- Goebbels used an assassination as an excuse to start the Kristallnacht 'pogrom'. During the night of 9-10 November 1938, all over Germany Jewish business premises, homes and synagogues were burned down or sacked. Jews were beaten up, close to a hundred

were killed and between 20,000 and 30,000 were sent to concentration camps.
- After Kristallnacht, Jewish businesses were confiscated and, in Germany forced emigration began (it had already started in Austria).
- Gypsies were registered and supervised. Some were sent to concentration camps before the outbreak of the Second World War.
- Homosexuals were persecuted before the outbreak of the Second World War. Many were sent to concentration camps. 'Asocials' were also sent to concentration camps. Those with certain illnesses and disabilities were sterilised.

Activity 6.5 Measures were taken against minorities 1933-39

ITEM 1 Arnold Biegeleisen

I was 25 years old and employed as a clerk when Hitler became Chancellor. On the whole, everyone was really nice to us. Besides myself, only one Jew was employed there. There was only one individual who caused us any problems - a former member of the SPD who had been one of the first to cross to the other side. Jewish stores and businesses were first boycotted on 1 April 1933. SA men stood in front of shops carrying signs which read 'Don't buy from Jews'. My mother, who didn't look Jewish at all, was stopped by an SA guard after leaving one of the shops. He said: 'You see the sign, but you go in anyway!' We didn't take the warnings and threats seriously. At that time we were still permitted to move round freely. One day, one of our customers from Munich showed up and saw me working there. I overheard him telling the company owner: 'Since you continue to employ Jews, we can no longer do business with you'. After that incident, my colleagues warned me every time they saw a customer coming and I would run and hide in the toilets. This continued until a day in April 1935 when the customer from Munich showed up again. I wasn't able to hide fast enough and he saw me. He roared at the management: 'If you think you're pulling the wool over my eyes, you're wrong. You are still allowing Jews to work here!'. The company let me work until December, but then the boss said I'd have to go. I received unemployment benefit for a while, but soon decided to leave Germany. In 1936, with 10 marks cash and 20 marks for my fare, I boarded ship to Argentina.

Arnold Biegeleisen was born in 1908. He was a Jewish clerk with good prospects until the Nazis came to power. He emigrated to Argentina and returned to Berlin after the Second World War.

A member of the SA stands outside a shop owned by Jews during the boycott of Jewish shops and businesses on 1 April 1933.

Adapted from Steinhoff, Pechel & Showalter 1991.

ITEM 2 Kristallnacht

Before November 1938, incidences of violence against the Jews were on a relatively small scale and were carried out in a fairly random fashion by the SA. All this changed with Kristallnacht. It began with an act of personal revenge by a Jew and ended in a state-sponsored orgy of violence against Jews and their property throughout Germany. The act of personal revenge took place in Paris on 7 November when Herschel Grynszpan, a 17-year-old Jew, shot and fatally wounded Ernst von Rath, a diplomat at the German Embassy. Rath died of his wounds on 9 November. Following the news of his death members of the SA and Nazi Party attacked and burned down Jewish synagogues, homes and businesses, killing 91 Jews in the process and imprisoning c.30,000. A major turning point in the Nazi policy towards the Jews seemed to have been reached. The Nazis attempted to portray Kristallnacht as a

This photo shows one of the many Jewish stored to be wrecked and looted during Kristallnacht. The photo was taken in Berlin.

popular, spontaneous reaction of outrage on the news of Rath's death. It was nothing of the sort. It was inspired by an inflammatory speech made by Goebbels on 9 November, with Hitler's approval. The aftermath was significant. At a meeting on 12 November, Göring announced plans to eliminate Jews from the German economy. In theory, insurance companies should have covered the costs of the destroyed Jewish businesses. It was agreed at the meeting that, to retain their credibility, insurers would pay for the damage. But the government would then confiscate the money. On the same day - 12 November - Göring also issued the Decree on the Penalty Payment by Jews who are German Subjects. This required Jews to pay 1 billion marks in a fine imposed because of their 'hostile attitude' towards the German state and people. A second decree excluded Jews from the retail trade, management of German companies, the selling of goods and services and employment as independent craftspeople. Intentionalist historians claim that the Nazis were working to a blueprint developed in the 1920s and suggest this was an important step on a road already mapped out. Structuralist historians, on the other hand, argue that there was no blueprint. Kristallnacht, they argue, was the product of a power struggle between Hitler's lieutenants and there was no inevitability that it would lead to the Holocaust. The main catalyst for that was the outbreak of the Second World War.

Adapted from Neville 1999.

ITEM 3 A historian's view

The Nazi intention to humiliate and dispossess Jews living in Germany is not in question. What has been hotly debated recently is whether the murder of European Jews was an objective that Hitler had in mind from early on or whether it was the result of improvisation. The passage of the Nuremburg Laws is a case in point. The restlessness of the Nazi rank-and-file may have been a contributory factor in Hitler's decision to announce new restrictions. Similarly when Hitler approved the policy of Jewish emigration in the mid-1930s this was not only due to a desire to rid Germany of Jews but also to the influence of Himmler who believed that the orderly expulsion of Jews rather than violent attacks on them would help to preserve Germany's image abroad. By 1937, 120,000 Jews had left Germany after being robbed of their possessions. This policy was intensified when the Germans took over Czechoslovakia and Austria. Finally, when a Jewish boy murdered a German embassy official in November 1938, it was Goebbels, anxious to curry favour with Hitler at the expense of Himmler and Göring who persuaded Hitler to

This photo shows pro-Nazis humiliating Jews. The photo was taken in the Austrian town of Linz the day after Kristallnacht. Three Jewish women have been made to sit on a platform. Their hair is about to be shaved off and they are forced to wear a sign which reads: 'I have been removed from the national community'.

approve of a large-scale pogrom against the Jews. The pogrom, which caused widespread horror abroad and disquiet among many Germans, was followed by a spate of anti-Jewish legislation which drove Jews out of commercial life. They were practically deprived of a means of livelihood. They could not enter cinemas, theatres or swimming pools. They could not own cars. Their children were expelled from school and university. It is important to remember other victims, too. The Nazis were determined to remove 'unsound racial elements'. By 1941, 200-350,000 Germans with a mental or physical disability had been compulsorily sterilised. Between 1939 and 1941, 80,000 mentally ill patients were murdered by gas or injections. Homosexuals, the work-shy, tramps, Jehovah's Witnesses and Gypsies were all persecuted.

Adapted from Carr 1991.

2.3 What led to the Holocaust?

A controversial area

Much controversy surrounds the Holocaust. There is even debate about how to define the word itself (from a Greek word meaning 'burnt offering'). Some historians apply it to all Nazi mass murder, including the mentally ill, the disabled, Gypsies and Slavs. Others, like Klaus Fischer and Yehuda Bauer, confine it to the Jews. Here, we take it to include all groups targeted by Nazi racialism and, at the same time, focus on the 6 million Jews who died throughout Europe. The section first covers the chronology of events, then the issues debated. An outline of the chronology is provided in Box 6.20.

The euthanasia programme

As noted in Section 2.2 above, some historians see a progression from sterilisation (1933-39) to euthanasia (1939-41), to the Holocaust (1941-5). The sterilisation programme is discussed in Section 2.2. According to Michael Burleigh, the Nazi euthanasia programme had less to do with mercy killing than with cutting costs and strengthening the 'Aryan race':

'The decision to kill the mentally ill and physically disabled was taken by Hitler in order to clear the decks for war, and was justified with the aid of crude utilitarian arguments. Many health professionals and psychiatrists accommodated themselves to policies which a few years later became one of the components of the "Final Solution of the Jewish Question".' (Burleigh 2000, p.45)

Henry Friedlander links the programme with ideology rather than practical considerations. He includes euthanasia victims in the Holocaust, arguing that:

'Anti-Semitism was only part of a larger world view which divided mankind into worthy and unworthy populations.' (Friedlander H. 2000, p.65)

In May 1939 the Chancellery of the Führer received a petition from the parents of a severely handicapped boy asking for permission to have him killed. Knowing Hitler's views, the Chancellery made this one of the few petitions to reach the Führer. Hitler granted permission and authorised the Chancellery to do so in similar cases. This quickly led to a programme in which 6,000 children were killed, including adolescents. Parents were promised advanced treatment for their children, but warned that they might not survive. 'Treatment' consisted of fatal medication.

Under the Nazis, mental asylums deteriorated. The

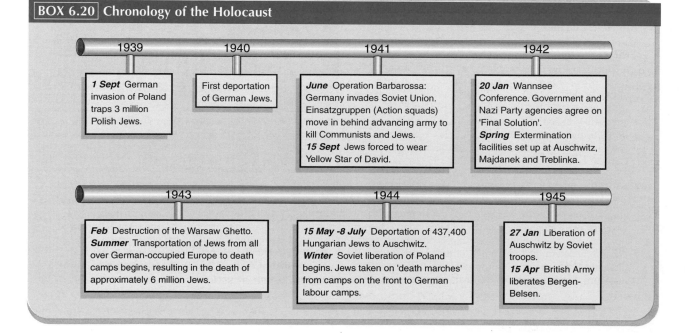

BOX 6.20 | Chronology of the Holocaust

1939
- **1 Sept** German invasion of Poland traps 3 million Polish Jews.

1940
- First deportation of German Jews.

1941
- **June** Operation Barbarossa: Germany invades Soviet Union. Einsatzgruppen (Action squads) move in behind advancing army to kill Communists and Jews.
- **15 Sept** Jews forced to wear Yellow Star of David.

1942
- **20 Jan** Wannsee Conference. Government and Nazi Party agencies agree on 'Final Solution'.
- **Spring** Extermination facilities set up at Auschwitz, Majdanek and Treblinka.

1943
- **Feb** Destruction of the Warsaw Ghetto.
- **Summer** Transportation of Jews from all over German-occupied Europe to death camps begins, resulting in the death of approximately 6 million Jews.

1944
- **15 May -8 July** Deportation of 437,400 Hungarian Jews to Auschwitz.
- **Winter** Soviet liberation of Poland begins. Jews taken on 'death marches' from camps on the front to German labour camps.

1945
- **27 Jan** Liberation of Auschwitz by Soviet troops.
- **15 Apr** British Army liberates Bergen-Belsen.

regime was reluctant to spend money on 'life unworthy of living'. Institutions became freak-shows, with 'Nazi formations being given tours to illustrate the inherent uselessness of the patients' (Burleigh 2000, p.48). In July 1939 Hitler said that he favoured euthanasia for seriously ill mental patients and commissioned a feasibility study. Viktor Brack, Deputy to the Head of the Führer Chancellery Philip Bouhler, took the initiative and gave Bouhler a plan to present to Hitler. Hitler then agreed to extend euthanasia to adults. Doctors suggested a target of 60,000 patients. However, to avoid negative public opinion, the operation was kept top-secret. Brack was put in charge of the organisation, code-named T4 after its address at Tiergartenstrasse 4, Berlin. Asylums completed forms giving patients' details, and these were given in batches of 200-300 to assessors who decided whether patients should live or die - without ever seeing them. Patients were killed mostly by carbon monoxide gas, though some were shot by SS squads. In occupied Poland, mobile gas vans were used (Kershaw 2000a, pp.259-61)

When information about what was happening eventually became public knowledge, there was a great deal of alarm. In a rare case of effective opposition to the regime, several church ministers protested. The most notable protest was by Bishop von Galen of Munster, who denounced the programme from the pulpit. The RAF even dropped copies of his sermon over German cities. When Hitler ended the programme - at least officially, it had already killed 70,000 people, exceeding its target. Most historians think that in reality it continued in even greater secrecy up to 1945 (Knopp 2001, p.91).

Deportations to ghettos

Klaus Fischer identifies four phases in the persecution of the Jews - (1) legalised discrimination (2) forced emigration (3) resettlement and ghettoisation (4) extermination. (Fischer K. 1995, p.390). Forced emigration had already begun in 1938 after Kristallnacht (see Section 2.2 above). When the Second World War broke out, this changed into 'deportation'. Jews (and other minorities) were rounded up and forcibly transported to ghettos - areas where they would be isolated from the surrounding population - and then to death camps. The situation was confused by the uncertainties of war. Klaus Fischer writes:

'Hitler's blitzkrieg campaigns were so rapid, the defeat of his enemies so unexpectedly [speedy], that the Nazis had no long-range plans to administer their conquered territories.' (Fischer K. 1995, p.479)

The German annexation of Poland trapped 3 million Jews there. The immediate policy was to dump over a million in an area of central Poland, administered by Hans Frank. This was to free the rest of Poland for resettlement by ethnic Germans.

By the time war broke out, the original population of Jews in Germany itself had been reduced by more than half. Shortly after the outbreak of war, there were around 190,000 Jews left in Germany. Deportation began to be undertaken on a huge scale in October 1941, organised by Eichmann (see Box 6.19 above). In three waves, over 100,000 Jews were deported to ghettos in Lodz, Riga and Minsk, and then to the death camps of Chelmno, Belzec and Auschwitz (Gellately 2001, p.142). The first 2,934 German Jews were shot by Einsatzkommando 3 in Lithuania on 25 November 1941 (Knopp 2001, p.97; see below for an account of the Einsatzgruppen). The first death camp, Chelmno, became operational on 8 December 1941, Belzec in spring 1942, and Auschwitz in the summer. The process of deportation is described in Box 6.21. It is important to note that, despite what went on once the Jews were inside the deportation centres, much was done to preserve an illusion of normality. The Jews were told they were going to be resettled in the East. The fact that they were told to take luggage reassured them.

The death camps were in remote parts of Poland, accessible by rail and yet away from population centres so they could be kept secret. Jews might have to travel first to a deportation camp such as Westerbork in Holland, from which 112,000 Jews were deported to the East, or they might go straight to a Polish ghetto. At any rate, they could expect a journey of several days, in a passenger train or cattle truck. Either would be very crowded, with little to eat or drink, and a bucket for a toilet. It might be freezing in winter or stifling in summer. People often died before arrival.

For Jews exempted for the time being, there was a process aimed at turning them into objects in the eyes of other Germans. They had to hand over their valuables, their phones were cut off, they were not allowed hot water and could not use balconies. Food was strictly rationed, and they could obtain no clothing. From 1940 they were conscripted for labour such as shovelling snow, and in 1941 they lost the last trace of employee protection and could only use public transport for long journeys if they had a work pass.

In May 1942, Goebbels pressed to have the last Jews deported from Germany. There were legal difficulties with those in 'mixed' marriages, and so the Gestapo was ordered to 'frame' these Jews. They were assisted by non-Jews, who according to Gellately were often keen to denounce them. On 19 September 1941, it became compulsory for Jews to wear a patch of yellow material in the shape of the Star of David to show that they were Jewish. Then, on 24 October 1941 a decree threatened any non-

BOX 6.21 | Deportation

Most German Jews perished in the concentration camps not long after they had been deported, the majority of deportations taking place between autumn 1941 and the summer of 1942. By the end of 1942, most of the deported Jews were already dead. Eyewitness accounts and other documents for the trial of the heads of the Cologne Gestapo in 1954 show how deportations were carried out. Around 11,500 Jews in the Cologne area were deported, beginning on 21 October 1941 with the deportation of 1,000 Jews to the Lodz ghetto. The final deportation took place on 1 October 1944. The greatest number took place in 1942. By the end of 1942, nearly 80% of Jews in the Cologne area had already been deported. The process was as follows. First, the Reich Central Security Office sent a written communication to the Head of the Cologne Gestapo ordering him to assemble a certain number of Jews of a specific type and age profile, to depart from Cologne on a specific date for a specific destination. The Head of the Gestapo then met with his department heads. Soon after this, the Head of the Gestapo's Jewish desk met with the leader of the local Jewish community and ordered him to prepare a list of Jews who were to be deported. When the time drew near, the Jews had to find their way to the Cologne-Deutz Congress Centre. Practically every member of the Gestapo was there to meet them. The Centre itself was sealed off with barbed wire and guarded by uniformed policemen and members of the SS. Inside, the Jews were herded like animals into a large unheated hall covered in sawdust. They were then registered and had their luggage searched (many of their possessions were simply confiscated by the Gestapo). Usually, they were only allowed to take 60 marks, some food, eating utensils and a small suitcase containing shoes, clothes, two blankets and food to tide them over. They were beaten, forced to undergo body searches and robbed of their cash and valuables. When the trains arrived, the guards pushed and clubbed the Jews onto them. The trains were mainly old freight trains with no toilet facilities. The Jews were forced to pay for their journey.

Adapted from Johnson 1999.

Jew displaying sympathy to a Jew with three months in a concentration camp. Despite plenty of evidence of individual acts of kindness by non-Jews towards Jews (and, at the same time, plenty of evidence of non-Jews insulting and assaulting those branded with the yellow stars), on just one occasion was there a public protest. In February 1943, when the last Berlin Jews were being deported, their non-Jewish friends and relatives protested for several days. This forced the regime to release 1,500 men and women from 'mixed marriages'.

Gypsies and other groups

Before the war, Gypsies had been confined to regimented camps and closely supervised. Himmler wanted to save at least some 'pure' Gypsies, as interesting specimens, but this was opposed by Hitler and Bormann. Klaus Fischer writes:

'It was probably at a conference in Berlin on September 21, 1939, chaired by SD Chief Heydrich, that a decision was made to carry out the measures that would lead to the "final solution" of the Gypsy question.' (Fischer 1995, p.387)

Dr Robert Ritter, a 'racial expert' claimed to have found pronounced criminal tendencies in Gypsies of mixed blood - supposedly about 90% of German Gypsies. Gellately writes that, on 24 January 1940, the Ministry of the Interior wrote to the police proposing sterilisation of Gypsies. However, this could not be agreed, and the first 2,500 were deported in mid-May 1940. Eventually:

- 18,000 German and Austrian Gypsies were murdered in Auschwitz and Chelmno
- 25,000 Polish Gypsies died under Nazi occupation
- at least 16,000 French Gypsies were killed (Knopp 2001, p.222).

Homosexuals and Jehovah's Witnesses were also deported, and many eventually murdered. Klaus Fischer gives a figure of 15,000 homosexuals sent to concentration camps, and Auschwitz certainly contained substantial numbers of both groups (Fischer K. 1995, p.388).

Ghettos

Deported German Jews who were not sent straight to concentration camps found themselves in Polish 'ghettos' along with millions of Jews from Poland and elsewhere - see Box 6.22. 'Ghettos' - special living areas for Jews - had existed in the past, but the ghettos set up by the Nazis were on a different scale and little more than prison camps. In the Warsaw ghetto, half a million people were crammed into 1.3 square miles. Most lived at least seven to a room. There was little food or running water. People supplemented their rations by black marketeering and sending children via the sewers to beg and steal food outside the ghetto. There was little work available and only a few people were permitted to work outside the ghetto. The Jews set up schools in secret, and practised their religion - though both were illegal. Overcrowding and lack of hygiene led to disease epidemics which killed thousands.

The Nazis set up the 'Judenrate', Jewish councils, through which they controlled housing and policing. Later these councils even provided lists of names facilitating transport to the concentration camps. They had little choice but to cooperate. When fewer and fewer names were put onto lists, the Nazis changed tactics. They simply rounded up all the

BOX 6.22 | The ghetto at Lodz

To the Jews coming from major German cities, the deportation to Lodz must have seemed like a journey back in time to the Middle Ages. Yet, apart from the name, the 'ghetto' that awaited them had nothing in common with the well-established Jewish quarters of the past. The ghettos set up by the Nazis were nothing more than prison camps - ante-rooms of death. In February 1940, the German Police Chief in Lodz decreed that three districts, which were particularly run-down, would become a ghetto area. Of the houses, mainly wooden shacks, 95% were without running water or main drainage. All non-Jewish residents of these districts were forced to leave their homes by 30 April. In their place, in addition to the 60,000 Jews already living there, 100,000 Jews from other districts and outer suburbs were moved in. Anybody who refused was threatened with death and, on the night of 6 March, 200 Jews were shot as a punishment for attempted escapes and delaying tactics. In order to create some separation from the adjacent residential areas, the German authorities ordered whole blocks of houses to be torn down and, in their place, set up a no-man's land with barbed wire, watch towers and checkpoints. From now on, it was a punishable offence for a Jew to leave the ghetto and anyone visiting it from the city needed a special permit. The loss of liberty went hand-in-hand with the confiscation of property. What was left behind was seized. Whatever Jews brought with them was confiscated. They were forced to exchange their property for a specially introduced ghetto 'currency'. All they had left was their ability to work. And that was mercilessly exploited. As the war went on, the ghettos were turned into workshops supplying uniforms, boots, weapon components and so on - producing products for the very organisation which was threatening to destroy them. In Lodz over 70,000 people were engaged in slave labour. In order to keep costs down, in December 1940, the German authorities set up communal kitchens which supplied the equivalent of prison food. Those working were on one diet (just enough to keep them alive and able to work), whilst others were given less food. As a result, everybody in the ghetto was constantly hungry.

Adapted from Knopp 2001.

Jews they could find in what was called an 'Aktion'. Aktions were well planned and thorough. They usually took place when a ghetto was being run down. Streets were blocked off and houses were cleared systematically using dogs to find anyone hiding. People found at home could take belongings. Others were sent straight to the station. Most went quietly, thinking this was their best chance of survival. When the final clearance of the Warsaw Ghetto took place, however, there was an uprising. Poorly armed Jews fought well-armed German soldiers for three weeks before the ghetto was burned down.

The Einsatzgruppen

The Nazi leadership dreamed of ethnically cleansing Eastern Europe and the Russian steppes, wiping out 30 million Slavs and turning the whole area into an Aryan 'Garden of Eden'. The plan was worked out six months before the invasion of the Soviet Union. This invasion, 'Operation Barbarossa', was launched in June 1941. Hitler had long been convinced that the Soviet Union was virtually a puppet state run by 'Jewish intelligentsia'. Therefore as the Wehrmacht (the German Army) made advances into the Soviet Union, including its non-Russian satellite states, they were closely followed by killing squads, the Einsatzgruppen (A, B, C and D), set up by Himmler and Heydrich. Their job was to murder leading Communists and intellectuals, and all Jews. Victims were made to dig their own mass grave, undress, and then line up by the grave, or in it, to be shot.

The killers were volunteers, largely from middle-class backgrounds. They were aided by the Waffen SS and the Orpo ('order police'), and frequently by the local population. At times even ordinary army battalions took part. Frequently they cooperated. Rarely, they protested. Guido Knopp writes:

'Units of the Wehrmacht were brought in to assist with mass shootings. At other places soldiers were witnesses - and more. Not all of them were guilty of these crimes, not a great many even, but too many - especially in the towns. Some reacted with horror, others with disgust. Only a few protested. Hardly anyone enquired about the reasons. Quite a number never heard anything about the crimes, being exclusively occupied with their own survival. Then again there were others who applauded the murderous activities of the Einsatzgruppen.' (Knopp 2001, p.xx)

On 13 May 1941, General Field Marshal Keitel decreed that the Russian population would no longer be protected by international law. In addition the definition of a partisan - an armed resistance fighter - was broadened to include unarmed 'agitators' or anyone suspected of being one. In effect this meant that soldiers 'could massacre civilians without having to answer to a German court martial' (Knopp 2001, p.19). Naturally this applied to Jews.

Scientific genocide

Men in the Einsatzgruppen were more often ardent Nazis and nationalists than psychopaths and sadists. As a result, many began to suffer psychologically from the effects of the mass shootings. In addition, this method of killing was uneconomical in terms of manpower, and slow. Himmler gave the task of finding an alternative to the head of the Einsatzgruppen, Arthur Nebe, who had helped develop killing methods in the T4 euthanasia programme. Experimenting with mental patients, Nebe first tried explosives. This worked, but had obvious disadvantages. He found that exhaust fumes were more effective. This led to the development of mobile gas vans, much used in the first death camp, Chelmno. Victims were loaded in the back and driven to a burial pit, the exhaust fumes gradually filling their compartment. By the time they reached the pit they were dead. Whilst Chelmno continued to use mobile gas vans, the other five death camps built gas chambers and used Zyklon B, an insecticide that produced cyanide gas. By the spring of 1942, gas chambers were in operation in all five of these death camps.

The death camps

By the end of the war, there were three distinct types of concentration camp:

- prison camps - eg Bergen-Belsen, Buchenwald, Dachau (these were not designed to kill large numbers)
- work camps - some were large industrial complexes (eg the IG Farben plant at Auschwitz III)
- death camps - Belzec, Chelmno, Sobibor, Treblinka were built to kill Jews, whilst two further death camps, Majdanek and Auschwitz, had work camps attached (Auschwitz was also used as the site for medical experimentation by Dr Mengele).

Box 6.23 describes the system that developed in the death camps.

The SS reaped considerable profits from the prisoners' belongings, clothes, gold teeth, and even their hair, which was used to make industrial felt. It also benefited from their labour, in mines, quarries and factories. Some were hired out to local factories and farmers. They were expected to live, on average, for nine months before dying of disease, slow starvation, brutal beatings and despair. There would be frequent 'selections' at which prisoners would be sorted into those still fit for work and those to be gassed.

Near the end of the war, as British and US troops moved in, surviving concentration camp inmates were led on gruelling death marches to Germany to be used as forced labour, and to conceal the atrocities in the camps from the Allies for as long as possible. Many died of exhaustion and hunger on the route, or were shot if they could not keep up. On a ten-day march from Danzig, for example, 700 prisoners out of a total 7,000 were shot. Eventually, survivors were just herded into the sea and murdered. The largest marches began in the winter of 1944-45, when German defeat was inevitable.

The main issues

The horror and enormity of the Holocaust can never be fully understood. Historians focus on several main questions:

BOX 6.23 | The death camps

The most horrific aspect of the Nazi death machine was the six purpose built death camps. These six camps have a special importance because they were dedicated to killing people the Nazis regarded as 'worthless'. By the spring of 1942, gas chambers, with adjacent crematoria, were operational in all the camps, except Chelmno which carried out killings with gas vans. All six death camps were located in Poland. The most renowned was Auschwitz-Birkenau which had four huge gas chambers with the technical capacity to kill 20,000 people per day. It appears the actual total was nearer 6,000 per day. The scale of the killing operation can be illustrated by the fact that it was served by 44 parallel railway tracks. Those arriving at Auschwitz came in sealed trains. On the platform, they were divided into those fit for slave labour and those - usually children, the sick and the elderly - to be sent straight to the gas chamber. Each Jew was tattooed on the arm with a number. A fit, especially a skilled, Jewish worker stood a chance of survival. Out of the 35,000 Jewish slave labourers hired by IG Farben, 10,000 survived. At Auschwitz-Birkenau, victims were fooled into thinking they were being taken for a shower. The gas chambers were innocent-looking buildings from the outside, surrounded by well-kept lawns and flower beds. The sign over the entry to the gas chambers read 'showers'. Inside, light music was played by a small orchestra of young women dressed in white blouses and navy blue skirts. Victims were told to undress. As they entered the large 'shower room' with 2,000 others, large doors shut behind them. The deadly pellets of Zyklon B (an insecticide) were dropped through vents above and entered the room as cyanide gas. It sometimes took 20-30 minutes for the screaming to stop. The task of piling the victims onto wagons and taking them to the crematorium was carried out by strong camp inmates who were promised survival in return. The total number killed between 1942 and 1944 (when the killing stopped) was 2.5 million executed by gassing, with a further 50,000 killed by shooting, disease and starvation.

Adapted from McDonough 1999.

- What were its origins?
- How central was Hitler's role?
- Did Hitler always plan to annihilate the Jews?
- Did Hitler order the Final Solution - and, if so, when?
- To what extent were ordinary Germans involved?

The origins of the Holocaust

The traditional view

Traditional explanations focus on anti-Semitism. As noted in Section 2.2 above, anti-Semitism had been widespread throughout Europe for centuries and it was far from being a uniquely German phenomenon. Raoul Hilberg has argued that none of the measures taken by Nazis against Jews was completely original. Box 6.24 shows what he means.

There was no organised attempt to eliminate the Jews before the Nazi era, but there had been many pogroms and expulsions of Jews - starting with their expulsion from Judea by the Romans in AD 70. Hilberg argues that the Jews did not resist the Nazis more because, over centuries, they had learned that the way to survive was to avoid confrontation (Hilberg 2000, p.21).

Daniel Goldhagen agrees that there is a long history of European anti-Semitism, but argues that a strong 'eliminationist' variant of it grew up in Germany. He says that it was widely assumed in late 19th-century Germany that there was a Jewish problem. In the early 20th century, he claims, Jews were generally seen as parasites and enemies of the state. He writes:

'A survey of the political and social life of Weimar reveals that virtually every major institution and group in Germany - including schools and universities, the military, bureaucracy, and judiciary, professional associations, the churches, and political parties - was permeated by anti-Semitism.' (Goldhagen 1997, p.82)

Saul Friedlander agrees that anti-Semitism became widespread in the late 19th century:

'Redemptive anti-Semitism, nurtured by the deep soil of Christian religious tradition, resurfaced in late 19th-century Germany as one of several ideologies of salvation brought forth by the forebodings of decline and catastrophe which had seeped into the imagination of the epoch.' (Friedlander S. 2000, p.83)

Friedlander says that this belief that Germany could be 'saved' only through ridding itself of the Jews became a religious-political standpoint. He sees this anti-Semitism, together with a crisis of German national identity and the growth of Völkisch ideology, as the basis upon which action leading to the Holocaust rested. He also points out that it was not just anti-Semitism, but a belief in eugenics and social engineering that combined to make the Holocaust possible. Anti-Semitism was just part of an overall racialist agenda. This is a viewpoint shared by Detlev Peukert, who points out that other groups were targeted, such as Gypsies. Peukert argues that Jews came to represent everything that many Germans hated and feared about modern society, including capitalism, liberalism and Marxism (Peukert 1987, pp.208-09).

The modernist thesis

Hilberg is actually best-known for his 'modernist' argument that the insane logic of the German bureaucracy helped to make the Holocaust possible. In this view, bureaucrats like Adolf Eichmann were part of a well-oiled machine that just needed a push to set the Holocaust in motion. Another 'modernist' viewpoint is presented by Götz Aly who has emphasised the importance of economists and social planners in calculating the cost-benefit of extermination. According to this view, the Final Solution was the first stage of a programme of economic rationality. In 1995, Aly revised this view, arguing that it was the huge transfers of population that led to the Holocaust (Aly 2000, pp.94-105). Friedlander calls this 'inadequate' because it does not explain why West European Jews were deported and killed (Friedlander S. 2000, p.88). Friedlander

---

BOX 6.24 | **Precedents for Nazi measures against the Jews**

Many of the measures the Nazis took against the Jews had precedents in the past - often in the distant past.

Measure taken by Nazis	Precedent
Law for the Protection of German Blood and Honour (15 September 1935)	The Synod of Elvira in CE 306 prohibited intermarriage and sex between Christians and Jews
Decree of 24 December 1940 lays down that Jews should pay tax in place of donations to the Nazi Party	The Synod of Genoa in CE 1078 laid down that Jews should pay the same tax to support Church as that paid by Christians
Decree of 15 September 1941 lays down that Jews were to wear the yellow Star of David	The Fourth Lateran Council of CE 1215 made it compulsory for Jewish clothes to have a badge
Order issued by Heydrich on 21 September 1939 ordered Jews to be confined to ghettos	The Synod of Breslau in CE 1267 ordered that Jews be confined to ghettos

Adapted from Hilberg 2000.

argues that the traditional and modern views are not mutually exclusive:

'With regard to the Nazi myth of the Jew, archaic religious themes and so-called modern scientific theories were interwoven in a multifaceted representation of the arch enemy of the Volk.' (Friedlander S. 2000, p.84)

How central was Hitler's role?

The question of Hitler's role brings us back to the intentionalism versus structuralism debate (see Unit 4, Section 1.1). In the extreme intentionalist view, the Holocaust happened because Hitler had always intended to annihilate the Jews (and perhaps other groups). He followed a plan and was always in charge. In other words - no Hitler, no Holocaust. The extreme structuralist view is that Hitler had no definite plans to murder the Jews or other groups and he was not fully in charge. As a result, the power structure of the Nazi regime enabled the Holocaust to evolve. There was no plan. The viewpoints of the intentionalists and structuralists are outlined in Box 6.25.

It should be noted that a few historians have suggested that Hitler did not genuinely hate Jews. They argue that he was just using them as a scapegoat. The conservative historian Ernst Nolte, for example, has suggested that Hitler's anti-Semitism was less important than his anti-Bolshevism (Nolte 1988). Coming from a very different political stance, Marxist historians have interpreted the Holocaust in class terms and reached similar conclusions to Nolte's. However, most historians accept that the anti-Jewish hatred expressed in Hitler's speeches and writings was genuine. Some have called it his only consistent guiding principle.

Hitler's decision?

Many historians have debated whether, or when, Hitler ordered the Final Solution. No definitive Hitler order has ever been found, nor is one likely to be found. Some historians argue that Hitler learned from his experience with the T4 euthanasia programme not to give written orders for which he could be held responsible (Knopp 2001, p.91). A few historians have argued that Hitler cannot be blamed for the Final Solution, but the vast majority, including the structuralists, agree that Hitler was responsible, even if by weight of influence and authority rather than by a direct order.

The meeting of the SS in January 1940

Ian Kershaw sees as a key moment, a meeting of top SS leaders in January 1940. This meeting agreed on a policy of ghettoisation for women, children and those unfit for work, and forced labour for others. Kershaw writes:

'The decision to murder millions had at this point still not been taken. But in thought and practice a

BOX 6.25 | How central was Hitler's role?

(i) The intentionalist viewpoint

Intentionalists, especially those who emphasise the totalitarian nature of the Nazi regime, say that the Jews were murdered because Hitler, the all-powerful dictator, had always wanted it. Daniel Goldhagen, for example, argues that Hitler was the driving force behind the anti-Jewish policy. In the first few years of his rule, he argues, Hitler settled for compromise 'solutions' to the 'Jewish problem' because of the apparent impossibility of 'solving' it as he might have wished. All of the 'solutions' that he and his subordinates came up with derived directly and immediately from the same diagnosis of the 'problem', namely that, ideally, Jews should wiped out. It should be noted that most intentionalists insist that regarding Hitler as central to the Holocaust does not mean that he was solely to blame. Knopp for example, argues that there is no doubt that Hitler was the prime mover. Without Hitler, he suggests, there would probably have been no invasion of the Soviet Union and no Holocaust. But, he goes on, this does not mean that the guilt can be shifted onto one individual. Hitler's criminal energy released the criminal energy of others.
Adapted from Goldhagen 1997 and Knopp 2001.

(ii) The structuralist viewpoint

Marxist Tim Mason argues that an overemphasis on Hitler means a failure to give due weight to the social, economic and political reasons for change. To interpret history merely in terms of key figures, he argues, encourages a false logic which rationalises events after they have happened in light of what we see as the intentions of those involved. In other words, just because Hitler wanted the Jews dead and it happened, that does not mean that Hitler alone made it happen. Hans Mommsen, agrees that the Final Solution cannot be explained by Hitler alone, nor solely by Nazi ideology. Rather, the way in which Hitler allowed rival agencies to improvise policies and to compete for his approval led to a 'cumulative radicalisation'. In Mommsen's view, though Hitler knew and approved of what was going on, the Holocaust evolved. It was not planned. Besides, Hitler avoided associating himself with potentially unpopular or incriminating policies - and the Holocaust fell into this category. Martin Broszat argues that, until the autumn of 1941, the aim was still to deport the Jews. It was only the failure of the Russian campaign and Nazis' inability to cope with the millions of deported Jews building up in Poland that led to initiatives which gained Hitler's approval. By this way of thinking, the Holocaust was the result of the regime's hasty search for a way out of a problem it had created for itself.
Adapted from Mason 1981, Mommsen 1991 and Broszat 1979.

step in that direction had been taken.' (Kershaw 2000, p.111)

Kershaw notes that, at this point, there were still major differences of opinion on how to deal with the Jews. Eichmann was still investigating the possibility of shipping them to Palestine. Himmler wanted to send them to a 'reserve' in Madagascar. This idea was finally scrapped in 1942.

The first mass shootings

In the spring of 1941 the first mass shootings of Russian Jews by the Einsatzgruppen marked a major development. Kershaw argues that:

'Most historians have accepted that some blanket empowering directive from Hitler to kill the Russian Jews lay behind Heydrich's verbal instructions.' (Kershaw 2000, p.117)

Göring commissioned Heydrich to prepare for 'a total solution of the Jewish Question' in German territory at the end of July 1941 and most historians think that Hitler made a decision to carry out the Final Solution in the spring or summer of 1941.

The Wannsee Conference, 20 January 1942

Further debate surrounds whether or not a decision had already been taken when Heydrich chaired a meeting of Nazi leaders at the Wannsee Conference on 20 January 1942. Some, including Ian Kershaw, think that they were still trying to agree on what form the Final Solution should take (Kershaw 2000, p.121). The majority think that the decision had already been taken. Significantly, Hitler himself was absent, which fits with his usual avoidance of possible blame. For Guido Knopp, the meeting was significant in that it spread responsibility:

'By the end of the Wannsee Conference, if not before, all the senior decision makers in the Reich were acquainted with and jointly responsible for the murder of the century. All were agreed that the shipping-off of the Jews should be forced ahead as rapidly as possible.' (Knopp 2001, p.105)

To what extent were ordinary Germans involved?

At one time most historians thought that ordinary Germans were largely ignorant of the Holocaust. However, research increasingly refutes this. Robert Gellately's work on denunciations to the Gestapo suggests that many ordinary Germans passively accepted or even approved of Jews being sent to concentration camps (Gellately 2001, pp.138-39). Goldhagen writes of the wide support for Nazi anti-Semitism, even among people who objected to other aspects of Nazism. He quotes diary entries from ordinary Germans talking about a probable Holocaust happening in the East (Goldhagen 1997, p.105). He also raises a point made by other historians, namely that the killings by the Einsatzgruppen, assisted by army and police units, must have been reported to their families in Germany, and that the knowledge would have spread throughout the army (Goldhagen 1997, p.111).

It has also been argued that the death camps involved so many workers, SS guards and local people, that word must have got back to Germany. Of course the remoteness of the camps would have helped people who chose not to think the unthinkable, and to deny the rumours. At any rate, there was little they could have done. Klaus Fischer writes:

'How secret was the Holocaust? The answer, as painful as it still may be to some Germans, is that it was an open secret. It was known not only to the circle of direct perpetrators – Hitler, Himmler, Heydrich, the SS executioners - but also to high-ranking members of the government...the party, and the Wehrmacht. Soldiers returning from the front who were exposed to the "terrible secret" spilled their knowledge to loved ones, friends, and acquaintances. By the middle of 1944 the secret was widely known.' (Fischer K. 1995, p.498)

MAIN POINTS - Section 2.3

- The euthanasia programme probably paved the way for the Holocaust. An important step towards it was the first mass killings carried out by the Einsatzgruppen who massacred Communists and Jews in the Soviet Union from the spring of 1941.
- Deportation of German Jews began to be undertaken on a huge scale in October 1941, organised by Eichmann. Jews were either deported to ghettos in Poland and then death camps or direct to death camps.
- By the spring of 1942, six death camps had been set up. These camps used gas to kill their victims.

- Historians see the origins of the Holocaust in terms of anti-Semitism, racialism, and difficulties in Germany adapting to modernisation.
- Intentionalists say Hitler was in charge and planned the Holocaust. Structuralists argue that the Holocaust evolved.
- Most historians say that if Hitler did order the Holocaust to take place, he did so in 1941. Historians increasingly think that ordinary Germans at least suspected that the Holocaust was taking place. Some argue that there was support for it among ordinary Germans.

Activity 6.6 The Holocaust

ITEM 1 Hitler and the Holocaust

(i) Anti-Semitism on purely emotional grounds will find its final expression in the form of pogroms. However, rational anti-Semitism must lead to a carefully planned legal curbing and eradication of Jewish privilege...though its final unalterable objective must be the removal of the Jews altogether.

Part of a letter written by Hitler in 1919, quoted in Knopp 2001.

(ii) In the course of my life I have very often been a prophet, and have usually been ridiculed for it. During the time of my struggle for power it was in the first instance only the Jewish race that received my prophecies with laughter when I said that I would one day take over the leadership of the state, and with it that of the whole nation, and that I would then among other things settle the Jewish problem. Their laughter was uproarious, but I think that for some time now they have been laughing on the other side of their face. Today I will once more be a prophet. If the international Jewish financiers in and outside of Europe should succeed in plunging the nations once more into a world war, then the result will not be the Bolshevising of the earth, and thus the victory of Jewry, but the annihilation of the Jewish race in Europe!

Part of a speech made by Hitler to the Reichstag on 30 January 1939, the anniversary of his appointment as Chancellor, quoted in Fischer K. 1995.

(iii) My prophecy will find its fulfilment in the fact that Aryan humanity will not be destroyed by this war, but the Jew will be exterminated. No matter what the struggle may bring, or how long it may last, that will be the ultimate result.

Hitler's message to Nazi Party members, 24 February 1942, quoted in Knopp 2001.

ITEM 2 The death camps

On 5 September 1941, in the sick bay in Auschwitz, a committee of SS doctors separated the sick from amongst a group of Polish prisoners. It was an arbitrary allocation to life or death purely on outward appearance. Those selected for death were instructed to stay where they were. Dressed only in shirts and underpants, they shivered in the cold. After an hour the order came. 'Get over to Block 11'. Konrad Sweda was working as an orderly in the sick bay. He remembers: 'We picked up a stretcher with one of the sick and went into the hall of the punishment block. From there, we were sent down into the cellar. I felt faint as I found myself in the evil-smelling dungeon. We laid the poor wretch on the cold concrete. A second man was immediately placed on top of him, then a third and a fourth. They were being stacked up while they were still alive. In a cell designed for one man, they packed in 30, 40, as many as 50 people.' When he asked what was going to happen he got no answer. Only a few hours later, he observed Russian POWs being forced to take the same route. When they reached Block 11, the guards shoved them into the already crammed cells. When the cell doors were slammed shut, those outside could hear a desperate moaning and screaming. The sounds grew fainter and soon nothing was heard. For the first time, in the early hours of 6 September 1941, the SS had tested a cyanide preparation known as Zyklon B on human beings. The trial had been 'successful' and the executioners declared themselves satisfied. About 600 Soviet soldiers and nearly 300 sick prisoners had been gassed to death. The means of mass murder in Auschwitz had been discovered. The advantage over mass shootings was obvious. Zyklon B killed more quickly and more cost effectively. It was also more 'humane' - for the perpetrators not the victims. The camp commandant, Rudolf Höss, later stated: 'I must say frankly that the gassing had a reassuring effect on me since, in the foreseeable future a start had to be made on the mass extermination of the Jews. I always dreaded the shootings. Now I was assured we would be spared all those blood baths'.

This photo was taken in Auschwitz after it was liberated by the Soviet troops in January 1945. It shows a human hand protruding from an incinerator in the crematorium.

Adapted from Knopp 2001.

ITEM 3 A historian's view

Words are quite inadequate to describe the enormity of a crime without parallel in the whole of history. Of Hitler's determination to be rid of the Jews 'one way or the other', there is no doubt. Nevertheless, it is by no means certain that he planned the Holocaust from his first entry into politics. More likely an element of improvisation characterised Nazi policy here, as elsewhere. During the Polish campaign, SS units murdered Jewish members of the Polish ruling class. When some Wehrmacht commanders tried to restrain the SS, Hitler deprived the army of any share in the administration of Poland, handing it over to the SS. Heydrich herded Polish Jews into ghettos and deportation from Germany began. After the fall of France, Nazi leaders toyed with the idea of settling 4 million Jews in Madagascar. But continued British resistance made this impossible. The attack on Russia sealed the fate of the Jews. Almost certainly, Hitler ordered the extermination of European Jews in the summer of 1941 when the Russian campaign was going well. The first phase was carried out by the Einsatzgruppen. The Wehrmacht was relieved that front-line soldiers had not been assigned this grisly task. Some of those working in the death camps were already practised murderers, having been engaged in the gassing of the mentally ill. When that operation was suspended in August 1941, these 'mercy killers' found new employment. Perhaps the most horrible feature of the death camps was the meticulous care and thoroughness with which camp staff disposed of personal effects. Clothes and shoes were carefully counted. Gold fillings (from teeth torn off after death) were sent to the Reichsbank. Hair was cut off and used for stuffing chairs. Bones were used for fertiliser. The fat of victims' bodies was boiled down and used in soap-making. Most Germans had little direct knowledge of what was going on. There were whispers of dreadful deeds, but the Nazis went to some pains to disguise the operation. Exposed to the pressures of wartime under a totalitarian regime, ordinary people suppressed their doubts and curiosity.

This photo shows a pile of shoes taken from inmates at Auschwitz concentration camp.

Adapted from Carr 1991.

Questions

1. Using Items 1-3 and your own knowledge, give arguments for and against the view that Hitler was directly responsible for the Holocaust.
2. How would (a) an intentionalist and (b) a structuralist historian interpret the passages in Item 1?
3. What do Items 2 and 3 tell us about the nature of the Holocaust?

3 Nazi society and economy

Key issues

1. What impact did did the Nazis make on German society?
2. How did the economy perform under the Nazis in the period 1933-45?

3.1 What impact did the Nazis make on German society?

The debate

Historians who have considered the impact that the Nazis made on German society have tended to focus on the following three key questions:

1. What impact did the Nazis make before, and after, 1945?
2. What changes would probably have occurred anyway?
3. Which changes were deliberate, and which were incidental?

Some historians claim that Nazism was revolutionary, others counter-revolutionary. Some argue that it was a modernising force, despite its traditionalist aspects, others that it was anti-modernist. It is also important to bear in mind that, although changes in income, employment or birth rate can be easily tracked in records, it is harder to assess how attitudes changed. A further complicating factor is that half of the regime's 12 years in power were spent at war, and war is itself a huge agent for change - though, as Geoff Layton notes, one could see war as 'a natural feature of Nazism' (Layton 2000, p.90).

Was Nazism a modernising force?

Some of the changes associated with modern industrial societies are:

- an increased range of goods and services
- greater division of labour and specialisation
- social mobility (the breaking down of class barriers)
- centralisation of government
- separation of state from religion
- urbanisation - a growth of cities
- democracy.

Clearly the Nazi Party was anti-democratic. On the other hand, it did centralise government, albeit as a means of control. Yet Nazi ideology was full of contradictions. The Nazi Party claimed to reject what it saw as the moral squalor of urban life and its propaganda idealised the peasant lifestyle, yet the regime actually did very little for the peasants. Moreover, Hitler's aims of rearmament and war demanded increased industrialisation, which made people move to the cities for work. Similarly, the Nazi Party claimed to uphold traditional moral values and yet it sought to undermine the churches. It claimed to support the family, yet it wanted people to put loyalty to the Führer, the Nazi Party and Germany first.

The Nazi impact on the class structure

In the 1960s, American historian David Schoenbaum analysed these contradictions. He argued that the Nazis were a strong modernising force, producing 'a double revolution...of means and ends. The revolution of ends was ideological - war against bourgeois [middle-class] and industrial society. The revolution of means was its [reverse]. It was bourgeois and industrial since, in an industrial age, even a war against industrial society must be fought with industrial means and the bourgeois are necessary to fight the bourgeoisie' (Schoenbaum 1966, pp.xxi-xxii). Schoenbaum's arguments and the responses to it are outlined in Box 6.26.

Impact on the working class

Marxist historians tend to analyse social change in terms of class struggle. So, historians in the GDR (Communist East Germany - the part of Germany controlled by the Soviet Union after the end of the Second World War) saw Nazism as a dictatorship of the most reactionary elements of the ruling class. It is therefore not surprising that they saw Nazism as incapable of producing real social change. Western Marxist historians such as Tim Mason, on the other hand, place emphasis on the ways in which the Nazis controlled the working class. In Ian Kershaw's words:

BOX 6.26 Schoenbaum's arguments and responses to them

Schoenbaum distinguished between 'objective social reality' and 'interpreted social reality'. The objective reality (how things actually were) was the opposite of what Hitler had promised - there was more urbanisation, industrialisation, economic inequality and a maintenance of the status quo. The interpreted reality (how Germans perceived Germany) was different. According to Schoenbaum, Germans thought they lived in a society united like no other in recent German history, a society of opportunities for young and old, classes and masses, a society that was New Deal and good old days at the same time. This perception was the basis of a new social mobility which led to a breakdown in the traditional class structure. German sociologist Ralf Dahrendorf agrees that the Nazi regime brought important change. He argues that Nazism enabled Germany to become a modern society, completing the revolution of 1918. It did this, he said, not intentionally, but by destroying the traditional loyalties and values of religion, region, family and the workplace, reducing the power of the élites and levelling social strata. By way of contrast, Ian Kershaw claims that there was little or no objective change in German society. He says that historians' previous beliefs that change had taken place were due to a naive acceptance of Nazi propaganda and to an incorrect assumption that changes post-1945 stemmed from the Nazi era. He thinks there was only a small increase in social mobility. He points out that élites still dominated in the army, the social make-up of the civil service and Big Business remained the same and education was still dominated by the middle and upper classes. What mobility there was, he claims, amounted to a slight acceleration of changes that had already begun in the Weimar Republic'. He also describes Schoenbaum's ideas about interpreted social reality as 'highly speculative and impressionistic', arguing that, in fact, most people were increasingly disillusioned with the regime. Henry Turner, on the other hand, takes Schoenbaum's paradox further, seeing Nazi ideology as a sincere attempt to use modern means to destroy modern society. Conquering new territory (ie the policy of Lebensraum) was supposed to make de-urbanisation and de-industrialisation possible, enabling urban Germans to return to the ideal peasant lifestyle. Kershaw considers that this gives the Nazi regime too much credit for logic and ignores the continued need for an arms industry in order to defend newly won territory.

Adapted from Schoenbaum 1966, Dahrendorf 1968, Turner 1972 and Kershaw 2000.

'Nazism destroyed working-class organizations reshaped class relations by greatly strengthening the position of employers, who were backed with all the weight of a repressive police state, and kept down living standards while providing for soaring profits.' (Kershaw 2000, p.165)

Mason also places an emphasis on working-class resistance to the Nazis. Other historians, including Kershaw, however, argue that there was widespread working-class support for the Nazis (Kershaw 2000, p.165). Yet, despite the propaganda ideal of the Völksgemeinschaft, Hitler's policies did not genuinely aim to improve the standard of life for the working class. Hitler quickly suppressed left-wing parties that stood for workers' rights, and in the 'Night of the Long Knives' he purged the more left-wing Nazi Party members, such as Gregor Strasser. It follows that there must have been other reasons for working-class support. These are considered in Box 6.27.

BOX 6.27 | **Reasons for working-class support of the Nazi regime**

The main attraction of the Nazi regime to the working class was economic. Almost everyone benefited to some extent from the end of the Depression. The economy revived, with both unemployment and inflation being drastically reduced. In 1933 over a third of the population was unemployed. This figure was reduced to 74,000 by 1939, by which time there were over a million job vacancies. Nazi propaganda claimed this as a resounding achievement for the regime, and many Germans looking back after the war continued to see it in this way. Lutz Niethammer's 1983 study, based on a university oral history project, shows that Germans recalled the 1930s as a time of order and economic miracle. However, it may be that people would inevitably compare this period with the chaos and hardship of the war and its aftermath. It is also questionable how far economic growth was achieved by the Nazis rather than by growth in the world economy (see Section 3.2 below for a more detailed study of economic developments). Ian Kershaw's view is that the working class were worse off under the Nazis. The unions were shut down. Members of the working class had no political representation, and they were subject to Gestapo repression. There was a slight rise in wages in the late 1930s, but this was coupled with longer hours and more pressure. Their class position remained the same, except that the most extreme exploitation was now of foreign workers. Geoff Layton notes that the working class benefited from employment, stable rents and increased wages (especially in the armaments industry). However, he adds that real wages (relative to inflation) rose above 1929 levels only in 1938 and that the average working week rose from 43 hours in 1933 to 47 hours in 1939.

Adapted from Welch 1993, p.58, Herbert 1986, Kershaw 2000 and Layton 2000.

Strength through Joy and Beauty of Labour

Opinion is divided on how far working-class families benefited from the Strength through Joy and Beauty of Labour organisations. Kershaw plays down the value of Strength through Joy for workers, as does Peukert, who sees it largely as a propaganda exercise:

'[It] organised holiday trips ranging from weekend excursions to health-cure visits to the Harz and the Black Forest, and Norwegian cruises. In reality, however, long-distance travel was restricted to a hand-picked minority, and most Germans spent their vacations at home or in the immediate vicinity.' (Peukert 1987, p.70)

Welch accepts that Strength through Joy did benefit workers, though not as much as the regime claimed. He quotes SOPADE reports (reports written for the SPD in exile) testifying to its popularity. These reports suggest that workers may well have been cynical about the organisation's intentions, yet prepared to take what it offered (Welch 1993, pp.58-59). Lisa Pine is slightly more positive about the effects of these welfare organisations, pointing out that in 1938, 10.3 million people went on Strength through Joy holidays (Pine 2002, p.3).

Peukert suggests that one lasting effect of Nazi repression may have been to make workers more self-seeking, since they could no longer make group demands. He also suggests that the 'retreat into the private sphere' forced by Nazi repression had a long-term depoliticising effect, helping to create a post-war consumer society (see Kershaw 2000, p.180). This is similar to the view of Michael Geyser, who argues that the Nazis destroyed 'bonds of solidarity, by fostering the egotism of both individuals and institutions, and by applauding as strong and healthy' people with no sympathy for others, and that, in this way, they created a more selfish, opportunist society (Geyser 1986, p.36).

Impact on farming communities

The Nazis had a mixed effect on farming communities. A substantial number of farm debts were written off and farmers benefited from increased food prices in 1933-36. But the Reich Food Estate's bureaucratic meddling was resented. For example, Layton cites the absurd Reich Food Estate ruling that each hen was to lay 65 eggs a year (Layton 2000, p.66). Another regulation prevented milk-producing farmers from selling direct to the consumer. Instead they had to sell to a central agency, which paid them less, again a source of resentment. The Reich Entailed Farm Law was also resented. This was meant to preserve rural life by giving security of tenure to occupiers of medium-sized farms. In practice, it meant that farmland could not be sold or divided up among a farmer's children, with the result that younger sons were dispossessed.

Impact on middle and upper classes

The lower-middle class ('Mittelstand' - small retailers and so on) were promised a great deal in 1933, but in fact were disappointed. It was more important to the regime to woo Big Business in order to rearm for war. On the other hand, retailers benefited from people having more money to spend. In addition, some middle-class men benefited from job opportunities in an expanded civil service while others were able to take jobs from which women had been removed - for example, in schools and universities. Another area of opportunity was in professions from which Jews were gradually being banned, especially medicine, commerce and the law.

The upper classes were largely unaffected. Hitler realised that he had to work with them. Big Business generally benefited from Nazi policies. The share index rose from 41 points in 1932 to 106 in 1940. Annual dividends to investors grew from an average of 2.83% to 6.60% during this period and average management salaries grew from 3,700 marks in 1934 to 5,420 marks in 1938. (Layton 2000, p.67).

The Nazi impact on the position of women

The First World War had created a labour shortage that had pushed women into factory work. There was also a surplus of 1.8 million marriageable women, most of whom needed to work to support themselves (Layton 2000, p.81). Added to this, in the 1920s there was an increased demand for non-manual labour and unskilled mass production workers. Meanwhile, the realisation that birth control, and smaller families, could improve standard of living meant that many women were able to have careers. When the Nazis came to power, women were becoming more educated and entering the professions. As Box 6.28 shows, this all changed under the Nazis.

Most historians agree with Klaus Fischer's assessment, namely that:

'The Nazis looked upon the family primarily as a reproductive unit furnishing soldiers for the Reich.'
As Box 6.28 suggests, they set about reversing female emancipation and turning women into baby machines to increase the population and justify the regime's demands for increased Lebensraum (living space). For the Nazis, a woman's place was in the home.

The Depression helped justify Nazi pressure on labour exchanges and employers to discriminate against women. As a result of these measures, although in 1932-37 female employment rose from 4.8 million to 5.9 million, this represented a fall from 37% to 31% of the total (Layton 2000, p.82). In the professions, women were banned from practising law in 1936, and there were strong efforts to keep them out of other professions. They were

| BOX 6.28 | The Nazi view of women |

The Nazis promised to restore the traditional balance between the sexes by encouraging women to celebrate their 'natural' domestic role as mothers and housewives. 'Equal rights for women', Hitler said, 'means that they receive the respect they deserve in the sphere nature has assigned them'. In particular, women were to become the focus of the Nazis' drive to boost the birth rate. At least in the early years of the regime they were systematically directed away from the idea of a full-time career towards starting or extending a family. To this end a generous system of marriage loans was introduced. Similarly, in education, the emphasis was moved away from developing 'unnatural' qualities such as engaging in academic study in favour of training for future maternal roles through compulsory courses in domestic science and biology. Women were also discouraged from using make-up and wearing 'decadent' foreign clothes. Attempts were made to create a new 'Germanic' style through a German Fashion Bureau set up in 1933 with Magda Goebbels (Josef Goebbels' wife) as Honorary President. There was also an increased emphasis on physical fitness. Women were encouraged to achieve the Reich Sport Medal. Smoking, especially when pregnant, was frowned upon. In marriage, the aim was for love to be replaced by Rassegefuhl - 'racial awareness'. Couples applying for a marriage loan were forced to go through a demanding medical examination, leading to a great fear of hereditary defects and a thriving black market in documents proving an Aryan ancestry. The future wives of SS men were subject to a particularly rigorous procedure. Those considered to be racially or socially undesirable were denied benefits. According to one estimate, 27,958 'undesirable' women had been forcibly sterilised by the end of 1934. Jewish women, in particular, were victimised. If an Aryan man was married to a Jew, he was encouraged to divorce her. In 1939, it was announced that the strict ban on abortion did not apply to Jews. Non-Jewish women who did not want to marry were subject to a different kind of harassment. The Nazi state showed little interest in the fate of single women beyond child-bearing age. They were often forced to seek the lowest paid and most monotonous work.
Adapted from Stibbe 1993.

also banned from jury service.

By 1937, rearmament and the introduction of conscription had created a labour shortage. Market forces meant that employers had to take on more women, a fact that Hitler reluctantly accepted. In 1937-39 female employment rose from 5.9 million to 6.9 million, representing an extra 2% of the total workforce. However, their long hours, coupled with family responsibilities, meant that this was not necessarily an improvement in their situation. In 1943, when Speer wanted to conscript women workers, Bormann and Hitler were opposed ideologically, but in the end they had to bow to the pressure of war.

Lisa Pine claims that, as a result of Nazi family policy, there was a slight increase in the German birth rate, but she argues that:

'This was not necessarily attributable to Nazi incentives to promote procreation. In fact it seems that many couples felt more secure about getting married and having children because the economic climate had improved.' (Pine 2000, p.24)

There were more marriages but not more children per marriage. Pine claims that, far from restoring the family, the Nazis undermined it because its members were obliged to go out and take part in official activities such as Hitler Youth, rather than staying at home. They also took away the family's educational role.

The regime also undermined the family by its encouragement of denunciations to the Gestapo. Gellately (2001) has shown that many denunciations were by individuals against members of their own family (see Unit 6, Section 2.1). However, as Kershaw points out, the family came nowhere near to breaking down (Kershaw 2000, p.179).

The Nazi impact on religion (see also Unit 5, Section 2.3)

Despite what one might expect of Christianity, there was a great deal of virulent nationalism, belligerence and racism - especially anti-Semitism - in the churches. This was not introduced by the Nazis, but they did encourage it. While claiming to stand for traditional German values, including Christian ones, the Nazis in reality only tolerated or used Christianity. Hitler saw it as incompatible with Nazi ideology. He was sensitive to popular opinion, but he tried to undermine Christian institutions and its calendar of festivals. In 1938, carols and nativity plays were forbidden in schools and the word 'Christmas' was replaced by 'Yuletide'. There is a debate over the extent to which the Nazi regime undermined traditional religious loyalties. This is explored in Box 6.29.

On the key moral question of anti-Semitism, many historians, including Gellately (2001), Goldhagen (1997) and Hilberg (2000), argue that it was deeply ingrained in German society long before the Nazis came to power. Kershaw writes that:

'Enhancement of existing prejudice against Jews and other racial minorities unquestionably occurred.' (Kershaw 2000, p.178)

But he adds that protest against the 'euthanasia action' and the Nazis' perceived need for secrecy over the Holocaust argue that Germans had not been won over to Nazi racial and eugenic ideology. Of course Nazi policies had a huge impact on the Jewish population (see Unit 6, Sections 2.2 and 2.3).

BOX 6.29 How far did the Nazis break down traditional religious loyalties?

Klaus Fischer argues that the churches survived Gleichschlatung (coordination - see Unit 5, Section 1.2) because the Nazis had no long-range plan concerning their role in the future Third Reich. Some Nazi Protestants formed the racist 'Positive German Christians'. Martin Niemoller, however, led the formation of a Pastoral Emergency Union when the Prussian general synod (which was composed of two-thirds Positive German Christians) ratified a proposal ruling that only those of Aryan origin could become priests. This led to the formation of the anti-Nazi Confessional Church. Kershaw argues that Ralf Dahrendorf overestimated the extent of the breakdown of traditional religious loyalties and that, in rural areas, loyalty often increased. He points out that the churches gained in influence after the Second World War. If anything, it could be argued that, by persecution and threat, the Nazis actually helped to strengthen the role of Christianity in Germany.
Adapted from Fischer 1995, Dahrendorf 1968 and Kershaw 2000.

The Nazi impact on cultural life (see also Unit 6, Section 1.1 above)

The Nazi approach to cultural life was that all art had to serve the Nazi cause - it was merely an aspect of propaganda and it certainly should not challenge the status quo. The regime was anti-intellectual and it scorned 'art for art's sake' as mere self-indulgence that went against the ideal of the Völksgemeinschaft.

Although under the Nazis some workers went to the theatre and cinema for the first time, with cheap tickets made available by Strength through Joy, most historians agree that cultural life was bland and unoriginal, consisting of lightweight distraction and heavy-handed propaganda. Detlev Peukert writes:

'Since National Socialism had no cultural vision of its own, its cultural policies, like its policies in other fields, were either destructive or parasitical.' (Peukert 1987, p.189)

Conclusion

Historians now generally argue that the Nazis had less impact on German society than was at one time thought to be the case. There is an increased understanding of the extent to which pre-1933 trends continued to develop under the the Nazis, and a new scepticism about Nazi propaganda claims. However, an important new perception, supported in Kershaw (2000) and Noakes & Pridham (2000) among others, is that Nazism did have quite unintended effects by virtue of its destructiveness. In so far as it succeeded in destroying German institutions, and in its waging of a war that bankrupted the country, it paved the way for a new Germany.

MAIN POINTS - Section 3.1

- East German Marxist historians claim that no significant social change took place under the Nazis. Others question how far Nazism was a modernising force. Dahrendorf and Schoenbaum claim that Nazism had a revolutionary impact. But Kershaw claims that there was little or no objective change in German society.
- Some historians say social mobility increased under the Nazis. Others argue that change to the class structure was minimal.
- Most historians agree that women were worse off under the Nazis, being limited to traditional roles. Some argue, however, that in some ways they were better off.
- Religious life continued, though people probably became more racist.
- Most historians agree that cultural life became bland and unoriginal.

Activity 6.7 What impact did the Nazis make on German society?

ITEM 1 Creating a Völksgemeinschaft

This photo shows two of the pages in a children's book produced in 1936. The picture shows a Jewish family reading a sign which says: 'Jews are not wanted here'. The text is a rhyme which says that Germans should be able to breath pure air (ie air which is not contaminated by Jews).

The Nazis employed a variety of propaganda and socialisation methods, underpinned by the threat or use of force, to reshape German society. In addition to propaganda in the media, the regime introduced significant changes to the educational system and to the school curriculum to ensure that Nazi ideas were reflected. Further, a host of Nazi organisations were set up to foster feelings of belonging, unity and conformity (eg the youth groups - the Hitler Youth and League of German Girls). The regime attempted to undermine sectional loyalties - to class, locality and family - and to replace them with a new national consciousness. It tried to reorder society to fit in with the Nazi idea of perfection. This meant the creation of types - the ideal 'national comrade' who belonged to society and the 'unfit' who did not. In the Third Reich a variety of measures were undertaken to turn the majority of Germans into reliable, fit and productive members of society and, at the same time, to exclude, terrorise and even annihilate those groups that did not conform to the Nazi ideal. The regime claimed that it had created a classless society in which class barriers were broken down and workers had new opportunities. In many ways, this seemed to be the case. What used to be middle-class pursuits - for example, taking a holiday or owning a car - came within the reach of the working class. Mass tourism was introduced under the Strength through Joy organisation. This arranged subsidised leisure cruises and holidays, car ownership and greater access to the theatre, cinema and other cultural activities. Such opportunities plus cosmetic improvements in working conditions were designed to appeal to workers. The main benefit, however, was the growth in employment. The regime's claims to have created a classless society were not wholly accurate. The Nazi regime succeeded neither in totally removing class barriers nor in destroying traditional class loyalties. Another means of rallying people to the national cause was foreign policy success. While foreign policy continued to succeed, the sense of national community (Völksgemeinschaft) was enhanced. Once the tide of war turned, however, Hitler's infallibility and the nation's strength began to be called into question.

Adapted from Pine 2002.

ITEM 2 Hitler on the classless society

I too am a child of the people. I do not trace my line from any castle. I come from the workshop. Neither was I a general. I was simply a soldier, as were millions of others. It is something wonderful that amongst us an unknown from the army of the millions of German people - of workers and of soldiers - could rise to be head of the Reich and of the nation. By my side stand Germans from all walks of life who today are amongst the leaders of the nation. Men who were once workers on the land are now governing German states in the name of the Reich. It is true that men who came from the middle class and former aristocrats have their place in this movement. But, to us, it matters nothing where they come from if only they can work to the profit of our people. That is the decisive test. We have not broken down classes in order to set new ones in their place. We have broken down classes to make way for the German people as a whole.

Part of a speech made Hitler, quoted in Baynes 1942.

ITEM 3 Women in the Third Reich

Jill Stephenson points out that the Nazis' policies towards women were in line with those of other European states in the inter-war years. Measures designed to curb abortions and contraception and a preoccupation with a declining birth rate among 'healthy' sections of society were common. France, for example, was particularly worried about the birth rate and in 1920 began the practice of rewarding women who had lots of children - the practice was then copied by the Nazis. Similarly, campaigns to remove married women from the labour market to make way for unemployed men was a Europe-wide response to the Depression. In Germany itself, measures to this end were introduced by Brüning. The significant break in the Nazis' stance towards women came, Stephenson argues, in 1936 when unemployment was

This photo shows German women working in a weapons factory in 1940.

down and the Nazis began to focus on rearmament. The increased need for female labour meant that, whatever leading Nazis' beliefs, they could only discriminate against women to a limited extent. Stephenson concludes that women under Nazism benefited both from a rise in the status and benefits given to mothers and housewives, whilst, at the same time, consolidating their position in employment outside the home. David Schoenbaum agrees, noting how economic pressure reduced the gap between men's and women's wages. Women, he argues, had no political power, but they had increased job opportunities and rising wage rates, as well as improved maternity benefits and services. This helps to explain why a number of leading figures in the pre-1933 women's movement came to support the Nazi regime. It should be noted, however, that, once women are no longer seen as passive victims of the Nazi regime, new controversies come to light. Koonz, for example, argues that women played a major role in supporting Nazi power. By surrendering their political rights in return for the honour and prestige bestowed on them as mothers in the fatherland, she argues, German women ultimately played an equal role in helping to make war and genocide possible. She points out, for example, that members of the Women's Bureau were expected to play an active role in spreading Nazi values, promoting eugenics and 'racial' awareness and collecting the names of those fit for the sterilisation or euthanasia programmes. While Nazi men launched their racially-charged war of conquest in the East, Nazi women busily created their own Lebensraum at home. It should be noted, however, that, although some women collaborated with the regime, there is a significant body of evidence to show that some did not.

Adapted from Stibbe 1993.

(ii) The mission of women is to be beautiful and to bring children into the world. This is not at all as rude and unmodern as it sounds. The female bird pretties herself for her mate and hatches the eggs for him. In exchange, the mate takes care of gathering food, and stands guard and wards off the enemy.

Goebbels, quoted in Fischer K. 1995.

Questions

1. Using Items 1-3 and your own knowledge, assess the impact that the Nazis made on German society.
2. a) What does Item 2 tell us about the nature of the German society that Hitler wanted to create?
   b) How successful was he in creating it? Use Item 1 in your answer.
3. Using Item 3, give arguments for and against the view that the position of women deteriorated under the Nazis.

3.2 How did the economy perform under the Nazis in the period 1933-45?

The economic position in 1933

The economic crisis which engulfed Germany from the late 1920s was a major cause of the collapse of the Weimar Republic and the rise to power of the Nazis (see Unit 3, Part 2 and Unit 4, Part 3). Although there were some signs of the beginning of a recovery in 1932, Richard Overy argues that eight million people were still unemployed when the Nazis came to power and that the economy was still in very poor shape:

'Over eight million people who had been employed in 1929 were without work (the conventional figure of six million unemployed in 1933 is derived from the official register - but by 1932 many had dropped off the register or had failed to register in the first place). Agricultural prices collapsed leaving peasants impoverished and in debt; artisan income was halved; even for those in employment, the Slump brought short-time working and temporary lay-offs. Investor confidence was at rock bottom. The value of trade was half that of 1929 and German capitalism appeared to be in terminal decline.' (Overy 1996, p.8)

It was in this economic context that the Nazis came to power with their promise of 'Bread and Work'. It is important to note that, although the Nazis promised 'Bread and Work', historians agree that no detailed economic programme had been drawn up. The following assessment is typical:

'It seems clear that, when he was appointed Chancellor in January 1933, Hitler had no clear idea of the kind of economic policy he would follow.' (Craig 1981, p.603)

Overy points out that some leading Nazis had come up with ideas which they hoped would lead to economic revival, but suggests that Hitler was reluctant to implement such ideas:

'Those few Nazis who did think about economic questions had a whole range of radical solutions - social control of industry, redistribution of wealth, attacks on "unproductive" finance capitalism - which Hitler was extremely reluctant to introduce because of the effect they would have on the German business community.' (Overy 1996, p.8)

Most historians agree that economic policy under the Nazis went through three key phases:

- Phase 1 (1933-36) - the first Four Year plan - the key aim was to reduce unemployment
- Phase 2 (1936-39) - the second Four Year Plan - the key aim was to rearm as quickly as possible
- Phase 3 (1939-45) - the wartime economy - the economy was focused exclusively on winning the war.

In the past, historians have argued that, as soon as he came to power, Hitler began to rearm Germany and that this emphasis on rearmament explains why the Nazis were able to turn around the German economy so quickly. Today, however, few historians accept such a point of view. Whilst they would agree that there was a clear focus on rearmament after 1936, most would argue that there was little effort to rearm before that date. These arguments are explored in Box 6.30.

BOX 6.30 **Economic policy and rearmament 1933-36**

It is sometimes argued that Hitler went for the easy option - rearmament from the start. Large quantities of military spending would somehow solve the problem and drag Germany out of recession. Very few historians now take that argument seriously, if only for one rather obvious reason. Rearmament might certainly have helped certain sections of German heavy industry, but it would have done little to solve the major structural problems facing Germany, namely:

- the balance of payments (ie the problem of ensuring that government expenditure balanced government income - in 1933, it did not, there was a large government deficit)
- the banking and finance structure (rearmament would not provide the investment needed to help the banks and financial institutions)
- low agricultural investment (rearmament would not help farmers) .

Indeed, so wide-ranging were the economic difficulties facing Germany in 1933 that it was extremely unlikely there would be a single cause of economic recovery. Recovery rested on a package of reforms and policies. Rearmament was certainly part of that package, but in the first two years of revival it was a relatively limited part. There were three critical factors. First, the government insisted on adopting a strategy of economic nationalism in its relations with other states. In the 1920s, Germany had been hostage to large loans from overseas. These contributed to the crisis in 1929 when other countries recalled their loans (see Unit 3, Section 2.1). After 1933, the Nazis were determined to reduce Germany's economic ties with other countries. They refused to pay reparations and other debts and introduced new regulations. Second, the government made strenuous efforts to stabilise Germany's credit structure. The state took over much of the banking system and took control of the capital market. And third, the state itself generated new investment and new demand in the economy by increasing the level of state spending. Rearmament was one area of state spending but it was only one. The state undertook a wide range of major projects to improve Germany's infrastructure.

Adapted from Overy 1996.

Phase 1 (1933-36)

It was as early as February 1933 that Hitler announced that he intended to reorganise the economy to ensure economic recovery by the means of two Four Year Plans:

'[In February 1933, Hitler] announced that the national government would "achieve the great task of reorganising the economy of our Volk by means of two great Four Year Plans: for the salvation of the German farmer in order to maintain the food supply and, in consequence, the very basis of the nation's life; for the salvation of the German worker, by means of a powerful and comprehensive attack upon unemployment". Apart from continuing the work creation policies of his predecessors, however, he did nothing to fulfil these pledges until he had solicited the advice of leading industrialists and it was not until the summer that a programme was inaugurated that could be described as National Socialist.' (Craig 1981, p.604)

In the summer of 1933, the Nazi government invested a billion marks in a programme of public works. This programme of road, canal and house building stimulated the economy and provided a great deal of employment. One scheme that proved particularly popular was the scheme to build a national network of motorways or 'autobahnen':

'The building of the autobahnen which not only provided jobs for thousands of construction workers and engineers and architects but also stimulated the automotive industry and allied trades struck the national fancy...Nazi propagandists pulled out all the stops in advertising this as dramatic proof of the energy and earnestness with which the regime was tackling the country's basic problems.' (Craig 1981, p.604)

The New Plan

It was noted in Box 6.30 above that the Nazi government insisted on adopting a strategy of economic nationalism in its relations with other states. To ensure that Germany did not fall into the trap of relying on foreign loans and foreign investment, Hjalmar Schacht, the President of the Reichsbank and, from the summer of 1934, Finance Minister, introduced the 'New Plan' in September 1934:

'In September 1934, comprehensive controls over foreign transactions were established in the so-called "New Plan" drawn up by Hjalmar Schacht, President of the Reichsbank and Minister of Economics. Imports could only be brought in under licence; capital could not be moved freely abroad; foreign earnings in Germany were kept in blocked accounts, to be spent only on German goods and services. Where feasible the government negotiated barter agreements with other traders in order to secure essential supplies of food and raw materials. Not surprisingly, foreign lending became insignificant in the 1930s.' (Overy 1996a, p.26)

The extent of recovery

Overy (2001) argues that six factors combined to ensure an economic recovery after the Nazis came to power:

- political stabilisation
- the crushing of the labour movement (ie the abolition of trade unions in May 1933)
- the continuation of policies begun under Brüning (such as the work creations schemes)
- the New Plan
- greater central control
- increased government spending, especially on large-scale projects designed to improve Germany's infrastructure.

Economic recovery after the Nazis came to power was swift. In particular, unemployment fell sharply. The extent of the economic recovery is outlined in Box 6.31.

BOX 6.31 The economic recovery, 1933-36

In the early years, Nazi economic policy was under the control of Hjalmar Schacht. This reflected the need of the Nazi leadership to work with the powerful forces of Big Business. Schacht was already a respected international financier because of his leading role in the creation of a new currency following the period of hyperinflation in 1923. By 1936, the economic recovery was well advanced. Nazi government investment in the first three years was directed to work creation schemes (reforestation, land reclamation), motorisation (developing the vehicle industry and the roads to go with it) and construction (housing and public buildings). The cumulative effect was to triple public investment between 1933 and 1936 and to increase government expenditure by nearly 70% over the same period. Yet even in 1936, the government deficit was certainly not out of control since Schacht maintained taxes at a relatively high level and encouraged private savings in state savings banks. Of more public note was the decline in unemployment to 2.1 million in mid-1935 from a peak of well over 6 million, an achievement which drew admiration from both home and abroad. Of course, it must be remembered that all this took place as the world economy began to recover and undoubtedly Schacht was aided by the natural upturn in the business cycle after it had reached its lowest point in the winter of 1932-33. Nevertheless, it is difficult to believe that such a marked turnaround in investment and employment could have been achieved regardless of Nazi economic policy. By mid-1936, unemployment had fallen to 1.5 million, industrial production had increased by 60% since 1933 and GNP (Gross National Product - the national income) had increased by 40%.

Adapted from Layton 2000.

Phase 2 (1936-39)

Most historians agree that a turning point in economic management came in 1936 when Hitler put Göring in charge of the second Four Year Plan:

'The real turning point in the development of both the German economy and the German military build-up came in 1936 with the announcement of the second Four Year Plan in October...The Plan ushered in a quite different phase of military expansion based upon the restructuring of the economy to meet the probable needs of war.' (Overy 1998, p.4)

Overy points out that the second Four Year Plan was launched after Hitler wrote a memorandum in which he made it clear that he believed that a war between Germany and the forces of 'Bolshevism and world Jewry' was inevitable and that, as a result, the German economy should focus on preparing for the forthcoming military struggle. This viewpoint, Overy notes, was not popular with some sections of the business community:

'By 1936, it was clear that the German economy was at a crossroads. Important elements in the business community and in German politics thought that the opportunity had now come to embark on a consumer boom at home, to produce increased living standards and to expand German trade abroad. Having stabilised the economy, many businessmen had no thought of war or war preparation at all - the last thing they wanted was a repeat of 1914. Most of them wanted a period of stabilisation and consolidation.' (Overy 1996, p.9)

One of those opposed to rearmament was Hjalmar Schacht. He argued that it was important that Germany should not build up too big a debt and that the way to reduce its debt was to cut rearmament. Hitler's memorandum was a response to Schacht's arguments and it led, eventually, to Schacht's resignation in November 1937.

The second Four Year Plan

The second Four Year Plan was launched in October 1936:

'The politico-economic crisis of 1936 was resolved by the introduction of the Four Year Plan under the control of Hermann Göring in October of that year. Its fundamental aim was to make the German armed forces and economy ready for war within four years. In order to achieve this, the Plan highlighted four objectives: an increase in agricultural production; the retraining of key sectors of the labour force; government regulation of imports and exports to satisfy strategic priorities; and, above all, the achievement of self-sufficiency in raw materials such as oil, rubber and metals - if necessary by the development of ersatz (synthetic) substitutes.' (Layton 2000, p.57)

Overy (1996) argues that the launching of the second Four Year Plan sent out two signals, namely that:

- the economy was going to be brought more closely under state supervision
- Germany was going to turn its back on the world economy and build up a siege economy.

One of the key aims of the second Four Year Plan was to avoid the threat of a blockade. This was to be achieved by the adoption of a policy of 'autarky':

'At the core of the Plan was a strategy of import-substitution, or autarky, designed to free Germany from the threat of blockade. Hitler was aware that the blockade had damaged Germany's war effort between 1914 and 1918 and he could see the recent efforts to impose League of Nations' sanctions on Italy for her invasion of Abyssinia [modern-day Ethiopia]. His answer was to rely on domestic production of vital war materials or, where this was not possible, to secure them in eastern or south-eastern Europe, safe from interference by other powers.' (Overy 1998, p.7)

Other aspects of the Four Year Plan are outlined in Box 6.32.

BOX 6.32 The Four Year Plan

It was not until 1938 that the political conflict generated by the introduction of the second Four Year Plan was finally resolved. In 1938, Göring effectively became economic dictator (by then he had been able to use the Four Year Plan organisation as a platform from which to defeat Schacht and other conservative critics). Under Göring, 6.4 billion marks were invested by state authorities and private companies in gigantic industrial ventures. In addition, in February 1938 Hitler himself became Supreme Commander of the Armed Forces and was able to bring both economic and military policy much more firmly under his control. In the period from 1938 to the outbreak of war, Germany's economy experienced one of the few sustained bursts of economic growth that it had had since 1914. Germany's GNP grew by almost a third more than it had reached in 1929. And almost all of the additional production went to the build-up of Germany's new military forces. In particular, it was spent on a vast investment programme in German heavy industry and engineering, designed to provide a foundation for Germany's future war effort. As a result, two-thirds of the industrial investment in Germany between 1936 and 1939 went directly into preparation for war - such sectors as the chemical industry, aluminium, aviation and electrical engineering. Indeed, by 1939, over a quarter of Germany's industrial workforce was working on orders from the Armed Forces, apart from all those workers who were busy building new chemical plants and aluminium works - which were seen as complementary to the development of weapons industries. Rearmament dominated Germany's economy between 1936 and 1939.

Adapted from Overy 1996.

How successful was the Four Year Plan?

Most historians agree that the adoption of the Four Year Plan made a significant impact on the German economy. Overy, for example, claims that there was a 'remarkable transformation' after 1936:

'In 1938, the German economy was almost 40% larger than it had been in 1928, at the peak of the previous boom, yet consumer expenditure per head grew by only 4% over the same period and exports declined by 57%. In other words almost all the additional growth in the economy was diverted to state spending, and most of that went on remilitarisation and economic preparations for war. The level of defence spending by the late 1930s...was in fact very high in relation to conventional peacetime spending. In 1938-39 the military budget took up 52% of state spending and 17% of the national product. In 1913, during the pre-war arms race, the German government spent only 24% of a much smaller budget on defence.' (Overy 1998, p.7)

Although there was a definite shift in priorities after 1936, there is evidence to suggest that the Four Year Plan was not a complete success. Overy points out that the outbreak of the Second World War came earlier than anticipated and planned. As a result, the transformation of the economy was not complete:

'By 1939, much of the programme set up in 1936 was underway, some of it completed. Hitler had said four years, but this was...not a firm plan complete with schedules and deadlines. Most of the capital projects could not be completed much before 1942, and the large arms programme followed on from their completion. In 1939 the German economy was not yet ready for a major war.' (Overy 1998, p.8)

This was not just a matter of time, it was also the result of cumbersome bureaucracy and inefficiency. The intervention of the state and the demands of the Armed Forces made it difficult for industry to maximise the resources at its disposal:

'[The military authorities]complained regularly that the Four Year Plan failed to do everything that the Armed Forces wanted, while the military authorities made things difficult for the Four Year Plan by imposing their own priorities on the arms industry - unnecessarily high standards of workmanship (which discouraged mass-production methods), constant technical refinements (which made forward planning of production almost impossible) and a refusal to integrate the production requirements of the three services (and thus avoid duplication of effort). The outcome was expensive and slow-moving production programmes.' (Overy 1998, p.8)

Phase 3 (1939-45)

Most historians agree that Hitler did not aim to go to war with Britain and France in 1939. As Overy puts it:

'When war broke out in 1939, it was not the war that Hitler had expected. He planned a localised war against Poland, for which he required only limited resources.' (Overy 1996, p.10)

Overy argues that, once war did break out with Britain and France, Hitler drew up targets for military production which were designed to push the German economy as far as it would go. The result was that:

'By the summer of 1941, almost two-thirds of Germany's industrial workforce was engaged in war-related activities and the figure even by 1944, at the height of the war, was not much greater. German consumption of civilian products declined by more than 20% between 1939 and 1941.' (Overy 1996, p.10)

Despite this, however, Germany still failed to produce weapons in sufficient quantities to guarantee military success. Overy argues that were two reasons for this:

- there was no central agency whose job was to look at the big picture and ensure that there was coherent planning - instead, there were many agencies, each with their own priorities
- by overseeing every stage of the production process, the Armed Forces ensured that planning was difficult and production inefficient.

Overy argues that:

'The tension was never really resolved until the spring of 1941 when Hitler enquired about aircraft and tanks for the invasion of the Soviet Union. When it was discovered that Germany hardly had any more tanks and aircraft to attack Russia than it had had to attack Poland two years before, Hitler was astonished. In May he set up an inquiry and soon discovered the cause: too many people in charge of the economy and excessive military intervention in industrial production.' (Overy 1996, p.11)

As a result, in February 1942, he appointed Albert Speer as Armaments Minister - see Box 6.33.

It should be noted that the use of forced and slave labour and the plundering of occupied land affected the German economy during the war. Carr argues that centralised planning only partly explains why the German economy was able to sustain the war effort for so long:

'The other half of the picture was the ruthless exploitation of occupied Europe; without food supplies from the East, German living standards would have fallen dramatically; and without Sauckel's brutal use of foreign labour and Göring's indiscriminate plundering of raw materials from all corners of Europe, the war machine would grind to a halt long before 1945.' (Carr 1991, p.335)

The reference to 'Sauckel' is a reference to Fritz

BOX 6.33 | Albert Speer, Minister of Armaments

By the end of 1941, Germany was at war with Britain, the Soviet Union and the USA and yet its armaments production remained inferior to that of Britain. Preparations for a new approach had begun in the autumn of 1941 and Hitler had issued a 'Rationalisation Decree' in December 1941, but it was the appointment of Albert Speer as Minister of Armaments in February 1942 which marked the real turning point. Speer was Hitler's personal architect and on very good terms with him. He now used the Führer's authority to cut through all the various interests to implement a programme of 'industrial self-responsibility'. Controls over industry and constraints were relaxed. In their place, a Central Planning Board was set up. This was supported by a number of committees, each looking after a key sector of the economy. This gave industrialists a considerable degree of freedom whilst ensuring that Speer could maintain overall control. Speer encouraged industrialists and engineers to join his ministerial team and, wherever possible, excluded military personnel from the production process. Over the next two years a quite remarkable transformation took place. Total arms production increased by 59% in the first six months alone and, by the second half of 1944, when German war production peaked, there had been more than a threefold increase since early 1942. But Speer's economic successes should not disguise the fact that Germany actually had the capacity to produce even more. Speer was not always able to counter the power of Nazi Party officials at a local level and the economic agencies of the SS remained a law unto themselves, especially in the conquered lands. And, above all, from 1943, Speer could not reverse the damaging effects of Anglo-American bombing. If it had not been for the destruction, breakdown in communications and the need to divert resources into the construction of anti-aircraft installations and underground industrial sites (all the result of the bombing), Germany could well have achieved a total war economy.

Adapted from Layton 2000.

Sauckel, the Gauleiter (ie Nazi chief) in Thuringia. In 1942, Hitler appointed Sauckel to a new office entitled 'Plenipotentiary for Labour Allocation':

'Sauckel's job was to procure, allocate and exploit all foreign labour and he did so with efficient cruelty. Sauckel's agents filled their quotas by rounding up foreigners in town squares, churches, cinemas and other places where people congregated in great numbers and shipping them back to Germany in freight cars. Within only a year, Sauckel managed to round up close to 2.1 million foreign workers, bringing the total to 7 million by the middle of 1944.' (Fischer K. 1995, p.487)

MAIN POINTS - Section 3.2

- **When the Nazis came to power, 8 million people were unemployed and the economy was in very poor shape. It is important to note that, although the Nazis promised 'Bread and Work', historians agree that no detailed economic programme had been drawn up.**
- **Most historians agree that Nazi economic policy went through three key phases - (1) 1933-36 - the first Four Year Plan - focus on reducing unemployment (2) 1936-39 - the second Four Year Plan - focus on rearming (3) 1939-45 - the wartime economy - focus on winning the war.**
- **In the past, historians have argued that, from 1933, the main focus was on rearmament and that rearmament explains the economic recovery. Today, however, few historians accept such a point of view.**
- **Six factors combined to ensure rapid economic recovery after the Nazis came to power - (1) political stabilisation (2) the crushing of the labour movement (3) the continuation of policies**

- begun under Brüning (4) the New Plan (5) greater central control (6) increased government spending, especially on large-scale work creation projects.
- **Most historians agree that a turning point came in 1936 when Hitler put Göring in charge of the second Four Year Plan. This ushered in a quite different phase of military expansion based upon the restructuring of the economy to meet the probable needs of war.**
- **In the first two years of the war, Germany failed to produce weapons in sufficient quantities to guarantee military success because (1) there was no central agency and (2) the interference by the Armed Forces ensured that planning was difficult and production inefficient.**
- **Weapons production increased significantly after Albert Speer became Minister of Armaments in February 1942. Bombing and some continued inefficiency, however, ensured that production did not meet its maximum capacity.**

Activity 6.8 The German economy 1933-45

ITEM 1 The economic recovery

	1928	1932	1933	1934	1935	1936	1937
Gross National Product (billion Reichmarks)	89.5	57.6	59.1	66.5	74.4	82.6	93.2
Registered Unemployed (millions)	1.4	5.6	4.8	2.7	2.2	1.6	0.9
State Investment (billion Reichmarks)	6.6	2.2	2.5	4.6	6.4	8.1	8.4
State Expenditure (national & local, billion Reichmarks)	23.2	17.1	18.4	21.6	21.9	23.6	26.9
Industrial Production (1928 = 100)	100	58	66	83	96	107	117
Real earnings (average of 1925-9 = 100)	106	91	87	88	91	93	96

This table shows how the German economy recovered after 1933.

1939	1940	1941	1942	1943
21.9	50.2	54.5	56.7	61.0

This chart shows the percentage of workers working on military contracts between 1939 and 1943.

Adapted from Overy 1996 and 1998.

ITEM 2 The autobahnen

In late September 1933, over 700 unemployed men in Frankfurt were informed that they were to be employed on the new Autobahnen (motorways). They swore an oath to the Führer, were presented with shovels and marched to their new workplace. Meanwhile, Hitler had flown in and was driven to the motorway building site. Two cubic tons of earth were dumped before his feet and he started shovelling until the first beads of sweat dripped to the ground. The spot where Hitler had shovelled then had to be roped off to deter workers taking handfuls of soil as relics. And so was born one of the most potent propaganda images of the Third Reich. The construction of a motorway system was part of a more comprehensive vision. A typically Nazi ad hoc agency, under the Swabian civil engineer Fritz Todt, assumed responsibility for the annual target of 1,000 km, with the start-up capital and much of the skilled workforce initially derived from the national railways. The motorways were a national prestige project which would literally bind the nation closer together, at the same time returning a 600,000 men to work. The scheme had many propaganda advantages over less visible work-creation schemes. The Adolf Hitler Highways promised a society in which goods would move by lorry or soldiers would be taken to foreign frontiers. Every family would own a car for picnics in scenic lay-bys, a tantalising prospect for people who rarely left their own villages or cities. Actually, the military preferred trains on the grounds that military vehicles would rip up the road surface and fracture bridges. They also worried that motorways would provide route maps for bombs targeted at German cities. But the motorways were a social rather than a military vision. Actually, nothing like 600,000 were employed. In 1936, an all-time maximum of 120,000 worked on the motorways. Put differently, 4-5% of the 6 million registered unemployed were in 1933 were so employed. Even if related industries employed double this number, the effect on unemployment was actually minimal. By 1941, almost 4,000 km had been built (the projected total was 20,000). The roads were deserted. In 1938, only 3% of goods were transported by road. Only a few hundred 'people's cars' were ever built before Volkswagen production turned to military uses.

Hitler at the new motorway building site in September 1933.

Adapted from Burleigh 2000.

ITEM 3 A historian's view

The nature of economic recovery which took place in Germany after 1933 illustrates not so much what ought to have been done by the Weimar Republic, but why it could not have done it. Although there is some evidence of increased production in the second half of 1932, there is little reason to believe that Germany would have recovered any more successfully than France, without the massive programme of state investment undertaken by Hitler. Between 1933 and 1938, 44-49% of investment came from the state. The lion's share had a military purpose, as the increase in military spending from just 1.5% of GNP in 1933, to 20% in 1938 suggests - though even this understates the importance of rearmament since much apparently non-military investment in transport and infrastructure (most famously, the Autobahnen) had strategic objectives. The results were impressive. Between 1928 and 1932, GNP had fallen by c.20% in real terms. Between 1932 and 1938, it increased by c.75%. Industrial output in the same periods fell by 42% and rose by 110%. Unemployment fell to just 400,000 in 1938. Yet there was only modest inflation. How was this possible? First, public spending went up by 120%. Second, although taxes were increased, the public debt went up from 14 billion marks to 42 billion. Third, the money supply expanded by 70%. But, prices were kept down - they rose by no more than 16% between 1933 and 1937. The main explanation for the relative success of Nazi economic policy lies in the fact that private consumption was restrained in a way that had been more or less impossible under Weimar. The bulk of production was in producer goods not consumer goods. As investment rose, private consumption as a percentage of national income fell from 83-59%. To give a striking example, beer consumption per capita in 1937 was 60% lower than ten years previously. Private consumption was reined in to allow rearmament to proceed with minimal inflation. Although many of the economic controls used by the Nazis had in fact been developed under Weimar, none of this would have been possible without a radical transformation of the political system. Hitler's earliest political statements show that he understood the need for political centralisation. The destruction of the trade unions and the creation in their stead of the Labour Front and the subordination of employers' associations to the Reich Estate of German Industry meant, for both organised labour and business, an end to independence. Hitler's declaration in the Four Year Plan memorandum - 'the job of the Reich Economics Ministry is simply to set out the national economic tasks; private industry has to fulfil them' - captures the subordination of economics to politics which had been achieved.

Adapted from Ferguson 1997.

Questions

1. Judging from Items 1-3 and your own knowledge, what was the nature of the economic recovery achieved by the Nazis after 1933?
2. a) Using Items 1 and 3 explain how the Nazis' economic achievements fitted in with their political aims.

b) What impact did the outbreak of war against Britain and France have on the German economy?
3. 'Work creation schemes, like the building of the Autobahnen, were the key to economic recovery'. Using Item 2, give arguments for and against this statement.

References

- **Aly (2000)** Aly, G., 'The planning intelligentsia and the "Final Solution"' in *Bartov (2000)*.

- **Barkai (1996)** Barkai, A., 'The German Völksgemeinschaft from the persecution of the Jews to the "Final Solution"' in *Burleigh (1996)*.

- **Bartov (2000)** Bartov, O. (ed.), *The Holocaust: Origins, Implementation, Aftermath*, Routledge, 2000.

- **Baynes (1942)** Baynes, N. (ed.), *The Speeches of Adolf Hitler*, Oxford University Press, 1942.

- **Bessel (1984)** Bessel, R., *Political Violence and the Rise of Nazism, the Storm Troopers in Eastern Germany 1925-34*, New Haven, 1984.

- **Bracher (1971)** Bracher, K.D., *The German Dictatorship: the Origins, Structure and Consequences of National Socialism*, Penguin, 1971.

- **Broszat (1979)** Broszat, M., 'Hitler and the genesis of the "Final Solution"', *Yad Vashem Studies 13, 1979* - see also, in *Koch (1985)*.

- **Bullock (1991)** Bullock, A., *Hitler and Stalin: Parallel Lives*, HarperCollins, 1991.

- **Burleigh (1996)** Burleigh, M., *Confronting the Nazi Past*, Collins & Brown, 1996.

- **Burleigh (2000)** Burleigh, M., 'Psychiatry, German society and the Nazi "euthanasia" programme' in *Bartov (2000)*.

- **Carr (1991)** Carr, W., *A History of Germany 1815-1990*, Edward Arnold, 1991.

- **Craig (1981)** Craig, G., *Germany 1866-1945*, Oxford University Press, 1981.

- **Dahrendorf (1968)** Dahrendorf, R., *Society and Democracy in Germany*, Weidenfeld & Nicolson, 1968.

- **Falter (1986)** Falter, J., 'How likely were workers to vote for the NSDAP?' in *Fischer, C. (1996)*.

- **Ferguson (1997)** Ferguson, N., 'The German inter-war economy: political choice versus economic determinism' in *Fulbrook (1997)*.

- **Fischer C. (1995)** Fischer, C., *The Rise of the Nazis*, Manchester University Press, 1995.

- **Fischer C. (1996)** Fischer, C. (ed.), *The Rise of National Socialism and the Working Classes in Weimar Germany*, Berghahn Books, 1996.

- **Fischer K. (1995)** Fischer, K.P., *Nazi Germany: a New History*, Constable and Company, 1995.

- **Frei (1993)** Frei, N., *Nationalist Socialist Rule in Germany: the Führer State 1933-45*, Blackwell, 1993.

- **Friedlander H. (2000)** Friedlander, H., 'Step by step: the expansion of murder, 1939-1941' in *Bartov (2000)*.

- **Friedlander (1997)** Friedlander, S., *Nazi Germany and the Jews*, HarperCollins, 1997.

- **Friedlander S. (2000)** Friedlander, S., 'The extermination of the European Jews in historiography: fifty years later' in *Bartov (2000)*.

- **Fulbrook (1997)** Fulbrook, M. (ed.), *German History since 1800*, Edward Arnold, 1997.

- **Geary (1993)** Geary, D. *Hitler and Nazism*, Routledge, 1993.

- **Gellately (2001)** Gellately, R., *Backing Hitler*, Oxford University Press, 2001.

- **Geyser (1986)** Geyser, M., 'The Nazi state: machine or morass?', *History Today, Vol.36, Jan. 1986*.

- **Goldhagen (1997)** Goldhagen, D., *Hitler's Willing Executioners*, Little Brown, 1997.

- **Gregor (2001)** Gregor, N., 'New perspectives on Nazi Germany', *Modern History Review, Vol.13.1, Sept. 2001*.

- **Herbert (1986)** Herbert, U., 'Life in the Third Reich: good time, bad times', *History Today, Vol.36, Feb. 1986*.

- **Hilberg (2000)** Hilberg, R., 'The destruction of the European Jews' in *Bartov (2000)*.

- **Hirschfeld & Kettenacker (1981)** Hirschfeld & Kettenacker (eds.), *Der 'Führerstaat': Mythos und Realität*, Klett-Cotta, 1981.

- **Hitler (1925)** Hitler, A., *Mein Kampf*, edition cited - Pimlico, 1992.

- **Housden (2000)** Housden, M., 'Lebensraum - policy or propaganda?', *History Review, September 2000*.

- **Johnson (2000)** Johnson, E., *The Nazi Terror*, John Murray, 2000.

- **Kershaw (1991)** Kershaw, I., *Hitler*, Pearson Education, 1991.

- **Kershaw (1998)** Kershaw, I., *Hitler: 1889-1936 - Hubris*, Penguin, 1998.

- **Kershaw (2000)** Kershaw, I., *The Nazi Dictatorship: Problems and Perspectives of Interpretation (4th edn)*, Arnold, 2000.

- **Kershaw (2000a)** Kershaw, I., *Hitler: 1936-1945 Nemesis*, Penguin, 2000.

- **Knopp (2001)** Knopp, G., *Hitler's Holocaust*, Sutton Publishing, 2001.

- **Koch (1985)** Koch, H.W. (ed.), *Aspects of the Third Reich*, Macmillan, 1985.

- **Layton (2000)** Layton, G., *Germany: the Third Reich 1933-45*, Hodder and Stoughton, 2000.

- **Mason (1981)** Mason, T., 'Intention and Explanation' in *Hirschfeld & Kettenacker (1981)*.

- **McDonough (1999)** McDonough, F., *Hitler and Nazi Germany*, Cambridge University Press, 1999.

- **Mommsen (1991)** Mommsen, H., *From Weimar to Auschwitz*, Oxford University Press, 1991.

- **Monteath (2000)** Monteath, P., 'Swastikas by the seaside', *History Today, Vol. 50, May 2000*.

- **Neville (1999)** Neville, P., *The Holocaust*, Cambridge University Press, 1999.

- **Niethammer (1986)** Niethammer, L., 'Life history and social culture in the Ruhr 1930-1960', *History Today, Vol. 36, February 1986*.

- **Noakes & Pridham (2000)** Noakes, J. & Pridham, G. (eds), *Nazism 1919-45: Volume 2: State, Economy and Society 1933-39 (2nd edn)*, University of Exeter Press, 2000.

- **Noakes & Pridham (2001)** Noakes, J. & Pridham, G. (eds), *Nazism 1919-45: Volume 3: Foreign Policy, War and Racial Extermination (2nd edn)*, University of Exeter Press, 2001.

- **Nolte (1988)** Nolte, E., *The European Civil War 1917-45*, London, 1988.

- **Overy (1996)** Overy, R., 'The Nazi economy: success or failure?', *Modern History Review, Vol.7.4, April 1996*.

- **Overy (1996a)** Overy, R., *The Nazi Economic Recovery: 1932-38 (2nd edn)*, Cambridge University Press, 1996.

- **Overy (1998)** Overy, R., 'The Nazi economy - was it geared to war?', *History Review, No.31, Sept 1998*.

- **Peukert (1987)** Peukert, D., *Inside Nazi Germany: Conformity and Opposition in Everyday Life*, Penguin, 1987.

- **Pine (1997)** Pine, L., 'Nazism in the classroom', *History Today, Vol. 47, April 1997*.

- **Pine (1999)** Pine, L., 'Girls in uniform', *History Today, Vol. 49, March 1999*.

- **Pine (2000)** Pine, L., 'Nazi family policy: towards "a strong and pure German nation"', *Modern History Review, Vol.11.4, April 2000*.

- **Pine (2002)** Pine, L., 'The impact of the Nazi regime upon German society', *Modern History Review, Vol.13.3, Feb. 2002*.

- **Reed-Purvis (1999)** Reed-Purvis, J., 'The Gestapo - the people's police force?', *Modern History Review, Vol.11.2, Nov. 1999*.

- **Rees (1997)** Rees, L., *The Nazis: a Warning from History*, BBC Publications, 1997.

- **Schleunes (1970)** Schleunes, K., *The Twisted Road to Auschwitz: Nazi Policy toward German Jews, 1933-1939*, University of Illinois Press, 1970.

- **Schoenbaum (1966)** Schoenbaum, D., *Hitler's Social Revolution*, Anchor, 1966.

- **Snyder (1976)** Snyder, L., *Encyclopedia of the Third Reich*, McGraw-Hill (USA), 1976.

- **Steinhoff, Pechel & Showalter (1991)** Steinhoff, J., Pechel, P. & Showalter, D., *Voices from the Third Reich*, Grafton Books, 1991.

• **Stibbe (1993)** Stibbe, M., 'Women and the Nazi state', *History Today, Vol.43, November 1993.*

• **Taylor (1964)** Taylor, A.J.P., *The Origins of the Second World War*, Penguin, 1964.

• **Turner (1972)** Turner, H., 'Fascism and modernization', *World Politics, Vol.24.4, 1972.*

• **Welch (1993)** Welch, D., *The Third Reich: Politics and Propaganda*, Routledge, 1993.

• **Zeman (1973)** Zeman, R., *Nazi Propaganda*, Oxford University Press, 1973.

Index

ACKNOWLEDGEMENTS

Dedication

To Claire, Jane, Sarah, Mick, Katie, Ruth, Lisa, Maisie and Esme

Acknowledgements

Cover design	Caroline Waring-Collins (Waring Collins Ltd)
Page design	Rebecca Leatherbarrow (Waring Collins Ltd)
Graphic origination	Derek Baker (Waring Collins Ltd)
Graphics	Tim Button (Waring Collins Ltd)
Reader	Wendy Janes

Picture Credits

AKG 10, 18, 26, 27, 35, 43, 52, 71, 72, 95, 121, 238, 239L&R, 240, 241, 243, 245, 250, 260, 261B&T, 270, 271, 276, 277, 283; Bildarchiv Preussicher 152, 158T, 178T&B, 180, 195, 198, 199, 213T ; British Film Institute 221; Centre for the Study of Cartoons and Caricature, Canterbury 213B; German Bundesarchiv 131T; Hoover Archives 191; Hulton Getty 9, 18, 53, 79, 97, 103, 112, 137, 142T&B, 150, 151T&B, 158B, 235 236; *Illustrierter Beobachter* 228R; David King Collection 228L; Mary Evans Picture Library 66R, 254; Punch Magazine 66L, 206R; Topham Picturepoint 42, 106, 109, 117, 125, 131B 136, 208; Weidenfeld Archives 244R; Weimar Archive 206L, 244L; Wiener Library 51; Jonathan Wright 102.

Cover pictures

Hulton Getty (children playing with money during the period of hyperinflation in 1923)
Hulton Getty (Bismarck)
Topham Picturepoint (Hitler practising his oratory)
AKG (propaganda poster showing an ideal Nazi family)

Every effort has been made to locate the copyright owners of material used in this book. Any omissions brought to the attention of the publisher are regretted and will be credited in subsequent printings.

British Library Cataloguing in Publication Data. A catalogue record for this book is available from the British Library.

ISBN 1 902796 20 9

Causeway Press Limited, PO Box 13, Ormskirk, Lancs, L39 5HP

© Steve Eddy, Tony Lancaster & Steve Lancaster
First impression, 2002

Printed and bound by LEGOPRINT SPA, Italy